Date:05/2012

PALM BEACH COUNTY
LIBRARY SYSTEM

**3650 Summit Boulevard
West Palm Beach, FL 33406**

HISTORICAL DICTIONARIES
OF WAR, REVOLUTION, AND CIVIL UNREST
Jon Woronoff, Series Editor

The United States–Mexican War, by Edward H. Moseley and Paul C. Clark Jr. 1997.

World War I, by Ian V. Hogg. 1998.

The United States Marine Corps, by Harry A. Gailey. 1998.

The Wars of the French Revolution, by Steven T. Ross. 1998.

The Spanish-American War, by Brad K. Berner. 1998.

The Persian Gulf War, by Clayton R. Newell. 1998.

The United States Air Force and Its Antecedents, by Michael Robert Terry. 1999.

World War II: The War Against Japan, by Anne Sharp Wells. 1999.

British and Irish Civil Wars, by Martyn Bennett. 2000.

The Cold War, by Joseph Smith and Simon Davis. 2000.

Ancient Greek Warfare, by Iain Spence. 2002.

The Civil War, by Terry L. Jones. 2002.

The Crimean War, by Guy Arnold. 2002.

The United States Army: A Historical Dictionary, by Clayton R. Newell. 2002.

The Chinese Civil War, by Edwin Pak-wah Leung. 2002.

The Crusades, by Corliss K. Slack. 2003.

Ancient Egyptian Warfare, by Robert G. Morkot. 2003.

The French Revolution, by Paul R. Hanson. 2004.

Arms Control and Disarmament, by Jeffrey A. Larsen and James M. Smith. 2005.

The Russo-Japanese War, by Rotem Kowner. 2005.

Afghan Wars, Revolutions, and Insurgencies, Second Edition, by Ludwig W. Adamec. 2005.

The War of 1812, by Robert Malcomson. 2006.

The Arab-Israeli Conflict, by P. R. Kumaraswamy. 2006.

Nuclear, Biological, and Chemical Warfare, by Benjamin C. Garrett and John Hart. 2007.

Civil Wars in Africa, Second Edition, by Guy Arnold. 2008.

The Northern Ireland Conflict, by Gordon Gillespie. 2008.

The Anglo-Boer War, by Fransjohan Pretorius. 2009.

The Zulu Wars, by John Laband. 2009.

Terrorism, Third Edition, by Sean K. Anderson with Stephen Sloan. 2009.

American Revolution, Second Edition, by Terry M. Mays. 2010.

"Dirty Wars," Second Edition, by David Kohut and Olga Vilella. 2010.

Korean War, Second Edition, by Paul M. Edwards. 2010.

Holocaust, Second Edition, by Jack R. Fischel. 2010.

United States Navy, Second Edition, by James M. Morris and Patricia M. Kearns. 2011.

The War in Vietnam, by Ronald B. Frankum Jr. 2011.

Historical Dictionary
of the War in Vietnam

Ronald B. Frankum Jr.

The Scarecrow Press, Inc.
Lanham • Toronto • Plymouth, UK
2011

Published by Scarecrow Press, Inc.
A wholly owned subsidiary of The Rowman & Littlefield Publishing Group, Inc.
4501 Forbes Boulevard, Suite 200, Lanham, Maryland 20706
http://www.scarecrowpress.com

Estover Road, Plymouth PL6 7PY, United Kingdom

British Library Cataloguing in Publication Information Available

Library of Congress Cataloging-in-Publication Data

Frankum, Ronald Bruce, 1967–
    Historical dictionary of the war in Vietnam / Ronald B. Frankum Jr.
        p. cm. — (Historical dictionaries of war, revolution, and civil unrest)
    Includes bibliographical references.
    ISBN 978-0-8108-6796-3 (cloth : alk. paper) — ISBN 978-0-8108-7956-0 (ebook)
    1. Vietnam War, 1961–1975—Dictionaries. I. Title.
    DS557.7.F735 2011
    959.704'303—dc22   2010052321

∞™ The paper used in this publication meets the minimum requirements of American
National Standard for Information Sciences—Permanence of Paper for Printed Library
Materials, ANSI/NISO Z39.48-1992.

Printed in the United States of America

This volume is dedicated to Jack Joseph Frankum.

Contents

Editor's Foreword

The Second Indochina War, or the Vietnam War, as it was called in the West, or again the American War, as it was known in Vietnam, was one of the fiercest, most frustrating, and also most futile wars in history. In it, a seemingly puny North Vietnam took on the world's most powerful nation, the United States—and beat it. But this took some doing. The North had to devote over a decade to ousting the U.S. and conquering the South, and these were years of intensive warfare with hundreds of thousands of troops in the field, fighting over territory often meter for meter, thus resulting in tens of thousands of military deaths and even more collateral ones as ordinary people got in the way, meanwhile wreaking havoc on the nation's economic foundation. The U.S., never expecting such ferocious resistance, poured in troops and national wealth as it almost bombed Vietnam out of existence, North and South. It was frustrated by its inability to make much headway, by repeated reverses, and by growing opposition at home, and it finally pulled out. That was in 1973, with the South falling in 1975. Why all this? Well, to defend a bastion of capitalism, which became a bastion of communism. That was then; what about now? In 1986, the Socialist Republic of Vietnam adopted a policy of *doi moi*, and since then it has been creating what? Well, basically a mixed economy with a strong capitalist tinge, dominated by the South, and whose main customer is the United States. Was it all worthwhile?

This *Historical Dictionary of the Vietnam War* does not tell us whether it was worthwhile or not; that is not its function. What it does explain, often in very significant detail, is how the war came about, how it was fought, how it infected the whole region including neighboring Laos and Cambodia, what efforts were made by all parties, and how it ended. This long period of war, and those before and after, are charted quite closely in the chronology, while the list of acronyms is a must in following the story. Most of the explaining is done in the dictionary section. In about 700 entries, this section focuses on the key players, these being the various nations involved, the political parties and governments thereof, an assortment of military commands and units, and a range of persons whose names are forever attached to that conflict. Other entries describe crucial events that were, then at least, regarded as major advances or setbacks. Some more are devoted to the aircraft, ships, and weapons used; to countless operations and projects; and to major cities and other locations. They cover all the warring parties and start with the First Indochina War, proceed with the backdrop to the Second, and continue until just after the fall of Saigon. The bibliography, which is a very important component of the book, permits readers to learn more about the war as a whole, the players, events, and so on.

This volume, which is a completely new edition, was written by Ronald B. Frankum Jr., who is rapidly emerging as one of the leading authorities on the Vietnam War. He teaches modern American foreign policy, military history, and the Vietnam War at Millersville University in Pennsylvania and has lectured at other schools. Most exceptionally, he has also conducted workshops in Vietnam in both Hà Nội and Hồ Chí Minh City. In less than a decade, he has produced four books, *Silent Partners: The United States and Australia in Vietnam*, *The Vietnam War for Dummies*, *Like Rolling Thunder: The Air War during the Vietnam War*, and *Operation Passage to Freedom: The United States in Vietnam, 1954–1955*, with this historical dictionary as the fifth, and this one is most certainly not addressed to dummies. That seems not to be enough, for he is now working on a study of Ngô Đình Diệm, the key figure in the South. With this sort of background, and with access to the essential information and documentation, he has done most of the hard work for us so that we can look up specific facts or cover the field more generally in our own attempts to make sense of what happened, and also, should that be our cast of mind, to attribute blame or praise.

Jon Woronoff
Series Editor

Preface

The challenge of presenting the history of the Vietnam War, with all of its intrigue, personalities, episodes, and events, is daunting. Wars are by definition complex events that when coupled with different perspectives make the challenge even greater. It was this challenge that compelled me to undertake this project. Vietnam War historiography is at a crossroads, as some scholars have begun to abandon the field to work on the new struggles of the 21st century while others struggle to accept new interpretations that bring in the Vietnamese voice but often at the expense of long-held beliefs that have been entrenched in that historiography since the publication of the Pentagon Papers. There is no question that professional and amateur scholarship will notice entries that are missing, question the importance of some that are included, and be wary of interpretations of the history when they are present. The study of the Vietnam War requires this type of scrutiny, while the potential for controversy is second nature. This volume represents the best attempt by one scholar to gather and explain why the Vietnam War matters and how it is significant in modern history. It is also an attempt to reflect the newer trends in the field that acknowledge that the boundaries of the war have moved beyond the Democratic Republic of Vietnam and the Republic of Vietnam, and even beyond Southeast Asia.

This edition of the *Historical Dictionary of the Vietnam War* represents a departure from the previous edition by Edwin Moïse. While many of the entry titles are the same, all have been rewritten, with new information and recently released documents and studies incorporated into the history. Several entries from the previous edition have been replaced with entries that reflect the changing nature of Vietnam War studies. There is a more significant emphasis on the international perspective of the war and an attempt to give the Vietnamese a greater voice in their history. This change is not a reflection on the quality of the previous edition, which was a comprehensive and well-crafted dictionary, but rather is a recognition of the ever-evolving nature of the study of the war.

The bibliography at the end of the volume focuses, for the most part, on American scholarship of the war, though there are expanded sections on allied accounts for both sides of the conflict. Because of the limitations of a single volume on the war, the bibliography excludes articles and non–manuscript length studies. The historiography of the Vietnam War could easily take over the entire volume if one were to include everything. Foreign language studies, save for a few important works that have been translated, were also left out because of space limitations. The bibliography has also been subdivided into categories, though scholars of the war will note that books could have been assigned to more than one category. The selection of works into categories was made, in part, based on the significance of the books or the number of available books in a particular category. This is a subjective process and certainly not perfect.

In many respects, this work is a culmination of 20 years of studying the Vietnam War and its influences on Southeast Asia and the United States. While the process has been challenging and not every day rewarding, it has brought an even greater respect by this scholar for the breadth, depth, and significance of the war. The men and women who served in Southeast Asia or who were directly or indirectly affected by the war deserve to have their history and experiences recorded as accurately and completely as possible. This work does not presume to fulfill the latter objective, as it would take more than a single volume, but every effort has been made to accomplish the former, as has the attempt to treat a variety of significantly different, and conflicting, subjects fairly.

This type of work cannot be accomplished alone. Several individuals have influenced this work, either knowingly or not, including Drs. William C. Stinchcombe, George C. Herring Jr., John Ernst, and James R. Reckner. My time at the Vietnam Archive at Texas Tech University was invaluable to this type of study, though I did not know I would be involved in its undertaking until six years after the fact. I am also indebted to Herb Pankratz at the Dwight D. Eisenhower Presidential Library and the wonderful staff at the John F. Kennedy Presidential Library for their assistance during my many visits. Both libraries and the Millersville University of Pennsylvania Faculty Grants Committee helped to defray expenses for this and other projects that helped in formulating this volume. Ms. Terri Monserrat provided the greatest source of support, critique, and humor during the time of researching, writing, and editing the work. While still at the beginning of her career as a historian, her work in this volume is immeasurable, as is her stamp on the project. This volume would not be nearly as complete or accurate without her diligence and detail to the history. She and others with whom I have consulted, however, are free from fault for any errors or omissions in this work. Should any type of error surface or varying interpretation need inclusion, those who discover the problem should contact the author directly.

Reader's Notes

In order to make the *Historical Dictionary* as easy to use whether one is a professional or amateur scholar of the Vietnam War, each entry has been cross-referenced throughout the dictionary section of the volume. Cross-referenced entries are in bold. While every effort has been made to avoid multiple cross-referenced entries next to one another, readers should be aware that there are a few such cases, such as **marine helicopters**, which denotes entries for both the marines and helicopters rather than a specific cross-reference to marine helicopters. It is also important to note in a few cases that the exact title of the entry is not always in bold in the cross-reference. For instance, **long-range reconnaissance patrols** is a cross-reference to the entry for long-range patrols.

Each acronym within the *Historical Dictionary* is always preceded by its full spelling, except for the United States, which is referred to as the U.S. after the first mention. While this might seem cumbersome, it allows those who are not familiar with the terminology of the war greater ease in understanding and avoids the constant flipping of pages back to the acronyms list at the beginning of the book. The volume also lists the English translation of most organizations followed by the actual name, usually in French or Vietnamese, followed by the most common acronym. An example of this style is, Cambodian Army (Force Armée Nationale Khmère/FANK). The exceptions are Vietnamese organization names that are common.

This new edition of the *Historical Dictionary* has also used Vietnamese diacritical marks throughout the text, with the exception of the word Vietnam and American titles that include Vietnamese names such as the Saigon Military Mission. This might seem confusing at first for some not familiar with the Vietnamese language who expect *Saigon* or *Hanoi* rather than *Sài Gòn* or *Hà Nội*, but this inconvenience is far outweighed by the need of a reference work to have the proper names included. This might create a complication for those who expect U.S. spellings and format, as words like *Dienbienphu* are properly spelled *Điện Biên Phủ*. Vietnamese is a monosyllabic language, and every effort has been made to retain that style and format. Other exceptions to the Vietnamese spelling occur, specifically in the bibliography, when there is doubt to exactly how a name should be spelled. In these cases, an Americanized version of the Vietnamese name is used.

Vietnamese names are also structured so that the family name comes first and the first name is last. The *Historical Dictionary* is formatted to follow this convention. Individuals searching for Ngô Đình Diệm or Phạm Văn Đồng would look under *N* and *P*, respectively. Laotian and Cambodian names follow a similar structure as the Vietnamese, and every attempt has been made to keep their mention consistent. Vietnamese names are fully spelled out in the work in order to avoid confusion, though American and European last names are used after the first full mention in an entry.

This edition of the *Historical Dictionary* uses the formal names or abbreviations of the organizations and countries. Thus, rather than seeing North Vietnam and South Vietnam, the Democratic Republic of Vietnam (DRV) and the Republic of Vietnam (RVN) appear. Rather than the common U.S. use of Việt Cộng, a contraction of Cộng Sản Việt Nam or Vietnamese Communist, a term credited by Ngô Đình Diệm to describe the southern insurgency, the National Liberation Front is utilized. The same is true for the People's Army of Vietnam and the Army of the Republic of Vietnam. The exception is when the people, rather than the country, are mentioned. North Vietnamese and South Vietnamese are used frequently and refer to the people of the DRV and RVN respectively.

Every effort has been made to determine the exact dates for significant events. In some cases, approximations were necessary in order to not misrepresent speculation as fact. Readers might find it confusing or frustrating to see a date like May 1937 rather than the exact day in May, but some information simply is not available or is still contested. When no date is available, the *Historical Dictionary* uses a question mark. This is done infrequently.

This edition of the *Historical Dictionary* uses the metric system, though an approximate conversion is offered in parentheses. For example, 915 meters (3,000 feet). However, an exact conversion would have 915 meters (3001.968 feet). Knowingly including this discrepancy seems reasonable when most of the measures within an entry provided are not exact science. For instance, not every 2,000-pound bomb weighed exactly 2,000 pounds, nor did every F-4 Phantom have an exact maximum speed of 1,600 kilometers (1,000 miles) per hour. Most conversions are given in inches, feet, miles, or pounds. One inch equals 2.54 centimeters. One foot equals 30.48 centimeters. Three feet or one yard equals .9144 meters. One pound equals .4536 kilograms. When tons are used, the short ton (2,000 pounds or 909.09 kilograms) is the standard. Nautical miles are also used and are the equivalent to 1.1508 miles or 1.852 kilometers. The exception to using the metric system is with some weapons and munitions. A 250-pound bomb is referred to as such, as is a 105-mm artillery gun or a 2.75-inch rocket.

Acronyms and Abbreviations

1ATF	1st Australian Task Force
ABCCC	Airborne Battlefield Command and Control Center
AC	Gunship
ACAV	Armored Cavalry Assault Vehicle
ACV	Air Cushioned Vehicle
AFVN	American Friends of Vietnam
AGM	Air-to-Ground Missile
AHC	Assault Helicopter Company
AID	Agency for International Development
AIM	Air Intercept Missile
APC	Armored Personnel Carrier
ARVN	Army of the Republic of Vietnam
ASHC	Assault Support Helicopter Company
CALCAV	Clergy and Laity Concerned About Vietnam
CAP	Combat Air Patrol
CAP	Combined Action Platoon
CAT	Civil Air Transport
CBS	Columbia Broadcasting System
CBU	Cluster Bomb Unit
CCTS	Combat Crew Training Squadron
CDNI	Committee for the Defense of National Interests
CIA	Central Intelligence Agency
CIDG	Civilian Irregular Defense Group
CNN	Cable News Network
CNO	Chief of Naval Operations
CORDS	Civil Operations and Revolutionary Development Support
COSVN	Văn Phòng Trung Ương Cục Miền Nam (Central Office for South Vietnam)
CPF	Catholic Peace Fellowship
CPK	Communist Party of Kampuchea
CTZ	Corps Tactical Zone
DAO	Defense Attaché Office

DAV	Diplomatic Academy of Vietnam
DEROS	Date Eligible to Return from Overseas
DMZ	Demilitarized Zone
DRV	Democratic Republic of Vietnam
EC	Electronics Aircraft
ELINT	Electronic Intelligence
FAC	Forward Air Controller
FAG	Forward Air Guide
FANK	Force Armée Nationale Khmère (Cambodian Army)
FM	Frequency Modulated Radio
FOR	Fellowship of Reconciliation
FSB	Fire Support Base
FULRO	Front Unifié de Lutte des Races Opprimées
FUNK	Front Uni National du Kampuchéa (National United Front of Kampuchea)
H&I	Harassment and Interdiction
HES	Hamlet Evaluation System
HF	High Frequency Radio
HUAC	House Un-American Activities Committee
ICC	International Control Commission
ICCS	International Commission of Control and Supervision
JCS	Joint Chiefs of Staff
JPAC	Joint POW/MIA Accounting Command
JTFFA	Joint Task Force—Full Accounting
KIA	Killed in Action
KPRP	Khmer People's Revolutionary Party
KWP	Khmer Workers' Party
LAW	Light Anti-Tank Weapon
LLDB	Lực Lượng Đặc Biệt Quân Lực Việt Nam Cộng Hòa (Vietnamese Special Forces)
LOH	Light Observation Helicopter
LORAN	Long-Range Radio-Navigation
LRP	Long-Range Patrol
LRRP	Long-Range Reconnaissance Patrol
LVTP	Landing Vehicle Tracked Personnel
LZ	Landing Zone
MAAG	Military Assistance Advisory Group
MACV	Military Assistance Command, Vietnam
MACV-SOG	Military Assistance Command, Vietnam–Studies and Observation Group
MAF	Marine Amphibious Force

MAP	Military Assistance Program
MAPC	Military Affairs Party Committee
MIA	Missing in Action
MiG	Mikoyan-Gurevich Fighter Aircraft
Mobe	National Mobilization Committee to End the War in Vietnam
MRF	Mobile Riverine Force
MSUG	Michigan State University Group
NATO	North Atlantic Treaty Organization
NCC	National Coordinating Committee to End the War in Vietnam
NLF	National Liberation Front
NSAM	National Security Action Memorandum
NSC	National Security Council
OCO	Office of Civil Operations
OSS	Office of Strategic Services
PACV	Patrol Air Cushion Vehicle
PAT	People's Action Teams
PAVN	People's Army of Vietnam
PBR	Patrol Boat, River
PHILCAG	Philippine Civil Action Group
POW	Prisoners of War
PRC	People's Republic of China
PRG	Provisional Revolutionary Government of the Republic of South Vietnam
PRU	Provincial Reconnaissance Unit
PSDF	People's Self-Defense Force
PT	Patrol Torpedo Boat
RAAF	Royal Australian Air Force
RAN	Royal Australian Navy
RLA	Royal Laotian Army
RLAF	Royal Laotian Air Force
RLP	Rally of the Lao People
ROC	Republic of China
ROCMACV	Republic of China Military Assistance Advisory Group, Vietnam
ROK	Republic of Korea
RPG	Rocket Propelled Grenade
RVN	Republic of Vietnam
RVNAF	Republic of Vietnam Air Force
SAM	Surface-to-Air Missile
SAR	Search-and-Rescue
SARTF	Search-and-Rescue Task Force
SC	Surveillance Aircraft

SDC   Self-Defense Corps
SDS   Students for a Democratic Society
SEAL   Sea, Air, and Land Team
SEALORDS   Southeast Asia Lake Ocean River Delta Strategy
SEATO   South East Asian Treaty Organization
SLAR   Side-Looking Airborne Radar
SLF   Special Landing Force
SMM   Saigon Military Mission
SOG   Studies and Observation Group
SRG   Strategic Resources Group
SRV   Socialist Republic of Vietnam
STRATA   Short-Term Roadwatch and Target Acquisition
TERM   Temporary Equipment Recovery Mission
TOW   Tube-launched, Optically-tracked, Wire data link guided missile
UHF   Ultra High Frequency Radio
UN   United Nations
UP   United Press
USAF   United States Air Force
USCG   United States Coast Guard
USMC   United States Marine Corps
USN   United States Navy
USSR   Union of Soviet Socialist Republics
VCI   Việt Cộng Infrastructure
VHF   Very High Frequency Radio
VIỆT MINH   Việt Nam Độc Lập Đồng Minh Hôi (League for the Independence of Vietnam)
VNA   Quân Đội Quốc Gia Việt Nam (Vietnamese National Army)
VVAW   Vietnam Veterans Against the War
WAC   Women's Army Corps
WAF   Women in the Air Force
WAVES   Women Accepted for Voluntary Emergency Service
WIA   Wounded-in-Action
WRL   War Resisters League

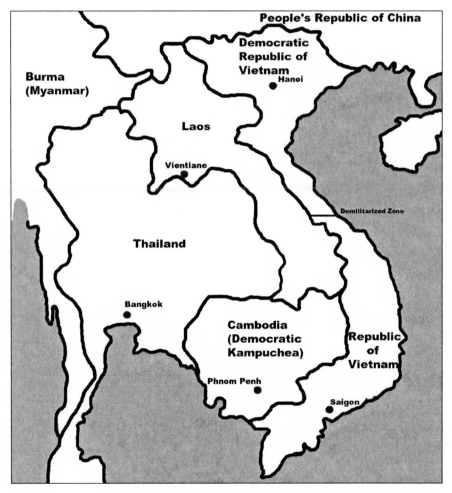

1. Southeast Asia during the war years

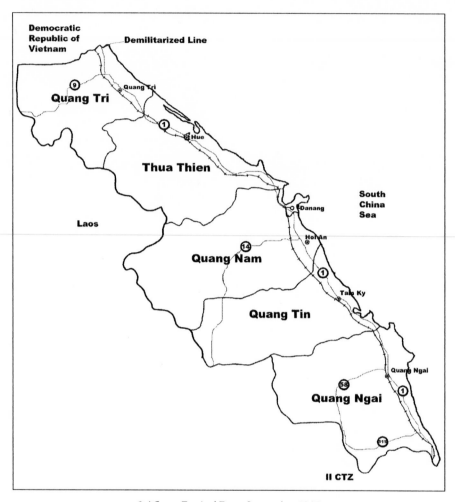

2. I Corps Tactical Zone, September 1967

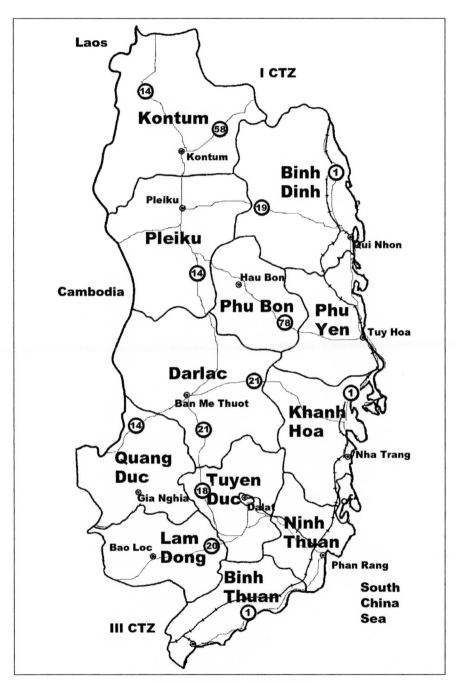

3. II Corps Tactical Zone, September 1967

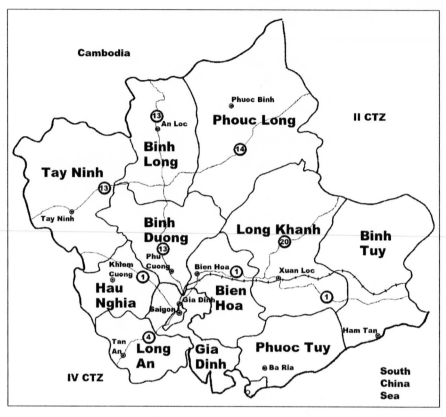

4. III Corps Tactical Zone, September 1967

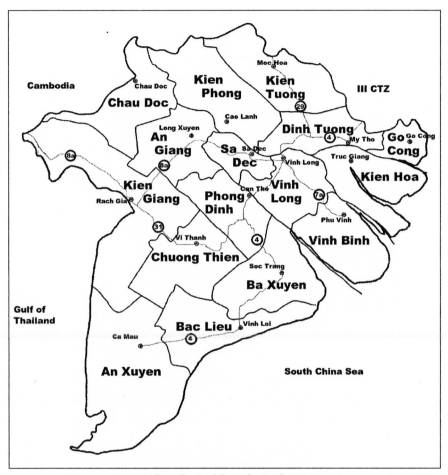

5. IV Corps Tactical Zone, September 1967

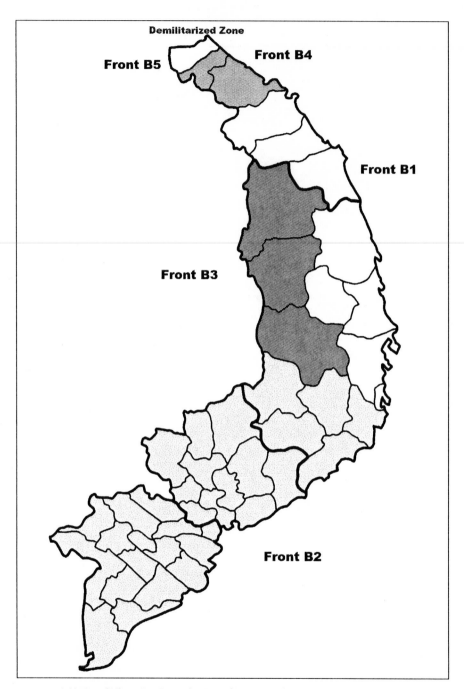

6. National Liberation Front division of Front B within the Republic of Vietnam

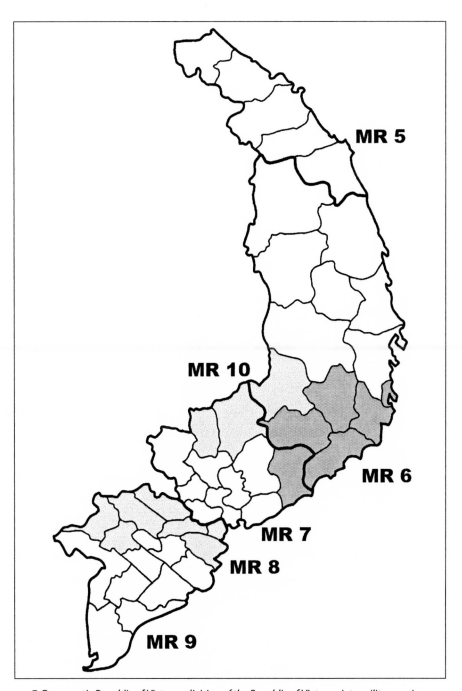

MR 5

MR 10

MR 6

MR 7

MR 8

MR 9

7. Democratic Republic of Vietnam division of the Republic of Vietnam into military regions

Chronology

1945   9 March: Japan orchestrates a coup d'état against the French in Indochina. **August:** Việt Minh uprising in Hà Nội. **25 August:** Bảo Đại abdicates Nguyễn Dynasty throne. **2 September:** Hồ Chí Minh establishes the Democratic Republic of Vietnam (DRV) with Hà Nội as its capital. World War II officially ends.

1946   March: France agrees to the March 1946 election of a National Assembly with Hồ Chí Minh as the head of government and Bảo Đại as the supreme adviser. **19 December:** Việt Minh attacks the French in Hà Nội in response to the 23 November French naval bombardment of Hải Phòng. This event was commonly thought of as the beginning of the First Indochina War.

1947   26 July: National Security Act of 1947 establishes the Central Intelligence Agency.

1949   Chinese civil war ends with a communist victory. **March:** National Army of Vietnam (Quân Đội Quốc Gia Việt Nam) organizes to protect the State of Vietnam. **8 March:** France recognizes the independence of the State of Vietnam with Bảo Đại as the Head of State and Sài Gòn as its capital.

1950   Pathet Lao established. **7 February:** U.S. recognizes the State of Vietnam, Laos, and Cambodia. **25 June:** Korean War begins. **17 September:** Military Assistance Advisory Group (MAAG), Indochina personnel arrive in Vietnam.

1951   Lao Động Party forms at the Second Congress of the Indochinese Communist Party. General Association of Buddhists organizes various Buddhist groups who oppose French colonial rule.

1952   March: French establish the Vietnamese Navy. **4 November:** Dwight D. Eisenhower wins the presidential election.

1953 French initiate what becomes known as the Navarre Plan in Indochina. **9 November:** Cambodia receives its independence from France.

1954 **April:** General John W. O'Daniel becomes the first chief of MAAG, Indochina. **7 May:** French fortress at Điện Biên Phủ falls to the Vietnamese. **8 May–21 July:** Indochina phase of the Geneva Conference produces an armistice and effectively ends the First Indochina War and French rule in Indochina. **16 June:** Ngô Đình Diệm returns to Vietnam from his self-exile. **7 July:** Ngô Đình Diệm forms his first government and becomes the president of the Council of Ministers for the State of Vietnam. **8 August–May 1955:** U.S. Navy's Operation Passage to Freedom transports 310,000 Vietnamese from the North to the South. **8 September:** Formation of the South East Asia Treaty Organization. **13 October:** Ngô Đình Diệm establishes the Vietnamese Marine Corps.

1955 **March:** Bình Xuyên, Cao Đài, Hòa Hảo sects attempt to overthrow Ngô Đình Diệm. **2 March:** Norodom Sihanouk abdicates the Cambodian throne to his father, Norodom Suramarit, and takes the position of prime minister. **April:** Ngô Đình Diệm establishes the Civil Guard. **15 May:** Ngô Đình Diệm abolishes Bảo Đại's Imperial Guard. **23 October:** Ngô Đình Diệm replaces Bảo Đại as the chief of state then proclaims the Republic of Vietnam (RVN) on 26 October.

1956 **February:** Vietnamese Special Forces is established as the First Observation Group. **26 October:** Army of the Republic of Vietnam (ARVN) organizes from the Vietnamese National Army. **2–14 November:** Residents of Nghệ An province in the DRV revolt against the Hà Nội government's land redistribution policy. The uprising is suppressed.

1957 **March:** Elbridge Durbrow becomes the U.S. ambassador to the RVN.

1958 **June:** Committee for the Defense of National Interests (CDNI) forms in Laos in response to the 4 May 1958 supplementary election in which the newly formed communist party Neo Lao Hak Xat wins 9 of the 21 seats contested. **15 September:** Bajaraka Movement uprising in the Central Highlands.

1959 **26 March:** Civil Air Transport operating in Southeast Asia changes its name to Air America. **May:** 559th Transport Group establishes to develop what becomes known as the Hồ Chí Minh Trail. **July–August 1961:** Agroville Program contests communist insurgency for control of the RVN countryside. **July:** Mobile training team from the 77th Special Forces Group trains the Royal Laotian Army in what becomes known as Project Hotfoot. **8 July:** The first U.S. combat deaths in Vietnam by hostile fire occur when two American Army advisers are killed in Biên Hòa province. **25 December:** The CDNI, led by General Phoumi Nosavan, completes a bloodless coup d'état of Premier Phoui Sananikone in Laos.

1960 **January:** The Students for a Democratic Society form in Ann Arbor, Michigan. **17 January:** Nguyễn Thị Định leads an uprising against Ngô Đình Diệm in Bến Tre province. **April:** The CDNI wins a landslide victory over the Neo Lao Hak Xat in the national election in Laos. **26 April:** The Bloc for Liberty and Progress issues the Caravelle Manifesto in protest of Ngô Đình Diệm rule and his handling of the insurgency. **9 August:** Kong Le orchestrates a coup d'état against the newly elected government in Laos. **September:** Lieutenant General Lionel McGarr replaces General Samuel T. Williams as head of the MAAG, Vietnam. The Khmer People's Revolutionary Party changes its name to the Khmer Workers' Party and allies itself with Norodom Sihanouk. The party will evolve into the Khmer Rouge. **11 November:** Abortive coup d'état against Ngô Đình Diệm in the RVN. **24 November:** Ngô Đình Thục, brother to Ngô Đình Diệm, becomes the archbishop of Huế. **December:** Boun Oum returns to power in Laos to head an anticommunist government. **20 December:** The National Front for the Liberation of South Vietnam (NLF) is created in Tây Ninh province.

1961 The DRV and NLF establish the headquarters for the Central Office for South Vietnam in Tây Ninh province. The Front B in RVN divides into two sections. Front B1 includes all of I CTZ and most of II CTZ, while the Front B2 consists of all III CTZ and IV CTZ and the three southern provinces of II CTZ. **19 January:** President Dwight D. Eisenhower meets with incoming President John F. Kennedy and maintains that Laos is the keystone to Southeast Asia. **21 January:** Robert McNamara becomes the secretary of defense. **April:** Project White Star begins in Laos. RVN conducts a national presidential election with Ngô Đình Diệm victorious. **14 April:** Project Jungle Jim is organized to train the RVN Air Force (RVNAF). **3 May:** Durbrow departs the RVN and is replaced by Frederick Nolting Jr. on 10 May. **16 May–23 July 1962:** The International Conference on the Settlement of the Laotian Question begins. **16 June:** Staley Mission travels to the RVN to assess the Vietnamese economy. **28 June:** NSAM 57 outlines how the U.S. would conduct paramilitary operations in the RVN. **July:** First use of herbicides in the RVN. **1 July:** General Maxwell Taylor accepts the position of military representative of the president. **October:** Project Pipe Stem begins to conduct reconnaissance missions over northern Laos. **11 October:** Start of Operation Farm Gate to train RVNAF personnel, which eventually will lead to American personnel involved in combat operations. **18–24 October:** General Taylor and Walt W. Rostow travel to the RVN and recommend escalation for the U.S. in Southeast Asia. **23 October:** The DRV creates the 759th Transport Group to infiltrate personnel and supplies by sea into the RVN. **November:** U.S. Special Forces detachments begin to train and equip members of the Civilian Irregular Defense Group (CIDG). **17 November:** Department of State issues an appeal to allied nations to participate in the defense of Southeast Asia. **29 November:** First class of 1,500 Vietnamese women begin their training under the guise of the Women's Solidarity Movement, which was organized by Madame Ngô Đình Nhu. **December:** Able Marble personnel redeploy from Don Muang Royal Thai Air Force Base to Tân Sơn Nhứt Air Base in Sài Gòn to assist RVN and U.S. advisers in gathering intelligence for military operations. **December:** First United States helicopters arrive in the RVN to conduct air mobility missions. **7 December:** Ngô Đình Diệm requests C-123s from the 315th Air Division to assist in military operations as part of Project Mule Train under Operation Farm Gate.

1962   The RVN creates the Rừng Sác Special Zone from Long An province. The area remains a safe haven for the NLF during most of the war. **12 January–7 January 1971:** The spraying of herbicides through Operation Ranch Hand. **8 February:** U.S. creates the Military Assistance Command, Vietnam (MACV), with General Paul D. Harkins as its first commander. **27 February:** RVNAF pilots attack the Presidential Palace in an attempt to kill Ngô Đình Diệm. **March:** First members of the SEALs arrive in the RVN. **April:** Creation of the Dirty Thirty, a group of U.S. airmen who train the RVN's 1st Transportation Group. Creation of the Trail Watchers program to monitor movement along the Hồ Chí Minh Trail. **May:** First Australian advisers arrive in the RVN. **June:** Ngô Đình Diệm terminates the RVN contract with the Michigan State University Group. **11 June:** Souvanna Phouma forms a new government in Laos with four members of the communist Neo Lao Hak Xat party in the government. **8 July:** The International Conference on the Settlement of the Laotian Question issues *The Declaration on the Neutrality of Laos*. **23 July:** Participants in the International Conference on the Settlement of the Laotian Question sign *The International Agreement on the Neutrality of Laos*. **October:** The NLF ambushes and decimates an ARVN Ranger platoon in the Mê Kông Delta.

1963   **2 January:** Battle of Ấp Bắc. **8 May:** Buddhist demonstrations in Huế against the Sài Gòn government result in nine deaths. **11 June:** Self-immolation of Thích Quảng Đức in protest of Ngô Đình Diệm's treatment of the Buddhists in the RVN. **21 August:** Ngô Đình Nhu authorizes a series of pagoda raids in the RVN to stop a possible coup d'état but severely damages the Sài Gòn government's standing with the Buddhists and Americans. **26 August:** Henry Cabot Lodge Jr. replaces Nolting as U.S. ambassador to the RVN. **September:** General Victor Krulak and Joseph Mendenhall travel to the RVN to assess Ngô Đình Diệm and the future of U.S.-RVN relations. **1 November:** Coup d'état removes Ngô Đình Diệm from power. **22 November:** Assassination of John F. Kennedy in Dallas.

1964 **24 January:** Studies and Observations Group initiates and coordinates covert operations in Southeast Asia. **30 January:** Nguyễn Khánh orchestrates a coup d'état against the Provisional Government of the Republic of Vietnam that had overthrown Ngô Đình Diệm. **February:** First group of MiG-17s arrives in Hà Nội. **16 March:** McNamara issues NSAM 288 which confirms People's Army of Vietnam (PAVN) and NLF use of Communist Chinese and Soviet weaponry. **April:** Laotian military officers overthrow the Phoumi Nosavan government. **23 April:** President Lyndon B. Johnson initiates the Show the Flag program to gather Third Country support in the RVN. **May:** MACV takes over all functions of MAAG, which ceases to exist. Creation of the Front B3 from Front B1 that includes the three western provinces of Darlac, Plei Ku, and Kon Tum in II CTZ, which make up the Central Highlands. **2 May:** Attack on the converted helicopter-carrying ship the U.S.S. *Card* docked in Sài Gòn Harbor. **15 May:** Project Leaping Lena begins training Vietnamese Special Forces and CIDG personnel in long-range reconnaissance patrols. **16 May:** Twelve War Resisters League members burn their draft cards in New York City. **June:** The first New Zealanders arrive in the RVN to assist the Sài Gòn government. **20 June:** General William C. Westmoreland assumes command of MACV. **30 June:** Admiral Ulysses S. G. Sharp becomes the commander-in-chief of all military forces in the Pacific Theater. **6 July:** Battle of Nam Đông results in Roger Donlan receiving the first Medal of Honor in the Vietnam War. **August:** The first contingent from the Philippines arrives in the RVN as a result of the Show the Flag program. **2 August:** First Gulf of Tŏn Kĭn Incident. **4 August:** Second Gulf of Tŏn Kĭn Incident is reported but is later called into question. **5 August:** The U.S. initiates Operation Pierce Arrow in response to the Gulf of Tŏn Kĭn Incidents. **7 August:** Gulf of Tŏn Kĭn Resolution approved. **September:** The United Front of Oppressed People (Front Unifié de Lutte des Races Opprimées) helps organize a rebellion near Ban Mê Thuột that includes personnel from the CIDG. **13 September:** The first Republic of Korea troops arrive in the RVN as a result of the Show the Flag program. **October:** Project Delta succeeds Project Leaping Lena. **8 October:** First contingent of the Republic of

China Military Assistance Advisory Group, Vietnam, arrives in the RVN. **November:** Women's Army Corps personnel arrive in Vietnam. **December:** War Resisters League organizes a larger demonstration against the war. **24 December:** Operation Barrel Roll begins in Laos. **28 December:** Battle of Bình Giã begins and results in a significant ARVN defeat.

1965   **7 February:** The NLF mortars Camp Holloway, near Plei Ku in the Central Highlands, killing eight Americans and wounding 128. **8 February:** Operation Flaming Dart responds to NLF attacks on U.S. personnel in the RVN. **10 February:** The NLF attacks an American billet in Qui Nhơn, killing 23 and wounding 21, which results in a second round of Operation Flaming Dart sorties. **21 February:** Nguyễn Cao Kỳ and Nguyễn Văn Thiệu lead a coup against Nguyễn Khánh. **2 March–31 October 1968:** Operation Rolling Thunder. **8 March:** Battalion Landing Team 3rd Battalion, 9th Marine Regiment lands on the beaches of Đà Nẵng, marking the first American combat troops in the RVN. **11 March:** Operation Market Time interdicts sea infiltration from the DRV into the RVN. **24 March:** First teach-in occurs at the University of Michigan in Ann Arbor. **April:** First Australian battalion arrives in the RVN. **3 April:** Operation Steel Tiger, an air campaign in Laos to interdict DRV personnel moving down the Hồ Chí Minh Trail, begins. **8 April:** Phạm Văn Đồng outlines four conditions for the DRV to negotiate an end to the war, one of which, the reunification of the country, the U.S. refuses to accept. **17 April:** The SDS organizes a major antiwar demonstration in Washington, D.C. **13–17 May:** The U.S. initiates the first of several bombing pauses. **7 June:** General Westmoreland requests an additional 35 battalions of combat troops and another 9 in reserve in order to stave off defeat in Vietnam. **18 June:** Arc Light missions begin. **28–30 June:** The 173rd Airborne Brigade engages in the first major combat operation of the war to the northeast of Sài Gòn in War Zone D. **1 July:** George Ball authors *A Compromise Solution for South Vietnam* in an attempt to persuade Johnson not to escalate in the RVN. **31 July:** U.S. Navy forms Task Force 115, the Coastal Surveillance Force, to better coordinate sea interdiction efforts. **August:** Iron Hand missions begin to eliminate SA-2 missile sites. **18–24 August:** III Marine Amphibious Force conducts Operation Starlite, the first amphibious operation of the war. **15–16 October:** First International Days of Protest. **November:** Operation Shining Brass launches reconnaissance missions into Laos to monitor the Hồ Chí Minh Trail. **14–18 November:** Battle of the Ia Đrăng Valley marks the first time U.S. combat troops engage PAVN forces. **6 December:** Operation Tiger Hound, an area carved out of Steel Tiger by Westmoreland, begins. **18 December:** Operation Game Warden interdicts PAVN and NLF movement on the inland waterways of the RVN. **31 December:** The number of U.S. personnel in Southeast Asia reaches 181,000.

1966   Hatchet Teams begin to operate along the Hồ Chí Minh Trail in Laos and Cambodia to ambush PAVN and NLF personnel. **11 January:** National Emergency Committee forms from the Catholic Peace Movement. **28 January–6 March:** Operation Masher/White Wing, the first major search-and-destroy operation, targets the NLF in the Bồng Sơn Plain. **February:** People's Action Teams evolve into 59-man mobile Revolutionary Development Cadre units and conduct pacification missions. **March:** Battle of A Shau. Buddhists rise up in I CTZ after the firing of the Buddhist general Nguyễn Chánh Thi. First PBRs arrive in the RVN under Task Force 116. **15 March:** Creation of I Field Force to coordinate military activities in II CTZ and II Field Force to coordinate military activities in III CTZ. **25–26 March:** Second International Days of Protest. **30 March–15 April:** Operation Abilene, a search-and-destroy operation, focuses in Phước Tuy province. **April:** Second Australian battalion arrives in the RVN and joins the 1st Australian Task Force with its base of operations in Phước Tuy province. Establishment of the Front B4 by removing the two most northerly provinces in I CTZ, Quảng Trị and Thừa Thiên, from the Front B1 area of operation. **1 April:** U.S. establishes the 7th Air Force in the RVN to better coordinate the various air campaigns in Southeast Asia. **May:** Clergy and Laity Concerned about Vietnam organizes. Mobile Riverine Force combines army and navy units to fight the NLF on the waterways of the RVN. **June:** Front B5 forms by taking the northern half of Quảng Trị that borders the Demilitarized Zone in the Front B4. **18 July:** Operation Tally Ho, an extension of Operation Tiger Hound, focuses on the area in the DRV north of the DMZ. **September:** Creation of the Recondo School from Project Delta. The Kampuchea Worker's Party secretly changes its name to the Communist Party of Kampuchea and becomes known as the Khmer Rouge. **14 September–24 November:** Operation Attleboro, a search-and-destroy mission, attempts to eliminate the NLF in War Zone C. **15 September:** Construction begins on what would become known as the McNamara Line with Project Practice Nine. **2–24 October:** Operation Irving, a search-and-destroy operation, targets the NLF in Bình Định province, north of Qui Nhơn. **25 October–31 October 1968:** The 7th Fleet raids DRV coastal position from the Demilitarized Zone (DMZ) to the 20th parallel in Operation Sea Dragon. **November:** Office of Civil Operations establishes controls over the civilian pacification effort in the RVN. **10 November:** Start of the Kit Carson Scout program. **31 December:** The number of U.S. personnel in Southeast Asia reaches 365,000.

1967   Another Mother for Peace organizes to educate women on antiwar activism. The Hamlet Evaluation System is conceived to measure six different factors that determine the security of hamlets throughout the Republic of Vietnam. Six veterans form the Vietnam Veterans Against the War (VVAW). **2 January:** Operation Bolo, an air operation designed to eliminate the MiG threat to the vulnerable F-105 bombers employed in Operation Rolling Thunder, begins. **8–28 January:** Operation Cedar Falls, a search-and-destroy operation, targets the NLF in the Iron Triangle. **10 January:** UN Secretary General U Thant openly criticizes U.S. actions in Southeast Asia at a press conference. **February:** Westmoreland creates Task Force Oregon to supplement the marine presence in I CTZ before it becomes the 23rd Division (Americal). **4 February:** The NLF attacks the ammunition depot at Long Bình and destroys an estimated 15,000 155-mm artillery shells. **22 February:** 2nd Battalion, 503rd Regiment, 173rd Airborne Brigade conducts the only parachute jump of the war during Operation Junction City. **March:** Operation Shining Brass changes its name to Prairie Fire after the operation is leaked by the media. **5 April–11 May 1973:** Ellsworth Bunker serves as U.S. ambassador to the RVN. **May:** The National Mobilization Committee to End the War in Vietnam organizes and coordinates monthly nationwide protests. **10 May:** U.S. establishes the Civil Operations and Revolutionary Development Support to coordinate civilian and military pacification efforts. **17 May:** Operation Commando Lava experiments with a project designed to disrupt movement down the Hồ Chí Minh Trail by dropping chemicals to break up the soil and create mud and landslides. **30 June:** Congress passes the Military Selective Service Act of 1967, which increases the range of potential inductees from 18 to 35 years of age. It retains student deferments, but this exemption terminates at the end of the four-year degree or when the individual turns 24. **August:** Senator John Stennis (D-Mississippi) conducts hearings through the Preparedness Investigating Subcommittee of the Senate Armed Services Committee and concludes that the Johnson administration has placed too many restrictions on the U.S. air campaign over the DRV. **September:** Operation Daniel Boone, designed to identify PAVN and NLF base areas in Cambodia, begins. The Short-Term Roadwatch and Target Acquisition (STRATA) program infiltrates into the DRV. **21 September:** Thailand's Queen's Cobra Regiment arrives in the RVN working with the 9th Division. **17 October:** The Baltimore Four enter the Selective Service headquarters located in the U.S. Customs House Building in Baltimore to destroy draft records. SDS participates in the melee against Dow Chemical representatives at the University of Wisconsin in Madison. **21 October:** Antiwar demonstration, known as the March on the Pentagon, occurs, during which time some of the protesters attempt to levitate the building. **25 October:** Citizens Committee for Peace with Freedom in Vietnam, a prowar organization, issues its statement of support for the Johnson administration. **31 October:** Nguyễn Văn Thiệu becomes RVN president with Nguyễn Cao Kỳ as his vice president. **9 December:** Operation Commando Vault, a project to test the use of heavy bombs for clearing areas previously inaccessible to helicopter landings, conducts its first successful test.

1968 McNamara authorizes the Department of Defense study, *United States-Vietnam Relations, 1945–1967: A Study Prepared by the Department of Defense*, known as the Pentagon Papers upon its unauthorized release. Third Country Forces in the RVN reach their peak strength of over 65,000. Over 43 countries make a contribution, but many are too insignificant to justify the success of the effort to garner allied support. **21 January–8 April:** Siege at Khe Sanh. **31 January:** Tết Offensive begins. **7 February:** Using PT-76 amphibious tanks, PAVN troops overrun the Special Forces camp at Lang Vei. **1 March:** Clark Clifford replaces McNamara as secretary of defense. **12 March:** Senator Eugene McCarthy finishes a close second to Johnson in the New Hampshire Democratic presidential primary. **16 March:** Mỹ Lai massacre. Senator Robert Kennedy announces his candidacy for the presidency. **31 March:** Johnson announces a partial bombing halt over the DRV and that he will not seek or accept the Democratic Party's nomination for the presidential election. **4 April:** Assassination of Martin Luther King Jr. **7 April–29 June:** Operation Truscott White, a joint U.S. Army and U.S. Air Force operation to interdict North Vietnamese supplies and personnel moving along the Hồ Chí Minh Trail in the area where the Democratic Republic of Vietnam, Laos, and Cambodia met, is conducted. **8 April:** The first of a series of ARVN operations under the name Toàn Thắng (complete victory) begins. **26 April:** Student Mobilization Committee coordinates a national strike in protest of the war. **May:** Second Tết Offensive. The Royal Laotian Air Force conducts is first missions without a U.S. presence. **17 May:** Catonsville Nine episode occurs when antiwar protesters break into the office of Local Draft Board 33 in Catonsville, Maryland, and destroy draft records using homemade napalm. **June:** The RVN creates the People's Self-Defense Force to ensure a military presence at the hamlet and village level. **6 June:** Senator Robert Kennedy dies from an assassin's bullet. **2 July:** General Creighton Abrams replaces Westmoreland as MACV commander. **August:** Third Tết Offensive. The Democratic Party National Convention in Chicago is witness to significant antiwar demonstrations. Thailand's Black Panther division arrives in the RVN. **1 October:** Admiral Elmo R. Zumwalt becomes the commander of U.S. Naval Forces, Vietnam. **18 October–April 1971:** Zumwalt initiates the South East Asia Lake Ocean

River Delta Strategy. **November:** Paris peace negotiations begin. This will last over four years until the Paris Peace Accords are signed in January 1973. **15 November–December:** Operation Commando Hunt absorbs operations Steel Tiger and Tiger Hound in Laos.

1969   **20 January:** Richard M. Nixon becomes the U.S. president. **22 January–18 March:** Operation Dewey Canyon I, a search-and-destroy operation, attempts to eliminate the NLF presence in the A Shau Valley. **March:** Prince Norodom Sihanouk announces that PAVN and NLF personnel are using Cambodia as a base of operations against the RVN. **3–4 March:** First and only U.S.-PAVN tank battle at Bến Hét. **18 March–26 May 1970:** Operation Menu, a secret bombing campaign in Cambodia, seeks to hamper PAVN and NLF movement between Cambodia's border and the RVN. **15 April–1 January 1971:** Operation Washington Green, a search-and-clear operation designed to improve pacification efforts in the An Lão Valley in Bình Định province, is conducted. **10 May–7 June:** Operation Apache Snow, search-and-destroy operation in the provinces of Thừa Thiên and Quảng Trị, is conducted. **10–20 May:** Battle for Hamburger Hill. **June:** U.S. reaches its peak strength of approximately 543,000 personnel in the RVN. **8 June:** Provisional Revolutionary Government of the Republic of South Vietnam is established. **25 July:** Nixon announces what becomes known as the Nixon Doctrine at a press conference in Guam, leading to Vietnamization in Southeast Asia. **14 August:** Sihanouk announces the formation of the Salvation Government in Cambodia with Lon Nol as prime minister and Prince Sisowath Sirik Matak as deputy prime minister. **2 September:** Hồ Chí Minh dies. **7–20 September:** Operation Defiant Stand, the 62nd and last amphibious operation of the 7th Fleet Special Landing Force, targets the NLF on the Barrier Islands south of Đà Nẵng. **15 October:** Moratorium Day demonstration against the war brings tens of thousands together across the U.S. **November:** Seymour Hersh exposes Mỹ Lai massacre after interviewing William Calley. **15 November:** National Moratorium Day demonstration brings hundreds of thousands together across the U.S. **26 November:** Nixon authorizes an amendment of the Military Selective Service Act of 1967 that establishes a lottery to randomly determine induction. **1 December:** First lottery for induction occurs.

1970   **15 February:** Last of the Philippine Civil Action Group contingent leaves the RVN. **March:** The Peers Commission issues its report on the Mỹ Lai massacre. **18 March:** Lon Nol and Sirik Matak lead a successful coup d'état against Sihanouk in Cambodia. **22 March:** The RVN terminates the CIDG program. **24 April:** Operation Patio begins in Cambodia as a precursor to the Cambodian Incursion. **30 April–30 June:** Cambodian Incursion. ARVN troops continue to operate in Cambodia until 31 July. **4 May:** Shootings at Kent State University. **14 May:** Shootings occur at Jackson State University. **30 May:** Operation Freedom Deal begins in Cambodia, though it is not officially named until 6 June. **18 June:** Operation Freedom Action begins in Cambodia. **24 June:** Senate repeals the Gulf of Tŏn Kĭn Resolution. **1 July:** Zumwalt becomes chief of naval operations. **1–23 July:** Siege of Fire Support Base Ripcord. **21 September:** The mobile Civil Action Program deactivates and absorbs into the Combined Action Groups. **November:** First contingent of Australian and New Zealand troops leave the RVN. **21 November:** Raid of the Sơn Tây prison camp. **22 December:** Cooper-Church Amendment passes in the House and Senate and is put into effect on 5 January 1971.

1971   **31 January–2 February:** VVAW organize the Winter Soldier Investigations in Detroit, Michigan. **February:** Operation Lâm Sơn 719, which was designed to cut the Hồ Chí Minh Trail at Tchepone, is conducted. **29 March:** William Calley is convicted of 22 counts of murder for his role in the Mỹ Lai massacre. **19–23 April:** Antiwar demonstration, known as Operation Dewey Canyon III, in Washington, D.C. **30 April:** U.S. dismantles I Field Force. **2 May:** U.S. dismantles II Field Force. **13 June:** Portions of the 1968 study, *United States-Vietnam Relations, 1945–1967: A Study Prepared by the Department of Defense*, also known as the Pentagon Papers, are released by the *New York Times*. **26–30 December:** Nixon orders Operation Proud Deep Alpha as a preemptive air strike against the DRV.

1972   **31 March–October:** Easter Offensive. **April:** Frederick Carlton Weyand replaces Creighton W. Abrams as commander, MACV. **6 April:** Operation Freedom Train begins in response to the PAVN Easter Offensive. **May:** U.S. initiates Project Enhance to replace the war materiel necessary to fight the PAVN and expand the size of the RVN Armed Forces. **1 May:** U.S. deactivates the Studies and Observation Group. **9 May–22 October:** U.S. conducts the air campaign Operation Linebacker I in response to the Easter Offensive. **12 August:** The last U.S. combat unit in Vietnam is deactivated. **20 October:** Secretary of Defense Melvin R. Laird initiates Project Enhance Plus, which sends nearly $2 billion of military equipment to the RVN. **18 December:** The last Australian advisers leave the RVN. **18–29 December:** Operation Linebacker II.

1973   **22 January:** Lyndon B. Johnson dies. **27 January:** Paris Peace Accords. **28 January:** Defense Attaché Office replaces MACV. **6 February–27 July:** U.S. conducts Operation End Sweep, an effort to clear mines in DRV waters. **19 June:** Congress passes the Case-Church Amendment. **21 June:** Graham Martin succeeds Ellsworth Bunker as U.S. ambassador to the RVN. **15 August:** U.S. air strikes stop after Congress enacts Public Law 93-53, also known as the Case-Church Amendment. **10 October:** Spiro Agnew resigns as vice president after a financial scandal. **7 November:** House Joint Resolution 542 (the War Powers Resolution) passes Congress. **6 December:** Gerald Ford is sworn in as vice president. **10 December:** Secretaries of state Henry Kissinger and Lê Đức Thọ win the Nobel Peace Prize for their work resulting in the Paris Peace Accords. Kissinger accepts the honor. Lê Đức Thọ refuses the award.

1974   **11 February:** William Calley petitions and receives habeas corpus. He is released on bail on 27 February, returns to jail on 13 June, and is finally released on 9 November 1974, having served less than three years under house arrest. **April:** A Laotian coalition government, which includes the Neo Lao Hak Xat, is formed. **June:** The last Air America personnel leave Laos. **9 August:** Ford is sworn in as president after Nixon resigns as a result of the Watergate scandal. **13 December–6 January 1975:** Battle for Phước Long begins the final DRV offensive against the RVN.

1975   **28 January:** Ford's request for a $300 million supplement for the RVN is rejected by Congress. An additional $722 million on 10 April is also turned down. **12 March:** Ban Mê Thuột falls to the PAVN, resulting in the abandonment of the Central Highlands by the RVN. **24 March:** The RVN abandons Huế. **30 March:** Đà Nẵng falls to the PAVN. **3–26 April:** Operation Babylift, an attempt to remove orphans from the RVN, is conducted. **3 April:** Cam Ranh Bay falls to the PAVN. **9–26 April:** Battle of Xuân Lộc. **12 April:** Operation Eagle Pull results in the U.S. evacuation of Phnom Penh. **17 April:** Phnom Penh falls to the Khmer Rouge. **21 April:** Nguyễn Văn Thiệu resigns as RVN president. Trần Văn Hương becomes the new president for a week. **28 April:** Dương Văn Minh returns as RVN president only to hand over the reins of government to the North Vietnamese as they enter Sài Gòn two days later. **29 April:** U.S. evacuates Sài Gòn under Operation Frequent Wind. **30 April:** Sài Gòn falls, marking the end of the war. **May:** Khmer Rouge initiates a four-year genocide in Cambodia that claims between 1.7 and 3 million people. **12 May:** Khmer Rouge seizes SS *Mayaguez* and holds the ship and crew hostage for three days. **2 December:** The Pathet Lao establishes Lao People's Democratic Republic.

1976   **5 January:** Cambodian monarchy is abolished with the passage of a new constitution that elects Pol Pot as the head of government while Cambodia is renamed the Democratic Republic of Kampuchea. **2 July:** The Socialist Republic of Vietnam (SRV) forms from the DRV and RVN.

1978 **December:** The SRV invades Kampuchea in response to border raids by the Khmer Rouge.

1979 **7 January:** SRV troops capture Phnom Penh.

1982 **23 January:** CBS airs the documentary *The Uncounted Enemy: A Vietnam Deception*, which argues that Westmoreland deceived the American people on the number of enemy dead and in the field during the war.

1984 *Westmoreland v. CBS* libel lawsuit.

1986 SRV introduces the economic policy of Đổi Mới.

1989 **September:** SRV troops withdraw from Cambodia.

1991 **7 July:** U.S. office for MIA Affairs opens in Hà Nội. **December:** U.S. lifts ban on American travel to the SRV.

1992 **February:** Joint Task Force–Full Accounting is established.

1994 **3 February:** President William J. Clinton lifts the U.S. trade embargo against the SRV.

1995 **11 July:** Clinton normalizes relations with the SRV. **6 August:** U.S. Embassy in Hà Nội opens.

1997 **10 April:** Douglas "Pete" Peterson, a Vietnam War veteran and former POW, becomes U.S. ambassador to the SRV.

1999 **August:** U.S. Consulate General opens in Hồ Chí Minh City.

2000 **16–20 November:** Clinton visits the SRV.

2002 **10 May:** Vice President Nguyễn Thị Bình visits the U.S.

2004 **11 December:** United Airlines' first flight from the U.S. into the SRV arrives in Hồ Chí Minh City.

2005 **19–24 June:** SRV Prime Minister Phan Văn Khải meets President George W. Bush in Washington, D.C.

2006 **17–20 November:** Bush visits the SRV to participate in the Asia-Pacific Economic Cooperation Leaders' meeting in Hà Nội.

2007 **24–29 September:** SRV Prime Minister Nguyễn Tấn Dũng attends the 62nd Session of the UN General Assembly. **16 October:** The SRV is elected as nonpermanent member of the UN Security Council for 2008–2009. **November:** Lê Công Phung is appointed as the SRV ambassador to the U.S.

2009 **6–7 April:** Senator, and former POW, John McCain visits Hà Nội.

2010 **25 March:** The SRV opens a consulate general in Houston, Texas. **10 April:** 113th Repatriation Ceremony held at Đà Nẵng Airport. **8–9 July:** The Vietnam Center at Texas Tech University and the Diplomatic Academy of Vietnam (DAV) hold an academic symposium titled "United States-Vietnam Relations: Toward a Brighter Future" at the DAV.

Introduction

War by any definition is a violent, complex set of actions and events that significantly impact, either directly or indirectly, all of those involved in the conflict. The Vietnam War, though perhaps it is better to expand the geographic limits to Southeast Asia, is no exception. For Southeast Asia, the war altered forever the history, topography, people, economy, and politics of the Democratic Republic of Vietnam (DRV), the Republic of Vietnam (RVN), Cambodia, and Laos. Other countries in the region were also affected, though not to the extent of the four mentioned above. That the war was controversial is an understatement, as is the notion that the war can be understood from any one perspective. There is no one way to examine it, nor is there a perfect organizational model. Each method and model is problematic in leaving out important individuals or events that helped to shape the image of the war in the minds of the participants and observers. For instance, coverage of the 1968 Tết Offensive, called by the North Vietnamese Cuộc Tổng Tiến Công Và Nổi Dậy (General Offensive and Uprising) or Tết Mậu Thân (Tết during the Year of the Monkey), could easily take up this entire introduction, or even most of the dictionary, should one attempt to examine it from all sides and perspectives.

The war was one with many beginnings and seemingly many ends. For the Vietnamese, the war for independence began against the French soon after they asserted their control in the 19th century, though the First Indochina War has a starting date in 1946 and ended with the signing of the July 1954 Geneva Agreements. The conflict began again when RVN president Ngô Đình Diệm refused to hold elections in July 1956 as stipulated by the Geneva Agreements. Many within the United States consider the "real" war to have begun on 8 March 1965 when the first combat troops arrived at Đà Nẵng, though American interests in Southeast Asia date back more than two decades. The American war ended on 27 January 1973 with the signing of the Paris Peace Accords, though the lingering controversy of the nearly 20-year involvement of the U.S. continues today.

On 30 April 1975, the official war ended with the fall of Sài Gòn and the surrender of the RVN government.[1] For many Vietnamese, the hardships

1

and turmoil of the conflict would not end until after they had safely escaped the newly formed Socialist Republic of Vietnam, and even then, for the Old Guard who had sacrificed everything for the RVN, the war will never end until Vietnam is free from outside interference and communist ideology. What the war was, how it impacted the lives of those it touched, and the consequences of the decades of conflict continue to elicit discussion and debate, acrimonious at times or filled with lament for what could have been. It was a war with many questions and few answers, and it greatly shapes the world today.

One way of understanding the Vietnam War is by marking its time with turning points, both major and minor, that involved events or decisions that helped to influence its course in the years to come. By examining a few of these turning points, an organizational framework takes shape that makes understanding the war more possible. One of the earliest turning points that included Americans and Vietnamese was in 1945 toward the end of World War II. During the course of that war, President Franklin D. Roosevelt had made it clear that French Indochina needed to be transformed from a colony to an independent state or series of states under an international trusteeship. He argued on more than one occasion that the French needed to establish themselves as honest citizens before they could retake the reins of world power status. Roosevelt argued that, after nearly one hundred years, French colonialism had left Indochina worse off. He maintained that the people in that region deserved something better than a return to it. Roosevelt's death on 12 April 1945 marked the beginning of the turning point as he was replaced by Vice President Harry S. Truman.[2]

Truman did not share Roosevelt's global approach to postwar politics and instead focused on the safety and stability of Western Europe as it confronted the Soviet Union. Truman called for containing communism, and with that strategy he needed a strong France to serve as a bulwark against the potential for communist encroachment into Western Europe. Truman focused on Europe rather than the world, which made Indochina a sacrifice to the greater threat of communism. This shift in U.S. policy denied the Vietnamese, Cambodian, and Laotian people the opportunity to work toward self-government under the auspices of the United Nations. It was the first of many opportunities lost. A few months later, the August Revolution (Cách Mạng Tháng Tám), initiated by Hồ Chí Minh and the Indochinese Communist Party, sought to take over Vietnam before the French could regain power. The League for the Independence of Vietnam (Việt Nam Độc Lập Đồng Minh Hôi, or Việt Minh) controlled much of the northern part of Vietnam, including Hà Nội and Hải Phòng, and they held other major cities, such as Huế and Sài Gòn for a time. On 2 September, Hồ Chí Minh proclaimed the DRV using words borrowed from the American Declaration of Independence. He appealed to U.S. sensibilities in the declaration, but his communist past and Truman's determination to aid France rather than continue Roosevelt's wartime policy marked another opportunity lost. These events resulted in the start of the First Indochina War, which would dominate Southeast Asia until the war's completion in 1954.

In Laos, France's early surrender during the war encouraged nationalists to push for independence, which King Sisavang Vong declared in 1945. In September 1945, the three sections of Laos fabricated by the French—Vientiane, Champassak, and Luang Prabang—reunited under the Lao Issara (Free Laos) in a move toward independence. As in Vietnam, the French military ended the independence movement. Cambodia was able to gain a degree of autonomy from France after World War II and remained relatively peaceful until the 9 November 1953 agreement in which France granted its independence.[3]

This war's end would not result in a satisfactory outcome for all those now interested in Southeast Asia. While there were several moments during the First Indochina War that were significant for both the French and the Vietnamese, it was the last year of the war, 1954, that marks the next major turning point. Three events make this year significant: the Battle of Điện Biên Phủ, the Geneva Conference, and the movement of Vietnamese between the two zones set up by the Geneva Agreements. These events ended the war for one country, began it for another, and established the division of Vietnam that would exist until 1975.

The road to the Battle of Điện Biên Phủ began when the commander of the French Union Forces in Indochina, General Henri Navarre, established a fortress near the village of Điện Biên Phủ in December 1953. He committed to this venture after his original plan to consolidate his troops in the Red River Delta was frustrated by the action of People's Army of Vietnam (PAVN) general Võ Nguyên Giáp. Navarre believed that his fortress, along Route 19, would force the Vietnamese to battle and allow the French to utilize their superior firepower, specifically artillery and airpower, to destroy his enemy. Instead, Navarre's plan had the opposite effect as the Vietnamese surrounded and isolated the French Union Forces and initiated a prolonged siege that resulted in the surrender of the troops and fortress on 7 May 1954, one day before the Geneva Conference in Switzerland took up the question of Indochina. The battle was a decisive victory for the Vietnamese, whose position at Geneva was strengthened. It provided the Vietnamese with the advantage, which they used to exact the July 1954 Geneva Agreements and the end of the French colonial experiment in Indochina.[4]

On 21 July, representatives from France and the DRV signed the 48-article agreement that outlined the end of the First Indochina War. The U.S. refused to sign but issued a statement offering to respect the agreements if all other parties did the same. The Geneva Agreements divided Vietnam into two temporary countries along a line near the 17th parallel and provided for a general election to occur within two years to unify the country. The conference was the last great chance for peace in Indochina. For the French, it confirmed their exit from Indochina, though they remained in the region through most of the 1950s. For the Vietnamese, it was a victory but one that was incomplete, as Vietnam was divided physically and ideologically. For the U.S., it signaled a change in its Vietnamese policy that would be enhanced by another of the conditions of the final agreements.

The Geneva Agreements stipulated that the Vietnamese would have the right to move freely between the two Vietnams for a period of 300 days without hindrance. In the South, the president of the Council of Ministers for the State of Vietnam, Ngô Đình Diệm, organized Operation Exodus. He also requested assistance from the U.S., which initiated Operation Passage to Freedom. The operation started on 8 August and lasted for 10 months. It involved over 100 ships from the U.S. Navy and the movement of 310,000 of the total 810,000 Vietnamese who relocated from the North to the South. The operation introduced American servicemen to Vietnam, its people, and its culture and had a profound impact on the sailors and officers as well as on the myriad of government officials who worked with the Vietnamese to resettle and rehabilitate the northern refugee population. As one U.S. official commented at the end of the operation, the U.S. had morally married itself to the Vietnamese and their future by encouraging and then participating in that exodus to the South. These three major events of 1954 make it a significant year in the war.[5]

As a result of the 1954 Geneva Conference, Cambodia agreed to remain neutral, but under the leadership of Norodom Sihanouk it began to side with the DRV as it appeared that they might win the war. Sihanouk, like his fellow Cambodians, had an inherent distrust of the Vietnamese people and quickly entered into confrontation with the RVN over the border between the two countries. Internally, Sihanouk consolidated his power with the creation of the Sangkum Reastr Niyum (People's Socialist Community), which became the dominant force in Cambodian politics and was only directly confronted by the Pracheachon, a political organization of communists and Democrats. It was also during this time that the Laotian Pathet Lao, under the leadership of Prince Souphanouvong, worked with the Việt Minh against the French. This helped to establish a North Vietnamese presence in the country that would remain well after the next war concluded.[6]

By the end of the calendar year, the French had been defeated and were on their way out of Indochina, the U.S. began its nearly 20-year commitment to the Vietnamese people, the North Vietnamese had made a significant move toward independence only to be thwarted by Cold War politics, and the South Vietnamese started their long journey to forging a Republic and staving off communist encroachment in the south.

The next major turning point in the war occurred during the year 1960. Following Ngô Đình Diệm's policies in the late 1950s that caused serious consternation for those opposed to the Sài Gòn government, the insurgents began to intensify their efforts to create instability in the RVN. The year began with a 25 January 1960 attack by a unit labeled the 2nd Liberation Battalion against the compound of the 21st Army of the Republic of Vietnam (ARVN) Division at Tây Ninh. With increased insurgent action, the intrigue within Sài Gòn politics intensified. On 26 April 1960, 18 members of the Bloc for Liberty and Progress issued a proclamation referred to as the Caravelle Manifesto because these individuals, who were anticommunist politicians, businessmen, and religious leaders, signed the document in the famous Caravelle Hotel. The document criticized Ngô Đình Diệm and called for greater action against the insurgency as well as significant reforms and a decrease in power held by the president.[7]

The manifesto and the individuals associated with it influenced Americans in Sài Gòn who had already begun to turn against Ngô Đình Diệm. Among them was U.S. ambassador Elbridge Durbrow, who expressed his disillusionment with Ngô Đình Diệm and failed to support the president during the aborted 11 November 1960 coup d'état attempt initiated by some dissatisfied Vietnamese paratroopers and other ARVN personnel. While the attempted coup d'état had some impact on Ngô Đình Diệm, it was the failure of his U.S. allies to unconditionally support him that began the slow disintegration of U.S.-Vietnamese relations.

As the pace of the war increased, the insurgency reorganized with the creation of the National Front for the Liberation of South Vietnam (NLF), referred to by the U.S. and the RVN as the Cộng Sản Bắc Việt (Việt Cộng). The NLF was formed on 20 December 1960 in Tây Ninh province in the RVN in response to a new direction that the war in Vietnam had taken. Lê Duẩn, the Vietnamese Communist Party general secretary, called for armed confrontation to achieve his party's goals against the Sài Gòn government. The creation of the NLF was significant in both the U.S. and Southeast Asia. For those who opposed the DRV, the NLF confirmed that the insurgency was under their control. For those who opposed U.S. action in Southeast Asia, the NLF gave credence to the claim that a civil war existed in the RVN with the goal of replacing the oppressive Sài Gòn government.

While the situation in the RVN deteriorated, American attention was firmly fixed on Laos when in August 1960 army captain Kong Le initiated a successful coup d'état and returned Souvanna Phouma to the head of the government.

Souvanna Phouma was quickly replaced by General Phoumi Nosavan, who had the backing of the U.S. This political infighting allowed the Pathet Lao time to organize and present a legitimate threat to the U.S. efforts of peace in the region. By the end of the year, the situation was so precarious that President Dwight D. Eisenhower would warn incoming president John F. Kennedy that Laos was the keystone to stability in Southeast Asia. Cambodia was peaceful in comparison to Laos and the RVN, but its role in harboring the military officers responsible for the abortive 11 November coup d'état helped to maintain the tension between Sài Gòn and Phnom Penh.

The year 1960 marked the beginning of a more intense effort by the insurgents, supported by the DRV, to create instability in the South. Whether intentional or not, this effort was aided by internal dissent within Sài Gòn and was multiplied by the principal representative of the U.S. and his staff in the embassy, who worked, deliberately or not, to distance themselves from Ngô Đình Diệm. Once the slow descent into chaos began, there was nothing to stop the inevitable conclusion three years later in what would become the next major turning point in the war.

The year 1963 began with a significant battle that established, or confirmed to many, the problems of the ARVN. The year continued with political and religious unrest and a growing schism between Ngô Đình Diệm and the Americans that culminated in a coup d'état that overthrew Ngô Đình Diệm. The year ended with the assassination of John F. Kennedy and the beginning of the fulfillment of the Americanization of the war that Kennedy had moved toward during his tenure in office. On 2 January 1963, the 7th ARVN Division engaged the 261st Main Force Battalion near Ấp Bắc and the 415th Regional Battalion in Ấp Tân Thôi in the Mê Kông Delta. The U.S. encouraged the ARVN mission in order to restore confidence in the South Vietnamese, who had been shaken by a series of defeats in the region. The American adviser to the 7th ARVN Division, Lieutenant Colonel John Paul Vann, believed that the enemy force was small and that the ARVN use of superior technology would ensure a victory.

The NLF troops were more numerous than expected and were better prepared for the ARVN assault. During the course of the day, the NLF practiced strict fire discipline that earned them the element of surprise, while the ARVN commanders failed to adjust to the changing nature of the battlefield, which brought Vann to openly criticize his South Vietnamese counterparts. The battle was significant not only because the NLF had won their first large-scale battle against the ARVN, but it also brought to the forefront a group of reporters who assessed the battle as Vann had seen it, in all of its pessimism, and rejected the official military version. These reporters would be at the core of those within the media who continued to reject the official version of events in Vietnam in what would grow into the credibility gap. They would also work toward pushing American public opinion against Ngô Đình Diệm as 1963 continued. On the heels of the often criticized 1962 Strategic Hamlet Program, these reporters had many adherents and seemingly endless avenues to criticize the Sài Gòn government.

The next major event to shape the year was the Buddhist Crisis, which was a result of two events. The first was related to the Episcopal silver jubilee for Ngô Đình Thục, the archbishop of Huế and Ngô Đình Diệm's older brother, who during the celebration flew the white-and-gold Catholic flag. Under a decree promulgated by Ngô Đình Diệm earlier, this action was prohibited, but the Sài Gòn government did not enforce it. On 7 May 1963, Buddhists in Huế, as a part of a celebration marking the 2,507th anniversary of the birth of Buddha, wanted to fly the Buddhist flag. The Sài Gòn government refused the request. A demonstration against this decision was met with force, resulting in a clash between Buddhists and Huế security forces and several casualties, including nine deaths.[8]

While Ngô Đình Diệm promised to investigate the incident and work with the Buddhist leaders toward reconciliation, his actions were too slow. The RVN exploded when, on 11 June, a Buddhist monk, Thích Quảng Đức, committed the act of self-immolation on a busy street intersection in Chợ Lớn, a suburb of Sài Gòn. This act turned many within the U.S. against the Sài Gòn government. The crisis continued to escalate, with Buddhist demonstrations, public statements by the Ngô family that inflamed the crisis, and a continued failure by Ngô Đình Diệm to assign any blame for the events to members of his government or family.

When his brother, Ngô Đình Nhu, orchestrated what he called a countercoup on 21 August that targeted Buddhist pagodas in Sài Gòn and Huế, resulting in the arrest of hundreds of protestors and bystanders and the disappearance of even more, U.S. officials began to publicly distance themselves from the RVN president. A change in ambassadors, from the pro-Ngô Đình Diệm Frederick E. Nolting Jr. to the fiercely anti-Ngô Đình Diệm Henry Cabot Lodge Jr., signaled a shift in American policy toward Vietnam. On 1 November, this policy was finalized with the coup d'état that resulted in the assassination of Ngô Đình Diệm and Ngô Đình Nhu and marked the beginning of a major shift in America's Vietnam experience. While the assassination was not directly linked to anything that Lodge did as ambassador, the appearance of U.S. duplicity in the event was clear at the time. As Admiral Lorenzo Sabin, who commanded Task Force 90 during Operation Passage to Freedom in 1954, would write in an unpublished manuscript in the days that followed the assassination, "Ngo Dinh Diem has been destroyed. The most indomitable foe of communism in all Southeast Asia was betrayed in a coup d'état with the connivance of our own government and for which some day we shall have to account before the bar of human justice. It will require a lot of explaining to justify our part in the overthrow of a duly constituted government which we were assisting in a war against a common enemy."[9]

While 1964 saw many significant events that helped to shape the actions in Vietnam, such as the incident in the Gulf of Tŏn Kĭn and the congressional resolution that followed, the increased movement of PAVN troops into the RVN and their more aggressive action against the Sài Gòn government, and the instability of that government as no one cabinet could stabilize the political situation, it is 1965 that serves as the next major turning point in the war. From an American perspective, the early months of 1965 were marked with escalatory moves that increased the U.S. military commitment to support the ARVN, who were struggling. The year began in similar fashion to 1963 as Vietnamese Rangers and Airborne Battalions suffered a humiliating defeat at the Battle of Bình Giã. Increased NLF attacks against American positions, such as the mortaring of Camp Holloway, near Plei Ku in the Central Highlands, on 7 February and the 10 February attack of the American billet in Qui Nhơn, led to retaliatory attacks by air. Operation Flaming Dart preceded Operation Rolling Thunder, a sustained air campaign against the DRV that signaled to the North Vietnamese that the U.S. was committed to defending the RVN and punishing the North for its support of the NLF.

The first American combat troops arrived on 8 March, several days after the first Rolling Thunder sorties hit selected targets north of the 17th parallel. By June, additional combat troops arrived, and the U.S. altered its strategy from protecting enclaves that supported the air war to search-and-destroy operations designed to kill more of the enemy in the field than he could replace from reinforcements from the North. The 173rd Airborne Brigade conducted the first major operation between 28 and 30 June. With this new strategy, General Westmoreland pressed for additional troops; the initial number was 44 battalions, including at least nine from allied nations. Australia was the first to respond when it committed a battalion in April.[10]

Within the RVN, internal tension led to Buddhist protests similar to 1963 and another change of government in January that brought Nguyễn Khánh to power. On 18 June, Air Marshall Nguyễn Cao Kỳ assumed power in Sài Gòn, the ninth government change since the assassination of Ngô Đình Diệm. Nguyễn Cao Kỳ began to mobilize the RVN for a prolonged war. He extended martial law and a curfew in the cities, imposed price controls, cut government salaries, and broke off diplomatic relations with France. He also encouraged his military to conduct more active operations against the PAVN and NLF that, when coupled with the American effort, slowly stemmed the tide of the DRV's successful actions.

For the DRV, military operations continued to draw allied forces into the field, though they were able to avoid major engagements until the November Battle of the Ia Đrăng Valley. Politically, 1965 saw the North Vietnamese establish preconditions for beginning negotiations to end the war. On 8 April, DRV premier Phạm Văn Đồng outlined four points as conditions for negotiations and peace. He demanded Vietnamese independence, the removal of all foreign powers, a political settlement of the disputes between North and South, and the reunification of the two Vietnams. These points would remain fixed for the remainder of the war. The last requirement was unacceptable for the U.S.

While the U.S. focused on the war in Vietnam, the situations in Laos and Cambodia were interlinked with their eastern neighbors. In Laos, the U.S. initiated Operation Steel Tiger on 3 April to interdict the flow of personnel and supplies coming down the Hồ Chí Minh Trail. The trail had become more significant after the U.S. launched Operation Market Time in March and stopped sea infiltration from the DRV to the RVN. On 6 December, Westmoreland carved out the eastern section of Steel Tiger from the DMZ southward and placed it under MACV control with Operation Tiger Hound. This move made it easier to coordinate military operations in the RVN with air interdiction in Laos.

In the northern section of Laos, the U.S. continued with Operation Barrel Roll in support of the Royal Laotian Army's efforts against the Pathet Lao in the Plains of Jars. The Laotian war, which remained secret because of the earlier signing of the 1962 Geneva Agreements on Laos, was governed by the terrain and weather. During the dry season, U.S. and Laotian forces fought a defensive war against the Pathet Lao, who were supported by the PAVN, and an offensive war during the monsoon season. Victory was measured by control of the Lima Sites throughout the Plains of Jars and avoiding collapse. This would be the nature of the war in Laos until the 1970s.

Sihanouk continued to proclaim Cambodian neutrality, but he secretly made arrangements with the PAVN and NLF to ignore their presence along the Cambodian-RVN border in exchange for money and military supplies. Sihanouk also opened up the port of Sihanoukville to neutral ships that carried weapons and munitions to these soldiers fighting against U.S. and ARVN troops. Using the Hak Ly Company, a front for the NLF, war material was shipped overland and divided between the Cambodians under Sihanouk and the Vietnamese in the base areas along the border.[11] Just as President Lyndon B. Johnson was reluctant to expose American personnel in Laos because of its neutrality, he made Cambodia off limits to the U.S. military for fear that U.S. action there would widen the war in Southeast Asia.

By the end of 1965, there were approximately 180,000 Americans in Vietnam, while nearly 1,350 had been killed and approximately 5,300 wounded.

The RVN had lost nearly 10 times that number and four times the number wounded. It is estimated that PAVN and NLF losses were nearly 35,000. The year 1965 was significant in the war, as it marked the beginning of the Americanization of the war, in which the U.S. took over the military responsibility from the RVN while committing itself to a conflict for which it had not formally or officially declared war. The war would continue to escalate, seemingly without end, until there were approximately 540,000 U.S. personnel and 65,000 Third Country forces by 1968.

The U.S. had conducted a series of major operations with the ARVN to destroy the PAVN and NLF forces operating within the RVN, and while the enemy had not been destroyed, General Westmoreland proclaimed in November 1967 that the U.S. had seized the initiative on the battlefield and that the PAVN and NLF could no longer mount an effective offensive against the Free World Forces. The year 1968 would prove that statement false and usher in the most significant turning point of the war, marking the beginning of the end of U.S. involvement in Southeast Asia.

The year 1968 began with all eyes focused on the marine base at Khe Sanh. Located in the northwestern section of the RVN and approximately seven miles from the Laotian border along Route 9, Khe Sanh was used as a base from which the marines could observe and interdict North Vietnamese personnel and supplies traveling down the Hồ Chí Minh Trail. Fighting between the marines and PAVN started in April 1967, and by early 1968, North Vietnamese general Võ Nguyên Giáp had decided to force the U.S. to react to his pressure against Khe Sanh. Because Võ Nguyên Giáp had been the commander during the 1954 Battle of Điện Biên Phủ, many in the U.S. made parallels between the two episodes, even though they were uniquely different. The real purpose of Khe Sanh was to distract the U.S. from a larger PAVN and NLF offensive against most of the major urban areas and military facilities in the RVN.[12]

The North Vietnamese sought to take advantage of U.S. attention focused on Khe Sanh to infiltrate its personnel into the cities and launch their offensive, with the hope of sparking a national uprising and the overthrow of the Sài Gòn government. If the U.S. and ARVN diverted their attention away from Khe Sanh to deal with the Tết Offensive, Võ Nguyên Giáp hoped to overrun Khe Sanh and force a Điện Biên Phủ-like political settlement, with the U.S. withdrawing from Southeast Asia. Khe Sanh was held, and the base was eventually relieved on 8 April. Ironically, the base was abandoned and destroyed in July when it was deemed no longer significant, as the PAVN and NLF changed their strategy and tactics.

On 31 January, while the drama of Khe Sanh was unfolding, the PAVN and NLF orchestrated the Tết Offensive, which began on the first day of the holiday. The objective of the operation was to cause as much damage as possible to U.S. and ARVN forces in the RVN and to encourage a general uprising of the people against the Sài Gòn government. PAVN and NLF forces attacked every significant urban center, including nearly all of the provincial capitals, with major thrusts against Sài Gòn and Huế. In Sài Gòn, they attacked the U.S. embassy, the presidential palace, the radio station, the MACV compound, and the Tân Sơn Nhứt airfield. These attacks failed, but fighting continued in Chợ Lớn, a suburb of Sài Gòn, until the end of February. The destruction done to the capital was significant, as was the effect on the thousands of the city's inhabitants who lost their homes, businesses, and family members. In Huế, the PAVN and NLF overran the University of Huế and occupied most of the citadel until it was recaptured at the end of February after an intense fight. In addition to the destruction of many of the historic buildings inside the citadel, the PAVN and NLF executed over 3,000 Vietnamese.

Another significant consequence of the offensive was the 31 March 1968 announcement by Johnson that he would not seek or accept his party's nomination for the presidency in the 1968 presidential election and his order to initiate a bombing pause north of the 19th parallel. In the fall, Johnson would announce the end of Operation Rolling Thunder. The U.S. would not initiate a sustained campaign against the DRV until late 1971 in response to PAVN preparations for the Easter Offensive.

For the North Vietnamese, the Tết Offensive was a military failure. The South Vietnamese did not rise up against the Sài Gòn government, nor was there even a groundswell of support for those engaged in the offensive. Their casualties were estimated at 45,000, while the U.S. and RVN lost approximately 4,300 killed and 16,000 wounded. Another significant feature of the offensive was the destruction of the NLF, which had exposed itself during the offensive with dire consequences. The infrastructure of the NLF would never recover, though its units would continue to exist, with a growing percentage of North Vietnamese filling the ranks. Võ Nguyên Giáp's gamble had failed, though the political fallout in the U.S. and the failure of the U.S. to take advantage of the political vacuum created by the destruction of the NLF did provide some positives for the North Vietnamese.

Two additional mini-Tết offensives later in the year also proved to be military and political failures. However, it was not until November 1968 that the South Vietnamese finally agreed to an attempt to regain the initiative with the approval of the Accelerated Pacification Campaign (APC). Carried out by William Colby, who headed Civilian Operations and Revolutionary Development Support, the APC's objective was to improve existing security in contested hamlets by coordinating military operations and pacification teams. The program successfully secured nearly 1,110 formerly contested hamlets.

The APC also worked to improve rural militias, such as the Regional Forces, Popular Forces, and People's Self-Defense Force by increasing their training, upgrading their weapons, and putting continuous pressure on the enemy. The program was effective, but it was too late, as many within the U.S. had turned against the war and simply wanted their soldiers to return home.

Within the U.S., 1968 defined the antiwar movement with a series of mass demonstrations against the war throughout the country.[13] The episode at the Democratic Party National Convention in Chicago in the summer highlighted the bankruptcy of the incumbent party while a shocked nation watched police clash with protestors outside the convention hall and throughout the city. The antiwar movement had gained considerable credibility after the Tết Offensive, which had proven the "light at the end of the tunnel" position of the Johnson administration to be false. With Johnson announcing his intention not to seek reelection and the entry of Robert Kennedy into the Democratic Party primaries as an antiwar candidate, joining Eugene McCarthy who had already fared well in the New Hampshire primary, the antiwar movement seemed to have unstoppable momentum. Activities such as the protests at the Democratic Party National Convention in August and the earlier episode in Catonsville, Maryland, when on 17 May 1968, nine antiwar activists had broken into the office of Local Draft Board 33 and destroyed draft records using homemade napalm showed the extent to which the antiwar movement had escalated, but internal divisions would soon fracture the alliance of those opposed to the war.

The Chicago riots and Johnson's war policies brought to the surface the notion that the Democratic Party no longer had control of the country. This allowed the Republicans to enter the presidential race with a real chance to win. Their nominee, Richard Nixon, had legitimate credentials as a foreign policy expert and alluded to a plan to end the war with honor. When Nixon gained the White House in November, the American role in the Vietnam War would begin to diminish. Unfortunately for those who had to fight and those who opposed the conflict, it would take over four more years before the U.S. could disentangle itself from Southeast Asia.

The Nixon administration had little patience for the antiwar movement, and the active cadre opposed to the war soon worked as hard to discredit Nixon as they had Johnson. While major events would occur in 1970, including the Cambodian Incursion and the explosion of antiwar activity as a result of that event, and in 1971, such as Operation Lâm Sơn 719 and a move by Congress to regain some control over American foreign policy, it was 1972 that served as the next major turning point in the war. That year marked another presidential election in the U.S. as well as the largest North Vietnamese offensive in the war.

The Easter Offensive, which began on 30 March 1972, was the first major offensive by a communist country since the Chinese entered the Korean War in 1950. The offensive involved more than 125,000 men with 80,000 in reserve as well as the North Vietnamese supply of tanks and artillery against an ARVN army that was spread out over the RVN and a diminished American fighting force that had been depleted as a result of Vietnamization.[14] The offensive was the culmination of fears expressed by the U.S. military since the 1950s that had trained and organized the ARVN for such an event. The North Vietnamese had three main objectives in the operation. The first was a direct frontal assault across the DMZ into Quảng Trị province with the purpose of decimating the RVN Armed Forces and causing chaos and confusion in an attempt to demoralize the military and civilian population. The second objective was an attack in Kon Tum province with the purpose of dividing the RVN into two parts. Traditional military strategy held that the division of the RVN near route 19 would cause the Sài Gòn government to fall. The final objective was the occupation of An Lộc and the establishment of the Provisional Revolutionary Government of South Vietnam, which was to signal the beginning of a national uprising.

With a limited number of American combat troops in Vietnam and a presidential election looming in the U.S., the North Vietnamese decided to risk an all-out attack in the South. They based their decision on a number of factors, including the war weariness evident in the U.S. and highlighted by the antiwar movement, the failure of the South Vietnamese to successfully mount the 1971 Lâm Sơn 719 operation into Laos, and the need to inflict a defeat against the remaining U.S. troops that might sway the November presidential election toward the Democratic Party and its candidate George S. McGovern, who voiced opposition to continued involvement in the war. The North Vietnamese also believed that the people in the South were ready to overthrow the Sài Gòn government and only needed a catalyst to begin the process. In almost all cases, the North Vietnamese underestimated the willingness of Nixon to respond, the resolve of the ARVN defenders, and the mood of the South Vietnamese people.

In the two northernmost prongs of the attack, the PAVN achieved a high degree of surprise and success against the ARVN. In I CTZ, PAVN forces drove the ARVN troops to the northern part of Huế before a new commander, General Ngô Quang Trưởng, stabilized the front and began a counterattack that drove the PAVN attackers back to a position near their starting point in March. By October 1972, the northern front had stabilized. In Kon Tum, a similar fate occurred as ARVN forces were defeated and on the brink of collapse before President Nguyễn Văn Thiệu replaced the commander in the field, Ngô Dzu, with General Nguyễn Văn Toàn, who also stabilized the situation in the first few weeks of May and went on the offensive, driving the PAVN forces out of the area by the end of June. In both cases, the ARVN forces were aided by U.S. air and sea firepower, as well as by American advisers on the ground who helped to direct attacks against the exposed PAVN forces.

In the third prong, the Battle for An Lộc, three NLF Divisions of Front B-2 surrounded the ARVN defenders, though most of the NLF troops were regular PAVN officers and men. The ARVN forces held the city despite a 95-day siege. Again, with the assistance of American firepower and advisers, the ARVN went on the counteroffensive and regained the initiative in June. The battle was over in July. The 1972 Easter Offensive demonstrated that the ARVN soldier, when properly led and supported by firepower, was more than a match for the PAVN. It is estimated that the DRV took 50 percent casualties and lost a significant portion of their tanks and heavy artillery. There was no uprising of the people, and the PAVN commander, Võ Nguyên Giáp, was quietly replaced by his deputy, Văn Tiến Dũng. Nixon was reelected by an overwhelming margin, and the antiwar movement was unable to capitalize on the escalation of events. The North Vietnamese gamble had failed.

The U.S. supported the ARVN in their defense with two major air campaigns. The first, Operation Linebacker, had the objectives of eliminating all supply routes between the People's Republic of China and the DRV, destroying the war materials stockpiled to support the offensive, and interdicting any supplies entering the South. Nixon vowed to bomb the DRV as they had never been bombed before, which was something the DRV had not anticipated. Supplementing the estimated 40,000 sorties flown and the more than 125,000 tons of bombs of the aerial bombardment was the U.S. Navy, which fired over 100,000 shells into the DRV. Because the North had exposed its war machine in this overt attack, it was extremely vulnerable and suffered as a result.

Nixon also authorized the mining of Hải Phòng harbor, which effectively cut off the ability of the North Vietnamese to obtain supplies by sea. The Linebacker operation ended on 22 October 1972 after the DRV offensive had faltered and the ARVN had regained most of their lost territory. The second bombing campaign, Operation Linebacker II, also known as the Christmas Bombings, began on 18 December 1972 and lasted until 29 December 1972, with a brief pause in the middle. Nixon authorized the operation to punish the North Vietnamese for their obstinacy at the negotiation table and to destroy all of the major targets around Hà Nội and Hải Phòng. The objective of Linebacker II was to force the DRV back to the negotiating table. The U.S. launched approximately 1,400 sorties and dropped nearly 20,000 tons of bombs in the 12 days of the campaign. On 26 December, the DRV agreed to resume negotiations, which began on 8 January 1973. On

27 January, the parties involved in the war signed the Paris Peace Accords, which marked the official beginning of the end of America's involvement in Southeast Asia.

By 1975, the last year of the war, the U.S. Congress had orchestrated its own coup d'état against the executive in their struggle for control over U.S. foreign policy. On 19 June 1973, the Case-Church Amendment prevented further U.S. military involvement in Southeast Asia on or after 15 August by restricting funds to support combat activities in, over, and off the shore of Southeast Asia. Congress also passed the War Powers Resolution of 1973 (Public Law 93-148), which took away the president's ability to deploy combat troops overseas for a long period of time without congressional support. With these congressional obstacles in place, the U.S. watched as the North Vietnamese launched their final offensive in 1975, which culminated in the fall of Sài Gòn on 30 April 1975.

Before the capital of the RVN fell, the U.S. Congress severely cut back on its military spending for the RVN, and the U.S. abandoned its facilities. President Nguyễn Văn Thiệu resigned on 21 April with a farewell message that lambasted the U.S. for its failure to live up to its agreements made to protect the RVN after the signing of the Paris Peace Accords. Two days later, the last real resistance against the PAVN forces collapsed as the 18th ARVN Division finally retreated from a position near Xuân Lộc, north of Sài Gòn in Long Khánh province, after fighting three PAVN divisions, the 341st, 6th, and 7th, for 12 days. The rugged defense by ARVN troops, led by Major General Lê Minh Đảo, offered a final hope for the RVN, but it was too little, too late.

As Xuân Lộc fell, President Gerald Ford, who had taken over after the resignation of Nixon as a result of the Watergate scandal, told an audience at Tulane University that the U.S. could return to a time before Vietnam, but not by fighting in the war that was over as far as the U.S. was concerned. Abandoned by the U.S. and led under a caretaker government headed ironically by General Dương Văn Minh, who had assumed control of the government after the assassination of Ngô Đình Diệm, the remnants of the Sài Gòn government waited for the PAVN and NLF as they crashed through the gates of the presidential palace on 30 April 1975 after having broadcast the surrender of the RVN Armed Forces earlier in the day. The war in Vietnam was over, as was the conflict in Cambodia, while the communist takeover in Laos would be complete by the end of the year. The war was over, but turmoil, confusion, instability, and despair for the people of Southeast Asia would continue for years to come.

NOTES

1. For a good account of the last days of war, see David Butler, *The Fall of Saigon* (Simon & Schuster, 1985); and Larry Engelmann, *Tears Before the Rain: An Oral History of the Fall of Saigon* (Oxford University Press, 1990).

2. Gary R. Hess, "Franklin Roosevelt and Indochina," *Journal of American History* 59, no. 2 (September 1972): 353–68.

3. Arthur J. Dommen, *The Indochinese Experience of the French and the Americans: Nationalism and Communism in Cambodia, Laos, and Vietnam* (Indiana University Press, 2001), 89–92.

4. George C. Herring and Richard H. Immerman, "Eisenhower, Dulles, and Dienbienphu: 'The Day We Didn't Go to War' Revisited." *Journal of American History* 71, no. 2 (1984): 343–63.

5. Ronald B. Frankum Jr., *Operation Passage to Freedom: The United States Navy in Vietnam, 1954–1955* (Texas Tech University Press, 2007), 207.

6. Dommen, *The Indochinese Experience of the French and the Americans*, 305–17.

7. Bernard Fall, *The Two Vietnams* (Praeger, 1964), 435–36.

8. Robert Scigliano, "Vietnam: Politics and Religion." *Asian Survey* 4, no. 1 (1964): 666–73; and Moya Ann Ball, "A Case Study of the Kennedy Administration's Decision-Making Concerning the Diem Coup of November, 1963." *Western Journal of Speech Communication* 54, no. 4 (1990): 557–74.

9. Unpublished article by Admiral Lorenzo S. Sabin, "The Tragedy of Ngo Dinh Diem," Folder 9, Box 1, Papers of VADM Lorenzo S. Sabin, USN, 1954–1967, Operational Archives, Naval Historical Center, Washington, D.C.

10. George Herring, *America's Longest War: The United States and Vietnam, 1950–1975* (McGraw-Hill, 2002), 155–67; and John M. Carland, *Stemming the Tide: May 1965 to October 1966* (Center of Military History, 2000), 113–50.

11. Ronald B. Frankum Jr., *Like Rolling Thunder: The Air War in Vietnam, 1964–1975* (Rowman & Littlefield, 2005), 133–34.

12. For a good account of the Tết Offensive, see James H. Willbanks, *The Tet Offensive: A Concise History* (Columbia University Press, 2006).

13. Charles DeBenedetti, with Charles Chatfield, *An American Ordeal: The Antiwar Movement of the Vietnam Era* (Syracuse University Press, 1990) offers a good account of the antiwar movement.

14. For a good overview of the Easter Offensive, see Dale Andradé, *Trial by Fire: The 1972 Easter Offensive, America's Last Vietnam Battle* (Hippocrene, 1995); Lâm Quang Thi, *Hell in An Loc: The 1972 Easter Offensive and the Battle That Saved South Viet Nam* (University of North Texas Press, 2009); and Gerald H. Turley, *The Easter Offensive* (Presidio Press, 1985).

NUMBERS

173RD AIRBORNE BRIGADE. Approximately 3,500 men of the 173rd Airborne Brigade, known as the "Sky Soldiers," arrived in Vietnam on 7 May 1965, serving primarily in III **Corps Tactical Zone** under the **II Field Force, Vietnam**. The 1st and 2nd Battalion, 503rd Infantry Regiment and elements of the 1st Australian Regiment were assigned to the 173rd Airborne Brigade. Between 28 and 30 June 1965, the unit conducted the first major combat operation of the war to the northeast of **Sài Gòn**, in **War Zone D**. This would be the first of hundreds of operations for the **United States** Armed Forces designed to search for and destroy the enemy.

The 2nd Battalion, 503rd Regiment was involved in a number of these types of operations and had the distinction of participating in the only parachute jump of the war on 22 February 1967 during Operation **Junction City**. The 173rd fought in **War Zone C** and **War Zone D**, to the northwest of Sài Gòn in an area commonly referred to as the **Iron Triangle**. The unit served in Vietnam until 1971 and was deactivated on 14 January 1972, though it would be reactivated in 2000. Approximately 1,800 men of the brigade were killed during the war. The unit received 13 Medals of Honor and 46 Distinguished Service Crosses. *See also* ARMY, UNITED STATES; ATTLEBORO, OPERATION; BIÊN HÒA; DECKHOUSE, OPERATIONS; WASHINGTON GREEN, OPERATION.

44 BATTALION DEBATE. On 7 June 1965, General **William C. Westmoreland** requested an additional 35 battalions of combat troops and another nine in reserve in order to stave off defeat in Vietnam and begin the process of regaining the initiative. This request initiated the 44 battalion debate within the **Lyndon B. Johnson** administration as it marked a distinct change in the **United States'** involvement in Vietnam. The debate served as the last real chance for the **Doves** to prevent the Americanization of the war.

559TH TRANSPORT GROUP. Established in the **Democratic Republic of Vietnam** (DRV) in May 1959, the 559th Transport Group was tasked with organizing the logistic system that would become known as the **Hồ Chí Minh**

Trail. Initially comprised of 24,000 men, most of whom had relocated to the North after the 1954 **Geneva Agreements**, the unit was spread along the trail that stretched from the DRV to the **Republic of Vietnam** (RVN) via **Laos** and **Cambodia**. The 559th Transport Group, under the command of Colonel Vo Bam, continued its missions throughout the war and was instrumental in frustrating the **United States'** attempts to end the North Vietnamese infiltration of personnel and supplies into the RVN. *See also* 759TH TRANSPORT GROUP; ĐỒNG SĨ NGUYÊN; HOÀNG VĂN THÁI.

7TH AIR FORCE. The **United States** 7th Air Force replaced the 2nd Air Division on 1 April 1966, paving the way for a larger commitment of air assets in Vietnam under a more unified command and control structure. The commander of the 7th Air Force reported directly to the Military Assistance Command, Vietnam, and to the commander-in-chief, Pacific Air Force, but did not have the expanded area of responsibility that the 2nd Air Division held. The 7th Air Force directed air operations from bases in the Republic of Vietnam while the 13th Air Force managed air operations originating in **Thailand**. *See also* AIR FORCE, UNITED STATES.

759TH TRANSPORT GROUP. In May 1959, the **Democratic Republic of Vietnam** (DRV) established the **559th Transport Group** to coordinate the movement of personnel and supplies from the North into the **Republic of Vietnam**. The DRV also attempted to infiltrate by sea but had limited success in 1959 and 1960. On 23 October 1961, the 759th Transport Group was established with the mission of sea infiltration. At first, the **National Liberation Front** was required to send its vessels north to receive supplies, but slowly the 759th Transport Group developed a fleet of vessels to assist in the process. The first successful shipment arrived at **Cà Mau** at the southern end of the **Mê Kông Delta** in September 1962. By the end of 1963, over 1,400 tons of supplies had been delivered, including heavy weapons. The DRV recognized that seaborne infiltration proved to be more efficient than land routes through **Laos**. On 24 January 1964, the 759th Transport Group was designated Group 125. Seaborne infiltration continued unabated until the **United States** initiated Operation **Market Time** in March 1965, which proved to be a most effective deterrent and forced the DRV to further develop the **Hồ Chí Minh Trail**.

I FIELD FORCE, VIETNAM. Corps-level field command established in **Nha Trang** on 15 March 1966 to coordinate **United States Army** activities in II **Corps Tactical Zone**. It was dismantled on 30 April 1971 when, as a result of **Vietnamization**, a majority of the U.S. Army ground combat troops had withdrawn from Vietnam. It was succeeded by the 2nd Regional Assistance Command.

II FIELD FORCE, VIETNAM. Corps-level field command established in **Long Bình** on 15 March 1966 to coordinate **United States Army** activities in III **Corps Tactical Zone**, which included the provinces around **Sài Gòn**. It was the largest Corps command in Vietnam. It was dismantled on 2 May 1971 when, as a result of **Vietnamization**, a majority of the U.S. Army ground combat troops had withdrawn from Vietnam. It was succeeded by the 3rd Regional Assistance Command.

A

A SHAU, BATTLE OF. A March 1966 battle in the A Shau Valley that resulted in the loss of a **United States Special Forces** camp and a significant number of **People's Army of Vietnam** (PAVN) forces. The A Shau Special Forces Camp was positioned in **Thừa Thiên** province near an infiltration point into the **Republic of Vietnam** from **Laos** along the **Hồ Chí Minh Trail**. The camp was manned by 10 U.S. Special Forces personnel and over 200 **Civilian Irregular Defense Group** personnel. In early March, the camp received **intelligence** that it was about to be overrun by elements of the 325th PAVN Division. On 7 March, seven additional Special Forces personnel and a Mobile Strike Force Command company, made up of **Montagnards**, reinforced the camp. Taking advantage of poor weather conditions, the PAVN attacked in the early hours of 9 March. The attack continued through 10 March, forcing the defenders to abandon camp by the early evening hours. The loss of the camp and the PAVN effort to overrun it reinforced the importance of the A Shau Valley to the North Vietnamese strategy. The A Shau Valley was the scene of many operations throughout the war.

ABILENE, OPERATION. A **search-and-destroy** operation centered in Phước Tuy province. It began on 30 March 1966 and lasted until 15 April 1966. The Free World Force consisted of elements of the 1st **Division** and 173rd Airborne Brigade with the 1st Battalion of the Royal Australian Regiment and the 161st **New Zealand** Artillery Battery against a **National Liberation Front** (NLF) battalion. While search-and-destroy was a significant part of the mission, the operation was also designed to eliminate known NLF bases in an area approximately 48 to 64 kilometers (30 to 40 miles) to the east of **Sài Gòn**. The **United States** and Australia claimed 81 NLF soldiers killed. The operation culminated on 11 and 12 April during the Battle of Xã Cẩm Mỹ when the NLF's D800 Battalion ambushed C Company, 2nd Battalion, 16th Infantry, 1st Infantry Division. The overnight battle cost the U.S. 38 killed and 71 wounded, which represented over 80 percent of the company. This battle soured any success achieved by the U.S. and Australia during the 45-day operation.

ABLE MARBLE, PROJECT. The name for a **United States** air **reconnaissance** task force deployed to the Don Muang Royal Thai Air Force Base in November 1961 to conduct reconnaissance flights over **Laos**. In December 1961, Able Marble personnel redeployed to Tân Sơn Nhứt Air Base in **Sài Gòn** and began assisting the **Republic of Vietnam** and U.S. **advisers** in gathering **intelligence** for military operations. Able Marble personnel remained in Vietnam and were eventually consolidated into the 460th Tactical Reconnaissance Wing after the introduction of U.S. ground troops.

ABRAMS, CREIGHTON WILLIAMS, JR. (1914–1974). Commander of the **Military Assistance Command, Vietnam** (MACV), and chief of staff of the **United States Army**. Abrams had a distinguished career in World War II in George Patton's 3rd Army. He served as a tank commander in the 1st Armored Division, a battalion commander in, and commander of, the 37th Armored Region, and on the Army General Staff at the end of the war. After the war, he served in a variety of positions including commander of the 2nd Armored Cavalry, chief of staff for the I, IX, and X Corps in Korea, and for the Armor Center at Fort Knox. He also was the deputy assistant chief of staff for reserve components, assistant division commander, and then commander, of the 3rd Armored Division, and assistant deputy chief of staff and director of operations in the Office of the Deputy Chief of Staff for Operations. Before the Vietnam War, he served as the acting vice chief of staff and vice chief of staff of the U.S. Army and was promoted to general in September 1964.

In Vietnam, Abrams served as the deputy commander MACV from 1967 to 2 July 1968 and replaced **William C. Westmoreland** as commander. He was responsible for initiating the **Accelerated Pacification Campaign** that attempted to take advantage of the **National Liberation Front** defeat as a result of the 1968 **Tết Offensive**. Abrams oversaw the completion of the **Vietnamization** program, the 1970 incursion into **Cambodia**, and the failed **Lam Sơn 719** operation in 1971. He commanded the remnants of the U.S. Armed Forces during the 1972 **Easter Offensive** and, as chief of staff of the army, managed the end of the draft and the reorganization of the U.S. Army. He served as commander until 12 October 1972, when he assumed the position of chief of staff of the U.S. Army, a title he would hold until his death on 4 September 1974. *See also* RECONDO SCHOOL; VIETNAMIZATION; WEYAND, FREDERICK CARLTON.

ACHESON, DEAN GOODERHAM (1893–1971). Secretary of state under Harry S. Truman. Acheson was educated at Yale and Harvard universities and entered public life as undersecretary of the Treasury in 1933, where he soon became acting secretary. He resigned that position in November 1933 because of a disagreement with President Franklin D. Roosevelt over financial policy. Acheson returned to public service in 1941 as an assistant secretary of state and worked toward the postwar peace by playing a role in the Bretton Woods Conference. In 1945, Acheson became undersecretary of the Department of State and was involved in many of the Cold War events in the postwar years. He replaced George C. Marshall as secretary of state on 21 January 1949 and remained in that position until 20 January 1953.

After the outbreak of the Korean War in 1950, Acheson pushed for **United States** recognition of the three Associated States and advocated sending military aid to **France** in its fight to hold on to Indochina. Acheson returned to his law practice during the Dwight D. Eisenhower administration. He was instrumental in assisting **John F. Kennedy** in his run for the White House in 1960. He served as an informal adviser and elder statesman during the Kennedy and **Lyndon B. Johnson** administrations even though he would turn against the war after the 1968 **Tết Offensive**. Before his death in 1971, Acheson also served as an adviser to the **Richard M. Nixon** administration. In 1970, he wrote his memoirs, *Creation: My Years in the State Department*, which won the Pulitzer Prize in History. *See also* CITIZEN'S COMMITTEE FOR PEACE WITH FREEDOM IN VIETNAM; RUSK, DAVID DEAN.

ADVISERS. The **United States** and **Third Country** forces provided both civilian and military advisers to the **Republic of Vietnam** (RVN) over a period of 25 years. The U.S. set up its **Military Assistance Advisory Group** (MAAG), Indochina, in 1950 as a result of the Korean War and the threat of communism in Asia. Advising efforts were minimal until after the 1954 **Geneva Conference**, which marked the beginning of the end of French involvement in Southeast Asia. During the 300-day period of **refugee** movement between the two temporary zones established by the Geneva Conference, U.S. advisers began to arrive in Vietnam to aid in the resettlement and rehabilitation of those who chose to move south. Members of the U.S. Overseas Mission and Special Technical and Economic Missions worked with MAAG personnel to fill the void left by the French.

The Geneva Conference limited the number of U.S. advisers in Vietnam to 342. The U.S. worked around this limit when, on 9 February 1956, it announced the creation of the **Temporary Equipment Recovery Mission** (TERM). In June 1956, TERM personnel began to arrive in Vietnam with two major objectives. Its public mission was supervising the recovery and removal of Mutual Defense Assistance Program equipment that the U.S. had provided to the French during the **First Indochina War**. Privately, its mission was also to improve the logistical capabilities of the newly created **Army of the Republic of Vietnam** (ARVN). The TERM increased the number of

U.S. personnel in Vietnam from 342 to 692. TERM personnel were assigned to ARVN military units and focused on logistics, medical, quartermaster, transportation, ordnance, engineer, and signal units. The **International Control Commission** never agreed to the TERM, and in December 1958 it passed a resolution that called for the mission to leave by 30 June 1959. In May 1960, the TERM was absorbed into the MAAG, making the temporary mission permanent while the U.S. ceiling for advisers rose to 685.

The number of U.S. advisers in Vietnam increased dramatically during the presidency of **John F. Kennedy**. Kennedy also authorized a changed role for these personnel who became more involved in combat operations. Advisers, such as the U.S. Army **Special Forces**, were charged with the creation of a counterpart and also helped to create the **Civilian Irregular Defense Group** while **Air Force** advisers arrived to help improve the **RVN Air Force**. Additional advisers joined Vietnamese navy and marine units while the number of U.S. personnel attached to ARVN units grew each month. **Australia** also began providing advisers in May 1962, followed by the **Republic of Korea**, **New Zealand**, and the **Philippines** within the year.

In 1965, the military mission of the U.S. changed from an advisory effort to one of Americanizing the war with the introduction of combat troops. The number of U.S. advisers, or Cố Vấn (counterpart), continued to increase during the 1960s, though the main American focus was on U.S. **search-and-destroy** operations. When President **Richard M. Nixon** announced the policy of **Vietnamization** in July 1969, marking the beginning of U.S. combat troop withdrawal, the number of advisers increased. By 1971, the estimated 14,000 advisers also began to withdraw, though their effectiveness remained. This was especially true during the 1972 **Easter Offensive** as advisers provided invaluable assistance to their ARVN units in successfully countering the massive **Democratic Republic of Vietnam** invasion.

The U.S. also provided advisers in **Laos** and **Cambodia** during the war. In Laos, the advisers who had arrived as early as 1959 were hampered by the secretive nature of the war in that country, while Americans in Cambodia did not arrive until late in the war and were unable to make a significant difference there. In December 1970, a revision of the **Cooper-Church Amendment** was attached to the Supplementary Foreign Assistance Act of 1970. Public Law 91-652 was put into effect on 5 January 1971, and while it was less restrictive than the original amendment, it did end the U.S. advisory effort in Cambodia.

The U.S. advisory effort in Southeast Asia had mixed results. Advisers followed the same **tour of duty** concept as the regular soldiers. They were rotated in their assignments every six months. This meant that it was difficult to sustain a relationship with the Vietnamese troops to which they were assigned. The language barrier and lack of trust were two major obstacles, as was the difference in objectives between U.S. and RVN officers. U.S. advisers spent a limited amount of time with their Vietnamese units and had a strong desire to make a positive and lasting effect, while the Vietnamese officers had been fighting for years before the adviser arrived and knew that the fighting would continue well after the adviser left for another assignment. This created the impression by some Americans that the RVN Armed Forces were lazy and did not want to fight for their country, as advisers were often ignored. The reality was that the RVN had been fighting for 10 years before the first U.S. combat troops arrived and would spend 20 years fighting a war for their own survival.

The DRV also received advisers from the **People's Republic of China** (PRC) and the **Soviet Union** during the war, though reliable estimates on the number of personnel involved are not available. The PRC advisers were involved in the battle as early as the 1950s. Advisers played a number of roles within the DRV but were mostly involved in military and political **propaganda** training. Like their PRC counterparts, the Soviet advisers assisted in teaching the PAVN forces how to operate the weapons systems delivered to the DRV. Because of the nature of the **air war** over the DRV, these advisers did experience combat, though the nature of that contact remains unclear. *See also* ABLE MARBLE, PROJECT; COUNTERINSURGENCY; HOTFOOT, PROJECT; LONG-RANGE PATROL; MÊ KÔNG DELTA; PACIFICATION; SELF-DEFENSE CORPS; WHITE STAR, PROJECT.

AERIAL REFUELING. During the **United States** air war over the **Democratic Republic of Vietnam** (DRV), it was necessary to refuel the aircraft conducting air strikes. In order to conduct aerial refueling, the U.S. used the KC-135 Stratotanker, which was a version of the Boeing 717. This aircraft made it possible for U.S. aircraft to **bomb** the DRV and avoid the most intense air defense pockets by taking a longer, more circumspect path to the target. *See also* AIRCRAFT (CARGO TRANSPORT), UNITED STATES.

AEROMEDICAL EVACUATIONS (MEDEVAC). The 315th Air **Division** and 834th Air Division were responsible for aeromedical evacuations. The units used **helicopters**, known as **Dustoffs**, which allowed them to transport the wounded from the battlefield quickly, in minutes rather than hours, to field hospitals where they were treated or stabilized. This gave the soldiers in the war a greater chance of surviving their wounds than in any previous war. The **United States** also used C-134 and C-141 aircraft to move more seriously wounded personnel to more permanent facilities in **Guam**, the **Philippines**, or Japan. *See also* TACTICAL AIRLIFT.

AGENT ORANGE. A herbicide used in Operation **Ranch Hand** that received its name by the colored band on the 55-gallon drums used to transport it. Each herbicide used had special advantages. Agent Orange was the most common herbicide used during the war, accounting for almost 60 percent of herbicides sprayed. Over 12 million gallons were dispersed during the war in an effort to destroy food crops used to support the **National Liberation Front** (NLF), to deny jungle coverage for **People's Army of Vietnam** (PAVN) and NLF forces, and to destroy vegetation near major roads and waterways from which the PAVN and NLF launched ambushes. Agent Orange, a mixture of 2,4-D (2,4, dichlorophenoxyacetic acid) and 2,4,5-T (2,4,5 trichlorophenoxyacetic acid), worked well on broadleaf vegetation, as did Agent White, also a mixture of 2,4-D (2,4, dichlorophenoxyacetic acid) and 2,4,5-T (2,4,5 trichlorophenoxyacetic acid), though it had a low volatility. Agent Blue consisted of sodium cacodylate and dimethylarsinic acid and was very effective on grass targets. It was a water-based desiccant and killed as it dried. Herbicides, like Agent Orange, used during the war were very controversial after the conflict was over, as they were sometimes linked to life-threatening illnesses. *See also* GUAM; ZUMWALT, ELMO RUSSELL, JR.

AGNEW, SPIRO THEODORE (1918–1996). Republican senator and **United States** vice president. Agnew received his education at Johns Hopkins University and the University of Baltimore. He served in the U.S. Army during World War II in the Western Theater, winning the Bronze Star. After the war, Agnew practiced law and entered politics in 1961 when he won an election to be a county executive. He became the first Republican to win election in Baltimore County in the 20th century. In 1966, Agnew was elected governor of Maryland where he earned his conservative credentials on a national scale, in part for his actions against **antiwar** activists and the more radical elements of the civil rights movement. In the election of 1968, Agnew supported Nelson Rockefeller before turning his support to President **Richard M. Nixon**, which earned him the vice presidency when Nixon won the election.

While in the executive branch, Agnew generated a high level of animosity from senators and White House officials who disagreed with his approach to politics and his perception of the role of the Office of the Vice President to initiate policy. Agnew became a focal point of criticism for the Nixon administration because of his outspoken disdain of the **media** and its reporting of Nixon's policies. Nixon unleashed Agnew on the media in order to focus its inevitable negative response on the vice president rather than the president and to vocalize the White House's disgust with the low level of professionalism exhibited by the press. Agnew's role as critic of the press and of the antiwar movement revitalized his political value in the White House.

While Agnew wanted to play a greater role in U.S. foreign policy, he was restrained by Nixon, who saw that as his own preserve. He assumed a more conservative, anticommunist position than Nixon, as the president sought to open relations with the **People's Republic of China** and the **Soviet Union**. Agnew's criticism of Nixon's policies eventually led Nixon to seek an alternative to the vice president, even if it meant forcing Agnew to resign, though this strategy would not work. Events would transpire that made it unnecessary for Nixon to force Agnew out of office. In April 1973, information surfaced that Agnew had engaged in questionable financial practices and actions as governor of Maryland.

Agnew eventually settled his financial issues by paying back taxes on income earned and paying a fine, and in turn he received a suspended sentence. On 10 October 1973, Agnew resigned, the first vice president to resign since John C. Calhoun in the 1830s. Agnew moved to California and engaged in international business. He isolated himself from discussions of his role in the White House and his legacy within the Nixon administration. *See also* CLIFFORD, CLARK MCADAMS; FORD, GERALD RUDOLPH.

AGROVILLE PROGRAM. A **pacification** program created as a response to the communist insurgent program of **Trụ Giãn** (targeted assassination) established by the **Ngô Đình Diệm** government in 1959. In a July 1959 radio broadcast commemorating the fifth anniversary of his rise to power, Ngô Đình Diệm announced the creation of the program, which was described as a plan to concentrate the people into protected villages. Agrovilles would have all the amenities that villages lacked. Peasants would have access to electricity, schools, medical facilities, and doctors, as well as other infrastructure that would markedly increase their quality of life. While not mentioned in the broadcast, another important goal of the Agroville Program was the creation of centers for the people, to protect them against the increased communist insurgent threat. The insurgents had preyed upon the people by taxing them, recruiting from their ranks, and receiving **intelligence** on the disposition of the **Army of the Republic of Vietnam** troops operating in their area. By denying the insurgency access to the people and providing the peasants with the benefits of modernization, Ngô Đình Diệm hoped to deny the insurgency its most potent resource.

While sound in theory, the Agroville Program was not well implemented. Because Agrovilles were placed in areas of strategic importance along major roads or waterways, the ground chosen was not always the most fertile for agriculture. Peasants were forced to move away from their ancestral lands to the agrovilles and oftentimes had to leave behind their cultivated crops. If they completed all of their required work in the agroville, the peasants had the opportunity to tend to their own crops, but without the protection offered in the agroville. This created hardships for many people, as did the implementation of the corvée labor system, which required communal work within the agroville before individuals could tend to their personal needs.

Another problem with agrovilles was security. A planned community would have some type of barrier around it made up of a mud wall, sharpened bamboo sticks, or barbed wire with sentry stations. These obstructions did not always provide more protection inside the agroville as opposed to outside the compound. This made it hard to return to old fields to maintain or harvest existing crops. It was also difficult for officials to travel between secured areas at night, when the insurgents operated. Ultimately, the Agroville Program failed to achieve its desired results, and no new agrovilles were begun after the middle of 1961. The next year, a modification of the program surfaced with the **Strategic Hamlet Program**. The Agroville Program failed to completely protect the people, it did not deliver on its promise of modernity, and ultimately it did not improve the lives of the people. While the theory behind the program was sound, it was not implemented properly, and as a result it incurred the resentment of the Vietnamese people and many **United States** officials in the **Republic of Vietnam**.

AIR AMERICA. An airline owned by the **Central Intelligence Agency** (CIA) that aided in the secret war in **Laos**. Air America's origins date back to 1950 when the CIA realized that it needed air assets to assist in covert operations in Asia. It purchased the Civil Air Transport (CAT), which had been operating in China. In May 1953, CAT aircraft and personnel were introduced into the **First Indochina War** to support French operations in Laos. Flying the C-119, CAT provided air missions until July 1953. CAT pilots returned to Indochina in March 1954 to aid the beleaguered French Union Forces at **Điện Biên Phủ** until the fortress's fall on 7 May 1954. CAT aircraft and personnel remained in Indochina and assisted in Operation Exodus, the Vietnamese evacuation of people from the **Democratic Republic of Vietnam** to the South.

CAT returned to Southeast Asia in September 1956 when it provided humanitarian relief to Laos. It returned to Laos permanently in July 1957 to aid the Royal Laotian Government in its fight against the **People's Army of Vietnam** and **Pathet Lao**. As the war intensified and the Vientiane government underwent a period of instability, the **United States** focused more resources and attention in Laos, which was paralleled by increased CAT involvement. On 26 March 1959, CAT changed its name to Air America in order to separate CAT's non-Southeast Asian operations from its work in Laos. Air America aircraft and personnel played a significant role in the war in Laos, providing such services as **search-and-rescue**, **airmobility**, air transport of personnel and materials, fire support missions, and training. Air America made it possible for the U.S. to conduct its war in Laos without drawing attention to America's increasing involvement in that neutral country. In April 1972, Director of Central Intelligence **Richard Helms** ordered the CIA to end its relationship with Air America. By June 1974, the last Air America personnel left Laos, though operations in the RVN continued until the fall of **Sài Gòn** in April 1975. Air America ceased to exist on 30 June 1976. *See also* AIRCRAFT (CARGO TRANSPORT), UNITED STATES; FORWARD AIR CONTROLLER.

AIR COMMANDOS. On 14 April 1961, the **United States** established the 4400th Combat Crew Training Squadron (CCTS) in response to the need for air commandos to assist in **counterinsurgency** operations around the world. Based on similar units employed during World War II, the 4400th CCTS included C-47, B-26, and T-28 aircraft and had an initial strength of 124 officers and 228 enlisted personnel. On 6 November 1961, Detachment 2 of the 4400th CCTS, with the code name Project **Jungle Jim** and under Operation **Farm Gate**, was ordered to Vietnam. The unit was stationed at **Biên Hòa** and trained the **Republic of Vietnam Air Force** in air operations. The detachment also helped to coordinate air activities outside of the **Military Assistance Advisory Group**. On 1 June 1963, the 4400th CCTS was redesignated the 1st Air Commando Squadron (Composite). It flew its first mission on 8 July 1963. The unit flew the C-47 gunship and transitioned from the B-26 and T-28 to the A-1 Skyraider. It moved to **Plei Ku** in February 1966 and was redesignated the 1st Air Command Squadron, Fighter in August 1967, and the 1st Special Operations Squadron in August 1968. The unit remained in Vietnam until 7 November 1972 and returned to Vietnam for a brief period from 15 December 1972 to 28 January 1973.

Additional air commando units arrived in Vietnam with the Americanization of the war. Starting in 1966, the 5th Air Commando Squadron conducted psychological warfare missions from **Nha Trang**, using C-47 and U-10 aircraft. It dropped pamphlets and broadcast messages to the **People's Army of Vietnam** and the **National Liberation Front** from loudspeakers as part of the **Chiêu Hồi** program and to warn civilians of impending military operations. Other air commando units flew from Nakhon Phanom, **Thailand**. The 56th Air Commando Wing was activated in March 1967 and redesignated the 56th Special Operations Wing in August 1968. It flew in missions over **Laos**, including Operation **Commando Lava**, with the objective of disrupting the **Hồ Chí Minh Trail** by breaking down the soil to cause excessive mud and landslides. It also assisted in **search-and-rescue** missions.

AIR FORCE, REPUBLIC OF VIETNAM (RVNAF). Known as the Không Quân Việt Nam, the RVNAF remained relatively small until the introduction of **United States** combat personnel in 1965. In the 1950s, U.S. **advisers** trained the RVNAF in the use of **helicopters**, including the H-19 and H-34. The first fixed-wing aircraft used by the RVNAF was the T-28 Trojan, though later in the war the Vietnamese employed the AC-47 and AC-119 gunships, A-1 Skyraider, A-37 Dragonfly, and the F-5 Freedom Fighters. These were among the more notable types of aircraft employed by the South Vietnamese. Though the RVNAF started with modest numbers, by 1972 it was one of the largest air forces in the world with nearly 1,500 fixed-winged aircraft and over 500 helicopters. Under the leadership of **Nguyễn Cao Kỳ** in its formative years, the RVNAF conducted tens of thousands of **sorties** during the war, including the second major strike against the **Democratic Republic of Vietnam** (DRV) in Operation **Flaming Dart**, which was the brief air campaign in response to February 1965 **National Liberation Front** attacks against American personnel and facilities in the **Central Highlands**.

As the ground and air war escalated, the RVNAF limited its sorties over the DRV, because of the MiG aircraft threat, and focused instead on air-to-ground support missions for the Republic of Vietnam Armed Forces. The RVNAF stationed its fixed-wing aircraft at **Đà Nẵng**, **Nha Trang**, Phan Rang, Bình Thủy, **Plei Ku**, **Biên Hòa**, Phu Cat, and **Tân Sơn Nhứt**. Its helicopter squadrons were located at Bình Thủy, Đà Nẵng, Nha Trang, Biên Hòa, Sóc Trăng, Plei Ku, Phu Cat, and Tân Sơn Nhứt. With **Vietnamization** beginning in July 1969, the RVNAF expanded its mission, but as the U.S. pulled out of the area, the RVNAF began to suffer from maintenance and supply issues. It was not able to make a significant impact in the final **People's Army of Vietnam** offensive in 1974–1975, with the exception of aiding the **Army of the Republic of Vietnam**'s 18th Division during its battle at **Xuân Lộc**.

AIR FORCE, UNITED STATES (USAF). **United States** air assets were involved in a variety of roles in Southeast Asia as early as 1954, though it was not until the reactivation of the **7th Air Force** on 28 March 1966 that a more formal command structure was put into place. The 7th Air Force was responsible for 10 bases in the **Republic of Vietnam** (RVN) and oversaw the **bombing** responsibilities for **Route Packages** V and VIa in Operation **Rolling Thunder**. It conducted a majority of the air **sorties** in the RVN. The 7th Air Force conducted hundreds of thousands of sorties during the war in Southeast Asia, with such missions as bombing, air-to-ground support, **reconnaissance**, **search-and-rescue**, transportation, and cargo lift. In March 1973, as a result of the agreements reached in Paris on 27 January 1973, the 7th Air Force's command was transferred to **Thailand**. It was deactivated on 30 June 1975.

AIR WAR • 31

The 13th Air Force operated from Thailand and was involved in similar operations as the 7th Air Force, though it concentrated on operations over the **Democratic Republic of Vietnam** (DRV), **Laos**, and **Cambodia**. The U.S. established nine major bases in Thailand to support the efforts of the 13th Air Force, as well as a series of minor installations that took care of the over 30,000 personnel officially assigned to the unit. Three chiefs of staff were involved during the most significant period of USAF involvement in Southeast Asia.

Curtis E. LeMay, who served as the USAF chief of staff from 30 June 1961 to 31 January 1965, advocated the heavy use of strategic bombing to pressure the DRV to end its support of the **National Liberation Front** and enter into negotiations toward a peaceful resolution. His successor, John P. McConnell, who served from 1 February 1965 to 31 July 1969, was also an advocate of bombing the DRV and oversaw Operation Rolling Thunder. McConnell called for increased bombing in order to limit the need for ground troops in the RVN. On 1 August 1969, John D. Ryan took over as chief of staff. Ryan was not as adamant in advocating the use of strategic bombing and in fact was involved in the controversy with General **John Lavelle**, the commander of the 7th Air Force, who had authorized air strikes against unauthorized targets claiming that the U.S. aircraft had been attacked first. Ryan remained the chief of staff until 31 July 1973. The other chiefs of staff to preside during the war were George S. Brown, who served between 1 August 1973 and 30 June 1974, and David C. Jones, who served from 1 July 1974 to 30 June 1978. Both also served as the chairman of the **Joint Chiefs of Staff**. *See also* AIR WAR; AIRBORNE BATTLEFIELD COMMAND AND CONTROL CENTERS; AIRCRAFT (BOMBERS), UNITED STATES; AIRCRAFT (CARGO TRANSPORT), UNITED STATES; AIRCRAFT (FIGHTER), UNITED STATES; AIRCRAFT (RECONNAISSANCE), UNITED STATES; ARC LIGHT MISSIONS; BOLO, OPERATION; BOMBING PAUSES; COMMANDO VAULT, OPERATION; DIRTY THIRTY; FACT SHEET, OPERATION; JUNGLE JIM, PROJECT; LINEBACKER I, OPERATION; LINEBACKER II, OPERATION; LORAN; NIAGARA, OPERATION; POPEYE, PROJECT; PROUD DEEP ALPHA; QUICK REACTION FORCE; RAVEN; STEEL TIGER, OPERATION; TAILWIND, OPERATION; TALLY HO, OPERATION; TIGER HOUND, OPERATION; TRUSCOTT WHITE, OPERATION; WATERPUMP, PROJECT; WOMEN, UNITED STATES.

AIR WAR. The air war in Southeast Asia was one of the longest and most intense efforts during the war. It encompassed missions over the **Democratic Republic of Vietnam** (DRV), the **Republic of Vietnam** (RVN), **Laos**, and **Cambodia**. It included flights originating from these countries, as well as **Thailand** and **Guam**, and from **United States** carriers in the Gulf of Tŏn

Kĭn and the South China Sea. While the DRV possessed an air force of MiG fighters, the vast majority of its aircraft **sorties** were confined to the DRV in an interceptor role to counter the U.S. Air Force (USAF) and **RVN Air Force** (RVNAF) campaigns to bomb and interdict the DRV. The DRV did build up an air defense system of MiG fighters, surface-to-air **missiles**, and **antiaircraft artillery** that was considered one of the strongest in the world by the late 1960s. U.S. air assets and **advisers** were present in Southeast Asia in the earlier 1950s. Americans and their aircraft were involved at the Battle for **Điện Biên Phủ** in 1954 and participated in the training of the RVNAF. The most significant operations of the air war occurred in the 1960s.

The most notable air operations occurred over the DRV. The U.S. initiated the **bombing** of the DRV in August 1964 in Operation **Pierce Arrow** in response to the **Gulf of Tŏn Kĭn Incident**. This was followed by Operation **Flaming Dart** in February 1965, which also served as a retaliatory strike for DRV support of **National Liberation Front** (NLF) activities against U.S. personnel. The longest campaign began on 2 March 1965 with Operation **Rolling Thunder**. Rolling Thunder had as its principal objective the reprimand of the DRV for its actions in the RVN. The **Joint Chiefs of Staff** maintained that the air operation would demonstrate to the North Vietnamese that the punishment for support of the NLF and continued action in the RVN would be far greater than the benefits of such support or involvement. The campaign was originally conceived as an eight-week program but was extended in two-week cycles for an additional three and a half years. The mission for Rolling Thunder expanded as the air campaign progressed. Interdiction of personnel from the **People's Army of Vietnam** (PAVN) and DRV supplies became a primary objective, as did the destruction of DRV infrastructure and industry that could be used to support the war effort. As the war progressed, Rolling Thunder was also used to force the DRV to the negotiating table to secure peace for Southeast Asia. Rolling Thunder sorties were supported by **Iron Hand** missions that had the objective of identifying and eliminating surface-to-air missile sites. The U.S. also launched **Blue Tree** missions that gathered **intelligence** to support Rolling Thunder sorties.

Rolling Thunder achieved success in its military objectives in that much of the DRV's infrastructure was destroyed, damaged, or dispersed by the time the operation ended. Rolling Thunder also caused the DRV to divert much more personnel and supplies to maintaining the **Hồ Chí Minh Trail**. However, restrictions on the air sorties allowed the DRV to take advantage of the situation and maintain its pressure against the RVN. Rolling Thunder did not force the DRV to the negotiating table, nor did it dissuade North Vietnamese support for the NLF. PAVN soldiers continued to flow into the South to fight the U.S. and the RVN Armed Forces for the duration of the war.

The next major air operation over the DRV consisted of operations **Linebacker I** and **Linebacker II**. Linebacker I was in response to the 1972 **Easter Offensive** and proved to be a significant air operation that caused tremendous damage to the PAVN forces that were exposed during the invasion. Linebacker II, or the Christmas bombings, did persuade the DRV to return to the negotiating table in late December 1972 and helped bring about the January 1973 **Paris Peace Accords**.

The U.S. was also heavily involved in air operations over the RVN, though the missions were more varied. The USAF and RVNAF employed the concept of **airmobility** to act as a troop multiplier by allowing the U.S. and its allies to move quickly, and in large numbers, throughout the RVN, bypassing difficult obstacles or inaccessible areas. The use of the **helicopter** and various fixed-winged aircraft made this possible. Ground support missions, or close air support, caused as many PAVN and NLF casualties as ground engagements. This aspect of the air war was credited with saving a significant number of U.S., RVN, and allied personnel. Airpower gave the allied forces an overwhelming advantage in firepower, including the use of the B-52 Stratofortress, which conducted **Arc Light** missions. The air war over the RVN also included interdiction and was coordinated with air operations in the southern end of the DRV, Laos, and Cambodia, while defoliation missions through Operation **Ranch Hand** killed vegetation with herbicides and exposed PAVN and NLF base camps, decreased the potential for ambushes, and denied the enemy their food source. The USAF and RVNAF also conducted **reconnaissance** missions to gather intelligence and locate the enemy, and provided **search-and-rescue** services for downed pilots and crew. One of the largest missions of the air war was **tactical airlift**, both within Southeast Asia and between that region of the world and the U.S.

There were several operations in Laos starting with Operation **Barrel Roll** in 1964. This campaign began with reconnaissance missions but soon expanded to include close air support for the beleaguered Royal Laotian Army and its allied forces against the PAVN and Pathet Lao. With the introduction of Operation **Steel Tiger** in April 1965, which focused on interdiction in the southern region of Laos in the area to the north and south of the **Demilitarized Zone**, Barrel Roll missions concentrated on northern Laos and would continue until 1973. Steel Tiger operations lasted until 1968, though its area of operation was divided in December 1965 with Operation **Tiger Hound**. In 1968, Operation **Commando Hunt** absorbed Steel Tiger, Tiger Hound, and the interdiction missions under Barrel Roll to maximize the limited resources available. The USAF and RVNAF were also involved in a variety of other missions; one of the more notable was support for the February 1971 Operation **Lam Sơn 719** that was designed to cut the Hồ Chí Minh Trail at **Tchepone**.

In Cambodia, the air war began in earnest in March 1969 when President **Richard M. Nixon** authorized Operation **Menu**. Its missions, Breakfast, Lunch, Supper, Dinner, and Dessert, were designed to harass the PAVN and NLF forces who had established base areas in neutral Cambodia along the Cambodian-RVN border. This campaign was conducted in secret until the May 1970 **Cambodian Incursion**. At this point, a new air operation, **Freedom Deal**, was initiated to support the results of the incursion and was later expanded in Operation **Freedom Action**.

In some aspects, the air war was successful for the U.S. and RVN. Their aircraft performed missions that allowed the military and politicians to conduct their strategy and tactics. U.S. strategy had no chance of success without the air war. The RVN would not have survived the 1960s without air assets, and the DRV would have been able to dominate the region had the USAF and RVNAF ceased to play a role in the war. It seems likely that the Laotian and Cambodian governments would have succumbed to their communist insurgencies much earlier without an active air war. But the air war also failed to convince the DRV that the war could not be won, and it did not dissuade the PAVN or NLF in their continued conflict against the U.S. and RVN. The DRV withstood everything that the USAF and RVNAF threw against it, while the North Vietnamese people not only endured the air campaigns but rallied behind the war. Like much of what occurred during the war, the air war was successful but in the end failed. *See also* AIRCRAFT (BOMBERS), UNITED STATES; AIRCRAFT (CARGO TRANSPORT), UNITED STATES; AIRCRAFT (FIGHTER), UNITED STATES; AIRCRAFT (RECONNAISSANCE), UNITED STATES.

AIRBORNE BATTLEFIELD COMMAND AND CONTROL CENTERS (ABCCC). The mission of the ABCCC was to manage air operations in **Laos**. The ABCCC served as a command post in the sky, using first the RC-47 and then the EC-130 to direct aircraft against **People's Army of Vietnam**, **National Liberation Front**, and **Pathet Lao** supply depots and personnel, as well as providing protection for **Free World Forces** engaged with the enemy. The RC-47 conducted missions, originating from Udorn, **Thailand**, and landed at Nakhon Phanom, Thailand, flying over Laos to assist in Operation **Steel Tiger**. These missions, known as Dogpatch, gathered **intelligence** from teams in Laos who watched the **Hồ Chí Minh Trail**, while Cricket missions provided information for Operation **Barrel Roll** in the northern part of Laos. ABCCC suffered from several difficulties, including language barriers, equipment issues, and the rugged terrain of Laos disrupting communications. **United States** ambassador to Laos, **William Sullivan**, also demanded control over U.S. airstrikes, which added a layer into the decision-making process and sometimes delayed hitting targets of opportunity. By 1967, additional ABCCC flights were originating from **Đà Nẵng** and handled day-time air sorties in Laos. The RC-47 was replaced with the EC-130.

AIRCRAFT (BOMBERS), UNITED STATES. The **United States** used a number of aircraft with the primary mission of bombing. The most notable of these aircraft included the B-26, B-52, B-57, and B-66. Built by Douglas, the B-26 Invader first saw service in Southeast Asia in 1951 when the U.S. provided France with five RB-26 (**reconnaissance**) and 24 B-26 aircraft. Use of the B-26 was ended by the French with the fall of **Điện Biên Phủ** but was reintroduced in 1961 when the U.S. sent four of the aircraft with the 4400th Combat Crew Training Squadron. The original purpose of the aircraft was as a trainer for the **Republic of Vietnam Air Force**, but as the number of American **advisers** increased, it was deployed into combat with American personnel. It was withdrawn in 1964 after the aircraft began to fail, but it once again returned in 1966 designed as the B-26K. It flew in Southeast Asia until 1969. The original B-26 carried up to 1,814 kilograms (4,000 pounds) of **bombs**; the B-26K could carry up to 3,628 kilograms (8,000 pounds).

Built by Boeing, the B-52 Stratofortress was designed as an intercontinental, high-altitude heavy bomber and proved to be a formidable weapon in the U.S. arsenal. Eight versions of the aircraft were developed from the first flight in 1952, each improving the payload, flight range, or other features of the previous model. The B-52H, powered by eight Pratt and Whitney engines, had a range of 16,000 kilometers (10,000 miles), though it also had the capability of in-flight refueling. The B-52D would accommodate 84 500-pound bombs in its bay and up to 24 750-pound bombs under its wings for a total of 27,215 kilograms (60,000 pounds). The G model added two GAM-77 air-to-surface missiles, while the H model added a multibarrel tail cannon and forward-firing penetration rocket launchers.

The B-52 had a top speed of 958 kilometers (595 miles) per hour, could fly at up to 16.7 kilometers (55,000 feet), and carried a crew of six. The **Democratic Republic of Vietnam** (DRV) air defense system was no match for the B-52 that struck at North Vietnamese targets without warning and with devastating effectiveness. The B-52 was also used in **Arc Light** missions in the **Republic of Vietnam** that caused a significant amount of destruction against the **National Liberation Front** (NLF) and allowed for greater effectiveness in the allied fighting force. Critics of the B-52 operations argued that the weapon was not designed for insurgency fighting and caused more damage around the targets than against it, but the aircraft proved itself to be one of the few weapons of the war that both the **People's Army of Vietnam** and the NLF feared.

Built by Martin, the B-57 Canberra was a tactical bomber that also could function as a reconnaissance aircraft. Five versions of the two-person bomber aircraft were built. The B-57B carried eight .50 caliber **machine guns** or four 20-mm cannons. It also had four **napalm** tanks and eight 12-centimeter (5-inch) high-velocity aircraft rockets in addition to its payload. Its bombs were released using a preloaded revolving bomb-bay door that allowed the aircraft the ability to maintain its speed when releasing its bombs. The B-57 had a maximum speed of over 965 kilometers (600 miles) per hour and a range of over 3,200 kilometers (2,000 miles), while it could fly at a height of 13.7 kilometers (45,000 feet). Later versions maintained these specifications. The B-57 was preferred for its ability to loiter over a target for a long period of time and for its large **bombing** capacity. The RB-57A served as the reconnaissance version of the aircraft and was used to photograph bombing damage done during Operation **Rolling Thunder**.

Built by Douglas, the B-66 Destroyer served several different roles during the war. The EB-66 provided electronic **intelligence** and served as an electronic countermeasures aircraft for bombing sorties over the DRV, while the RB-66 conducted reconnaissance missions. The B version was produced for night photographic reconnaissance, while the C model was an all-weather aircraft. The B-66 also had a model designed for weather reconnaissance, known as the WB-66. The aircraft had a crew of three and was powered by two Allison turbojet engines with a maximum airspeed of 1,125 kilometers (700 miles) per hour and a range of over 2,400 kilometers (1,500 miles) before in-flight refueling. It housed two 22-mm cannons in a tail ball turret. The reconnaissance model housed three K46 night cameras, a K38 day camera, and photoflash bombs. The bomber version of the aircraft carried a payload of 6,800 kilograms (15,000 pounds). *See also* AIR WAR.

AIRCRAFT (CARGO TRANSPORT), UNITED STATES. The **United States** used a number of cargo transport aircraft, with the designation of C before the model number, to move personnel and supplies to Southeast Asia and within the theater during the war. These aircraft made it possible for the U.S. to fight a war so far from its shores. Cargo transport aircraft flew the most **sorties** of any other type of aircraft during the war. The aircraft were also modified to conduct a number of other types of missions.

Built by Douglas and designated as the C-54 by the **United States Air Force**, the DC-4 Skymaster served as a transport aircraft, primarily for **Air America** in **Laos** and **Cambodia**, to perform such duties as airlift and psychological warfare. The aircraft was powered by four Pratt and Whitney engines and was designed to accommodate heavy loads of either supplies or personnel.

The C-7 Caribou, built by DeHavilland, served as a light transport aircraft for the U.S. Army, though the 134 still in service in 1967 were transferred to the USAF. The aircraft was powered by two Pratt and Whitney engines with a maximum level speed of 345 kilometers (214 miles) per hour and a climb rate of 413 meters (1,355 feet) per minute. The Caribou had a range of 2,100 kilometers (1,307 miles) unloaded and a maximum payload of 4,000 kilograms (8,740 pounds), though 2,700 kilograms (6,000 pounds), or two fully loaded jeeps, were its normal cargo. It was a useful aircraft during the war because of its ability to take off and land on short runways, which were numerous in Vietnam. It carried a crew of two or three and could normally transport 32 troops; 26 paratroopers; or 22 stretcher patients, 4 sitting **casualties**, and 4 attendants.

Built by Curtiss, the C-46 Commando was a twin Pratt and Whitney engine transport designed to move either military personnel or cargo. The aircraft was used by Air America during the war and was built to house a crew of four. The Commando was an older aircraft but was still capable of transporting approximately 6,800 kilograms (15,000 pounds), with an overload weight capacity of 9,000 kilograms (20,000 pounds). It had a maximum speed of 425 kilometers (265 miles) per hour. The aircraft had a greater capacity than the C-47 but was more difficult to maintain.

Built by Douglass, the C-47 Skytrain operated primarily as a transport during the war, though it also was modified as a surveillance aircraft (SC), an electronics aircraft (EC), and a gunship (AC). It had a crew of three and was powered by two Pratt and Whitney engines, capable of 368 kilometers (229 miles) per hour and a range of 2,400 kilometers (1,500 miles). It could transport up to 3,900 kilograms (8,600 pounds), though a normal load was 2,700 kilograms (6,000 pounds), or 28 fully equipped soldiers. The AC-47 (Spooky) had three 7.62-mm miniguns that could fire as fast as 6,000 rounds per minute. It was also used as a flare ship to illuminate the night over besieged villages, **fire support bases**, or troops in the field.

Built by Fairchild, the C-119 Flying Boxcar, with its crew of up to five, was a twin-engine cargo and troop transport and later was modified as a gunship during the war. The aircraft had a normal payload capacity of between 12,500 and 12,700 kilograms (27,500–28,000 pounds). It had a cruising speed of 322 kilometers (200 miles) per hour and a rate of climb of approximately 228 meters (750 feet) per minute, with a range of between 1,950 and 2,280 kilometers (1,211–1,416 miles), depending upon the model. The first AC-119 gunships were modified from the G model and included four 7.62-mm miniguns, a flare launcher, and a sighting system. The AC-119K had an additional two 20-mm cannons and more-power turbojet engines with a greater speed and range.

The C-121 Constellation, built by Lockheed, served as a long-range cargo and troop transport and was modified as a **reconnaissance**, early-warning, electronic surveillance, and **intelligence** aircraft. The aircraft was powered by four Wright turbojet engines that could reach a maximum speed of 566 kilometers (352 miles) per hour when fully loaded and had a range of 7,750 kilometers (4,820 miles). With a minimum crew of at least four, the Constellation accommodated between 75 and 94 personnel depending upon the model, or had a payload capacity of approximately 9,000 kilograms (20,000 pounds). The two RC-121 versions carried reconnaissance equipment and early-warning radar, while the EC-121 version provided electronic surveillance and intelligence for fighters that might engage MiGs over the **Democratic Republic of Vietnam**. A later version, the C-121J, flew over Vietnam with equipment that provided for television and radio transmission, as well as relaying equipment. These Blue Eagles, as they were known, were capable of broadcasting on two television stations and on shortwave and FM radio; they were also able to conduct live broadcasts. The Constellation served a variety of roles during the war, including assisting in operations such as **aerial refueling** and **search-and-rescue** missions.

Built by Fairchild, the C-123 Provider served as an assault transport for troops and cargo, though it was also modified as the UC-123 for use in the dispersal of herbicides in Operation **Ranch Hand** sorties. The aircraft was powered by two Pratt and Whitney engines with a maximum speed of 394 kilometers (245 miles) per hour and a range of 2,365 kilometers (1,470 miles). The C-123 carried a crew of two and was capable of carrying 60 fully equipped troops or just under 6,800 kilograms (15,000 pounds) in a normal cargo.

Built by Douglas, the C-124 Globemaster, also known as "Old Shakey," was a troop and cargo transport capable of carrying 200 troops or, when serving as an ambulance carrier, 127 stretchers and 52 sitting patients. It had a payload capacity of 22,680 kilograms (50,000 pounds). The Globemaster had a crew of five, plus space for a relief crew. The aircraft had a maximum range of 3,500 kilometers (2,175 miles), making it suitable for the transpacific flight.

Built by Lockheed, the C-130 Hercules served a variety of roles during the war. As a transport, the C-130 went through a series of versions. The C model had a maximum payload capacity of nearly 20,000 kilograms (44,000 pounds), though 11,340 kilograms (25,000 pounds) was a normal load, with a cruising speed of 621 kilometers (386 miles) per hour and a maximum range of 4,000 kilometers (2,487 miles). The aircraft had room for a crew of five with relief quarters for a second crew. The U.S. **Navy** used a version of the EC-130 for electronic surveillance, while the HC-130, with an expanded range and a crew of between 7 and 10, coordinated search-and-rescue missions with its high frequency (HF), very high frequency (VHF), ultra high frequency (UHF), and frequency modulated (FM) radios in its role as mission control. This version of the C-130 also served as the refueling tanker for the HH-53 **helicopters**. The C-130 was also modified as a reconnaissance aircraft, weather aircraft, and tanker. Its most notable modification was as a gunship. The AC-130 Spectre was armed with four 20-mm and four 7.62-mm multibarrel guns, though 40-mm guns sometimes replaced the 20-mm ones. Along with the other gunships in the U.S. arsenal, the AC-130 was very effective in armed reconnaissance and was especially capable against enemy vehicles and personnel aboveground.

Built by Lockheed-Georgia, the C-141 Starlifter was developed as a long-range troop and cargo transport. The four-engine aircraft, with a crew of four, could accommodate 154 troops, 123 fully equipped paratroopers, or 80 stretchers and 16 sitting patients. It had a maximum payload capacity of 32,140 kilograms (70,850 pounds), a maximum speed of 919 kilometers (571 miles) per hour, and a range of 6,381 kilometers (3,965 miles) with a normal payload. The C-141 made trips to and from Vietnam almost every day during the war.

Built by Boeing, the KC-135 Stratotanker was the primary aerial refueling aircraft used during the war. The four-person crew, four-engine aircraft had a range of over 17,700 kilometers (11,000 miles) and a maximum fuel capacity of 31,200 gallons, or approximately 54,430 kilograms (120,000 pounds) of fuel. It had a maximum speed of 856 kilometers (532 miles) per hour and a range of 1,850 kilometers (1,150 miles). *See also* AIR WAR.

AIRCRAFT (FIGHTER), UNITED STATES. The **United States** employed a number of different aircraft during the war in Southeast Asia in missions that ranged from fighter/interceptor to **bombing**, **reconnaissance**, and cargo transport. U.S. aircraft were used in all countries in the Southeast Asian theater. Aircraft were identified by a letter that designated its function and number. Letters included *A* for attack aircraft, *B* for bomber, *C* for Cargo, *F* for fighter, *O* for observation, and *T* for trainer. While this type of identification helped to distinguish the primary mission of the aircraft, many of them had more than one role in the air war. Some of the more numerous of the attack aircraft included the A-1, A-6, and A-37.

Built by the Douglas Company, the A-1 Skyraider used in Vietnam was the sixth version of the AD series. It was originally conceived as a 1945 replacement for the SBD dive-bomber, with a 453-kilogram (1,000-pound) payload, but it carried 10 times that amount by the time of the Vietnam War. The aircraft supported a 15.5-meter (50 feet, 9 inch) wingspan with a maximum overload capacity of 6,550 kilograms (14,450 pounds). The AD-6 version housed a 2,700-hp engine with a maximum speed of 587 kilometers (365 miles) per hour, a climb rate of 869 meters (2,850 feet) per minute, and a combat radius of 2,400 kilometers (1,500 miles). It was armed with four 20-mm cannons and had 15 different areas under its wings for weapons that included **bombs**, rockets, **napalm, cluster bomb units, mines**, grenades, flares, and smoke. The Skyraider was considered a very reliable fighting craft that could sustain a significant amount of damage before being forced out of the air. It was the preferred aircraft for **search-and-rescue** missions because of its ability to loiter over crash sites. The A-1 saw service in Vietnam with the **U.S. Navy, U.S. Air Force**, and **Republic of Vietnam Air Force** (RVNAF), who used the Skyraider as their principal propeller-driven aircraft. As the A-1 were released from U.S. service, they were transferred to the RVNAF. By November 1972, all A-1 aircraft in Vietnam were flown by the Vietnamese.

Built by Grumman, the A-6 Intruder was flown by the U.S. Navy and **Marine Corps** during the war. It was designed as a low-level attack bomber capable of carrier takeoffs and landings. The A model was the primary one used during the war, though models through E saw action. The A-6A had a payload of 7,840 kilograms (17,280 pounds), and the maximum speed was 1,042 kilometers (648 miles) per hour, with a combat range of between 3,100 and 4,700 kilometers (1,925–2,900 miles), depending on armaments, conditions, and the use of external fuel tanks. Other versions of the A-6 included the EA-6 Prowler, which retained some of its armaments but was designed as a strike support aircraft, in order to diminish the enemy's electronic air defense capabilities. It also carried sophisticated navigation, photographic, and bombing equipment that allowed it to improve the accuracy of the **Rolling Thunder** and **Linebacker** missions as well as aerial reconnaissance missions. The KA-6D served as a flight fuel tanker and had the ability to refuel other aircraft from its reserve of up to 9,525 kilograms (21,000 pounds) of fuel depending on conditions and distance to the transfer point. The A-6 crew consisted of a pilot and a navigator/bombardier.

Built by Cessna, the A-37 Dragonfly was originally designed to be an armed **counterinsurgency** light attack aircraft. Two models were used in the war in this type of mission. The A-37A entered service in 1963, while the model B became active in 1967. Powered by two General Electric turbojets, the Dragonfly had a maximum speed of 843 kilometers (524 miles) per hour, with a climb rate of 2,130 meters (6,990 feet) per second. With a maximum payload, it had a range of 740 kilometers (460 miles), though that was extended to 1,625 kilometers (1,012 miles) when equipped with four 100-gallon drop tanks. The Dragonfly carried a number of possible armament combinations that could handle up to 1,860 kilograms (4,100 pounds) of munitions, including 500- to 1,000-pound bombs, rocket pods, MK-81 or MK-82 bombs, BLU-32 fire bombs, gun pods, cluster-bomb units, demolition bombs, canister clusters, or flare launchers. Each aircraft was also armed with a 7.62-mm minigun installed in its forward fuselage. For aerial reconnaissance, the Dragonfly could also be equipped with a gun or strike camera. The A-37 was a two-seat aircraft, flown by the USAF and RVNAF, with more than 165,000 **sorties** to its credit in Southeast Asia.

Fighter aircraft included the F-4, F-5, F-100, F-101, F-102, F-104, F-105, and F-111. These aircraft flew a variety of different missions, including bombing and reconnaissance, though their primary mission was engaging the enemy's aircraft. Built by McDonnell Douglas, the F-4 Phantom was a heavily used all-weather fighter that also saw action as a reconnaissance aircraft. The F-4 was a twin-engine, two-seat aircraft that could reach a maximum speed of over two times the speed of sound, with a range of between 1,450 and 1,600 kilometers (900–1,000 miles) depending on its mission. It carried six Sparrow III **missiles** or four Sparrow III and four Sidewinder missiles. The aircraft could also be used as a bomber and could handle an additional 7,250 kilograms (16,000 pounds) of ordnances, including 680-pound, 750-pound, and 1,000-pound bombs, or smoke or napalm bombs. The F-4 was involved in the **Wild Weasel** program, where it was modified to include electronic countermeasure warning sensors, chaff, and jamming pods. It also participated in the successful Operation **Bolo** and various bombing campaigns in Southeast Asia. The RF-4 carried side-looking radar, forward and side-looking cameras, and infrared detectors.

Built by Northrop, the F-5 Freedom Fighter served as a light tactical fighter. In 1967, the RVNAF received its first F-5 as it transitioned to a jet air force. The earlier models of the aircraft sent to Vietnam accommodated a single pilot, though there were fighter-trainer models that seated two. The F-5 could reach between Mach 1.34 and 1.4 depending on the model, while its cruising speed was just below the speed of sound. It had a range of between 2,200 and 2,600 kilometers (1,350–1,600 miles) depending on model, payload, and whether external fuel tanks were added. It carried two 20-mm cannons and had five pylons for bombs, air-to-air or air-to-surface missiles, gun packs, or external fuel tanks, for a maximum payload of 2,500 kilograms (5,500 pounds). The aircraft made the RVNAF a formidable force, but in the final months of the war, many of the aircraft were grounded because of maintenance issues. The number of available F-5 aircraft was not enough to strengthen the South Vietnamese defensive positions against the North Vietnamese invasion in 1975.

Built by North American, the F-100 Super Sabre was the USAF's first supersonic fighter and was also utilized as a reconnaissance aircraft. The aircraft had a maximum speed of 1,323 kilometers (822 miles) per hour with afterburners, and a combat range of 925 kilometers (575 miles). It was the first operational aircraft to fly faster than the speed of sound. The Super Sabre flew bombing missions, MiG **combat air patrol**, reconnaissance, and **forward air controller** missions. It was a single-seat aircraft, though the F model was a two-seat version. It had four 20-mm M39E cannons and six under-wing pylons that could handle 42 2.75-inch rockets, 2,700 kilograms (6,000 pounds) of munitions, or napalm bombs. The RF-100, a reconnaissance version of the aircraft, carried cameras and equipment under its wings. The F-100 saw significant action during the war and was involved in most of the major air campaigns in Southeast Asia.

Built by McDonnell, the F-101 Voodoo was a supersonic twin-engine escort turned fighter-bomber that was also modified as a reconnaissance aircraft. It had a cruising speed of approximately 885 kilometers (550 miles) per hour, with a range of 4,500 kilometers (2,800 miles) with external fuel tanks. The F-101A carried four 20-mm M39A cannons, three Hughes GAR-1 Falcon missiles, and 12 rockets, or approximately 725 kilograms (1,600 pounds) of munitions. The RF-101 was based on the A and C models with cameras and equipment in the nose of the aircraft. The aircraft had a crew of one.

Built by Convair, the F-102 Delta Dagger was a supersonic, one-person, all-weather interceptor used against the **Democratic Republic of Vietnam** (DRV). With a maximum speed of over Mach 1.25 and a ceiling limit of 16.5 kilometers (54,000 feet), it was faster than the North Vietnamese MiGs, though it was less maneuverable than its modern adversaries. It was armed with six Hughes GAR-1D/2A Falcon air-to-air guided missiles and carried 24 2.75-inch rockets. The aircraft was used to provide air support for bombing sorties during the air campaigns against the North.

Built by Lockheed, the F-104 Starfighter was a single-engine interceptor used in Operation Rolling Thunder. The aircraft was originally conceived as an answer to the MiG-15, which was matched with the F-86 during the Korean War. It had a trapezoidal, small, straight wing that earned the aircraft the nickname, "Missile with a Man." It saw limited action in Vietnam, used primarily for air-to-air combat, though it was involved in no kills and rarely engaged MiG aircraft over North Vietnam. The F-104 was used between July 1965 and July 1967, flying more than 5,200 sorties. A total of 14 aircraft were lost during the war to a combination of MiG fighters, ground fire, surface-to-air missiles, collisions, and engine failure. The aircraft was eventually phased out for the F-4 Phantom aircraft.

Built by Republic, the F-105 Thunderchief was a supersonic single-seated fighter-bomber that also served as an interceptor. With a maximum speed of Mach 2.25 at 11.6 kilometers (38,000 feet) and a maximum range of 3,330 kilometers (2,070 miles), it was a much-used aircraft in the bombing of the DRV. It was armed with one M61 20-mm Vulcan automatic multibarrel gun and could deliver up to 5,440 kilograms (12,000 pounds) of bombs or a combination of fuel tanks, nuclear missiles, sidewinder missiles, fire bombs, mines, and rockets.

Built by General Dynamics, the F-111 Farm Gate, sometimes known as the Aardvark, was created to fulfill the role as an all-weather, day-and-night fighter-bomber. The aircraft was modified to provide electronic countermeasures and could also serve as a reconnaissance aircraft if needed. The F-111 was created to be the all-encompassing aircraft for the USAF. It was a two-seat variable-geometry aircraft; that is, the outer portion of the wings swept back to allow it a high rate of climb. The F-111A was armed with an M61 multibarrel 20-mm gun or up to 680 kilograms (1,500 pounds) of bombs. It had a maximum speed of Mach 2.2 and was very involved in the **Linebacker II** bombing campaign.

Built by North American, the T-28 Trojan was used primarily as a training aircraft. The two-seat aircraft had duplicate flight controls and was powered by a Wright radial air-cooled engine. It had a maximum speed of 459 kilometers (285 miles) per hour and a range of 1,700 kilometers (1,060 miles). The T-28 could be armed with bombs, rockets, and .50 caliber **machine guns**. The T-28D Nomad was modified for the war and served as a trainer, for armed reconnaissance, and as an air support aircraft. It had a maximum speed of 612 kilometers (380 miles) per hour and a range with a full weapons load of 800 kilometers (500 miles), though that could be extended with external fuel tanks to 1,930 kilometers (1,200 miles), at the expense of munitions. It had two .50 caliber guns and carried up to 816 kilograms (1,800 pounds) of bombs, napalm, or rockets. *See also* AIR WAR; ENHANCE, PROJECT; ENHANCE PLUS, PROJECT; PIPE STEM, PROJECT.

AIRCRAFT (RECONNAISSANCE), UNITED STATES. The U.S. relied on observation and **reconnaissance** aircraft for **intelligence** on the enemy's location and movement, for assessing bombing damage, and for working with ground forces to provide air-to-ground fire support. While some aircraft with a C or F designation conducted this type of **sortie**, there were specific aircraft designed for these requirements.

Cessna built two types of observation aircraft. The O-1 Bird Dog was a single-engine, two-seat observation, light reconnaissance, and **forward air controller** aircraft. It had a maximum speed of 185 kilometers (115 miles) per hour and a range of 850 kilometers (530 miles). The aircraft carried no weapons, though it had the ability to deploy smoke to identify targets for fighters and bombers. The O-2 Skymaster was a twin-engine aircraft that had many defined roles during the war. It served as a forward air controller, observation, psychological warfare, and reconnaissance aircraft. The Skymaster had a crew of two with space for an additional four passengers when needed. The aircraft had a maximum cruising speed of 315 kilometers (196 miles) per hour and a range of 1,250 kilometers (780 miles) without extra fuel reserves.

The Skymaster's tractor-pusher propeller allowed it to sustain greater ground fire than the O-1, while its four wing pylons could carry rockets, flares, smoke, or 7.62-mm minigun pods.

North American also built two observation aircraft. The OV-1 Mohawk was a two-seat observation and surveillance aircraft used during the war. The U.S. used four different models of the Mohawk with a maximum cruising speed of between 443 and 489 kilometers (275–304 miles) per hour and a range with external tanks of between 1,980 and 2,270 kilometers (1,225–1,400 miles). The Mohawk carried two KA-60C 180-degree panoramic cameras and one KA-76 serial frame camera. Other equipment included side-looking airborne radar (SLAR) that could map terrain by sending pulses that bounced off the terrain and other objects and then were translated into photographic images. The OV-1B had an onboard film processor that allowed the crew to see the photographs while still in the air. The OV-1C was equipped with infrared radar to detect objects on the ground, while the OV-1D had the ability to use either SLAR or infrared radar depending on the mission. Some O-1s in Vietnam were also armed with **bombs** and were used for armed reconnaissance when the situation arose.

The OV-10 Bronco was a two-seat, twin-engine aircraft used for armed reconnaissance, counterinsurgency operations, **helicopter** escort, and forward air controller sorties. A few of the aircraft were equipped with a night periscopic site, laser rangefinder and target illuminator, and **LORAN** receiver for nighttime armed reconnaissance. It had a maximum speed of 727 kilometers (452 miles) per hour and a range of 367 kilometers (228 miles) with weapons and no loitering time over the target. Auxiliary fuel tanks could extend the range to 2,300 kilometers (1,428 miles). It could carry up to 1,630 kilograms (3,600 pounds) of bombs and had four 7.62-mm M60C **machine guns**. It could also be modified to carry sidewinder **missiles**, rocket pods, flare pods, and free-fall ordnance. The Bronco had the additional capacity to hold up to 1,450 kilograms (3,200 pounds) of equipment, five paratroopers, or two stretcher patients and a medic.

There were two high-altitude reconnaissance aircraft employed in the war, both built by Lockheed-Martin. The U-2 Dragon Lady was a single-seat, high-altitude reconnaissance aircraft with a ceiling of 21.3 kilometers (70,000 feet) and a maximum speed of 850 kilometers (528 miles) per hour. Its sorties started in 1964, with the aircraft first operating from **Biên Hòa** airbase and then U-Tapao, **Thailand**. It provided both day and night reconnaissance over the **Democratic Republic of Vietnam** (DRV) during the war. It carried up to five 70-mm cameras along with other equipment that allowed it to record radio and radar transmissions.

The SR-71 Blackbird served as a strategic photographic and reconnaissance aircraft over the DRV. It was noted for its high rate of speed, which was estimated at over Mach 3, and for its operational ceiling of over 24.4 kilometers (80,000 feet). The Blackbird had a range of 1,930 kilometers (1,200 miles) but could refuel in flight. The crew of two had a variety of equipment at their disposal, including sophisticated navigational devices that provided continuous and automatic star tracking and high-performance equipment for photographic reconnaissance and intelligence gathering. *See also* AIR WAR; AIRCRAFT (FIGHTER), UNITED STATES.

AIRCRAFT, DEMOCRATIC REPUBLIC OF VIETNAM. The North Vietnamese provided a three-layered air defense to counter U.S. **bombing** campaigns. One layer of this defense was interceptor aircraft. The **Democratic Republic of Vietnam** (DRV) used four different types of Mikoyan-Gurevich (MiG) aircraft built in the **Soviet Union**.

The MiG-15, known as the Fagot, was one of the early aircraft used by the North Vietnamese Air Force in the war. It was armed with two 23-mm cannons and one 37-mm cannon and could carry rockets or two 100-kilogram **bombs**. It had a cruising speed of 837 kilometers (520 miles) per hour and a maximum speed of nearly 1,078 kilometers (670 miles) per hour, and a range of 804 kilometers (500 miles), which could be increased by 50 percent with external tanks. The MiG-15 was not a great threat to U.S. fighters.

The MiG-17 Fresco was a greater threat. In February 1964, the first group of 36 MiG-17 arrived in **Hà Nội** after Vietnamese pilots had received training in the **People's Republic of China** and the Soviet Union, and it earned its first confirmed kill on 3 April 1965 when it downed an F-105. Like its predecessor, the MiG-17 carried two 23-mm cannons and one 37-mm cannon, but it had the capacity to carry a greater bomb load of 500 kilograms (1,100 pounds) or 16 rockets. It had a maximum speed of 1,144 kilometers (711 miles) per hour and a range of 1,030 kilometers (640 miles), which could be increased by just less than 40 percent with external fuel tanks. The MiG-17 was more maneuverable than the MiG-15 and was reportedly preferred over the MiG-19 and MiG-21 for the same characteristic, even if it was slower than these two aircraft.

The MiG-19, known as the Farmer, was the first supersonic fighter introduced into the North Vietnamese Air Force, with a maximum speed of just over 1,448 kilometers (900 miles) per hour. The MiG-19 entered into service for the DRV in 1969 with the formation of the 925th Fighter Regiment and was considered a real threat during the **Linebacker** campaigns. The Farmer was armed with three 30-mm cannons. It had a range of approximately 2,090 kilometers (1,300 miles), depending on conditions, and a crew of one.

The MiG-21, known as the Fishbed, was the most advanced aircraft in the North Vietnamese Air Force. Courtesy of the Soviet Union, who delivered the

MiG-21 to the DRV as a gift to the people, the aircraft saw action in the war in April 1966. The MiG-21 did not have the technological advancement of its American adversaries, but it did pose a constant threat to Operation **Rolling Thunder** and the two Linebacker operations. Of the 17 North Vietnamese aces claimed during the war, 14 of them flew the MiG-21. The Farmer was armed with one 23-mm cannon and carried two air-to-air **missiles**. It had a maximum speed of Mach 2.2 and a range of just over 1,200 kilometers (750 miles). Like the MiG-19, it had a crew of one.

AIRMOBILITY. Airmobility evolved dramatically during the Vietnam War. In previous wars, aviation units had been instrumental in **reconnaissance** and directing **artillery**. During the Korean War, airmobile units were involved in **search-and-rescue** and **aeromedical evacuation** missions, both of which would continue in Vietnam. Encouraged in part by Secretary of Defense **Robert McNamara**, the first airmobile unit was established during the **John F. Kennedy** administration. Airmobile units were organized under the army, with responsibilities in troop transport, aerial fire support, reconnaissance, and resupply. The first **helicopters** dedicated to airmobility arrived in Vietnam in December 1961 to assist **Army of the Republic of Vietnam** troops. While the results were initially unsuccessful, the concept became integrated into the American strategic plan. There were two airmobile divisions, 1st Cavalry and the 101st Airborne, which relied on airmobility in fighting the enemy, while aviation battalions were employed through the four **Corps Tactical Zones**, including the **Assault Helicopter Company** and the **Assault Support Helicopter Company**.

Another category of airmobility was the Air Cavalry regiment, which was separate from the 1st Cavalry Division. Because of Vietnam's diverse and rugged terrain and the enemy's strategy and tactics dedicated to **guerrilla warfare**, airmobility provided a degree of mobility that ground forces lacked, it added an element of surprise in many of the operations, and it served as a troop multiplier against an elusive enemy. Airmobility allowed **United States** and Vietnamese forces to go anywhere at any time, and provided increased flexibility in operations by allowing resupply for prolonged operations in isolated and vulnerable areas. Airmobility provided a distinct advantage for the U.S. and Vietnamese but was never effective enough to be decisive in the war. *See also* AIR WAR.

AMERICAN FRIENDS OF VIETNAM (AFVN). Established in 1955, the AFVN was a political lobbying group made up of Americans who supported **Ngô Đình Diệm**. The organization held a number of conferences designed to inform the American people about Vietnam's plight and educate them on Vietnam's potential. In addition to its formal and informal lobbying efforts in

Washington, D.C., the AFVN raised money to support humanitarian efforts in the **Republic of Vietnam**. After the assassination of Ngô Đình Diệm in November 1963, the AFVN's influence diminished as its membership dwindled and the organization divided over supporting the Americanization of the war. By the end of the war in 1975, the AFVN had ceased to play any significant role. *See also* CONGRESS, UNITED STATES; KENNEDY, JOHN FITZGERALD; O'DANIEL, JOHN WILSON.

AMPHIBIOUS OPERATIONS, UNITED STATES. Throughout the war, the **United States Navy** possessed an overwhelming superiority of force over the North Vietnamese. The 7th Fleet dominated its adversary's small coastal fleet, and as a result, the U.S. and Task Force 76, which carried out many of the amphibious attacks, was free to move personnel and supplies anywhere and at any time in the **Republic of Vietnam** (RVN). The first U.S. Navy action occurred on 8 March 1965 with the landing of the Battalion Landing Team, 3rd Battalion, 9th Marine Regiment on the **Đà Nẵng** beaches as part of a two-battalion deployment to the RVN, an event that marked the first American combat troops in Southeast Asia. The first amphibious operation in which U.S. forces sought to engage the enemy began with Operation **Starlite** from 18 to 24 August 1965, an attempt by the III Marine Amphibious Force to destroy the 1st **National Liberation Front** (NLF) regiment in **Quảng Trị**. In a similar type of mission, operations **Blue Marlin** I and II, between 10 and 12 November and between 16 and 18 November 1965, targeted the NLF near Tam Kỳ and Hội An. In the 28 January to 28 February 1966 Operation **Double Eagle**, the U.S. **Marine Corps** conducted a **search-and-destroy** mission near Quảng Ngãi City and Tam Kỳ, while Operation **Defiant Stand** used **Republic of Korea** troops and American marines to clear the Barrier Island off the coast of Đà Nẵng.

The ability to have free and safe access in the open seas allowed the U.S. and its allies a distinct advantage. Amphibious operations could quickly move large numbers of troops along the Vietnamese coastline. Some military officers questioned the need for amphibious assaults, arguing that the beach landings of a World War II variety did not conform to the **People's Army of Vietnam** (PAVN) and NLF style of fighting and pointed to the less-than-desirable results of the many amphibious assaults. Still, the limitless opportunities to land troops along the coastline did force the PAVN and NLF to abandon that area as a safe haven. When the PAVN and NLF tried to reestablish control along the coast, they often found themselves surrounded and were rendered ineffective.

AMTRAC. The Landing Vehicle Tracked Personnel (LVTP) referred to as the Amphibious Tractor, or Amtrac, was originally designed to transport **marines**

to landing beaches in amphibious assaults. In Vietnam, the **United States** Marine Corps (USMC) used the LVTP-5A1. It carried a crew of three (crew chief, driver, and machine gunner) and normally transported 34 personnel, though that number could be expanded to 45 in an emergency. The vehicle had a maximum speed of 48 kilometers (30 miles) per hour on land and approximately 10.6 kilometers (6.6 miles) per hour on water, which made it a versatile weapon in the war. The major drawback with the LVTP-5A1 was the position of its 12 cells that held up to 456 gallons of fuel, which were located in the hull of the vehicle, making them vulnerable to land **mines**. During the war, the LVTP-5A1 was used primarily to transport personnel and supplies for the USMC, though it was also utilized as a medevac carrier in combat areas.

ANGEL'S WING. An area in **Cambodia** bordering **Tây Ninh** province in the **Republic of Vietnam** that was used by the **People's Army of Vietnam** and the **National Liberation Front** in their war against **Sài Gòn**. The Angel's Wing was directly south of Tây Ninh City and was traversed by **Route 1**, just north of the formation known as the **Parrot's Beak**.

ANOTHER MOTHER FOR PEACE. Founded in 1967, Another Mother for Peace was organized as an **antiwar** group to educate women on how to become antiwar activists. The organization believed war was obsolete and focused much of its effort on a letter-writing campaign to elected officials who supported this position. The campaign began with a Mother's Day card to members of **Congress** and the president calling for an end to the killing and the start of negotiations toward peace.

ANTIAIRCRAFT ARTILLERY. The **Democratic Republic of Vietnam** (DRV) and the **National Liberation Front** (NLF) used a variety of antiaircraft artillery during the war to offset the significant advantages of **United States** and **Free World Forces** aircraft. The smallest caliber weapon, the 12.7-mm and 14.5-mm **machine guns**, were used by the NLF. They did not present much of a threat to the faster-flying jets, though they were more effective against slower-moving aircraft and **helicopters**. The North Vietnamese also used the smaller-caliber weapons but relied more on the 23-mm and 37-mm machine guns for lower-flying aircraft, while the 57-mm and 100-mm artillery reached much higher altitudes. The Type 59 57-mm AAA was developed by the **People's Republic of China** from the S-60 model developed by the **Soviet Union**. It was more effective against aircraft flying between 457 and 1,524 meters (1,500–5,000 feet), though it did have an effective range of 6,553 meters (21,500 feet) if radar guided and 4,572 meters (15,000 feet) if optically guided. It could fire a sustained rate of 70 rounds per minute, thought it could fire as much as 120 rounds per minute for a short period of time.

The Soviet-built KS-19 was a 100-mm AAA that fired 15 rounds per minute with a maximum range of just short of 15.2 kilometers (50,000 feet) with a proximity fuse. By the late 1960s, the DRV had one of the most sophisticated air defense systems in the world. Coupled with the SA-2, a surface-to-air missile, and the MiG-fighter, the AAA provided a protective blanket across all of the strategic areas of the DRV. Despite this sophistication, the U.S. was able to bomb the DRV whenever and wherever it wished. *See also* AIR WAR; BOLO, OPERATION; COMBAT AIR PATROL; LONG BIÊN BRIDGE (PAUL DOUMER BRIDGE); LORAN; TCHEPONE; TRUSCOTT WHITE, OPERATION.

ANTIWAR MOVEMENT. While an antiwar movement existed in the 1950s, its focus was against violence in general rather than specific **United States** action in Southeast Asia. Organizations such as the **Fellowship of Reconciliation** and the **War Resisters League** (WRL) voiced opposition to American military **advisers** working in the **Republic of Vietnam** (RVN) after 1955, and a few individuals were concerned about the number of U.S. dollars being spent on nation building and the war against the communist insurgency. It was not until the presidency of **John F. Kennedy** that criticism against the war emerged, but even that opposition was tempered.

Individuals who spoke out against American action in the RVN were less critical of U.S. military action and were more focused on the rule of **Ngô Đình Diệm** and his response to the 1963 **Buddhist Crisis**. Elder statesman **W. Averell Harriman** advocated the removal of Ngô Đình Diệm and his brother **Ngô Đình Nhu**, while others in the Kennedy administration expressed some apprehension about U.S. escalation. This type of criticism was reinforced in **media** reporting as individuals like **David Halberstam**, **Neil Sheehan**, and **Malcolm Browne** made sure that Americans received only negative reports about the actions of the **Sài Gòn** government.

After the assassinations of Ngô Đình Diệm and Kennedy in November 1963, the antiwar movement began to organize as President **Lyndon B. Johnson** continued Kennedy's policies of escalation in 1964. **Phillip Berrigan** founded the **Emergency Citizens' Group Concerned about Vietnam** in Newburgh, New York, and cofounded with his older brother, David, the **Catholic Peace Fellowship**. The Fellowship of Reconciliation, headed by **A. J. Muste**, organized an October 1964 demonstration against the increasing numbers of American advisers in Southeast Asia by calling for resistance to the draft. Earlier, David Dellinger led the WRL in a May 1964 demonstration during which 12 men burned their draft cards. At the end of the year, in

December 1964, the WRL conducted the first national demonstration against U.S. action in Vietnam, though the turnout was minimal.

The antiwar movement was emboldened in March 1965 after Johnson authorized the sustained **bombing** of the **Democratic Republic of Vietnam** and the deployment of two battalions of **marines** to **Đà Nẵng**. The **Students for a Democratic Society** (SDS) took an early leadership position in the movement. Headed by Tom Hayden, the organization sponsored **teach-ins** and coordinated the signing of "We Won't Go" petitions for men who were eligible for the draft. Modeled on the nonviolent civil rights sit-in activities of the early 1960s, the first teach-in occurred at the University of Michigan in Ann Arbor on 24 March 1965. The two-day event was attended by approximately 2,500 participants. The SDS also organized a major antiwar demonstration in Washington, D.C., on 17 April 1965, which numbered approximately 20,000. An additional teach-in at the University of California, Berkeley, starting on 21 May, attracted an estimated 30,000 people. These types of activities organized students around the college campus and helped to increase the numbers in the antiwar movement throughout the year.

The **National Coordinating Committee to End the War in Vietnam**, which was established to coordinate the dozens of antiwar organizations founded in 1965, met in Washington in August 1965 to discuss its future action. It helped to organize the 15–16 October 1965 International Days of Protest, an event that had been initiated by the Berkeley Vietnam Day Committee. As more antiwar organizations were formed, the movement found a willing ally in the church.

In October 1965, approximately 100 clergy members met in New York City to organize religious opposition to the war. On 11 January 1966, the group formally created the National Emergency Committee in order to relegitimize an antiwar movement that had gained a reputation for being too radical. In May 1966, the group organized the Clergy Concerned about Vietnam, whose name was changed to the **National Emergency Committee of Clergy and Laymen Concerned about Vietnam**, when the committee opened its membership to all people regardless of religion.

The National Coordinating Committee to End the War in Vietnam organized a Second International Days of Protest on 25–26 March 1966 that attracted more than 100,000 people. In addition to the nationwide protest movements, there were countless local demonstrations and specific organizations founded around the U.S. against the war. **Another Mother for Peace** was one such organization. It was established in 1967 to educate women on how to become antiwar activists. It focused on a letter-writing campaign to elected officials who agreed that war had become obsolete and called for an end to the killing and the start of negotiations toward peace.

In 1967, the **Spring Mobilization to End the War in Vietnam** was established with the objective of coordinating mass demonstrations against the war. It organized its first nationwide protest on 25 April 1967 that brought 130,000 protestors to New York City and half that number to San Francisco. In May 1967, the organization changed its name to the **National Mobilization Committee to End the War in Vietnam** (Mobe). Mobe organized its first major protest on 21 October 1967 in Washington, D.C., which led to a march on the Pentagon building. The SDS joined in that protest but was also involved in the controversial 17 October demonstration turned melee against Dow Chemical at the University of Wisconsin in Madison. As the war progressed without end, the antiwar movement experienced more radical actions.

On 17 October 1967, Philip Berrigan, Thomas Lewis, and David Eberhardt entered the **Selective Services** headquarters located in the U.S. Customs House building in Baltimore and poured duck's blood on draft records while James Mengel passed out pamphlets that explained their actions. The group became known as the **Baltimore Four**. Berrigan and Lewis were sentenced to six years in federal prison, Eberhardt was sentenced to three years, and Mengel's sentence was postponed. On 17 May 1968, nine individuals, including Phillip and **David Berrigan** and four other Catholic priests broke into the office of Local Draft Board 33 in Catonsville, Maryland, and removed draft records. The group, known as the **Catonsville Nine**, burned the draft records in a parking lot near the office using homemade **napalm**. The group was convicted of mutilating and destroying government records and of obstructing the duties of the Selective Service program in a trial that attracted approximately 1,500 protestors and 200 police to protect the proceedings.

Despite the radicalization of the movement, there were many national leaders who lent legitimacy to the antiwar protestors and countered the more radical elements within the movement. **Martin Luther King Jr.** did not immediately oppose the war, but he began to publicly advocate a reassessment of the U.S. military policy, which relied on airpower to force negotiations and **search-and-destroy** missions that emphasized the attrition strategy. King opposed the indiscriminate use of American firepower in fighting the Vietnamese, arguing that the U.S. role in Vietnam was becoming one of a colonialist power. He opposed spending more money on fighting a war to destroy a nation thousands of miles away than on improving the social, economic, spiritual, and cultural environment at home. On 4 April 1968, King was assassinated as he stood on the balcony of the Lorraine Motel in Memphis, Tennessee.

There were also many congressmen who spoke out against the war. Early opposition by senators **Wayne Morse** (D-Oregon) and Ernest Gruening (D-Alaska), both of whom voted against the **Gulf of Tŏn Kĭn Resolution** in August 1964, was joined by others in **Congress** who became concerned about the nature of U.S. action in Southeast Asia. In 1966, Republican Mark Hatfield won a Senate seat from Oregon on an antiwar platform. He received support in the election from his Democratic counterpart, Senator Morse. Democratic senators **Mike Mansfield** (Montana), **Frank Church** (Idaho), **J. William Fulbright** (Arkansas), **George McGovern** (South Dakota), Edward Kennedy (Massachusetts), and **Eugene McCarthy** (Minnesota) joined Republican senators George Aiken (Vermont), Clifford Case (New Jersey), and Jacob Javits (New York) in opposing the war as American escalation continued through 1966 and 1967.

In the presidential election of 1968, Johnson received a challenge in the 12 March New Hampshire primary in which antiwar candidate Eugene McCarthy finished a strong second to the incumbent president. This encouraged Senator **Robert Kennedy** (New York) to announce his candidacy for the Democrats in the election four days later. Kennedy had supported the war effort but in 1967 began to change his stance by arguing for a **bombing pause** to encourage negotiations. Like King, Kennedy argued that America's resources and personnel were being diverted to Southeast Asia instead of being used to help improve conditions within the U.S. Kennedy ran an effective campaign and seemed close to the White House after a 4 June primary win in California. He was assassinated that evening.

The loss of King and Kennedy, coupled with the fiasco at the 1968 Democratic National Convention in Chicago, helped to break apart what was left of the cohesion within the antiwar movement. Earlier in the year, the SDS organized the "Ten Days of Resistance" and worked with the Student Mobilization Committee to coordinate antiwar demonstrations, including the 26 April 1968 national strike. In 1969, the antiwar movement was fully engaged in demonstrations against the war. The New Mobilization Committee to End the War in Vietnam helped coordinate the Moratorium Day demonstration on 15 October 1969, which numbered in the tens of thousands, and the 15 November 1969 National Moratorium Day, whose participants numbered in the hundreds of thousands. In November 1969, the antiwar movement was energized by the revelations regarding the **Mỹ Lai** massacre when Seymour Hersh published an article based on an interview with **William Calley**, who was one of the principal instigators of the incident. Monthly demonstrations continued to attract a significant number of people.

By the end of 1969, the antiwar movement was at its peak, but the organization lacked leadership and cohesion. The movement was fractured by the nature of the war, the varied perspectives and interests represented within the movement, and the election of **Richard M. Nixon**. Nixon announced in July 1969 that the U.S. would begin the policy of **Vietnamization**. This plan for disengagement took some of the focus out of the antiwar movement, but the events of Mỹ Lai and 1970 provided a last push for the protestors.

At the end of April 1970, Nixon announced the **Cambodian Incursion**. Though the operation would last only 60 days, those who had opposed the war believed that Nixon had betrayed Vietnamization with the escalatory move. The incursion resulted in nationwide protests that closed many college campuses down at the end of their spring term. It also resulted in the shooting of four individuals on the campus of **Kent State University** by national guardsmen sent to the campus to quell the demonstrations. The events of 4 May shocked the nation and inflamed the antiwar movement for a period of time though the galvanizing affect of the shootings led to the fracturing of the antiwar movement as many of the aggressive groups used the Kent State University episode as justification for more militant action. Ten days following the Kent State University incident, another shooting occurred on the campus of **Jackson State University**.

In 1971, the **Vietnam Veterans Against the War** (VVAW), an organization that was established in 1967, sponsored the 31 January–2 February **Winter Soldier investigation** in Detroit, Michigan. During the investigation, veterans and others made claims against U.S. action in Vietnam that included rape, murder, torture, and other unseemly actions. The VVAW also coordinated the 19–23 April 1971 protest in Washington, D.C., known as **Dewey Canyon** III. More than 1,000 veterans and others joined in the protests that took place in front of the White House, Congress, the Pentagon, the Supreme Court, and the gates of the Arlington Cemetery. It organized a march from Concord, Massachusetts, to Boston on Memorial Day 1971, retracing the steps of the 1775 Minutemen campaign that opened the military phase of the American Revolution, but the march was stopped before it could begin. On 26 December 1971, members of the VVAW barricaded themselves in the Statue of Liberty facility to gain attention for their cause. They remained for two days.

Another major event for the antiwar movement was the June 1971 publication of part of the 1968 study, *United States-Vietnam Relations, 1945–1967: A Study Prepared by the Department of Defense*, often referred to as the **Pentagon Papers**, by the *New York Times*. The portions of the study were given to the *New York Times* by **Daniel Ellsberg**, a former RAND employee who worked on it. The Nixon administration tried to suspend the release of the pages, but a 30 June Supreme Court decision allowed the publication to continue. Senator Mike Gravel (D-Alaska), who was chairman of the Subcommittee on Public Buildings and Grounds, also entered a significant portion of the study into the Congressional Record, making its publication guaranteed. Ellsberg became a folk hero for the antiwar movement as the Nixon administration attempted to discredit him, including his arrest under the Espionage Act of 1917.

By 1972, the number of combat troops in Vietnam had decreased significantly. Most Americans were eager to move beyond the war years. Americans generally approved of the Nixon administration's response to the 1972 **Easter Offensive** and criticized such actions as **Jane Fonda**'s trip to the DRV in July 1972 during which she was photographed in the seat of an **antiaircraft artillery** gun while the U.S. was conducting Operation **Linebacker I**. Fonda also issued statements about the treatment of American prisoners of war that contradicted the prisoners' own statements about torture during their imprisonment.

The influence of the antiwar movement ended with the 1972 presidential election. Senator George McGovern ran against Nixon on an antiwar platform. McGovern had run in 1968 and after that election became one of the leading critics of the war. His platform called for immediate withdrawal from Vietnam and a reduction of the U.S. military. Nixon soundly defeated McGovern, and after a prolonged period of negotiations, the hostile parties in the conflict signed the January 1973 **Paris Peace Accords**. The end of the U.S. participation in the war took away the main impetus for the antiwar movement, though a few radical elements, such as the Weathermen, continued to use the war to justify criminal action.

The impact of the antiwar movement in the war's outcome remained controversial. Those involved in the movement argued that they helped to end the war and change American foreign and military policy. Those who opposed the antiwar movement maintained that it prolonged the war by giving the DRV and **National Liberation Front** encouragement to continue the fight against overwhelming odds. Like much in the war, both sides offered legitimate evidence to support their contention, but neither side will ever be able to convince the other of their point. *See also* AGNEW, SPIRO THEODORE; AMERICAN FRIENDS OF VIETNAM (AFVN); BALL, GEORGE WILDMAN; CITIZENS COMMITTEE FOR PEACE WITH FREEDOM IN VIETNAM; CLERGY AND LAITY CONCERNED ABOUT VIETNAM; DRINAN, ROBERT FREDERICK; VIETNAM MORATORIUM COMMITTEE.

ẤP BẮC, BATTLE OF. On 2 January 1963, the 7th Division of the **Army of the Republic of Vietnam** (ARVN) engaged the 261st Main Force Battalion near the village of Ấp Bắc and the 415th Regional Battalion in Ấp Tân Thôi. The American **adviser** to the 7th ARVN Division, Lieutenant Colonel **John Paul Vann**, had encouraged the move in order to achieve a quick and decisive victory against an enemy that had hurt the morale of the ARVN forces earlier in an October 1962 defeat of an ARVN Ranger platoon. Vann, who expected a smaller number of the enemy around Ấp Bắc, believed that the 7th ARVN Division was capable of achieving that victory. In previous encounters with **helicopters**, the troops of the **National Liberation Front** (NLF) had fled or exposed themselves to ground and air fire with sporadic gunfire against the aircraft. Vann believed it would be no different with the CH-21 helicopters involved in the operation. In this instance, the NLF practiced strict fire discipline and stood its ground along a tree and canal line, maintaining a strong defensive position. After one battalion of ARVN troops disembarked from the helicopters, the NLF engaged them. The second battalion, which could have reinforced the first, was not delivered to the battlefield. Vann maintained that it was the incompetence of the ARVN commander that resulted in this failure as well as the botched attack at Ấp Bắc. It was not until the early evening that the ARVN forces reinforced the troops fighting on the ground to such an extent that they forced the NLF to leave the battlefield. Only after they left did the ARVN troops secure their objective.

Ấp Bắc was a lesson for the South Vietnamese military and American advisers who were filled with frustration at opportunities lost. It also marked the beginning of more pronounced **media** criticism of the ARVN and the American military role in the war after **Military Assistance Command, Vietnam**, commander General **Paul Harkins** declared that the operation was a success, because the ARVN had secured Ấp Bắc. Reporters **David Halberstam**, **Neil Sheehan**, and **Malcolm Browne**, who were on the scene the next day, rejected this pronouncement after they learned of Vann's version of the battle. *See also* KENNEDY, JOHN FITZGERALD; LÝ TÒNG BÁ; NGÔ ĐÌNH DIỆM; NOLTING, FREDERICK ERNEST, JR.

APACHE SNOW, OPERATION. A **search-and-destroy** operation in the provinces of **Thừa Thiên** and **Quảng Trị** conducted between 10 May and 7 June 1969. The primary objective of Apache Snow was to eliminate the **People's Army of Vietnam** (PAVN) presence in the A Shau Valley, in which it had moved personnel and supplies from the **Hồ Chí Minh Trail** in **Laos** to the **Republic of Vietnam**. The **United States** had initiated a series of operations in the A Shau Valley previous to Apache Snow with limited success. PAVN forces had used the rugged terrain to their advantage to hide from U.S. forces. Apache Snow involved battalions for the 101st Airborne **Division** and the 3rd Regiment of the **Army of the Republic of Vietnam**'s 1st Division. Like its predecessors, the operation achieved limited success, as the A Shau Valley continued to be a contested area. During the operation, the Battle for **Hamburger Hill** (Hill 937) occurred, which helped to galvanize congressional opposition to the war and served as a reminder of the difficult nature of the conflict for the U.S.

ARC LIGHT MISSIONS. In 1964, the Strategic Air Command promulgated Operation Plan 52-65, which called for conventional **bombing sorties**

against predetermined targets. Arc Light missions, as they would become known, used the B-52 Stratofortress bomber to deliver a significant amount of munitions in a short period of time to support ground troops and to disrupt or destroy enemy supply depots, logistics infrastructure, and lines of communication. While Arc Light missions, which began on 18 June 1965, provided a potent weapon for the **United States**, their effectiveness was governed by U.S. adherence to the laws of war. Missions were formulated on the requirement that they avoid noncombatant **casualties**, monuments, temples, and other historical landmarks if the destruction of those structures would cause political problems. Missions in **Laos** also needed the approval of the American ambassador in Vientiane.

Another constraint to the operations was the B-52 point of origin for its mission. The aircraft operated on **Guam**, which translated to 12 hours in the air and a 24-hour turnaround when a target was nominated. This obstacle was overcome with the establishment of a **Quick Reaction Force** and the **Ground Diverted Force concept**. The **U.S. Air Force** also established the Kadena Air Base at Okinawa, Japan, and the U-Tapao Royal Thai Air Force Base in **Thailand** capable of handling the B-52s. While the sortie rate for Arc Light missions averaged between 200 and 300 per month in 1965, it achieved its desired rate of 1,800 per month in March 1968. Ground commanders argued that Arc Light missions were so significant that they altered North Vietnamese and Việt Cộng strategy and tactics. This benefit outweighed any of the political problems associated with saturation bombing. Critics of the **air war** maintained that Arc Light missions were too indiscriminate in their destruction and killed too many civilians or damaged nonmilitary targets. The mission ended in August 1973 after U.S. combat troops had left the **Republic of Vietnam**. The controversy surrounding the nature of the B-52 missions continued beyond the war's end and served to shape future U.S. military strategy and tactics. *See also* AIRCRAFT (BOMBERS), UNITED STATES; COMMANDO HUNT, OPERATION; CONSTANT GUARD, OPERATION; TIGER HOUND, OPERATION; TRUSCOTT WHITE, OPERATION.

ARIZONA TERRITORY. An area that was located to the southwest of **Đà Nẵng** in **Quảng Nam**. Named after the famed Arizona Territory of the 19th century in the **United States** that had gained a reputation for lawlessness and conflict, this area in the **Republic of Vietnam** was continuously contested between the **People's Army of Vietnam**, the **National Liberation Front**, the U.S. **Marine Corps**, and the **Army of the Republic of Vietnam**.

ARMORED PERSONNEL CARRIERS (APC). The **United States**, the **Army of the Republic of Vietnam** (ARVN), and **Third Country** forces employed the M113 APC in Southeast Asia. The Food Machinery Corporation produced the first version of the M113 in 1960 as a lighter-weight version of the M75 APC, which could not be transported by air. The M113 first arrived in Vietnam in March 1962 and was incorporated into two ARVN mechanized rifle companies. It had a crew of two and could carry 11 soldiers. Fully loaded, the M113 weighed approximately 10,660 kilograms (23,500 pounds). It had a cruising range of around 320 kilometers (200 miles) with a top speed of 60 kilometers (37 miles) per hour using a gasoline engine. The M113 had a .50 caliber **machine gun** as its primary weapon.

The first M113s were used in the field on 11 June 1962 and were quickly nicknamed Green Dragons by the **National Liberation Front**. The initial surprise and advantage of the M113 was overcome by the end of the year. At the **Battle of Ấp Bắc**, the M113's light armor and exposed firing position revealed its weakness, and the weapon underwent a reevaluation by both the U.S. and the ARVN. A new version of the APC was developed in 1963. The M113A1 had some major changes from the original model. The M113A1 was about 453 kilograms (1,000 pounds) heavier than the M113 and switched to a diesel engine. The top speed remained the same, but the range of the APC increased by 160 kilometers (100 miles). The M113A1 also had a tighter turning radius and faster acceleration. It also had a shield for the turret of the .50 caliber M2 machine gun. Two .30 caliber machine guns were mounted on the sides as the U.S. Army developed their own version of the M113A1 with the Armored Cavalry Assault Vehicle (ACAV). The ACAV was a more complete fighting vehicle, but it still possessed light armor that was vulnerable to land **mines**.

The APC was used in a variety of roles during the war. It was employed in **search-and-destroy** and reconnaissance-in-force missions. While critics of the APC argued that it did not possess enough armor to protect the troops it transported, it did serve as the primary vehicle for moving personnel and supplies throughout the rugged countries of Southeast Asia.

ARMY OF THE REPUBLIC OF VIETNAM (ARVN). The ARVN served as the main fighting force for the **Republic of Vietnam** (RVN) during the war. On 26 October 1956, the ARVN formed from the **Vietnamese National Army**, which had been created by **Bảo Đại** in 1949. Its early combat operations against the communist insurgency were marked with difficulties as the organization continued to train its officers and men who had not received adequate instruction from the French during the colonial period. ARVN forces did manage to keep the insurgency off balance until 1959, when the North Vietnamese fully committed to the war in the South, but they never were able to gain the initiative against their elusive enemy.

In November 1963, ARVN general **Dương Văn Minh** became president of the RVN after the coup d'état and assassination of **Ngô Đình Diệm**, which set up the precedent of military leadership in the RVN that lasted until the end of the war. As the war escalated and the **United States** assumed more responsibility for the direction of combat operations, ARVN forces continued to develop and engage the **People's Army of Vietnam** (PAVN) and the **National Liberation Front** (NLF). While there were instances of incompetence and corruption within its ranks, ARVN soldiers proved to be good fighters when properly led, though the common perception of the American soldier was that the ARVN were not committed to the war and preferred to have the U.S. assume the burden. The estimated 1,100,000 ARVN **casualties**, including over 250,000 killed, belie this allegation.

There were 11 ARVN divisions created during the course of the war, either from the original Vietnamese National Army or as a result of the need for additional units after 1956. ARVN soldiers fought in most of the major **search-and-destroy** operations and demonstrated their skills during the **Cambodian Incursion** and the 1972 **Easter Offensive**. While the ARVN did suffer from desertion and, in some cases, an unwillingness to engage the enemy, these instances did not represent the entire organization during the course of the war. After President **Richard M. Nixon** initiated his **Vietnamization** program, ARVN soldiers assumed the burden of fighting the PAVN and NLF and suffered an estimated 22,000 casualties per year from 1969 to 1971. The ARVN also completed more operations than the U.S. during the course of the war.

When the U.S. left Vietnam, ARVN soldiers continued to fight despite a shortage of equipment and ammunition. Even when the North Vietnamese launched their final offensive in 1975, many ARVN soldiers fought gallantly in defense of their country, including a major engagement at **Xuân Lộc**, though **media** images received in the U.S. were of ARVN soldiers fleeing the battlefield and hiding themselves within the civilian population. The ARVN ceased to exist after the fall of **Sài Gòn** in April 1975, while ARVN officers and soldiers suffered in reeducation camps in the postwar period as they accounted for their support for the RVN. *See also* ÁP BẮC, BATTLE OF; DEWEY CANYON II, OPERATION; HOÀNG XUÂN LÃM; HUẾ; LAM SƠN 71; TAYLOR-ROSTOW MISSION; TOÀN THẮNG, OPERATIONS.

ARMY, UNITED STATES. The **United States** Army bore the brunt of the fighting during the Vietnam War and provided the majority of the troops who saw service in Southeast Asia. Of the 58,183 listed as killed during the war, 38,209 belonged to the U.S. Army. The U.S. Army presence in Vietnam began in the early 1950s with military **advisers** to the State of Vietnam and then the **Republic of Vietnam** (RVN) after 1955. The **Military Assistance Ad-**

visory **Group** (MAAG) and the **Military Assistance Command, Vietnam** (MACV), were both led by U.S. Army generals throughout their existence.

Before 1965, the U.S. Army provided training and assistance to the RVN Armed Forces. U.S. strategy in the 1950s focused on large unit action. As a result, the U.S. Army organized the **Army of the Republic of Vietnam** (ARVN) along a similar line with the main objective of withstanding an invasion from the **Democratic Republic of Vietnam**. The MAAG leadership, which included Lieutenant General **John W. O'Daniel, Samuel T. Williams**, and **Lionel C. McGarr**, emphasized this type of training and advocated an increase in the size of the ARVN. Williams was the most outspoken of the three and often came into conflict with the U.S. ambassador to the RVN, **Elbridge Durbrow**, who preferred to use military assistance as leverage to force **Ngô Đình Diệm** to enact political, economic, and social reforms. Williams and the other MAAG commanders also clashed with Ngô Đình Diệm, who used the ARVN for static or **pacification** missions rather than as a deterrent to the DRV.

The role of the U.S. Army began to change in the early 1960s as the DRV began sending **People's Army of Vietnam** (PAVN) personnel to aid in the struggle of the **National Liberation Front** (NLF). President **John F. Kennedy** brought with him a policy of flexible response that allowed for a response to **guerrilla warfare** by using **Special Forces**. The U.S. Army continued to offer advice, but it also became involved in combat operations within that advising role, which led to American deaths on the battlefield. The number of U.S. Army advisers dramatically increased during the Kennedy administration, as did the overall size of the army.

When **Lyndon B. Johnson** entered the White House in November 1963, the situation in Vietnam was deteriorating. With the advice of the MACV commander, General **William C. Westmoreland**, and the **Joint Chiefs of Staff**, Johnson ordered military units to the RVN in 1965. The first army combat unit to arrive was the **173rd Airborne Brigade**. It followed the establishment of the 1st Logistical Command, which Westmoreland had requested in late December 1964. The 173rd Airborne Brigade established a base at **Biên Hòa**. The American approach was to concentrate in strategic enclaves near the coast, around cities, and at military bases in a defensive posture. Several enclaves were established in 1965.

As additional U.S. combat units arrived in Vietnam, the strategy of the U.S. Army shifted to more offensive actions designed to **search-and-destroy** the PAVN and NLF. This type of operation, which relied on a strategy of attrition to measure success, required additional combat units. The U.S. Army would end up supplying approximately 65 percent of the total U.S. personnel in Southeast Asia. When the U.S. decided to increase its military presence in the RVN, its total worldwide strength was just under one million men. The Johnson administration decided not to mobilize the U.S. Army Reserves or conduct a major call-up of the National Guard to fill the ranks in Vietnam. Instead, the U.S. employed the **Selective Service System** to meet the requirements. This strategy helped to erode public support for the war as **casualties** mounted and no end was in sight. The failure to employ the Reserves also meant that a large pool of talented officers and noncommissioned officers was not utilized. As the war progressed, the morale and cohesion of the U.S. Army began to decline. This became especially true after President **Richard M. Nixon** announced the policy of **Vietnamization**, which started the withdrawal of American troops from Vietnam but also required a brief period of escalatory action and additional casualties to allow the ARVN forces to take over combat responsibilities.

There were nine U.S. Army chiefs of staff from 1955 to 1975. Most notable were generals **Harold K. Johnson**, who served from 3 July 1964 to 2 July 1968 and presided over the period of U.S. escalation, and Westmoreland, who replaced Johnson after leaving command of the MACV and remained until 30 June 1972. The three chiefs of staff who followed Westmoreland had to deal with a U.S. Army that had been damaged as a result of its Vietnam experience as military discipline waned, drug abuse increased, and racial tension threatened to tear apart cohesion within the ranks. On 12 August 1972, the last U.S. Army combat unit in Vietnam was deactivated, though the war would continue for nearly three more years, and the U.S. Army would take much longer to recover from its time in Vietnam. *See also* ABRAMS, CREIGHTON WILLIAMS, JR.; I FIELD FORCE, VIETNAM; II FIELD FORCE, VIETNAM; IA ĐRĂNG VALLEY, BATTLE FOR; MỸ LAI; TRUSCOTT WHITE, OPERATION; VANN, JOHN PAUL; WEYAND, FREDERICK CARLTON; WHEELER, EARLE GILMORE.

ARTILLERY. Artillery was used on both sides of the war, though the **United States** relied on it as a primary means of firepower. A typical U.S. Army artillery battalion had 18 guns, usually divided into three groups of six. At the height of U.S. involvement in the war, it deployed 57 artillery battalions in Vietnam. There were six main types of artillery used by the U.S. and the **Republic of Vietnam** Armed Forces.

The M101A1 howitzer was initially deployed to Vietnam and served as the primary general-purpose field artillery weapon. It was considered light, at just less than 2,267 kilograms (5,000 pounds), and could be towed. The barrel of the M101A1 was 105 mm. It could fire at a sustained rate of just under three rounds per minute, though it had a maximum rate of fire of 10 rounds per minute. The M101A1 fired a 15-kilogram (33-pound) shell that contained approximately 2.2 kilograms (4.8 pounds) of explosives nearly 11.2 kilometers (7 miles). In March 1966, the M101A1 was replaced by the M102. The M102 was of a similar caliber but weighed significantly less at 680 kilograms (1,500 pounds). This made it easier to transport by **helicopter** or by smaller truck, though one of the main complaints about it in comparison with the M101A1 was the lower ground clearance when being towed. It fired the same shell as the M101A1 but at a slightly greater distance. The M101A1 and M102 were the most common types of artillery piece used by the U.S. in Vietnam.

The M108 self-propelled howitzer was a large artillery gun that mounted a 105-mm gun on the body of an M113 armored personnel carrier. It weighed approximately 19,000 kilograms (42,000 pounds), which made it impossible to transport by helicopter but the vehicle did have a range of 362 kilometers (225 miles) and a maximum speed of 56 kilometers (35 miles) per hour. The M108 carried a crew of five and could fire four rounds per minute at a range of between 11.2 kilometers (7 miles) and 14.4 kilometers (9 miles).

The U.S. used two primary weapons at the 155-mm caliber. The M109 was a self-propelled medium howitzer that was considered highly mobile. It had a similar range and speed as the M108 and weighed 25,000 kilograms (55,000 pounds) when fully loaded. It had a sustained rate of fire of one round per minute, though the average fell after the first hour, with a maximum rate of fire of four rounds per minute for three minutes. The maximum range of fire for the M109 was between 17.7 kilometers (11 miles) and 21.7 kilometers (13.5 miles).

The M114A1 howitzer was also a 155-mm caliber medium artillery piece that weighed almost 5,900 kilograms (13,000 pounds). It fired a 43-kilogram (95-pound) shell approximately 14.4 kilometers (9 miles) and had a sustained rate of fire of two rounds per minute, though that number decreased after the first 15 minutes. The weapon could fire 40 rounds per hour in a prolonged barrage. The M114A1 had a crew of 11. In addition to the two 155-mm used by the army, the **marines** also employed the M53 155-mm self-propelled gun that had a longer range than the M114A1 howitzer.

The U.S. used two heavy guns during the war, which were usually mixed together in the same artillery battalion. The M107 was a 175-mm self-propelled artillery piece that fired a 147-kilogram (323-pound) shell approximately 33.8 kilometers (21 miles). It weighed 28,300 kilograms (62,400 pounds) and needed a crew of 13, though the vehicle had a capacity for only five. It could fire less than one round per minute, while its barrel needed to be changed every 400 rounds. The M107 had a range of 724 kilometers (450 miles) and a maximum speed of approximately 80 kilometers (50 miles) per hour. The M107 was comparable to the longest-range artillery piece used by the **Democratic Republic of Vietnam** (DRV).

The M110 was an 8-inch howitzer that was also self-propelled. It weighed approximately the same as the M107, though its caliber was slightly larger at 203 mm. It needed a crew of 13 to fire its 90-kilogram (200-pound) shell nearly 16.9 kilometers (10.5 miles). It had a range of 523 kilometers (325 miles) and a maximum speed of 55 kilometers (34 miles) per hour.

The U.S. maximized its use of field artillery during the war in a number of missions, including ground support, harassment, and interdiction. Artillery pieces made a significant difference during many of the major engagements between the U.S., the RVN, the **People's Army of Vietnam** (PAVN), and the **National Liberation Front** (NLF). This was especially true when the U.S. and ARVN engaged the PAVN and NLF forces in fixed positions such as the siege of Khe Sanh, the 1968 Tết Offensive, and the 1972 Easter Offensive.

PAVN forces employed several types of artillery during the war. It used the **Soviet**-built 85-mm artillery field gun as well as captured 75-mm and 105-mm guns. The main long-range weapon was the 122-mm M1938 field howitzer. A similar weapon, known as the Type 54, was produced by the **People's Republic of China**. It weighed approximately 2,450 kilograms (5,400 pounds) and required a crew of eight. The M1938 could fire between five and six rounds per minute at a maximum range of 11.7 kilometers (7.3 miles).

The PAVN also used the 130-mm M1954 field gun, which was also known as the M46. The Chinese version was the Type 59-1. It was a towed weapon that weighed approximately 7,700 kilograms (17,000 pounds) and required a crew of eight. It could sustain a rate of fire of five rounds per minute with bursts of up to eight rounds per minute. It had a maximum range of 27.3 kilometers (17 miles).

One of the largest artillery pieces used by the PAVN was the Soviet-built 152-mm M1955 howitzer, which was a towed field gun, also known as the M37 or D-20. The Chinese version of the weapon was known as the Type 66. It weighed 5,670 kilograms (12,500 pounds) and required a crew of eight. It had a sustained rate of fire of one round per minute, though it could fire bursts of up to six rounds. It had a maximum range of 24.1 kilometers (15 miles), though it began to lose effectiveness after 17.7 kilometers (11 miles). *See also* CLUSTER BOMB UNIT; ENHANCE, PROJECT; MORTAR; ONTOS.

ASSAULT HELICOPTER COMPANY (AHC). The AHC was the main aviation unit in the war. Typically there were two companies per division or 10 per **Corps Tactical Zone**. While the AHC had a variety of missions, its principal responsibility was air assault in support of ground troops. Other missions included armed **reconnaissance**, support of units who were responding to enemy operations, and airlift operations. The AHC employed UH-1B and UH-1C model Iroquois **helicopters** and the AH-1G Cobra helicopter. The

AHC also transported armed platoons into combat or, when it was not carrying troops, was also effective in fire support missions. The AHC conducted "white" team operations which involved light observation helicopters (LOH) for visual reconnaissance and **hunter-killer** teams that used the strategy of offering the LOH as bait for the enemy and using the AH-1G Cobra helicopter, with its superior firepower, to destroy the enemy once he was exposed. The AHC averaged 2,800 hours of flying time per month and was responsible for creating the image of Vietnam as the helicopter war. *See also* AIR WAR; AIRMOBILITY.

ASSAULT SUPPORT HELICOPTER COMPANY (ASHC). The ASHC provided medium and heavy-lift capability, which included the transportation of troops, ammunition, and other supplies to **fire support bases** or camps isolated from the main roads or inaccessible without the use of a **helicopter** or fixed-wing aircraft. *See also* AIRMOBILITY.

ATTLEBORO, OPERATION. A **search-and-destroy** operation conducted by the 196th Light Infantry Brigade in **War Zone C** in **Tây Ninh** province. The operation began on 14 September 1966 but experienced little initial contact with the 9th **Division** of the **National Liberation Front** (NLF). After significant contact in October, the operation was expanded to include elements from the **United States'** 1st, 4th, and 25th divisions as well as the **173rd Airborne Brigade**, the 11th Armored Cavalry, and **Army of the Republic of Vietnam** units. The operation ended on 24 November 1966 with an estimated 500 **People's Army of Vietnam** and NLF killed, over 1,110 wounded, and 155 allied soldiers killed. The NLF also lost an estimated 2,400 tons of rice and over 25,000 grenades, 127 guns, 19 crew-served weapons, and over 453 kilograms (1,000 pounds) of war-related material. The U.S. also destroyed nine base camps, 124 **tunnels** or caves, and 502 bunkers. The operation was considered a success, though it did not eliminate the NLF presence in Tây Ninh. *See also* IRON TRIANGLE.

AUSTRALIA. In November 1961, the State Department issued an appeal to its allies to join in the fight to keep the **Republic of Vietnam** (RVN) free. Australia responded in May 1962 by sending 30 **advisers**, the first of several hundred that would make up the Australian Army Training Team, Vietnam. By April 1964, when President **Lyndon B. Johnson** had initiated the "**Show the Flag**" or "Many Flags" program in Vietnam, there were nearly 200 Australian advisers in Vietnam. With the Americanization of the war in 1965, Australia responded by sending the 1st Battalion, Royal Australian Regiment, which arrived in time to conduct a major **search-and-destroy** operation with the **173rd Airborne Brigade** in November. A second battalion arrived in April 1966, which combined with the first battalion committed in April 1965 to create the 1st Australian Task Force (1ATF). The 1ATF had as its area of responsibility the province of Phước Tuy. A third battalion was added in 1967. The Australians were well trained in jungle warfare and conducted a number of operations within the province to eliminate the **National Liberation Front** (NLF). On 18 August, near Long Tân, the Australians fought their most notable battle against the NLF and suffered the largest number of **casualties** for any one day in Vietnam. Eighteen Australians died, while an estimated 250 NLF were killed.

The Royal Australian Air Force (RAAF) was also present in Southeast Asia in 1962 when the reconstituted No. 79 Squadron deployed to Ubon, **Thailand**. The RAAF grew in size as the number of advisers and then combat troops increased. During the war, the RAAF had three primary missions: airlift, air-to-ground support, and **bombing**. The RAAF transported over a million passengers to, from, and within Vietnam during the war in approximately 318,000 **sorties**. It was responsible for delivering 27,000 tons of **bombs** on enemy targets in nearly 12,000 sorties.

The Royal Australian Navy (RAN) played a limited role in Vietnam, which included providing transport and logistics support for the army in Phước Tuy. This mission was best symbolized by the HMAS *Sidney*, nicknamed the "Vung Tàu Ferry," and support for operations **Sea Dragon** and **Market Time**. From May 1967, the RAN contributed at least one destroyer during Sea Dragon until the end of the operation, firing an estimated 101,000 4.5-inch and 5-inch shells on the enemy. It also worked with Task Force 115 to stop the infiltration of personnel and supplies by sea.

The Australian contingent began to withdraw in November 1970 with the last army troops leaving Phước Tuy in November 1971. The final advisers left on 18 December 1972, and combat operations ceased on 11 January 1973. The final Australian combat troops left at the beginning of July 1973 only to return in March 1975 to oversee the evacuation of the remaining Australians in the RVN. Approximately 50,000 Australians served in Vietnam during the country's 10-year involvement in the war. There were 521 Australians killed in action and nearly 2,400 wounded. The Australian contribution to the war effort may have been considered small by American standards, but the commitment fulfilled Australia's responsibilities as one of the **United States'** most stalwart allies in the conflict. *See also* ĐIỆN BIÊN PHỦ, BATTLE OF; DOMINO THEORY; NEW ZEALAND; SOUTH EAST ASIAN TREATY ORGANIZATION; THIRD COUNTRY FORCES; UNITED ACTION.

B

BABYLIFT, OPERATION. In early April 1975, when it became clear that the **Republic of Vietnam** would not be able to withstand the **Democratic Republic of Vietnam** offensive, international relief groups organized the evacuation of Vietnamese orphans, many of whom were the children of **United States** servicemen and Vietnamese women. Operation Babylift lasted between 3 April and 26 April 1975. It consisted of 30 C-5A Galaxy aircraft flights and removed approximately 2,000 children to the U.S. and 1,300 children to Europe, **Canada**, and **Australia**. The operation was marred by disaster in its first flight when on 4 April a C-5A crashed shortly after taking off at **Tân Sơn Nhứt**. Of the approximately 330 aboard the flight, 154 were killed. Babylift flights would also become controversial later on when accusations were made suggesting that not all of the children were orphans.

BẮC BỘ. Also known as Bắc Kỳ or Bắc Phần but commonly referred to as Tŏn Kĭn, Bắc Bộ was the northernmost Vietnamese province of French Indochina, created in the first decade of the 19th century. **France** created Bắc Bộ and the two other areas, An Nam and Cochin China (Nam Kỳ), in order to exert its control over the Vietnamese people and accentuate the natural divisions that existed among the Vietnamese. Even though some North Vietnamese referred to the **Democratic Republic of Vietnam** (DRV) as Bắc Bộ, the actual territory covered an area greater than the DRV. It ceased to exist as an administrative area at the end of the **First Indochina War**. *See also* NORTH VIETNAM.

BAHNAR. Located in and around **Kon Tum** province, the Bahnar speak a dialect of the Mon-**Khmer** language. A unique feature of the Bahnar village is the Rông (communal house), whose roof sometimes reaches 30.5 meters (100 feet) in height. Bahnar are animist and worship trees and were often mistreated by the **People's Army of Vietnam**, the **National Liberation Front**, and the **Republic of Vietnam**. *See also* BAJARAKA MOVEMENT; PLEI KU; SEDANG.

BAJARAKA MOVEMENT. An independence movement that included participants from the four major **Montagnard** tribes in the Central Highlands of the **Republic of Vietnam**. The name's origin comes from the first two letters, or first syllable, of the **Bahnar, Jarai**, Rade, and Kaho people. The people worked toward their independence from the **Sài Gòn** government, starting in 1954 with the goal of establishing their own administration and army. The movement formalized in 1957 after the Montagnard people were pushed from lands they had called their own as a result of **Ngô Đình Diệm**'s efforts to resettle North Vietnamese **refugees** who had fled during Operation Exodus and Operation **Passage to Freedom** in 1954–1955. The Bajaraka Movement was not only dedicated to preserving their land from the northern refugees but also resisted attempts by the Sài Gòn government to assimilate them into the republic.

On 15 September 1958, the movement organized an uprising, but it was quickly suppressed by the **Army of the Republic of Vietnam**, killing or capturing most of the leadership. The Bajaraka Movement continued to operate after the failed uprising but was less effective with its leadership removed. It was not until 1964 that those leaders who had been imprisoned were released. The Montagnard people were not able to gain autonomy during the remainder of the war and continued to be suppressed by the new **Hà Nội** government after 1975. *See also* Y-BIH ALEO.

BALL, GEORGE WILDMAN (1909–1994). Undersecretary of state in the **John F. Kennedy** and **Lyndon B. Johnson** administrations and critic of American escalation during the war. Ball started his political career during the Great Depression and rose to the second highest post in the State Department by 1961. He argued against Kennedy's decision to introduce additional **advisers** into Vietnam because he believed that the **United States** needed to focus on Europe rather than Southeast Asia in the Cold War. Ball played a significant role in a variety of crises during the Kennedy administration, including Cyprus, Pakistan, the Congo, and the 1962 Cuban missile crisis. During his five-year tenure in the State Department, he was consistent in his opposition of escalation in Vietnam, culminating in his 1 July 1965 memorandum to Johnson titled, *A Compromise Solution for South Vietnam*, in which he argued that the **Republic of Vietnam** was losing the war and that the U.S., even with hundreds of thousands of troops, would not be able to defeat the **National Liberation Front** or to negotiate a favorable end to the war. Despite his criticism of the war, Ball did not advocate the **antiwar** position of abandonment as the war became more unfavorable, though he did represent the **Dove** position within the Johnson administration. He argued for a political settlement and a policy that would eventually become **Vietnamization**. Ball resigned as undersecretary of state in 1966 but returned to public life in May 1968 as the U.S. delegate to the **United Nations** until the beginning of the **Richard M. Nixon** administration.

BALTIMORE FOUR. On 17 October 1967, **Philip Berrigan**, Thomas Lewis, and David Eberhardt, entered into the **Selective Service** headquarters located in the **United States** Customs House building in Baltimore and poured duck's blood on draft records of men from 17 of the city's 26 local draft boards. James Mengel, who was with the group, chose not to participate in the event but instead passed out pamphlets that explained their actions and equated the blood with that which was lost in Vietnam. Berrigan and Lewis were jailed after refusing to sign a pledge to appear in court. The group became known as the Baltimore Four. They were convicted of mutilating and destroying government records and obstructing the duties of the Selective Service program. On 24 May 1968, Berrigan and Lewis were sentenced to six years in federal prison, Eberhardt was sentenced to three years, and Mengel's sentence was postponed. This sentencing occurred seven days after Berrigan and Lewis were involved in the **Catonsville Nine** episode. *See also* ANTI-WAR MOVEMENT.

BAN MÊ THUỘT. Ban Mê Thuột was the capital of Darlac province in the Central Highlands in II **Corps Tactical Zone** and also the name for the largest district in the province. The city was located on **Route** 14, south of Route 21, approximately 127 kilometers (80 miles) to the northwest of **Cam Ranh Bay**. Ban Mê Thuột was the largest city in the Central Highlands and home to the **Rhadé**, a **Montagnard** tribe. It was the site of the **Front Unifié de Lutte des Races Opprimées** (FULRO) uprising. In September 1964, FULRO helped to organize a rebellion near Ban Mê Thuột that included personnel from the **Civilian Irregular Defense Groups**, whose membership included a number of **Cham** and **Khmer**. While the uprising failed, it was not until 1967 that the two sides agreed to focus their attention against the common threat of the **Democratic Republic of Vietnam**.

Ban Mê Thuột was also one of the capitals targeted by the **People's Army of Vietnam** (PAVN) and the **National Liberation Front** during the January 1968 **Tết Offensive**. The attack began on 30 January 1968, a day before the scheduled offensive, but was beaten back quickly. In 1975, Ban Mê Thuột was again the site of heavy fighting when the North Vietnamese launched what would become known as the Hồ Chí Minh Campaign. On 10 March, the 320th PAVN Division attacked Ban Mê Thuột and its defenders, the 23rd **Army of the Republic of Vietnam** (ARVN) Division, capturing the town by 12 March. President **Nguyễn Văn Thiệu** had planned to recapture the city by taking the 22nd ARVN Division from **Kon Tum** and **Plei Ku** to join what was left of the 23rd ARVN Division, but instead he ordered the abandonment of the Central Highlands, which set in motion the final collapse of the **Republic of Vietnam**. After the war, the city's name was changed to Buôn Mê Thuột, and the province expanded. *See also* MNONG.

BẢO ĐẠI (1913–1997). Born Nguyễn Phúc Vĩnh Thụy, Bảo Đại was the last emperor of the Nguyễn Dynasty, ruling from 1926 until 25 August 1945, when he abdicated the throne. Bảo Đại struggled to maintain Vietnamese autonomy at the end of the French colonial era and during the Japanese occupation of World War II. He was a collaborator with French colonial rule and with the brutal Japanese occupation. As a result, Bảo Đại was never able to assume a prominent role in the postwar effort to gain Vietnamese independence or stave off communist domination. He served as the supreme adviser to the **Democratic Republic of Vietnam** from 1945 to 1949, though he had very little real power or influence. Bảo Đại lived abroad until 1949, when the French convinced him to return to Vietnam as the chief of state.

After the fall of the fortress at **Điện Biên Phủ**, Bảo Đại moved to **France** and ruled from abroad. He retained this position until the October 1955 referendum that was orchestrated by **Ngô Đình Diệm** to remove him from power. Bảo Đại stayed in France for the remainder of his life and never became involved in the public debate that raged over the war until 1972 when he issued a statement calling for an end to the war. He then took an anti-**United States** and anti-**Nguyễn Văn Thiệu** position, advocating for a neutral Vietnam in the Cold War. After the end of the war in 1975, Bảo Đại returned to a quieter political life, though he did visit Vietnamese communities in the U.S. in 1982. *See also* BÌNH XUYÊN; ĐÀ LẠT; GENEVA CONFERENCE, 1954; HUẾ; LÊ VĂN VIỄN; PHAN HUY QUÁT; REPUBLIC OF VIETNAM; SÀI GÒN; TRẦN VĂN CHƯƠNG; VIETNAMESE NATIONAL ARMY.

BARREL ROLL, OPERATION. Air operation designed to harass and interdict the **People's Army of Vietnam** (PAVN) and **Pathet Lao** in **Laos**. Initiated on 24 December 1964, the first **sortie** of Barrel Roll provided support for the forces under **Vang Pao**. Barrel Roll missions consisted of up to four F-105s on **bombing** missions twice per week. Restrictions on targets hampered the effectiveness of the Barrel Roll missions in its early stages. Target selection had to go through a myriad of approvals, with the final authorization coming from the **United States** embassy in Vientiane.

Barrel Roll missions followed the monsoon season. During the dry season from November to April, U.S. aircraft supported the defense-minded Laotian forces against a numerically superior PAVN and Pathet Lao force. During the wet season from April to November, U.S. aircraft, with tactical air support and airlift, supported Laotian operations to regain ground lost in the previous PAVN and Pathet Lao offensive. The ebb and flow of the battle as dictated by the monsoon season meant continuous combat over the same terrain for nearly a decade. In April 1965, as the air war in Vietnam escalated and the situation in Laos intensified, the U.S. divided the air war in Laos into two separate campaigns. Barrel Roll continued to operate in the northern part of the country with a focus on providing air support for ground troops until 1973, while operations **Steel Tiger**, **Tiger Hound**, and **Commando Hunt** covered the southern area. *See also* AIRBORNE BATTLEFIELD COMMAND AND CONTROL CENTERS; PLAIN OF JARS; SULLIVAN, WILLIAM HEALY; WATERPUMP, PROJECT; YANKEE TEAM.

BARRIER REEF, OPERATION. Fourth **United States Navy** operation that made up the attempt under the **SEALORDS** strategy to interdict the **People's Army of Vietnam** and **National Liberation Front** infiltration of the waterways between **Cambodia** and the **Republic of Vietnam** (RVN). Spurred by the success of operations **Search Turn**, **Foul Deck** renamed to Trần Hưng Đạo, and **Giant Slingshot**, Admiral **Elmo R. Zumwalt Jr.** initiated Operation Barrier Reef on 2 January 1969 to complete the line of interdiction from Rạch Giá on the Gulf of **Thailand** to the north of **Sài Gòn**. This barrier offered a continuously patrolled line of over 400 kilometers (250 miles). The U.S. manned the barrier system until April 1971, when it handed over its vessels to the RVN's navy as part of **Vietnamization**.

BẾN HÉT. Located to the west of **Đắk Tô** in **Kon Tum** province, the **fire support base** at Bến Hét was established in 1967 at the junction of the **Republic of Vietnam**, **Laos**, and **Cambodia**. The next year, the base housed a **Special Forces** camp. Bến Hét was significant because it lay in the path of the **Hồ Chí Minh Trail**, where by that time the North Vietnamese were sending a steady flow of personnel and supplies to support the war in the South. Because of the significance of Bến Hét's location, it was both strongly defended and aggressively attacked in 1969. On 3 March 1969, the North Vietnamese sent armor to attack the camp, which marked the first time that armor from both sides engaged one another in battle. The North Vietnamese Front B-3, equipped with PT-76 light amphibious **tanks**, engaged the Company B, 1st Battalion, 69th Armor, which used the M48 tank. In the battle, the North Vietnamese lost two PT-76s, while the **United States** had one M48 damaged.

In 1969, the North Vietnamese besieged Bến Hét from 5 May until 29 June. The **Army of the Republic of Vietnam** (ARVN) bore the brunt of the 55-day siege, as the U.S. 4th Infantry **Division**, which had operated in the area, had been removed earlier in April. The U.S. supported the ARVN troops with approximately 500 artillerymen, air support, and an additional 500 combat engineers at Đăk Tô, but the relationship between ARVN and U.S. troops was strained. During the siege, the U.S. lost 19 killed and 120 wounded. By June, the North Vietnamese had surrounded Bến Hét, but a relief force of approximately 1,500 ARVN troops battled up **Route** 512 to relieve the troops near the end of June. It was estimated that the North Vietnamese lost 1,800 **casualties**; there were no reliable numbers of ARVN casualties. At the end of December 1971, Bến Hét became an ARVN Ranger camp. It was overrun by the **People's Army of Vietnam** and ceased to exist on 13 October 1972.

BẾN TRE. Capital of Kiến Hoa province in IV **Corps Tactical Zone**, located on one branch of the **Mê Kông River** as it flows into the delta. The city became known for two significant events during the war. The first occurred on 17 January 1960 with an uprising against **Ngô Đình Diệm** led by **Nguyễn Thị Định**, who would later become a founding member of the **National Liberation Front**. The city was also known for the Peter Arnett question to Major Chet Brown, "So you had to destroy the village in order to save it?" on 7 February 1968 in reference to the destruction of Bến Tre earlier during the 1968 **Tết Offensive**. Later the quotation was attributed incorrectly to Brown and served as an example of the folly and futility of war.

BERRIGAN, DANIEL JOSEPH (1921–). Antiwar leader and founder of several protest groups during the war. Berrigan was born in Virginia, Minnesota. He trained with the Jesuits and was ordained as a priest in 1952. He was a member of the New Catholic Left and opposed war. Berrigan and his younger brother Phillip were involved in a number of peace organizations and helped to organize resistance against the war. He was one of the founders of the Catholic Peace Movement in 1965, which assisted those who opposed the war and did not wish to serve in combat. He also served as the assistant director of Cornell United Religious Work from 1966 to 1970. As a result of his antiwar activities, Berrigan was arrested in 1967. In early 1968, he traveled to **Hà Nội** and helped to bring back three POWs. While these were the first POWs returned during the war, the North Vietnamese exploited the event for its **propaganda** value.

On 17 May 1968, Berrigan was involved in the destruction of draft files in Catonsville, Maryland, where he was arrested, as one of the **Catonsville Nine**, for conspiracy and destruction of government property and sentenced to three years in prison. Upon his release in 1972, Berrigan traveled to Paris to continue his antiwar activities. During the course of the war, Berrigan authored two books and received the **War Resisters League** Peace Award. After

Vietnam, he continued his protests against war, nuclear power, and American foreign policy in general. *See also* BERRIGAN, PHILIP FRANCIS.

BERRIGAN, PHILIP FRANCIS (1923–2002). Antiwar leader and participant in several protest activities during the war. Berrigan was born in Two Harbors, Minnesota. He served in World War II toward the end of that conflict, which influenced him toward a career in religion. Berrigan was ordained as a priest in the Saint Joseph's Society of the Sacred Heart in 1955, a group formed after the American Civil War to assist newly freed slaves. Berrigan also was a member of the New Catholic Left and was active in the civil rights movement in the 1950s and 1960s. As the war in Southeast Asia intensified, Berrigan focused his energy and attention toward the antiwar movement.

In 1964, he founded the **Emergency Citizens' Group Concerned about Vietnam** and cofounded with his older brother, Daniel, the **Catholic Peace Fellowship** in 1964. His antiwar activities became more radical as the war progressed. On 17 October 1967, Berrigan became one of the **Baltimore Four** who symbolically poured duck's blood on **Selective Service** records in the city's customs house. On 17 May 1968, he joined his brother and others in destroying draft files in Catonsville, Maryland. While in jail for his actions as one of the **Catonsville Nine**, Berrigan was also involved in the Harrisburg Seven plot to kidnap **Henry Kissinger**. Berrigan inspired a generation of antiwar protestors whose actions became more radical as the war progressed. He continued to protest war, civil injustice, and American foreign policy until his death. *See also* BERRIGAN, DANIEL JOSEPH.

BIÊN HÒA. Biên Hòa province was located to the east of **Sài Gòn**, while its capital of the same name was situated along **Route** 1 to the northeast. The original province included territory that connected it to the sea, but that area was transferred to **Gia Định** in the 1960s. During Operation **Passage to Freedom**, immediately after the signing of the 1954 **Geneva Agreements**, Biên Hòa experienced a population explosion as northern **refugees** were resettled in the province. As a result, Biên Hòa became a strategic area for the **Republic of Vietnam**, given its proximity to Sài Gòn, its position on Route 1 and the major railway in the South, and the new South Vietnamese citizens. During the 1950s, the **United States** directed a significant amount of resources to the area in order to rehabilitate the population and provide protection against the growing insurgency movement. On 8 July 1959, two American Army **advisers** were killed, which marked the first U.S. combat deaths in Vietnam by hostile fire.

Biên Hòa continued to play a strategic role in the 1960s. The U.S. established a major air base north of the capital from which the **U.S. Air Force** began its long war against the **National Liberation Front** and the **Democratic Republic of Vietnam**. The air base would become the largest U.S. facility in Southeast Asia and one of the busiest airfields in the world. In addition to the air base, Biên Hòa also housed **II Field Force, Vietnam**, headquarters and the U.S. Army base of **Long Bình**, which included the infamous Long Bình Jail. It was also the home of the **173rd Airborne Brigade** upon its arrival in 1965 and of the 1st U.S. **Division** for a brief time in late 1965. The province was one of the last to hold out before the fall of Sài Gòn in April 1975. *See also* AIR COMMANDOS; AIR FORCE, REPUBLIC OF VIETNAM; ARMY, UNITED STATES; INTERNATIONAL COMMISSION OF CONTROL AND SUPERVISION; JUNGLE JIM, PROJECT; REPUBLIC OF KOREA.

BÌNH ĐỊNH. Bình Định province was located on the coast of the **Republic of Vietnam** with its capital at **Qui Nhơn**. It was the home of the 1st Cavalry **Division**, based at An Khê, and the **Republic of Korea**'s Capital Division based in Qui Nhơn. The province was witness to several major **search-and-destroy** operations during the war, including operations **Masher/White Wing, Thayer,** and **Irving** in 1966. Bình Định was also the origin of the Tây Sơn Rebellion that began in 1770. *See also* BỒNG SƠN PLAIN; LÝ TÒNG BÁ; MARINE CORPS, VIETNAMESE; WASHINGTON GREEN, OPERATION.

BÌNH GIÃ, BATTLE OF. On 28 December 1964, elements of the 9th **Division** of the **National Liberation Front** (NLF) attacked an **Army of the Republic of Vietnam** (ARVN) unit at Bình Giã in Phước Tuy province. The attack was a part of a larger effort to strike at the **Republic of Vietnam** (RVN), which was still reeling from the effects of the coup d'état against **Ngô Đình Diệm** over a year earlier. The NLF overwhelmed the 65 militia men protecting the village and defeated two ARVN companies that had been called in for assistance. The next day, almost a battalion of ARVN Rangers arrived, but most of the force was immediately pinned down by the NLF. A battalion of Vietnamese **marines** arrived on 30 December and secured Bình Giã, which led to the fiercest day of fighting on 31 December, when nearly 400 marines forced their way to the site of a **helicopter** crash from the previous day with four Americans aboard and an isolated company of rangers.

By 1 January, an additional two battalions of rangers joined the battle, but the NLF had made the decision to leave the battlefield. The next day, the marines at Bình Giã linked up with the ARVN Rangers to police the battlefield. The battle pitted approximately 1,500 NLF soldiers against four ARVN Ranger battalions, three airborne battalions, and the marine battalion. The

RVN lost nearly 150 men with over 100 wounded and 165 missing. The battle was a military failure for the RVN and exposed how weak the ARVN really was when compared to frontline NLF troops.

BÌNH XUYÊN. The Bình Xuyên originated in the 1920s when a series of organized crime groups and pirates began to terrorize civilians and the military to the south of **Sài Gòn**. The group eventually threatened Sài Gòn in the late 1940s until **Ngô Đình Diệm** eliminated any real power the group possessed in 1955. It was led by Bảy Viễn, whose real name was **Lê Văn Viễn**. During the late 1940s, the Bình Xuyên and **Bảo Đại** worked out an agreement by which the group had free rein in Sài Gòn. The Bình Xuyên controlled gambling, prostitution, the drug trade, and the police force in return for the support of Bảo Đại's rule in Vietnam. The Bình Xuyên also enjoyed the support of the French as they exited the country after the 1954 **Geneva Agreements**.

In April 1955, the Bình Xuyên joined with the **Hòa Hảo** to form the United Front of Nationalist Forces. On 20 April, the United Front of Nationalist Forces attempted to overthrow Ngô Đình Diệm. The Bình Xuyên forces did not expect the swift and efficient reaction by the **Army of the Republic of Vietnam** forces in Sài Gòn and were beaten. By early May, the Bình Xuyên ceased to be an effective fighting force, as those not killed or captured fled the city to the Rừng Sác region south of Sài Gòn. Many later joined the insurgents, while Bảy Viễn fled to **France**. The defeat of the Bình Xuyên allowed Ngô Đình Diệm to abolish Bảo Đại's Imperial Guard and orchestrate a referendum on 23 October 1955 that allowed him to officially replace Bảo Đại as the head of state. *See also* COLLINS, JOSEPH LAWTON; LANSDALE, EDWARD GEARY; NGUYỄN CHÁNH THI; NGUYỄN HỮU HẠNH; RỪNG SÁC SPECIAL ZONE.

BLUE MARLIN, OPERATION. A joint **United States Marine Corps** (USMC) and **Republic of Vietnam** Marine Corps **search-and-destroy** operation in Quảng Tín province. The first phase of the operation, Blue Marlin I, began on 10 November 1965 with the marines landing 24 kilometers (15 miles) to the north of **Chu Lai** and working their way southward along **Route** 1. In the two-day phase, which involved the first joint U.S.-Vietnamese amphibious landing, there was no major contact with the enemy. Phase two of the operation, Blue Marlin II, began on 16 November 1965 and lasted for three days. Centered on the provinces of **Quảng Nam** and Quảng Tín, it involved the USMC and **Army of the Republic of Vietnam** (ARVN) Rangers who moved up both sides of the Trường Giang River to the Cầu Dai River, approximately 21 kilometers (13 miles) to the south of **Đà Nẵng**. Some 25 enemy soldiers were killed, with 15 captured and another 79 detained, while two ARVN soldiers were killed. *See also* AMPHIBIOUS OPERATIONS, UNITED STATES; NAVY, UNITED STATES; WALT, LEWIS W.

BLUE TREE. These were the air **reconnaissance** missions associated with Operation **Rolling Thunder** and the **Iron Hand sorties**, with the objective of gathering **intelligence** to support **bombing** missions. Blue Tree missions included all of the **Democratic Republic of Vietnam** except for restricted areas around **Hà Nội** and on the Chinese border. *See also* AIR WAR.

BLUE-WATER NAVY. Term used to describe **United States Navy** ships that operated in the South China Sea, the Gulf of Tŏn Kĭn, and the Gulf of Thailand. The blue-water navy consisted of capital ships, such as cruisers, aircraft carriers, and a battleship. There were also **coast guard** cutters and destroyers. The blue-water navy was involved in Operation **Market Time**, the interdiction campaign to stop North Vietnamese efforts to supply its forces in the **Republic of Vietnam** by sea. It also participated in Operation **Sea Dragon**, the naval complement to the air campaign Operation **Rolling Thunder** against the **Democratic Republic of Vietnam**. The blue-water navy was instrumental in helping thwart the 1972 **Easter Offensive** conducted by the North Vietnamese. *See also* BROWN-WATER NAVY.

BỜI LỜI WOODS. A forest located to the southeast of **Tây Ninh** city in Tây Ninh province, III **Corps Tactical Zone**. The woods bordered the **Iron Triangle** and served as a major stronghold for the **National Liberation Front** throughout the war. *See also* SHERWOOD FOREST, OPERATION.

BOLO, OPERATION. An air operation designed to eliminate the North Vietnamese MiG fighter threat to the vulnerable F-105 bombers employed in Operation **Rolling Thunder**. As Operation Rolling Thunder ended its second year, the North Vietnamese had developed a three-tiered air defense system of **antiaircraft artillery**, SAMs, and MiG fighters. On 2 January 1967, Colonel Robin Olds led a group of F-4Cs in an air strike using a similar formation and radio transmissions associated with the F-105. The North Vietnamese fell for the feint, losing seven aircraft in less than 15 minutes. The **United States** suffered no **casualties**. A similar mission on 6 January resulted in two additional MiG losses and forced the North Vietnamese to stand down their fighter force until May 1967. Operation Bolo provided the **U.S. Air Force** with much needed relief from one of the three significant weapons used by the North Vietnamese in their air defense. *See also* AIR WAR; AIRCRAFT (FIGHTER), UNITED STATES.

BOMBING PAUSES. On 12 February 1965, the Joint Chiefs of Staff forwarded to Secretary of Defense **Robert McNamara** an air campaign program to increase the pressure on the **Democratic Republic of Vietnam** (DRV) to stop the infiltration of personnel and supplies into the **Republic of Vietnam** (RVN). Operation **Rolling Thunder** began on 2 March and had as its objectives the reduction or elimination of military support received by the DRV, the destruction of infrastructure used to support the war, and the interdiction of personnel and supplies into the RVN. The **United States** hoped that the air campaign would convince the DRV that the U.S. was committed to the RVN and that the air strikes would lead to negotiations. The DRV argued that negotiations could not commence until the bombing stopped.

On 11 May 1965, the U.S. announced its first bombing pause to begin two days later. This decision was based upon indications that the DRV was willing to discuss a peaceful resolution to the growing conflict. During the pause, the U.S. conducted **reconnaissance** missions over the DRV. The halt lasted only five days when it became apparent that the DRV had no interest in negotiating toward an agreeable peace. Operation Rolling Thunder resumed on 18 May. During the five-day halt, U.S. reconnaissance aircraft confirmed that the DRV had redoubled its air defenses, including the introduction of the SA-2 air defense missile, and had repaired facilities that had been damaged since the beginning of the air campaign. The first pause set a precedent for the U.S. and the DRV.

For the **Lyndon B. Johnson** administration, bombing pauses, along with the threat of resumption, became a negotiating tool. The U.S. believed that this carrot-and-stick approach would force the DRV to realize that it had no choice but to submit to U.S. demands to end the war. The bombing pauses frustrated many within the military who believed that the ploy would not work, and it lessened the confidence of the **Sài Gòn** government as to the resolve of the U.S. to win the war. For the DRV, the bombing pauses were not seen as a carrot-and-stick strategy but rather as an indication that there was division within the Johnson administration that could be exploited by continued resolve to endure the Rolling Thunder **sorties**.

During the 46th and 47th cycle of Rolling Thunder in December 1965, the U.S. announced that it would begin a second major bombing pause to observe Christmas and the Tết holiday. While the U.S. had no indication from the DRV that it was willing to negotiate in good faith, the Johnson administration, and specifically McNamara, hoped the gesture would allow the DRV to reconsider its support for the **National Liberation Front**. The second bombing pause began on 24 December 1965. The U.S. continued to fly reconnaissance over the DRV and observed significant efforts to repair and rebuild damaged roads, railways, and bridges. The DRV air defense also received a major improvement. The pause lasted until 30 January 1966, after the end of Tết and as a result of the DRV's unwillingness to negotiate.

On 31 March 1968, President Lyndon B. Johnson stunned the nation when he announced that he would not seek or accept his party's nomination for the presidential candidacy in the 1968 national election. Johnson also announced that he authorized the end of Rolling Thunder operations north of the 20th parallel starting on 1 April. On 3 April, he ordered the end of air strikes north of the 19th parallel. This action was seen as a bombing pause by most in the U.S., but in reality the U.S. had not significantly decreased the number of air sorties over the DRV but had simply concentrated U.S. airpower over **Route Package** 1, 2, and part of 3. In the second quarter of 1968, the **United States** flew 27,406 sorties over the DRV, which was nearly double that of the first three months of the year. On 31 October 1968, Johnson ordered an end to Rolling Thunder to begin on 1 November. His critics argued that the halt was designed to help the presidential campaign of **Hubert Humphrey**, but it really served as a preliminary move to prepare for negotiations in Paris.

President **Richard M. Nixon** continued the bombing pause in his presidency, allowing for only **protective reaction strikes**. In late 1971, it became apparent that the DRV was organizing for a major offensive. As a result, Nixon ordered Operation **Proud Deep Alpha** in December 1971 to destroy DRV stockpiles of material south of the 20th parallel. When the DRV launched the 1972 **Easter Offensive**, the U.S. responded with operations **Freedom Train** and **Linebacker I**. A bombing pause began on 22 October 1972, officially ending Linebacker I, but bombing sorties were resumed on 18 December with the initiation of **Linebacker II**. The final halt occurred on 30 December. The January 1973 **Paris Peace Accords** ended U.S. bombing in the **Republic of Vietnam**. In April, U.S. air operations ended in **Laos**, and on 15 August, the last U.S. combat sorties in **Cambodia** were flown. *See also* AIR WAR; ANTIWAR MOVEMENT; CANADA; KENNEDY, ROBERT FRANCIS; RABORN, WILLIAM FRANCIS; UNITED NATIONS.

BOMBS. The **United States** used a series of different types of bombs during the war, of which the most common type were the dumb bombs, identified as the Mark bomb, which ranged from 250 to 2,000 pounds. The Mark bombs were either general purpose or high-explosive weapons. The U.S. also employed fuel-air explosives such as **napalm** and experimented with guided bombs.

There were many varieties of Mark bombs used in Vietnam. The Mark-82 (Mk-82) was a free-fall 500-pound bomb designed to provide extensive damage. It carried an explosive charge of 87 kilograms (192 pounds) in a casing 1.68 meters (66 inches) long and with a diameter of 37 centimeters

(14.5 inches). The Mk-83 weighed approximately 1,000 pounds with a 200-kilogram (445-pound) explosive charge and was housed in a 3-meter (120-inch) long and 36-centimeter (14-inch) diameter shell. It was used primarily by the U.S. **Navy**. The Mk-84 weighed 2,000 pounds with an explosive charge of 428 kilograms (945 pounds). The Mk-84 was 3.28 meters (129 inches) long and 46 centimeters (18 inches) in diameter. The Mk-118 was the largest bomb in the Mark series used in Vietnam, with a weight of 3,000 pounds and an explosive charge of 880 kilograms (1,945 pounds). The U.S. also used the Mk-20/CBU-100 **cluster bomb unit**, which had been designed as an antitank weapon but proved effective against the **Democratic Republic of Vietnam**'s air defense systems.

Laser-guided weapons were also employed in Southeast Asia during the war. Among the more popular were the AGM-62 Walleye I and Paveway I **missiles**. The Walleye was introduced in 1967 as an electro-optically guided air-to-ground missile. It was a glide missile with a television camera mounted to its front and steered to its target by the pilot of the aircraft that delivered it or by a trailing aircraft. The weapon had limited usage during Operation **Rolling Thunder** but was used with greater frequency in operations **Linebacker I** and **Linebacker II**. The Paveway I was a modified Mk-117 that was a highly accurate laser-guided bomb used briefly before the end of Operation Rolling Thunder and more extensively during the Linebacker operations. It was credited with the destruction of the **Thanh Hóa bridge**, which had been a difficult target to hit.

The U.S. also used larger bombs for a number of missions in Southeast Asia during the war. The BLU-82, known as the Daisy Cutter, was a 15,000-pound weapon with approximately 5,700 kilograms (12,600 pounds) of explosives. It was first experimented with in Operation **Commando Vault** to create instant **landing zones** in the thick jungles of Southeast Asia, though the weapon's value increased because of its large blast radius and the tremendous shock from the explosion after impact. One of the more effective and controversial types of bombs was delivered by the BLU-118, which served as the canister for the 500-pound napalm bomb. *See also* AIR WAR; AIRCRAFT (BOMBERS), UNITED STATES; BOMBING PAUSES.

BỒNG SƠN PLAIN. Located in **Bình Định** province in II **Corps Tactical Zone**, north of **Qui Nhơn**, the Bồng Sơn Plain was a heavily populated area that had been a stronghold for the **National Liberation Front** (NLF) as well as the **Việt Minh** before them. The area was under the operational control of the 1st Cavalry **Division** in late 1965 and was witness to a series of **search-and-destroy** operations designed to clear the area of **People's Army of Vietnam** (PAVN) and NLF influence. The first major operation was **Masher/**

White Wing, which lasted from 28 January to 6 March 1966 and also included the 22nd **Army of the Republic of Vietnam** (ARVN) Division, the **Republic of Vietnam** Airborne Brigade, and the 1st Regiment of the **Republic of Korea**'s Capitol Division. These forces were aligned against the 3rd PAVN Division as well as NLF regiments. This was followed by Operation Bee Bee, which lasted from 26 April to 28 April 1966 and involved the 3rd Brigade, 1st Cavalry Division. Two concurrent operations followed. Operation Crazy Horse, from 16 May to 5 June 1966, involved the 1st Brigade, 1st Cavalry Division, Republic of Korea Capitol Division and ARVN forces in a search-and-destroy operation and also served as a spoiling attack planned by the NLF against the **Civilian Irregular Defense Group** (CIDG) camp at Vĩnh Thành, while Operation Davy Crockett, which lasted from 4 to 27 May 1966, involved the 3rd Brigade, 1st Cavalry Division and the 22nd ARVN Division around the Bồng Sơn **Special Forces** camp and was a continuation of the Masher/White Wing search-and-destroy concept.

The next major operation occurred in 1967. Operation Bullseye, which lasted from 27 January to 31 January 1967, involved the 2nd Brigade, 1st Cavalry Division and the 40th ARVN Regiment. The operation was really a reconnaissance-in-force and was coordinated with Operation **Thayer** II, an operation that combined elements of the 1st Air Cavalry Division, 3rd ARVN Airborne Brigade and the 41st ARVN Regiment in a sweep of the Kim Sơn Valley. The final major operation occurred in 1968. Operation Đàn Sinh 22-6 started on 22 August and lasted until 12 December 1968. It involved the **173rd Airborne Brigade** and the 22nd ARVN Division in a reconnaissance-in-force operation. Despite the attention paid to the Bồng Sơn Plain, the 3rd PAVN Division, consisting of the 2nd, 18th, and 22nd regiments, continued to operate in the area throughout the war.

BOOBY TRAPS. The **People's Army of Vietnam** (PAVN) and the **National Liberation Front** (NLF) used a variety of booby traps during the war in order to inflict **casualties** on the **Free World Forces**. Booby traps came in a variety of types and sophistication. One of the simplest traps was the use of panji sticks, sharpened to a point and inserted into a pit dug in the ground. Panji sticks or other sharpened objects were also used to create an injury when stepped on. In both cases, the victim of the trap would receive a wound to the foot or leg. To make the wound more serious, the objects often had fecal matter spread over them to cause infection. Other simple traps used sharpened objects with a counterweight that was triggered by movement to cause injury to the head or face. Trip wires also set off booby traps designed with panji sticks, arrows, logs embedded with bamboo pikes (known as mace traps), stinging insects, reptiles, or explosives. The PAVN and NLF used discarded or dud weapons, such as grenades, cartridges, or **artillery** shells, as booby traps. Trails and areas where the enemy was expected to travel were frequently booby trapped. These areas were often identified with some type of marker that enabled friendly forces to bypass dangerous areas. On the other hand, the **United States**, the **Army of the Republic of Vietnam**, and other **Free World Forces** used booby traps, though they did not compare in their simplicity with those used by the PAVN and NLF. *See also* GUERRILLA WARFARE; TUNNEL RATS; U MINH FOREST.

BOUN OUM, PRINCE (1912–1980). Twice prime minister of **Laos** and also referred to as Boun Oum Na Champassak, he was the son of Laotian king Ratsadanay, who was from the southern part of Laos, formerly known as the Kingdom of Champassak. Boun Oum was educated at the Wat Liep Monastery School and the École de droit in Laos. In 1946, his father died, and Boun Oum assumed the position of head of the House of Champassak. During the **First Indochina War**, Boun Oum sided with **France**. He served as the first prime minister of an independent Laos from March 1949 to February 1950 until he was ousted by his cousin **Souvanna Phouma**, who organized a neutralist government. Boun Oum returned to power in December 1960 to head an anticommunist government but was again removed from power as a result of the 1962 **Geneva Conference** on Laos. Boun Oum joined Souvanna Phouma in organizing a government of national union, with Souvanna Phouma as the prime minister and Boun Oum as the inspector general of the kingdom. During the war, Boun Oum represented the pro-Western faction in Laos, while his cousin Souvanna Phouma led the neutralists and Prince **Souphanouvong** headed the communist groups. Boum Oum left Laos in 1974 as the **Pathet Lao** increased their power in Laos. He moved to **Thailand** and then settled in Paris.

BROTHERHOOD, OPERATION. In 1954, the **Philippines** Junior Chamber of Commerce organized a group of medical professionals to aid the State of Vietnam, which had just finished the **First Indochina War**. Vietnam was beginning to feel the effects of the northern **refugee** population who were arriving in the South as a result of Operation Exodus and Operation **Passage to Freedom**. Under the name Operation Brotherhood, the Philippines, guided by President Ramon Magsaysay, worked with the Vietnamese people to provide medical care and supplies necessary for survival. The first group of Filipinos arrived in October 1954. In 1955, Operation Brotherhood was selected as a Junior Chamber International project, and Jaycees from 18 countries as well as private and governmental organizations and individuals contributed money and supplies for the relief effort. By the time the members of Operation Brotherhood left the **Republic of Vietnam** (RVN) in December 1967, it was estimated that they had treated nearly 750,000 people. The Philippines continued to provide aid to the RVN, eventually committing, in 1966, a 2,000-person task force to conduct a civic action campaign in the Thanh Điền forest.

BROWN-WATER NAVY. Term used to describe the naval craft and vessels that operated in the waterways of inland Vietnam during the war. As the name implies, it operated in the brown water of Vietnam, which included its rivers, streams, and canals. These forces operated mainly in IV **Corps Tactical Zone**, though the presence of the brown-water navy was seen throughout the **Republic of Vietnam**. Two of the main vessels used in brown-water navy operations were the **patrol boat, river**, and the **swift boat**, though the navy also employed monitors, barges, and some more traditional vessels in its arsenal. The brown-water navy was instrumental in the success of Operation **SEALORDS** and in the ability to sustain pressure against the **National Liberation Front** forces to the west and south of **Sài Gòn**. *See also* BLUE-WATER NAVY; NAVY, REPUBLIC OF VIETNAM.

BROWNE, MALCOLM WILDE (1931–). Journalist and Pulitzer Prize recipient, Browne served in the **United States Army** from 1956 to 1958 and, after being stationed in Korea, became a reporter for *Stars and Stripes*. He joined the Associated Press in 1960 and in the fall of 1961 became a correspondent for Indochina. On 11 June 1963, Browne was informed that a significant event would occur on a crowded street in **Sài Gòn**. He arrived in time to take photographs of the self-immolation of **Thích Quảng Đức**, which would win him a Pulitzer Prize. The photograph served as a catalyst for the growing U.S. opposition to the rule of **Ngô Đình Diệm** that culminated in his overthrow and assassination in November 1963. Browne later joined the *New York Times* as a foreign correspondent and then as a science reporter. He also served as the senior editor for *Discover* magazine. He authored *The New Faces of War* in 1965 and wrote his autobiography, *Muddy Boots and Red Socks*, in 1993. *See also* ANTIWAR MOVEMENT; NGUYỄN NGỌC LOAN.

BRU. A **Montagnard** tribe that lived in **Quảng Trị** and in the provinces bordering it in Laos and **Thailand**. The Bru speak the Mon-**Khmer** language and practice slash-and-burn agriculture.

BUDDHIST CRISIS, 1963. The **Buddhist** Crisis resulted from **Ngô Đình Diệm**'s reaction to two events in 1963. The first was related to the Episcopal silver jubilee for Ngô Đình Thục, the archbishop of **Huế** and Ngô Đình Diệm's older brother, who during the celebration flew the white-and-gold Catholic flag. Under a decree promulgated by Ngô Đình Diệm earlier, this action was prohibited, but the **Sài Gòn** government did not enforce it. On 7 May 1963, Buddhists in Huế, as a part of a celebration marking the 2,507th anniversary of the birth of Buddha, wanted to fly the Buddhist flag. The Sài Gòn government refused the request. This resulted in a demonstration the next day against Ngô Đình Diệm's arbitrary and contradictory decision and a clash between the Buddhist protesters and local security forces in Huế, led by Major Đặng Sỹ.

The security forces tried to disperse the Buddhists with fire hoses and tear gas, but Đặng Sỹ issued live ammunition and grenades to his troops after the demonstrators failed to disband. At the end of the day, nine Vietnamese were dead and several others wounded. Both the Buddhist leaders and the Ngô Đình Diệm government claimed that the deaths were the responsibility of the other side. Neither side was willing to reconcile their differences, and as a result tensions mounted. On 11 June, a Buddhist monk, **Thích Quảng Đức**, committed self-immolation on a busy street intersection in **Chợ Lớn**, a suburb of Sài Gòn. This act turned many within the **United States** against Ngô Đình Diệm and his brother, **Ngô Đình Nhu**.

Both Ngô Đình Diệm and the U.S. mismanaged the crisis. Ngô Đình Diệm stubbornly held to his family loyalties and supported Ngô Đình Thục and Ngô Đình Nhu, even though Ngô Đình Diệm disagreed with Ngô Đình Thục's violation of the decree. The **John F. Kennedy** administration placed increasing pressure on Ngô Đình Diệm to resolve the crisis and failed to consider it an internal matter. American **media** outlets helped to keep the issue alive in the U.S. and intensified their criticism of Ngô Đình Diệm's rule and his adherence to his family. Early in the crisis, Ngô Đình Diệm made some moves toward reconciliation, but he was never able to satisfy the Buddhist leaders. As the crisis deepened, the Buddhist leaders called for his removal, which prompted Ngô Đình Diệm to claim that the communists had infiltrated the Buddhist movement. As the crisis continued through the summer, Ngô Đình Nhu became increasingly paranoid that the Buddhists were planning a coup d'état against his brother. On 21 August, he authorized a series of raids on pagodas in Sài Gòn and Huế, resulting in the arrest of hundreds of protestors and bystanders. The most famous raid occurred at the **Xá Lợi Pagoda** in Sài Gòn.

By the end of August 1963, few in Washington supported Ngô Đình Diệm. The new ambassador, **Henry Cabot Lodge Jr.**, who replaced **Frederick E. Nolting Jr.** on 26 August, had a decidedly anti-Ngô Đình Diệm stance and did little to restore confidence in the **Republic of Vietnam** president. **W.**

Averill Harriman further complicated matters when, at a 28 August press conference, he asserted that the U.S. had put Ngô Đình Diệm in power and had been betrayed by that decision. The crisis continued into the fall without an end in sight. It would serve as one of the more significant justifications for the U.S. decision not to impede the talk of a military-initiated coup d'état, which eventually took place on 1 November 1963, resulting in the assassination of Ngô Đình Diệm and Ngô Đình Nhu, and it marked the beginning of a major shift in America's Vietnam experience. *See also* NGÔ ĐÌNH CẨN; THÍCH TRÍ QUANG; TÔN THẤT ĐÍNH.

BUDDHIST RELIGION. Buddhism was introduced to Vietnam at some point in the 2nd century. The Vietnamese Buddhists were influenced by various versions of the religion. Most Vietnamese practiced a Mahayana form of Buddhism, which has its origins in **India** and was introduced in Vietnam from the North. Another form of Buddhism, Theravada, had a following in Southeast Asia and was brought to Vietnam through **Thailand, Laos**, and **Cambodia**. Theravada Buddhism was practiced by the **Khmer** in Cambodia, the **Lao** in Laos, and the **Khmer Krom** in the **Mê Kông Delta**, among others.

The Buddhist religion was recognized during the Đinh Dynasty at the end of the 10th century, while the religion flourished under succeeding Vietnamese dynasties. Buddhists did protest continued French rule in the region, and in 1951, the General Association of Buddhists was created to reorganize their religious activities. Buddhist leaders were involved with the **Hòa Hảo**, which threatened the internal stability of the State of Vietnam in 1954–1955. During the early 1960s, Vietnamese Buddhists attempted to undermine the rule of **Ngô Đình Diệm**, who had failed to eliminate earlier French colonial anti-Buddhist decrees. In 1963, the **Buddhist Crisis** served as a catalyst for the removal of Ngô Đình Diệm from office and his assassination.

The coup d'état against Ngô Đình Diệm ushered in an era of more active Buddhist leadership in political and military decisions. Buddhists protested against the government of **Nguyễn Khánh** and **Trần Văn Hương** in 1964 and staged a significant uprising in March 1966 in I **Corps Tactical Zone** against the removal of Buddhist general **Nguyễn Chánh Thi**. The religious activities of the Vietnamese Buddhists in the **Democratic Republic of Vietnam** were suppressed, but after the reunification of the two Vietnams into the Socialist Republic of Vietnam in 1976, the Buddhist influence has slowly regained prominence on a national scale. *See also* FRANCE.

BUFFALO HUNTER. Code name for **United States** air **reconnaissance drones** that flew over the **Democratic Republic of Vietnam** (DRV) during the war. One drone used in project Buffalo Hunter was the AQM-34L Firebee.

It was a remotely piloted vehicle used in reconnaissance of DRV targets that had been struck but still posed a danger to manned reconnaissance flights because of **antiaircraft artillery**. Launched and controlled from a DC-130 Hercules cargo aircraft, the Firebee provided low-level photography. The drone had a maximum speed of 1,030 kilometers (645 miles) per hour and a range of 1,200 kilometers (750 miles), with a maximum ceiling of 15.2 kilometers (50,000 feet). The drone was equipped with Doppler-radar, a **LORAN** navigation system, a River Bounder Electronic Countermeasures system that could jam surface-to-air missile radar, and real-time photography retrieval. Its length ranged from 7.9 meters (26 feet) to 9.7 meters (32 feet), depending on the model used. When the Firebee finished its mission, it was recovered by **helicopter** in the air, on land, or in the water. The U.S. conducted approximately 35 Buffalo Hunter missions.

BUNDY, MCGEORGE (1919–1996). National security adviser and younger brother to **William Bundy**, McGeorge Bundy was born in Boston and educated at the Groton School and at Yale University where he graduate first in his class. He became a junior fellow at Harvard in 1941 and joined the Office of Facts and Figures in Washington after the **United States** entered World War II in December 1941. He entered the U.S. Army and was aide to Rear Admiral Alan J. Kirk. By the time the war ended, he had risen to the rank of captain. After the war, he turned to international relations, eventually joining the Council on Foreign Relations in 1949, and was involved in studying the Marshall Plan. Also in 1949, he joined the faculty of Harvard University as a professor of political science and in 1953 became chairman of the department. That fall, he became the dean of the Faculty of Arts and Sciences. In 1961, President **John F. Kennedy** appointed him as his assistant to the president for national security affairs. He served as the national security adviser from 20 January 1961 to 28 February 1966. Bundy was involved in all of the significant foreign policy events during the Kennedy administration. He was one of the leading proponents of escalation in Vietnam, including sustained **bombing**.

It was Bundy and Secretary of Defense **Robert McNamara** who pushed for the air campaign against the **Democratic Republic of Vietnam**. Bundy would eventually shift his opinion away from escalation in Vietnam but voiced his doubt too late. After he left the White House, he became the president of the Ford Foundation. He remained in that position until 1979. Bundy returned to academia as a professor of history at New York University for the next decade and as a scholar-in-residence at the Carnegie Foundation from 1990 until his death in 1996. *See also* NATIONAL SECURITY ACTION MEMORANDUM 328; ROSTOW, WALT WHITMAN.

BUNDY, WILLIAM PUTNAM (1917–2000). Assistant secretary of state and older brother to **McGeorge Bundy**. Bundy was born in Boston and educated at the Groton School, where he graduated at the top of his class, and at Yale University. He earned an MA in history at Harvard and started law school before the **United States** entered World War II. In 1941, he entered the U.S. Army and joined the Signal Corps as a code breaker in Great Britain. By the time the war ended, he had risen to the rank of major. After the war, Bundy finished his law degree. He joined the **Central Intelligence Agency** after the start of the Korean War and became chief of staff for the preparation of National Intelligence Estimates and supported the activities of the **National Security Council**.

When **John F. Kennedy** was elected to the White House, Bundy served as the deputy assistant secretary of defense for international security affairs until November 1963, and then as assistant secretary of defense for international security affairs until 14 March 1964. On 16 March, President **Lyndon B. Johnson** promoted him to the assistant secretary of state for far eastern affairs (a position renamed assistant secretary of state for East Asian and Pacific affairs). He remained there until 4 May 1969. Early in the war, Bundy favored an international settlement to the conflict rather than a slow escalation leading to combat troops, but he was one of the individuals who drafted the August 1964 **Gulf of Tŏn Kĭn Resolution**. Despite his **Dove** tendencies, Bundy did not join Undersecretary of State **George Ball** in his July 1965 attempt to end escalation, though he did call for moderation. After his public service with the Kennedy and **Johnson** administrations, Bundy joined the Center for International Studies at the Massachusetts Institute of Technology. His public service record followed him to Massachusetts where he was singled out by **antiwar** demonstrators. From 1972 to 1984, he served as the editor for the influential journal *Foreign Affairs*. He also taught at Princeton University.

BUNKER, ELLSWORTH (1894–1984). United States ambassador to the **Republic of Vietnam** (RVN) from April 1967 to May 1973. Bunker entered public life during the Harry S. Truman administration, when he was appointed as ambassador to Argentina in 1951. In 1952, he became the ambassador to Italy. He remained in that position until 1953. In 1956, President Dwight D. Eisenhower appointed him as ambassador to **India**. He remained in that post until 1961, overseeing an intense period of tension between India and its neighbor, the **People's Republic of China**. He helped to broker a settlement between **Australia** and Indonesia over the problem of West New Guinea in 1962 and then became ambassador to the Organization of American States in 1964.

On 5 April 1967, President **Lyndon B. Johnson** appointed Bunker as ambassador to the RVN to replace **Henry Cabot Lodge Jr.** He remained in that position until 11 May 1973 where he fulfilled the objectives of the Johnson and **Richard M. Nixon** administrations in their prosecution of the war, which included convincing RVN president **Nguyễn Văn Thiệu** to sign the January 1973 **Paris Peace Accords.** After the war, Bunker helped work out the 1977 Torrijos-Carter Treaties that handed over operation of the Panama Canal to Panama. His diplomatic career was one of conflict resolution, though the resolution he helped to bring about in Vietnam did not last for more than two years before the country fell to communism in April 1975. *See also* MARTIN, GRAHAM ANDERSON.

C

C-4. A plastic explosive, primarily from cyclotrimethylene trinitramine, used by **United States** and allied personnel in the war for a number of missions. It was lightweight and very stable; it would not explode without a detonation device. C-4 would work when wet and was malleable, which allowed it to be used for more than just military missions. C-4 was used to detonate **mines** and fixed targets, but because of its slow-burning properties, it was also used as a fuel to heat rations or to keep warm. *See also* MINES, LAND.

CÀ MAU. Located in An Xuyên province (previously a part of Bạc Liêu) in IV **Corps Tactical Zone**, Cà Mau served as the capital of the province. It was situated between **Route** 12, which terminated at the southernmost city in the **Republic of Vietnam** (RVN), Năm Căn, and Route 4, which went north to Sóc Trăng. This area was also known as the Cà Mau Peninsula. The peninsula is bordered by the Gulf of Thailand to the west and the South China Sea to the east. The Cà Mau Peninsula was heavily contested by the **Việt Minh** and the **National Liberation Front** during the **First Indochina War** and the **Second Indochina War**. One of its prominent features was the U **Minh Forest** located between the borders of Kiên Giang and An Xuyên provinces, which included swamplands that made it almost inaccessible, and therefore it often served as a safe haven for those forces battling the **Sài Gòn** government.

CALLEY, WILLIAM LAWS, JR. (1943–). Principal participant in the **Mỹ Lai** massacre. Calley was educated at Miami Edison High School and dropped out of Palm Beach Junior College after one year. He held a variety of jobs until he enlisted in the **United States Army** in July 1966. After basic training at Fort Benning, he received advanced individual training as a company clerk. He was accepted to Officer Candidate School and completed the course in September 1967. Calley was commissioned as a second lieutenant and was assigned to Company C, 1st Battalion, 20th Infantry Regiment, 11th Infantry Brigade, which became a part of the 23rd **Division**, also known as the Americal Division. Calley's record as an officer was uneven; he was both liked and disliked. Calley became one of the leading participants in an event that came to symbolize the negative aspects of the war and served as a rallying point for **antiwar** activists. Calley's company was operating around the village of Sơn Mỹ. The U.S. had been operating in the area for much of the war and had suffered significant **casualties** as a result of **booby traps** and **mines**.

On 16 March 1968, Calley ordered his men into the hamlets of Mỹ Lai and My Khe to round up and kill the inhabitants. This episode, which was originally covered up, became known as the Mỹ Lai massacre, after journalist Seymour Hersh uncovered the story in November 1969. Twenty-six Americans were charged with various crimes. The charges and Hersh's story led to a U.S. Army official investigation directed by General William Peers which in March 1970 reported on the massacre and cover-up. Calley's trial began on 17 November 1970 with charges of premeditated murder of 104 Vietnamese. On 29 March 1971, Calley was convicted of 22 counts of murder. He was sentenced to life at hard labor at Fort Leavenworth on 31 March. The only other case that went to trial was for Brigade Commander, Colonel Oran K. Henderson, who was acquitted in December 1971.

The Calley trial received much attention, and while Calley became the target for antiwar protestors, there were many in the U.S. who believed that he was made a scapegoat for the crimes of other men. There were state and national demonstrations in support of Calley, many of which argued that Calley had been convicted only for doing his job, which unfortunately resulted in the death of civilians caught in the cross fire of battle. The day after his conviction, President **Richard M. Nixon** authorized the transfer of Calley from Fort Leavenworth to Fort Benning as Calley's appeals were heard. On 20 August 1971, Calley's sentence was reduced to 20 years by the commanding general at Fort Benning. In 1973, it was further reduced to 10 years.

On 11 February 1974, Calley petitioned and received habeas corpus, which led to his release on bail on 27 February. The case was reversed by an appeals court, and Calley returned to jail at Fort Leavenworth on 13 June. He was finally released on 9 November 1974, having served less than three years under house arrest while at Fort Benning and as a prison laborer (clerk-typist) at Fort Leavenworth. Calley's public appearances were few, and he refused to discuss the events of Mỹ Lai unless significantly paid. On 19 August 2009, Calley allegedly apologized for the Mỹ Lai massacre at a meeting of the Kiwanis Club of Greater Columbus. His mea culpa was greeted with outrage by the veteran community, which still suffered the effects of the Mỹ Lai massacre that marred the honorable service of so many American veterans of the war.

CAM RANH BAY. Located in Ninh Thuận province in III **Corps Tactical Zone** along the South China Sea and nearly 290 kilometers (180 miles) to the north-northeast of **Sài Gòn**, Cam Ranh Bay became one of the major logistic centers of the **United States** after 1965. Cam Ranh Bay was preferred because of its deep-water inlet that was able to accommodate all U.S. ships. It was also easily protected and was located very close to **Route** 1, which stretched from Sài Gòn to the **Demilitarized Zone**, making the water port accessible to all parts of the **Republic of Vietnam** (RVN). While the U.S. built up its naval facilities at Cam Ranh Bay in 1965, the area had been used by both the French and the Japanese. It was not considered important in the earlier period of American involvement until the U.S. initiated Operation **Market Time** and began its gradual escalation of troops and aircraft in the RVN.

Because of the strategic location of Cam Ranh Bay, an airbase was also established near the city of Cam Ranh, as was the Joint Service Ammunition Depot, which supplied ammunition to Task Force 115, Task Force 116, and Task Force 117, as well as to many of the naval ships involved in Operation **Sea Dragon**. The air base was used by the U.S. after 8 November 1965. It housed the 12th Tactical Fighter Wing, the 412th Munitions Maintenance Squadron, the 1512th Support Squadron of the Military Air Transport Service, the 9th Aeromedical Evacuation Group, the 14th Aerial Port Squadron and the 608th Military Airlift Support Squadrons of the Military Airlift Command, the 483rd Tactical Airlift Wing, and additional aircraft involved in special operations. The facilities at Cam Ranh Bay were eventually turned over to the RVN during the later stages of **Vietnamization**. It was captured by the **People's Army of Vietnam** on 3 April 1975 during the final offensive.

CAMBODIA (DEMOCRATIC KAMPUCHEA). Situated to the west of the **Republic of Vietnam** (RVN) and south of **Laos**, Cambodia was one of the three countries that made up French Indochina before it received its independence in November 1953. The country, with its capital at **Phnom Penh**, is approximately 181,100 square kilometers (69,900 square miles), with a population that numbered between six and seven million during the war. In addition to the capital, the other major city in Cambodia was **Sihanoukville**, which possessed the major port for the country. The Tonlé Sap (Great Lake), **Mê Kông**, and Bassac rivers were the major waterways in the country, while mountains dominated the north and southwest part of the country. Like most of Southeast Asia, Cambodia is also governed by **climate**, with tropical monsoon rains during the summer and early fall. Most of the people in the country during the war were **Khmer**, which is also the official language, but a small Vietnamese population was also present along the border between the two countries, which often led to border disputes and accusations of kidnapping during the 1950s and early 1960s. Lao, **Chams**, and **Montagnards** also inhabited Cambodia. The majority of Cambodians practice Theravada **Buddhism**, though there is a small Islamic and Christian population.

The dispute over borders between Cambodia and the RVN preceded the **First Indochina War** as the Vietnamese people carved out the southern part of their country from the Khmer Kingdom of Angkor, which had fallen into disarray in the 15th century. Cambodia fell quickly into the French colonial empire in the 19th century and remained a colony until it was able to gain a degree of autonomy from **France** after World War II, culminating in a 9 November 1953 agreement that gave Cambodia its independence. As a result of the 1954 **Geneva Conference**, Cambodia agreed to remain neutral, but under the leadership of **Norodom Sihanouk**, it began to side with the North Vietnamese as it appeared that they might win the war. Sihanouk, like his fellow Cambodians, had an inherent distrust of the Vietnamese people and quickly entered into confrontation with RVN president **Ngô Đình Diệm** over border raids between the two countries, and over Cambodia's harboring, or at least negligence in allowing, the communist insurgents who used that country to launch attacks against the **Sài Gòn** government. Internally, Sihanouk consolidated his power with the creation of the Sangkum Reastr Niyum (People's Socialist Community), which became the dominant force in Cambodian politics and was only directly confronted by the Pracheachon, a political organization of communists and Democrats.

While the Cambodian border area with the RVN grew into a significant safe haven for **People's Army of Vietnam** (PAVN) and **National Liberation Front** (NLF) personnel during the 1960s, it was the unintended consequences of the **United States'** effort to interdict the flow of personnel and supplies by sea that pushed Cambodia further into the war. The success of Operation **Market Time**, which began on 11 March 1965, effectively cut off the sea route and forced the North Vietnamese to find another way to support its war in the South. While it developed the **Hồ Chí Minh Trail** through Laos and the northeastern part of Cambodia, the North Vietnamese needed an efficient way to move the supplies necessary to sustain the war. The solution to Market Time was to bypass the sea interdiction, which stretched to 240 kilometers (150 miles) off of the RVN coastline, and send neutral shipping into Sihanoukville. The North Vietnamese formed the **Hak Ly Company** as a front for transfer of these supplies from Sihanoukville, through Phnom Penh, along Highway 4, to Kampong Speu where they divided the materials between the PAVN and NLF and the Cambodia Army at Lovek. In an obvious act of duplicity, Sihanouk maintained a public stance of neutrality in the war but clearly failed to live up to that policy.

Sihanouk continued to look the other way as the North Vietnamese moved troops into his country and the PAVN and NLF operated from secured bases against U.S. and **Army of the Republic of Vietnam** (ARVN) troops. Cambodia became a sanctuary for the PAVN and NLF force, which frustrated the U.S. because it could not move into the neutral country. By 1969, PAVN and NLF base areas along the border consisted of established training areas, rest and relaxation camps, hospitals, forward bases, and a series of bunker complexes, while the number of Vietnamese soldiers in Cambodia was estimated at 40,000. Whereas the **Lyndon B. Johnson** administration failed to escalate the war by eliminating the Vietnamese threat in Cambodia, the **Richard M. Nixon** administration exposed the failure of Cambodian neutrality and worked to end that annoyance.

Nixon's more aggressive strategy was countered by the PAVN and NLF, which started to show signs of violating their long-standing agreement with Phnom Penh by collecting taxes from Cambodians under their control and conscripting them to build roads, camps, and other facilities for their use. The North Vietnamese also encouraged a black market for rice by paying a higher-than-market value for the food, which undermined the already fragile Cambodian economy. Added to these measures was the North Vietnamese support of the **Khmer Rouge**, a small but growing communist insurgency in Cambodia under the leadership of Saloth Sar (**Pol Pot**), which sought to overthrow the government and initiate a social and economic revolution.

Nixon authorized a secret **bombing** campaign against PAVN- and NLF-held territory in Cambodia that began on 18 March 1969. The operation, known as **Menu**, with missions titled Breakfast, Lunch, Supper, Dessert, and Snack, was designed to stave off a 1969 PAVN and NLF offensive directed against Sài Gòn similar to the 1968 **Tết Offensive**. The operation had the immediate effect of throwing the North Vietnamese off balance and continued until 26 May 1970. The secret nature of the bombing was exposed by a *New York Times* article on 2 May 1970 after the U.S. initiated the **Cambodian Incursion**. Menu delivered an estimated 120,000 tons of **bombs**. In conjunction with Menu, Sihanouk publicly announced that the PAVN and NLF were present in Cambodia and had established a base area to support their war against the RVN. While the confirmation of what the U.S. already knew was appreciated, Sihanouk's action of restricting the shipment of weapons from Kampong Speu and Lovek to the base areas was significant.

In August 1969, under increasing political pressure from the anticommunist factions within Cambodia, Sihanouk created the Salvation Government with former army commander-in-chief **Lon Nol** as prime minister and Prince **Sisowath Sirik Matak**, Sihanouk's cousin, as deputy prime minister. Both men were anticommunist and strongly opposed the presence of PAVN and NLF troops in Cambodia. Cambodia was, however, too important to the **Democratic Republic of Vietnam** (DRV) in its war against the RVN. **Hà**

Nội began to pressure Sihanouk to relax his position and return to the pre-March 1969 status quo. In September, Sihanouk agreed and authorized the release of approximately 5,000 tons of material. In return, he was financially compensated and received a guarantee from the DRV that it would limit the use of its base areas, vacate them when there was no longer a need, and stop aiding the Khmer Rouge.

Neither Lon Nol nor Matak concurred and began to work against Sihanouk's rule. After the death of his wife, Lon Nol left for France in October 1969, and Matak took over the government. His relationship with Sihanouk had always been strained, but Sihanouk's September decision further deteriorated the association. When Sihanouk left for France on 6 January 1970 for health reasons, Matak and Lon Nol, who had returned to Cambodia on 18 February 1970, took advantage of the situation.

Factions that supported the position of Lon Nol and Matak organized public demonstrations for 8 March against the PAVN and NLF in several border towns. Protestors destroyed the North Vietnamese and **Provisional Revolutionary Government of the Republic of South Vietnam** embassy while Cambodia forces fired on PAVN and NLF base areas. A few days after the demonstrations, Lon Nol ordered PAVN and NLF troops out of Cambodia and issued a proclamation returning his country back to strict neutrality. Sihanouk, who was still overseas, opposed this new policy, which led Lon Nol and Matak to call for Sihanouk's removal from office. On 18 March 1970, the Cambodian national assembly met and voted in secret to replace Sihanouk as the head of state.

The bloodless coup d'état forced Sihanouk into a more permanent exile in the **People's Republic of China**, where he broadcast from Radio Peking an appeal to the people to rise up and overthrow Lon Nol. In April, Sihanouk aligned himself with the Indochinese People's United Front, a communist coalition from Vietnam, Cambodia, and Laos, and on 5 May, he announced the Royal Government of National Union as the legitimate government of Cambodia. He also publicly supported the Khmer Rouge, which gave that organization the legitimacy it had lacked to that point, even though his position and influence within the group never amounted to much.

Between March and April 1970, with the political crisis as a backdrop, PAVN and NLF forces increased their activity along the border but began to push west toward Phnom Penh rather than east toward Sài Gòn. The Vietnamese also increased their support for the Khmer Rouge and organized pro-Sihanouk rallies in an effort to undermine Lon Nol and Matak. PAVN and NLF forces even engaged the Cambodian Army (Force Armée Nationale Khmère/FANK) during the growing crisis, which culminated in a 13 April appeal by Lon Nol to all nations of the world to come to Cambodia's aid against communism. Cambodia's neutral position was pushed aside for a pro-U.S. policy that expected the same type of American aid as was given to Sài Gòn. Nixon obliged as the U.S. helped equip the expansion of FANK and made plans for an American and South Vietnamese incursion into the base area in Cambodia, long considered out of bounds.

The Cambodian Incursion would last 60 days for the U.S. and 90 for the RVN, with mixed results. U.S. and ARVN forces did not fully engage the PAVN and NLF in a large-scale battle, though much of the facilities that had existed in the base areas were destroyed. The incursion did set off a new round of U.S. aid to Cambodia that allowed FANK to continue its fight against the Khmer Rouge, although the communists were able to use the incursion to rally the people to their cause. The Khmer Rouge, now with active North Vietnamese help, maintained a stronghold in the northeast part of the country and over the next few years expanded their control in the north and in the countryside. American aid and a sustained bombing campaign, under operation **Freedom Deal** and **Freedom Action**, could not eliminate the Khmer Rouge presence or influence.

As a result of the January 1973 **Paris Peace Accords**, a ceasefire went into effect in Vietnam while foreign military activities in Cambodia ended. The U.S. was obligated to a total withdrawal of its armed forces, weapons, and war materials from the country. In the spirit of the accord, Lon Nol agreed to a suspension of FANK offensive action starting on 29 January, and the U.S. decreased its air **sorties** within Cambodia until it was clear that the Khmer Rouge would not respond in kind to Lon Nol's actions. On 18 March, Lon Nol declared a state of siege in Phnom Penh, and intense U.S. air strikes helped to stop the Khmer Rouge from overrunning the capital. U.S. air strikes increased over the next few months but were forced to stop after **Congress** imposed a termination on 15 August 1973 with Public Law 93-53, also known as the **Case-Church Amendment**. With the U.S. out of Cambodia, the Khmer Rouge was able to consolidate its power and resume its push toward Phnom Penh. By 1974, FANK forces controlled only urban areas and small strategic pockets of land. The Khmer Rouge had access to the people in the countryside and was set to overrun the capital in 1975. The final offensive began on 1 January 1975 and lasted until 17 April when Khmer Rouge forces entered Phnom Penh. Pol Pot consolidated his power within the Khmer Rouge, eliminating his rivals, and began the process of eliminating Western influence in a renovated Cambodia that would return to its agrarian roots. A new constitution was drafted, and Cambodia was renamed Democratic Kampuchea. While Pol Pot promised peace and prosperity, he initiated a genocide that killed an estimated 1.7 to 3 million Cambodians through forced labor, starvation, disease, and execution in what would become known as the killing fields.

The genocide only ended after the Socialist Republic of Vietnam invaded in December 1978 and Pol Pot was forced to flee. The Vietnam-Cambodian war caused further suffering for Cambodia that was not rectified when the Vietnamese withdrew in September 1989. In September 1993, Cambodia established a constitutional monarchy, though forces loyal to Sihanouk and Pol Pot continued to fight. Khmer Rouge forces operated for another six years, attempting to take back control, but they were finally eliminated in 1999, two years after a government amnesty program allowed the fighters to return to their homes. Sihanouk abdicated the throne on 7 October 2004, and Pol Pot had died earlier in 1998. As a result of over 50 years of war, Cambodia became one of the most impoverished nations in Asia and is still recovering from the war, the Khmer Rouge, and the killing fields. *See also* ANGEL'S WING; COOPER-CHURCH AMENDMENT; DANIEL BOONE, OPERATION; DEWEY CANYON II, OPERATION; FISHHOOK; KHMER KROM; KHMER SEREI; MAYAGUEZ INCIDENT; PATIO, OPERATION; PLAIN OF REEDS; PRAIRIE FIRE; SIHANOUK TRAIL; SPIKE TEAMS; TRUSCOTT WHITE, OPERATION.

CAMBODIAN INCURSION. In March 1969, Prince **Norodom Sihanouk** announced that **People's Army of Vietnam** (PAVN) and **National Liberation Front** (NLF) soldiers were using Cambodia as a base of operations against the **Republic of Vietnam** (RVN). This was a major admission, as Sihanouk had denied aiding the North Vietnamese even though the **United States** had evidence to the contrary. At this time, there were approximately 40,000 PAVN and NLF soldiers in Cambodia along the border with the RVN operating in established training areas, rest and relaxation camps, hospitals, forward bases, and bunker complexes. Sihanouk's first official recognition of this threat that had plagued the RVN for the entire Vietnam War set in motion a series of events that led to a joint U.S.-**Army of the Republic of Vietnam** (ARVN) incursion into Cambodia to destroy the enemy soldiers and their sophisticated bases. Sihanouk's declaration also occurred as the U.S. began Operation **Menu**, the secret **bombing** of the PAVN and NLF base area in Cambodia. The incursion was the culmination of a political crisis that grew out of the March 1969 declaration between Sihanouk, Prime Minister **Lon Nol**, who was the former army commander-in-chief, and Deputy Prime Minister Prince **Sisowath Sirik Matak**. President **Richard M. Nixon** took advantage of the political crisis and the preexisting American action to strike at the PAVN and NLF at the invitation of Lon Nol.

The U.S. phase of the operation began on 1 May in III **Corps Tactical Zone** (CTZ) when a 15,000-man force, which included the U.S. 11th Armored Cavalry Regiment and 1st Cavalry **Division**, surrounded an area known as the **Fishhook**. The force encountered only sporadic contact with the enemy, who had fled the area. Another force, which included an ARVN task force and members of the U.S. 25th Division, encircled PAVN and NLF base camps in the **Parrot's Beak**, meeting stiff resistance before the enemy fled. A third thrust across the border occurred in II CTZ, west of **Plei Ku**, involving the U.S. 4th Infantry Division, elements of the 101st Airborne Division, and the 22nd ARVN Division. Here, too, the enemy fled. While the combined U.S.-ARVN force severely disrupted and killed an estimated 11,000 soldiers, an unintended result of the incursion was to push the PAVN and NLF into the northern provinces of Cambodia and force them to increase their support for the **Khmer Rouge**, the insurgents fighting the Royal Cambodia Government.

The Cambodia Incursion was the first real test of Nixon's **Vietnamization** program, a plan designed to slowly disengage American combat troops from Southeast Asia and replace them with ARVN personnel. Even if the main force of the PAVN and NLF was not destroyed, the incursion did disrupt plans for a 1970 offensive against **Sài Gòn** and took from the enemy an amount of rice estimated to feed almost 38,000 soldiers for one year as well as enough weapons to supply over 50 NLF infantry battalions. For a period of time, the incursion eliminated Cambodia as a viable sanctuary for the PAVN and NLF to escape U.S. and ARVN operations and created disorder along the Cambodia portion of the **Hồ Chí Minh Trail**.

While Nixon would announce on 30 June that the incursion had bought time for the South Vietnamese to strengthen themselves, it came with a heavy political price. The **antiwar movement** in the U.S. exploded, leading to a series of strikes at college campuses in May, the tragedy at **Kent State University**, and the Senate's repeal of the **Gulf of Tŏn Kĭn Resolution** on 24 June 1970. The incursion also served as a catalyst for the eventual passing of the **Cooper-Church Amendment** to the Foreign Military Sales Bill, which began **congressional** efforts to take from the executive the right to make foreign policy decisions. *See also* ĐỖ CAO TRÍ; FREEDOM DEAL, OPERATION; MANSFIELD, MICHAEL JOSEPH; MARINE CORPS, VIETNAMESE; NGUYỄN VĂN HIẾU; TOÀN THẮNG, OPERATIONS.

CẦN LAO PARTY. The Personalist Labor Revolutionary Party (Cần Lao Nhân Vị Cách Mạng Đảng/Cần Lao Party) was established by **Republic of Vietnam** (RVN) president **Ngô Đình Diệm** and his brother **Ngô Đình Nhu** in 1956 with the assistance of the **United States**. The Cần Lao, whose membership was secret, used the political philosophy of personalism (Nhân Vị) as a counter to communism, while the party's organization was similar to that of the Communist Party in the North. Ngô Đình Nhu used the Cần Lao Party to ensure loyalty within the RVN, which led to accusations of favoritism and excessive corruption and abuse. Even though the U.S. fully supported the organization at its inception, American officials opposed to Ngô Đình Diệm in the early 1960s pointed to the Cần Lao Party as an example of the corrupt, authoritarian nature of his presidency and as a reason why the U.S. needed to support a change of government in 1963. After the assassinations of Ngô Đình Diệm and Ngô Đình Nhu, the party ceased to function.

CẦN THƠ. Located on the south bank of the Hậu Giang River, approximately 160 kilometers (100 miles) from **Sài Gòn**, at the convergence of a number of waterways leading into the South China Sea, Cần Thơ was the largest city in the **Mê Kông Delta** and the capital of Phong Dinh province. It was also home to the **Army of the Republic of Vietnam** headquarters for IV **Corps Tactical Zone** as well as the center for **United States Navy** and **Republic of Vietnam** activities in the Mê Kông Delta.

CANADA. The Canadian role in the Vietnam War followed a tight line between supporting the **United States** in its fight against communism around the world and engaging in nonmilitary involvement in order to maintain stability in contested areas. Canada's involvement in Southeast Asia began in the early 1950s when the U.S. pressured it to contribute to the defense of the French at **Điện Biên Phủ** through **United Action** at the end of the **First Indochina War**. The Canadians refused but did become a part of the **International Control Commission** (ICC) with Poland and **India** to ensure that the 1954 **Geneva Agreements** were followed. Canadian efforts to maintain the peace and stability sought by the Geneva Agreements were continually frustrated by the **Democratic Republic of Vietnam** and the southern communist insurgency on one side, and the **Republic of Vietnam** (RVN) and the U.S. on the other. Both sides accused the other of violating the agreements, while each loosely interpreted the agreements to suit their own objectives. The Canadians were also frustrated by the Polish, and sometimes Indian, representatives, who worked against the RVN and U.S. in maintaining the agreements.

As the conflict progressed, Canada continued its representation on the ICC, but it also began to provide humanitarian aid to the RVN. When the U.S. started to insert military **advisers** and then combat troops into Southeast Asia, the Canadians attempted to mediate a resolution to the growing conflict, but many Canadians began to criticize how the U.S. was fighting the war in Southeast Asia. The first significant public criticism by a high-ranking Canadian official occurred on 2 April 1965 when Prime Minister Lester Pearson gave a speech at Temple University in which he called for a **bombing pause**. While Pearson's speech was supportive of the U.S. stand against communism, his suggestion of a bombing pause earned the private ire of President

Lyndon B. Johnson. The criticism became more pronounced as American escalation continued, though public relations between the two governments remained cordial until the U.S. air campaigns in response to the 1972 **Easter Offensive**. This did not stop the U.S. from requesting Canadian contributions as part of the larger movement to garner **Third Country** support.

Tension between Canada and the U.S. also occurred as a result of American draft dodgers or deserters from the U.S. Armed Forces seeking refuge in Canada. Not all Canadians agreed with the policy of admitting such individuals into their country, though Canadian laws allowed American citizens to immigrate so long as they did not pose a threat to Canada. The exact number of Americans who immigrated to Canada because of the war is not known, though an estimate of around 30,000 is generally accepted. Some sources offer numbers that reach four times that amount. The U.S. did provide the largest group of immigrants into Canada during the war years. While Canada did not officially participate in the war, there were Canadians who volunteered to fight. Estimates of Canadians who volunteered for service in Southeast Asia numbered around 30,000, including many Native Americans. The number of Canadian citizens who died in the war was 110.

In January 1973, the International Control Commission was disbanded with the signing of the January 1973 **Paris Peace Accords**. A newly formed **International Commission of Control and Supervision** (ICCS) was created and included Canadian representatives, but they pulled out after two of its members were detained by communists and one ICCS **helicopter** was shot down by a surface-to-air missile. Representatives from Iran replaced the Canadians. After the war ended in April 1975, thousands of Vietnamese settled in Canada, including several hundred children who were airlifted through Operation **Babylift**.

CAO ĐÀI. The Cao Đài Tiên Ông Đài Bồ Tát Ma-ha-tát, usually shortened to Cao Đài, was a religious group that originated in **Tây Ninh** City, near the Cambodian border, in 1926. The group opposed French colonial rule and allied loosely with the **Việt Minh** during the **First Indochina War**. In 1947, the organization split with the Việt Minh by choosing neutrality, because that was more in line with its religious philosophy. The Cao Đài continued this neutral stance to the end of the conflict but offered only lukewarm support for **Ngô Đình Diệm**, who would eventually split the group and reduce its influence with promises of power and bribery. While Cao Đài influence diminished during the war, it continues to function in Vietnam today despite the fact that members are persecuted for their religious beliefs. *See also* CARAVELLE MANIFESTO; LANSDALE, EDWARD GEARY; NGÔ ĐÌNH DIỆM; PHAN KHẮC SỬU.

CAO VĂN VIÊN (1921–2008). Army of the Republic of Vietnam general and chief of the Joint General Staff. Cao Văn Viên was born in Vientiane, **Laos** and migrated to the **Mê Kông Delta** in the 1930s. He received his education at **Sài Gòn** University. In 1949, he was commissioned as a second lieutenant from Cap Saint Jacques Military School. He served in a variety of positions during the **First Indochina War**, including chief of the press and information section in the Ministry of Defense in 1951 and commander of the 10th Battalion in 1953 and 56th Battalion in 1954. He rose to the rank of major by the end of the war. In 1956, he was promoted to lieutenant colonel and assumed the role of chief of staff of the special military staff and then to colonel and commander of the airborne brigade in 1960. During this time, he received military training at the Command and General Staff College in Fort Leavenworth, Kansas as well as training in airborne operations and **helicopter** piloting.

After the **Ngô Đình Diệm** coup d'état, he rose to the rank of brigadier general and chief of staff of the Joint General Staff and then commander of the III Corps in 1964. Cao Văn Viên did not participate in the coup d'état but was spared a fate similar to Ngô Đình Diệm because of his military record. He continued to serve as chief of staff of the Joint General Staff and, from January to October 1967, served as the minister of defense. He was the **Republic of Vietnam**'s (RVN) only four-star general and was heavily decorated for his military record and service to the RVN. He fled Vietnam with the fall of Sài Gòn in 1975 and resettled in the **United States** where he became a citizen in 1982. Cao Văn Viên wrote of his military experience for the office of the U.S. Army official historian.

CARAVELLE MANIFESTO. On 26 April 1960, 18 members of the Bloc for Liberty and Progress issued a proclamation, known later as the Caravelle Manifesto because it was signed at that famous hotel in **Sài Gòn**. The manifesto called for reforms within the **Ngô Đình Diệm** regime and paved the way for the possibility of a new government to head the **Republic of Vietnam** (RVN). The signatories of the document were either former politicians or prominent members of the **Cao Đài** or **Hòa Hảo** that Diem had defeated in 1955. The Caravelle Manifesto represented a legitimate threat to Ngô Đình Diệm and raised questions about the nature of the rule of the RVN president that the **United States** ambassador to Vietnam **Elbridge Durbrow** had long believed valid. The language of the manifesto in many ways echoed the communist **propaganda** that had been directed toward Ngô Đình Diệm and his ascension to power. It was a very critical and influential document in the reinvention of U.S.-Vietnamese relations for the year. *See also* PHAN KHẮC SỬU.

CARVER, GEORGE ALEXANDER, JR. (1930–1994). Central Intelligence Agency (CIA) officer. Carver graduated Phi Beta Kappa from Yale University in 1950 and earned a PhD from Oxford University in 1953, after which he joined the CIA. He served in Taiwan and the **Republic of Vietnam** but was forced to leave **Sài Gòn** after his association with Phan Quang Đán, an opponent of **Ngô Đình Diệm**, became known following the abortive coup d'état on 11 November 1960. He served as a member of the Vietnamese Affairs Staff in the CIA until September 1966 and then became a special assistant for Vietnamese affairs in 1966, under **Richard Helms**, director of central intelligence, and continued in that position until 1973, also serving under directors James R. Schlesinger and **William Colby**. Carver supported President **Lyndon B. Johnson**'s handling of the war until the 1968 **Tết Offensive**.

In the fall of 1967, Carver helped to author a study for Secretary of Defense **Robert McNamara** that listed alternatives to the policy as it was being enacted. This study, and the effects of the Tết Offensive, pushed Carver to become more instrumental in changing Vietnam policy in the months following the Tết Offensive. He retired from the CIA in 1979 and joined the Center for Strategic and International Studies. After the war, Carver was involved in the 1984 *Westmoreland v. CBS* case involving body counts after CBS aired the documentary *The Uncounted Enemy: A Vietnam Deception* in 1982. The documentary suggested that Westmoreland had deceived the American people on the number of enemy dead and in the field during the war.

CASE-CHURCH AMENDMENT. Introduced into **Congress** in 1972 by **Frank Church** (D-Idaho) and Clifford Case (R-New Jersey), the Case-Church Amendment sought to end American financing of combat activities conducted by **United States** military forces in the **Democratic Republic of Vietnam**, the **Republic of Vietnam** (RVN), **Laos**, and **Cambodia**. Unlike the earlier **Cooper-Church Amendment**, whose language did not cover every contingency, the Case-Church Amendment was very clear in its pronouncement, which prohibited any continued American combat in Southeast Asia. The initial amendment was rejected by the U.S. Senate in August 1972 by a close margin but was reintroduced just before the final signing of the **Paris Peace Accords**. Despite significant lobbying from the White House and State Department, both of whom argued that the amendment would severely limit the American ability to conduct any meaningful foreign policy in Southeast Asia, Congress passed the amendment on 19 June 1973. The House of Representatives approved the amendment by a vote of 278 to 124, while the Senate passed it by a 64-to-26 margin, making the amendment veto proof. President **Richard M. Nixon** threatened to veto the amendment in order to secure an extended deadline for the prohibition to take place. However, the

White House did secure a deadline of 15 August 1973, which allowed for additional **bombings** and for equipment to arrive in the RVN and Laos. As the war deteriorated through 1974–1975, the **Gerald R. Ford** administration would point to the amendment as the major cause of its inability to support the **Sài Gòn** government when the North Vietnamese blatantly violated the Paris Peace Accords.

CASUALTIES. The figures for casualties depend on the sources used and when one begins or ends the conflict. Using the most reliable sources, it was estimated that the **United States** lost 58,193 personnel in the war. The majority of these personnel killed during the war served with the **Army** (38,209), followed by the **Marine Corps** (14,838), **Air Force** (2,584), **Navy** (2,555), and **Coast Guard** (7). The average age of death was between 20 and 21, with the majority of the casualties (22,378) within this age range. The majority of casualties were killed-in-action (38,502), with the next highest total resulting from nonhostile action from other causes, illness, injury, or while missing (10,787), followed by death while missing (3,524) and death while captured (116).

Most of the American casualties occurred in the **Republic of Vietnam** (RVN) (55,629), followed by the **Democratic Republic of Vietnam** (DRV) (1,124), **Laos** (733), **Cambodia** (520), **Thailand** (177), and the **People's Republic of China** (10). One of the false assumptions about the war was that it was fought only by single men, though 29.4 percent (17,215) were married at the time of their death. The vast majority were enlisted (50,312) and white (50,120), while most were in service with the regular military (34,475). The majority of the casualties, some 39,361, occurred between 1967 and 1972, and the highest number of casualties came from California (5,573), New York (4,121), Texas (3,415), Pennsylvania (3,144), and Ohio (3,096). The U.S. lists eight **women** killed from the 58,193 total.

The RVN lost an estimated 260,000 killed-in-action, though that number has been listed as low as 216,000 and as high as over 300,000. The RVN also suffered over 1,100,000 wounded. The **Republic of Korea** lost an estimated 5,100 killed-in-action, with over 11,000 wounded. **Australia** lost 426 killed-in-action, with just less than 3,000 wounded. Thailand lost 351 killed-in-action, with approximately 1,350 wounded. **New Zealand** lost 55 killed-in-action, with just over 200 wounded. The **Philippines** lost seven killed-in-action.

The DRV claimed over 1,100,000 combat deaths, with an additional 65,000 civilian deaths, while the **National Liberation Front** lost an estimated 250,000 killed. There were also confirmed reports of **People's Republic of China** and North Korea personnel deaths, though there are no reliable numbers.

CATHOLIC PEACE FELLOWSHIP. The Catholic Peace Fellowship (CPF) was formed in 1965 by **Daniel** and **Phillip Berrigan** and Jim Forest. Forest and the Berrigan brothers were inspired by their involvement with the **Fellowship of Reconciliation** and the need to galvanize Catholics into action against the war by working with conscientious objectors and others who chose not to participate in combat. The group provided educational, counseling, and advocacy services for those who wished to resist war. The organization still exists. *See also* ANTIWAR MOVEMENT.

CATONSVILLE NINE. On 17 May 1968, nine individuals, including **Phillip** and **David Berrigan** and four other Catholic priests, broke into the office of Local Draft Board 33 in Catonsville, Maryland, and removed draft records. The group, which also included Tom Lewis, who with Philip Berrigan had been convicted of an earlier incident in the **Selective Service** office in the **United States** Customs House in Baltimore, then burned the draft records in a parking lot near the office using homemade **napalm**. As the trial commenced, the Catonsville Nine, as they became known, refused to participate in the selection of juries, citing their lack of faith in the judicial process. Nearly 200 police had to surround the courthouse to hold back an estimated 1,500 protestors, counterprotestors, and onlookers. On 10 October 1968, the group was convicted of mutilating and destroying government records and obstructing the duties of the Selective Service program. A conspiracy charge to commit the above acts was dropped in order to expedite the trial. Philip Berrigan and Lewis received a sentence of three and a half years in jail, while the others received sentences between two and three years. *See also* ANTIWAR MOVEMENT; BALTIMORE FOUR.

CEDAR FALLS, OPERATION. A **search-and-destroy** operation in the **Iron Triangle**, to the northwest of **Sài Gòn**, that lasted from 8 to 28 January 1967. The operation was centered in the Thanh Điền Forest Reserve, where the **National Liberation Front** (NLF) headquarters for **Military Region 4** was located, with the objective of eliminating the enemy from the area northwest of Phú Cường. Cedar Falls was the largest ground operation of the war, involving over 30,000 **United States** troops under the II Field Force and **Army of the Republic of Vietnam** (ARVN) troops against an unknown number of NLF. It was also the first major operation of 1967, during which time General **William C. Westmoreland** planned to go on the offensive to drive the **People's Army of Vietnam** and NLF soldiers away from major urban centers. The operation also sought to create **New Life Villages** in the area that had been heavily concentrated with NLF personnel and supporters. This involved massive relocation of the peasantry, defoliation of useable vegetation, and the creation of **free-fire zones**, in which any individual discovered was considered an enemy and a legitimate target.

While the operation was deemed a success, in that it achieved its limited objectives, the NLF were not confronted in a major battle and thus were not eliminated from the region, nor were the people cut off from NLF influence. The methods employed in the operation were roundly criticized by the U.S. **media** and by others opposed to the war. When the operation ended, the U.S. tallied impressive statistics to justify the claims of victory. It estimated nearly 750 NLF killed, 280 detained, and almost 550 **Hồi Chánh** defectors under the **Chiêu Hồi** program. Tens of thousands of rounds of ammunition and hundreds of weapons were also captured. The U.S. lost 72 killed-in-action and 337 wounded, while the ARVN lost 11 killed-in-action and 8 wounded. *See also* DIVISION, UNITED STATES.

CENTRAL HIGHLANDS. Also known as Tây Nguyên or Cao Nguyên Trung Phần, the Central Highlands made up the western provinces of **Plei Ku**, **Kon Tum**, Darlac, Phú Bồn, Quảng Đức, Lâm Đồng, and Tuyên Đức and comprised some 52,000 square kilometers (20,000 square miles). The area was very important during the war because of its proximity to the southern corner of **Laos** and the northern third of **Cambodia** that bordered the **Republic of Vietnam**. The Central Highlands was an area of infiltration from the **Hồ Chí Minh Trail** that ran through Laos and Cambodia. It was populated by ethnic minorities such as the **Jarai**, **Bahnar**, and K'hor, who spoke either a variation of the Malayo-Polynesian or Mon-**Khmer** languages. *See also* CIVILIAN IRREGULAR DEFENSE GROUP; ĐÀ LẠT; ĐẮK TÔ; IA ĐRĂNG VALLEY, BATTLE FOR; MONTAGNARDS.

CENTRAL INTELLIGENCE AGENCY (CIA). The National Security Act of 1947 created the CIA on 18 September with the mission of gathering information for the **National Security Council** and the executive branch to use in determining **United States** foreign policy. As the Cold War continued through the 1950s, the role of the CIA expanded to include covert operations, and it generally served as the organization capable of providing an alternative, secret, and sometimes unsavory option for the U.S. government in its efforts to contain or eliminate communist influence throughout the world.

The CIA's predecessor, the Office of Strategic Services, had a history in Southeast Asia during World War II, but the CIA would not become interested in the region until after the fall of China in 1949 and the outbreak of the war in Korea in 1950. CIA activities were limited to supporting the French Union Forces during the **First Indochina War**, though during the culminating battle of that war, the 1954 Battle for **Điện Biên Phủ**, the CIA employed civilian pilots, most of whom were a part of the Civil Air Transport, to move a portion of the daily 170 tons of ammunition and 32 tons of food needed for the fortress to maintain the fight. The U.S. flew 1,800 airlift **sorties** during the battle.

After the conclusion of the 1954 **Geneva Conference** that marked the end of **France**'s influence in Indochina, the CIA sponsored the **Saigon** Military Mission (SMM) under the leadership of **Edward Lansdale** to conduct psychological warfare in the **Democratic Republic of Vietnam** (DRV) in order to damage the northern Vietnamese reputation and encourage the flight of Vietnamese from the North to the South. The SMM had actually entered Vietnam before the fall of Điện Biên Phủ with the mission of assisting the Vietnamese in conducting unconventional warfare. Its numbers were too small to make a difference before the French fortress fell and the 1954 Geneva Conference was concluded. The SMM also helped **Ngô Đình Diệm** consolidate his power in Vietnam, which eventually led to the establishment of the **Republic of Vietnam** in October 1955.

During the remainder of the 1950s, the CIA was involved in covert and psychological operations in Southeast Asia designed to harass the DRV and its southern allies. It assisted in the creation of the **First Observation Group**, which was organized in February 1956 under the command of Colonel **Lê Quang Tung**. The First Observation Group trained to conduct guerrilla operations against the **People's Army of Vietnam** (PAVN) in the event of a DRV invasion. When that invasion failed to materialize, the CIA helped personnel from the First Observation Group conduct limited covert raids against the DRV and **Laos** in the late 1950s. The raids expanded as the communist insurgency intensified in the early 1960s.

The CIA was also heavily involved in the Civil War in Laos in the late 1950s and early 1960s. The Civil Air Transport (CAT) returned to Southeast Asia in September 1956 when it provided humanitarian relief to Laos. It began to operate in Laos permanently in July 1957, aiding the Royal Laotian Government in its fight against the PAVN and **Pathet Lao**. On 26 March 1959, CAT changed its name to **Air America** in order to separate its non-Southeast Asian operations from its work in Laos. Air America aircraft and personnel played a significant role in the war in Laos, providing such services as **search-and-rescue**, **airmobility**, air transport of personnel and materials, fire support missions, and training. Air America made it possible for the U.S. to conduct its war in Laos without drawing attention to America's increased involvement in the neutral country.

The CIA also provided financial support for **Phoumi Nosavan**, leader of the **Committee for the Defense of National Interests** (CDNI). Phoumi and the CDNI represented the right wing of the political spectrum in Laos and opposed the **Neo Lao Hak Xat**, the political front for the Laos communist insurgency, the Pathet Lao. The CIA funded Project **Hotfoot** in 1959, which trained members of the **Lao Theung** population group in **counterinsurgency** operations. The program evolved into Operation **White Star** in 1961 and included the **Hmong** people. The CIA-sponsored programs continued until the signing of the 1962 **Geneva Accords**. It also supported General **Vang Pao**, an ethnic Hmong, whose private army battled the PAVN, the **National Liberation Front**, and the Pathet Lao during the war. Vang Pao, whose forces were often outnumbered, was loyal to the crown and an anticommunist, though his legacy in Laotian resistance was marred by accusations of drug trafficking.

The image of the CIA suffered a setback early in the **John F. Kennedy** administration after the failure of the Bay of Pigs operation in 1961. One result of this failure was the creation of **National Security Action Memorandum (NSAM) 57** on 28 June 1961. NSAM 57 outlined how the U.S. would conduct paramilitary operations to produce the most effective results. The document called for the U.S. to assist, overtly or covertly, friendly governments or insurgents seeking to overthrow an enemy government. It also authorized the Department of Defense to oversee all paramilitary operations, with the CIA in a supporting role. This document would play a part in many of the programs initiated in the RVN and Laos in the early 1960s, including the **Civilian Irregular Defense Group** (CIDG), **Trail Watchers**, White Star, and **Mountain Scouts**. These programs were transferred to the **Military Assistance Command, Vietnam**, through Operation **Switchback**, which was completed on 1 July 1963. In January 1964, the CIA handed over covert operations, which resulted in the creation of the Studies and Observation Group.

The CIA was generally supportive of Ngô Đình Diệm. During the November 1960 abortive coup d'état, **William Colby**, who was the CIA station chief in Sài Gòn, backed the RVN president even though the U.S. ambassador, **Elbridge Durbrow**, had made his displeasure known. The CIA did not support the Department of State position to remove Ngô Đình Diệm from power, and it generally opposed the November 1963 coup d'état, though one of its members, Lucian Conein, who had been Lansdale's second in the Saigon Military Mission, did act as a liaison between the military officers who executed the coup d'état and the U.S. ambassador to the RVN at the time, **Henry Cabot Lodge Jr.**

After the change in the Sài Gòn government, the CIA helped to create the People's Action Teams (PAT) and the Provincial Reconnaissance Units (PRU) in 1964. The former was an early effort in **pacification**, while the latter continued the practice of covert raids into the DRV. While the PAT program eventually transferred to the military as stipulated by NSAM 57, the PRU remained under the control of the CIA and would play a significant role in later pacification efforts. Also in 1964, the CIA sponsored the training of Vietnamese **Special Forces** and CIDG personnel in **long-range reconnaissance**

patrols in Project **Leaping Lena**. While the effort would not be successful, it did lead to the creation of Project Delta in October 1964 and the establishment of the **Recondo School** in September 1966.

The CIA helped to fund the **Office of Civil Operations** (OCO), which was organized in November 1966 in an effort to improve the efficiency of pacification efforts. It coordinated all civilian efforts related to pacification in the RVN. The OCO was eventually absorbed into the **Civil Operations and Revolutionary Development Support** (CORDS) when that organization was established on 10 May 1967. Under the leadership of **Robert Komer**, who was succeeded by William Colby, CORDS dramatically improved the U.S. pacification effort. Colby would eventually become the director of Central Intelligence. The CIA worked with CORDS and would become implicated in the **Phoenix Program**, which, among other things, was involved in targeted assassinations of key members of the **Việt Cộng** infrastructure.

Directors of Central Intelligence during the wars in Southeast Asia included Allen Dulles (26 February 1953–29 November 1961), **John McCone** (29 November 1961–28 April 1965), **William Raborn** (28 April–30 June 1966), **Richard Helms** (30 June 1966–2 February 1973), James Schlesinger (2 February 1973–2 July 1973), and William Colby (4 September 1973–30 January 1976). *See also* CARVER, GEORGE ALEXANDER, JR.; ORDER OF BATTLE DISPUTE; SHEEP DIPPING; SPECIAL FORCES, UNITED STATES; STUDIES AND OBSERVATION GROUP.

CENTRAL OFFICE FOR SOUTH VIETNAM (COSVN). Known as the Văn Phòng Trung Ương Cục Miền Nam, which was loosely translated as the Central Office of the Southern Region, this organization served as the headquarters for the political and military effort in the southern region of the **Republic of Vietnam** (RVN) from 1961 to 1975. It was commonly referred to as COSVN by the **United States**. An earlier version of COSVN was established at the end of the **First Indochina War** in the southern third of the RVN, known by the **Democratic Republic of Vietnam** (DRV) as Nam Bộ. Its importance diminished through the rest of the 1950s until the DRV made the decision to intensify the war in the south. In 1961, the headquarters for COSVN was established in **Tây Ninh** province with the combination of the southern departments of the **Lao Động** Party and the existing political branch of the **National Liberation Front** (NLF). Its operational area covered what would become known as **Front** B2, which included the military regions designated by the DRV as 6, 7, 8, 9, and 10, or the southernmost part of Trung Bộ and all of Nam Bộ. This area was the equivalent to III and IV **Corps Tactical Zones** (CTZ) and the five southernmost provinces in II CTZ. COSVN directed the escalation of NLF operations in the early 1960s. (*See* map 7.)

Nguyễn Văn Linh served as the general secretary for COSVN, and in October 1963 he also led the Military Affairs Party Committee (MAPC). In 1964, **Nguyễn Chí Thanh** took control of COSVN and ran the organization through the Americanization of the war. He died while on a trip to **Hà Nội** in July 1967. He was replaced by **Phạm Hùng**, who was the general secretary to both COSVN and the MAPC until the end of the war. COSVN was a highly mobile and flexible organization. While it was primarily based in **Tây Ninh** province, it was not located in a single fixed facility. Rather, COSVN consisted of a series of bunkers and gathering spots around the province that were easily accessible by bicycle or motorbike but were isolated enough to avoid detection by the U.S. or the **Army of the Republic of Vietnam** (ARVN). Around 1967, it moved near the Cambodian border, in the area known as the **Fishhook**, and during the 1970 **Cambodian Incursion** it relocated to Kratie in **Cambodia**. At the end of the war, COSVN was located west of Lộc Ninh. Its mobility and decentralized command allowed it to remain hidden from the U.S. and ARVN.

During the presidency of **Lyndon B. Johnson**, the COSVN easily avoided detection by taking advantage of neutral Cambodia. During the Johnson administration, the U.S. military launched a number of **search-and-destroy** missions into **War Zone C**, where the COSVN headquarters was located, but it failed to find and eliminate the enemy. When **Richard M. Nixon** became president, he ordered the **bombing** of the border area between the RVN and Cambodia, with the specific mission of destroying the **People's Army of Vietnam** and NLF personnel in the region and disrupting COSVN operations. Operation **Menu** lasted between 18 March 1969 and May 1970, when its name changed to Operation **Freedom Deal** with the 1970 Cambodian Incursion. Neither the incursion nor the targeted air campaign was able to destroy the COSVN. It continued to function until the end of the war. *See also* LÊ DUẨN; TRẦN NAM TRUNG; TRẦN VĂN QUANG; TRẦN VĂN TRÀ.

CHAMS. Originally people of the Champa Kingdom who were conquered by the Vietnamese at the beginning of the 15th century, the Chams were an ethnic minority that was centered between Kampong Cham province in **Cambodia** and the **Central Highlands**. The Cham people fought for their independence, at one time joining the **Front Unifié de Lutte des Races Opprimées** (FULRO), during the war. They were both aided and persecuted by the **National Liberation Front** and the **Sài Gòn** government. The Cambodian Chams were targeted for execution during the **Khmer Rouge** reign of terror after 1975 and today are the target of scorn by the **Hà Nội** government for their unique cultural beliefs and independent mindset. *See also* BAN MÊ THUỘT.

CHIÊU HỒI. The Chiêu Hồi, or "Open Arms," program was initiated by the **Republic of Vietnam** (RVN) as a way to demoralize the **National Liberation Front** (NLF) and encourage defections to the South Vietnamese side. Variations of the program had been around since the 1950s, though the Chiêu Hồi program started in 1963. Through the program, the RVN distributed leaflets and posters and ran a campaign of radio and broadcast slogans showing the advantages of working with, rather than opposing, the **Sài Gòn** government. Safe-conduct passes ensured that any defectors in the program were guaranteed good treatment if they turned themselves in to an allied or South Vietnamese official. Individuals who took advantage of the program were known as **Hồi Chánh**, or returnees. Some of these Hồi Chánh joined the South Vietnamese Armed Forces or served as **Kit Carson Scouts** for **United States** forces. There were many NLF who took advantage of the Chiêu Hồi and then returned to the insurgency. While the success of the program was controversial, it did remove tens of thousands of NLF from the field and provided the RVN with one of its few **propaganda** successes during the war. *See also* KOMER, ROBERT WILLIAM; OFFICE OF CIVIL OPERATIONS; PACIFICATION; PHOENIX PROGRAM.

CHINA, PEOPLE'S REPUBLIC OF. Mention of the Vietnamese first appeared in official Chinese annals as a minority people in the kingdom of Nam Việt, known in Chinese history as Nan Yüeh in 208 BC. The origin of Vietnam, from a section of China, set the tone for the relationship between the two countries. It was one of interaction and alliance, with episodes of conflict and violence. In 111 BC, the Han Dynasty extended its power southward and absorbed Nam Việt into the Chinese empire. This began 1,000 years of occupation as well as the creation of an entrenched Vietnamese mentality to resist foreign invaders regardless of the cost, which would benefit them during the **First Indochina War** and the **Second Indochina War**.

Chinese involvement in Vietnam also gave birth to early martyrs in the Vietnamese nationalist movement, including Trưng Trắc and Trưng Nhị. These two sisters helped to organize a rebellion army of approximately 80,000 men and women that fought the Chinese. The Trưng sisters continued their fight between AD 39 and 42, eventually succumbing to the Chinese, and opted for suicide by drowning themselves in a river rather than submitting to Chinese rule. The Chinese also made a martyr of Phùng Thồ Chính, who led one of the Trưng Sisters' armies and reportedly gave birth at the battlefront, put her baby on her back, and continued to fight until the end.

China's involvement in Vietnam ebbed and flowed over the next few centuries. The Vietnamese learned to be submissive when the Chinese dynasties were strong, and aggressive in seeking independence when they were weak. It was not until 939 that the Vietnamese were able to assert their independence from the Chinese with the autonomous Vietnamese kingdom under the rule of the Ngô Quyền Dynasty. China influenced the development of Vietnamese culture and society with the creation of a civil service under the control of Vietnamese mandarins who were knowledgeable of the Chinese language and culture, and the Vietnamese absorbed Chinese characteristics, advancements, and institutions that suited them while rejecting those things that did not.

Between 1407 and 1428, the Chinese attempted to regain control of Vietnam, though they were defeated by Lê Lợi. The Chinese would make an additional attempt in 1789 during the Tây Sơn conflict, but they failed to gain a foothold before the Nguyễn Dynasty under Gia Long, with French assistance, consolidated control in 1802. China would not play a major role in Vietnam for another 150 years.

In 1949, the Chinese Civil War concluded with the victory of the Communist Party under the leadership of Mao Zedong. The new People's Republic of China defeated the nationalist forces under Chiang Kai-shek, which retreated to Taiwan to reform the Republic of China. Communist China was diplomatically and economically isolated from the West by the **United States**. The Americans believed that China was now a satellite of the **Soviet Union** and had designs to spread communism throughout Asia and the Pacific. This Cold War mentality was reaffirmed in American eyes after the Chinese attacked **United Nations** forces in November 1950 during the Korean War.

China provided some aid to the **Việt Minh** during the First Indochina War and was influential in convincing the Vietnamese to accept the terms of the 1954 **Geneva Conference** rather than prolonging the war and possibly involving the U.S. in Southeast Asia on a larger scale. After the Geneva Conference, the Chinese encouraged the **Democratic Republic of Vietnam**'s (DRV) land reform program that had begun in Vietnamese-controlled territory before the end of the war. The Chinese also provided relief to the DRV after this land reform program failed to achieve results and led the country to the brink of disaster. For the remainder of the 1950s, China supplied **advisers** and assistance to the DRV while Mao Zedong encouraged his Vietnamese allies to begin preparations for increased aggression in the **Republic of Vietnam**. This directly confronted the Soviet Union position of peaceful coexistence between the two sides of the Cold War.

By the end of the 1950s, the Chinese advocated overt aggression in the RVN to counter the gains made by RVN president **Ngô Đình Diệm**. This led to a split among the Vietnamese communists. Some continued to maintain the Soviet position and supported a low-intensity struggle to win the Vietnamese people to the DRV position, while others followed the Chinese model that called for conflict leading to the overthrow of the **Sài Gòn** government.

The Chinese position, supported by **Nguyễn Chí Thanh, Lê Duẩn, Lê Đức Thọ**, and for a time **Trường Chinh**, won out, and the Vietnamese stepped up their attacks in the South. As a result, Chinese weapons began to flow into the DRV. The majority of **People's Army of Vietnam** (PAVN) and **National Liberation Front** (NLF) personnel used the Chinese-made Type 56 **rifle**, an exact copy of the AK-47 rifle. On 16 March 1964, Secretary of Defense **Robert McNamara** issued a memorandum confirming that the PAVN and NLF were using Chinese-built 57-mm and 75-mm recoilless rifles, heavy **machine guns**, 90-mm rocket launchers and **mortars**, rocket-propelled grenades (**RPG-2**), and the Type 56 rifle. There were also Chinese advisers in the northern part of the DRV and in the northwestern section of **Laos**.

In Laos, the Chinese participated in the International Conference on the Settlement of the Laotian Question, as it was formally titled, between 16 May 1961 and 23 July 1962, but it rejected the 1962 **Geneva Accords** that evolved from the conference. As a result, the Chinese encouraged the Vietnamese and **Pathet Lao** to avoid negotiations with the U.S., Sài Gòn, or Vientiane governments, which resulted in increased tensions in Southeast Asia and the emerging war in Vietnam. The Sino-Soviet split continued to cause trouble for the Vietnamese, but in 1964, after the **Gulf of Tŏn Kĭn Incident**, Vietnamese-Soviet relations improved. China continued to play a major role in supporting the PAVN forces, but Soviet and Eastern Bloc weapons became crucial to the DRV's survival. This was especially true in the air war as Soviet-built SA-2 missiles; heavy, **antiaircraft artillery**; and MiG fighters made up the DRV's air defense system. The Chinese role in the war continued to include some weaponry, especially small arms and ammunition, but it also involved a significant number of engineers to improve infrastructure and antiaircraft units to free up PAVN forces to move southward. Most importantly, China served as a deterrent against a possible U.S. invasion of the DRV, as it had tried to do with the North Koreans in 1950. The Chinese provided similar aid to the Pathet Lao in Laos, though on a smaller scale.

During the height of the Vietnam War, from 1966 to 1968, China underwent the Great Proletarian Cultural Revolution, which began on 16 May 1966 when Mao Zedong argued that the Chinese Communist Party, and Chinese society in general, had been too greatly influenced by a liberal bourgeoisie element that sought to restore capitalism to the country. Mao responded to the threat by appealing to Chinese youth to form the Red Guard and eliminate this dangerous element in China. The Cultural Revolution divided China and caused untold misery for much of its population. The movement officially ended in 1969, though its immediate effects continued through the early 1970s. Despite the turmoil, China continued to support the DRV in the war even as border skirmishes with the **Soviet Union** threatened to escalate into overt war.

The U.S. had viewed China as a threat in the region since its origins in 1949. China was able to check U.S. action against the DRV up to the **Lyndon B. Johnson** administration, but in 1969, when **Richard M. Nixon** entered the White House, the U.S. relationship with Asia began to change. On 9 July 1971, National Security Adviser **Henry Kissinger** feigned illness during a trip to Islamabad, Pakistan, and boarded a plane to Beijing. Kissinger set into motion a historic 1972 trip by Nixon to China in which Nixon announced that he had plans to normalize relations between the two adversaries. During Nixon's visit, the Vietnam War came up repeatedly. The U.S. wanted China to intervene to mediate an end to the war or to put pressure on the DRV to seriously negotiate an end to the conflict. The Chinese skirted the issue or offered noncommittal responses to American requests. While China refused to deliberate on the DRV or the war, Nixon's visit lessened tensions and made it possible for him to authorize operations **Linebacker I** and **Linebacker II** in response to the 1972 **Easter Offensive** and the failure of the DRV to negotiate in Paris in good faith, without the fear of overt Chinese intervention.

China acknowledged the 1973 **Paris Peace Accords**, but it continued to provide aid to the DRV from 1973 to 1975. When the war ended and the Vietnamese united as the Socialist Republic of Vietnam (SRV), the relationship between the two countries became strained. The Vietnamese were more supportive of the Soviet model, and after their invasion into **Cambodia**, which had been renamed Democratic Kampuchea, in December 1978 in response to **Khmer Rouge** border raids into the SRV, the Chinese entered the conflict against the Vietnamese. The Chinese attacks failed, and its troops were forced to retreat back to China while Vietnam remained in Kampuchea until September 1989.

CHINA, REPUBLIC OF (ROC). In 1949, after the Kuomintang troops were defeated by the communists and forced to retreat from mainland China, the ROC was reestablished. The government continued to function from Taiwan and a series of smaller islands between Taiwan and China. The **United States** supported the ROC during its struggle against the **People's Republic of China** (PRC) in the 1950s and 1960s while the ROC government supported U.S. efforts to defend the **Republic of Vietnam** (RVN). ROC activities in the RVN, however, were limited because of the traditional tension that had developed over a period of two thousand years and the fear that any overt support by the ROC would be matched by the PRC.

ROC president Chiang Kai-shek offered personnel and resources to the RVN in the 1950s only to be rejected by President Dwight D. Eisenhower and Secretary of State **John Foster Dulles**. Similar proposals were submitted to President **John F. Kennedy**. In February 1964, ROC minister of defense

Yu Ta-Wei renewed the effort to involve his country's personnel in Southeast Asia. President **Lyndon B. Johnson**, also wary of the political and diplomatic side effects of ROC involvement, moved to limit its involvement. When Johnson initiated the **Show the Flag** program in April 1964, the ROC was not among the nations that the U.S. believed should come to the aid of the RVN through a Free World effort, though Johnson eventually agreed to military **advisers**. On 8 October 1964, the first contingent of the Republic of China **Military Assistance Advisory Group**, Vietnam (ROCMACV), arrived in the RVN with the mission of offering advice on political warfare, the **refugee** situation, and medical needs.

ROC military advisers served in all four **Corps Tactical Zones** and had specific involvement with the Republic of Vietnam Armed Forces Political Warfare College in **Đà Lạt** and the Armed Forces General Political Warfare Directorate in **Sài Gòn**. A seven-man provincial health assistance team worked at the provincial hospital at Phan Thiết. By the end of 1965, ROC personnel numbered approximately 100, in addition to two C-46 aircraft and crew. The next year, the ROC contingent increased as the U.S. received six LST (landing ship, tank) vessels and their crew for service in the RVN. General **William C. Westmoreland** requested ROC combat troops in June 1966, but his efforts were thwarted by the U.S. embassy in Sài Gòn because of the political sensitivity of such a move. ROC involvement increased in 1967 with additional medical personnel and technical advisers. The size and structure of the ROCMACV remained essentially the same until 1970. During this period, the ROC provided over $3 million dollars in aid to the RVN, including a series of emergency gifts in rice and other desperately needed material after the 1968 **Tết Offensive**. As the U.S. finalized **Vietnamization**, ROC personnel began disengaging from the RVN with mixed feelings. The Chinese government had a strong desire to assist the U.S. in its struggle against communism in Southeast Asia, but the U.S. was never able to fully realize that commitment because of the politics and diplomacy involved in accepting a greater role from that country. The ROC situation became synonymous with the U.S. struggle in Southeast Asia, as too many good intentions were pulled in different directions in order to accommodate varying points of view.

CHỢ LỚN. Translated as "big market," Chợ Lớn is the name for the Chinese section of **Sài Gòn** located on the west side of the Sài Gòn River. The area was originally settled by a group of Chinese who fled reprisals by the Tây Sơn in the late 18th century. It formed as its own city in the late 19th century, merged with Sài Gòn in the early 1930s, and then was absorbed into Sài Gòn in the year following the creation of the **Republic of Vietnam**. Chợ Lớn suffered damage during the 1968 **Tết Offensive** and was the temporary home for many of the **refugees** of the war in the late 1960s and early 1970s. Throughout the war, it remained an area of intrigue and one that served as a source of opposition to the Sài Gòn government.

CHU HUY MÂN (1913–2006). People's Army of Vietnam (PAVN) general and Politburo member, Chu Huy Mân was born in Nghệ An province. His rise to power was due in part to his association with **Võ Nguyên Giáp**, commander of the armed forces in the **Democratic Republic of Vietnam**. He served as a member of the Communist Party of Vietnam Central Committee, a Politburo member, and a member of the National Assembly. During the war, Chu Huy Mân commanded the PAVN forces during the Battle of the Ia Đrăng Valley in November 1965, as well as during the Battle of Bồng Sơn. In 1977, he ran PAVN's general political department and remained in that position until he was forced out in 1986. Chu Huy Mân was also removed from the Politburo, in which he held the eighth highest position, at the same time as the Socialist Republic of Vietnam replaced many of its old guard. Before 1986, he also served as the vice president of the State Council and as deputy secretary of the Military Party Central Committee. For his service to Vietnam, he was awarded the Gold Star Order, the highest award in the country.

CHU LAI. Located on the coast of the **Republic of Vietnam** approximately 80 kilometers (50 miles) to the south-southeast of **Đà Nẵng** in **Quảng Nam**, Chu Lai served as an airfield for the **United States Marine Corps** (USMC) from 1 June 1965 until the USMC departed on 3 September 1970. Chu Lai was the home of the 1st Marine **Division** in 1966 and the 23rd Infantry Division from 1967 to 1971. Chu Lai also housed **swift boats**, Navy Seabees, and other naval support units. *See also* OREGON, TASK FORCE.

CHURCH, FRANK FORRESTER (1924–1984). United States senator (D-Idaho) and advocate of restraining presidential authority to conduct foreign policy in Southeast Asia. Church enlisted in the U.S. Army in 1943 and served as an intelligence officer in the China-Burma-India Theater during World War II. After the war, he graduated from Stanford University in 1947 and from Stanford Law School in 1950. He practiced law in Boise, Idaho, until his election to the U.S. Senate in 1956, where he served until 3 January 1981. He served on a number of committees, including the Committee on Foreign Relations.

Church clashed with Senate majority leader **Lyndon B. Johnson** in his early career, but his advocacy of civil rights eventually solidified their association in the late 1950s. Their relationship was strained when Church began to oppose the Vietnam War in 1966–1967. In 1970, Church, with

Senator **John Sherman Cooper** (R-Kentucky), introduced an amendment to the Foreign Military Sales Act (HR 15628) in response to the 1970 **Cambodian Incursion**. The original amendment prohibited combat troops in **Cambodia** after 1 July 1970 and challenged the president's ability to commit troops in the future. When this amendment failed to garner enough support, a revised amendment was introduced to the Supplementary Foreign Assistance Act of 1970, which passed in both the House of Representatives and the Senate on 22 December 1970 as Public Law 91-652. In 1972, Church and Senator Clifford Case (R-New Jersey) introduced an amendment to end American financing of combat activities conducted by U.S. military forces in the **Democratic Republic of Vietnam**, the **Republic of Vietnam** (RVN), **Laos**, and Cambodia. Unlike the earlier **Cooper-Church Amendment**, the **Case-Church Amendment** clearly prohibited any continued American combat in Southeast Asia. The Senate rejected the original amendment, but it was reintroduced in the days before the signing of the **Paris Peace Accords**. **Congress** passed the amendment on 19 June 1973 after President **Richard M. Nixon** threatened to veto it. The White House did secure a later deadline of 15 August 1973 for the amendment's implementation, which allowed for additional **bombings** and equipment to arrive in the RVN, Cambodia, and Laos.

After the war, Church continued in the Senate and even ran for the Democratic nomination for president in 1976, winning four primaries before withdrawing and supporting James E. Carter. Church's antiwar record and support for James E. Carter's foreign policy led to his defeat for a fifth term to a conservative Republican congressman. Church returned to his practice of law before cancer took his life. *See also* ANTIWAR MOVEMENT.

CITIZENS COMMITTEE FOR PEACE WITH FREEDOM IN VIETNAM. A national, nonpartisan committee of individuals who issued a policy statement on 25 October 1967 calling for continued support of the **United States**' effort in assisting the **Republic of Vietnam** in their war against the North. The group supported President **Lyndon B. Johnson**'s uncompromising position in Vietnam as well as the U.S.-backed resistance to northern aggression. The group opposed surrender in Vietnam but cautioned for a U.S. policy that lay in the middle ground between capitulation and the indiscriminate use of military power. The group advocated a debate on the nature of the war in Vietnam but wanted to make sure that the majority voice, those who supported the war, had a forum from which they could disseminate their view. Prominent members of the group included presidents Harry S. Truman and Dwight D. Eisenhower, as well as former secretary of state **Dean Acheson** and former secretary of defense Thomas S. Gates. The group represented the feelings of what President **Richard M. Nixon** would call the "silent majority" during his tenure as president.

CIVIL GUARD. Officially established by **Ngô Đình Diệm** in April 1955, the Civil Guard was organized as a paramilitary organization to assist the **Army of the Republic of Vietnam** (ARVN). The concept of the Civil Guard had actually been created by the French during the **First Indochina War**. The Civil Guard existed in nearly every district of each province in the **Republic of Vietnam** (RVN). It, along with the **Self-Defense Corps**, was responsible for internal security. Both the Civil Guard and the Self-Defense Corps were led by ARVN officers, but the troops were generally poorly trained and were not as well equipped as the ARVN. Their purpose was to patrol the countryside within a limited area and keep the insurgents off balance. When they engaged a superior force, the Civil Guard called in the ARVN to assist in operations. As a result, the Civil Guard and Self-Defense Corps bore the brunt of attacks on a daily basis. Because of their quality of training and equipment, they were not able to eliminate the threat to the people. Another problem with the Civil Guard was that it was under the Ministry of the Interior rather than the Ministry of Defense. This made it difficult for the **United States** to provide aid through the Military Assistance Program (MAP). Most of the aid for the Civil Guard came through the **Michigan State University Group** that had been contracted to help the **Sài Gòn** government in the 1950s.

Another problem with the Civil Guard was how it was employed in the field. In the late 1950s, Ngô Đình Diệm used the Civil Guard as an extension of the ARVN because the ARVN force was not large enough to combat the communist insurgency, which had intensified its efforts against the Sài Gòn government. While the **Military Assistance Advisory Group** under generals **Samuel T. Williams** and **Lionel C. McGarr**, along with Ngô Đình Diệm, argued that the ARVN needed to be increased in order to change the mission of the Civil Guard, the U.S. ambassador to the RVN, **Elbridge Durbrow**, argued that Ngô Đình Diệm was misusing the Civil Guard in order to increase American aid to the RVN and increase the size of the ARVN.

Durbrow was in constant conflict with Ngô Đình Diệm about various issues in the late 1950s and into 1960. He preferred to use promises of additional funding for the ARVN and the Civil Guard as a carrot in order to force Ngô Đình Diệm to initiate political, social, and economic reforms expected by the U.S. embassy. As a result, delays in increasing the ARVN and a failure to properly equip the Civil Guard resulted in increased instability in the countryside and the growth of the insurgency into the **National Liberation Front** (NLF) after its formation in December 1960. Ngô Đình

Diệm initiated some of the reforms for the Civil Guard. After the failed 11 November 1960 coup d'état against him, Ngô Đình Diệm did issue Decision Number 272-NV on 22 November, which placed the Civil Guard temporarily under the responsibility of the Ministry of Defense, allowing that ministry to reorganize, train, and equip the Civil Guard. The switch was made permanent, though Durbrow continued to worry that the decree would not go far enough in removing the Interior's control over the individual units, which also made it difficult for the U.S. to provide MAP equipment to it. The Civil Guard was an integral part of the network of units protecting the villages from the NLF. It required MAP equipment, but it also needed to have better coordination with ARVN commanders.

Durbrow was correct in that the final reform was not totally complete, as province chiefs still had access to the Civil Guard, though coordination between military region commanders and the Civil Guard did increase. Ngô Đình Diệm argued that too many ARVN forces were organized in large units, which made it difficult to combat the small-sized NLF units roaming about the countryside. Additionally, he lamented the fact that many of his Civil Guard units, the force best suited for antiguerrilla activity, were preoccupied with staff or specialist duties, or were in static defensive positions. In short, the **Republic of Vietnam** Armed Forces were not being utilized to their fullest.

On the American side, Durbrow maintained that American **advisers** should train the Civil Guard in antiguerrilla tactics, while General **Edward Lansdale**, who was well respected by Ngô Đình Diệm, suggested that counterguerrilla tactics would be more appropriate. What on the surface appeared to be a question of semantics was really a symptom of the larger disagreement between the two men. For Lansdale, Durbrow's antiguerrilla operations meant training the Civil Guard to protect the rear areas from NLF threat. The focus was on missions such as protecting truck convoys from ambush. Lansdale's counterguerrilla training would allow the Civil Guard to conduct operations against the NLF. Where Durbrow wanted to apply a passive approach, Lansdale preferred something more active. All of these conflicts resulted in further delays in the appropriate use of the Civil Guard. It was not until mid-1962 that the Civil Guard began to receive more modern weapons and some additional training. However, the countryside had changed dramatically from the late 1950s as the NLF had become much more coordinated and effective in combating the ARVN and Civil Guard. With the 1963 **Buddhist Crisis**, the focus moved away from the fight in the countryside, and the Civil Guard languished. Eventually the concepts of the Civil Guard and Self-Defense Corps were absorbed into the **Regional** and **Popular forces** after the coup d'état against Ngô Đình Diệm. *See also* PHẠM NGỌC THẢO.

CIVIL OPERATIONS AND REVOLUTIONARY DEVELOPMENT SUPPORT (CORDS). An organization created by the **United States** in order to coordinate the many military and civilian **pacification** activities in the **Republic of Vietnam**. CORDS was established on 10 May 1967 with **Robert Komer** at its head. He held the rank of ambassador, or the military equivalent of a three-star general. CORDS was placed under the **Military Assistance Command, Vietnam**, and Komer reported directly to General **William C. Westmoreland**. This allowed Komer the authority to bypass those civilians who opposed committing resources to military pacification. As a result, Komer was able to use CORDS to link together the numerous and varied pacification efforts, which included political, economic, and military programs. The organization was seen as successful in its ability to get the most out of the existing programs, but its implementation occurred too late for it to be as effective as envisioned.

CORDS confirmed that pacification was more than just a civilian or military effort. It required a combination of resources and a compromise of competing ideas in order to be successful. Komer oversaw CORDS until November 1968 when **William Colby** took over the organization. Colby headed CORDS during the period of **Vietnamization**. In June 1971, Colonel George Jacobson assumed command until the organization was disbanded in 1973. *See also* NEW LIFE VILLAGES; OFFICE OF CIVIL OPERATIONS; PHOENIX PROGRAM.

CIVILIAN IRREGULAR DEFENSE GROUP (CIDG). In late 1961, **United States Special Forces** detachments began to train and equip members of the CIDG, a militia made up initially of Vietnamese minorities that were directly threatened by the **National Liberation Front** (NLF). The effort to organize the **Montagnards** in the **Central Highlands** region started with the **Rhadé** tribesmen in the village of Buon Enao, near **Ban Mê Thuột**, Darlac province, in October 1961. The Special Forces helped to develop the CIDG program by experimenting with different strategies and tactics to fight the communist insurgency. The primary goal became area development, which was the process of securing an area and developing independent self-defense programs so that villagers could defend themselves. Over 80 of these programs were created during this period. By 1964, CIDG units were conducting operations against NLF bases and areas of operation. In 1965, concurrent with the beginning of American escalation, the CIDG program took on a more offensive role in the war. They were no longer defenders of village and home but conducted operations to destroy the NLF.

There were attempts to disband the CIDG or absorb it into the **Regional Forces** in 1967, but the move was deemed premature given the success of the units. With **Vietnamization**, a combined Joint General Staff–Military Assistance Command planning committee recommended the termination of the CIDG program on 20 March 1970. The CIDG camps were converted for army use while the CIDG men were either absorbed into the **Army of the Republic of Vietnam** or recruited to the Vietnamese Army Rangers. Many former CIDG members chose to conduct operations aimed at border control with the Vietnamese Special Forces. *See also* A SHAU, BATTLE OF; CENTRAL INTELLIGENCE AGENCY; FRONT UNIFIÉ DE LUTTE DES RACES OPPRIMÉES; LANG VEI; LEAPING LENA; TRAIL WATCHERS.

CLAYMORE MINE. *See* MINES, LAND.

CLERGY AND LAITY CONCERNED ABOUT VIETNAM (CALCAV). An **antiwar** organization established in May 1966 when the Clergy Concerned about Vietnam allowed nonclergy to participate in their organization. The new organization, CALCAV, actively opposed the **United States'** involvement and escalation of the Vietnam War. CALCAV sponsored several events, including **Martin Luther King Jr.**'s Vietnam Summer designed to increase awareness about the war and increase antiwar activism. CALCAV began to engage in more militant tactics such as draft resistance and protests against the contributions of Dow Chemical and Honeywell to the war effort. In 1971, CALCAV focused on issues other than Vietnam and eventually dropped "about Vietnam" from its organizational title.

CLIFFORD, CLARK MCADAMS (1906–1998). Counselor to President Harry S. Truman, chairman of the Foreign Intelligence Advisory Board during the **John F. Kennedy** and **Lyndon B. Johnson** administrations, and secretary of defense under Johnson. Clifford was involved in many of the critical events of the Cold War, including the 1945 Potsdam Conference, the formation of the 1947 Truman Doctrine, the Marshall Plan, the recognition of Israel, and the National Security Act.

Clifford became secretary of defense on 1 March 1968, replacing **Robert McNamara**. While Clifford was an early supporter of the war, he worked toward ending it after the beginning of the significant American escalation of combat troops in 1965. It was Clifford who counseled President Lyndon B. Johnson to reject General **William C. Westmoreland**'s request for an additional 206,000 troops after the 1968 **Tết Offensive**, which began the process of easing Westmoreland out of command. Though Clifford and Johnson disagreed on America's Vietnam policy, Johnson did award him the Medal of Freedom with Distinction, the highest award given to civilians in the **United States**. Though he was out of public office during the **Richard M. Nixon** administration, he worked toward ending the war but succeeded only in earning the wrath of President Nixon and Vice President **Spiro T. Agnew**. Clifford served as an adviser to the James E. Carter administration but later became embroiled in the Bank of Credit and Commerce International scandal that tarnished his reputation.

CLIMATE, SOUTHEAST ASIA. Monsoon winds dictated the climate in Vietnam, **Laos**, and **Cambodia**. These winds, from the southwest and northeast, determined cloud coverage and precipitation. Cool, dry air passing over the Asian continent directed the winter northeast monsoon, while the reverse occurred in the summer as the winds shifted to the southwest and forced warm, moist air to move inland from the ocean. The summer monsoon was characterized by significant rain in the interior of Vietnam, Laos, and Cambodia, with cloud coverage prevalent over the **Red River Delta** in the North and the **Central Highlands**. There was normally a quick transition from summer to winter monsoon winds that brought turbulent weather to the Gulf of Tŏn Kĭn and precipitated heavy thunderstorms and typhoons in the center of the two Vietnams. While the winter monsoons produced less rain to the outer regions, it did result in significant concentrations of clouds, fog, and light drizzle or rain. Known as the Crachin, this weather pattern was normal around **Hà Nội** and forced adjustments to the **United States'** air campaigns against the **Democratic Republic of Vietnam**. The same was true in Laos, where weather played a predominant role in determining offensive and defensive campaigns during the war. *See also* POPEYE, PROJECT.

CLUSTER BOMB UNIT (CBU). The CBU was made up of canisters, **bombs**, or rockets that carried multiple bomblets that, when exploded, scattered the contents over a wide area. The CBU contained bomblets of metal darts, nails, or shards that were most effective against personnel targets and were normally delivered by aircraft or **artillery**. In **Laos**, postwar estimates claim that the **United States** dropped nearly 13,500 CBU-26, with each CBU-26 delivering over 650 bomblets. In the **Democratic Republic of Vietnam**, the U.S. used the CBU against air defense positions because of the wide area covered by a single unit and the fact that the aircraft delivering the munitions did not have to fly very low over the target. The CBU caused serious damage to any personnel exposed to its explosion. The weapon, however, could not discriminate between enemy and civilian and was often the source of controversy throughout the war.

COAST GUARD, UNITED STATES (USCG). The USCG became involved in the war with the establishment of Task Force 115, the Coastal Surveillance Force, which participated in Operation **Market Time**. On 29 April 1965, with the formation of USCG Squadron One, USCG vessels participated in the interdiction campaign to deny the North Vietnamese the ability to move personnel and supplies by sea. The USCG initially provided 17 patrol boats for the operation, which came under the operational control of Task Force 115 when it was established on 31 July 1965. The USCG boats worked from bases at **Đà Nẵng, Qui Nhơn, Nha Trang**, Vũng Tàu, and An Thới and searched Vietnamese vessels, especially the numerous fishing vessels that frequented the waterways under the jurisdiction of Task Force 115. Within the first year of operations, the ships of Squadron One had inspected over 30,000 Vietnamese vessels and boarded an additional 35,000. It captured over 100 tons of war-related supplies. When the last of the USCG ships from Squadron One left Southeast Asia in August 1970, they had boarded over 235,000 Vietnamese vessels and inspected more than 280,000.

In 1967, the USCG was asked to provide more assets in support of Market Time. As a result, Squadron Three was formed and began operations on 4 April 1967. When the last ships of Squadron Three left Southeast Asia, they had conducted over 200 Market Time patrols, inspected approximately 50,000 Vietnamese vessels, and boarded over 1,000. USCG cutters also supported Operation **Sea Dragon** fire support missions, and coast guard units were involved in Civil Action Projects, Medical Civil Action Projects, and other humanitarian missions. The USCG contributed to the destruction of 10 larger Soviet-built trawlers from May 1966 to April 1971. Seven members of the USCG were killed-in-action in the war, and 59 were wounded-in-action. *See also* BLUE-WATER NAVY; NAVY, REPUBLIC OF VIETNAM.

COLBY, WILLIAM EGAN (1920–1996). Director of central intelligence. Colby graduated from Princeton University in 1940 and joined the **United States Army** as a second lieutenant in August 1941. In 1943, he entered into service with the Office of Strategic Services and worked in the European Theater in covert operations behind German lines and with the French resistance. After the war, in 1947, Colby earned a law degree from Columbia University. He practiced law in New York between 1947 and 1949 and then joined the **Central Intelligence Agency** (CIA) in 1950. He was involved in Cold War activities in Sweden from 1951 to 1953 and in Italy from 1953 to 1958. In 1959, Colby was introduced to Southeast Asia when he became the CIA station chief in **Sài Gòn**. In this capacity, he worked closely with **Republic of Vietnam** (RVN) president **Ngô Đình Diệm** and his brother **Ngô Đình Nhu**. During the abortive November 1960 coup d'état, Colby ran afoul of Ngô Đình Nhu, though he was generally trusted and was seen as a supporter of the Sài Gòn government. He was involved in a number of activities in the RVN, including the beginning of clandestine operations against the **Democratic Republic of Vietnam** authorized by President **John F. Kennedy**.

In 1962, Colby left his Sài Gòn position and became the head of the Far East Division for the CIA. He remained in that position until 1967 when he became the deputy director of the **Civil Operations and Revolutionary Development Support** (CORDS) and then director of CORDS in 1968. Colby was responsible for many programs under CORDS, including the **Phoenix Program**, the **People's Self-Defense Force** project, and improvement of the **Regional** and **Popular forces**. Colby remained with CORDS until 1971. While Colby and the U.S. would be maligned for the Phoenix Program, which critics of the war labeled an assassination program, Colby defended his decisions given the nature of the war in Vietnam.

His work at CORDS brought a number of improvements to the people of Vietnam, who had long suffered from the effects of the **National Liberation Front** and the **People's Army of Vietnam**. Because of CORDS, the South Vietnamese were in a better position to defend themselves and their families than they had been before the 1968 **Tết Offensive** that ravaged the countryside. Colby became the executive director-comptroller of the CIA from 1972 to 1973 and served concurrently as the deputy director for operations from 2 March to 24 August 1973.

On 10 May 1973, President **Richard M. Nixon** appointed Colby as the director of central intelligence. He was confirmed on 1 August and sworn in on 4 September 1973, replacing James R. Schlesinger. While director, Colby witnessed the fall of Sài Gòn and was involved in a number of post-Vietnam decisions that were guided by Cold War policies. On 30 January 1976, President Gerald Ford replaced him. The move was considered political given the political climate in Washington, D.C., in the immediate post–Vietnam War period. Colby published his memoir, *Honorable Men*, in 1978. He published *Lost Victory* in 1989, which focused in more depth on his time in Vietnam. He remained involved in international affairs during his retirement, working as a risk management consultant. Colby died while canoeing on the Potomac River near his home at Rock Point, Maryland. *See also* KOMER, ROBERT WILLIAM; PACIFICATION.

COLLINS, JOSEPH LAWTON (1896–1987). Collins graduated from the **United States** Military Academy in 1917 and quickly rose through the ranks of the U.S. Army. He taught chemistry at West Point from 1921 to 1925 and graduated from a number of military courses and school during the interwar years. He entered World War II with the temporary rank of colonel but was quickly promoted to the temporary rank of brigadier general in February 1942 and major general in May 1942. He served as chief of staff of the Hawaiian

Department between 1941 and 1942 and commanded the 25th Infantry Division during the battle for Guadalcanal in 1942 and 1943, where he earned the nickname "Lightning Joe" for his work against the Japanese. Collins commanded the VII Corps during the Normandy invasion in 1944. In April, he was promoted to temporary lieutenant general and was made a permanent brigadier general in June 1945.

After the war, Collins served in a variety of positions of increasing importance, including as director of information of the army (1945–1947), deputy and vice chief of staff of the army (1947–1949), and chief of staff of the army (1949–1953) during the Korean War, before which he was made a permanent major general. In 1954, President Dwight D. Eisenhower appointed Collins as a special representative of the U.S. in Vietnam with the rank of ambassador. He traveled to Vietnam to assess the status of the State of Vietnam and its political leader **Ngô Đình Diệm**. Collins concluded that Ngô Đình Diệm was not suitable for Vietnam and argued that he should be replaced. Ngô Đình Diệm, however, managed to retain his position and consolidated his power after defeating the **Bình Xuyên** and **Hòa Hảo** who had joined to form the United Front of Nationalist Forces in April 1955. Collins continued to report that the Vietnamese premier was useless and needed to be replaced. Collins left Vietnam on 14 May 1955 and retired from active military service in March 1956.

COMASS LINK SATELLITE TRANSMISSION SYSTEM. One of the difficulties in air photographic **reconnaissance** was the transit time necessary to send an image to the **United States** for evaluation and authorization for a **bombing** mission. In July 1967, the U.S. introduced the COMASS LINK Satellite Transmission System, which was comprised of three 40-foot vans located at Tân Sơn Nhứt, Hawaii, and Washington, D.C. The **U.S. Air Force** transmitted 11.4 × 11.4 cm (4.5 × 4.5 inch) black-and-white photographs using a laser light source. The image data was then translated by a photo multiplier tube into an electronic signal and sent via satellite to another van in Hawaii, where it strengthened the signal and resent the image to Washington, D.C. The image was finally reproduced at 30 lines per millimeter with up to 16 shades of gray. With this technology, the U.S. could analyze photographic reconnaissance in minutes rather than hours or days, allowing for quicker reaction time and authorization of bombing **sorties**.

COMBAT AIR PATROL (CAP). After the **United States** initiated air operations over the **Democratic Republic of Vietnam**, the North Vietnamese countered with a sophisticated air defense system that included **antiaircraft artillery**, surface-to-air **missiles**, and MiG fighters. The U.S. responded to the

MiG threat with CAP missions, sometimes referred to as MiGCAP missions. CAP missions used fighter aircraft to engage any MiG interceptors over a target while bombers delivered their munitions on a selected target. The CAP aircraft would fly patterns around the bombers at varying altitudes in order to detect the MiGs more quickly. CAP missions also included support for **search-and-rescue** and other **sorties** that might be threatened by MiG interceptors. *See also* BOLO, OPERATION; FIREFLY, PROJECT.

COMBAT SKYSPOT. Working in conjunction with Operation Commando Nail technology, ground-based radar sites, known as Combat Skyspot, were developed at the end of Operation **Rolling Thunder** to increase the flexibility and efficiency of the **bombing** campaign. The radar facilities identified targets and helped direct aircraft to their intended target. The combined use of these two programs allowed the **United States** to hit North Vietnamese targets that had previously been immune from air attack during the monsoon season. Unfortunately, the technology arrived too late to alter the outcome of Operation Rolling Thunder. *See also* HOTSPOT.

COMBINED ACTION PLATOON (CAP). The CAP used **United States Marines** and Vietnamese from the **Popular Forces** to provide assistance to the Revolutionary Development program in previously contested territory in the **Republic of Vietnam**. CAP teams entered villages after they had been cleared of **People's Army of Vietnam** or **National Liberation Front** personnel by the U.S. military or the **Army of the Republic of Vietnam**. The teams helped to organize local defense. The U.S. Marine Corps (USMC) helped to train the Popular Forces personnel involved in the CAP missions, providing logistical support, airpower, and reinforcements if the Popular Forces engaged with the enemy. CAP missions also allowed for humanitarian programs to proceed.

The CAP missions were a response to the nature of the war in Vietnam, which was fought primarily at the village and hamlet level rather than on grand battlefields. Starting in 1965, the concept of the CAP team began to be implemented as selected marines were assigned to villages to assist Popular Forces units in their protection. Generally, one 25-man USMC rifle squadron would join with local Popular Forces of varying strength to form a platoon-strength force. By pairing marines with the Popular Forces, the result was considered a troop multiplier for the marines, who were at times overstretched because of the number of hamlets and villages. The program continued unofficially until February 1967 when Major General **Lewis W. Walt**, commander of the III Marine Amphibious Force (MAF) and 3rd Marine **Division**, formally established the program. Lieutenant Colonel William R. Corson was selected as the III MAF deputy director for combined action.

The CAP units received training in **Đà Nẵng** where they learned a little about the Vietnamese language and culture and the basic procedures for CAP operations. Critics of the program argued that CAP personnel were not effective and that the U.S. was expending too many resources for little return. The concept, however, continued to receive support from within the Marine Corps, which had expanded the number of units to over 100 by 1969 and had a presence in all the provinces of I **Corps Tactical Zone** (CTZ) in 1970. By this time, CAP units had been formed into Combined Action Groups, of which there were four in I CTZ. The marines had committed 2,000 men to the program. Originally CAP units were assigned to a fixed point, but by 1968, as a result of the **Tết Offensive**, the marines began to experiment with mobile CAP units in order to keep the enemy guessing as to their location and provide greater protection to a larger number of Vietnamese.

The mobile CAP concept was fully implemented by 1970, but with **Vietnamization** underway, the CAP program felt the effects of the American withdrawal from Southeast Asia. On 21 September 1970, the program was deactivated and absorbed into the Combined Action Groups. In its five years of operation, the CAP program provided an example of how to fight the war in Vietnam, focusing on winning the "hearts and minds" of the Vietnamese people while also providing them with an opportunity to train for their own defense. In some cases, the program worked well, though in others it merely highlighted one of the major problems of the American war in Vietnam, which was the overreliance of the Vietnamese on the U.S. to provide for their protection.

COMMANDO HUNT, OPERATION. Air interdiction campaign in southern **Laos** that began on 15 November 1968. Commando Hunt resulted from the increased requirement to stop infiltration down the **Hồ Chí Minh Trail** and the need to utilize air assets made available after President **Lyndon B. Johnson**'s 1 November 1968 decision to cease the sustained **bombing** campaign against the **Democratic Republic of Vietnam** (DRV). Commando Hunt targeted Laotian territory between the 16th and 18th parallel, with a special emphasis on the southern mountain passes between Laos and the DRV. Using data gathered from **Igloo White**, the **7th Air Force** concentrated on truck parks and storage facilities as well as known congested areas of the trail.

The initial phase of Commando Hunt proved very successful as **United States intelligence** sources estimated that the **People's Army of Vietnam** (PAVN) took twice as long to get supplies down the trail after the operation began. When the PAVN reacted to the first phase by stationing repair crews along the trail and creating a series of bypasses around the bottlenecked areas, Commando Hunt entered its second phase, which focused on armed **recon-**

naissance based upon known enemy movement. The U.S. also employed Special **Arc Light** Operating Areas with lenient restrictions for the B-52 **sorties**, which allowed for restrike without authorization and immediate reaction to confirmed intelligence.

By the end of the third phase in April 1969, the U.S. had flown 67,094 tactical air and 3,811 Arc Light sorties, with an estimated 4,300 trucks destroyed and 1,600 vehicles damaged. U.S. intelligence estimated that Commando Hunt resulted in less than one-fifth of the supplies that started the journey from the North reaching their destination in the South. While Commando Hunt did not stop the flow of personnel and supplies down the Hồ Chí Minh Trail, it made it much more difficult for the DRV to support the war in the South and provided extra time for President **Richard M. Nixon**'s **Vietnamization** program to become effective. The operation ended in April 1972 when the air assets committed to it were required to respond to the PAVN **Easter Offensive**. *See also* AIR WAR; STUDIES AND OBSERVATION GROUP.

COMMANDO LAVA. A project designed to disrupt movement down the **Hồ Chí Minh Trail** by dropping chemicals to break up the soil and create mud and landslides. The project was initiated on 17 May 1967 in **Laos** when three C-130 aircraft from the 41st Tactical Airlift Squadron flew from Udorn Royal Thai Air Base in **Thailand**. The initial results appeared to be successful, but there was political controversy around the flights as Laos was still considered to be neutral in the war. This was made apparent when, one day before the operation, a **reconnaissance** aircraft was forced to land in Laos because it had not carried enough fuel for its mission and uniformed American personnel were seen refueling it.

The C-130 aircraft dropped a chemical mixture, produced by Dow Chemical, that consisted of Trisodium Nitrilotriacedic Acid and Sodium Tripolyphosphate placed in cloth bags that broke on impact. The white powder resembled soap, which when mixed with water caused the soil to become unstable. This process earned the operation the slogan, "Make mud, not war." Two more missions, which were less successful, were flown over the A Shau Valley before the mission was canceled. The dangers inherent in the operation outweighed the benefits.

COMMANDO VAULT, OPERATION. Program designed to test the use of heavy **bombs** for clearing areas previous inaccessible to **helicopter** landings. The first test of this concept occurred on 9 December 1967 when the **United States Air Force** (USAF) exploded a 3,000-pound M118 bomb near **Đắk Tô**. The bomb cleared an area approximately 46 meters (150 feet) wide and detonated prepositioned **booby traps**. Commando Vault originated from the need to develop, test, and assess larger bombs. At the beginning of Commando Vault, in December 1968, the 834th Air Division based at Tân Sơn Nhứt Air Base tested a 10,000-pound M121 bomb under the code name Combat Trap. It produced a blast area of 2,800 square meters (30,000 square feet). When the USAF depleted its stock of M121 bombs, it switched to the 15,000-pound BLU-82/B, with a blast area of 4,800 square meters (15,700 square feet), which proved to be as effective as the M121. By October 1970, the 834th Air Division detonated 323 bombs, usually dropped from a C-130 aircraft and glided down on a parachute, to create **landing zones** and assist in the construction of firebases. Commando Vault proved successful in establishing landing zones in inaccessible areas and was equally successful in seriously injuring enemy soldiers who were unlucky enough to be within the blast area radius. In a country where the terrain was inhospitable to U.S. weapons, Commando Vault offered one solution to overcome these obstacles.

COMMITTEE FOR THE DEFENSE OF NATIONAL INTERESTS (CDNI). A group of military and civilian leaders who organized in June 1958 as a response to the 4 May 1958 supplementary election in **Laos** in which the **Neo Lao Hak Xat**, the newly formed **Pathet Lao** political organization, won 9 of the 21 seats contested. The CDNI was very conservative and supported the anticommunist elements in Laos. While it maintained that it was not a political party but rather a group organized to influence politics, it acted very much like a political party. The CDNI had three basic tenets that guided its policies. It was anticommunist, it was against corruption, and it was organized to build a stronger Laos from its colonial past. In late December 1959, the group, led by General **Phoumi Nosavan**, carried out a bloodless coup d'état against Premier Phoui Sananikone. Phoumi Nosavan formed a new political party after the April 1960 elections. His Paxa Sangkhom (Social Democrats) was an offshoot of the CDNI, which ceased to play a significant role in Laotian politics. *See also* CENTRAL INTELLIGENCE AGENCY; RALLY OF THE LAO PEOPLE.

CONGRESS, UNITED STATES. After **United States** recognition of the State of Vietnam in 1950, Congress paid very little attention to the events in Indochina. In 1954, when Secretary of State **John Foster Dulles** attempted to organize **United Action** in defense of the beleaguered French Union Forces at **Điện Biên Phủ**, both he and President Dwight D. Eisenhower consulted congressmen on the proposal. When Congress refused to support United Action without the active participation of the British, the plan failed to materialize. For the remainder of the 1950s, as the U.S. engaged in nation building in the **Republic of Vietnam** (RVN), Congress did little more than send members to Indochina to assess the **Ngô Đình Diệm** government and respond to such pro-RVN groups as the **American Friends of Vietnam**.

Among the active supporters of U.S. policy during this period were senators **John F. Kennedy** (D-Massachusetts), **Lyndon B. Johnson** (D-Texas), and **Michael Mansfield** (D-Montana). During the Kennedy presidency, some within Congress began to voice concern over U.S. policy in Southeast Asia. Most of the opposition stemmed from U.S. support for Ngô Đình Diệm. Many congressmen were convinced that the RVN president was leading his country away from U.S. goals. Senator **George McGovern** (D-South Dakota) joined others in protesting the **Sài Gòn** government's response to the 1963 **Buddhist Crisis**. Kennedy's escalatory moves did attract the attention of Mansfield and others who argued that the U.S. should not become too involved with personnel in the region. Most of the concern was never made public, as the members of Congress preferred to maintain a united front against the threats of communism abroad.

In 1964, Congress had its first real chance to debate American involvement in Vietnam when, in August, the **Gulf of Tŏn Kĭn Incident** occurred. In response to the alleged 4 August 1964 North Vietnamese action against the U.S.S. *Maddox* (DD-731) and U.S.S. *Turner Joy* (DD-951), the White House urged the Senate and House of Representatives to approve Joint Resolution of Congress H.J. RES 1145, which they did on 7 August 1964. The **Gulf of Tŏn Kĭn Resolution** approved and supported any presidential act deemed necessary to protect U.S. forces in Southeast Asia. The resolution also called upon the U.S. to take necessary steps to assist states of the **South East Asian Treaty Organization** who were threatened, with an implied reference to the RVN. The resolution was originally to be in effect until the president determined that it was not necessary or until Congress passed a concurrent resolution to end the authorization. Only two senators, **Wayne Morse** (D-Oregon) and Ernest Gruening (D-Alaska), opposed the resolution, while all present in the House of Representatives approved it. The Gulf of Tŏn Kĭn Resolution became President **Lyndon B. Johnson**'s justification for American escalation in Vietnam, which eventually led to the Americanization of the war.

By the mid-1960s, a majority of Congress still supported the war in Southeast Asia. There were also those in the extreme who maintained that the Johnson administration was not doing enough to prosecute the war. In August 1967, Senator **John Stennis** (D-Mississippi) conducted hearings through the Preparedness Investigating Subcommittee of the Senate Armed Services Committee. Stennis concluded that the Johnson administration placed too many restrictions on the U.S. air campaign over the **Democratic Republic of Vietnam** (DRV). As the Stennis report made its way to the public, other congressmen began to voice their opposition to the war.

McGovern, Gruening, and Morse were joined by Mansfield, **Frank Church** (D-Idaho), **J. William Fulbright** (D-Arkansas), **Robert Kennedy** (D-New York), and **Eugene McCarthy** (D-Minnesota). Within the Republican ranks, Senators George Aiken (Vermont), Clifford Case (New Jersey), and Jacob Javits (New York) opposed Johnson's handling of the war. In 1966, Republican Mark Hatfield won a Senate seat from Oregon because of his **antiwar** platform. These senators were joined by state governors, including New York's Nelson Rockefeller and Pennsylvania's William Scranton. House of Representatives opposition also began to rise as the war lingered without end and the number of **casualties** increased.

When President **Richard M. Nixon** entered the White House in 1969, many within Congress opposed the war, believing that they had been lied to by the Johnson administration about the Gulf of Tŏn Kĭn Incident. There was a move to have Congress regain control over American foreign policy. In response to the 1970 **Cambodian Incursion**, Senators **John Sherman Cooper** (R-Kentucky) and Frank Church (D-Idaho) introduced an amendment to the Foreign Military Sales Act (HR 15628) that sought to limit the ability of the president to deploy combat troops in Southeast Asia. The original version of the amendment prohibited U.S. combat troops in **Cambodia** after 1 July 1970 as well as forbade any other military personnel or activity supported by the U.S. without congressional approval.

The House of Representatives rejected this version of the amendment after Nixon warned that he would veto HR 15628 if it contained any proviso outlined in the **Cooper-Church Amendment**. Cooper and Church introduced a revision of the original amendment to the Supplementary Foreign Assistance Act of 1970, which passed in both the House of Representatives and the Senate on 22 December 1970. Public Law 91-652, put into effect on 5 January 1971, was less restrictive of air operations.

After the failure of the 1971 Operation **Lam Sơn 719**, senators Church and Case introduced an amendment to end American financing of combat activities conducted by U.S. military forces in the DRV, RVN, **Laos**, and Cambodia. Unlike the earlier Cooper-Church Amendment, the language of which did not cover every contingency, the **Case-Church Amendment** was very clear in its pronouncement that prohibited any continued American combat in Southeast Asia. The initial amendment was rejected by the Senate in August 1972 by a close margin but was reintroduced just before the final signing of the **Paris Peace Accords**.

Despite significant lobbying from the White House and State Department, Congress passed the amendment on 19 June 1973. The House of Representatives approved the amendment by a vote of 278 to 124, while the Senate passed it by a 64-to-26 margin, making the amendment veto proof. Nixon still threatened to veto the amendment in order to secure an extended deadline for when the prohibition would take place. The White House did obtain a deadline of 15 August 1973, which allowed for additional **bombings** and equipment to arrive in the RVN and Laos before funds were cut off.

Congress's next act to regain authority over American foreign relations occurred in July 1973 when Congress initiated House Joint Resolution 542, known as the **War Powers Resolution**. The resolution was Congress's attempt to curb the power of the presidency to introduce American troops into a foreign country for a prolonged period without congressional approval. The resolution reaffirmed the role of Congress in foreign policy decisions that was perceived to have been lost with the Gulf of Tŏn Kĭn Resolution and the escalation in Vietnam. The resolution required the president to report to Congress within 48 hours if he committed U.S. troops to a foreign conflict or if he "substantially" increased the number of combat troops in a foreign country. These troops were required to be withdrawn unless Congress approved the president's action within 60 days. Both the House of Representatives and Senate passed the resolution on 7 November 1973 by a two-thirds majority. Nixon vetoed it, but the veto was overturned. The resolution hampered the ability of President **Gerald R. Ford** to aid the RVN in 1974 and 1975.

Congress's final act in the war was its 1975 decision not to grant Ford's request for supplements to the $1.45 billion in military aid asked for in the last year of the Nixon administration. Congress had authorized only $700 million of the Nixon request for fiscal year 1975. On 28 January 1975, Ford requested a $300 million supplement, but it was rejected. He requested an additional $722 million on 10 April but was again turned down by Congress. The congressional refusal to come to the aid of its 25-year ally caused many within the U.S. to argue that Congress had cut off all funds to the RVN and had allowed it to fall. In reality, U.S. assistance continued to flow to Sài Gòn until the fall of the capital on 30 April 1975, but the amount of U.S. dollars in aid was not enough to stop the momentum of the DRV offensive. Only U.S. personnel and hardware could have made a difference, but Congress had made sure that the executive would not be able to repeat its actions of 1964. *See also* ANOTHER MOTHER FOR PEACE; CREDIBILITY GAP; PARIS PEACE ACCORDS; SELECTIVE SERVICE SYSTEM; UNITED ACTION; WAR POWERS RESOLUTION.

CONSTANT GUARD, OPERATION. Three phased air operations that anticipated the 1972 **Easter Offensive** and worked toward the interdiction of North Vietnamese supplies to the **Republic of Vietnam**. In early February 1972, the Tactical Air Command initiated Operational Plan 100, known as Constant Guard. The first phase of Constant Guard began on 7 April with the deployment of two F-4E squadrons and one F-105G squadron to airfields in Vietnam and **Thailand**, all of which arrived in April after the offensive began. Eight EB-66s used for electronic countermeasures in **Arc Light** missions joined the first phase. The second phase added two additional squadrons of F-4Es to Udorn, Thailand, on 2 May. The final phase saw the deployment of the 49th Tactical Fighter Wing with an additional four squadrons of F-4 aircraft. These aircraft were supplemented with B-52 bombers flying from Thailand and **Guam**, as well as the 1st Marine Air Wing and four aircraft carriers at **Yankee Station** in the Gulf of Tŏn Kĭn. In total, Constant Guard moved 12 squadrons and approximately 200 aircraft in an operation that lasted until 13 May 1972.

COOPER, JOHN SHERMAN (1901–1991). Republican **United States** senator from Kentucky. Cooper graduated from Yale and attended Harvard Law School from 1923 to 1925. He served in the Kentucky House of Representatives from 1928 to 1930 and then as a judge of Pulaski County, Kentucky, until 1938. During World War II, Cooper served in the U.S. Army, reaching the rank of captain. He was elected to the U.S. Senate in 1946, filling a vacancy by resignation. He was not reelected in 1948. In 1949, Cooper served as delegate to the General Assembly of the **United Nations** and as an alternate delegate the next two years. In 1952, he was elected to the Senate, filling a vacancy by death. Again, he was unsuccessful in his reelection attempt in 1954. In 1955, Cooper became the ambassador to **India** and Nepal until elected to the Senate in 1956 to fill another vacancy by death. This time he would remain until 1973.

In the late 1960s, Cooper became one of many in **Congress** who opposed **Lyndon B. Johnson** and American escalation in Vietnam. In 1970, in response to the **Cambodian Incursion**, Cooper joined Senator **Frank Church** (D-Idaho) in introducing an amendment that would prohibit American combat troops in **Cambodia** after 1 July 1970. When the amendment was rejected by the House of Representatives, Cooper and Church introduced a revision of the original amendment to the Supplementary Foreign Assistance Act of 1970, which passed in both the House of Representatives and the Senate on 22 December 1970. Public Law 91-652, put into effect on 5 January 1971, was less restrictive than the original but did serve as one of the early, important pieces of congressional legislation designed to regain control over American foreign policy from the executive. After the Senate, Cooper served as ambassador to the German Democratic Republic from 1974 to 1976 and then resumed his law practice until his death.

COOPER-CHURCH AMENDMENT. Introduced by senators **John Sherman Cooper** (R-Kentucky) and **Frank Church** (D-Idaho), the Cooper-

Church Amendment, which was attached to the Foreign Military Sales Act (HR 15628), responded to the May 1970 **Cambodian Incursion** and sought to limit the ability of the president to deploy combat troops in Southeast Asia. The original version of the amendment prohibited **United States** combat troops in **Cambodia** after 1 July 1970 as well as forbade any other military personnel or activity supported by the U.S. without congressional approval. The House of Representatives rejected this version of the amendment after President **Richard M. Nixon** warned that he would veto HR 15628 if it contained any proviso outlined in the Cooper-Church Amendment. Cooper and Church introduced a revision of the original amendment to the Supplementary Foreign Assistance Act of 1970, which passed in both the House of Representatives and the Senate on 22 December 1970. Public Law 91-652, put into effect on 5 January 1971, was less restrictive of air operations. At this point, the Cambodia Incursion had ended, though the U.S. was still engaged in air operations in Cambodia.

COR. A small group of **Montagnards** who live in Quảng Ngãi province and whose language falls into the Mon-**Khmer** family. On 28 August 1959, a group of Cor rose up against the **Ngô Đình Diệm** government, and the group changed their surname to **Hồ Chí Minh**'s upon his death on 2 September 1969.

CORPS TACTICAL ZONE (CTZ). The **Army of the Republic of Vietnam** divided the **Republic of Vietnam** into four CTZs in order to better organize its efforts during the war. I CTZ comprised the five northern provinces and included such strategic cities as **Huế** and **Đà Nẵng**. It bordered the **Demilitarized Zone**. II CTZ was directly south of I CTZ and included 12 provinces, including areas such as **Đà Lạt** and **Cam Ranh Bay**. III CTZ also comprised 12 provinces and included **Sài Gòn** and Vũng Tàu, while IV CTZ comprised the **Mê Kông Delta**, with the significant cities of **Cần Thơ** and Mỹ Tho.

COUNTERINSURGENCY. During the **John F. Kennedy** administration, the **United States** military incorporated counterinsurgency into its response to the Vietnam situation. Counterinsurgency, which focused on protecting the Vietnamese people from the **National Liberation Front**'s (NLF) tactics and influence, was seen as the solution to the growing problem in Southeast Asia. During the 1950s, the U.S. military had trained and equipped the **Army of the Republic of Vietnam** to fight a conventional war with division-size units, with the anticipation that the **Democratic Republic of Vietnam** would launch an overt invasion from the north similar to what had been done in

Korea in 1950. The growth of the communist insurgency in the **Republic of Vietnam** (RVN) under the leadership of the NLF forced the Kennedy administration to change its tactics.

Using **Special Forces** personnel and military **advisers**, the U.S. helped to develop counterinsurgency techniques in the RVN to take the initiative away from the NLF. Counterinsurgency strategy focused on winning the hearts and minds of the Vietnamese by protecting them from the terror employed by the NLF and by allowing them to realize the benefits offered by the **Sài Gòn** government and the U.S. Most counterinsurgency operations were small in scale, where a few men or **women** could operate in a specific region with a high degree of flexibility. While counterinsurgency strategy was used by all branches of the U.S. Armed Forces and by civilian agencies such as the **Central Intelligence Agency**, it was stressed in missions by the U.S. Army Special Forces and the U.S. **Marine Corps**. *See also* AIR COMMANDOS; LANSDALE, EDWARD GEARY; SPECIAL FORCES, VIETNAMESE; VANN, JOHN PAUL.

CREDIBILITY GAP. Term used to explain the difference between the **John F. Kennedy**, **Lyndon B. Johnson**, and **Richard M. Nixon** administration's explanations and justifications of the events that occurred in Southeast Asia, especially Vietnam, in comparison to **media** coverage of the war and the observations of those with firsthand experience in Southeast Asia. The credibility gap came to denote a cynical explanation for how the American people and **Congress** were deceived into supporting the Americanization and escalation of the war. The American public continued to support the war as a result of early credibility given to Washington officials, but the support gradually eroded over time, as the perceived reality of the situation in Southeast Asia moved further away from the official position as explained in Washington. *See also* ẤP BẮC, BATTLE OF; HALBERSTAM, DAVID.

CRONKITE, WALTER LELAND, JR. (1916–2009). Journalist and television personality. Cronkite received some education at the University of Texas at Austin before getting his first job in the **media** as a reporter for the *Houston Post*. He also worked as a sportscaster in Oklahoma City before being hired by United Press in 1939. Cronkite covered the European Theater during World War II as part of a group informally known as the "Writing 69th." In 1950, he moved to the Columbia Broadcasting System (CBS) and started to report for television. Cronkite thrived in the new media that many believed would never replace radio or print journalism. He hosted a number of shows until 1962 when CBS made him the anchor of the *CBS Evening News* and the managing editor in 1963 when the program expanded from 15 to 30 minutes. Cronkite became one of the leading stars in television news during his 20-year career at CBS and reported such monumental stories as the assassination of President **John F. Kennedy**, the civil rights movement, the landing on the moon, Watergate, and Vietnam. His catchphrase, "And that's the way it is," was known in a majority of the households in the **United States**. He entered into the Vietnam arena in September 1963 when he interviewed Kennedy.

Cronkite visited Vietnam on a number of occasions and was generally positive about American involvement in the war through the 1968 **Tết Offensive**. Before the Tết Offensive, his stories focused on the American soldier doing his job, characterized by his report from a B-57 Canberra bomber on an air-to-ground fire support mission. Cronkite reported on the Tết Offensive after it began and continued a positive spin on the fighting from his position in **Huế**. He, however, argued that even though the Tết Offensive had ended in a military disaster for the North Vietnamese and the **National Liberation Front**, the best the U.S. could do was achieve a stalemate. Critics of the media in Vietnam held that Cronkite turned against the war with his Tết broadcast. Cronkite argued that the U.S. had not been defeated but was mired in stalemate. For a nation reeling from the Tết Offensive and President **Lyndon B. Johnson**'s 31 March 1968 television broadcast in which he announced that he would not seek or accept his party's nomination for the presidential election, Cronkite's words were perceived as defeatism.

It was alleged that Johnson responded to Cronkite's assessment with the notion that if he had lost Cronkite, he had lost middle America. Whether or not the Johnson statement was actually made, the sentiment was real. Cronkite was considered one of the most trusted individuals on television, and his opinion carried much weight. Cronkite reported the war until its end. He retired in 1981 and produced a few programs for CBS. In 1996, he published his autobiography, *A Reporter's Life*.

CỦ CHI. Located to the northwest of **Sài Gòn** in Hậu Nghĩa, Củ Chi district was a major stronghold for the **National Liberation Front** (NLF) during the war. It was made famous by the extensive network of **tunnels** under the district used by the NLF to evade **Army of the Republic of Vietnam** (ARVN) and **United States** forces throughout the war. The NLF used the tunnel complex system as a base of operations against Sài Gòn and the Capital Military Region. The U.S. stationed the 25th Infantry **Division** in Củ Chi near **Route** 1. The division was in constant contact with the NLF from 1965 to the time of its withdrawal in 1971.

The U.S. tried unsuccessfully to eliminate the tunnel system but was frustrated by how well they were concealed and the extensive nature of the system. Between 8 and 14 January 1966, the **173rd Airborne Brigade** and 1st Battalion of the Royal Australian Regiment conducted Operation Crimp in the Củ Chi area. The operation failed to eliminate the NLF threat, but it did expose the extent to which the NLF had dug into the ground. In Operation **Cedar Falls**, from 8 to 28 January 1967, U.S. and ARVN troops attempted to eliminate the NLF threat in the area but again failed to permanently remove the NLF from Củ Chi. The NLF used the Củ Chi base as a staging area for the 1968 **Tết Offensive**. After Tết, the U.S. authorized B-52 bomber **sorties** against NLF strongholds, which resulted in significant damage but did not end the use of the tunnel system for the remainder of the war.

D

ĐÀ LẠT. Capital of Tuyên Đức province and the largest city in the southern part of the **Central Highlands**. The town is noted for its cool weather in comparative terms to the rest of the **Republic of Vietnam**. During World War II, it served as the capital of Indochina and a resort home for Emperor **Bảo Đại**. The area housed a French military academy, established in 1951, based on the Saint Cyr Military Academy in **France**. The school later trained officers for the **Army of the Republic of Vietnam**. There were 31 classes that graduated from it between 1951 and 1975. For the most part, Đà Lạt remained outside the war except during the 1968 **Tết Offensive**. The city was also known for a small nuclear physics research center that remains active today, though most of the material available for use dates from the 1950s.

ĐÀ NẴNG. Located in **Quảng Nam** in I **Corps Tactical Zone**, Đà Nẵng, also known as Tourane during the French rule in Indochina, was a major port city, military base, and air base during the war. The city was located next to the Song Hào (Tourane or Đà Nẵng River), which flowed into Đà Nẵng Bay and the South China Sea. In 1961, President **John F. Kennedy** authorized the establishment of a long-range radar facility in Đà Nẵng to provide **intelligence** on **Soviet** air activity over **Laos**, with **United States** personnel arriving in 1962 under Project Mule Train. Đà Nẵng was also used by U.S. **Special Forces** to train South Vietnamese to watch the **Demilitarized Zone** (DMZ) for infiltration in the Trail Watchers project and the Mountain Scout program that organized small teams of **Montagnards** to patrol in the jungle. Đà Nẵng also housed U.S. and South Vietnamese personnel that were involved in **OPLAN 34A** missions into the **Democratic Republic of Vietnam** (DRV).

On 8 March 1965, two **marine** battalions arrived in Đà Nẵng, marking the introduction of American combat troops in the **Republic of Vietnam** (RVN). Đà Nẵng developed into a significant U.S. military and air base. The 3rd Marine **Division** was based in Đà Nẵng from May 1965 to October 1966, and the 1st Marine Division operated from Đà Nẵng from November 1966 to April 1971. A number of major operations were focused on the areas around Đà Nẵng, including the November 1965 Operation **Blue Marlin** II. In 1966,

Đà Nẵng witnessed a general uprising of **Buddhists**, students, and other civilians that occurred after the commander of I Corps, **Nguyễn Chánh Thi**, was dismissed from service by **Nguyễn Cao Kỳ**. Đà Nẵng was also one of the first areas attacked during the 1968 **Tết Offensive**. The force assaulting the Americans during the offensive struck the day before the general offensive was to begin. Đà Nẵng was also one of two areas targeted for the third, and final, Tết Offensive that occurred in August 1968. This offensive, like the first, failed to destroy the U.S. forces. In August 1968, after the Tết offensives were over, a riot occurred at the marine prison in Đà Nẵng, followed by a more significant riot at **Long Bình** Jail.

A major air base was located near Đà Nẵng, which housed aircraft of both the RVN and the U.S. The air base was located less than 145 kilometers (90 miles) from the DMZ, making it the northernmost air base in the RVN. It was first organized in 1957 and was developed into a modern airfield with a long runway. The **Republic of Vietnam Air Force** (RVNAF) stationed the 41st Wing at Đà Nẵng in 1964, and aircraft from there launched their first air strikes against the DRV on 8 February 1965 as part of Operation **Flaming Dart**. After the U.S. joined the RVNAF at Đà Nẵng, a second runway was added in 1966. This made it the second busiest airfield in Southeast Asia.

The RVNAF 1st Air Division was headquartered at Đà Nẵng. It included the 41st Tactical Wing, the 51st Tactical Wing, and the 61st Tactical Wing, as well as several **helicopter** squadrons. The U.S. had a significant presence as well, starting in 1962 with Project Mule Train. In August 1963, the 777th Troop Carrier Squadron arrived at Đà Nẵng to assist the Special Forces.

In May 1972, American forces, mostly from the **U.S. Air Force**, began withdrawing from Đà Nẵng after the city was secured from the North Vietnamese who had earlier launched the **Easter Offensive**. The last units left at the end of June 1972. The city and military base remained in South Vietnamese hands until the final North Vietnamese offensive in 1975. After the abandonment of the **Central Highlands** in March 1975, Đà Nẵng's fate was sealed. On 28 March 1975, the 1st RVNAF Air Division left Đà Nẵng, two days before the **People's Army of Vietnam** took the city and military bases and nearly 200 aircraft, fuel, and munitions.

DAGGER THRUST. Mission name for an operation designed to attack the **National Liberation Front** (NLF) near the coast of the **Republic of Vietnam**. Dagger Thrust missions, which were approved in July 1965 and started in September 1965, were carried out in support of Operation **Market Time** activities that had begun in March 1965. Dagger Thrust missions called upon the **United States Marines**' Special Landing Force to strike quickly at areas believed to have a high concentration of NLF forces or in areas of suspected supply depots. The first series of Dagger Thrust missions began on 28 September and consisted of three raids in succession. The target included the Vùng Mù Peninsula, south of **Qui Nhơn**, and an area approximately 80 kilometers (50 miles) south in the Bèn Gọi area. The next set of Dagger Thrust missions occurred in late November 1965 after the completion of Operation **Blue Marlin**. The first target was in III **Corps Tactical Zone**, approximately 145 kilometers (90 miles) east of **Sài Gòn**. The fifth and final Dagger Thrust raid occurred on 5 December, 64 kilometers (40 miles) north of Qui Nhơn.

ĐẮK TÔ. Located to the north of **Kon Tum**, Đắk Tô is situated on **Route 14** in the Đắk Tô district of Kon Tum province. It was located approximately 24 kilometers (15 miles) to the east of the border between the **Republic of Vietnam** (RVN), **Cambodia**, and **Laos**. In 1962, an airstrip was built at Đắk Tô to support **United States Army Special Forces** A-Team operations. The **United States** also assisted a contingent of the **Civilian Irregular Defense Group** (CIDG) at Đắk Tô, one of many along the western border with Laos and Cambodia to stop the infiltration of personnel and supplies coming into the RVN through the **Hồ Chí Minh Trail**.

Starting in the summer of 1967, the **People's Army of Vietnam** (PAVN) initiated a series of battles in Kon Tum province designed to take pressure off the infiltration points into the RVN from the Hồ Chí Minh Trail. The U.S. responded to these attacks by introducing elements of the 4th Infantry **Division** and **173rd Airborne Brigade** in Operation Greeley. Đắk Tô was targeted in November 1967 when four PAVN regiments sought to destroy the Americans at the camp. To disrupt the PAVN plan, the U.S. initiated Operation MacArthur with existing forces plus the 1st Brigade, 1st Air Cavalry on 3 November. The Battle of Đắk Tô lasted 19 days, with several intense firefights in the surrounding foothills and rocket and mortar fire on the camp and airstrip. When the battle ended on 22 November, the U.S. had lost 376 killed and over 1,400 wounded, while the **Army of the Republic of Vietnam** had lost 79 killed. Over 1,000 PAVN soldiers were killed, making the 1st PAVN Division ineffective until it could be replenished.

Đắk Tô became the scene of additional fighting in 1969 when two regiments of PAVN laid siege to the CIDG camp. The camp was surrounded from 5 May to 29 June and was subject to constant rocket and mortar fire while the roads leading to it, as well as the camp at **Bến Hét**, were cut. The siege was lifted at the end of June when the PAVN retreated back into Cambodia. During the 1972 **Easter Offensive**, the North Vietnamese overran Đắk Tô, though the camp was retaken in October after intense fighting. It was eventually abandoned when the **Sài Gòn** government chose to surrender the **Central Highlands** during the final 1975 PAVN offensive.

DANIEL BOONE, OPERATION. Operation designed to identify **People's Army of Vietnam** and **National Liberation Front** base areas in **Cambodia** that originated in April 1967. The first missions began in September 1967 and involved small teams of 12 men conducting reconnaissance missions into Cambodia, which had proclaimed neutrality in the war. Similar reconnaissance missions over the next two years would confirm the extent to which the North Vietnamese had taken over the border between the **Republic of Vietnam** and Cambodia and had worked out a compromise with Prince **Norodom Sihanouk** to move supplies from **Sihanoukville**, via the **Hak Ly** Company, to the established base areas.

The missions were under the operational control of the **Studies and Observation Group** (SOG) and paralleled similar SOG missions under Operation **Shining Brass** into **Laos**. Daniel Boone missions were secret, which meant the reconnaissance teams were not provided with air support for insertion or extraction, or if they became engaged with the enemy in Cambodian territory. While mission objectives did not include engaging the enemy, teams were allowed to place antipersonnel devices in Cambodia after the operation had been established. In 1969, Operation Daniel Boone was renamed Salem House. After the **Cambodian Incursion**, **United States** personnel no longer participated in reconnaissance missions into Cambodia and instead assisted the South Vietnamese in what became known as Operation Thốt Nốt in April 1971. *See also* PRAIRIE FIRE; SIHANOUK TRAIL.

DECKHOUSE, OPERATIONS. A series of six different operations involving the Special Landing Force (SLF) of the **United States Marines** that made use of the amphibious advantage the U.S. possessed over the **People's Army of Vietnam** (PAVN) and the **National Liberation Front** (NLF). Deckhouse I, centered in Phú Yên province, involved the 3rd Battalion, 5th Marines in support of the 1st Cavalry **Division** in Operation Nathan Hale. The operation lasted from 17 to 30 June 1966. Deckhouse II involved the same unit in a similar supporting role. This time the SLF supported Operation Hastings in **Quảng Trị** from 16 to 30 July 1966. In Deckhouse III, from 16 to 20 August 1966, the 1st Battalion, 26th Marines conducted a joint operation with the **173rd Airborne Brigade** in Operation Toledo along the Vũng Tàu Peninsula. Deckhouse IV lasted from 15 to 18 September 1966 and involved the same unit plus the 3rd Marine Reconnaissance Battalion just south of the **Demilitarized Zone**. During the first week of January 1967, the 1st Battalion, 9th Marines joined the Vietnamese Marines in Deckhouse V. The operation focused on capturing NLF suspects in Bình Tuy and Kiến Hoa province. It ended on 16 January 1967. The final Deckhouse operation began on 16 February 1967 and lasted until 3 March 1967. It also focused on the provinces of Bình

Tuy and Kiến Hoa but expanded into Quảng Ngãi province. This operation involved the 1st Marine Division Headquarters and the 1st Battalion, 4th Marines. The Deckhouse operations demonstrated the complete advantage held by the **Free World Forces** in moving troops by sea. There was no area connected to the coast that was accessible to amphibious assault that remained safe for the PAVN and NLF during the American phase of the war.

DEFENSE ATTACHÉ OFFICE (DAO). Activated on 28 January 1973, the DAO replaced the **Military Assistance Command, Vietnam** (MACV), after the signing of the **Paris Peace Accords**. It assumed the responsibilities of MACV, though on a much smaller scale and focused on the coordination of **United States** aid to the South Vietnamese. The DAO used the former MACV compound at **Tân Sơn Nhứt** with personnel in **Đà Nẵng**, **Plei Ku**, **Qui Nhơn**, **Nha Trang**, **Biên Hòa**, **Long Bình**, Nhà Bè, Đồng Tâm, Bình Thủy, and **Cần Thơ**. The Paris Peace Accords limited the strength of the DAO to 50 military personnel, though the group was supplemented with over 1,000 civilian personnel. Major General John E. Murray commanded the DAO until 1974 and was replaced by Major General Homer D. Smith until the fall of **Sài Gòn** on 30 April 1975.

Another responsibility of the DAO was to assess the strength of the forces of the **Army of the Republic of Vietnam** and the **People's Army of Vietnam**. It issued quarterly reports that provided a threat assessment examining the status of the North Vietnamese Armed Forces, a detailed analysis of the South Vietnamese position in each of the military regions, an assessment of the **intelligence** capability and force structure of the **Republic of Vietnam** (RVN) Armed Forces, and a detailed report on the Vietnamese Army, **Navy**, **Air Force**, **Marine Corps**, and Territorial Forces, which included the **Regional Forces**, **Popular Forces**, and the **People's Self-Defense Force**. The DAO also assessed South Vietnamese communications capability, training, planning, morale, and command and control. The final quarterly report also included a section on the possible evacuation of Sài Gòn. Both Murray and Smith constantly alerted their superiors that the South Vietnamese were much weaker than they appeared and warned of the growing strength of the North Vietnamese, but they were often overruled by the U.S. ambassador to the RVN, **Graham Martin**. DAO personnel were among the last to evacuate in April 1975, and it ceased operations after Sài Gòn fell. *See also* FREQUENT WIND, OPERATION.

DEFIANT STAND, OPERATION. The 62nd, and last, **amphibious operation** of the 7th Fleet Special Landing Force (SLF). Defiant Stand began on 7 September 1969 when the 1st Battalion, 26th **Marine** Regiment, in a joint operation with the 3rd Brigade of the Korean Marine Corps (Blue Dragon), conducted a **search-and-destroy** mission against the southern part of Barrier Island, 55 kilometers (34 miles) south of Đà Nẵng. Defiant Stand was the first amphibious assault in the war for the **Republic of Korea** troops. Preceding the operation, the Vietnamese navy blocked off the water escape routes while the American SLF attacked by air. Prior to the initial amphibious assault, HMM-265 transported part of the **United States** and Korean force, using CH-46D **helicopters**, to the island to set up blocking positions. The operation, the third such attack against the area in 1969, achieved limited results. The **National Liberation Front** avoided the allied forces, with the exception of a few ambushes and rearguard actions, as they retreated away from the area of operation. The U.S. recorded 293 enemy killed. The operation, known as Seung Yong 15-1 by the Republic of Korea, ended on 20 September 1969.

DEMILITARIZED ZONE (DMZ). The DMZ between the **Republic of Vietnam** (RVN) and the **Democratic Republic of Vietnam** was established as a result of the 1954 **Geneva Agreements** that ended the **First Indochina War**. The area was created from a swath of land just south of the 17th parallel on either side of the Bến Hải River, from the beaches of the South China Sea to the border between **Laos** and the two Vietnams. The DMZ was put into place as French and Vietnamese forces regrouped. Its purpose was to ensure that no further outbreak of war would come to Vietnam. It was a temporary zone that was meant to fade away soon after the elections outlined in the Geneva Agreements had occurred. They were required to take place within two years of the signing of the documents on 21 July 1954. When the RVN refused to follow through with elections, the DMZ became a more permanent fixture and remained the RVN's first line of defense throughout the war. Fighting along the DMZ was at times fierce, as the two sides used **mortar, artillery**, and raiding parties to harass one another. It saw heavy fighting in the months preceding and during the 1968 **Tết Offensive** and 1972 **Easter Offensive**, both initiated by the **People's Army of Vietnam** and **National Liberation Front**.

DEMOCRATIC REPUBLIC OF VIETNAM (DRV). Established on 2 September 1945 by **Hồ Chí Minh**, the DRV (Việt Nam Dân Chủ Cộng Hòa), or North Vietnam, was created as a state for all Vietnamese people in their bid for independence. The French agreed to the March 1946 election of a National Assembly, with Hồ Chí Minh as the head of government and **Bảo Đại** as the supreme adviser. When the **First Indochina War** broke out between the French and Vietnamese later in the year, Bảo Đại rejected the DRV and, with **France**'s assistance, became the leader of the State of Vietnam. The

DRV was the government most recognized with the opposition to French colonialism and in support of Vietnamese nationalism. With the end of the First Indochina War and the signing of the 1954 **Geneva Agreements** that partitioned Vietnam along a **Demilitarized Zone** near the 17th parallel, the DRV assumed control of the northern territory, while Bảo Đại and then **Ngô Đình Diệm** controlled the South, which would become known as the **Republic of Vietnam** in October 1955.

Hồ Chí Minh served as the first president of the DRV until his death on 2 September 1969. He was replaced by Tôn Đức Thắng. **Phạm Văn Đồng** served as the premier of the DRV and held the primary power in the DRV as leader of the Politburo of the **Lao Động** Party. Its first secretary was **Lê Duẩn**. Both Phạm Văn Đồng and Lê Duẩn served in their positions until the DRV was renamed the Socialist Republic of Vietnam in 1976.

DESOTO PATROLS. Electronic **intelligence** mission against the **Democratic Republic of Vietnam** (DRV) beginning in the fall of 1963, which led to the **Gulf of Tŏn Kĭn Incident** and **Resolution** in August 1964. The mission usually consisted of a single destroyer advancing deep into the contested waters off the coast of the DRV in order to activate the electronic defense systems. The destroyer would then gather as much information as possible from this electronic data to use for further operations, including South Vietnamese **OPLAN 34A** missions designed to take the war to the North. The North Vietnamese considered these missions to be an overt act of aggression, while the **United States** insisted that the ships involved in the missions were in international waters. The U.S. also countered that the DeSoto missions confirmed the movement of personnel and supplies from the DRV to the **Republic of Vietnam**, which it considered an act of war.

DEWEY CANYON I, OPERATION. **United States Marine Corps** operation in the A Shau Valley designed to eliminate **People's Army of Vietnam** (PAVN) and **National Liberation Front** (NLF) access to the civilian populations in the Đa Krông Valley and to confront a believed buildup of enemy troops in Base Area 611 along the Laotian border. The operation ran from 22 January to 18 March 1969. It involved battalions from the 3rd and 9th Marines, who had been fighting a limited offensive war up to that point as they manned the **McNamara Line**. The highlight of the operation was a limited raid into Base Area 611 that bordered the **Republic of Vietnam** and **Laos**, which included the movement of **United States** troops into Laos to engage the PAVN soldiers who had been using the country's neutrality to their advantage. Like many **search-and-destroy** operations during the war, Dewey Canyon I was considered a success even though the main PAVN and

NLF units were not destroyed and, as a result, continued to pose a threat to the civilian population. During the course of the operation, 121 marines were killed-in-action, and 803 were wounded. The PAVN killed were estimated at approximately 1,500. The U.S. captured or destroyed nearly 500 tons of war-related supplies. *See also* DEWEY CANYON II, OPERATION.

DEWEY CANYON II, OPERATION. Operation conducted by the 5th Infantry and 101st Airborne **Division** and the 2nd battalion, 17th Cavalry Regiment in support of the February 1971 **Army of the Republic of Vietnam** (ARVN) operation into **Laos**, known as **Lam Sơn 719**. Because the **United States** was restricted from participating in military operations that involved troops entering into **Cambodia** or Laos as a result of the 5 January 1971 Public Law 91-652, known as the **Cooper-Church Amendment**, the U.S. could only play a supporting role to the ARVN operation. U.S. forces helped to reopen the old **marine** base at **Khe Sanh**, which provided **artillery** support for the ARVN forces, and **Route** 9 to the Laotian border. The U.S. was successful in completing its objectives, though Operation Lam Sơn 719 would end in disaster for the ARVN forces involved in the operation. *See also* DEWEY CANYON I, OPERATION.

DEWEY CANYON III, OPERATION. Between 19 and 23 April 1971, the **Vietnam Veterans Against the War** (VVAW) staged an **antiwar** demonstration in Washington, D.C. On 19 April, a little more than 1,000 veterans led by Gold Star mothers (women who had lost their son in war) marched across the Lincoln Memorial Bridge to the gates of Arlington Cemetery. After a ceremony honoring those who had died in Vietnam, a small group of Gold Star mothers and veterans tried to lay wreaths inside the cemetery but were denied entry. The group then marched back across the bridge and set up camp on the Mall, where it presented its demands to **Congress** and continued to protest the war. On 20 April, some veterans then lobbied Congress while others marched back to Arlington Cemetery and were allowed to enter. For the next two days, the veterans continued to lobby Congress while future senator John Kerry testified in front of the Senate Foreign Relations Committee on 22 April. The protest culminated on 23 April when the veterans threw their medals and ribbons on the steps of the Capitol Building. Opponents of the VVAW argued that not all of the participants were veterans, nor were all of the medals genuine. Regardless, the protest, dubbed Dewey Canyon III, keep the antiwar movement in the press and on the minds of those who were becoming war weary.

ĐIỆN BIÊN PHỦ, BATTLE OF. After being frustrated in his attempt to consolidate his forces in the **Red River Delta**, the commander of the French

Union Forces in Indochina, General **Henri Navarre**, established a fortress near the village of Điện Biên Phủ, which was located in a valley in the northwestern section of Vietnam. Navarre maintained that the overwhelming preponderance of firepower the French could bring to battle, coupled with a strong defensive position along strategic **Route** 19, would force the Vietnamese under **Võ Nguyên Giáp** to fight and would ultimately result in a decisive defeat for the Vietnamese opposed to French colonialism in Indochina. In December 1953, Navarre procured 25 C-47 transport aircraft from the **United States** to begin establishing the fortress. The early battle focused on the roads leading to the fortress, which served as the main source of resupply. When the Vietnamese cut the roads, the French were forced to resupply by air. By January 1954, the French Union Forces required 20 C-119 and 50 C-47 transport **sorties** per day to maintain an adequate supply level.

When ground relief efforts failed to reopen the highways and the Vietnamese damaged the only usable airstrip in the valley in March, the situation became critical for the French. The French had not anticipated the Vietnamese ability to move **artillery** pieces up the rugged terrain surrounding the valley and had underestimated the Vietnamese determination to take the fortress. While French airpower proved an equalizer, it became difficult to maintain the required sortie rate due to attrition from **antiaircraft artillery** and normal wear and tear. With the situation deteriorating, the French government requested American aircraft and pilots. The U.S. loaned a number of B-26 bombers and 12 additional C-119 transports but refused the inclusion of American pilots because of the high risk of **casualties**. The **Air Force** section of the **Military Assistance Advisory Group** sent 200 technicians to **Hà Nội** to service the aircraft and keep the French air campaign going. There were also American civilian pilots, most employed by the Civil Air Transport, which included former World War II pilots brought in by the **Central Intelligence Agency**. These pilots volunteered to transport some of the daily 170 tons of ammunition and 32 tons of food required at the fortress. The U.S. flew 1,800 airlift sorties in Indochina, but it was not enough to alter the outcome of the battle.

The Vietnamese continued to press their advantage and eventually surrounded the French Union Forces at Điện Biên Phủ. They weakened the defenders with constant harassment while the French were forced to live in squalid conditions. As the situation became critical, French political and military leaders requested American assistance to avoid defeat. In March 1954, General Paul Ely, commander-in-chief of the French Union Forces, requested from the chairman of the **Joint Chiefs of Staff**, Admiral Arthur Radford, a U.S.-led bombing campaign to reverse the situation. The plan that originated from the request, Operation **Vulture**, called for 60 B-29 aircraft to saturate the Vietnamese position around the fortress with **bombs**. The plan was ultimately rejected by the U.S. because few believed the operation would reverse the battle or the war against the Vietnamese. As the battle waged into April, another strategy was developed to aid the French. Known as **United Action**, this plan called for a coalition of forces, led by the U.S. and Great Britain, to introduce ground troops into Indochina to relieve the pressure at Điện Biên Phủ and in the Red River Delta. United Action failed after Great Britain, later joined by **Australia** and **New Zealand**, refused to become involved in a colonial war that had little chance of success.

As France negotiated with the U.S. and Great Britain for possible intervention in Indochina, the conditions at Điện Biên Phủ continued to deteriorate. The French fortress fell on 7 May 1954, one day before the question of Indochina was to be discussed at the **Geneva Conference** in Switzerland. This further weakened the French position in Indochina and ultimately led to the armistice that ended the **First Indochina War** and the French colonial experience in Indochina. *See also* ĐỒNG SĨ NGUYÊN; DULLES, JOHN FOSTER; HOÀNG VĂN THÁI; NAVARRE PLAN; NGÔ ĐÌNH DIỆM; PEOPLE'S ARMY OF VIETNAM; TRẦN NAM TRUNG; TRẦN VĂN QUANG; VĂN TIẾN DŨNG.

DIKES. Earthen works designed to keep water contained in or out of a certain area. Dikes dotted the landscape of Indochina. During the war, the dike system around **Hà Nội** became the focus of much speculation and controversy. Because parts of Hà Nội were below sea level, the city was protected by a complex series of dikes that kept the waters of the Red River at bay. Hà Nội had been off limits to Operation **Rolling Thunder** sorties, but in 1972, during the **Linebacker** operations, the **United States** bombed the city. In June, the North Vietnamese accused the U.S. of targeting the 4,000 kilometers (2,500 miles) of earthen dikes in order to cause as much misery as possible to the civilian population in the **Democratic Republic of Vietnam**'s capital. The damage to the dikes was confirmed by the Swedish ambassador and journalists in Hà Nội, while critics of American efforts in Vietnam, such as **United Nations** secretary General Kurt Waldheim and actress **Jane Fonda** publicly voiced their opposition to the **bombings**.

U.S. officials argued that the North Vietnamese had placed elements of their air defense system on the dikes in order to force the U.S. to ignore these legitimate targets. This action made what was once a civilian target a military one, though it was difficult to convey this to the international community, despite aerial **reconnaissance** photography that showed what the North Vietnamese had done. That the U.S. did not completely destroy the dike system in Hà Nội when it had the capability to do so in a matter of days suggests that it was not a target of Linebacker **sorties**. The battle of public relations and international **propaganda** during the 1972 controversy demonstrated how successful the North Vietnamese had been in achieving the advantage. It moved military targets to civilian areas that would not normally have been legitimate targets. When the U.S. refrained from destroying the dike system, it was still condemned by the **antiwar movement** and the international community for recklessness, even though it caused minimal damage. Given the number of sorties flown and munitions dropped during the various air campaigns, the U.S. should have been commended for avoiding this type of target even though North Vietnamese actions had turned what had once been a civilian target into a military one.

DIRTY THIRTY. The creation of the **Republic of Vietnam Air Force** (RVNAF) 2nd Fighter Squadron at the **Biên Hòa** airbase took experienced pilots away from the RVNAF's 1st Transportation Group. This meant that the 1st Transportation Group did not have enough pilots to fly their C-47 aircraft. The **Military Assistance Advisory Group** recommended that **United States** pilots replace the Vietnamese and serve as copilots until more Vietnamese could be trained. In April 1962, 30 **U.S. Air Force** pilots were temporarily assigned to fly with the 1st Transportation Group and train their Vietnamese counterparts in the C-47. The American pilots remained under U.S. commanders but were integrated into the RVNAF structure. On call 24 hours a day, they earned the nickname "the Dirty Thirty" after a reporter wrote about their always-dirty uniforms. The first group of USAF personnel was replaced by a second contingent in early 1963. This group was eventually reassigned in December 1963. The Dirty Thirty logged over 25,000 flying hours with the Vietnamese and enabled many of the Vietnamese to transition to fighter aircraft.

DIVISION, UNITED STATES. The U.S. used a number of divisions during the Vietnam War. A typical division consisted of three infantry brigades, each of which had three infantry battalions. The divisions also included a number of **artillery** battalions, as well as at least one battalion of **helicopters** and medical, signal, supply and transport, engineer, and maintenance battalions. It also had military police, reconnaissance, and **intelligence** units.

The 1st Infantry Division, nicknamed the Big Red One arrived in the **Republic of Vietnam** (RVN) in July 1965. It participated in approximately 25 named operations by the end of 1965. The first major action was Operation Checkerboard I, a **search-and-destroy** mission, in Bình Dương province, and it participated in over 100 named operations before it left in April 1970. The division was involved in some of the most significant operations during the war, including a search-and-destroy mission in **War Zone C** under Operation

Attleboro between 14 September 1966 and 24 November 1966. The division also participated in the major search-and-destroy missions in 1967, including operations **Cedar Falls** and **Junction City**. During the 1968 **Tết Offensive**, the 1st Infantry Division secured **Tân Sơn Nhứt** Air Base. The division served in III **Corps Tactical Zone** (CTZ), with its headquarters at Dĩ An and Lai Khê in Bình Dương province. The division suffered 6,146 killed-in-action (KIA) and 16,019 wounded-in-action (WIA) during the war.

The 1st Cavalry Division (Airmobile), oftentimes called the 1st Cavalry, 1st Air Cavalry, or just the Cav, was established in July 1965 from elements of the 11th Air Assault Division and was deployed to An Khê in **Bình Định** province. Its first action was in support of the **Special Forces** camp at Plei Me, which evolved into the Battle of the Ia Đrăng Valley in November 1965. It was involved in Operation Pershing in 1967, a major search-and-destroy in II CTZ, and it participated in the clearing of **Huế** during the Tết Offensive and in relieving the U.S. **Marine Corps** (USMC) base of **Khe Sanh**. In late 1968, the division moved to III CTZ near the Parrots Beak on the Cambodian border, and in 1970 it was involved in the **Cambodian Incursion**. Most of the division left the RVN in April 1971, though the division was not completely withdrawn until the summer of 1972. The division suffered 5,444 KIA and 26,592 WIA.

The 4th Infantry Division, known as the Ivy Division, deployed to the RVN in September 1966 and remained until 8 December 1970, though one brigade would continue to operate independently until January 1972. The division was primarily in the Central Highlands, with its headquarters at either **Plei Ku**, **Đắk Tô**, or An Khê. It was also involved in operations Attleboro and Junction City and participated in the Cambodian Incursion. In August 1967, the 3rd Brigade, 4th Infantry Division switched with the 3rd Brigade, 25th Infantry Division, which was participating in **Task Force Oregon**. The brigades were switched back by the end of 1970. The division suffered 2,531 KIA and 15,229 WIA.

The 5th Infantry Division (Mechanized), known as the Red Diamond or the Red Devils, sent its 1st Brigade to the RVN in March 1968. The entire division never deployed to the RVN. It operated in **Quảng Trị** and was involved in a number of operations, including Operation **Dewey Canyon** II. By August 1971, the brigade had left the RVN.

The 9th Infantry Division, nicknamed the Old Reliables, arrived in the RVN on 16 December 1966. It spent a considerable amount of time in the **Mê Kông Delta**, though it was assigned to the III CTZ. It operated in Định Tường and **Long An** provinces. Its 2nd Brigade worked with the **Mobile Riverine Force** in IV CTZ and was involved with the **Patrol Air Cushion Vehicle** experiment. It left the RVN on 12 October 1970, though its 3rd

Brigade continued to work with the 25th Infantry Division within Long An province in III CTZ.

The 23rd Infantry Division, known as the Americal, was reactivated in the RVN in September 1967 from elements that made up **Task Force Oregon**, which had been created by bringing together troops from the 25th Infantry Division, the 101st Airborne Division, and the 196th Light Infantry Brigade. It was headquartered at **Chu Lai** in IV CTZ and operated in Quảng Ngãi and Quảng Tín provinces. The 23rd Infantry Division was involved in the 16 March 1968 **Mỹ Lai** massacre and was marred by **fragging** and combat refusal incidents. Two of its brigades withdrew from Vietnam in November 1971, though the 196th Infantry Brigade remained and was reconstituted as an independent brigade. It started its withdrawal from the RVN on 29 June 1972.

The 25th Infantry Division, known as Tropic Lightning, sent personnel to the RVN in 1963, though it was not until August 1965 that the main division began to arrive. It was stationed in Hawaii with specific training in tropical warfare. Its engineering battalion helped construct **Cam Ranh Bay**. Its 3rd Brigade arrived in December 1965 and worked in the Central Highlands. By March 1966, the rest of the division arrived. The 25th Infantry Division operated near **Củ Chi** in III CTZ, though it participated in limited operations in the IV CTZ. The division was involved in operations Cedar Falls and Junction City in 1967, and during the Tết Offensive, it helped to defend **Sài Gòn**. It also played a major role in the Cambodian Incursion. Most of the division left in December 1970, though its 2nd Brigade remained until April 1971.

The 82nd Airborne Division, known as the All American Division, arrived in the RVN in January 1968. Its 3rd Brigade operated near Huế and Phú Bài in I CTZ. It also operated in IV CTZ and near the Cambodian border and **Iron Triangle**. The division suffered 227 KIA and 1,009 WIA.

The 101st Airborne Division, nicknamed the Screaming Eagles, first entered the RVN in July 1965 when its 1st Brigade was deployed. The rest of the division arrived in November 1967. It operated in I CTZ and was involved in interdiction operations near the Laotian border and in the A Shau Valley. It was involved in several major engagements including the 1969 Battle of **Hamburger Hill** and the 1970 Fire Support Base **Ripcord** siege. The 101st Airborne Division also supplied the helicopters and pilots for the failed 1971 Operation Lam Sơn 719. It suffered 4,011 KIA and 18,259 WIA, which represented the third highest total behind the 1st Cavalry Division and the 25th Infantry Division. The division left between December 1971 and January 1972.

The USMC had two divisions deployed to the RVN. The 1st USMC Division arrived in 1966 and established its headquarters at Chu Lai. It operated in I CTZ in Quảng Ngãi and Quảng Tín provinces. In November 1966, it moved its headquarters to **Đà Nẵng**. The division left the RVN in

April 1971. When Vietnamese began to flee after the fall of Sài Gòn in April 1975, the 1st USMC Division provided relief for the **refugees** at Camp Pendleton, California.

The 3rd USMC Division arrived at Đà Nẵng on 6 May 1965 and completed its deployment by the end of 1965. It moved to Phú Bài in October 1966. In late 1967, the division moved to Quảng Trị. It withdrew from the RVN in November 1969. *See also* CASUALTIES.

DIXIE STATION. Located in the South China Sea, Dixie Station was the southern equivalent of the **Yankee Station** in the Gulf of Tŏn Kĭn. Established on 15 May 1965, an aircraft carrier located at Dixie Station provided close air support for allied forces engaged with the **People's Army of Vietnam** and the **National Liberation Front** in the **Republic of Vietnam**. A **United States** aircraft carrier operated from Dixie Station until 3 August 1966.

ĐỖ CAO TRÍ (1929–1971). Army of the Republic of Vietnam (ARVN) general, division, corps, and **Corps Tactical Zone** (CTZ) commander. Đỗ Cao Trí joined the military in 1947 and rose through the ranks to become the first commandant of the airborne. In 1949, he attended the French infantry and airborne schools, and in 1953 he attended the Vietnamese command and staff school in **Hà Nội**. He also received training at the **United States** command and general staff school at Fort Leavenworth, Kansas, in 1958. During the **First Indochina War**, he participated in combat jumps in the Nasan and in Operation Lạng Sơn in 1951. Toward the end of this war, he also fought in operations **Rừng Sác** and Đinh Tiên Hoàng. Đỗ Cao Trí was considered a very capable commander, though his reputation earned him enemies, including Air Marshall **Nguyễn Cao Kỳ**. He was accused of corruption on more than one occasion even though his family was already wealthy. On 5 August 1968, he assumed command of III Corps and III CTZ from General **Lê Nguyên Khang**, where he oversaw operations for the 5th, 18th, and 25th ARVN Divisions. During the **Cambodian Incursion** in April–June 1970, he was able to coordinate ARVN forces with U.S. forces around the **Parrot's Beak**. During the 1971 Operation Lam Sơn 719, Đỗ Cao Trí died in a **helicopter** crash on his way to assuming command of I Corps from General **Hoàng Xuân Lãm**. At the time of his death, Đỗ Cao Trí was the most decorated ARVN combat soldier. He represented what good leadership could do for the ARVN, and his loss was a severe blow when the **People's Army of Vietnam** launched its **Easter Offensive** the next year.

DOGS. There were an estimated 3,500 dogs that went to Southeast Asia with the **United States** Armed Forces, mostly in the **army** and **air force**. The majority of these were German shepherds. Dogs had certain advantages over humans in the jungles of Southeast Asia, especially the senses of hearing and smell. Dogs and their handlers received training at Fort Benning, Georgia, with some taking additional training in Malaysia.

Dogs performed a number of different missions during the war. Sentry dogs walked with personnel to guard military and civilian bases, facilities, and other buildings and were trained to bark or growl to warn their handler of unknown personnel near their position. Scout dogs received similar training to sentry dogs, but they were also taught how to locate enemy personnel silently. Patrol dogs served the same function but also walked point with troops operating in the field. Dogs helped decrease the likelihood of ambush because they could detect Vietnamese personnel at over 914 meters (3,000 feet). Dogs were also trained to locate and inspect **tunnels** that were used by the **National Liberation Front** (NLF) in areas like Củ Chi. The NLF feared the ability of dogs to detect the tunnel complexes and used a number of techniques, including stealing soap from U.S. military bases and spreading it around the openings, to confuse the dogs. Few dogs returned from the war, as the U.S. military decided to euthanize rather than transport them back to the U.S.

DOMINO THEORY. An idea that originated from the Cold War mentality that existed in the 1950s and 1960s. As an extension of the containment doctrine that called upon the **United States** to counter any communist efforts to encroach upon Free World or neutral countries, the domino theory argued that the fall of one country would lead to further destabilization in that country's region and the fall of additional, neighboring countries. In the case of the **Republic of Vietnam**, the theory suggested that its fall would lead to instability in Indochina, which would result in the loss of **Cambodia** and **Laos** to communism. With Indochina under communist rule, **Thailand** would have little chance to resist, and its fall would lead to the loss of Burma and Malaya/Malaysia. The loss of Southeast Asia would isolate many of the island nations in the Pacific, which could lead to a takeover of **Australia** and **New Zealand**, and eventually to communist influence reaching the shores of California.

The domino theory was an effective tool in justifying U.S. action during the Cold War, as it simplified the consequences of U.S. inaction in the world. In relation to Southeast Asia, the theory was first introduced to the American public by President Dwight D. Eisenhower at a presidential press conference on 7 April 1954.

ĐÔNG HÀ. Located on the Cam Lộ River in **Quảng Trị** in the northern part of the **Republic of Vietnam** (RVN), Đông Hà was the nearest city of significance to the **Demilitarized Zone**, at approximately 19.3 kilometers

(12 miles) away. Đông Hà served as the intersection for **Route** 1 and Route 9; its importance was confirmed by the presence of a **United States Marine** combat base and, after the 1968 **Tết Offensive**, the 3rd Marine **Division**. Đông Hà was overrun in the 1972 **Easter Offensive**, though the bridge that connected the two banks of the Cam Lộ River was blown up by U.S. **advisers**, which delayed briefly the **People's Army of Vietnam tanks** that were used in the opening weeks of the attack. As the northernmost town in the RVN, Đông Hà suffered a disproportionate amount of damage during the war, though its postwar recovery was hastened by its strategic location along the two major highways.

ĐỐNG SĨ NGUYÊN (1923–). People's Army of Vietnam general and vice chairman of the Council of Ministers and also known as Nguyễn Hữu Vũ and Nguyễn Văn Dong. Đông Sĩ Nguyên joined the Communist Party in 1939 and fought against **France** during the **First Indochina War** in Quảng Bình province. He served in **Laos**, during the Battle for **Điện Biên Phủ**, and was known for his anti-Catholic stand. He went south in 1965 to become a political officer for **Military Region** 4 and commanded the **559th Transport Group** on the **Hồ Chí Minh Trail** from January 1967 to 1975. After the war, he served as a member of the Communist Party Central Committee until 1991, as an alternate member of the Politburo from 1982 to 1986, and as a full member from 1986 to 1991. He also held the position of vice chairman of the Council of Ministers during this time and spent a period as the minister of transportation and communication, replacing Đinh Đức Thiện, the brother of **Lê Đức Thọ**. In 1999, he authored a book about his experiences on the Hồ Chí Minh Trail titled, *Đường Xuyên Trường Sơn.*

DONLAN, ROGER H. C. (1934–). Donlan was awarded the first Medal of Honor during the Vietnam War for his action during the 6 July 1964 battle at Nam Đông, 56 kilometers (35 miles) west of Đà Nẵng. As commander of Detachment A-726, C Company of the 7th **Special Forces** Group (Airborne), Donlan organized his American and **Australian advisers**, South Vietnamese troops, and **Nùng** militia against a reinforced **National Liberation Front** battalion. Despite serious wounds to his stomach, left shoulder, leg, and face, Donlan stayed in command of his troops and offered a spirited defense. For his action, President **Lyndon B. Johnson** awarded him the Congressional Medal of Honor on 17 December 1964. He retired from the army as a colonel on 14 December 1988.

DOUBLE EAGLE I, OPERATION. An **amphibious** and land-based operation that began on 28 January 1966 in southern Quảng Ngãi province, which involved the III Marine Amphibious Forces and elements of the 7th Fleet. Double Eagle was one of many operations that used the overwhelming superiority of naval forces to place troops at any position at any time on the coast of the **Republic of Vietnam**. In a typical **search-and-destroy** mission against an estimated force of 2,000 **People's Army of Vietnam** and **National Liberation Front** (NLF) personnel, four Marine Battalion Landing Teams were disembarked near Đức Phổ and moved inland to meet up with elements of the 1st Cavalry **Division** and the 22nd **Army of the Republic of Vietnam** Division. The troops were supported by a **helicopter** company and **artillery** battery. A navy detachment from the Beach-Jumper Unit also provided psychological support for the campaign. The operation was not considered a great success even though the amphibious portion of the operation was flawless. Most of the NLF in the area managed to escape the trap, though the **United States** claimed approximately 440 killed, with only six U.S. personnel killed and approximately 430 wounded. The two-phase operation ended on 28 February 1966.

DOUBLE EAGLE II, OPERATION. An operation, known by the **Army of the Republic of Vietnam** (ARVN) as Liên Kết 24, that succeeded Operation Double Eagle I. It began on 19 February 1966 during the final days of Operation **Double Eagle I**. This **search-and-destroy** mission involved the **United States Marine Corps** (USMC), the 501st Aviation Battalion, and the two divisions of the ARVN operating in the **Quế Sơn Valley**. The objective was to destroy the 1st Regiment of the **National Liberation Front** (NLF). When the operation ended on 28 February, the USMC estimated 75 to 125 enemy personnel killed and approximately 25 captured, plus a significant amount of rice and weapons confiscated. Four U.S. and four ARVN soldiers were killed. The operation failed to destroy the NLF in the operation's area.

DOVE. Term used to denote individuals who believed the **United States** should not be militarily involved in Vietnam. Some Doves shared the **Hawk** point of view that the U.S. had an obligation to improve the lives of the Vietnamese people through humanitarian and nonmilitary projects. Doves preferred American withdrawal from Southeast Asia and an end to the war through negotiations or any other means. *See also* 44 BATTALION DEBATE; BALL, GEORGE WILDMAN; BUNDY, WILLIAM PUTNAM; TRƯƠNG ĐÌNH DZŨ.

DRINAN, ROBERT FREDERICK (1920–2007). Roman Catholic priest, member of the House of Representatives (D-Massachusetts), and law professor. Drinan received a BA and MA from Boston College in 1942 and a law degree from Georgetown University in 1950. He was ordained a Catholic priest in the Jesuit Order in 1953 and earned a PhD in theology from the Gregorian University in Rome, Italy, in 1954. He returned to Massachusetts in 1956 and became the dean of the Boston College Law School until 1970, when he was elected to the House of Representatives on an **antiwar** platform. Drinan's election represented a change in the support of the war since he defeated the influential and respected Philip Philbin, who had chaired the House Armed Services Committee in the Democratic primary and was an influential member of **Congress**.

Drinan remained in the House until 1981 and was the first Roman Catholic priest to serve in Congress. He opposed President **Richard M. Nixon** and his policies in Southeast Asia, chaired the Subcommittee on Criminal Justice of the House Judiciary Committee, and in 1973 introduced a resolution calling for Nixon's impeachment for the secret **bombing** of **Cambodia** during the 1969–1970 Operation **Menu**. When Nixon was finally impeached, Drinan's charge was dropped from the articles. After adhering to the pope's call for an end to priests participating in electoral politics, Drinan taught at Georgetown University Law Center, founded the Georgetown *Journal of Legal Ethics*, and published several books and articles.

DRONES. Unmanned drones were used in the war to conduct air **reconnaissance** over the **Democratic Republic of Vietnam** (DRV) and **Laos**. The drone missions fell under the command of Strategic Air Command because they were considered part of the national reconnaissance mission. The first mission began in 1964 with the code name Bumble Bug. Drones were programmed to fly prearranged flights over the DRV and then return south of the **Demilitarized Zone**. The drones, whose construction was based on the Ryan Aeronautical Company's 1951 model, proved valuable during the **air war** by locating **surface-to-air missiles** and radar sites used to enhance the DRV's air defense system. During the monsoon season, drones were often the only available means to conduct air reconnaissance. The 100th Strategic Reconnaissance Wing at U-Tapao Royal Thai Air Force Base was responsible for launching the drones for missions over Laos and the DRV.

The **United States** utilized two types of drones during the war. The low-altitude model, used in **Buffalo Hunter** missions, was launched from a modified DC-130 and flew at an altitude of between 61 meters (200 feet) and 609 meters (2000 feet) to reach its target. It provided clear and detailed images but sacrificed area coverage for quality of image. High-altitude missions sacrificed quality for greater area coverage. Between 1969 and 1970, the U.S. **Navy** developed its own drone program know as Belfry Express. Drone missions gathered a large quantity of photographs and provided **intelligence** that allowed the U.S. to make more informed decisions on whether to bomb or rebomb targets over the DRV and Laos. The technology associated with the drones continued to improve throughout the war while its applications helped to revolutionize the technology after the war.

DƯ QUỐC ĐỐNG (1923–2008). Army of the Republic of Vietnam (ARVN) general. Dư Quốc Đống was **Nùng**, born in the northern part of Vietnam. His early military career was not marked by any remarkable event, though he was promoted to general in 1964 and commanded the ARVN Airborne Division. Dư Quốc Đống supported **Republic of Vietnam** president **Nguyễn Văn Thiệu** and continued to command as a result of his patronage. He was involved in the February 1971 Lam Sơn 719 operation into **Laos** that resulted in disaster, and he led the Airborne Division in the retaking of **Quảng Trị** during the 1972 **Easter Offensive**. In November 1972, he assumed command of the Capital Military District and, in February 1973, became the chief ARVN representative to the Joint Military Commission created as a result of the January 1973 **Paris Peace Accords**. Dư Quốc Đống was assigned to command Military Region 3 on 30 October 1973. Exactly one year later, now Lieutenant General Dư Quốc Đống, he also became the commander of the III Army Corps. In February, he was replaced by General Nguyễn Văn Toàn after the failure of the 13 December 1974–January 1975 Battle for Phước Long. *See also* YOUNG TURKS.

DULLES, JOHN FOSTER (1888–1959). Secretary of state during the Eisenhower administration. John Foster Dulles rose to the rank of major in the **United States Army** Intelligence Service during World War I. He then worked in both the private and public sector in jobs related to American foreign relations. He held positions as counsel to the American Commission to Negotiate Peace after World War I, was involved in the 1921–1922 Washington Naval Conference, served on the Reparations Commissions in the 1920s, was U.S. representative to the Berlin Debt Conferences in 1933, and was a member of the U.S. delegation to the San Francisco Conference on World Organization in 1945 that helped create the **United Nations**. Dulles was a representative to the United Nations General Assembly from 1946 to 1949 and was appointed as a Republican to the U.S. Senate when Robert F. Wagner resigned. He served in the Senate from 7 July 1949 to 8 November 1949 and then returned as the U.S. representative to the Fifth General Assembly of the United Nations in 1950.

Dulles consulted with the secretary of state in 1951–1952 and was appointed to that office by President Dwight D. Eisenhower in 1953. He remained secretary of state until his resignation on 15 April 1959 to deal with the cancer that would eventually take his life on 24 May. Dulles was instrumental in early U.S. policy toward Vietnam. He advocated increased American action to stave off French defeat at **Điện Biên Phủ** in early 1954. A Cold Warrior by experience, Dulles supported American efforts at nation building in Vietnam and believed that the U.S. had a responsibility to thwart communist aggression against the **Republic of Vietnam** (RVN). During his time in the State Department, Dulles helped to create the **South East Asia Treaty Organization**, which included protection for the RVN even though it was not a signatory.

Dulles practiced the policy of brinksmanship, or pushing American foreign policy to the brink of war with its adversary to force the other side to relinquish control and seek compromise rather than engage in a nuclear exchange. While this policy helped to contain the **Soviet Union**, it was less effective against the **Democratic Republic of Vietnam** and the communist insurgents in the South. Dulles' resignation and subsequent death preceded the intense North Vietnamese and **National Liberation Front** activity in the RVN that served as the catalyst for a change in American strategy in Vietnam. This included the assassination of **Ngô Đình Diệm** in 1963 and the Americanization of the war in 1965.

DƯƠNG VĂN MINH (1916–2001). Vietnamese general, politician, and briefly president of the **Republic of Vietnam** (RVN). Known as "Big Minh" because of his size, Dương Văn Minh began his military career with the French Union Forces. He was one of the few Vietnamese to receive a commission in the French Army and was one of the most experienced Vietnamese officers of the **Army of the Republic of Vietnam** (ARVN) when it was formed. Dương Văn Minh played a significant part in the defeat of the United Front of Nationalist Forces when it conspired to overthrow **Ngô Đình Diệm** in April 1955. Even though Dương Văn Minh played a major role in the ARVN as it developed throughout the 1950s and served as Ngô Đình Diệm's military adviser, he became one of the coup d'état planners that led to the assassination of Ngô Đình Diệm in November 1963.

Dương Văn Minh was the chairman of the Executive Committee of the Revolutionary Council and president of the Provisional Government of the Republic of Vietnam that ruled the country after the coup d'état and lasted until his government was overthrown by **Nguyễn Khánh** on 30 January 1964. He served as the head of state of the RVN from 8 February 1964 until 26 October 1964 under Nguyễn Khánh's rule. Dương Văn Minh then went into exile in **Thailand** only to return in 1968 when he reentered politics and became a potential presidential candidate against **Nguyễn Văn Thiệu** in 1971. He withdrew his candidacy because he believed the elections would be rigged against him. He returned to politics in 1973 with a plan to compromise with the **National Liberation Front** and even made contact with the North Vietnamese, but he was never able to get his program endorsed. On 28 April 1975, Dương Văn Minh returned to the presidency only to hand over the reins of government to the North Vietnamese as they entered **Sài Gòn** and ended the war on 30 April. Dương Văn Minh lived in isolation at his home for eight years after the war and left for **France** in 1983. He moved to California in the 1990s where he died on 6 August 2001. *See also* YOUNG TURKS.

DURBROW, ELBRIDGE (1903–1997). United States ambassador to the **Republic of Vietnam** (RVN). Durbrow received his education at Yale University, Stanford University, and the University of Chicago, as well as several international schools. He began his public service as vice consul in the U.S. embassy in Warsaw and then rose in rank through his service in embassies in Romania, Italy, and the **Soviet Union**. During World War II, he worked at the Department of State and was involved in many of the wartime diplomatic events that marked the period. He returned to Moscow after the war to become first the counselor of the embassy and then deputy chief of missions. During these years, Durbrow refined his Cold War philosophy and became an advocate of the containment doctrine.

Before becoming the RVN ambassador in 1957, Durbrow worked for the National War College, was director of the Foreign Service's personnel division, and served as deputy chief of mission in the U.S. embassy in Italy. When Durbrow arrived in **Sài Gòn** in March 1957, he was able to employ his Cold War philosophy in a country beset by a communist insurgency. At first, Durbrow worked with RVN president **Ngô Đình Diệm** in building up the country's infrastructure, military, and government. By 1959, he began to run afoul of Ngô Đình Diệm and his brother **Ngô Đình Nhu**, whom Durbrow believed needed to be removed from the country. Durbrow's reports to Washington increasingly criticized the Ngô family rule and advocated using American assistance and aid as leverage to enact political, economic, and social reforms.

In November 1960, a significant turning point occurred between Durbrow and Ngô Đình Diệm when the ambassador failed to clearly support the Vietnamese president during and after a failed coup d'état. As Ngô Đình Diệm moved against Durbrow and refused to heed his advice, Durbrow worked to not only remove Ngô Đình Nhu but also Ngô Đình Diệm. Durbrow argued that Ngô Đình Diệm was corrupt, inefficient, and obstinate in his rule. When **John F. Kennedy** entered the White House, a reassessment of American policy in the RVN occurred that placed Durbrow against General **Edward Lansdale**, who had known Ngô Đình Diệm and Vietnam since 1954 when he was involved in the Saigon Military Mission. In the course of the debate, Lansdale called for Durbrow's removal. Durbrow was rotated out of the embassy and left Vietnam on 3 May 1961. He was replaced by **Frederick E. Nolting Jr.**

Durbrow exemplified one of the main problems that the U.S. would experience during the war. He failed to understand the difference between the Vietnamese people and the U.S. His actions reversed positive U.S.-Vietnamese relations at a critical time in South Vietnamese history and helped push Ngô Đình Diệm down the path that would result in his assassination in November 1963. Before retiring in 1968, Durbrow worked as a U.S. representative to the North Atlantic Treaty Organization, returned to the National War College, and spent time at the Air University.

DUSTER. The M42A1, often referred to as a Duster, was a self-propelled 40-mm **antiaircraft gun system**. It carried a crew of six, though four personnel were more common in combat. The Duster was armed with twin 40-mm cannons and one 7.62-mm machine gun. It was over 5.8 meters (19 feet) long and less than 3.4 meters (11 feet) wide, with a range of approximately 160 kilometers (100 miles) and a road speed of 72 kilometers (45 miles) per hour. With the advent of the jet aircraft and the HAWK **missile** system, the Duster was retired from service in 1963. In 1966, the Duster returned to service in the war because of the poor performance of the HAWK. It was the primary weapon of the Air Defense Artillery battalions in Vietnam. The last Dusters were withdrawn from Vietnam in 1972. The weapon system was finally retired in 1988.

DUSTOFF. Term used to describe the medical evacuation of wounded soldiers by army **helicopters** during the war. The term derived from a 1963 radio call sign.

E

EAGLE PULL, OPERATION. Air operation designed to evacuate non-combatants from **Phnom Penh, Cambodia**. When it became clear that the Cambodian National Army (Forces Armées Nationales Khmères) was on the verge of collapse, the **United States** revisited its plan to evacuate American and allied personnel from the country. Operation Eagle Pull was conceived in early March 1975 and put into practice on 12 April 1975 after the **Khmer Rouge** had surrounded, and were poised to enter, Phnom Penh. The U.S. employed a combination of fixed-wing aircraft, such as the C-130, and U.S. **Marine Corps helicopters** to evacuate approximately 287 personnel from Phnom Penh in less than two hours. An additional group of approximately 900 Cambodians had earlier been evacuated to **Thailand**.

EASTER OFFENSIVE. A 1972 North Vietnamese three-pronged attack against the Republic of Vietnam Armed Forces that resulted in a significant military defeat for the **People's Army of Vietnam** (PAVN). The offensive was the most significant attack of communist forces since the Chinese entry into the Korean War in 1950. It involved over 125,000 men, with approximately 80,000 in reserve, with the objective of destroying the **Army of the Republic of Vietnam** (ARVN), embarrassing the **United States** and damaging the credibility of President **Richard M. Nixon** during an election year, and the conquest of the **Republic of Vietnam** (RVN). The North Vietnamese decided to launch the offensive as a result of a number of factors. The American election year was central, as was the fact that the U.S. had, through **Vietnamization**, nearly completed its withdrawal from Southeast Asia. There was a strong belief that the offensive would be the last chance to humiliate the Americans before they were completely out of war. The North Vietnamese had also observed the failure of the ARVN during the 1971 **Lam Sơn 719** operation that had ended in disaster. These two factors led many within the North Vietnamese leadership to believe that the people of the RVN would rise up against the **Sài Gòn** government after the early success of the PAVN troops.

The northernmost prong focused on **Quảng Trị**. The initial attack began on 31 March 1972. By 1 April, the 3rd ARVN Division had been forced out of its defensive positions, losing two regiments. Augmented by **marines** and rangers, the 3rd ARVN Division regrouped for a time around Quảng Trị by the middle of April. Quảng Trị City was abandoned on 1 May, and the 3rd ARVN Division ceased to function. With PAVN forces moving into **Thừa Thiên** province toward **Huế**, President **Nguyễn Văn Thiệu** replaced his I Corps commander, Lieutenant General **Hoàng Xuân Lãm**, with Lieutenant General **Ngô Quang Trưởng**, who arrived on 2 May and reorganized his forces. On 28 June, Ngô Quang Trưởng launched a counteroffensive with the aid of the Airborne Division and a significant amount of U.S. air and naval gun firepower. The counteroffensive slowly regained much of Quảng Trị. Quảng Trị City was retaken on 16 September, and much of the territory lost at the beginning of the battle was regained by the end of October.

The next prong of the attack focused on **Kon Tum** and **Plei Ku** provinces. The attack began on 12 April with three PAVN divisions seeking to cut **Route** 19. It was believed that this road held the key to the offensive, as it would have denied the South Vietnamese the ability to effectively move personnel and supplies to and from I **Corps Tactical Zone** (CTZ). On 15 April, the camps at **Đắk Tô** and Tân Cảnh were placed under siege. Tân Cảnh fell on 23 April. By 4 May, Kon Tum was defenseless, and the 3rd PAVN Division had succeeded in cutting Route 1 just north of Route 19. Similar to the situation in I CTZ, President **Nguyễn Văn Thiệu** replaced the II Corps commander, Lieutenant General Ngô Dzu, with Major General Nguyễn Văn Toàn, who stabilized the situation and on 28 May began the slow process of clearing the enemy out of Kon Tum. This part of the offensive was over by the end of June.

The final prong of the attack focused on the Lộc Ninh and An Lộc in Bình Long province. An Lộc was approximately 24 kilometers (15 miles) to the north of Sài Gòn along Route 13. The two cities were attacked by Front B2, made up of three **National Liberation Front** (NLF) divisions, though they were mostly North Vietnamese troops. The attack began on 2 April with the 5th NLF Division attacking Lộc Ninh to protect the northern flank while the 7th NLF Division cut Route 13 to protect the southern flank. The 9th NLF Division, the first formed in the RVN, would have the honor of taking An Lộc and establishing the **Provisional Revolutionary Government of the Republic of South Vietnam**. While there was early success in Lộc Ninh and cutting Route 13, the ARVN troops in An Lộc were able to hold out for 95 days until reinforced. The ARVN forces then launched a counterattack that drove the NLF out of the province.

In all three prongs, the ARVN were supported by massive U.S. firepower that helped to turn the tide of battle in each case. The U.S. also launched Operation **Linebacker I** in response to the Easter Offensive and dropped more than 125,000 tons of munitions on the **Democratic Republic of Vietnam** (DRV). Nixon had responded to the offensive in a more aggressive manner than expected. Linebacker I lessened the restrictions of earlier air campaigns against the DRV and mined **Hải Phòng** harbor, which effectively cut off the ability of the North Vietnamese to receive supplies by sea. The operation had the objectives of closing the DRV's land and rail lines of supply from the **People's Republic of China**; destroying the stockpiles of oil, war materials, and food; and interdicting North Vietnamese supply lines to the South. It ended on 22 October when the North Vietnamese appeared to be amenable to peace negotiations. When this proved premature, the U.S. launched Operation **Linebacker II**, also known as the Christmas **bombing**. From 18 to 29 December, the U.S. bombed **Hà Nội** and Hải Phòng until the North Vietnamese agreed to negotiate in good faith, which eventually led to the signing of the **Paris Peace Accords** on 27 January 1973.

The North Vietnamese failed in the 1972 Easter Offensive. It was estimated that it lost 50 percent of its personnel to **casualties** and had 50 percent of its armor destroyed. The U.S. responded in a different manner than expected, and **Richard M. Nixon** easily won the 1972 presidential election. The South Vietnamese people did not rise up against the Sài Gòn government, and the architect of the offensive, General **Võ Nguyên Giáp**, the hero of **Điện Biên Phủ** and military leader since 1945, was quietly eased out of power. The offensive was a military disaster for the North Vietnamese, who were able to learn from their mistakes and, with time, rebuild their forces for the final 1975 offensive.

ELLSBERG, DANIEL (1931–). Employed by RAND Corporation as a military analyst who leaked portions of the study, *United States-Vietnam Relations, 1945–1967: A Study Prepared by the Department of Defense* to the *New York Times* in 1971. Ellsberg was an early advocate of the war. He turned against it in the late 1960s, believing that the **United States** could not win in Vietnam while the American presence only resulted in further destruction of the country. After working for the Department of Defense and the Department of State, which included time in Vietnam, Ellsberg joined the RAND Corporation and was a member of the team that prepared Secretary of Defense **Robert McNamara**'s study on how the U.S. became involved in Vietnam. His experience in Vietnam and his reading of the secret documents that made up the study moved Ellsberg to turn against the war. After attending some **antiwar** rallies, Ellsberg decided to illegally copy portions of the Department of Defense study and release them to the public.

When Ellsberg failed to elicit the help of antiwar senators, he turned to the *New York Times*, which began to print portions of the study on 13 June 1971.

The **Richard M. Nixon** administration moved to suspend the release of the document, but a 30 June Supreme Court decision allowed the publication to continue. This occurred after Senator Mike Gravel (D-Alaska) entered a significant portion of the study into the Congressional Record. Gravel was the chairman of the Subcommittee on Public Buildings and Grounds at the time. The released portions of the study became commonly known as the **Pentagon Papers** and were published in book form in various versions. The Pentagon Papers damaged the credibility of the Nixon White House even though he was not implicated in the study. The Nixon administration's attempts to suppress the publication of the study and to discredit Ellsberg, including his arrest under the Espionage Act of 1917 which was later dismissed in court, elevated Ellsberg in the antiwar movement and forced many Americans to re-examine the U.S. war in Vietnam. *See also* ORDER OF BATTLE DISPUTE; SHEEHAN, NEIL.

EMERGENCY CITIZENS' GROUP CONCERNED ABOUT VIET-NAM. Founded in 1964 by **Phillip Berrigan** in Newburgh, New York, the Emergency Citizens' Group Concerned about Vietnam was one of many **antiwar** groups that protested the **United States** escalation of the war and was especially concerned with Operation **Rolling Thunder** and the introduction of combat troops in March 1965.

ENCLAVE STRATEGY. Strategy introduced into the **Republic of Vietnam** (RVN) in April 1965 with the beginning of Operation **Rolling Thunder**. The enclave strategy replaced a more cautious strategy of using **United States Marines** to guard military bases. It called for American personnel to protect major urban populations and military bases, especially airfields, from direct attack by the **People's Army of Vietnam** (PAVN) and **National Liberation Front** (NLF). These enclaves, situated for the most part on the coast, represented a defensive strategy in the South. They allowed a more offensive air campaign in the North to convince the North Vietnamese to terminate their support for the southern insurgency. The plan called for the **Army of the Republic of Vietnam** to assume the burden of fighting the PAVN and NLF soldiers in the countryside.

The U.S. ambassador to the RVN, **Maxwell D. Taylor**, was a strong advocate of the plan, while **Military Assistance Command, Vietnam**, commander **William C. Westmoreland** wanted to use the enclaves to conduct **search-and-destroy** missions to take the battle to, and regain the initiative from, the enemy. One of the consequences of the enclave strategy was the introduction of additional American combat personnel to protect the areas. This caused Westmoreland to call for additional troops, leading to the **44 battalion**

debate and the switch over from the enclave strategy to search-and-destroy operations and the Americanization of the war.

ENDSWEEP, OPERATION. As a result of the 27 January 1973 **Paris Peace Accords**, the **United States** agreed to clear the naval **mines** it had deployed during Operation **Pocket Money** in response to the 1972 **Easter Offensive**. The U.S. **Navy** formed Task Force 78, which combined surface ships and aircraft to locate and dispose of the Mark-36 and Mark-52 naval mines. Operation Endsweep began on 6 February 1973. **Hải Phòng** harbor was reopened in the first week of March. Operation Endsweep officially ended on 27 July 1973, and Task Force 78 disbanded. U.S. naval ships conducted over 3,500 minesweeping missions while aircraft flew over 600 **sorties**. The U.S. lost three **helicopters** but none due to naval mines.

ENHANCE, PROJECT. As a result of the 1972 **Easter Offensive**, the **Republic of Vietnam Armed Forces** had suffered serious losses in weapons and equipment that greatly affected its ability to defend against the **People's Army of Vietnam** (PAVN). The **United States** initiated Project Enhance to replace the war materiel necessary to fight the PAVN and expand the size of the RVN Armed Forces. Project Enhance began in May 1972. It included 175-mm **artillery**, M48 **tanks**, UH-1H and CH-47 **helicopters**, A-37 and C-130 aircraft, AC-119 gunships, O-1 and O-2 **reconnaissance** aircraft, and other equipment needed during the offensive. It was eventually phased out as the Easter Offensive diminished in intensity and was replaced with **Project Enhance Plus**.

ENHANCE PLUS, PROJECT. By the fall of 1972, the **United States** and **Democratic Republic of Vietnam** were engaged in negotiations in Paris to end the war. On 3 October, Secretary of State **Henry Kissinger** instructed the commander of the **Military Assistance Command, Vietnam**, **Frederick C. Weyand**, to develop a plan that would supply the **Republic of Vietnam Armed Forces** with a significant amount of weapons, munitions, and other war materiel in the very likely event that the impending **Paris Peace Accords** prohibited the introduction of new equipment. On 20 October 1972, Secretary of Defense **Melvin R. Laird** initiated Project Enhance Plus, which sent nearly $2 billion of military equipment to the **Republic of Vietnam** (RVN). The first shipment of equipment arrived on 23 October, and shipments continued until 12 December. By the end of the project, the RVN had the 4th largest army in the world, with over one million men in uniform. It had the 4th largest air force in the world, with over 2,000 aircraft and **helicopters**. Included in the deliveries were F-5A jets in addition to A-37, A-1, and C-130 aircraft and UH-1H helicopters. It also possessed the 5th largest navy, with over 1,500 ships and vessels.

The U.S. upgraded much of the RVN weapons but also made sure that as much equipment as possible was in place before the agreements were signed. Broken or damaged weapons could be replaced on a one-for-one basis under the terms of the agreement, which meant that the RVN could replace the damaged goods for new after 1973. While the project was not a violation of the 1973 Paris Peace Accords, it did call into question the U.S. interpretation of the spirit of the agreements. *See also* ENHANCE, PROJECT.

EXODUS, OPERATION. *See* PASSAGE TO FREEDOM, OPERATION.

F

FACT SHEET, OPERATION. Air mission associated with Operation **Rolling Thunder** designed to utilize psychological warfare against the **Democratic Republic of Vietnam** (DRV). Operation Fact Sheet dropped leaflets over the DRV that justified Rolling Thunder and offered suggestions on how the North Vietnamese people could end the **bombings** by turning against their government. Some leaflets warned the North Vietnamese to stay away from military facilities, while others highlighted the benefits of living in the **Republic of Vietnam**. The first mission occurred on 14 April 1965 when the **Republic of Vietnam Air Force** (RVNAF) dropped over 1 million leaflets on North Vietnamese cities with military facilities while the **United States Air Force** dropped 1.2 million leaflets. Additional million-plus leaflet **sorties** occurred on 28 April, 20 May, 22 May, and 23 May. Despite results that were less than expected, the U.S. and RVNAF dropped almost 5 million more leaflets in June and nearly 10 million in July. The leaflets had no effect on North Vietnamese strategy, but they did result in a few civilians moving away from military facilities.

FARM GATE, OPERATION. Operation designed to introduce American air assets into the **Republic of Vietnam** under Project **Jungle Jim**. On 11 October 1961, the **United States** deployed eight T-28, four RB-26, and four SC-47 aircraft, all of which had **Republic of Vietnam Air Force** (RVNAF) markings on them, to assist the RVNAF. The **John F. Kennedy** administration also provided 156 **U.S. Air Force** personnel under the operation. While the initial mission was training RVNAF personnel, it quickly expanded when American **advisers** recognized that the RVNAF required more hands-on experience in air operations to improve air support of ground troops. As a result, American personnel engaged in combat operations even though such activity was not a part of the original order. The number of Farm Gate missions increased despite the fact that the presence of U.S. personnel and aircraft was a violation of the 1954 **Geneva Agreements**. *See also* TACTICAL AIRLIFT.

FAST BUCK, OPERATION. Operation proposed by the **Joint Chiefs of Staff** to encourage North Vietnamese pilots to defect with their aircraft. Fast

Buck was modeled after Operation Nolah, used in the Korean War, and offered $100,000 for the aircraft, with a $50,000 bonus for the first defector and a $25,000 bonus for the second defector. North Vietnamese pilots who jettisoned their aircraft into the sea and were rescued by the Americans were offered $25,000. The operation hoped to capture more modern MiG fighters, increase **intelligence** on the North Vietnamese air defense system, increase distrust among the North Vietnamese, decrease MiG **sorties**, and disparage the North Vietnamese military image by increased defections. The operation was never implemented.

FELLOWSHIP OF RECONCILIATION (FOR). Founded in December 1914 in London with a **United States** branch opening in 1915, the Fellowship of Reconciliation had a long history of pacifism. During the early part of the war, the organization was led by **A. J. Muste** and was one of the first to protest against the war. In October 1964, Muste and the FOR called for draft resistance and warned against increasing American personnel in Vietnam. The organization was active in **antiwar** demonstrations and in counseling individuals who wished to dodge the draft. Its effectiveness was limited by internal squabbling as membership divided between American withdrawal from the **Republic of Vietnam** and support for the **Buddhist** Third Force movement.

FIRE SUPPORT BASE (FSB). A more permanent base used by the **United States**, South Vietnamese, and **Free World Forces** to provide fire support for troops operating within the range of its **artillery**. The FSB normally housed at least one battery of artillery, usually a 105-mm or 155-mm gun, **mortars**, a **landing zone**, and facilities to support the troops in the field such as medical treatment stations, communications, and support troops. Larger FSBs, many near the **Demilitarized Zone**, had multiple batteries of artillery and more troops to protect the perimeter.

FIREFLY, PROJECT. Project in which Thai pilots supplemented Americans responsible for **combat air patrol** and **search-and-rescue** missions in **Laos** in support of Operation **Barrel Roll**. There was a real concern that American pilots involved in air operations in Laos who were captured would prove to be an embarrassment for the **United States**, as Laos was still considered a neutral country. To limit this possibility, the U.S. employed pilots from the Royal Thai Air Force 223rd Squadron, the first five of which arrived on 27 May 1964 and flew their initial combat mission on 1 June. The U.S. contracted the Thai pilots to a six-month tour or 100 **sorties**. All of the Thai were volunteers who were paid a greater sum than their normal salary in **Thailand**. The project ended in 1973. *See also* WATERPUMP, PROJECT.

FIRST INDOCHINA WAR. Name often given to the war between the French and **Việt Minh** that occurred between 1946 and 1954. After the end of World War II, the Vietnamese attempted to negotiate with the French to gain their independence. **Hồ Chí Minh**, the political leader of the Việt Minh, had proclaimed the establishment of an independent **Democratic Republic of Vietnam** on 2 September 1945. Over the next year, negotiations in **France** failed to reach a compromise, and on 19 December 1946, the Việt Minh attacked the French in **Hà Nội** after an earlier 23 November naval bombardment of **Hải Phòng** by French naval forces. The majority of the war was fought in the northern region of Tŏn Kĭn and was primarily a protracted guerrilla fight, with the initiative held by the Việt Minh. The final major battle, at **Điện Biên Phủ**, which ended on 7 May 1954, convinced a war-weary France that the war could not be won without an increased commitment of personnel and resources beyond its limit of endurance. The war lasted nearly eight years and concluded with the 1954 **Geneva Agreements**. It officially was over on 1 August 1954 when the last phase of the armistice took place.

FIRST OBSERVATION GROUP. Organized in February 1956 under the command of Colonel **Lê Quang Tung**, the First Observation Group (Liên Đội Quan Sát) consisted of personnel who were trained to conduct guerrilla operations against the **People's Army of Vietnam** in the event that the **Democratic Republic of Vietnam** (DRV) invaded the **Republic of Vietnam** (RVN). All of the First Observation Group personnel were volunteers, and most of them had been **refugees** from the DRV as a result of the 1954 **Geneva Agreements**. The First Observation Group was under the nominal supervision of the RVN Armed Forces, though it was controlled by the Presidential Liaison Office under **Ngô Đình Diệm**, who authorized their training and mission. The personnel involved in the group received instruction from the **United States Special Forces** at its training center in **Nha Trang**. They were equipped through Military Assistant Program aid and received additional equipment and training from the **Central Intelligence Agency**. When the invasion from the DRV did not materialize, the group was used for limited covert raids against the DRV and **Laos** in the late 1950s.

In 1960, First Observation Group personnel were used against communist insurgency activity, which had increased during that year. In July 1961, the First Observation Group had approximately 340 personnel divided into 20 teams of 15 men, with two radios per team, and administrative and support staff. In July 1961, it underwent an expansion to over 800 men. The First Observation Group would eventually be absorbed into the Vietnamese Special Forces.

FISHHOOK. An area in **Cambodia** that borders the provinces of **Tây Ninh** and Bình Long in the **Republic of Vietnam**. It was used by the **People's Army of Vietnam** and the **National Liberation Front** (NLF) in their war against **Sài Gòn**. The Fishhook received its name based on the geographical shape of the border between the two countries. It was the reported seat of the NLF headquarters during the war. It was also a frequent target for Operation **Menu sorties** in 1969–1970 and an area of concern during the 1970 **Cambodian Incursion**.

FLAMING DART, OPERATION. An operation conducted in response to **National Liberation Front** (NLF) attacks on **United States** personnel and facilities. On 7 February 1965, the NLF mortared Camp Holloway, near **Plei Ku** in the **Central Highlands**, killing eight Americans and wounding 128. The attack also destroyed 16 **helicopters** and eight fixed-wing aircraft. President **Lyndon B. Johnson** used this attack to order a retaliatory air strike against the **Democratic Republic of Vietnam** (DRV). Operation Flaming Dart focused on seven previously identified targets: the barracks at Đồng Hới, Vit Thù Lù, Chap Le, Chánh Hòa, and Vu Con, as well as the **Thanh Hóa bridge** and the Quàng Khè naval base.

The American response occurred the same day when 24 A-4C and nine A-4E aircraft, all from the U.S. **Navy** (USN), supported by another 30 aircraft, attacked the Dong Hoi barracks, headquarters of the 325th **People's Army of Vietnam** Division. The mission destroyed 16 buildings and damaged another six. One A-4E was lost and another seven were damaged. Poor weather conditions forced the cancellation of the other planned air strikes. On 8 February, the **Republic of Vietnam Air Force** (RVNAF) attacked the Chap Le barracks with 30 A-1H and A-1E aircraft, led by Air Vice Marshall **Nguyễn Cao Kỳ**.

The initial attacks did not deter the NLF, who on 10 February attacked an American billet in **Qui Nhơn**, killing 23 and wounding 21. Approximately 100 USN aircraft conducted another series of Flaming Dart missions against the Chánh Hòa barracks while the RVNAF attacked the Vu Con barracks. This would be the last Flaming Dart mission as the U.S. moved to a more sustained, systematic **bombing** campaign against the DRV with Operation **Rolling Thunder**.

FLECHETTES. A small, nail-like object that could be fired from a shotgun or inserted into a missile or bomb that exploded before impact to cause maximum coverage. The flechette was an antipersonnel weapon designed to cause serious injury or kill the enemy. Because it could penetrate the jungle canopy, it was a valuable weapon against the **People's Army of Vietnam** and the **Na-**

tional Liberation Front, who used that coverage to hide and for protection. *See also* GRENADE LAUNCHER.

FONDA, JANE (1937–). Actress and **antiwar** protestor. Fonda, who was often referred to as Hanoi Jane, was one of the more famous of the antiwar activists during the war. She began a successful career as an actress in 1960 with her debut film, *Tall Story*, though she was more famous for her role in *Period of Adjustment* and *Barbarella*. Fonda, the daughter of actor Henry Fonda, was educated at Vassar College and was politically active in a number of causes, including the civil rights movement, Native American rights, and opposition to the Vietnam War. In the 1960s, she participated in the Free the Army Tour with Donald Sutherland, an antiwar variety show that mirrored Bob Hope's USO work. She also helped the **Vietnam Veterans Against the War** in its campaign to expose what it considered to be violations of international law by the **United States** in Vietnam.

In July 1972, Fonda traveled to the **Democratic Republic of Vietnam** where she spoke out against Operation **Linebacker I** and accused the U.S. of targeting the **dike** system around **Hà Nội** to spread misery to the civilian population. Her most famous act while in Hà Nội was being photographed in the seat of an **antiaircraft artillery** piece, though she would later admit that the act was a mistake. Fonda would also regret statements that contradicted American **prisoners of war** who spoke of North Vietnamese torture during their imprisonment.

Fonda remained active in the antiwar movement, organizing the Indochina Peace Campaign, until the fall of **Sài Gòn** in April 1975. Fonda was married several times, including to Tom Hayden, the former president of **Students for a Democratic Society** and antiwar activist and **media** entrepreneur Ted Turner. In 2005, she published her autobiography, *My Life So Far*.

FOO GAS. *See* MINES, LAND.

FOOTBOY. After a leak in the **United States** press in 1967 that identified the code name for the covert operations conducted in **Laos**, the U.S. decided to rename its various secret operations. The code name given to operations against the **Democratic Republic of Vietnam** (DRV) was Footboy. Footboy included four different missions: Plowman focused on maritime issues, Midriff concentrated on air operations, Humidor centered on psychological operations, and Timberwork attempted to insert agents into the North. Short-Term Roadwatch and Target Acquisition (**STRATA**) missions were also conducted by Vietnamese forces. Footboy was primarily an **intelligence** operation designed to disrupt the DRV war operations and cause instability within the North Vietnamese population. It ended on 1 November 1968.

FORCE ARMÉE NATIONALE KHMÈRE (FANK). The FANK was the primary fighting force for the Royal Cambodian Government between 1970 and 1975. It succeeded the Force Armée Royale Khmère, which had existed since 1954. The creation of FANK reflected the change in direction of the **Phnom Penh** government after **Lon Nol** replaced Prince **Norodom Sihanouk** on 18 March 1970 in a bloodless coup d'état. FANK forces fought the **People's Army of Vietnam** (PAVN), the **National Liberation Front** (NLF), and the **Khmer Rouge**, who sought to destabilize the government and return **Cambodia** to its neutral state, though that neutrality favored the continued use of the country by PAVN and NLF forces in their war against the **Republic of Vietnam**. As a result of the 1973 **Paris Peace Accords**, the **United States** limited its support for FANK operations, which severely affected its ability to fight the enemy. By 1975, FANK forces were on the defensive. On 1 April, Lon Nol resigned, which effectively ended the FANK. Phnom Penh was soon overrun by the Khmer Rouge, which sparked a genocide in Cambodia that claimed between 1.7 and 3 million of its citizens.

FORD, GERALD RUDOLPH (1913–2006). United States president. Educated at the University of Michigan at Ann Arbor where he also had a promising career as a professional football player, Gerald R. Ford graduated in 1935 and entered law school at Yale University. He received his law degree in 1941. During World War II, Ford joined the U.S. **Navy** and became a physical training officer at the University of North Carolina. After numerous attempts to join a unit in combat, he was finally sent to the Pacific Theater. He served as a physical education officer on the U.S.S. *Monterey*, a light aircraft carrier. Ford left the naval service as a lieutenant commander having experienced considerable combat.

After the war, he returned to law practice but ran for office in the House of Representatives as a Republican in 1948. He won the election and served in the House until 1973. Ford's record in the House was very positive even though his critics argued that he had never authored a major program of legislation on his own. Ford served on the Appropriations Committee and in 1963 became the chairman of the House Republican Conference. In 1965, he became the minority leader. He also served on the Warren Commission, which investigated the assassination of President **John F. Kennedy**. Ford worked tirelessly as the minority leader.

On 10 October 1973, after Vice President **Spiro T. Agnew** resigned, Ford learned that he was being considered as the next vice president. On 11 October, he accepted the offer from President **Richard M. Nixon**. Ford's nomination was confirmed on 6 December 1973, with only three opposed in the Senate and 35 in the House. In less than nine months, Ford would assume the presidency, the first to reach that office who had not been elected in a popular vote. Ford assumed the Office of the Presidency after the resignation of Nixon, taking the oath of office on 9 August 1974.

He inherited a Vietnam policy in disarray. **Congress** had exerted an extraordinary amount of energy and attention to regaining control of American foreign policy. In Southeast Asia, the **Case-Church Amendment** and **War Powers Resolution** made it nearly impossible for the U.S. to fulfill its unofficial promise to come to the aid of the **Republic of Vietnam** (RVN) in the event of North Vietnamese violations of the January 1973 **Paris Peace Accords**. Ford watched helplessly as Congress was unwilling to come to the aid of the South Vietnamese during the final offensive in 1975. Ford was outmaneuvered by Congress in his attempts to maintain the flow of resources to the RVN and **Cambodia**, though he did work to allow **refugees** from the Southeast Asian war to enter the U.S. Days before the fall of **Sài Gòn**, Ford spoke at Tulane University where he argued that the Vietnam War was over for the U.S. and that the nation needed to look forward rather than dwell in the past. For the Sài Gòn government, and those in the U.S. who had committed their lives and resources toward a free and independent Vietnam, these words were an act of betrayal. Ford served out the remainder of Nixon's term and was involved in controversial acts such as Nixon's pardon, the move to return the Panama Canal to the Panamanians, and failure to directly address the genocide in Cambodia.

Ford ran for the presidency in 1976, with Nelson Rockefeller as his vice president, but lost to James E. Carter and Walter Mondale. He was not able to distance himself from Nixon or the pardon, the Republican reputation, or the Vietnam War. He was even the target of two unsuccessful assassination attempts. Ford continued to be involved in public life as an elder statesman. In 1979, he authored his autobiography, *A Time to Heal*. At one point in 1980, Ford was considered for the vice presidency under Ronald W. Reagan, but he declined the offer and instead campaigned for Reagan and George H. W. Bush. In addition to many public speeches, Ford also taught at the University of Michigan and was involved in fund-raising efforts for the Republican Party.

FORRESTAL, MICHAEL VINCENT (1928–1989). Lawyer and Southeast Asian expert in the **John F. Kennedy** administration. Forrestal, the son of James V. Forrestal, the first **United States** secretary of defense, was commissioned as a second lieutenant in the U.S. **Navy** in 1946 and worked as the assistant naval attaché to the U.S. ambassador to the **Soviet Union, W. Averill Harriman**. Forrestal served as the secretary to the Quadripartite Naval Directorate of the Allied Control Council and the Tripartite Naval Commission in Berlin. In 1948, he became the deputy director of the East-West Trade Division of the U.S. European Cooperation Administration while also attending Princeton University. He earned a law degree from Harvard University in 1953, after which he practiced law until John F. Kennedy asked him to serve in his administration.

In 1962, Forrestal joined the senior staff of the **National Security Council** and specialized in Asia. During his time in the Kennedy administration, Forrestal became one of the leading opponents of the continued rule of **Ngô Đình Diệm** and a proponent of the coup d'état that ended the **Republic of Vietnam** president's life on 2 November 1963. After the assassination of Kennedy three weeks later, Forrestal remained in his position, though the influence he had enjoyed earlier waned under the new president, **Lyndon B. Johnson**, who did not support the overthrow of Ngô Đình Diệm. He resigned in 1965. Forrestal returned to his law practice and made only temporary forays into American foreign policy in the years that followed. He served as the president of the Board of Trustees of Phillips Exeter Academy as well as other philanthropic endeavors related to the performing arts.

FORWARD AIR CONTROLLER (FAC). The first FACs arrived in 1961 and increased in numbers as the **United States** air commitment to Southeast Asia escalated. FACs participated in operations involving all branches of the armed forces from the U.S., the **Republic of Vietnam**, and the **Free World Forces**. FACs were normally assigned to the same territory in order to become familiar with the area's unique characteristics. This allowed the FAC the ability to detect changes in the area of operation and gain information on where and how the enemy might travel or establish a base area. FACs flew a number of aircraft, including the O-1 Bird Dog which was the most common slow-moving observer, the O-2 Skymaster, the OV-10 Bronco, the F-100 Super Sabre (call sign Misty), and the F-4 (call sign Wolf).

These aircraft were equipped with either FM or UHF radio to communicate with ground forces and other aircraft. In addition to identifying the enemy on the ground, the FAC directed aircraft and **artillery** fire, as well as poststrike **reconnaissance** to determine damage. FACs were also involved in the air war in **Cambodia** (call sign Rustic) and **Laos**, while the U.S. employed nonmilitary FACs in Laos to work with **Air America** (call sign Butterfly). FACs played a significant role in the air war, ensuring the maximum amount of fire power for its troops engaged on the ground and working to make sure that ground troops were not exposed to friendly fire. *See also*

AIRCRAFT (FIGHTER), UNITED STATES; AIRCRAFT (RECONNAIS-SANCE), UNITED STATES; RAVEN; SHINING BRASS, OPERATION.

FORWARD AIR GUIDE (FAG). Vietnamese, Laotian, or Cambodian personnel who were responsible for directing air **sorties** against enemy positions, used as early as 1963. The FAGs operated both in the air and on the ground and were responsible for calling in air strikes conducted by **United States** aircraft, which sometimes resulted in difficulties in communication. This problem was outweighed by the intimate knowledge these indigenous personnel had of their area of operation. FAGs were used in most air campaigns outside of the **Democratic Republic of Vietnam**.

FOUL DECK, OPERATION. Second naval operation that made up the attempt under the **SEALORDS** strategy to interdict the **People's Army of Vietnam** and **National Liberation Front** infiltration of the waterways between **Cambodia** and the **Republic of Vietnam**. Following the success of Operation **Search Turn** that formed a barrier against infiltration from Cambodia between Rạch Giá and Long Xuyên, the November 1968 Operation Foul Deck expanded the barrier to the Giang Thành–Vĩnh Tế canal system in IV **Corps Tactical Zone**. In December 1968, the operation was renamed Trần Hưng Đạo in honor of the South Vietnamese contribution to the operation and in recognition of **Vietnamization**. *See also* BARRIER REEF, OPERATION; GIANT SLINGSHOT, OPERATION.

FRAGGING. This name derived from the use of a fragmentation grenade to complete the act of attacking a superior officer. While grenades were used frequently, those involved in fragging incidents also used other available weapons. During the war, fragging occurred with greater frequency after the announcement of **Vietnamization** in 1969. **United States** troops, most of whom were conscripted, did not want to be the last man killed in Vietnam, nor did they see the value in risking their lives for a cause that many believed lost.

Typical targets for this act included superior officers or noncommissioned officers, most of whom were considered lifers; that is, they had made the military their career. Officers who were not popular, were perceived to be incompetent, or were too aggressive were the main targets. While the number of reported fragging incidents was relatively low, the threat of fragging served as an informal way of persuading some junior officers to limit their aggressiveness. As American soldiers were withdrawn and support for the war within the military waned, soldiers sometimes published newspapers or pamphlets to promote fragging against officers, which served as another means of controlling the intensity of the war.

FRANCE. The first French contact with the people of Southeast Asia occurred in the 17th century when Jesuits visited the region. The French had limited interaction, usually in the form of trade, with the Vietnamese people until the 18th century, when France intervened in the Vietnamese civil war and helped reestablish the Nguyễn Dynasty after the Tây Sơn Rebellion. In 1802, the Nguyễn emperor Gia Long used the French to rid Vietnam of the Tây Sơn and in return gave the French trading rights in Tourane (**Đà Nẵng**). The French began to increase their influence in the region during the first decades of the 19th century by training Vietnamese in military strategy and tactics. When Gia Long died in 1820, the French fell out of favor with the Nguyễn emperors, who argued that the Jesuits were too dangerous to be given free rein in Southeast Asia.

The Vietnamese move against Catholicism failed to deflect French efforts at conversion, which resulted in increased tension between the Vietnamese and French people. The Nguyễn emperors attempted to form alliances with other European powers but failed to make diplomatic progress. By the mid-19th century, the French introduced naval units into Southeast Asia, which culminated in the 15 April 1847 naval battle at Đà Nẵng. The French then began a series of expeditions in Vietnam that lasted over the next two decades. In 1859, the French captured **Sài Gòn**, and despite Vietnamese attempts to regain the city, they were forced to sign the 13 April 1862 Treaty of Sài Gòn. With this treaty, and the one that followed at **Huế** the next year, the French consolidated their control over the southern half of Vietnam.

In 1864, the French renamed this southern territory Cochin China. The French continued to expand their control over territories in Vietnam, and in 1874, with another Treaty of Sài Gòn, the Vietnamese acknowledged French rule in Cochin China. Within the next decade, France would add the territories of Annam and Tŏn Kĭn. The French captured **Hà Nội** in 1882, and in 1883 a new Treaty of Huế gave the French formal control over most of these three regions. At the end of the year, the French fought to consolidate the remaining lands in Tŏn Kĭn, and in October 1887 they officially formed French Indochina, with Jean Antoine Ernest Constans as the first governor-general. The area that comprised **Laos** was incorporated into French Indochina in 1893.

The French ruled in Indochina until 1954, though they suffered from a Japanese occupation from 1940 to 1945, even if Indochina remained nominally controlled by the Vichy government. During the period from 1887 to 1954, France governed Indochina as a colonial possession. The Vietnamese people suffered under French colonialism even if the French did provide some improvements to the region. The Vietnamese nationalists started to protest French rule almost from the beginning of French Indochina but failed to make major inroads. It was not until after the end of World War II that the Vietnamese resistance became more effective. On 2 September 1945, the Vietnamese, under the leadership of **Hồ Chí Minh** and **Võ Nguyên Giáp**, declared independence, and both leaders attempted to negotiate the removal of the French from the region. When they failed, the Vietnamese initiated what would become known as the **First Indochina War** in 1946.

The French fought the **Việt Minh** from 1946 until 1954, when they lost at the Battle of **Điện Biên Phủ**, which ended the day before the convening of the 1954 **Geneva Conference**. France experienced tremendous strain as a result of the war, and its relations with such allies as the **United States** suffered when the Americans refused to become involved in the defense of Điện Biên Phủ even though they had been helping to defray the cost of the war since 1950. The last major French effort in Vietnam occurred during Operation Exodus, when it participated in the removal of 810,000 Vietnamese from the **Democratic Republic of Vietnam** to the South. In addition to these Vietnamese, the French and the U.S. transported French Union Forces and military and civil equipment within the 300-day period stipulated by the 1954 Geneva Agreements. The French removed their combat forces from Vietnam though they continued to influence events, including support for the attempted ouster of **Republic of Vietnam** prime minister **Ngô Đình Diệm** in 1955. The last of the French advisers did not leave until 1957.

In the post–First Indochina War period, the French continued to provide council with the Vietnamese and offered advice, sometimes solicited, to the U.S. when it became more involved in the Vietnam War during the administrations of **John F. Kennedy** and **Lyndon B. Johnson**. French president Charles De Gaulle cautioned the American leaders against escalation and grew critical of U.S. military and diplomatic policy in Southeast Asia in the 1960s. France's position led Prime Minister **Nguyễn Cao Kỳ** to break off diplomatic relations between the two countries in 1965.

Even though the French had been removed from Vietnam and were critical of U.S. policy, they continued to provide assistance to the Republic of Vietnam. France contributed nearly $155 million in nonmilitary aid, while French civilian advisers helped to train the Vietnamese in the fields of agriculture and education. The French also provided loans to various projects to enhance Vietnamese infrastructure and the medical profession. In 1968, the French offered Paris as a location for peace negotiations, which occurred off and on until the signing of the **Paris Peace Accords** on 27 January 1973.

FREE WORLD FORCES. *See* THIRD COUNTRY FORCES.

FREEDOM ACTION, OPERATION. Extension of Operation **Freedom Deal**, designed to target **People's Army of Vietnam**, **National Liberation**

Front, and **Khmer Rouge** forces operating in **Cambodia**. Freedom Action began on 18 June 1970, with the first B-52 air strikes occurring on 20 June. It lasted until the **United States** withdrew from Cambodia at the end of June.

FREEDOM DEAL, OPERATION. Air operation organized to target the **People's Army of Vietnam** (PAVN) and the **National Liberation Front** (NLF), who had concentrated in the northern province of **Cambodia** in response to the May 1970 **Cambodian Incursion**. Begun on 30 May, though not officially named until 6 June, Freedom Deal was the last significant air operation in Cambodia before that country fell to the **Khmer Rouge** in 1975. Seen as an extension of Operation **Steel Tiger** in **Laos**, Freedom Deal focused on interdiction and ground support for Force Armée Nationale Khmère troops engaged with the enemy. During the operation, the **United States** also placed MK-36 **mines** in the Se Kong and Se San, two of the major rivers in Cambodia, to deter their use as supply routes. On 18 June, as more **intelligence** was gathered on the disposition of PAVN, NLF, and Khmer Rouge forces, the operation was expanded and renamed **Freedom Action**. The air operation continued until the end of the U.S. incursion into Cambodia on 30 June 1970. *See also* MENU, OPERATION; PATIO, OPERATION; SIHANOUK TRAIL.

FREEDOM TRAIN, OPERATION. After the DRV initiated the **Easter Offensive** on 30 March 1972, the **United States** responded on 6 April with its first major air operation over the **Democratic Republic of Vietnam** since President **Lyndon B. Johnson** ended **bombing** north of the 17th parallel on 1 November 1968. Freedom Train concentrated on the exposed **People's Army of Vietnam** soldiers; on major petroleum, oil, and lubricant storage and transportation facilities; and on other infrastructure, such as lines of communication, railways, and bridges, which aided the North Vietnamese offensive. While Freedom Train was the first sustained bombing campaign against the North Vietnamese since **Rolling Thunder**, it was a very different type of operation. Freedom Train was an intense bombing campaign without the same political concerns that protected some targets in the North. Within two weeks, it was estimated that Freedom Train **sorties** had destroyed half of the petroleum products storage in **Hà Nội** and **Hải Phòng** while severely hampering the ability of the North Vietnamese to get much-needed supplies to the front to continue their offensive. The air operation lasted until 7 May, when it was absorbed into Operation **Linebacker I**, which was officially named on 10 May. *See also* PROTECTIVE REACTION STRIKES.

FREE-FIRE ZONES. Areas created by the **United States** Armed Forces, considered absent of civilians, into which military personnel could fire their available weapons without clearance or approval. These zones were set up near air bases early in the war for emergency munitions release from aircraft as well as for testing weapons systems. The location of the zones expanded during the course of the war to other areas where the enemy operated. Military personnel were encouraged to engage any individual or object moving through a free-fire zone. The use of free-fire zones was controversial, in that some civilians were killed or wounded by U.S. aircraft and personnel when they strayed into one of these areas unintentionally or without knowledge of their free-fire zone status. *See also* CEDAR FALLS, OPERATION.

FREQUENT WIND, OPERATION. In 1975, the **People's Army of Vietnam** (PAVN) launched its final offensive against the **Republic of Vietnam**. As the attack gained momentum, the **United States** began to plan for the evacuation of its personnel from **Sài Gòn**. The **Defense Attaché Office**, which had replaced the **Military Assistance Command, Vietnam**, on 28 January 1973, initiated Operation Frequent Wind in April 1975. The decision was made after the PAVN troops began to send rockets into **Tân Sơn Nhứt** Air Base, which effectively shut down fixed-winged aircraft evacuation. The operation, which was similar to Operation **Eagle Pull**, the evacuation of **Phnom Penh** that occurred two weeks earlier, commenced on 29 April 1975. During the course of the two-day operation, the U.S. evacuated 122 military personnel and approximately 7,000 American and Vietnamese civilians in just under 200 **helicopter sorties**. Two marine embassy guards were killed on the ground, and two marine CH-46 helicopters and crew were lost at sea. Operation Frequent Wind marked the end of America's 25-year presence in Southeast Asia.

FRONT (CHIẾN TRƯỜNG). Term used to denote the communists' divisions within Southeast Asia. The **Democratic Republic of Vietnam** was labeled Front A, the **Republic of Vietnam** (RVN) was Front B, **Laos** was Front C, and **Cambodia** was Front D, though it was later changed to Front K. The division within the RVN, or Front B, was the most commonly recognized during the war. In 1961, Front B in RVN was originally divided into two sections. Front B1 included all of I **Corps Tactical Zone** (CTZ) and most of II CTZ, while Front B2 consisted of all of III CTZ and IV CTZ and the three southern provinces of II CTZ. In May 1964, Front B3 was carved out from Front B1 and included the three western provinces of Darlac, **Plei Ku**, and **Kon Tum** in II CTZ that made up the Central Highlands. In April 1966, Front B4 was established by removing the two most northerly provinces in I CTZ, **Quảng Trị** and **Thừa Thiên**, from the Front B1 area of operation. Front B5 further divided Front B4 in June 1966 by taking the northern half of **Quảng Trị** that bordered the **Demilitarized Zone**. (*See* map 6.)

FRONT UNIFIÉ DE LUTTE DES RACES OPPRIMÉES (FULRO). The United Front of Oppressed People (Mặt Trận Thống Nhất Đấu Tranh Của Các Sắc Tộc Bị Áp Bức) was an organization developed in the 1960s to create an independent state within **Republic of Vietnam** and **Cambodian** territory for a group of indigenous people, including the **Cham** and **Khmer**. In September 1964, FULRO helped to organize a rebellion near **Ban Mê Thuột** that included personnel from the **Civilian Irregular Defense Groups** whose membership included a number of Cham and Khmer. The organization continued to resist the **Sài Gòn** government until an understanding was reached in 1967 that focused on the common threat of the **Democratic Republic of Vietnam**. Members of FULRO resisted the communists after the fall of Sài Gòn in April 1975. This action only brought unwanted attention from the new Socialist Republic of Vietnam (SRV), which continued to oppress the people, and the **Khmer Rouge** in Cambodia who targeted the Cham living in their country during the 1975–1979 genocide. After a series of failed attempts at resisting the Vietnamese, FULRO members disbanded and returned to their villages or fled to the **refugee** camps on the Thai-Cambodian border. In 1992, the organization ceased to exist, though forms of passive resistance by the former members of FULRO continued to plague the SRV's attempts to introduce communism and modernism into the region. *See also* MONTAGNARDS.

FULBRIGHT, JAMES WILLIAM (1905–1995). Fulbright started his political career in 1943 after being elected as a Democratic member of the House of Representatives for Arkansas. He then entered the **United States** Senate in 1944, where he served until December 1974. Fulbright had a number of key positions in the Senate, including the chairmanships of the Committee on Banking and Currency and the Committee on Foreign Relations. It was in this capacity that Fulbright supported the efforts of President **Lyndon B. Johnson** to defend the **Republic of Vietnam** against aggression from the **National Liberation Front** and North Vietnamese. Fulbright sponsored the August 1964 **Gulf of Tŏn Kĭn Resolution** that marked the beginning of a new phase of U.S. escalation in the war. After he learned more about the incident, Fulbright worked to repeal the resolution and became a leading spokesperson against the unlimited American escalation, including televised hearings in 1966. In that same year, Fulbright published a book, *The Arrogance of Power*, that criticized **Congress**, himself included, for not establishing goals and limits on American involvement in Southeast Asia and that openly called into question the Gulf of Tŏn Kĭn Resolution. Fulbright remained a critic of American policy as it related to Vietnam until the end of his Senate career.

G

GAME WARDEN, OPERATION. A naval interdiction operation to stop the North Vietnamese from using the inland waterways of the **Republic of Vietnam** to move personnel and supplies in support of their war against the **Sài Gòn** government. Operation Game Warden began on 18 December 1965 with the creation of the **River Patrol Force** (Task Force 116). The need for Operation Game Warden became clear as the **United States** escalated its involvement in Vietnam. The introduction of Operation **Market Time** in March 1965 had proven effective in ending North Vietnamese use of the sea as a transportation route, but that operation did not effectively extend into the inland water passages that stretched for more than 3,000 nautical miles (5,556 kilometers).

Operation Game Warden was an ambitious plan in that the **People's Army of Vietnam** (PAVN) and the **National Liberation Front** (NLF) used the myriad of streams, canals, rivers, and other waterways regardless of time of day or their remoteness, depth, or coverage of vegetation to the waterline. To deal with these many problems, the U.S. **Navy** introduced the **patrol boat, river** (PBR), which was a lightweight fiberglass-hulled boat built for speed, maneuverability, and capacity to travel in very shallow water. The PBRs, which searched all types of boats for illegal supplies, participated in ambushes, and provided fire support for allied troops, were aided by a naval squadron of UH-1B Iroquois **helicopters** (Seawolves) and a squadron of heavily armed OV-10 Broncos aircraft (Black Ponies).

U.S. Navy **SEAL** teams assisted Game Warden's objectives through reconnaissance patrols, ambushes, and raids. Game Warden disrupted the PAVN and NLF in the Mekong Delta, though it never was able to fully stop the flow of personnel and supplies coming from the communist bases in **Cambodia**. Despite the U.S. Navy's best efforts, the area of coverage was too great, and the enemy was elusive. In total, Operation Game Warden employed 120 PBRs, 20 LVCPs, eight UH-1Bs, and four modified LSTs (landing ships, tank). When the **SEALORDS** concept was established in October 1968, Operation Game Warden greatly expanded as Task Force 116 was absorbed into the new Task Force 194. Missions similar to Game Warden would continue until the U.S. Navy handed over responsibility for control of the waterways to the South Vietnamese as part of **Vietnamization** in 1971. *See also* PATROL AIR CUSHION VEHICLE.

GATE GUARD. Air mission in 1966 directly connected to Operation **Rolling Thunder** and designed to concentrate air **sorties** against specific transportation choke points between **Laos** and the **Democratic Republic of Vietnam** in **Route Package** 1. Daytime Gate Guard missions focused on interdiction of static targets, while nighttime missions involved armed **reconnaissance**. While Gate Guard did not cut off the infiltration of personnel and supplies traveling through Laos to the **Republic of Vietnam**, it did force the North Vietnamese to spend a considerable amount of resources to maintain its southern strategy.

GENEVA CONFERENCE AND AGREEMENTS, 1954. The 1954 Geneva Conference was held to discuss the military and political situation in Asia. The conference was divided into two sections. The first phase of the conference dealt with the armistice that ended the Korean War, while the second phase, which began on 8 May, the day after the surrender of the French garrison at **Điện Biên Phủ**, lasted until 21 July. The original intent of the second phase of the conference was to negotiate peace for Indochina, but it concluded with an agreement that put an end to nearly 100 years of **France**'s colonial rule in Indochina.

On 21 July, the two warring sides signed a 48-article agreement that ended the **First Indochina War**. Brigadier General Delteii signed for the commander-in-chief of the French Union Forces in Indochina, while Vice Minister of National Defense Tạ Quang Bửu signed for the **Democratic Republic of Vietnam** (DRV). The **United States** representative to the conference at that time, Undersecretary of State **Walter Bedell Smith**, was under instruction by Secretary of State **John Foster Dulles** not to sign the document. Instead, he submitted a statement by Dulles that supported the intent of the agreements and promised not to interfere or violate them unless compelled to do so.

The Geneva Agreements divided Vietnam into two temporary countries along the Sông (river) Bến Hải to Bô Hô Sứ, and from there due west to the Laotian border near the 17th parallel. The agreement also provided for a general election to occur within two years to unify the country. The northern part of Vietnam, known as the DRV, was led by **Hồ Chí Minh**. The southern section was known as the State of Vietnam but became the **Republic of Vietnam** in October 1955 after **Ngô Đình Diệm** forced the last Nguyen emperor, **Bảo Đại**, out of power in a national referendum. There were several key agreements in the 48-article document that brokered the armistice and determined U.S. action in the months and years to follow. Perhaps the most important article restricted the quantity and type of American assistance to the Vietnamese, while articles 12 through 16 created the situation that lead to Operation **Passage to Freedom** and a more active American role in Vietnam.

The 1954 Geneva Agreements would later become a source of frustration and complaint for all of the parties involved in Southeast Asia, as each side pointed to a series of violations caused by the other side in their attempt to jockey for advantage in the post–French colonial era. Nonetheless, the 1954 Geneva Agreements accomplished some significant things that could have led to a peaceful solution for Indochina had all of the parties involved in the conference respected the agreements.

GENEVA CONFERENCE AND ACCORDS OF 1962, IN REGARD TO LAOS. On 19 January 1961, President Dwight D. Eisenhower met with in-coming President **John F. Kennedy** to discuss the foreign policy concerns of the outgoing administration. Within the region of Southeast Asia, Eisenhower focused on the situation in **Laos** in which he stressed the importance of that country for the security of Southeast Asia. The communist insurgency in Laos had intensified in the last years of the Eisenhower administration, and political instability had caused the military situation to become precarious. Faced with the deteriorating situation in Laos, Kennedy decided to settle the situation through negotiations rather than commit American personnel to the country as he would in the **Republic of Vietnam** (RVN). The result was a 1962 Geneva Conference.

The International Conference on the Settlement of the Laotian Question, as it was formally titled, began in Geneva, Switzerland, on 16 May 1961 and ended on 23 July 1962. It brought together 14 concerned and involved nations to discuss the situation. The concept had support within the **United States**, especially by such individuals as Ambassador-at-Large **W. Averill Harriman**, while RVN president **Ngô Đình Diệm** rejected the conference as a means of dealing with the communist forces. The *Declaration on the Neutrality of Laos*, issued on 8 July 1962, allowed for the Laotians to maintain a coalition government with three political parties at odds with one another. One faction supported the U.S., another supported the communist **Pathet Lao**, and the third called for neutrality in the Cold War conflict. The *International Agreement on the Neutrality of Laos*, signed on 23 July 1962, affirmed that the 14 nations at the conference would respect Laotian neutrality by ending direct or indirect interference in Laotian internal affairs and keeping Laos out of military alliances.

The declaration and agreement did not last long, as the **Democratic Republic of Vietnam** became dependent upon the **Hồ Chí Minh Trail**, which ran through Laos, to keep its forces in the RVN supplied. With North Vietnamese violations of Laotian neutrality established, the U.S. and RVN would engage in their own actions counter to North Vietnamese moves. The result was a prolonged war, albeit on a smaller scale than the one in Vietnam, which consumed the country over the next 13 years.

GIA ĐỊNH PROVINCE. Province consisting of nine districts that surrounded **Sài Gòn**. The capital of the province was the city of Gia Định, located to the north of Sài Gòn. Gia Định began to serve as a suburb of Sài Gòn as more and more Vietnamese moved to the city to escape the war in the countryside. It was expanded in the 1960s to include two districts from **Biên Hòa** province, Xuyên Quảng and Cần Giờ, which had been a part of the **Rừng Sác Special Zone**.

GIANT SLINGSHOT, OPERATION. Third naval operation that made up the attempt under the **SEALORDS** strategy to interdict the **People's Army of Vietnam** (PAVN) and **National Liberation Front** (NLF) infiltration of the waterways between **Cambodia** and the **Republic of Vietnam**. Spurred by the success of operations **Search Turn** and **Foul Deck**, Admiral **Elmo R. Zumwalt Jr.** initiated Operation Giant Slingshot on 6 December 1968 in order to extend the barrier, which stretched from Rạch Giá to the Giang Thành–Vĩnh Tế canal system. The new barrier would include the area around the formation in Cambodia known as the **Parrot's Beak**, located in III **Corps Tactical Zone**. Giant Slingshot focused on the Vàm Cỏ Đông and Vàm Cỏ Tây rivers. This was an area of high infiltration for the PAVN and NLF during the war and a necessary barrier to protect **Sài Gòn**.

GOLDWATER, BARRY MORRIS (1909–1998). United States senator. Goldwater was born in the Arizona Territory, three years before it became a state. He attended the University of Arizona but left school in his first year after his father's death in 1929. He went to work in the family mercantile store, M. Goldwater and Sons, and stayed with the store until after World War II. During the conflict, Goldwater, an avid flyer, failed to gain entrance into combat flying but was accepted by the Ferry Command. In that capacity, he flew aircraft and supplies around the world during the war. After the war, he decided to run for public office and served on the Phoenix City Council in 1949. Goldwater decided to run for the U.S. Senate in 1952 in part because of President Harry S. Truman's policies during the Korean War. He took advantage of President Dwight D. Eisenhower's victory and won the seat from the Democratic incumbent and Senate majority leader, Ernest W. McFarland.

Goldwater earned a reputation in the Senate as a small government, anti-communist proponent. He easily won reelection in 1958 as a conservative and even received votes at the 1960 Republican Presidential National Convention. Goldwater served as the chairman of the Republican Senatorial Campaign Committee in 1960, which helped him increase his name recognition within the party. By 1962, he had decided to run for president against **John F. Kennedy** in the 1964 presidential election. When Kennedy was assassinated in November 1963, he considered withdrawing from contention but decided to oppose President **Lyndon B. Johnson**.

Goldwater lost early primaries to **Republic of Vietnam** ambassador **Henry Cabot Lodge Jr.** in New Hampshire, and to New York governor Nelson Rockefeller in Oregon, but he rebounded with a series of smaller state victories and a win in California, which solidified his nomination. During the campaign, Johnson was able to portray Goldwater as the more militant candidate, even though Johnson had slowly been escalating American advisory efforts in Southeast Asia. Goldwater helped to cultivate his **Hawkish** image with public statements that seemed extreme to many within the U.S., such as his suggestion of using a low-yield atomic bomb to defoliate the Vietnamese jungles and expose the **Hồ Chí Minh Trail**.

Goldwater argued that Johnson's Vietnam policy would not result in a victory. He advocated expanding the air war into the **Democratic Republic of Vietnam** and mining **Hải Phòng** harbor. Goldwater lost the election and, because he did not seek another senatorial term while running for the presidency, was without office for four years. He returned to the Senate in 1969 for another three terms before deciding not to run again for health reasons. At the time of his retirement, he served as the chairman of the Senate Armed Services Committee and the Senate Intelligence Committee. In 1979, Goldwater published his memoir, *With No Apologies*.

GRAVEL MINES. *See* MINES, LAND.

GREAT BRITAIN. Great Britain balanced its support for **United States** policy in Southeast Asia between encouraging independence for the former French colony of Indochina and maintaining its own colonial empire. As a result, Britain never supported the U.S. with military troops in Vietnam, but it did provide humanitarian aid and acted as a mediator in the various attempts at peace in the region. The first convergence between these competing interests occurred in 1954 during the Battle for **Điện Biên Phủ**. The British refused to support Operation **Vulture**, which would have seen a massive American bombardment of the forces following General **Võ Nguyên Giáp** who had surrounded the French at the fortress. The British also refused to become involved in the U.S.-sponsored plan of **United Action** that would have internationalized the war and allowed **France** to retain its Indochina colony. Britain did accept the 1955 **South East Asian Treaty Organization**.

After the defeat of the French at Điện Biên Phủ, the British participated in the 1954 **Geneva Conference**. As the cochair with the **Soviet Union**, the British helped to steer through the 48-article agreement that ended the **First Indochina War**. After the war, the British maintained a low profile in Southeast Asia, oftentimes mediating between the **Democratic Republic of Vietnam** (DRV) and the **Republic of Vietnam** (RVN), which was now the recipient of increased U.S. aid and assistance. The British had both an embassy in the RVN and a consul general in the DRV. Because of its alliance with the U.S. and recognition of the RVN, the British sent humanitarian aid to the Vietnamese. In 1963, they provided medical equipment for **Sài Gòn** and Huế University and instruments and implements for the Meteorological Service and the Agricultural School at Sài Gòn. They also supported the Atomic Research Establishment at **Đà Lạt**. British doctors and nurses served in Vietnam as civilians, while **advisers**, teachers, and technical experts assisted in nonmilitary projects. Total British aid to the RVN ran into the millions of dollars.

The British resisted U.S. attempts to get them to include combat soldiers in Vietnam, even after the November 1961 move by President **John F. Kennedy** and President **Lyndon B. Johnson**'s **Show the Flag** program, which started in April 1964. The British offered the expertise of Sir **Robert Thompson**, who had been successful during the Malayan Emergency in the 1950s, to serve as a special adviser for **counterinsurgency** and a consultant for the RVN's **Strategic Hamlet Program**. In October 1966, General **William C. Westmoreland** made plans to incorporate personnel from the British Gurkha Brigade into Vietnam as the unit was phased out of existence. While the plan never materialized, in part because the British rescinded the order to dissolve the brigade, the U.S. continued to pressure the British for greater involvement in Southeast Asia. Though the British refused all U.S. attempts to garner additional troops, it did remain a faithful ally as it balanced a precarious diplomatic line between being a strong ally, a cochair of the Geneva Conference, and a former colonial power.

GRENADE LAUNCHER. The M79 grenade launcher was a single-shot, breach-loaded weapon that fired a 40-mm round. It was known as the thumper, thump-gun, blooper, or bloop tube. It weighed a little less than three kilograms (6.5 pounds) when loaded and could fire six rounds per minute. The maximum range of the weapon was 396 meters (1,300 feet), though its effective range was 350 meters (1,150 feet). It could fire a grenade, smoke, **flechettes**, illumination, or antipersonnel shell, which made it very versatile, easy to operate, and well liked among **Free World Forces**.

GROUND DIVERTED FORCE CONCEPT. The Ground Diverted Force concept was a solution to the difficulties associated with long turnaround times for B-52 **Arc Light missions**, which originated in **Guam**. The concept called for the diversion of a preplanned strike to another target opportunity should the mission need to be changed. Rather than canceling the original mission, which proved to be costly and inefficient, the Ground Diverted Force concept enabled a higher completion rate for Arc Light missions.

GUAM. Guam is the largest of the Mariana Islands and is an organized, unincorporated territory of the **United States** dating back to the Spanish-American war of 1898. It is located in the Western Pacific, approximately 4,000 kilometers (2,500 miles) from **Sài Gòn** and 4,200 kilometers (2,600 miles) from **Hà Nội**. Guam was important in the air war because it housed B-52 Stratofortress bombers, which had replaced the B-47, and KC-135 Stratotankers at Andersen Air Force Base. B-52s used Guam as a base of operations to conduct **Arc Light missions** during the war. Other targets included **Laos, Cambodia**, and the **Democratic Republic of Vietnam**. B-52s also flew from U-Tapao in **Thailand**. The U.S. also stored its herbicides, including **Agent Orange**, in Guam.

The island was the location of President **Richard M. Nixon**'s announcement of his **Nixon Doctrine** in July 1969. After Sài Gòn fell in April 1975, Guam became a staging area for Vietnamese fleeing the communists. Nearly 150,000 Vietnamese **refugees** made their way to other nations via Guam after 1975.

GUERRILLA WARFARE. The **Việt Minh** used this strategy to fight against a numerically superior French Union Force during the **First Indochina War**, while the **National Liberation Front** (NLF) employed guerrilla warfare against the **United States** during the **Second Indochina War**. Guerrilla warfare allowed the Vietnamese to determine the level and intensity of fighting against the enemy. By resisting the temptation to engage in set-piece battles or prolonged military skirmishes, the Vietnamese determined the number and severity of **casualties**. This enabled the numerically and technologically inferior Vietnamese forces to withstand the military might of both **France** and the U.S.

During the American war in Vietnam, guerrilla warfare was primarily in the form of hit-and-run tactics that involved ambushes and brief firefights to cause as many casualties as possible. It was not a formula for military victory but rather a means to achieve a political victory by outlasting the U.S. In the NLF's guerrilla warfare strategy, it used the **topography** and terrain of the **Republic of Vietnam** (RVN) to its advantage. The NLF went underground and established a series of **tunnel** complexes that allowed it to hide from patrolling U.S. and **Army of the Republic of Vietnam** (ARVN) forces. The NLF also used the dense and hard-to-penetrate jungles and mountains in the country to elude its enemy, or based itself in an area like the **Rừng Sác Spe-**

cial **Zone** south of **Sài Gòn** or the **U Minh** Forest in IV **Corps Tactical Zone**, which made it difficult for the U.S. or ARVN to conduct operations against it. The **People's Army of Vietnam** (PAVN) and the NLF also used neutral **Cambodia** and **Laos** as base areas of operation to conduct missions against the RVN. The Vietnamese would disperse if engaged with superior numbers or technology and let their **booby traps** or snipers harass the invaders.

In addition to effectively using topography, the terrain, and low-level conflict, guerrilla warfare called for small-unit action and taking advantage of weather conditions and the night to negate the advantages of mobility, technology, and numbers possessed by the U.S. and the ARVN. For the PAVN and NLF, guerrilla warfare meant controlling the countryside and providing a presence among the people in order to discredit the Sài Gòn government and maintain instability among the villages, which would gradually force the people to abandon their support for Sài Gòn and become either actively or passively supportive of the insurgency.

There were three major exceptions to the employment of guerrilla warfare during the wars in Vietnam. The first occurred in 1954 at the Battle for **Điện Biên Phủ**; the second occurred during the 1968 **Tết Offensive**, and the final exception was the 1972 **Easter Offensive**. While the 1954 example was successful, the other two ended in military disaster for the PAVN and NLF, which only reinforced the decision to maintain the guerrilla warfare strategy until the final offensive against the RVN in 1975.

GULF OF TỒN KĨN INCIDENT. The Gulf of Tồn Kĩn Incident involved two pitched battles—the first of which was confirmed, while the second has been held in doubt—between the **United States** and the North Vietnamese Navy on 2 August and 4 August 1964. On 2 August, the U.S.S. *Maddox* (DD-731), a destroyer involved in a **DeSoto** mission off the coast of the **Democratic Republic of Vietnam** in the Gulf of Tồn Kĩn, was collecting electronic **intelligence** when it was engaged by North Vietnamese torpedo boats. The North Vietnamese were at a heightened state of awareness regarding American activity as a result of a late July **OPLAN 34A** mission that had struck at the North Vietnamese facilities at Hòn Mê and Hòn Ngư. Three North Vietnamese P-4 motor torpedo boats attacked the *Maddox* with torpedoes and machine-gun fire, though none of the torpedoes struck, and only one bullet hit the destroyer. The *Maddox* returned fire, as did F-8 aircraft from the U.S.S. *Ticonderoga* (CVA-14). One P-4 was seriously damaged, while the other two moved out of range. The *Maddox* was then ordered out of the Gulf of Tồn Kĩn, and President **Lyndon B. Johnson** issued a public note of protest based on the claim that the *Maddox* was in international waters.

The *Maddox* returned to the Gulf of Tổn Kỉn to continue the DeSoto mission on 3 August but was reinforced with the U.S.S. *Turner Joy* (DD-951). On the night of 4 August, the two destroyers reported a second attack, though it was not clear that the attack actually took place. Data and evidence at the time suggested that the North Vietnamese had attacked, and the next day Johnson ordered a retaliatory air strike. Operation **Pierce Arrow** used aircraft from the U.S.S. *Ticonderoga* and U.S.S. *Constellation* (CVA-64) against the oil storage facility at Vinh and against various naval facilities along the coast.

The second alleged incident also prompted Johnson to push forward a resolution to **Congress** authorizing the use of force, if necessary, to protect American military personnel and facilities against attack. The 7 August **Gulf of Tổn Kỉn Resolution**, as it would become known, served as justification for an escalation of U.S. involvement in Vietnam. The fact that evidence of the second attack was very circumstantial and controversial would later plague the Johnson administration and eventually led to a Senate repeal of the Gulf of Tổn Kỉn Resolution on 24 June 1970.

GULF OF TỔN KỈN RESOLUTION. In response to the alleged 4 August 1964 North Vietnamese action against the U.S.S. *Maddox* (DD-731) and U.S.S. *Turner Joy* (DD-951) operating in the Gulf of Tổn Kỉn, the **United States** Senate and House of Representatives, at the urging of the White House, approved Joint Resolution of **Congress** H.J. RES 1145 on 7 August 1964. In what become known as the Gulf of Tổn Kỉn Resolution, the document provided approval and support for the president to act as he deemed necessary to protect U.S. forces in Southeast Asia. The resolution also called upon the U.S. to take necessary steps to assist members of protocol states of the **South East Asian Treaty Organization** who were threatened, with an implied reference to the **Republic of Vietnam**.

The resolution was originally to be in effect until the president determined that it was not necessary or until Congress passed a concurrent resolution to end the authorization. Only two U.S. senators, **Wayne Morse** (D-Oregon) and Ernest Gruening (D-Alaska), opposed the resolution, while all present in the House of Representatives approved it. The Gulf of Tổn Kỉn Resolution became President **Lyndon B. Johnson**'s justification for American escalation in Vietnam, which eventually led to the Americanization of the war. The Senate repealed the resolution on 24 June 1970 as a consequence of the growing **antiwar** movement in Congress and as a response to the **Richard M. Nixon** administration's incursion into **Cambodia**.

H

HÀ NỘI. During the time of Chinese occupation, Hà Nội was known as Tống Bình until it was renamed Thăng Long (ascending dragon) in the first decade of the 10th century. It would have many names over the next millennium. In 1831, the Nguyễn Dynasty emperor Minh Mạng renamed Thăng Long to Hà Nội. Hà Nội served as the capital for French Indochina from 1902 to 1954. From 1954 to 1976, it served as the capital of the **Democratic Republic of Vietnam** (DRV). Hà Nội was located in the **Red River Delta**, approximately 1,775 kilometers (1,100 miles) from **Sài Gòn** and 95 kilometers (60 miles) from the Gulf of Tŏn Kĭn.

In August 1945, Hà Nội was the scene of a **Việt Minh** uprising that coincided with the end of World War II and was the location of **Hồ Chí Minh**'s Declaration of Independence on 2 September 1945. It continued to serve as a focal point throughout the **First Indochina War** until it was handed over to the Vietnamese on 10 October 1954 per the 1954 **Geneva Agreements**. After March 1965, when the **United States** initiated Operation **Rolling Thunder**, the bombing of Hà Nội became a controversial question. President **Lyndon B. Johnson** refused to authorize the bombing of the city because of the fear that it would induce the **People's Republic of China** to overtly escalate its involvement in the conflict and would create a public relations nightmare with the loss of civilian life and the destruction of civilian property. Johnson was also concerned with damaging neutral-country property in the city and with killing or wounding non-Vietnamese residents.

Johnson established a restrictive zone around the city that measured 30 nautical miles, or just short of 55 kilometers (35 miles). U.S. air strikes within this circle could only be approved by Johnson or his representative. The U.S. did strike within the restricted area in 1966, which led to a series of critical newspaper articles by the *New York Times*' **Harrison Salisbury**, who was invited to the city to see for himself the damage caused by the U.S. against the civilian population. Until 1968, the U.S. limited its air **sorties** over the restricted area, attacking only the **Long Biên Bridge** (Paul Doumer Bridge) with force. Hà Nội was spared air attacks from the end of Operation Rolling Thunder on 1 November 1968 to the initiation of Operation **Linebacker I** as a response to the 1972 **Easter Offensive**. Linebacker I still employed some restrictions in attacking Hà Nội, but the December 1972 **Linebacker II** attacks eased these restrictions even if they did not target the city's center. Neither Linebacker operation caused as much damage as had other air campaigns.

After the reunification of the DRV and the **Republic of Vietnam**, Hà Nội became the capital of the Socialist Republic of Vietnam.

HẢI PHÒNG. Located approximately 96 kilometers (60 miles) from **Hà Nội** and on the coast in the **Red River Delta**, Hải Phòng was the most significant seaport in the **Democratic Republic of Vietnam** (DRV). The city was founded after the failed rebellion led by the Trưng sisters. The French used the city as a naval base, as did the Japanese during their occupation of Indochina during World War II. The people of Hải Phòng revolted against the French in 1945, and Hải Phòng was believed to be the location of the first military action that started the **First Indochina War**. The city played a major role in that war, as well as the one against the **United States**, but was also prominent during the 1954–1955 U.S. **Navy** operation **Passage to Freedom**. After the 1954 **Geneva Agreements** were implemented, Hải Phòng became the principal point of embarkation for Vietnamese and Chinese **Nùng** who wished to depart the North for the South. This became especially true after October 1954, when Hà Nội was handed over to the Vietnamese who had defeated the French.

Hải Phòng also became the main point of debarkation for materiel provided by the DRV's allies. For almost the entire war, ships under communist or neutral flags offloaded equipment and supplies used by the **People's Army of Vietnam** (PAVN) and the **National Liberation Front** (NLF) to fight the U.S. and the **Republic of Vietnam**. While the city's harbor was not bombed by the U.S. during Operation **Rolling Thunder** for fear that the **People's Republic of China** or the **Soviet Union** would use that event as a pretext for overt escalation, it still developed one of the most sophisticated and concentrated air defense systems within the DRV. The U.S. did target facilities around Hải Phòng during Operation Rolling Thunder, but the **Lyndon B. Johnson** administration and the Department of Defense refused repeated requests to mine Hải Phòng harbor, even though surveys taken during Operation Passage to Freedom revealed that the sinking of even one major ship would cause a significant bottleneck from the harbor to the open sea.

It was not until 1972, in response to the **Easter Offensive**, that Hải Phòng was **bombed** and mined. On 16 April, B-52 bombers attacked the harbor and damaged or destroyed sections of the port facilities, in addition to striking four Soviet ships. In the opening phase of Operation **Linebacker I**, on 11 May, Hải Phòng harbor was mined. This action ended shipping in and out of the harbor until after the 1973 **Paris Peace Accords**, which had stipulated that the U.S. was required to help clear the waterways of **mines** it had dropped.

Hải Phòng and its harbor were the lifeblood of the DRV during the war. The ability of the PAVN and NLF to operate against the U.S. and RVN was assured when President Lyndon B. Johnson refused to take measures to close the facility to shipping. President **Richard M. Nixon**'s decision to do so proved effective, but it also arrived too late to change the course of the war. *See also* ENDSWEEP, OPERATION.

HAIG, ALEXANDER MEIGS, JR. (1924–). General, White House chief of staff, and secretary of state. Haig graduated from the **United States** Military Academy in 1947 and was assigned to General Douglas MacArthur's staff in Japan. He served with the X Corps during the first year of the Korean War and earned two Silver Stars for heroism. He continued his military career after the war, serving as a staff officer in the Office of the Deputy Chief of Staff for Operations in the Department of Defense between 1962 and 1964 and then becoming the military assistant to the secretary of the army in 1964 and military assistant to the secretary of defense until he entered combat in Vietnam as a battalion commander in the 1st Infantry **Division** at the rank of lieutenant colonel. Haig continued to earn distinction in battle, including the Distinguished Service Cross, the Distinguished Flying Cross, and a Purple Heart.

After his **tour of duty**, Haig became the commander of the 3rd Regiment of the Corps of Cadets at West Point, and in 1969 he was appointed the military assistant to **Henry Kissinger**, the presidential assistant for national security affairs. In 1970, President **Richard M. Nixon** promoted Haig to deputy assistant to the president for national security affairs, during which time he was involved in the Paris negotiations that led to the January 1973 **Paris Peace Accords**. After the war, he served as the vice chief of staff of the army and then as chief of staff of the army in the waning days of the Nixon administration and during the **Gerald R. Ford** administration, until September 1974. In the postwar period, Haig served as the supreme commander of the North Atlantic Treaty Organization from 1974 to 1979. He retired from the army as a four-star general in 1979. He served as secretary of state under Ronald W. Reagan from 22 January 1981 to 5 July 1982. After this time, he tried his hand at politics, hosted television shows on business and business education, and actively participated in organizations and conferences related to foreign policy. In 1992, he published his memoirs, *Inner Circles: How America Changed the World*.

HAK LY COMPANY. Company established by the **Democratic Republic of Vietnam** to move supplies received at the port of **Sihanoukville** in **Cambodia**

to aid **People's Army of Vietnam** (PAVN) and **National Liberation Front** (NLF) forces operating in the **Republic of Vietnam**. From Sihanoukville, the Hak Ly Company moved supplies to Kampong Speu where they were divided between the PAVN and NLF and the Cambodian Army at Lovek, with the full knowledge and consent of Prince **Norodom Sihanouk**. The Hak Ly Company legitimized, by appearance, the North Vietnamese presence at Sihanoukville but also called into question Cambodia's neutrality during the war.

HALBERSTAM, DAVID (1934–2007). Pulitzer Prize–winning journalist and author. Halberstam was educated at Harvard University, where he edited the student newspaper, *The Crimson*. He graduated in 1955 and wrote for two southern newspapers, focusing on the civil rights movement. In 1960, he joined the *New York Times* as a foreign correspondent and worked in the Congo. In 1962, he was transferred to the **Republic of Vietnam**.

He was one of the first reporters in the war and made his mark by criticizing the **Sài Gòn** government and its military leadership. He disagreed with the way the war was being fought and focused on the rule of **Ngô Đình Diệm** in 1962 and 1963. Halberstam described the failures of the **Strategic Hamlet Program** in 1962 and arrived on the scene of the **Battle of Ấp Bắc**, albeit a day after the real battle was fought, to tell a different story from the official military version of events. He was one of the first reporters to argue that a **credibility gap** existed between what officials in Washington and Sài Gòn argued and what was happening on the ground in Vietnam. He was particularly critical of the first **Military Assistance Command, Vietnam**, General Paul D. Harkin.

In 1964, Halberstam shared the Pulitzer Prize for his article describing the 11 June 1963 self-immolation of **Thích Quảng Đức**, which served as a catalyst for those who opposed Ngô Đình Diệm to seek his removal from office. Halberstam remained cautious and critical of the **United States'** policy in Vietnam for the remainder of the war, though he would leave Southeast Asia for Eastern Europe as the Americanization of the war began. He authored several books on the subject, including *The Making of a Quagmire* (1965) and *The Best and the Brightest* (1972), which sought to explain how the U.S. failed, as well as a number of other books on war, politics, American society and culture, and sports. *See also* MEDIA, UNITED STATES.

HAMBURGER HILL, BATTLE OF. A 10 to 20 May 1969 battle to take Ap Bia Mountain (Đồi A Bia), known as Hill 937 in the A Shau Valley, which was near the Laotian border in **Thừa Thiên** province. During Operation **Apache Snow**, a **search-and-destroy** operation, the forces of the **United States** followed up on earlier successes by the U.S. **Marine Corps** in Operation **Dewey**

Canyon to eliminate the threat of the **People's Army of Vietnam** (PAVN) in the A Shau Valley and interdict infiltration through the valley from **Laos** into the **Republic of Vietnam** along the **Hồ Chí Minh Trail**. On 10 May, three U.S. battalions from the 101st Airborne **Division**, elements of the 9th Marine Regiment, and the 3rd Battalion, 5th Cavalry Regiment, participated in an air assault into the valley to push the PAVN forces, estimated at three regiments, toward a blocking position near the Laotian border. Two **Army of the Republic of Vietnam** battalions blocked the highways into the valley and cut off other lines of retreat.

On 11 May, the 3rd Battalion, 187th Regiment moved against Hill 937. In the course of the battle, it was mistakenly fired upon by AH-1 Cobra **helicopters** and forced to retreat. The unit resumed the assault on 13 May after probing the PAVN defense following the initial contact, but they failed to complete the mission due to difficulties in the **topography** of the area. Another battalion from the 101st Airborne Division, the 1st Battalion, 506th Regiment, joined the assault on Hill 937, securing nearby Hill 916, but was not ready to combine its force with the 3rd Battalion, 187th Regiment until 18 May. By that time, the 3rd Battalion, 187th Regiment had already attempted to take Hill 937 on several different occasions but met stiff resistance from well-positioned and fortified PAVN troops who used the terrain to their advantage.

The tactics of the U.S. forces against Ap Bia Mountain played into the PAVN defense, as there were limited areas in which an assault force could maneuver for attack, and all of these avenues were well defended. The Battle of Ap Bia Mountain earned the name the Battle of Hamburger Hill after an Associated Press correspondent visited the battlefield and interviewed soldiers who made parallels to the Battle for Pork Chop Hill during the Korean War. The U.S. forces continued to assault the hill on 18 and 19 May, with a final assault on the morning of 20 May. During this last attack, which was preceded by an **artillery** bombardment and air attack, Hill 937 was finally taken by the 3rd Battalion, 187th Regiment. The U.S. suffered 72 killed and 372 wounded during the 10-day battle, while it claimed over 600 PAVN dead. The U.S. discovered a series of **tunnels** and base areas on the hill. News of the battle **casualties** served as a catalyst for **antiwar** critics to continue their fight against the war's continuation. This included specific reference to the battle and its losses by senators Edward Kennedy and **George McGovern**. On 5 June 1969, the U.S. abandoned the hill.

HAMLET EVALUATION SYSTEM (HES). In 1967, the **United States** created this program to measure six different factors that determined the condition of hamlets throughout the **Republic of Vietnam** (RVN). These factors included the following: **National Liberation Front** (NLF) military activity;

NLF political and subversive activity; friendly defensive and security capabilities; administrative and political capabilities; health, education, and welfare capabilities; and economic development. Based on a set of quantitative requirements, each of these factors was given a grade of V (controlled by the NLF), E, D, C, B, or A (controlled by the **Sài Gòn** government).

These scores were then combined to give the hamlets an overall grade based on the same criteria. Problems arose in the program as HES evaluators often came to different conclusions in these subjective measurements. The HES provided a means to assess the effectiveness of **pacification** in the RVN, but the quantitative nature of the program was endemic to the larger problem of the U.S. during the war. It used quantitative analysis to determine success or progress in a war where victory was not determined by numbers.

HARASSMENT AND INTERDICTION (H&I). A type of gunfire, usually from **artillery** or naval guns, that targeted an area with the hope of catching the enemy in the vicinity. H&I usually targeted known enemy positions or routes, oftentimes at night, and relied more on surprise and luck than actual military **intelligence**. This type of indiscriminate fire was roundly criticized by **antiwar** protestors who believed that H&I caused needless civilian **casualties**. American proponents of H&I argued that the element of surprise, coupled with target selection of known **People's Army of Vietnam** and **National Liberation Front** areas, kept the enemy off balance. The **United States** began H&I in 1965, while the **Republic of Vietnam** had employed the practice since 1962.

HARKINS, PAUL DONALD (1904–1984). First commander of **Military Assistance Command, Vietnam** (MACV). With the escalation of the war during the **John F. Kennedy** administration, the need to create a more structured military command became evident. In 1962, the MACV was established to eventually take over American control of the war from the Military Assistant Advisory Group, Vietnam. Harkins assumed command of MACV on 8 February and quickly became a source of controversy as he continued to report on the improvement of the military situation in Vietnam while others, including many members of the **media**, offered the opposing view. Harkins was particularly attacked by **David Halberstam** and **Neil Sheehan**, both of whom argued that the general was out of touch with what was happening in the war.

While Harkins did provide a positive image of the **counterinsurgency** campaign, he was not as optimistic as the newspapermen of the time indicated. As a result of the tension raised by the media, Harkins was never able to fully utilize the press to his advantage, and they, in turn, worked to undermine the general's credibility until he left Vietnam on 20 June 1964.

Harkins was succeeded by General **William C. Westmoreland**, who oversaw the introduction of combat troops and the escalation of American forces to 543,000 by June 1969. *See also* ẤP BẮC, BATTLE OF; MCGARR, LIONEL CHARLES; VANN, JOHN PAUL.

HARRIMAN, WILLIAM AVERELL (1891–1986). Politician and diplomat. Harriman was educated at Yale University and graduated in 1913. In 1922, he established W. A. Harriman and Company with money from his father, who had been very successful in the railroad industry. The company focused on the banking industry. Harriman continued in the business, which changed its name in 1927 to Harriman Brothers and Company, through the 1920s and the Great Depression. In 1931, the company merged with another to form Brown Brothers Harriman and Company. The company continued to grow, with interests in a number of railroads, banks, shipping lines, and other entities, including a successful horse racing business.

After the outbreak of war in Europe in 1939, Harriman served as a special envoy to Europe for the **United States** and became the U.S. ambassador to the **Soviet Union** in 1943. He served in that position until 1946 when he became the ambassador to Great Britain. After the war, Harriman continued to serve in the Harry S. Truman administration as secretary of commerce and one of the leaders of the Marshall Plan, and in 1954 he became governor of New York for one term. After Truman announced his intention not to seek reelection in the 1952 presidential election, Harriman attempted to gain the Democratic Party nomination but failed, then and in 1956. On 3 February 1961, after **John F. Kennedy** assumed the White House, Harriman was appointed an ambassador-at-large. During this time, he was involved in the formation of the International Conference on the Settlement of the Laotian Question, which commenced on 16 May 1961. He remained in that position until 3 December 1961, when he became the assistant secretary of state for far eastern affairs.

While in this position, he also became the chairman of the Task Force on Southeast Asia. Harriman pushed for Laotian neutrality, which was realized in theory with the *International Agreement on the Neutrality of Laos*, signed on 23 July 1962. During this time, Harriman became one of the leading critics of **Ngô Đình Diệm** within the Kennedy administration and helped to influence American policy toward the **Republic of Vietnam** president that ultimately led to the 1 November 1963 coup d'état.

On 3 April 1963, Harriman became the undersecretary of state for political affairs and chairman of the Special Group for Counterinsurgency. He remained in that position until 17 March 1965, when he returned to the job of ambassador-at-large. He headed the U.S. delegation to the Paris Peace Talks on Vietnam until 17 January 1969, when **Richard M. Nixon** was elected to the presidency. Harriman was never able to move the negotiations in a positive direction, as the North Vietnamese continually frustrated the U.S. delegation. After his retirement from politics in 1969, Harriman was awarded the Presidential Medal of Freedom. While he did not serve in the public arena again, Harriman continued to be an elder statesman and at times an influential adviser for the U.S. on American foreign relations.

HARVEST MOON, OPERATION. A December 1965 Operation in the **Quế Sơn Valley**, also known as Núi Lộc Sơn, the name of the dominant mountain in the area, which was situated between Quảng Nam and Quảng Tín in the southernmost part of I **Corps Tactical Zone**. After a 17 November attack by the 1st Regiment of the **National Liberation Front** (NLF) against the **Army of the Republic of Vietnam** (ARVN) headquarters in Hiệp Đức district in Quảng Nam, it became clear to the **United States** and ARVN forces that a major **search-and-destroy** operation was necessary to regain the initiative in the area. In early December, the U.S. and the South Vietnamese agreed to a joint operation to be known as Harvest Moon (Liên Kết 18). The operation involved elements of the 2nd Battalion, 7th **Marines**; 3rd Battalion, 3rd Marines; and 2nd Battalion, 9th Marines, with the Special Landing Force in reserve. The marines were joined by the ARVN Headquarters Group; the 3rd Battalion, 1st ARVN Regiment; the 1st Battalion, 5th ARVN Regiment; the 1st Battalion, 6th ARVN Regiment; and the 11th ARVN Ranger Battalion. The operation began on 8 December 1965, with the ARVN force moving down the Thăng Bình–Hiệp Đức road into the Quế Sơn Valley.

Harvest Moon lasted until 20 December 1965. It accounted for 407 **People's Army of Vietnam** and NLF personnel killed and 33 captured, while the marines lost 45 killed and 218 wounded. ARVN losses were 90 killed and 141 wounded, most occurring during the first two days. Airpower played a significant role in the operation, and the Marine Corps gained valuable experience in air-to-ground support. Harvest Moon was significant in the war as it marked one of the first major operations that indicated the transition of the American military tactic from the enclave to the search-and-destroy strategy.

HATCHET TEAMS. Small groups of South Vietnamese, usually **Nùng** or **Montagnard**, under **United States** leadership within the operational control of the **Studies and Observation Group**. The teams operated along the **Hồ Chí Minh Trail** in **Laos** and **Cambodia** starting in 1966. The teams of approximately 20 to 50 personnel ambushed the **People's Army of Vietnam** and **National Liberation Front** troops with whom they came into contact and engaged in special missions such as **search-and-rescue**. Hatchet teams included more personnel than **spike teams**. They provided special services to the secret war in Laos and Cambodia and struck at the elusive enemy where normal operations were prohibited. *See also* PRAIRIE FIRE; TAILWIND, OPERATION.

HẬU NGHĨA. Located approximately 48 kilometers (30 miles) to the west of **Sài Gòn** in III **Corps Tactical Zone**, Hâu Nghĩa was created by **Ngô Đình Diệm** in 1963 by carving out space from the provinces of **Long An**, **Tây Ninh**, and Bình Dương. The provincial capital was Khiêm Cường, which had originally been the small hamlet of Bàu Trai. Hâu Nghĩa was one of the most contested provinces in the **Republic of Vietnam**, in part because it bordered **Cambodia** near the **Parrot's Beak**, an area known to house a major **National Liberation Front** base area. The **Củ Chi** tunnels were also located in Hâu Nghĩa. In 1965, the **United States** initiated a review of its Vietnam policy to gauge how best to combine its superior firepower with the strategy of **pacification**. The team put together to write the study, which would eventually become the Program for the Pacification and Long-Term Development of South Vietnam, assessed the battle for Hâu Nghĩa because it represented the worst case scenario up to that point in the war.

HAWK. Term used to denote individuals who argued for a greater military presence in Vietnam, without restrictions on tactics employed or strategies utilized. The group was largely composed of conservative Republicans and Democrats who believed that the **United States** needed a military presence in Southeast Asia to prevent a communist takeover. Hawks supported the military war as opposed to their counterparts, the **Doves**. *See also* AGNEW, SPIRO THEODORE; HÉBERT, FELIX EDWARD; LEMAY, CURTIS EMERSON; MOORER, THOMAS HINMAN; SHARP, ULYSSES SIMPSON GRANT.

HÉBERT, FELIX EDWARD (1901–1979). Hébert was born in New Orleans and educated at Tulane University, graduating in 1924. He worked in the newspaper industry and in 1936 was on the Louisiana governor's staff. In 1940, Hébert was elected to the House of Representatives as a Democrat. He served in **Congress** from 3 January 1941 to 3 January 1977. During his time in Congress, he chaired the Committee on Armed Services in 1971.

Hébert supported President **Lyndon B. Johnson**'s handling of the war and was considered a **Hawk**. He advocated greater escalation of the war than Johnson authorized after the 1964 **Gulf of Tŏn Kĭn Incident**. He was also on the subcommittee of the Armed Services Committee that investigated the 1968 **Mỹ Lai** massacre. Hébert was critical of how the U.S. Army handled the situation. He showed more sympathy for the soldiers under investigation and worked to ensure that the prosecution of the men was difficult. He was criticized by opponents of the war for this position. He published his memoir, *Last of the Titans: The Life and Times of Congressman F. Edward Hébert of Louisiana*, in 1976.

HELICOPTER. One of the most enduring images of the Vietnam War was the helicopter, a rotary-wing aircraft that was capable of hovering over a single area and carrying a significant payload. It was during the war that this weapon became indispensible to how the **United States** and its allies fought. The helicopter was involved in many missions, including air-to-ground fire support, **airmobility**, **search-and-rescue**, and **aeromedical evacuation**. The helicopter was also used in such experimental projects as creating **landing zones** using 15,000 BLU-82B **bombings** in Operation **Commando Vault** and spraying herbicides in the early days of Operation **Ranch Hand**.

There were a number of different types of helicopters used in Southeast Asia after their initial introduction in December 1961. The helicopters were identified by a two-letter designation followed by a number. The second letter, H for helicopter, was commonly used in identifying helicopters during the war, though the first letter provided relevant information. *A* stood for attack, *C* for cargo, *O* for observation, and *U* for utility.

The UH-1 Iroquois, often referred to as the Huey, was perhaps the most recognizable symbol of the war. It was built by Bell. There were five versions of the UH-1 used in the war, which were involved in a variety of missions, including transportation, general purpose and utility, air assault, armed **reconnaissance**, reconnaissance, medical evacuation, and search-and-rescue, to name but a few. The first Iroquois arrived in Vietnam with the Utility Tactical Transport Company and carried 16 2.75-inch rockets as well as two .30-inch **machine guns**. The B model replaced these helicopters, with improved speed and space. It had a crew of two and could handle a normal payload of seven troops, or three litters and two walking wounded along with one medical personnel. The UH-1B was capable of carrying a 40-mm **grenade launcher** and two 30-mm cannons.

In 1965, the C model began to replace the B models and featured increased speed and maneuverability. The final version used by the U.S. Army was the F model, which was based on the UH-1B but could carry 1,815 kilograms (4,000 pounds), or the crew and 10 troops. The **U.S. Marines** (USMC) employed the UH-1E during the war, which was similar to the B and C models and could carry up to 1,815 kilograms (4,000 pounds), or a crew and eight troops. It was armed with two fixed 7.62-mm M60 machine guns and could carry two rocket pods and up to 36 rockets. Because of the versatility of the helicopter and the conditions experienced in Southeast Asia, from an unforgiving terrain, oppressive **climate**, and elusive enemy, the UH-1 proved to be a deciding factor in many operations and missions during the war.

The AH-1 Huey Cobra, also built by Bell, served as a close support and attack helicopter in the war. The U.S. Army employed the model G, which was initially armed with a GAU-2b/A 7.62 **minigun** but was later upgraded to a combination of two M28 miniguns, firing up to 4,000 rounds per minute, or one 40-mm grenade launcher. The cobra could also carry four separate external munitions, such as 72 2.75-inch rockets or two M18E1 minigun pods. The helicopter had a crew of two, could travel up to 566 kilometers (352 miles) per hour, and had a range of 574 kilometers (357 miles). The Cobra was an effective and versatile weapon in the **counterinsurgency** war because of the intense firepower it could bring to the battlefield. It also conducted armed reconnaissance and was involved in search-and-rescue missions.

The HH-3 Jolly Green Giant was originally designed as a medium assault helicopter but performed as an amphibious transport helicopter and was the first combat helicopter to engage in search-and-rescue operations during the war. It was built by Sikorsky. The helicopter saw action in Vietnam starting in 1967 from bases in Udorn, **Thailand**, and **Đà Nẵng**. The HH-3E had a crew of three, could carry two .50 caliber or 7.62-mm machine guns, and was equipped with self-sealing fuel tanks and armor for dangerous combat rescue missions such as the ones that took it into North Vietnamese territory. It had a rescue hoist and forest penetrator for difficult extractions. The Jolly Green Giant had a range of approximately 1,255 kilometers (780 miles) when equipped with external fuel tanks, and it had the ability to be refueled in flight. It had a cruising speed of 247 kilometers (154 miles) per hour and a payload capacity of over 10,000 kilograms (22,000 pounds). The U.S. **Navy** (USN) used the SH-3, a version of the HH-3, for search-and-rescue missions in the Gulf of Tŏn Kĭn and along the coast. The SH-3 carried a crew of four.

The OH-6 Cayuse was a light observation helicopter used in a variety of missions, including "**hunter-killer**" teams with the AH-1 Cobra. It was built by Hughes. The helicopter served as bait to draw gunfire, after which the Cobra would unleash its firepower on the exposed enemy. The helicopter had a crew of two and could carry either XM-72 7.62-mm machine guns or XM-75 grenade launchers. It had a cruising speed of 216 kilometers (134 miles) per hour and a range of 611 kilometers (380 miles). The Cayuse replaced the H-13 Sioux, which was built by Bell, early in the war. Other observation helicopters included the Hiller-built OH-23 Raven, whose use was minimal during the war, and the OH-58 Kiowa, also built by Bell, which entered service in Vietnam in May 1969.

Built by Boeing-Vertol, the CH-21 Shawnee, often called the Flying Banana because of its shape, was designed to serve in a variety of roles in Vietnam. It entered Southeast Asia in December 1961 and was used for search-and-rescue, medevac, and transport missions. The helicopter carried 22 equipped troops or 12 stretchers and attendants for a payload capacity of approximately 2,800 kilograms (6,250 pounds). It could be armed with either 7.62-mm or .50-inch machine guns mounted on the doors. The CH-21 had a maximum speed of 205 kilometers (127 miles) per hour. It was eventually replaced by the UH-1 Huey and the CH-47 Chinook, both of which were faster and had better range.

The CH-34 Choctaw, built by Sikorsky, served as a transport and general purpose helicopter for the U.S. Army during the war. It had a crew of two and could seat between 16 and 18 troops or 12 passengers. The helicopter had a maximum cruising speed of 156 kilometers (97 miles) per hour and a range of 397 kilometers (247 miles) and could carry approximately 2,700 kilograms (6,000 pounds) in addition to its equipment. The CH-34 was also used by the USN, designated the LH or SH Seabat depending on the mission, and by the USMC, designated the UH or VH Seahorse.

The CH-37 Mohave, sometimes known as the Deuce, was used by the USMC. It was built by Sikorsky. It was originally designed as a troop transport but was primarily used as a cargo transport. Only a limited number of the helicopters were built, and few were used in Vietnam.

The HH-43 Huskie was a heavily used helicopter during the war. It was built by Kaman. It had a crew of four, including one or two pilots—the second pilot for night and instrument flying—one or two firefighters, one medical technician, and the crew chief. The helicopter had a normal cruising speed of 177 kilometers (110 miles) per hour with a range of 804 kilometers (500 miles). The HH-43 was also equipped with a 217-foot jungle penetrator cable. The Huskie backed up the H-53 Jolly Green Giant in combat rescue missions and was also involved in crash fire-suppression missions. Two models of the Huskie flew in Southeast Asia: the B and the F. The models were similar, though the F model had more sophisticated communications equipment than the B model, as well as armor to protect the crew, and a maximum payload of between 1,760 and 1,800 kilograms (3,870–3,960 pounds).

The CH-46 Seaknight was a twin-engine medium-lift assault helicopter that moved troops for the USN and USMC. It was built by Boeing-Vertol. It could handle a crew of three and had room for 25 troops as well as 680 kilograms (1,500 pounds) of equipment, for a total capacity of approximately 5,900 kilograms (13,000 pounds). It also had a 4,500-kilogram (10,000-pound) capacity hook for external transport. With a cruising speed of between 236 and 249 kilometers (146–154 miles) per hour and a range of approximately 1,054 kilometers (655 miles), the Seaknight was a versatile helicopter that was used in a variety of missions during the war.

The CH-47 Chinook, built by Boeing-Vertol, served as a medium-lift helicopter for the U.S. Army. It had a crew of two and a payload capacity of 3,175 to 3,625 kilograms (7,000–8,000 pounds) depending on the terrain. The CH-47 arrived in Vietnam with the 1st Cavalry **Division** in 1965. It was armed with either one or two 7.62-mm M60 machine guns. The U.S. used three versions of the CH-47 during the war: models A, B, and C. The CH-47 had a maximum gross weight of approximately 20,800 kilograms (46,000 pounds), depending on the model. The helicopter carried a hoist and cargo hook when needed for carrying external loads, such as **artillery** for transport to isolated firebases or equipment recovery. The helicopter was heavily used during the war and was considered a reliable aircraft for transportation.

Built by Sikorsky, the CH-53 Sea Stallion served as a heavy assault transport helicopter for the USN and USMC in Southeast Asia. It carried a crew of three and could accommodate 37 equipped troops or 24 stretchers and four attendants, depending on the mission. The helicopter had a normal load capacity of approximately 9,000 kilograms (20,000 pounds), a normal cruising speed of 278 kilometers (173 miles) per hour, and a range of 869 kilometers (540 miles). In addition to transportation operations, the helicopter also participated in search-and-rescue operations.

The HH-53 Stallion or Buff, though commonly referred to as the Super Jolly Green Giant, was built by Sikorsky and served as a search-and-rescue helicopter in Aerospace Rescue and Recovery Squadrons during the war. It carried a crew of five: pilot, copilot, flight engineer, and two para-rescue personnel who were protected by armored plating. The HH-53B was armed with three 7.62-mm machine guns and was equipped with a 250-foot external hoist with a capacity of 9,000 kilograms (20,000 pounds). It could transport 38 fully equipped troops or 22 stretcher patients and four medical personnel, for a total of 8,400 kilograms (18,500 pounds). The helicopter was credited with many successful search-and-rescue missions during the war, including several dangerous missions deep in North Vietnamese territory to rescue downed pilots or prisoners of war.

The CH-54 Skycrane, also built by Sikorsky, served primarily as a heavy-lift crane helicopter, but it could also be modified for troop transport, minesweeping, recovery operations, and field hospital operations. It carried a pilot and copilot, with space for a third pilot who faced backward and controlled loading and unloading operations. The Skycrane had a cruising speed of 169 kilometers (105 miles) per hour, with a range of approximately 370 kilometers (230 miles). It was capable of lifting over 9,000 kilograms (20,000 pounds), but in 1971, a single CH-54B lifted over 18,000 kilograms

(40,000 pounds) in a test. The helicopter was also involved in the testing of BLU **bombs** and often carried the 10,000-pound version of the weapon in Commando Vault missions. *See also* ASSAULT HELICOPTER COMPANY; ASSAULT SUPPORT HELICOPTER COMPANY; DUSTOFF.

HELICOPTER VALLEY. Nickname for the Sông Ngàn Valley located in **Quảng Trị**. On 15 July 1966, during Operation Hastings, the **United States** attempted to engage the **People's Army of Vietnam** 324B Division, which was operating to the northwest of **Huế** across the **Demilitarized Zone**. At **Landing Zone** Crow, to the north of Camp Carroll and northeast of the **Rockpile**, three CH-46A **helicopters** collided with one another. This crash, plus the additional loss of a helicopter as a result of enemy gunfire, earned the valley its nickname.

HELMS, RICHARD MCGARRAH (1913–2002). Born in Pennsylvania and raised in New Jersey, Helms was educated in Switzerland and at Williams College. After college, he became a journalist and covered the 1936 Berlin Olympics for United Press and reported on Europe on the eve of World War II. During the war, Helms served in the **United States Navy** until 1943, when he joined the Office of Strategic Services (OSS) because of his knowledge of French and German, which he had learned while in Switzerland. He continued to work with the OSS and its successor, the **Central Intelligence Agency** (CIA). Helms was promoted to the position of deputy director for plans, which was involved in clandestine operations. He became the deputy director of central intelligence on 28 April 1965, where he remained until 30 June 1966 when he became the director of central intelligence until 1973. During his time in the CIA, Helms was involved in a number of significant and controversial events in American diplomatic history, including the Cuban Missile Crisis, the building of the Berlin Wall, the assassination of **Ngô Đình Diệm**, the Americanization of the Vietnam War, and the intensification of the Cold War.

Helms had a good working relationship with the other branches of government and the press, who considered him honest and professional. In 1973, Helms defied President **Richard M. Nixon**'s efforts to cover up the Watergate scandal, which enhanced Helms' reputation but also resulted in Nixon replacing him with James Rodney Schlesinger on 2 February 1973. Helms became the ambassador to Iran in 1973. In 1977, Helms was called to testify in front of the Senate Select Committee on Intelligence, where the role of the CIA in attempting to assassinate world leaders, including Fidel Castro of Cuba and President Salvador Allende of Chile, was publicized and condemned. Helms was also criticized by the Rockefeller Commission that was charged with investigating Watergate because he allegedly destroyed material that might have been beneficial to the investigation.

As a result of the multiple investigations, Helms resigned as ambassador and pleaded no contest to charges that he had lied to **Congress** in 1973 on the CIA's involvement in the assassination of Allende and the overthrow of the Chilean government. Helms was sentenced to two years in prison and a fine, but the sentence was suspended. He retired from public life after the resolution of the congressional issue and wrote his memoir, *A Look Over My Shoulder: A Life in the Central Intelligence Agency*, published in 2004 after his death.

HILSMAN, ROGER (1919–). Hilsman was educated at the **United States** Military Academy and graduated in 1943. During World War II, he was attached to the Office of Strategic Services after being wounded in battle a week into his service with Merrill's Marauders. He continued to work for that organization as it was transformed into the **Central Intelligence Agency** in 1947. Hilsman earned an MA in 1950 and a PhD in 1951 from Yale University, after which he served on the Joint American Military Advisory Group, London, and in the International Politics Branch, U.S. European Command Headquarters. In 1953, he returned to the U.S. and was employed by Princeton University, first at the Center for International Studies for a year, and then at the Woodrow Wilson School for an additional year. Between 1956 and 1958, he worked for the Foreign Affairs Division of the Legislative Reference Service in the Library of Congress and then returned to academia until 1961.

Hilsman became the director of the Bureau of Intelligence and Research in the Department of State on 19 February 1961 until he was promoted to assistant secretary of state for far eastern affairs on 25 April 1963. He remained in that position until 14 March 1964. Hilsman supported the political war in the **Republic of Vietnam** (RVN) and was an advocate of the **Strategic Hamlet Program**. The failure of the program and the 1963 Buddhist Crisis caused Hilsman to become disenchanted with **Ngô Đình Diệm** and his brother **Ngô Đình Nhu**. As the assistant secretary of state for far eastern affairs, Hilsman was one of the principal architects of the infamous 24 August 1963 telegram to the U.S. ambassador to the RVN, **Henry Cabot Lodge Jr.**, which authorized him to sound out the likelihood of a coup d'état against Ngô Đình Diệm.

The telegram had the approval of Secretary of State **Dean Rusk** and Secretary of Defense **Robert McNamara**, though that approval was questionably obtained by Hilsman. Lodge's initial actions upon receiving the telegram set in motion the events that would eventually lead to the 1 November 1963 coup d'état that toppled the **Sài Gòn** government. Hilsman returned to academia again as a professor of the Institute of War and Peace Studies at Columbia

University. He has published 11 books on foreign policy and politics, including the 1967 work, *To Move a Nation: The Politics of Foreign Policy in the Administration of John F. Kennedy*, that established the argument that President **John F. Kennedy** would have withdrawn American troops from Southeast Asia had he not been assassinated in November 1963.

HMONG. A large mountain tribe that was located in the northern section of **Laos** during the war. Hmong were sought after during the war by the North Vietnamese and **Pathet Lao**, as well as by the Royal Laotian Government and the **United States**. The U.S. helped, through the **Central Intelligence Agency** and other private means, to fund a large army made up of mostly Hmong under the leadership of **Vang Pao**. This group conducted operations against the **Hồ Chí Minh Trail**. Because the U.S. fought a secret war in Laos in order to stave off accusations of violations of the 1954 **Geneva Agreements** and the 1962 **Geneva Accords**, it was never able to publicize its role with the Hmong.

The plight of the Hmong was exposed by Dr. Thomas Dooley in his firsthand account of his time in Laos, titled *The Night They Burned the Mountain*. Dooley provided many Americans with their only understanding of the Hmong people and their culture. It was estimated that nearly 12,000 Hmong were killed in combat during the war. When the Pathet Lao assumed control of Vientiane, many of the Hmong fled to escape persecution for their wartime alliance against the communists. Large groups immigrated to the U.S., **Australia**, **France**, and **Thailand**. Those Hmong who did not flee resisted the Pathet Lao and the Socialist **Republic of Vietnam** but were not strong enough to effect change. *See also* MONTAGNARDS; REFUGEES.

HỒ CHÍ MINH (1890–1969). Hồ Chí Minh was born Nguyễn Sinh Cung in Hoàng Trù village and grew up in Nghệ An province in the northern part of Vietnam. His father, an ardent nationalist and anti-French spokesman, influenced Hồ Chí Minh in his early life. He changed his name to Nguyễn Tất Thành and was educated at the Quốc Học in **Huế** but left school either for anticolonial activities or because of a poor academic record. In 1911, Hồ Chí Minh left Vietnam aboard a French ocean liner and worked as a cook's apprentice. He traveled to the **United States**, London, and Paris, arriving in the capital of **France** toward the end of World War I, where he experienced firsthand the devastating effects of that war and underwent a reevaluation of his views of the West.

In Paris, Hồ Chí Minh changed his name to Nguyễn Ái Quốc (Nguyễn the Patriot) and submitted a proposal for Vietnamese independence from France to Woodrow Wilson who had argued for self-determination at the

Versailles Conference in 1919. Rebuffed by Wilson, Hồ Chí Minh helped found the French Communist Party in 1920 and became an expert on colonial issues. He received additional training and indoctrination in Moscow in 1923 and attended the 5th Communist International in June 1924 before being sent to China later that year, where he organized the Viêt Nam Thanh Niên Cach Mênh Dông Chi Hôi (Revolutionary Youth League of Vietnam). This organization would later become the foundation for the Indochinese Communist Party. In 1931, Hồ Chí Minh began a decade of travel, preaching the communist ideology and publicizing the Indochinese plight under French colonialism.

Hồ Chí Minh returned to Vietnam in 1941 and helped to organize the Viêt Nam Độc Lập Đồng Minh Hôi (League for the Independence of Vietnam), commonly referred to as the **Việt Minh**. He used the Việt Minh to rally support against the French and sided with the U.S., specifically personnel from the Office of Strategic Services, to provide intelligence on the Japanese Armed Forces occupying Indochina and to rescue downed pilots. In addition to making contact with the Americans, Hồ Chí Minh was arrested by the Nationalist Chinese because of his communist connections when he traveled to China. After his return to Vietnam in 1942, he nearly died from malaria and dysentery. As the war ended, Hồ Chí Minh made plans to proclaim Vietnam's independence from the French. In August 1945, he and the Việt Minh led a revolution culminating in the proclamation of the **Democratic Republic of Vietnam** (DRV) on 2 September 1945. It was around this time that he took on the pseudonym Hồ Chí Minh.

The French refused to recognize the new country even though Hồ Chí Minh was able to convince Vietnamese emperor **Bảo Đại** to abdicate, and the Vietnamese people clearly supported the move. Hồ Chí Minh and his military leader, **Võ Nguyên Giáp**, began to consolidate their power in the North as the French started to return to Indochina. After a failed French attempt to peacefully restore control of Indochina using Nationalist Chinese and British troops, Hồ Chí Minh and Võ Nguyên Giáp led the Việt Minh against the French, starting the nearly nine-year **First Indochina War**. In 1954, after the defeat of the French at **Điện Biên Phủ** and the **Geneva Agreements**, Hồ Chí Minh moved closer to his dream of an independent Vietnam, free of foreign interference. His communist background and the fear of a communist takeover of Southeast Asia, made more intense after the 1949 fall of China to communism, made this dream unrealistic.

The U.S. and the newly formed **Republic of Vietnam** worked against Hồ Chí Minh's vision of the DRV ruling over all of Vietnam. Hồ Chí Minh continued to lead his party and people in the **Second Indochina War**, which resulted in the Americanization of the war in 1965. He remained as president and leader of the Communist Party though many of the day-to-day activities of running the DRV and the war fell to others within the party.

After 1965, there was much speculation about Hồ Chí Minh's health. By this time, he was in his 70s and was relegated to public appearances to bolster the morale of the Vietnamese people who had to endure the U.S. bombing as well as the escalation of the war in the South, which was beginning to take a growing portion of the DRVs away. Hồ Chí Minh continued to meet with prominent leaders and visiting media but refrained from discussing politics. Because he did not meet with all of the important visitors to Hà Nội in the waning years of his life, it was believed that Hồ Chí Minh was not always lucid, though this too became a controversial point. He worked to maintain his image as "Uncle Hồ" and left the day-to-day decisions to the younger members of the Vietnamese Communist Party.

Hồ Chí Minh died on 2 September 1969. Until his death, he remained the most popular individual in the DRV and continues today to be held up by the Communist Party and those who fought for Vietnamese independence as the model all should emulate. He was often referred to as Bác Hồ (Uncle Hồ) to reinforce his image as a man of the people, a mythology he helped to create and maintain during his time after World War II. When the North Vietnamese overran **Sài Gòn** in April 1975, the South Vietnamese capital was renamed Hồ Chí Minh City.

HỒ CHÍ MINH CITY. Name given to the former capital of the **Republic of Vietnam** (RVN), **Sài Gòn**, after it fell to the North Vietnamese on 30 April 1975. The city was renamed in honor of Hồ Chí Minh, the political leader of the **Democratic Republic of Vietnam** from its founding until his death on 2 September 1969. Former leaders and residents of the RVN found the name change insulting. It also served as a reminder that the country may have been reunified, but the North Vietnamese controlled their future. Many of the residents of Hồ Chí Minh City continued to refer to it as Sài Gòn, while such things as intercity buses and the international airport designation still use the old name.

HỒ CHÍ MINH TRAIL. A system of paths and roads that was used by the North Vietnamese to support the war in the South. The Hồ Chí Minh Trail started in the **Democratic Republic of Vietnam** and traveled through **Laos** and **Cambodia** before exiting in the **Republic of Vietnam**. While the trail was heavily used after 1959, it had been established during the Japanese occupation in World War II from traditional pathways used by the local population. It was slowly expanded during the **First Indochina War**. It was not until the creation of the **559th Transport Group** in 1959 that the Hồ Chí

Minh Trail took on a greater importance in the northern strategy to defeat the **Sài Gòn** government.

The Americanization of the war in 1965 changed the significance of the trail to North Vietnamese strategy as the **United States** focused on interdiction. Operation **Market Time** effectively shut off the sea routes and forced the North Vietnamese to find alternative ways to support the war in the South. This action resulted in the North Vietnamese expanding the trail and devoting more resources to keep up the flow of personnel and materials. Throughout the 1960s and early 1970s, the trail evolved from a series of paths, roads, and makeshift shelters to paved roads, of varying degree, under cover of the canopy jungle, with all of the amenities necessary for making the trip.

The U.S. initiated a series of air campaigns, such as **Steel Tiger**, **Tiger Hound**, and **Commando Hunt**, designed to cut the trail, making the area one of the most heavily **bombed** in the 20th century. In order to interdict the trail, the U.S. also experimented with weather modification projects such as **Popeye**, electronic sensors in operations like **Igloo White**, and defoliation. While U.S. efforts caused the North Vietnamese to allocate more and more resources to the trail, the U.S. was never able to effectively cut the supply line.

HỒ TẤN QUYỀN (1927–1963). Hồ Tấn Quyền was a loyal supporter of **Ngô Đình Diệm** who served as the commander of the **Republic of Vietnam Navy** from 1959 to 1963. During the abortive coup d'état on 11 November 1960, Hồ Tấn Quyền led a company of Vietnamese **Marines** to the presidential palace to defend Ngô Đình Diệm. He also came to Ngô Đình Diệm's defense during the 27 February 1962 air force attacks against the presidential palace. During the 1 November 1963 coup d'état, Hồ Tấn Quyền, while driving toward **Sài Gòn** along the **Biên Hòa** highway, was assassinated by his junior officers, Trương Ngọc Lực and Nguyễn Kim Hương Giang, because of his loyalty to Ngô Đình Diệm and the fear that he would rally pro-government forces against the coup plotters.

HÒA HẢO. Founded by **Huỳnh Phú Sổ** in 1939 while on a pilgrimage to the sacred mountains of That Son and Ta Lon near the Cambodian border, the Hòa Hảo has its roots in **Buddhist** philosophy but concentrates on the individual peasant and revolves around home life and the village rather than rituals, rites, and structures. The Hòa Hảo opposed the **Việt Minh** during World War II because of their anticommunist views. During Bảo Đại's reign, the Hòa Hảo gained a degree of autonomy in return for support of the emperor. It created an army to help manage affairs, and after **Ngô Đình Diệm** returned to Vietnam in 1954, it began to oppose his attempts to re-exert authority in their territory.

In April 1955, the Hòa Hảo joined the **Bình Xuyên** to form the United Front of Nationalist Forces. On 20 April, they conspired to overthrow Ngô Đình Diệm. Ngô Đình Diệm, however, had split the front through cajoling and bribery, and after defeating the Bình Xuyên in **Sài Gòn**, he decimated the remnants of the Hòa Hảo army and publicly executed its leader, Lê Quang Vinh, known as Ba Cụt, in July 1956. The Hòa Hảo split between support for Ngô Đình Diệm and the communist insurgency, though more would later join the **National Liberation Front**. *See also* CARAVELLE MANIFESTO.

HOÀNG MINH THẢO (1921–2008). People's Army of Vietnam (PAVN) general. Hoàng Minh Thảo, who was born Tạ Thái An, was raised in the Tõn Kĭn region of French Indochina. He studied military science in China and was considered one of the better PAVN generals. He commanded the 304th PAVN Division from 1950 to 1953 during the **First Indochina War** and served as the deputy commander, then commander, of **Front** B3, which included the **Central Highlands** in the **Republic of Vietnam** (RVN), from 1966 to 1974. In August 1974, he commanded **Military Region** 5 and then returned to Front B3 for the final offensive against the RVN in March 1975. He commanded the attack against Buôn Mê Thuột that resulted in the South Vietnamese abandonment of the Central Highlands, and he led the flank attack from Phan Rang province against **Sài Gòn**.

Hoàng Minh Thảo was a member of the Vietnamese Communist Party for 63 years and was with the PAVN for 51 years. He was a highly decorated general, awarded the Hồ Chí Minh Order, the Independence Order First Class, the Military Order First Class, and party badges for 40 to 60 years of service. He authored several books on military strategy and, after the war, was involved in training the Socialist Republic of Vietnam's military commanders. He was in charge of the Infantry Institute, and in 1990 he became the rector of the Military Strategy Institute.

HOÀNG VĂN THÁI (1915–1986). People's Army of Vietnam (PAVN) general. Born Hoàng Văn Xiêm in Thái Bình province in the **Red River Delta**, Hoàng Văn Thái joined the Indochinese Communist Party in 1938. He fought with the Vietnamese nationalists against the Japanese during World War II and was one of the original members who oversaw the establishment of the PAVN. In 1945, he served as the first chief of staff for the PAVN and was closely allied with **Võ Nguyên Giáp**. He was replaced by **Văn Tiến Dũng** in November 1953. During the Battle of **Điện Biên Phủ**, Hoàng Văn Thái served as a special chief of staff to Võ Nguyên Giáp. Between 1960 and 1965, he held the position of cochairman of the Committee for Physical Training and Sports, which was involved in military training, and in 1966 he served briefly as the commander of **Military Region 5**. In 1967, he was assigned to the **Central Office for South Vietnam** and served as the commander of the People's Liberation Army. He remained in that position until 1973. In April 1974, he was promoted to the rank of lieutenant general and again served as the deputy chief of staff until 1981.

HOÀNG VĂN THÁI (1920–2000). People's Army of Vietnam (PAVN) general. Hoàng Văn Thái was born Huỳnh Đức Tui in **Quảng Nam**. He joined the Indochinese Communist Party toward the end of World War II and was involved in the May 1945 demonstration in Thuận Lí that served as a catalyst for the **Việt Minh** takeover of Quảng Bình province. He enlisted in the Việt Minh in 1947 and served with the 325th Division in a variety of positions, including the political commissar of Regiment 101 during its operations in **Laos** during the **First Indochina War**.

In December 1962, he became the deputy political commissar for Military Zone 4. In January 1965, he was promoted to the position of vice chairman for logistics, and in that capacity he commanded the **559th Transport Group** that had developed the **Hồ Chí Minh Trail** through Laos and **Cambodia**. In 1969, he remained involved with the 559th Transport Group as its deputy commander and also became the deputy commander and head of logistics for the Trị Triên Military Region. In 1972, he added the responsibility of the vice chairman for the Ministry of General Logistics. He remained in all of these positions until 1974, when he became the commander of the newly organized 2nd PAVN Corps. After the war, Hoàng Văn Thái served as the vice chairman for State Engineering and as the acting chair of that organization from 1986 to 1989.

HOÀNG XUÂN LÃM (1928–). Army of the Republic of Vietnam (ARVN) general, corps and **Corps Tactical Zone** (CTZ) commander. Hoàng Xuân Lãm served in the Vietnam National Army during the **First Indochina War**. He began as an armored platoon leader in the 1st Armored Company and rose in rank to commander of the 4th Armored Company by the 1954 **Geneva Agreements**. Hoàng Xuân Lãm commanded the Armored Cavalry Training Center at the Thủ Đức Reserve Officers' School from 1955 to 1957, as well as serving as armor officer for the 1st Military Region and as commander of the Armor Cavalry. In 1957, he was promoted to chief of the Armor Branch on the Joint General Staff until he assumed the position of director of instruction and chief of arms and services at the Command and Staff School in **Đà Lạt** in 1960.

He took over the 23rd ARVN Infantry Division in 1963 and transferred to the 2nd ARVN Infantry Division in 1964. In 1966, Hoàng Xuân Lãm was raised to the rank of commander of I Army Corps and I CTZ, and he also served as the government delegate to Central Vietnam's Coastal Area. Hoàng Xuân Lãm oversaw the 1971 Operation Lam Sơn 719 that ended in disaster for the South Vietnamese, and he was eventually replaced as commander of I Corps and I CTZ during the 1972 **Easter Offensive** when he proved unable to stem the North Vietnamese tide. **Republic of Vietnam** president **Nguyễn Văn Thiệu** promoted him to minister of defense in part because of his allegiance to the president, though he did not escape severe criticism from his fellow ARVN officers for his inaction during the opening days of the offensive.

HỒI CHÁNH. Name given to Vietnamese individuals who defected from the **National Liberation Front** (NLF) to the **Republic of Vietnam** (RVN) under the **Chiêu Hồi** program. These individuals sometimes served in the RVN Armed Forces or as **Kit Carson Scouts** for the **United States** military. There were an estimated 40,000 to 60,000 individuals who became Hồi Chánh, though critics of the program and the war argued that many simply returned to the NLF or worked as double agents.

HOTFOOT, PROJECT. Starting in July 1959, a mobile training team from the 77th **Special Forces** Group started to train personnel from the Royal Laotian Army (RLA) in what would become known as Project Hotfoot. The Special Forces personnel involved in the project were **sheep dipped**, which was the process of having them resign their commission in the **United States Army** to become civilians, since it was illegal to have uniformed Americans in neutral **Laos**. The U.S. justified Hotfoot personnel as a counter to the assistance provided to the communist insurgency, the **Pathet Lao**, by the **Democratic Republic of Vietnam**. In 1961, the project was renamed Monkhood and was again changed in April 1961 to project **White Star** when the U.S. organized the Military Assistance Command, Laos, and determined that it was acceptable to acknowledge that it had military **advisers** assisting the RLA in violation of the 1954 **Geneva Agreements**. *See also* CENTRAL INTELLIGENCE AGENCY.

HOTSPOT. Technique introduced into northern **Laos** in 1970, based on the **Combat Skyspot** model used during **Rolling Thunder**, to increase the accuracy of air strike missions against the **People's Army of Vietnam** and **Pathet Lao**. Hotspot utilized radar to guide air **sorties** to their target and then assisted with the timing for **bomb** release. Hotspot had many problems in the early stages, such as antenna site problems and poor mapping, but during the wet season, with the continuous and low cloud cover, it was the most effective way of targeting the enemy.

HRÊ. An ethnic minority tribe that was one of many that made up the **Montagnard** people. The tribe was located in the provinces of Bình Định and Quảng Ngãi and spoke the Mon-**Khmer** language. The Hrê allied with the **United States** Armed Forces, though their numbers were small.

HUÉ. A city that became the original imperial capital of Vietnam during the Nguyễn Dynasty from 1802 to 1945 when Emperor Gia Long consolidated his power with the help of the French over the feuding powers that had been engaged in civil war. Huế is located on the Perfume River (Sông Hương) in **Thừa Thiên** province in I **Corps Tactical Zone** (CTZ). In 1945, Huế ceased to be the capital of Vietnam when the **Việt Minh** established **Hà Nội** as its capital. In 1949, when **Bảo Đại** reestablished the State of Vietnam, **Sài Gòn** was chosen as the capital over Huế.

Huế played a major role in military and political affairs during the **First Indochina War** and the **Second Indochina War**. In the summer of 1963, it was at the center of the **Buddhist Crisis** that eventually led to the coup d'état against **Ngô Đình Diệm** in November 1963. A similar Buddhist Crisis in 1966 used Huế as a rallying point. Huế was also the scene of intense fighting during the 1968 **Tết Offensive**, which resulted in a prolonged struggle for the citadel and the massacre of over 3,000 Vietnamese who had been targeted because of their loyalty to the Sài Gòn government.

Huế continued to be a focal point in the post-1968 Tết Offensive as the fighting in I CTZ intensified. After the January 1973 **Paris Peace Accords**, **Republic of Vietnam** (RVN) president **Nguyễn Văn Thiệu** made the defense of Huế a priority until March 1975, when it became clear that the **Army of the Republic of Vietnam** would not be able to hold I CTZ against the advance of the **People's Army of Vietnam** (PAVN). When **RVN Marines** evacuated **Quảng Trị** to the north of Huế, the civilian population panicked and flooded into the former imperial capital, making it indefensible. Huế was abandoned on 24 March 1975 and was occupied by the PAVN on 26 March. *See also* HUÉ MASSACRE.

HUÉ MASSACRE. During the 1968 **Tết Offensive**, the **National Liberation Front** (NLF) attacked the ancient imperial city of **Huế** among many other targets. In Huế, the NLF focused on control of the citadel, the old imperial palace with high, thick walls, which bordered the Perfume River and covered approximately 5.18 square kilometers (2 square miles). On 31 January, the first day of the offensive, the NLF took over most of the citadel and parts of the city. They entered the city with lists of individuals who were targeted for assassination. During the course of the battle for the city, the NLF rounded up and killed an estimated 3,000 Vietnamese in what became known as the Huế Massacre. The victims of the massacre were buried in shallow mass graves, which were discovered by the Vietnamese and Americans after the city and citadel were recaptured at the end of February. *See also* TRẦN VĂN QUANG.

HUMPHREY, HUBERT HORATIO, JR. (1911–1978). Democratic senator for Minnesota, vice president, and presidential candidate. Humphrey was a stalwart supporter of the **John F. Kennedy** and **Lyndon B. Johnson** administrations' Vietnam policy. He joined the Johnson ticket for the 1964 presidential election and took the oath of office on 20 January 1965. Despite some private disagreements about the decision to Americanize the war, Humphrey publicly supported President Lyndon B. Johnson's decisions to escalate the war. This caused many within the Democratic Party to turn against Humphrey as they lost faith in Johnson. When Johnson announced his March 1968 decision not to seek or accept his party's nomination for the presidency, Humphrey became the party's choice when he announced his candidacy in April.

He faced a serious challenge from **antiwar** candidates Senator **Eugene McCarthy** of Minnesota and Senator **Robert Kennedy** of New York. During the Democratic Party nominating process, Humphrey was plagued by the antiwar movement and his close ties to Johnson. A series of events, including the assassination of Kennedy, antiwar demonstrations, riots surrounding the Democratic National Convention in Chicago, and the addition of southern Democrat and former Alabama governor George Wallace as a third candidate tainted Humphrey's run at the presidency after he won his party's nomination. Humphrey lost the election to **Richard M. Nixon**. After the failed election, Humphrey returned to Minnesota and taught at Macalester College and at the University of Minnesota before being reelected to the Senate in 1970, where he served until his death on 13 January 1978.

HUNTER-KILLER. Technique developed by the **United States** to expose and eliminate the enemy. Of the variety of combinations utilized in this tactic, the most common was for an OV-1 aircraft to play the role of the hunter, seeking targets of opportunity with the use of side-looking airborne radar or infrared heat-detecting devices. Once identified, the OV-1 directed gunships to the target to act as the killer.

HUỲNH PHÚ SỔ (1919–1947). Founder of the **Hòa Hảo**, who was sometimes referred to as Phật Thầy. Huỳnh Phú Sổ trained with a mystic in Núi Cấm and became a religious leader after a spontaneous, miraculous cure of an illness in May 1939. Huỳnh Phú Sổ organized his teaching to appeal to peasants. He offered a simple religion void of ceremonies and strict doctrines. His teachings, combined with his nationalist zeal, earned Huỳnh Phú Sổ trouble with the French. This anti-French position, and a series of correct predictions, earned him the following of thousands of Vietnamese. **France** responded to Hòa Hảo's growing power by exiling him to **Laos** in 1942. He was returned to **Sài Gòn** by the Japanese in 1945 but was kept under control until the end of the war.

Huỳnh Phú Sổ's Hòa Hảo not only gained adherents but also organized a militia that confronted the French. The Hòa Hảo, however, did not follow the **Việt Minh**, and the two armies clashed in the immediate post–World War II period. Throughout the early **First Indochina War**, the Việt Minh failed to gain an alliance with the Hòa Hảo, and the two factions targeted each other's members for execution. Because of Hòa Hảo's obstinacy toward the Việt Minh, Huỳnh Phú Sổ became a liability to the communist insurgents. He was captured in April 1947 and executed.

HUỲNH TẤN PHÁT (1913–1989). Huỳnh Tấn Phát earned his degree in architecture from **Hà Nội** University in the 1930s. He started active participation in anti-French activities in 1936 and edited the journal *Jeunesse*, an anti-French publication. He also was one of the founders of the Vanguard Youth movement. During the August 1945 revolution, Huỳnh Tấn Phát joined the fighting in **Sài Gòn** and was arrested for the first of many times, which ultimately forced him to go into hiding in 1949. He served with the **Việt Minh** as the director of the Information Service and on the Resistance and Administrative Committees in Sài Gòn.

At the end of the **First Indochina War**, he set up practice as an architect, though he remained a member of the insurgency. He was forced to go into hiding again in 1959 as a result of **Ngô Đình Diệm**'s anticommunist policies and later joined the Central Committee of the **National Liberation Front** (NLF). He would hold the office of secretary general and vice chairman of the Presidium within the NLF. In 1968, he became the chairman of the Alliance of National Democratic and Peace Forces, an organization created and supported by Hà Nội to help destabilize southern politics. In June 1969, Huỳnh Tấn Phát was elected the president of the **Provisional Revolutionary Government of the Republic of South Vietnam** until its dissolution in 1976. After the war, he became a vice premier, and in 1982 he served as the vice chairman of the Council of State. He was one of the few individuals from the South to hold a position of power in the Socialist **Republic of Vietnam** and within the Vietnamese Communist Party.

HUỲNH VĂN CAO (1927–). Army of the Republic of Vietnam (ARVN) general and **Republic of Vietnam** (RVN) senator. Huỳnh Văn Cao was born and educated in **Huế**. He graduated from the Army Officer School in Huế in 1950 and became a platoon leader until his promotion to commander in 1951. After completing the Command and Tactics School in **Hà Nội** in 1952, he served as a battalion commander until the end of the **First Indochina War**. Between 1955 and 1957, Huỳnh Văn Cao served as the chief of the Special Staff for **Ngô Đình Diệm**. He assumed the position of commander of the ARVN 13th Division in 1957, and after graduating from the Command and General Staff College in the **United States** in 1958, he took over the 7th ARVN Division and the Tiền Giang Tactical Zone. He served in this command between 1959 and 1962.

Huỳnh Văn Cao supported Ngô Đình Diệm and in December 1962 was given command of IV **Corps Tactical Zone** (CTZ) and was promoted to brigadier general in order to control ARVN troops loyal to the **Sài Gòn** government. After the November 1963 coup d'état against Ngô Đình Diệm, Huỳnh Văn Cao was dismissed from command, though he would become the chief negotiator for the Vietnamese delegation during its meetings with Cambodian representatives on the border disputes between the two countries. On 4 May 1964, he was chosen to become the general commissioner for the Popular Complaints and Suggestions Office, and in 1965 he was promoted to chief of the General Political Warfare Department.

Huỳnh Văn Cao tried to stay away from the rivalry that existed between factions that supported **Nguyễn Cao Kỳ** or **Nguyễn Văn Thiệu** and was rewarded for his efforts with the brief command of the I CTZ during the March 1966 **Buddhist** uprising. He was accused of supporting the Buddhists during the crisis and was forced to resign from the military as a major general. In 1967, Huỳnh Văn Cao entered politics and was elected as a senator representing the Social Democrat Bloc in the 1967 national elections. He served as the chairman of the Foreign Affairs and Information Committee, and after his reelection in 1970, he became the first deputy chairman until 1971. He served in the Senate until the fall of the RVN in April 1975 and spent 12 years in prison after the war. He immigrated to the U.S. in 1990. *See also* VANN, JOHN PAUL.

IA ĐRĂNG VALLEY, BATTLE FOR. First large-scale battle in the American war, which pitted units from the **United States Army** against the **People's Army of Vietnam** (PAVN) and lasted between 14 and 18 November 1965. The battle was part of a larger U.S. campaign to rid the **Central Highlands** of the PAVN and **National Liberation Front**, which had been steadily infiltrating into the region since 1964, culminating in an attack of the **Special Forces** camp at Plei Me on 19 October 1965. As a result of the attack and the need to test the newly developed **airmobility** tactics that had been designed to seize the initiative from the enemy, the U.S. decided to pursue the Plei Me attackers who had moved south and west of **Plei Ku**. On 14 November 1965, the 1st Battalion, 7th Cavalry was airlifted to an area near the Ia Đrăng River next to Chư Pơng mountains, about 22.5 kilometers (14 miles) to the northwest of Plei Me at a place designated **Landing Zone** (LZ) X-Ray.

At a little before 11:00 a.m., the leading elements of the battalion arrived and took up a defensive position while more troops were moved in by **helicopter**. The PAVN began attacking around 1:00 p.m., causing significant **casualties** on both sides as the U.S. force was caught with only a portion of its personnel on the ground. As the day progressed, the remainder of the U.S. force was put into the field as PAVN units attacked repeatedly in heavy frontal assaults. As evening approached, leading elements of the 2nd Battalion, 7th Cavalry began to arrive at the battle and reinforced the 1st Battalion. The PAVN probed the American lines but only assaulted one platoon that had been separated from the rest of the U.S. troops very early in the battle.

Fighting resumed the next morning with additional frontal assaults by the PAVN that risked overrunning the American position. The commander in the field, Colonel Hal Moore, transmitted a "Broken Arrow" message that called in airstrikes on the American position that had been infiltrated with PAVN soldiers. The airstrikes and concentrated fire from **artillery**, along with the stubborn defense by the units of the 7th Cavalry, finally forced the PAVN to withdraw from the field of battle around 10:00 a.m. The 2nd Battalion, 5th Cavalry reinforced the American position, and the units received only snipers and sporadic fire from the PAVN position for the rest of the day. On the morning of 16 November, the PAVN launched additional attacks but were beaten off with well-placed artillery and a stronger defensive position.

The PAVN withdrew completely from the battlefield after these attacks. By the end of the battle at LZ X-Ray, the U.S. had suffered 85 killed-in-action and 121 wounded. With LZ X-Ray secured, the U.S. began to withdraw its troops from the area the next day. What was left of the 1st Battalion was airlifted out on 16 November, and the 2nd Battalions of the 5th and 7th Cavalry moved overland to a new LZ, designated Albany, on 17 November while B-52s bombed the Chu Pong mountains.

After the lead elements of the U.S. troops reached LZ Albany, the PAVN ambushed the column, which had been spread out during the march, causing significant **casualties** to the American force. American air and artillery power were once again brought into the battle, as was a portion of the 1st Battalion, 5th Cavalry, in order to stabilize the situation, but the ambush had severely bloodied the U.S. force, which lost 155 killed-in-action and 124 wounded. Many of the Americans killed had been wounded on the field and shot by PAVN soldiers. The U.S. military considered the Battle of the Ia Đrăng Valley a success. The Americans controlled the battlefield at the end of the day, they had demonstrated the effectiveness of air and artillery power against the PAVN, and they had killed a significant number more of the enemy than the U.S. had lost. The estimated numbered of PAVN killed was around 1,000.

The battle served as a model for future engagements that would rely on firepower and mobility to keep the enemy off balance and cause damage when they chose to fight. For the PAVN, the battle was a reminder that the U.S. possessed superior firepower, and it reinforced the notion that direct, prolonged exposure in firefights was not a sound strategy. The PAVN would allow few such instances until the 1968 **Tết Offensive.**

IGLOO WHITE. United States program connected to the **McNamara Line** that was developed to enhance reconnaissance efforts and gather **intelligence** on the personnel and supplies moving down the **Hồ Chí Minh Trail.** Igloo White experimented with sensors to detect movement down the trail. The sensors transmitted their data to the Infiltration Surveillance Center where it was analyzed and used to direct aircraft to intercept and destroy the targets of opportunity. The program was initiated at the beginning of 1968 and lasted until the end of 1972. *See also* COMMANDO HUNT, OPERATION.

INDIA. At the end of the **First Indochina War,** India joined the **International Control Commission** (ICC), which was responsible for enforcing the 1954 **Geneva Agreements. Canada** represented the West, and Poland supported the East, while the Indian delegation spoke for the neutral nations and often served as the deciding vote in matters brought to the ICC. The ICC proved to be ineffective in the 1950s while India, which engaged in a border skirmish with the People's Republic of China in 1962, moved toward the Canadian position. This pro-West position did not help the **United States** or the **Republic of Vietnam** (RVN) because, by this time, neither side of the conflict paid much attention to the work of the ICC.

When the U.S. began to escalate its involvement in Southeast Asia after 1965, India continued to remain neutral, though its leaders voiced opposition to Operation **Rolling Thunder** and to the perceived indiscriminate **bombing** of civilian populations in the **Democratic Republic of Vietnam**. India was also critical of the **search-and-destroy** missions in the RVN that often negatively affected civilians caught up in the war. In 1971, India played a significant role in the formation of an independent Bangladesh. When the U.S. supported Pakistan in that struggle, the Indian government moved closer to the communist bloc, and as a result its support for the DRV increased as its anti-American rhetoric intensified. India continued to play a role in the ineffectual ICC until it was disbanded as a result of the January 1973 **Paris Peace Accords**. It did not participate in the **International Commission of Control and Supervision** that oversaw compliance with that agreement.

INTELLIGENCE. Intelligence played a major role in the Vietnam War. For the **United States**, the need for accurate and up-to-date intelligence on the activities of the **People's Army of Vietnam** (PAVN) and the **National Liberation Front** (NLF) was critical to the success of its strategy and tactical operations. The U.S. gathered its intelligence in a number of different ways. Because of the **topography** and **climate** of Vietnam, air reconnaissance offered the easiest way to collect information, though the PAVN and NLF were able to overcome this American technological advantage by going underground. The U.S. also engaged in numerous ground-based operations to gather intelligence on the movements of the enemy. While U.S. intelligence efforts depended more upon technology, the **Democratic Republic of Vietnam** (DRV) relied on human intelligence.

In October 1961, the U.S. used an air show in **Sài Gòn** as cover to send four RF-101 aircraft to conduct air **reconnaissance** missions. After the air show was over, the RF-101 aircraft remained in the Republic of Vietnam and, under project **Pipe Stem**, began photographing evidence of Soviet assistance to the **Pathet Lao** in northern **Laos**. Pipe Stem was followed by Project **Able Marble**, which conducted similar missions from **Thailand** and Sài Gòn. In May 1964, the U.S. conducted air reconnaissance over southern Laos to detect PAVN and NLF movement in the area that would become the **Hồ Chí**

Minh Trail. This mission, known as **Yankee Team**, eventually evolved into Operation **Barrel Roll**.

Other examples of air reconnaissance missions included **Blue Tree** missions, which were associated with Operation **Rolling Thunder** and involved gathering information about the bombing damage done by air **sorties**. The U.S. used aircraft throughout Southeast Asia to gather intelligence on the disposition of the PAVN and NLF forces. The U.S. also used air reconnaissance to gather information about POW camps in the DRV. Under Operation **Kingpin** in May 1970, the U.S. learned of the camp at **Sơn Tây**, to the west of **Hà Nội**, and attempted to raid the camp to release the prisoners. Though the raid was not successful, it did demonstrate the importance of intelligence-gathering operations in the war.

The U.S. also used unmanned **drones** in air reconnaissance missions over the DRV and Laos in **Buffalo Hunter** missions. The drones were launched from modified DC-130 aircraft. The U.S. **Navy** developed its own drone program known as Belfry Express between 1969 and 1970. Drone photography provided intelligence that allowed the U.S. to make more informed decisions about whether to bomb or rebomb targets over the DRV and Laos in areas that were heavily defended against air attack.

The U.S. also engaged in electronic intelligence missions against the DRV from the sea in **Desoto Patrols**. These missions usually consisted of a single destroyer advancing deep into the contested waters off the coast of the DRV in order to activate the electronic defense systems. The destroyer would then gather as much information as possible from this electronic data to use for further operations, including South Vietnamese **OPLAN 34A** missions designed to take the war to the North. Technology played a key role in intelligence gathering whether on land, in the air, or on the sea.

The U.S. relied on technology to locate and destroy PAVN and NLF forces. In addition to various forms of radar, the U.S. experimented with the "sniffer," a sensor that detected ammonium and other chemicals that indicated human habitation. The sniffer was placed in a helicopter that would fly over an area of suspected PAVN or NLF activity. When a positive reading was detected, the area was marked for either artillery or air strikes. The U.S. also experimented with sensors designed to detect movement through vibration. In Operation **Igloo White**, a program connected to the **McNamara Line** lasting from 1968 to 1972, the U.S. dropped sensors along the Hồ Chí Minh Trail that transmitted data to the Infiltration Surveillance Center. When the sensors indicated activity, air strikes were sent to intercept and destroy the targets of opportunity.

The U.S. developed a number of ground programs to gather intelligence on PAVN and NLF movement. In April 1962, the **Central Intelligence Agency** trained **Montagnards** to observe North Vietnamese movement down the Hồ Chí Minh Trail in the **Trail Watcher** program. This force was eventually absorbed into the **Special Forces**–authorized Border Surveillance–Control Operating concept. In May 1964, in Project **Leaping Lena**, Special Forces personnel trained Vietnamese Special Forces and **Civilian Irregular Defense Group** personnel how to conduct **long-range reconnaissance patrols**. The teams gathered intelligence in Laos, though early experiments in this type of intelligence-gathering missions failed to yield positive results. Another source for ground intelligence was the **Roadrunner** project that the U.S. Special Forces helped to established. These small reconnaissance teams, usually made up of Montagnards, provided intelligence on PAVN and NLF movements within the RVN. Both Leaping Lena and Roadrunner personnel were brought into Project Delta in May 1964 and into projects Omega and Sigma in August 1966.

The **Studies and Observation Group** also ran several projects whose objective was the gathering of intelligence on the PAVN and NLF. One such program was the **spike teams** that consisted of a small group of South Vietnamese under U.S. Special Forces leadership who conducted their missions in **Laos** and **Cambodia**. The CIA was also heavily involved in intelligence-gathering missions. In addition to the Trail Watchers, it sponsored the **Mountain Scouts** program, which operated within the RVN against PAVN and NLF positions in the **Central Highlands**.

One of the most effective forms of gathering intelligence was the use of long-range reconnaissance patrols (LRRPs). LRRPs consisted of small teams of personnel who were specially trained to evade the enemy while conducting reconnaissance in contested areas through the **Republic of Vietnam**. The teams went into enemy-controlled territory to locate PAVN and NLF base areas and personnel and then directed **artillery** and air strikes against them. The LRRP concept was integrated throughout the U.S. **Army** by the late 1960s, and despite the high risk and stress of the missions, it provided much-needed intelligence, allowed invaluable guidance of artillery and air strikes, and had an extremely high kill ratio.

The RVN also developed programs to gather intelligence that were separate from the U.S. During the **Ngô Đình Diệm** era, the South Vietnamese efforts were led by **Ngô Đình Nhu**, who headed the Social and Political Research Department. In 1964, the RVN organized the Central Intelligence Office, though it competed with the Vietnamese military for resources from the Sài Gòn government. The RVN and the U.S. also organized the Open Arms (**Chiêu Hồi**) program to encourage defections from the PAVN and NLF. These defectors (**Hồi Chánh**) did provide human intelligence, but it was not always accurate or timely.

The DRV also engaged in intelligence-related activities, though it relied more on its human agents, including **women**, than on technology. PAVN and NLF personnel infiltrated the American military in the RVN and the Sài Gòn government. Some of the more notable spies included **Nguyễn Hữu Hạnh**, **Phạm Ngọc Thảo**, and Phạm Xuân Ăn. The DRV effectively employed these spies at every level within the RVN.

Intelligence played a key role in the war, and both sides sought to acquire an advantage over the other. The significance of intelligence was seen on a daily basis, though such events as the 1968 Tết Offensive, when the U.S. failed to identify the major offensive, and the DRV's overestimation of South Vietnamese unity in overthrowing the Sài Gòn government made it clear how significant intelligence was during the war. *See also* AIRBORNE BATTLEFIELD COMMAND AND CONTROL CENTERS (ABCCC); AIRCRAFT (BOMBERS), UNITED STATES; AIRCRAFT (CARGO TRANSPORT), UNITED STATES; AIRCRAFT (RECONNAISSANCE), UNITED STATES; FAST BUCK, OPERATION; FOOTBOY; GULF OF TỐN KỈN INCIDENT; HARASSMENT AND INTERDICTION (H&I); IRON HAND; KIT CARSON SCOUTS; LIMA SITES; ORDER OF BATTLE DISPUTE; PHOENIX PROGRAM.

INTERNATIONAL COMMISSION OF CONTROL AND SUPERVISION (ICCS). Established as a result of the 27 January 1973 **Paris Peace Accords**, the ICCS was responsible for monitoring adherence to the agreements. The agency, whose 26 teams were divided into seven regions in the **Republic of Vietnam**, supervised the implementation of the agreements and investigated any violations of its provisions that it was responsible for observing. Teams were established in **Huế**, **Đà Nẵng**, **Plei Ku**, Phan Thiết, **Biên Hòa**, Mỹ Tho, and **Cần Thơ**. An additional 3 teams were placed in **Sài Gòn-Gia Định**, 12 teams were stationed near military facilities, and 7 teams were placed near ports of entry, with an additional 7 teams for dealing with the return of captured or detained personnel.

Personnel from Hungary, Poland, **Canada**, and Indonesia made up the teams, though the Canadian representatives pulled out after two of its members were detained by communists for over a month and one ICCS **helicopter** was shot down by a surface-to-air missile. Representatives from Iran replaced the Canadians. The teams were extremely busy, as both sides violated the cease-fire. The ICCS was powerless to enforce the protocols in the document. The 18 articles that created the ICCS provided little authority for the organization to enforce the accords, even when violations were blatant. By the time the North Vietnamese began their final offensive in 1975, the ICCS had ceased to be a functioning entity.

INTERNATIONAL CONTROL COMMISSION (ICC). The ICC was responsible for enforcing the 1954 **Geneva Agreements**. It was comprised of representatives from **Canada**, Poland, and **India**. The Canadians were responsible for representing the West, Poland represented the communist interests, and India spoke for the neutral nations. The ICC was supposed to act as a neutral organization to see that the articles of the Geneva Conference were adhered to, though from the first days after implementation, Canada sided with the **United States** and the **Republic of Vietnam**, Poland sided with the **Democratic Republic of Vietnam** (DRV), and India provided inconsistent representation. Each country also provided one-third of the personnel used to monitor and investigate complaints.

The ICC proved to be ineffective in overseeing the agreements in Vietnam, **Laos**, or **Cambodia**. It issued several reports of agreement violations but did not have the enforcement machinery to correct the problems. As the war escalated in the 1960s, the ICC continued to function in Southeast Asia, though its role had been reduced from monitoring and investigation to mediation and facilitation of communication between the warring sides. The ICC helped transport Western journalists and visitors to the DRV, but it really served no other useful purpose. The ICC was disbanded with the signing of the January 1973 **Paris Peace Accords**, and monitoring of the peace fell to the **International Commission of Control and Supervision**, which included representatives from Hungary, Poland, Canada, and Indonesia. The Canadians resigned when it became clear that the DRV was not adhering to the treaty, and they were replaced by personnel from Iran.

IRON HAND. Begun in August 1965, these air missions were associated with Operation **Rolling Thunder**. The primary objective was to identify and eliminate surface-to-air missile (SAM) sites. The **United States Air Force** employed the RB-66 electronic intelligence (ELINT) system to intercept enemy radar signals, including the guidance system used by the SA-2. In addition to ELINT, Iron Hand used photographic **reconnaissance** and **Blue Tree** missions to identify SAM sites and then immediately target them for destruction. If no SAMs were located at the identified sites, the air **sorties** were switched over to Rolling Thunder targets.

IRON TRIANGLE. Located in Bình Dương province to the northwest of **Sài Gòn**, the Iron Triangle was an area of approximately 155 square kilometers (60 square miles) that served as a safe haven for communist insurgents during the **First Indochina War** and the **Second Indochina War**. The area was located between the villages Bến Súc, Bến Có, and Bến Cụt, east of the Sài Gòn River, west of the Tinh River, and north of the provincial capital of

Phú Cường. Both the French and the **United States** tried to secure the area from the Vietnamese insurgents, but neither could neutralize the threat. Three major U.S. operations, **Attleboro**, **Cedar Falls**, and **Junction City**, swept the area without success because the National Liberation Front used their familiarity with the land and an extensive **tunnel** system, including the famous tunnels of Củ Chi, to elude the enemy. Operations within the Iron Triangle symbolized the frustration of fighting an elusive enemy. The French, Americans, and South Vietnamese knew where the enemy was located but could never completely eliminate them from the area.

IRVING, OPERATION. Search-and-destroy operation in **Bình Định** province, north of **Qui Nhơn**, referred to by the **Army of the Republic of Vietnam** (ARVN) forces as Operation Đại Bàng and by the **Republic of Korea** as Mang Ho 6. The operation began on 2 October 1966, with units from the 1st Air Cavalry **Division**, the 22nd ARVN Division, and the Republic of Korea's Capital Division working together to destroy the 610th Division of the **People's Army of Vietnam** (PAVN) along the coast. With the 1st Air Cavalry Division transporting two of its brigades by air into the Irving area, the Korean and ARVN troops established blocking positions in the southern part of the battlefield while ARVN units attacked from the northeast. The **United States Navy** and Vietnamese Junk Fleet cut off any sea escape.

As the allied units engaged the enemy, B-52 air strikes hit the suspected PAVN and **National Liberation Front** (NLF) command area in the Núi Miêu Mountains. The operation included a number of intense firefights with the PAVN and NLF forces and the discovery of a significant **tunnel** complex in the Núi Miêu Mountains, as well as other tunnel systems throughout the area that were cleared by **Tunnel Rats**. The operation ended on 24 October. Operation Irving was noted for its use of **airmobility** and its abundant use of firepower to destroy the enemy. The allied forces claimed 681 PAVN and NLF killed and 741 captured. The success of the operation allowed for greater **pacification** efforts in Bình Định for a time. *See also* THAYER, OPERATIONS.

J

JACKSON STATE UNIVERSITY. On 14 May 1970, riots broke out at Jackson State University when it was rumored that Mayor Charles Evers and his wife had been killed. Students, already inflamed by the institutional racism that pervaded Jackson, Mississippi, and the tragedy at **Kent State University** earlier in the month, immediately protested. When police were called to the scene, the protest intensified, leading to several alleged gunshots aimed at the police and the destruction of public property. The Fire Department responded to the riots to put out fires started by the students but were met with open hostility. The situation escalated and led to police dispersing the crowd of approximately 100 with gunfire, though the officers alleged that they had been fired upon first. Two black students were killed, one an innocent bystander, and 14 were injured. The incident, on the heels of the Kent State University shooting, served as a catalyst for continued student unrest, which focused on protesting the war but also included the social injustice occurring in the **United States** at the time. *See also* ANTIWAR MOVEMENT.

JARAI. One of the many ethnic groups of **Montagnard** who live in the **Central Highlands** of Vietnam. The group speaks Jarai, which is closely related to the **Cham** and Malayo-Polynesian language. The Jarai live in and around Kon Tum province. Jarai are animist, though many were converted to Christianity by American missionaries toward the end of the war. The Jarai were leaders in the Montagnard movement to create an independent state separate from the **Republic of Vietnam** (RVN). As a result, many Jarai were arrested, and the people were persecuted. The Jarai made a significant contribution to the **Civilian Irregular Defense Groups**, but when that program was terminated in 1970, a number of Jarai whose land transcended **Cambodia** and the RVN were recruited into the **Khmer Rouge**. *See also* BAJARAKA MOVEMENT.

JOHNSON, HAROLD KEITH (1912–1983). **United States Army** general. Johnson was born in North Dakota, was educated at the U.S. Military Academy, and graduated in 1933. He served with the 57th Infantry Regiment immediately before and during World War II and was promoted quickly through the ranks to lieutenant colonel.

He was involved in the Bataan Death March in 1942 after the U.S. surrender on the Bataan Peninsula. Johnson remained a prisoner of Japan until the war ended. After the war, Johnson taught at the Armed Forces Staff College. He also served in the Korean War as commander of the 5th and 8th Cavalry and was promoted to the temporary rank of colonel. He became a permanent colonel in 1956 and was also promoted to the temporary rank of brigadier general, which became permanent in 1960. In 1957, Johnson became the U.S. 7th Army's chief of staff, and in 1959 he became the chief of staff of the North Atlantic Treaty Organizations' Central Army Group in West Germany. He held the position of commandant of the Command and General Staff College from February 1963 to August 1966 and succeeded General **Earl G. Wheeler** as U.S. Army chief of staff from 1964, with the rank of a four-star general. He remained in that position until 2 July 1968, with a brief stint as chairman of the **Joint Chiefs of Staff** in 1967.

Johnson oversaw the Americanization of the war in Vietnam and was instrumental in carrying out the orders of President **Lyndon B. Johnson** and ensuring that General **William C. Westmoreland**, commander of the **Military Assistance Command, Vietnam**, received the personnel and resources he needed to fight the war. Johnson advocated for a greater mobilization of American resources than President Johnson was willing to provide. General Johnson called for the use of U.S. reserves in Vietnam and was sometimes at odds with President Johnson and Secretary of Defense **Robert McNamara** in their gradual approach to escalation and the strategies that involved quantification to determine progress in the war. Johnson retired from active service in July 1968 and was succeeded by Westmoreland. He became the president of the Herbert Hoover Presidential Library Association in 1969 and also served as a consultant to several defense corporations until his death.

JOHNSON, LYNDON BAINES (1908–1973). 36th President of the **United States**. Johnson was born in Stonewall, Texas, and was the first of five children. In 1913, his family moved to Johnson City, where he graduated from its high school in 1924. In 1927, he entered the Southwest Texas State Teachers College at San Marcos, Texas, but dropped out of school to teach and serve as the principal at a Mexican-American school in Cotulla. Johnson did earn his undergraduate degree in 1930 and taught public speaking at a high school in Houston, Texas. He entered politics after the 1931 election of Richard Kleberg to the House of Representatives. He served as Kleberg's secretary for three years and attended, for a short period of time, the law school at Georgetown University. On 25 July 1935, Johnson accepted the post as the Texas director of the National Youth Administration, one of the many New Deal programs designed to train and employ disadvantaged youth.

In 1937, he resigned from this position to run for the House of Representatives after the death of the congressman from the 10th district of Texas. With President Franklin D. Roosevelt's support, Johnson was elected on the Democratic ticket and continued to support New Deal programs in his district. He remained in the House until 1948, though he did fail to win a senate seat in a special election in 1941. With the U.S. declaration of war in December 1941, Johnson volunteered for active duty. Earlier, in June 1940, he had been appointed as a lieutenant commander in the U.S. Naval Reserve. Johnson was the first member of **Congress** to join the military in World War II. He fought in the Pacific Theater and earned the Silver Star before Roosevelt ordered all congressmen in the armed forces to return to Washington. Johnson ended his military service on 16 July 1942.

In 1948, Johnson won a seat in the U.S. Senate, earning the nickname "Landslide Lyndon" for his very close victory in the Democratic primary. He was elected the majority whip of the Senate in 1951, minority leader in 1953, and majority leader in 1955. Johnson was noted for his skill in working legislation through the Senate. He helped to secure passage of the 1957 Civil Rights Act and the 1958 National Aeronautics and Space Act. He also chaired the Senate Preparedness Investigating Subcommittee after the **Soviet Union** launched its Sputnik satellite into space. In 1960, Johnson was nominated for president at the Democratic National Convention but accepted the vice presidential nomination with **John F. Kennedy** as president. The Democratic ticket won a close race against **Richard M. Nixon** and **Henry Cabot Lodge Jr.** Johnson also won another term as senator but resigned his seat after taking the oath of office.

As vice president, Johnson served in a variety of positions. He visited Vietnam between 11 and 13 May 1961 and proclaimed his support for **Ngô Đình Diệm**. Johnson opposed the U.S. move to replace Ngô Đình Diệm in a coup d'état in November 1963 but accepted the decision once it had been made. On 22 November 1963, Kennedy was assassinated in Dallas, Texas, and Johnson became the 36th president. Johnson inherited a Vietnam policy in disarray, with no stable government in **Sài Gòn** and the likelihood of an American decision to either withdraw or continue to support its ally. Johnson also inherited a White House shocked and angered by the Kennedy assassination and lived under the shadow of Kennedy until he was elected to his own term of office in November 1964. Johnson was most focused on domestic issues during the remainder of Kennedy's term. He launched his Great Society program and ensured the passage of a series of domestic legislation that had been stalled during Kennedy's presidency, including the 1964 Civil Rights Act.

Because Johnson was committed to continuing the U.S. policy in Southeast Asia and defending the **Republic of Vietnam** (RVN) against communism, he became tied to further escalation. Throughout 1964, there was evidence that the North Vietnamese and **National Liberation Front** (NLF) were intensifying their efforts in the South, aided by the **People's Republic of China**, to take advantage of the political instability that followed the assassination of Ngô Đình Diệm. On 2 August and allegedly on 4 August, the North Vietnamese attacked U.S. naval ships in the Gulf of Tŏn Kĭn. Johnson used the events to push through Congress a resolution that allowed him to retaliate and provided justification for additional American personnel in Vietnam. He signed the **Gulf of Tŏn Kĭn Resolution** on 7 August, and within seven months he had agreed to a sustained air campaign against the **Democratic Republic of Vietnam**, known as **Rolling Thunder**, and to the introduction of combat troops into **Đà Nẵng**. Johnson followed the **enclave strategy** in Vietnam until convinced by General **William C. Westmoreland**, commander of the **Military Assistance Command, Vietnam**, that the U.S. needed to take a more active role in the war and suggested changing the strategy to **search-and-destroy**.

By the end of 1965, Johnson had authorized over 180,000 troops for Vietnam, a number that would double by the end of 1966. As Johnson continued to push through his Great Society programs, his administration became mired in the war in Southeast Asia while the growing **antiwar movement** consumed him. His presidency continued to accomplish some of his domestic goals, but the war distracted from this agenda, and members of Congress, both Republican and Democrat, began to voice their opposition to the American war in Vietnam.

At the end of 1967, Westmoreland advised Johnson that the U.S. had seized the initiative in the fighting and that the NLF was no longer capable of mounting a sustained offensive. This pronouncement occurred approximately three months before the 1968 **Tết Offensive** that engulfed the RVN and led many in the U.S. to agree with **Walter Cronkite**'s assessment that the war could only end in stalemate. On 31 March 1968, Johnson informed a televised audience that he would neither seek nor accept the Democratic Party's nomination in the 1968 presidential election. He left Washington, D.C., on 20 January 1969 after the inauguration of President **Richard M. Nixon** who defeated Johnson's vice president Hubert Humphrey. Johnson remained somewhat secluded after his retirement from public life. He worked to create his presidential library on the campus of the University of Texas at Austin, which was dedicated in 1971, and wrote his memoirs, *The Vantage Point*. He died on 22

January 1973, a week before the signing of the 1973 **Paris Peace Accords**. Despite the success of his domestic agenda, Johnson's legacy remained the Vietnam War. Ironically, it was the one event that he worked hard to avoid but was compelled to confront.

JOINT CHIEFS OF STAFF (JCS). The JCS was officially established as part of the National Security Act of 1947. The group includes high-ranking officers from the four major branches of the **United States** Armed Forces. Included in the group are the **Army** chief of staff, the **Air Force** chief of staff, the chief of naval operations, and the commandant of the **Marine Corps**. The group is lead by a chairman, who is chosen from the four representatives. The JCS advises the president and his administration on military matters and carries out the orders of the president.

After the Americanization of the war, the JCS called for increased support for the commander of the **Military Assistance Command, Vietnam** (MACV), and a loosening of the political restrictions that hampered the **air war** over the **Democratic Republic of Vietnam** (DRV), as well as the **mining** of **Hải Phòng** harbor and other North Vietnamese ports, in order to restrict the ability of resupply to the DRV from external sources. The JCS also called for a loosening of restrictions on operations in **Laos** and **Cambodia**. While the JCS was not as actively involved in Southeast Asia during the Dwight D. Eisenhower administration, it was very active during the **Lyndon B. Johnson** administration, and the JCS often were in conflict with Secretary of Defense **Robert McNamara** and members of the State Department who were interjecting politics into military strategy that forced the JCS and MACV to fight a different type of war than they were prepared to conduct.

JUNCTION CITY, OPERATION. On 22 February 1967, the **United States** was involved in the first and only major airborne assault in the war, and the first since the Korean War, when 700 paratroopers from the **173rd Airborne Brigade** jumped into the **Iron Triangle**, or **War Zone C**, to the northwest of **Sài Gòn** in a **search-and-destroy** mission that sought to eliminate the headquarters for the **National Liberation Front** shadow government in the **Republic of Vietnam**, the **Central Office for South Vietnam** (COSVN). The mission also dropped 189 tons of heavy equipment and 24 tons of supplies in the three-phased operation, which lasted until 14 May 1967. Operation Junction City, which also involved the **Army of the Republic of Vietnam**, was considered a success by the U.S. even though COSVN was not destroyed and the area continued to be contested after the operation was complete. The U.S. claimed over 1,700 enemy killed at a cost of 282 killed and over 1,000 wounded.

JUNGLE JIM, PROJECT. The 4400th Combat Crew Training Squadron (CCTS), nicknamed Jungle Jim, was created by the **United States Air Force** on 14 April 1961 to provide training and combat support for the allies. Between November and December 1961, Detachment 2 of the 4400th CCTS arrived at **Biên Hòa** to train and assist the **Army of the Republic of Vietnam** and the **Republic of Vietnam Air Force** to participate in Operation **Farm Gate**, first in a training role and eventually in combat operations.

K

KENNEDY, JOHN FITZGERALD (1917–1963). 35th president of the **United States**. Born in Massachusetts and educated briefly at Princeton University and then at Harvard University, John Fitzgerald Kennedy graduated cum laude in 1940. His senior thesis, *Appeasement in Munich*, was published in 1941 under the title *Why England Slept*. Kennedy enrolled in the Stanford Graduate School of Business for the fall 1940 semester but joined the **United States Navy** in 1941 after unsuccessfully volunteering for the U.S. Army earlier. Kennedy worked in public affairs until the attack on Pearl Harbor on 7 December 1941. After completing courses at the Naval Reserve Officer Training Corps and the Motor Torpedo Boat Squadron Training Center, Kennedy was assigned to Panama and then as commander of a patrol torpedo (PT) boat. He would then be transferred to the Pacific Theater.

On 2 August 1943, Kennedy's PT-109 was rammed and sunk by a Japanese destroyer. He and most of his men survived the ordeal and were eventually rescued on a Pacific island. Kennedy was honored for his actions and was considered by many as a war hero, though Kennedy maintained that the status was involuntary and was a result of circumstances rather than action. In October 1943, Kennedy moved to PT-59, which had been converted to a gunboat. He continued to serve until being honorably discharged in early 1945.

In 1946, Kennedy entered politics and won a seat in the House of Representatives as a Democrat from Massachusetts. He served three terms in the House before winning one of Massachusetts' Senate seats from the Republican incumbent, **Henry Cabot Lodge Jr.**, in 1952. During his first term, Kennedy published another book, *Profiles in Courage*, which earned him a Pulitzer Prize in 1957, though it was later revealed that Kennedy's speech writer and longtime political ally, Theodore Sorenson, penned much of the book. Kennedy was considered for the vice presidential nomination under Adlai Stevenson in the 1956 presidential election but was beaten by Senator Estes Kefauver of Tennessee. Kennedy did win a second senatorial term in 1958. While in the Senate, Kennedy became aware of the plight of the **Republic of Vietnam** (RVN) and **Ngô Đình Diệm** through the **American**

Friends of Vietnam (AFVN). He was an early supporter of U.S. attempts at nation building in the RVN.

On 2 January 1960, Kennedy announced his candidacy for the Democratic nomination in the 1960 presidential election. During the campaign season, he defeated senators **Hubert Humphrey** (Minnesota), **Wayne Morse** (Oregon), and **Lyndon B. Johnson** (Texas). With Johnson as his running mate, Kennedy ran against and narrowly defeated Vice President **Richard M. Nixon** in the November presidential election to become the 35th U.S. president.

When Kennedy met with outgoing President Dwight D. Eisenhower on 19 January 1961, he was informed that **Laos** was the most significant problem in Southeast Asia, which had recently undergone a coup d'état that had put in a pro-U.S. government under **Phoumi Nosavan**. A few days later, Kennedy was briefed by **Edward Lansdale** on the situation in the RVN and learned of the critical situation in that country. Kennedy chose to support the RVN with a series of escalatory moves, which further entrenched American personnel in Southeast Asia, while opting for neutralism in Laos. The former resulted in the introduction of additional military **advisers, helicopters,** and support units; the creation of the **Military Assistance Command, Vietnam** (MACV); increasing the size of the **Army of the Republic of Vietnam** and **Civil Guard**; and more aggressive rhetoric designed to warn the **Soviet Union**, the **People's Republic of China,** and others to refrain from supporting the **Democratic Republic of Vietnam** and the **National Liberation Front** (NLF). The Laotian situation resulted in the International Conference on the Settlement of the Laotian Question from 16 May 1961 to 23 July 1962 and the signing of the *International Agreement on the Neutrality of Laos*, also known as the 1962 **Geneva Accords.**

Kennedy continued to increase U.S. involvement in the RVN in 1962 as the U.S. inserted itself into the internal affairs of the **Sài Gòn** government. The significant event of the year was the creation of the **Strategic Hamlet Program**, which was designed to transfer the better qualities of the earlier, but unsuccessful, **Agroville Program** into a new **pacification** effort to protect and mobilize the Vietnamese people and to deny the NLF access to this principal resource. The U.S. supported a Strategic Hamlet Program based on the model used by Sir **Robert Thompson**, the British counterinsurgency specialist who had been successful in quelling the communist insurgency during the Malayan Emergency in the 1950s. Thompson, however, clashed with **Ngô Đình Nhu**, who headed the Vietnamese program. The overall failure of the program resulted in Kennedy beginning to doubt the legitimacy of the Sài Gòn government even though he had retained a long-held respect for Ngô Đình Diệm.

Kennedy received conflicting opinions on the situation in the RVN from both his military and civilian advisers. The U.S. ambassador to the RVN,

Frederick E. Nolting Jr., and the MACV commander, **Paul Harkins**, remained optimistic about the chances of the Sài Gòn government overcoming its deficiencies and defeating the NLF. Joseph Mendenhall, who had been involved in the U.S. embassy under **Elbridge Durbrow** and **W. Averell Harriman**, led the critics, who were gaining in influence in Washington. In the middle of these two groups were individuals such as General **Maxwell D. Taylor**, who served as a special assistant to the president, and **Walt W. Rostow**, who held a number of different positions in the Department of State. Kennedy balanced the two conflicting sides through 1962 but began to lean toward the critics as 1963 unfolded.

For Kennedy, the great crisis in Vietnam occurred in the summer of 1963 when the Buddhists protested the Sài Gòn government. The pretext for the protests was an 8 May 1963 incident that resulted in the deaths of nine demonstrators who attended a rally against the perceived discrimination by the Catholic Ngô Đình Diệm–led government against the Buddhist majority in the RVN. The **Buddhist Crisis** escalated as a result of Buddhist intrigue and a series of poor decisions by the Sài Gòn government, which included pagoda raids in August 1963 authorized by Ngô Đình Nhu that were justified as a counter coup d'état. Supporters of Ngô Đình Diệm were slowly replaced during this time.

Henry Cabot Lodge became the new ambassador while Harkins was discredited in the **media** and within Washington for his optimism after the disaster at the **Battle of Ấp Bắc**. The crisis allowed military officers who had opposed Ngô Đình Diệm to organize and present plans for their own coup d'état to more willing Americans. The result was the 1 November 1963 overthrow of Ngô Đình Diệm and his assassination the next day. While there was no evidence available to suggest that Kennedy supported the coup d'état, and an even stronger unlikelihood that he encouraged the assassination, the Kennedy administration did acquiesce to the change in government. Three weeks later, Kennedy would be assassinated by Lee Harvey Oswald in Dallas, Texas.

Kennedy's legacy left over 16,000 military advisers in the **Republic of Vietnam** and a government and country in turmoil. He chose escalatory options for America's role in Southeast Asia, though the historical debate remains divided on exactly what Kennedy would have done had he not been killed. Those who support Kennedy's Vietnam decisions suggest that he would have withdrawn American personnel from Southeast Asia instead of escalating the U.S. role, as was done under the Lyndon B. Johnson administration. Critics of Kennedy argue that President Johnson was merely continuing Kennedy's Vietnam policy, just as he honored the president by making sure that his domestic legislation was passed. Regardless, Kennedy's role in Vietnam was significant for the U.S., as it moved from a purely humanitarian and advisory role under President Dwight D. Eisenhower to a full-fledged military intervention under Johnson.

KENNEDY, ROBERT FRANCIS (1925–1968). Attorney general of the **United States** and senator from New York. Kennedy was born in Brookline, Massachusetts, and was the younger brother of President **John F. Kennedy**. He was educated at Harvard University but left school in 1944 to join the U.S. **Navy**. He served as a seaman second class in the Caribbean. After the war, he returned to Harvard to finish his degree in 1948 and earned a law degree at the University of Virginia in 1951. He worked for the criminal division of the Department of Justice until he became the campaign manager for his brother, John F. Kennedy, who ran for the U.S. Senate. After the successful campaign, Robert became an assistant counsel to the Senate Permanent Subcommittee on Investigations, which was under the leadership of Senator Joseph R. McCarthy. Kennedy grew disenchanted with the committee and resigned in mid-1953 but rejoined in 1954 as counsel for the Democratic minority and then chief counsel and staff director after McCarthy had been replaced. In January 1957, he became the chief counsel of the Senate Select Committee on Improper Activities in the Labor or Management Field but left in 1959 to serve as campaign manager for John F. Kennedy when he successfully ran for the presidency.

Robert Kennedy served as the attorney general under his brother. In that capacity, he was involved in most of the major decisions of the U.S. at the time, including such events as the Cuban Missile Crisis and the civil rights movement. Kennedy stayed in the White House after his brother was assassinated on 22 November 1963, even though he and the new president, **Lyndon B. Johnson**, were often in conflict. He resigned on 3 September 1964 when he decided to run for a U.S. Senate seat in New York. Kennedy defeated incumbent Republican Kenneth B. Keating. He served in the Senate from 3 January 1965 until 6 June 1968, when he was assassinated while campaigning for the presidency.

Kennedy supported the U.S. role in Vietnam while attorney general and in his early days as senator. Like his brother, he was a Cold War warrior who believed that the **Republic of Vietnam** (RVN) was worth saving, and he was committed to using American resources and personnel to ensure that the RVN was given an opportunity. In 1966, Kennedy began to turn against Johnson's handling of the war. Kennedy called for negotiations with the **National Liberation Front** (NLF), though his ideas for the terms of negotiations were nowhere near close enough to induce the NLF to the negotiation table. In 1967, he softened his position and called for the end of Operation **Rolling Thunder**, the sustained bombing campaign of North Vietnam. Kennedy believed a **bombing pause** could lead to successful negotiations. By the end of 1967, he grew bolder in his **antiwar** position and had moved into opposition with Johnson.

Kennedy believed that too many of America's resources and personnel were being diverted to Southeast Asia instead of being used to help improve conditions within the U.S. In early 1968, Kennedy declared that he would not run for president, but after the 12 March New Hampshire primary in which antiwar candidate **Eugene McCarthy** finished a strong second to Johnson, Kennedy decided to announce his candidacy on 16 March. When Johnson announced on 31 March that he would neither seek nor accept his party's nomination for another term, Kennedy became the front-runner in the Democratic Party. He campaigned on a platform that included ending the war in Vietnam and conducting diplomacy that was less aggressive than his predecessor or his Republican opponent, **Richard M. Nixon**, while calling for a continuation of the domestic policies of his brother and Johnson. After winning the California primary on 4 June, Kennedy left a rally at the Ambassador Hotel in Los Angeles, California, in the early morning of 5 June and was shot by a Palestinian named Sirhan Sirhan, who opposed Kennedy and his support for the Israelis during the June 1967 Six-Day War against Egypt, Jordan, and Syria. He died the next day.

KENT STATE UNIVERSITY. When the **United States** initiated its incursion into **Cambodia** on 30 April 1970, participants of the growing **antiwar movement** were outraged by the apparent duplicity of the escalation in the war when President **Richard M. Nixon** had promised disengagement. Students on college campuses around the U.S. intensified their protests against the war. At Kent State University, protests started on 1 May. After a day of violence mixed with peaceful protests, the National Guard was called out to help quiet the more violent protesters. The troops arrived late on 2 May to see nearly 1,000 protesters on the university commons and the ROTC building, which was adjacent to the commons, burned to the ground. By 4 May, the National Guard had established themselves on campus, which served as a catalyst for the more militant protesters who organized another rally.

This demonstration brought 2,000 to 3,000 protesters to the commons, even though the University had prohibited it. Around 12:00 p.m., the 100-strong National Guard, equipped with M1 **rifles**, were ordered to disperse the crowd on the commons. In the ensuing melee, which involved protesters throwing rocks and verbally abusing the guardsmen, a number of the troops opened fire. Four Kent State University students were killed, two of whom were not involved in the demonstration, and nine students were wounded. The events of 4 May shocked the nation and inflamed the antiwar movement for a period of time, though the galvanizing effect of the shootings led to the fracturing of the movement, as many of the aggressive groups used the Kent State University episode as justification for more militant action. Ten days following the Kent State University shootings, another shooting occurred on the campus of **Jackson State University**.

KHE SANH. Khe Sanh, in the northwestern section of the **Republic of Vietnam** and approximately 11 kilometers (7 miles) from the Laotian border along **Route** 9, served as a combat base for the **United States Marine Corps** (USMC) during the war, though the genesis of the base, its airfield, had been constructed in September 1962. It served as a base for a **Civilian Irregular Defense Group** and, in November 1964, as an outpost for the Green Berets. It was also the point of origin of the **Studies and Observation Group**, which used the base to infiltrate the **Hồ Chí Minh Trail** in **Laos**. In 1967, Khe Sanh was utilized as a base from which the marines could observe and interdict North Vietnamese personnel and supplies traveling down the Hồ Chí Minh Trail. In April, fighting broke out between the USMC and the **People's Army of Vietnam** (PAVN) in what became known as the Hill Fights. PAVN activity increased around Khe Sanh as the year progressed.

The marine base became the focal point for the **Lyndon B. Johnson** administration, the military, and the home front toward the beginning of 1968. The PAVN surrounded the base, which prompted many to make parallels with the 1954 Battle of **Điện Biên Phủ**, even though the two situations were uniquely different. North Vietnamese general **Võ Nguyên Giáp** hoped to convince the U.S. into thinking that Khe Sanh was his objective in early 1968 as he orchestrated the largest North Vietnamese offensive to date during the **Tết** holiday. If the U.S. focused on Khe Sanh, it would leave other areas unprotected and increase North Vietnamese chances of a nationwide victory and national uprising. If the U.S. sacrificed Khe Sanh to protect the rest of the country, Võ Nguyên Giáp hoped for the political and psychological effects of a Điện Biên Phủ–type victory during a presidential election year.

Khe Sanh, under the command of Colonel David E. Lownds, was reinforced with approximately 6,000 marines, for a total of five battalions, as well as the 37th **Army of the Republic of Vietnam** (ARVN) Ranger Battalion. It was estimated that Võ Nguyên Giáp had amassed a force of between 20,000 and 40,000 PAVN and **National Liberation Front** (NLF) troops during the siege. The North Vietnamese initiated their attack on 21 January and briefly penetrated the Khe Sanh perimeter but were beaten back. They then began a prolonged and intense **mortar** and rocket barrage on the marine base hitting the main ammunitions depot. On 24 January, the PAVN added heavy **artillery** to the barrage as well as snipers to harass the marines in the base which was now isolated by land. The marines had already dug in for a siege and were resupplied by the 109th Quartermaster Battalion by air, which technically meant that the base was not under a total siege, even if **media** reports back in the U.S. made it seem so. The U.S. also responded to the North Vietnamese action with Operation **Niagara**, one of the most concentrated air campaigns of the war that brought some relief to the marines.

As the focus became Khe Sanh, the North Vietnamese launched their **Tết Offensive** on 31 January. The marines at Khe Sanh remained on full alert through the offensive, even though the base was not attacked in force again. Khe Sanh continued to be mortared, snipped at, and barraged through February and March. On 1 April, Operation **Pegasus**, the overland effort to relieve the marines, began. By 8 April, elements of the 2nd Brigade, 1st Air Cavalry entered the combat base, officially ending the siege. The two marine regiments that had defended the base departed, leaving the defense of Khe Sanh to the 1st Marine Regiment, which had been a part of the relief force. The U.S. lost 730 killed-in-action and 2,642 wounded. The ARVN suffered 229 killed-in-action and 436 wounded, while the PAVN and NLF had an estimated 15,000 **casualties**.

William C. Westmoreland, who had argued that a presence at Khe Sanh continued to be necessary, was replaced by General **Creighton W. Abrams** at the end of June. Abrams ordered the evacuation and destruction of Khe Sanh, which was completed by 5 July. The abandonment of the combat base brought media criticism as it questioned why the marines had been put in such danger if the base was of no real importance. The justification, that the enemy had changed his tactics and created new infiltration routes, did not satisfy many within civilian and military circles who, after the siege of Khe Sanh, the Tết Offensive, and the 31 March announcement by President Lyndon B. Johnson that he would not seek or accept his party's nomination for the presidency, had grown tired of the war and the way it was being conducted.

During the February 1971 Operation Lam Sơn 719, Khe Sanh was again utilized as a forward base for a failed ARVN attempt to interdict the Hồ Chí Minh Trail. The camp was abandoned again the next year, though the airstrip was used by the North Vietnamese from 1973 until the end of the war. The old combat base now houses a museum dedicated to the North Vietnamese effort during the Battle of Khe Sanh, while much of the surrounding area has been developed into a coffee plantation.

KHMER. The Khmer people make up the majority of the population of **Cambodia** and are a part of the larger Mon-Khmer language family. Khmer groups are also present in the **Socialist Republic of Vietnam (Khmer Krom)** and in **Laos (Lao Theung)**, and smaller groups live in the **United States**,

Canada, and **France**, though a significant majority of the people reside in Cambodia. The Khmer practice a form of Theravada **Buddhism** that includes elements of Hinduism and ancestor-spirit worship. Most Khmer in Cambodia work in agriculture. Khmer language, culture, and practices have influenced the peoples of **Thailand**, Laos, and southwestern Vietnam. The Khmer people suffered as a result of the genocide initiated by **Pol Pot** and the **Khmer Rouge** from 1975 to 1979, when an estimated 1.7 to 3 million Cambodians were killed. *See also* KHMER KROM.

KHMER KROM. A group of **Khmer** people who lived in the **Mê Kông Delta** in the **Republic of Vietnam** (RVN). The group inhabited the area long before the Vietnamese migrated into the area in the 17th century. The Khmer Krom was one of the many ethnic minorities who lived in the RVN who practiced Theravada **Buddhism**. The **Sài Gòn** government heavily recruited Khmer Krom to serve in the **Civilian Irregular Defense Group** (CIDG). In 1970, when **Lon Nol** assumed leadership of **Cambodia** after a coup d'état replaced Prince **Norodom Sihanouk**, the Khmer Krom joined the Cambodian Royal Army in its effort to battle the **Khmer Rouge**, **People's Army of Vietnam**, and **National Liberation Front** forces operating in Cambodia.

One of the more famous Khmer Krom was **Sơn Ngọc Thành** who was born in Vietnam and led the **Khmer Serei**, a group dedicated to opposing the rule of Prince Norodom Sihanouk. Sơn Ngọc Thành was involved in recruiting Khmer Krom into the CIDG and in the transfer of CIDG members to the Cambodian Royal Army after 1970. The Khmer Krom suffered after the fall of the RVN because of their support for the Sài Gòn government throughout the war.

KHMER ROUGE. Cambodian insurgents during the **First Indochina War** and the **Second Indochina War** and the ruling party from 1975 to 1979. The Communist Party of Kampuchea, or Khmer Rouge, has its origins after World War II as Cambodians began to join the Indochinese Communist Party. In the midst of the First Indochina War, the Communist Party split into three factions based on region. In **Cambodia**, the Khmer People's Revolutionary Party (KPRP) formed in 1951 and was made up of the communist Khmer Issarak groups that had begun forming as early as 1947. The KPRP did not play an active role in resisting the French in the early 1950s. Instead, they were stationed in the **Democratic Republic of Vietnam** (DRV) or worked within the political system in Cambodia by forming the Pracheachon, an opposition party that contested national elections. The Pracheachon also worked toward the removal of Prince **Norodom Sihanouk** and his political organization, the Sangkum. Other future leaders of the Khmer Rouge found their political expression while students in Paris. They organized demonstrations, created organizations, and established literature that trained them as leaders of the organization when they returned to Cambodia in the 1960s.

In September 1960, the KPRP changed its name to the Khmer Workers' Party (KWP). With that change, there also came a policy of cooperating with Sihanouk, as he exhibited a decidedly favorable disposition toward the DRV in its intensifying conflict with the **Republic of Vietnam**. Tou Samouth, one of the leading advocates of working with Sihanouk, was elected general secretary of the new organization, while Saloth Sar, who would later become known as **Pol Pot**, was placed in the Political Bureau. When Tou Samouth was killed by government officials on 20 July 1962, Pol Pot took over leadership of the KWP and consolidated his power through a series of moves that eliminated the opposition and installed his allies in positions of power within the organization. Pol Pot avoided demands by Sihanouk to pledge his loyalty to the government in 1963.

In September 1966, the KWP secretly changed its name to the Communist Party of Kampuchea (CPK). The organization recruited from areas neglected by Sihanouk or occupied by the **People's Army of Vietnam** and the **National Liberation Front**. It fought against the **Army of the Republic of Vietnam** and the Americans but had no success in removing Sihanouk and spreading communism in Cambodia. Its 1967 offensive against **Phnom Penh** failed, but the 1968 offensive served as the beginning of the Khmer Rouge's struggle to overthrow Sihanouk. The Khmer Rouge, supported by the North Vietnamese, gained in popularity and confidence as it fought against the Royal Cambodian Army over the next two years.

On 18 March 1970, **Lon Nol** replaced Sihanouk as head of state, which forced Sihanouk to ally with the Khmer Rouge, adding to the organization's already growing popularity and influence. Sihanouk became the head of a government in exile that was supported by the Khmer Rouge as the fighting shifted to overthrowing Lon Nol and his soon-to-be ally, the **United States**. While Lon Nol authorized the American-led two-month **Cambodian Incursion** at the end of April 1970, it failed to destroy the Khmer Rouge. In fact, the opposite occurred as more Cambodians turned against the government to support Sihanouk and the Khmer Rouge.

By 1973, the Khmer Rouge had control or influence over most of Cambodia, despite American efforts to support the government and continue a sustained bombing campaign that had begun in 1969 with Operation **Menu**. The U.S. continued its air campaign after the Cambodian Incursion with operations **Freedom Deal** and **Freedom Action** in 1970. On 17 April 1975, two weeks before the fall of **Sài Gòn**, the Khmer Rouge captured **Phnom Penh** and took over leadership of the country, which it renamed Democratic

Kampuchea, and then began a revolution, which had the main objective of returning the people to the soil. The new government eliminated foreign contact with its people; ended education and any industry, idea, or function that had its origins in the West; abolished religion; confiscated all property; and started a program of forced labor.

Under Pol Pot, Cambodia experienced a genocide that destroyed a generation of people with an estimated 1.7 to 3 million executed or killed through neglect or torture as the leadership methodically turned the younger generation against the old to remake the country into a classless society. The educated, or anyone who had experienced Western ideas, were killed, as were those who showed signs of resistance. It was not until an invasion by the Socialist Republic of Vietnam in late 1978 that the genocide abated. Even though the Vietnamese captured Phnom Penh on 7 January 1979, the Khmer Rouge clung to power, retaining its seat in the **United Nations** until 1982. The organization split with Vietnam after the war and never regained the influence it had in the 1970s. By 1999, after nearly 20 years of opposing the post–Pol Pot government, the Khmer Rouge all but ceased to exist. It left a legacy of devastation that created one of the most impoverished nations in Asia.

KHMER SEREI. A group founded in 1954 by **Sơn Ngọc Thành** after King **Norodom Sihanouk** gained **Cambodian** independence from **France**. Sơn Ngọc Thành established the Khmer Serei (Free Khmer) in opposition to Sihanouk and the influence of the French in Cambodian politics. The Khmer Serei, who were mostly recruited from the **Khmer Krom** which lived in the **Mê Kông Delta** in the **Republic of Vietnam** (RVN), were an irregular force who established bases near the Cambodian-**Thailand** border and were supported by both the Thai and RVN governments. The Khmer Serei was not a powerful force in Cambodian politics, though it did maintain pressure on Sihanouk, who authorized repression of the group after it publicly criticized his rule. In November 1963, the Khmer Serei broadcast radio reports that were decidedly anti-Sihanouk. Sihanouk blamed the **United States** and Thailand for providing the technology to allow the broadcasts to occur and stopped economic relations with the U.S.

The U.S. supported the Khmer Serei, providing both weapons and training. The total force was less than 8,000 personnel at its height in 1968. After Sihanouk was replace by **Lon Nol** on 18 March 1970, the Khmer Serei increased in prestige, and Sơn Ngọc Thành became a senior adviser in the government and eventually was selected as prime minister from 18 March to 15 October 1972. Lon Nol never trusted the Khmer Serei, believing that Sơn Ngọc Thành would make a bid to take over. As a result, the Khmer Serei was used in a number of combat operations against the **People's Army of Vietnam**, the **National Liberation Front**, and the Khmer Rouge, which decimated the effectiveness of the organization as a fighting unit. When Sơn Ngọc Thành was replaced as prime minister in 1972, he went to the RVN, along with the remaining Khmer Serei. After the end of the war, Sơn Ngọc Thành was imprisoned, and the remaining Khmer Serei personnel in Vietnam were disbanded. The Khmer Rouge eliminated the Khmer Serei who remained in Cambodia. Sơn Ngọc Thành died in 1977, and the remaining Khmer Serei operated against the Khmer Rouge from **refugee** base camps near Thailand.

KING, MARTIN LUTHER, JR. (1929–1968). Civil rights leader and **anti-war** activist. Born in Georgia, he was educated at Morehouse College, graduating in 1948. Earlier, in 1947, King became an ordained Baptist minister. He received a Bachelor of Divinity from Crozer Theological Seminary in 1951 and a PhD in theology from Boston University in June 1955. King became involved in the civil rights movement in the 1950s and was involved in organizing the Montgomery Improvement Association during the bus boycott in that city in 1955. As a result of this episode, he became a leader in the modern civil rights movement. King's political philosophy was shaped by Mohandas Karamchand Gandhi, the leader of the movement to free **India** from British colonial rule, who was an advocate of passive resistance.

King was also influenced by Bayard Rustin, who was a proponent of nonviolence as a means to achieving an end. King's activism in civil rights continued until his death. He led the Southern Christian Leadership Conference and organized civil rights activities in Albany, Georgia, and Birmingham and Selma, Alabama. King played a prominent role in the movement, delivering an influential speech during the march on Washington on 28 August 1963, which helped inspire the Civil Rights Act of 1964 and the Voting Rights Act of 1965. King was awarded the Nobel Peace Prize on 14 October 1964 for his civil rights activities and nonviolent resistance philosophy.

King's focus on civil rights and nonviolence eventually translated into his opposition to the Vietnam War. He did not immediately oppose the war during the initial period of American escalation, though he began to privately, and then he publicly advocated a reassessment of the **United States** military policy, which relied on airpower to force negotiations and **search-and-destroy** missions that emphasized the attrition strategy. King's opposition focused on a number of issues that related to his political philosophy and his position in the civil rights movement.

He opposed the indiscriminate use of American firepower in fighting the **People's Army of Vietnam** and the **National Liberation Front**, and toward the end of his life, he argued that the U.S. role in Vietnam was becoming one of a colonialist power. King argued that the U.S. was diverting too many resources to the fighting in Southeast Asia, which could have been used to enhance President **Lyndon B. Johnson**'s Great Society programs that helped people in the U.S. who needed assistance. King opposed spending more money on fighting a war to destroy a nation thousands of miles away than on improving the social, economic, spiritual, and cultural environment at home, and he argued that a disproportionate number of African Americans served and sustained casualties in the war, even though statistics developed after the war showed that 7,241 African Americans were killed-in-action out of the total 58,190, or 12.4 percent. The percentage of African Americans in the U.S. in 1970 was 11.1 percent. While the numbers do not support King's assertion, his argument was taken seriously given the political and social climate of the 1960s.

King was severely criticized by many within the U.S., in addition to those southerners who had resisted the civil rights movement. He was accused of repeating the rhetoric of the **Democratic Republic of Vietnam** and of aiding the enemy in the war. He was later charged with promulgating communist ideology and a redistribution of wealth to better help those in need as he continued his opposition to the war. He furthered the growing schism between himself and mainstream America when he highlighted the irony of African Americans fighting for the independence of the **Republic of Vietnam** and for Vietnamese civil rights when those same soldiers were denied the same rights in the U.S. He continued his outspoken criticism of the war and the inconsistencies of U.S. policy to the end of his life. On 4 April 1968, King was assassinated as he stood on the balcony of the Lorraine Motel in Memphis, Tennessee, after delivering a speech to the Mason Temple, the world headquarters of the Church of God in Christ.

KINGPIN, OPERATION. In May 1970, aerial **reconnaissance** over the **Democratic Republic of Vietnam** (DRV) identified at least two prisoner-of-war camps near **Hà Nội**. One of the camps was located at **Sơn Tây**, west of the capital. Further **intelligence** suggested that the camp at Sơn Tây was expanding and that **United States** servicemen were being held there in captivity. The U.S. decided to conduct a rescue mission at Sơn Tây despite further reconnaissance in October which confirmed that the camp was emptying. Colonel Arthur D. "Bull" Simons organized a group of 100 **Special Forces** volunteers to conduct the raid, of whom 56 would actually participate.

On 21 November 1970, the operation was launched. A small assault force in an HH-3H **helicopter** crash-landed inside the prison while two additional HH-53s disembarked outside the compound to penetrate the perimeter. As the raid commenced, the U.S. orchestrated a series of diversionary attacks throughout the DRV, including an F-105 **Wild Weasel** mission to destroy surface-to-air missile sites that could threaten the helicopters after the rescue. Despite a few problems, the raid proceeded, but after entering the compound, the Special Forces discovered that there were no prisoners left at Sơn Tây. The Americans did engage a large number of North Vietnamese guards, though, killing an estimated 50 of them during the intense firefight.

After realizing that the prisoners had already been transferred, the raiders left. The entire operation took only 27 minutes. While no Americans were rescued—it turned out that the prisoners had been moved because of a lack of available water in the camp—they did hear the commotion related to the raid from their new camp at Đông Cao, approximately 24 kilometers (15 miles) to the east. The effort, even though it was a failure, did raise morale among the prisoners, who knew that they had not been forgotten. No Americans were killed in the rescue attempt. After the raid, prisoners of war were concentrated in several camps in Hà Nội to ensure that another rescue attempt would not occur.

KISSINGER, HENRY ALFRED (1923–). Secretary of state during the **Richard M. Nixon** administration, chief negotiator for the **United States** during the Paris Peace negotiations, and Nobel Peace Prize recipient. Kissinger immigrated to the U.S. before the start of World War II and was naturalized as a citizen in 1943. He received his PhD from Harvard University in 1954 and served on its faculty until 1971 in the Department of Government and at the Center for International Affairs. Before entering public life, he worked for the Council on Foreign Relations and the Rockefeller Brothers Fund in addition to his service at Harvard. He also authored many influential books on American foreign policy for which he received several honors and awards, including the Presidential Medal of Freedom in 1977. While Kissinger served as consultant for the Operations Research Office, the **National Security Council**, the Department of State, RAND Corporation, and the U.S. Arms Control and Disarmament Agency, his public life began when he was selected as President Nixon's national security adviser on 2 December 1968. He remained in that position until 3 November 1975. Kissinger also served as secretary of state from 22 September 1973 until 20 January 1977 under Nixon and President **Gerald R. Ford**.

Kissinger worked to end the war while Nixon pursued **Vietnamization** and "peace with honor" for the U.S. To this end, Kissinger opened negotiations with the North Vietnamese in Paris in 1968 and worked for five years to achieve peace, though his critics argued that he only achieved what was considered a decent interval between the American withdrawal from Vietnam and the fall of **Sài Gòn**. His most severe critics labeled that interval indecent and placed a significant amount of blame on the U.S. for its failure to back its allies in a time of need. Kissinger and Lê Đức Thọ, the chief negotiator for the North Vietnamese, jointly received the Nobel Peace Prize on 10 December 1973 for their efforts, though Lê Đức Thọ refused to accept it. In the years following the fall of Sài Gòn, Kissinger defended his record on Southeast Asia, though it continued to be a source of contention and sensitivity for him. *See also* PARIS PEACE ACCORDS.

KIT CARSON SCOUTS. Former **People's Army of Vietnam** (PAVN) or **National Liberation Front** (NLF) soldiers who participated in the **Chiêu Hồi** program and who, as **Hồi Chánh**, made the decision to join the war against their erstwhile comrades. The Kit Carson Scout program was organized by the **United States Marine Corps** and was inaugurated on 10 November 1966. The former U.S. enemies provided **intelligence** and training in countering PAVN and NLF strategies and tactics by providing realistic demonstrations for incoming soldiers to Vietnam and by participating in **search-and-destroy** operations. The early success of the program resulted in General **William C. Westmoreland** calling for Kit Carson Scouts in every division, even though critics of the program and the war argued that many of the defectors were double agents. Kit Carson Scouts provided an added dimension to the American war that had been absent in the early years. The scouts offered a new perspective on PAVN and NLF personnel and allowed the U.S. to better understand its enemy and coordinate a more effective strategy for countering PAVN and NLF tactics.

KOHO. Montagnards associated with the Mon-**Khmer** language group who lived in the **Central Highlands** region of the **Republic of Vietnam** to the southwest of **Đà Lạt**. The Koho were slash-and-burn farmers and were considered one of the poorer people in the region. Koho soldiers fought on the **United States'** side during the war, though the **Army of the Republic of Vietnam** did not consider them worthy of attention.

KOMER, ROBERT WILLIAM (1922–2000). Born in Chicago and educated at Harvard University, Komer was in Army Intelligence in Italy during World War II. He joined the **Central Intelligence Agency** in 1947 and worked in the Office of National Estimates. He became a member of the **National Security Council** staff in the **John F. Kennedy** administration where he focused on Europe and the Middle East. Komer remained on the staff of the National Security Council until September 1965 and then served as the deputy special assistant to the president for National Security Affairs until March 1966. On 28 March 1966, Komer became the special assistant to the president and was charged with dealing with the politics of the war.

On 10 May 1967, he took over as deputy for **Civil Operations and Revolutionary Development Support** (CORDS) to the commander of the **Military Assistance Command, Vietnam** (MACV), and served as a special assistant to the ambassador to Vietnam. He was given the rank of ambassador with the equivalent authority as a three-star general. Komer reported directly to MACV Commander **William C. Westmoreland**. This allowed him to begin the tasks outlined for CORDS. Komer sought to combine U.S. civilian and military **pacification** efforts with those of the **Republic of Vietnam** in order to more effectively provide security for the people of Vietnam. While in charge of CORDS, Komer helped to oversee programs such as **Chiêu Hồi**, Revolutionary Development, **New Life Villages**, and other pacification efforts. He was also involved in the creation of the **Phoenix Program**. He remained with CORDS until 28 October 1967, when President **Lyndon B. Johnson** selected him as the U.S. ambassador to Turkey. He was replaced by his deputy, **William Colby**. Komer worked for the RAND Corporation and then served as the undersecretary of defense for policy in the James E. Carter administration. During his time in Vietnam, Komer was given the nickname "Blowtorch Bob" for his forceful nature and ability to argue.

KON TUM. Kon Tum province was located in the northernmost part of II **Corps Tactical Zone** (CTZ), with its capital at Kon Tum City. It bordered both **Laos** and **Cambodia**. Kon Tum was considered one of the most strategic provinces in II CTZ because of its location and was heavily contested throughout much of the war. It was the home of a number of **Montagnard** tribes including the **Sedang, Bahnar**, and **Jarai**. The **United States** worked with these tribes, through the **Studies and Observation Group**, to establish infiltration teams into both Laos and Cambodia.

Kon Tum witnessed a number of significant battles and operations during the war. In November 1967, the **People's Army of Vietnam** (PAVN) attacked the U.S. forces at **Đắk Tô** in a battle that would last for 19 days and resulted in 376 Americans killed with over 1,400 wounded, while the **Army of the Republic of Vietnam** (ARVN) lost 79 killed. The PAVN lost over 1,000 troops. On 3 March 1969, PT-76 light amphibious **tanks** engaged U.S. M48 tanks at the **Special Forces** camp at **Bến Hét**, located to the west of Đắk Tô, in a rare armored battle. Between 5 May and 29 June, the PAVN besieged both Bến Hét and Đắk Tô.

During the 1972 **Easter Offensive**, the PAVN concentrated one of its thrusts against the provinces of Kon Tum and **Plei Ku**. On 15 April, the camps at Đắk Tô and Tân Cảnh were placed under siege. Tân Cảnh fell on 23 April. By 4 May, Kon Tum was defenseless, and the 3rd PAVN Division had succeeded in cutting **Route** 1 just north of Route 19 in Plei Ku. After **Republic of Vietnam** president **Nguyễn Văn Thiệu** replaced the II Corps commander, Lieutenant General Ngô Dzu, with Major General Nguyễn Văn Toàn, the ARVN went on the offensive and slowly drove the PAVN forces out of Kon Tum.

The province was abandoned during the final PAVN offensive in 1975 when President Nguyễn Văn Thiệu ordered the ARVN to retreat from the **Central Highlands** to defend the lower part of II CTZ and points south.

KONG LE (1934–). Born in Savannakhet province in **Laos** and a member of the **Lao Theung**, Kong Le joined the Royal Lao Army in 1952. He served with the 2nd Parachute Battalion during the **First Indochina War**, sometimes as acting commander, and helped to shape the battalion into one with a solid reputation. Kong Le was involved in Laotian politics throughout the 1950s and, on 25 December 1959, helped to orchestrate a coup d'état that placed a more conservative faction in Laos in power under the leadership of **Phoumi Nosavan**. On 9 August 1960, Kong Le led another coup d'état in Laos that placed the neutralist leader **Souvanna Phouma** in power. This event ushered in years of civil war in Laos that drew attention away from fighting the communist insurgency, the **Pathet Lao**, and toward internal conflict and instability.

In the August 1960 coup d'état, Kong Le called for an end to Laotian internal conflict and government corruption and for a move toward international neutrality. He received guarantees from King Sir Savang Vatthana; General Ouane Rattikone, the spokesperson for the old government; and Premier Prince Somsanith, and on 16 August he officially ended the coup d'état. In November, a coalition government was formed that included neutralists, communists, and conservatives. This coalition did not last long. On 8 December 1960, Souvanna Phouma relieved Kong Le from command and was promptly overthrown by Kong Le. This instability allowed Phoumi Nosavan, who had **United States** support, to return to power while Kong Le allied with the Pathet Lao and the **Democratic Republic of Vietnam** (DRV).

As a result of the 1962 **Geneva Accords** on Laos, a second coalition government was formed, and Kong Le found his **Soviet** and DRV support weakened. He returned to service under the Laotian government, but his effectiveness was diminished by internal conflict in his command. He became the chief of the Laotian Army on 27 November 1962. Internal conflict continued in Laos, and many of Kong Le's closest supporters were targeted for assassination. Kong Le's army defeated a 31 January 1965 coup d'état attempt led by Phoumi Nosavan, and on 15 November 1966, Kong Le was dismissed as chief of the army after the military reacted negatively to Souvanna Phouma's 7 October 1966 dissolution of Parliament. He fled Laos in 1967, and his supporters joined both the Royal Lao Army and the Pathet Lao. After the communists' political takeover of Laos in December 1975, Kong Le tried to rally the Laotian people against the new government but failed to gain any momentum.

KRULAK, VICTOR HAROLD (1913–2008). United States Marine Corps (USMC) general nicknamed "Brute." Krulak was born in Colorado, educated at the U.S. Naval Academy, and graduated in 1934. He served in a number of positions before World War II, including time on the U.S.S. *Arizona* and in China with the 4th Marines. He served as an aide to General Holland M. Smith who commanded the Amphibious Corps in the Atlantic Fleet, and after parachute training he was transferred to the Pacific Theater as commander of the 2nd Parachute Battalion in the 1st Marine Amphibious Corps. He fought, as a lieutenant colonel, on Choiseul Island in 1943, during which he won the Navy Cross and a Purple Heart, and at Okinawa in 1945.

After the war, Krulak became the assistant director of the Senior School at the USMC Base in Quantico and regimental commander of the 5th Marines at Camp Pendleton. He served as the chief of staff of the 1st Marine **Division** during the first year of the Korean War and became the secretary to the General Staff at Headquarters Marine Corps and chief of staff of the Fleet Marine Force, Pacific, from 1951 to 1955. In July 1956, as a new brigadier general and the youngest to that date, Krulak served as the assistant commander of the 3rd Marine Division, and from 1957 to 1959, he was the director of the Marine Corps Educational Center at Quantico. In November 1959, Krulak became a major general.

In 1962, Krulak worked for the **Joint Chiefs of Staff** as a special assistant for counterinsurgency activities. Krulak traveled to Vietnam in September 1963 with Joseph Mendenhall to assess the war and the rule of **Ngô Đình Diệm**. Krulak supported the **Republic of Vietnam** (RVN) president and the war's progress, while Mendenhall provided the opposite assessment, leading President **John F. Kennedy** to ask if they had visited the same country. In December 1963, Krulak became involved in an interdepartmental group that studied covert operations against North Vietnam. He became the commanding general of the Fleet Marine Force, Pacific, on 1 March 1964 and was promoted to lieutenant general. He stayed in this command until 1 June 1968 upon his retirement.

Krulak advocated small-unit action in the RVN, with the focus on the village and villager. He was also a proponent of **airmobility** and the offensive use of the **helicopter**. His strategy was overruled by General **William C. Westmoreland**. After his retirement from the Marine Corps, Krulak worked for Copley Newspapers and wrote three books, including one titled *First to Fight: An Inside View of the U.S. Marine Corps*. He remained involved with the USMC in his retirement.

L

LAIRD, MELVIN ROBERT (1922–). Republican member of the House of Representatives from Wisconsin and **United States** secretary of defense. Laird received his education at Carleton College. In 1942, he joined the U.S. **Navy**, becoming an ensign in 1944 and serving on a destroyer. In 1946, he left the Navy and became a state senator in Wisconsin, taking over his father's vacancy after his death. In 1952, he was elected to the U.S. House of Representatives where he served from 3 January 1953 to 21 January 1969, when he became President **Richard M. Nixon**'s secretary of defense. Laird served as secretary of defense from 22 January 1969 to 29 January 1973. Laird supported the war but was critical of both former Secretary of Defense **Robert McNamara** and President **Lyndon B. Johnson** for their handling of the escalation, charging both with deceiving the American people on the cost of the war and their gradual approach in introducing combat troops to Vietnam. As secretary of defense, Laird followed the Nixon policy of **Vietnamization**, for which he was a strong advocate, as well as oversaw an armed forces that had been damaged as a result of the events in Southeast Asia. He was responsible for a number of reforms within the Department of Defense that reflected the changing times in the U.S.

Laird's work as secretary of defense, which focused on fiscal responsibility and an effort to regain the trust of **Congress**, coupled with his veteran status, did much to rehabilitate the Pentagon, even though the policies and actions of Nixon and **Henry Kissinger** during the 1970 **Cambodian Incursion** and the 1971 Operation **Lam Sơn 719** were very controversial. Laird visited Vietnam several times to assess Vietnamization as well as to determine how the U.S. could best serve its ally, the **Republic of Vietnam**. Laird also oversaw the reduction of the U.S. Armed Forces from 3.5 million in 1969 to fewer than 2.3 million in 1973. While the end of the American war was one of Laird's major accomplishments, he was also involved in developing new weapons systems, supporting arms reduction negotiations, and ending conscription. In June 1973, Laird returned to the White House as a counselor in the Nixon administration, but he resigned in February 1974 as the Watergate scandal began to dominate the presidency. He joined *Reader's Digest* as a senior counselor for national and international affairs. Laird is the author of several books and articles and has served on numerous boards of directors.

LAM SƠN 719. A 1971 ground operation in **Laos** designed to cut the **Hồ Chí Minh Trail** and test the effectiveness of **Vietnamization**. As a result of the positive effects of the May 1970 **Cambodian Incursion**, the **United States** and the **Army of the Republic of Vietnam** (ARVN) decided to make an additional incursion into the southern part of Laos to end the infiltration of personnel and supplies coming down the Hồ Chí Minh Trail. The U.S. had already had some success cutting off the sea routes with Operation **Market Time**, while the ARVN performance in **Cambodia** a year earlier showcased the success of Vietnamization. Unlike the Cambodia experience, however, the U.S. had additional restrictions placed on it. The December 1970 **Cooper-Church Amendment** to the military appropriations bill forbade the introduction of American combat troops into Laos and prohibited U.S. **advisers** from accompanying the ARVN troops on the operation.

Lam Sơn 719 was divided into four phases. The first phase, which began on 30 January 1971, sought to secure the area east of the operation by reopening the old **Khe Sanh** base and clearing **Route 9**. The **U.S. Air Force** redeployed approximately 10,000 ARVN troops to the staging area in what became known as Operation **Dewey Canyon** II. On 8 February, the second phase began on the ground and with an air attack toward the objective of the city of **Tchepone**, after which the third phase would initiate **search-and-destroy** operations to identify and destroy any remaining enemy personnel and supplies. Some 18,000 ARVN troops participated in the operation. The final phase would see the withdrawal of the attacking force.

The operation began smoothly but was soon mired in miscommunication, poor leadership, and distrust. The **Republic of Vietnam Air Force** lacked the necessary training and equipment to support the operation, which demanded American attention to save the situation. As the operation commenced, President **Nguyễn Văn Thiệu** ordered a change to the plan that forced his troops to stop short of their objective. The commanding Vietnamese general, **Hoàng Xuân Lãm**, who owed his military position to his political loyalty to Nguyễn Văn Thiệu, obeyed. This resulted in the **People's Army of Vietnam** (PAVN) being able to recover from the initial surprise and reinforce its troops in the area. By 18 February, the 70B Corps of the PAVN, with T-34 and T-54 medium **tanks**, heavy **artillery**, and **antiaircraft guns**, closed in on the beleaguered ARVN forces. By the third week in February, the ARVN faced a force that was nearly five times its own depleted strength of 8,000.

With the precarious position of the ARVN forces clearly understood by all, Nguyễn Văn Thiệu authorized the continuation of phase 2, and an ARVN regiment was transported by **helicopter** to Tchepone, which it found deserted. After occupying the city, the **Sài Gòn** government proclaimed Lam Sơn 719 a success. This senseless move nearly cost the South Vietnamese the entire regiment as the PAVN encircled it. Only after a risky and costly extraction by U.S. helicopters were the South Vietnamese soldiers saved from disaster. The enduring image of Lam Sơn 719 was of ARVN soldiers hanging on to the skids of American helicopters fleeing from the battlefield, and through implication deserting their fallen and wounded comrades to the enemy. The ARVN forces suffered nearly 50 percent **casualties**, while the U.S. lost 108 helicopters destroyed and 618 damaged. Moreover, 215 Americans were killed in an operation for which they had been prohibited to participate by the U.S. **Congress**. The operation failed to cut the trail and exposed the flaws of Vietnamization, and when President **Richard M. Nixon** went on the air on 7 April and proclaimed Lam Sơn 719 a success, it severely damaged his credibility. Lam Sơn 719 encouraged the PAVN to mount a major operation the next year, the 1972 **Easter Offensive**, designed to test the determination and skill of the ARVN forces as well as America's resolve to continue fighting in Vietnam.

LANDING ZONE (LZ). Term used to describe the area used to land aircraft, usually **helicopters**. Because of the nature of the terrain in Vietnam, **airmobility** became an important part of the **United States** strategy. Airmobility served as a troop multiplier, in that the U.S. could move its personnel throughout Vietnam to apply pressure on the enemy whenever and wherever it chose. It also provided for quick and efficient resupply and **aeromedical evacuation**, which allowed the U.S. to determine the length and intensity of its operations. Landing zones were required to give airmobility a chance to work as a strategy.

The U.S. often cleared areas within the Vietnamese jungle to create LZs. This was done by chopping down foliage or using explosives to blow down trees. The U.S. also experimented with larger 10,000-pound and 15,000-pound **bombs** to clear larger areas under Operation **Commando Vault**. Once a temporary LZ was ready for extraction, the troops on the ground used smoke grenades to mark the area. Permanent LZs were used for longer operations, usually constructed with defensive obstacles such as sandbags or barbed wire, and often defended by **artillery** and **mortars** within a **fire support base**.

LANG VEI. Established on 21 December 1966, the camp at Lang Vei served as a base for a **Civilian Irregular Defense Group** (CIDG) and **Special Forces** Detachment A-101. The camp was located to the southwest of **Khe Sanh** near the Laotian border. After a failed 4 May 1967 attempt to overrun the camp, it was relocated nearer to the Laotian border, approximately half a mile to the west of the old camp, while its defenses were strengthened. Early on the morning of 7 February 1968, while the siege of Khe Sanh was going on and the **Tết Offensive** had taken the focus off of the activity around the area, the camp was attacked by 12 PT-76 amphibious **tanks** from the 202nd **People's Army of Vietnam** (PAVN) Armored Regiment, followed by elements of the 304th PAVN Division. The camp was overrun within a few minutes, though the 24 Americans and approximately 500 CIDG forces fought for a few hours. The CIDG suffered 40 percent **casualties** while 10 **United States** personnel were killed-in-action and 11 were wounded.

LANSDALE, EDWARD GEARY (1908–1987). United States Air Force (USAF) general. Lansdale was born in Detroit, Michigan, attended the University of California at Los Angeles, and left in 1931 to work in advertising. He joined the Office of Strategic Services in 1943 and, as a lieutenant in the U.S. Army, worked in military intelligence. Lansdale rose through the ranks and in 1945, as a major, was transferred to Headquarters Air Forces Western Pacific. He served as the chief of the Intelligence Division. Lansdale was stationed in the **Philippines** at the end of the war and continued to help develop the military intelligence organization within the Philippines Army after the war ended.

With the creation of the USAF in 1947, Lansdale received a commission as a captain with the temporary rank of major. He remained in the Philippines until 1948 when he became an instructor at the Strategic Intelligence School on the Lowry Air Force Base in Colorado. He was then assigned to the Office of Policy Coordination, the covert action arm of the new **Central Intelligence Agency**. Lansdale was given a temporary promotion to lieutenant colonel in 1949. In 1950, he was transferred to the Joint **United States** Military Assistance Group, Philippines, at the request of Philippines President Elpidio Quirino. Lansdale advised the Filipino Armed Forces intelligence services in their struggle against the communist Hukbalahap guerrilla insurgency as the liaison officer to Secretary of National Defense Ramon Magsaysay. While in the Philippines, Lansdale earned a reputation as someone who could get the job done as he helped to create psychological operations, develop a civic action program, and encourage Huk defections that diminished the communist insurgency's strength. He was again promoted in 1951 to the temporary rank of colonel.

Lansdale was transferred to the **Military Assistance Advisory Group**, Indochina, in 1953, though he returned briefly to the Philippines to help Magsaysay win the presidential election in 1954. On 1 June 1954, Lansdale joined the **Saigon** Military Mission. Lansdale advised the State of Vietnam in counterinsurgency strategy and became the confidant of **Ngô Đình Diệm**, who served as the president of the Council of Ministers for the State of

Vietnam until he proclaimed a republic in October 1955 and served as its president until his assassination in November 1963. Lansdale focused on psychological operations, military **intelligence**, and the development of a loyal political party to support Ngô Đình Diệm in his struggle to develop an independent Vietnam.

Lansdale continued to support Ngô Đình Diệm even when others in the U.S., including General **J. Lawton Collins**, who served as President Dwight D. Eisenhower's special representative of the U.S. in Vietnam with the rank of ambassador, turned against the **Republic of Vietnam** (RVN) president. When the French-supported **Bình Xuyên** and elements of the **Cao Đài** and **Hòa Hảo** sects attempted to overthrow Ngô Đình Diệm in March 1955, Lansdale worked to secure his safety and ensure that Ngô Đình Diệm would win and consolidate his power. While Lansdale was very effective in the RVN, his unorthodox style and commitment to Ngô Đình Diệm earned him adversaries in Washington.

Lansdale left the RVN in 1957 and worked briefly at the headquarters of the USAF and, in June 1957, for the Office of the Secretary of Defense, where he became the deputy assistant to the secretary of defense for special operations. In April 1960, he was temporarily promoted to brigadier general. Lansdale continued to be a supporter of Ngô Đình Diệm even as the U.S. ambassador to the RVN, **Elbridge Durbrow**, became increasingly frustrated with his inability to control the RVN president. When **John F. Kennedy** entered the White House in January 1961, Lansdale was sent to the RVN to resume his relationship with Ngô Đình Diệm and assess the situation in the RVN. He recommended that Durbrow be replaced and that the U.S. return to the practice of working with the Vietnamese rather than dictating what they could or could not do with U.S. assistance.

Though Lansdale had aspirations of becoming the next ambassador to the RVN, **Frederick E. Nolting Jr.** was selected. Instead, Lansdale became the deputy assistant for special operations to the secretary of defense and then, in May 1961, the assistant for special operations to the secretary of defense. He served as a member of the Presidential Task Force on Vietnam between April and May 1961. Lansdale also joined the **Taylor-Rostow Mission** to the RVN in October 1961, though his access to the president diminished as members of the State Department took control of a U.S.-Vietnam policy that sought to flex its power at the expense of Ngô Đình Diệm.

Lansdale opposed the U.S. policy in the RVN that moved away from working with Ngô Đình Diệm and toward replacing him. He was excluded from the decision-making process that led to the November 1963 coup d'état. Lansdale retired from the USAF in 1963 as a major general. He would return to Vietnam as a special assistant to Ambassador **Henry Cabot Lodge Jr.** on

16 August 1965 where he worked with the Vietnamese involved in **pacification** efforts. Lansdale advocated pacification rather than the Americanization of the war. He remained involved in the Vietnam War until 1968 when he retired from government service. He published his memoirs, *In the Midst of Wars: An American's Mission to Southeast Asia*, in 1972, though the book only examined his career up to 1956.

LAO. Ethnic group in **Laos** associated with the Mon-**Khmer** language group who lived primarily in northern Laos and practiced Theravada **Buddhism**. The Lao people made up a majority of Laos. *See also* LAO THEUNG.

LAO ĐỘNG PARTY. Established by **Hồ Chí Minh**, the Vietnam Workers' Party (Đảng Lao Động Việt Nam/Lao Động Party) was formed in 1951 at the Second Congress of the Indochinese Communist Party at Tuyên Quang in the northern part of Vietnam. It replaced the Indochinese Communist Party, which had been founded in 1930. It served as the main Communist Party organization in Vietnam until 1976 when its name was changed. The main purpose of the Lao Động Party was to bring together the people of Vietnam against first the common threat of **France**, and then the **Republic of Vietnam** (RVN) and the **United States**. It sought to liberate the Vietnamese people from colonialism and Western imperialism and to usher in a social and economic revolution that would transform the country.

The Lao Động Party was led by a general secretary until 1960 when the title was changed to first secretary. The first general secretary of the Lao Động Party was **Trường Chinh**. Hồ Chí Minh served as the general secretary from 1956 to 1957, and **Lê Duẩn** took over in 1957 and remained in that position until 1986. The general secretary or first secretary oversaw an organization that included a Politburo, which contained a select membership of communist leaders, and the Central Committee with an expanded membership. Hồ Chí Minh served as the president (or chairman) of the Central Committee until his death in 1969.

The Third Congress met in **Hà Nội** in 1960. It was at this congress that the decision was made to intensify the communist insurgency in the RVN, which led to the formation of the **National Liberation Front** in December 1960. By the time of the Fourth Congress in 1976, when the Lao Động Party was renamed the Communist Party of Vietnam, its membership was estimated at over 1.5 million members.

LAO THEUNG. The Lao Theung was one of three major population groups in **Laos**. The other two were the Lao Loum and Lao Sung. The Lao Theung lived in the hill country of Laos and spoke languages in the Mon-

Khmer group. They lived in communal houses and practiced slash-and-burn agriculture. The Lao Theung were considered the first inhabitants of Laos but were pushed out of their lands by the Lao Loum who gave them the name Kha (slave). That name remained during the French colonial period. A number of Lao Theung joined the communist insurgency movement, the **Pathet Lao**, but were also recruited by the **United States** in the late 1950s and early 1960s.

In 1959, the U.S. initiated Project **Hotfoot** and began recruiting Laotians for **counterinsurgency** operations. The program, which was funded by the **Central Intelligence Agency**, was renamed Operation **White Star** in 1961. U.S. **Special Forces** trained Lao Theung and **Hmong** personnel, but the operation was controversial because of Laotian neutrality and the lack of support from the **Military Assistance Advisory Group**. The operation ended as a result of the 1962 **Geneva Accords** on Laos, and the troops were withdrawn by October 1962. Lao Theung were again recruited after 1965 to provide reconnaissance along the **Hồ Chí Minh Trail**, but the U.S. was not able to expand this project because of the objections of the Vientiane government. Elements of the Lao Theung supported the Pathet Lao throughout the war, and after the December 1975 communist victory, the Lao Theung were rewarded with greater involvement in the governance of the country.

LAOS. Situated to the west of the **Democratic Republic of Vietnam** (DRV), east of **Thailand**, and north of **Cambodia**, Laos was one of the three countries that made up French Indochina during the colonial period. The country, with its capital at Vientiane, is approximately 236,800 square kilometers (91,430 square miles), with a population of around two million during the war. In addition to the capital, other major cities in Laos include Savannakhet and Luang Prabang. Like most of Southeast Asia, Laos is governed by **climate**, with tropical monsoon rains during the summer and early fall. The major ethnic group is the **Lao**, from the Tai-Kadai language family, which is comprised of several ethnic groups, while Theravada **Buddhism** is the predominant religion. Most of the Laotian people live in the **Mê Kông River** valleys and tributaries, with the remainder living in tribes in the mountains, often isolated. Lao is the official language, though French was spoken by many of the ruling class. Laos has primarily a basic agrarian economy.

Official Laotian history dates to 1353 during the Kingdom of Lan Xang. The kingdom flourished for nearly three centuries until the Thai empire absorbed and reapportioned it. During the end of the 19th century, **France** entered the region and exerted its influence. The French signed the Franco-Siamese Treaty of 1907 with the Thai, which created the western border of Laos. The French ruled Laos, dividing it into three sections—Vientiane,

Champassak, and Luang Prabang—as part of French Indochina until World War II, when the area was occupied by the Japanese. France's early surrender during the war encouraged Laotian nationalists to push for independence, which King Sisavang Vong declared in 1945. In September 1945, the three sections were reunited under the Lao Issara (Free Laos), but the return of the French military in 1946 temporarily ended the independence movement. As the **First Indochina War** raged in the late 1940s until 1954, Laotians played a limited role. It was during this time that the **Pathet Lao**, under the leadership of Prince **Souphanouvong**, worked with the **Việt Minh** against the French, but the Laotians did not gain their independence until after the 1954 **Geneva Agreements**.

Laos held elections in 1955 that put Prince **Souvanna Phouma** in power. His government depended upon other parties joining a coalition, which was a tenuous position at best. In 1958, his coalition failed, and a more right-wing government took over. In the election, the **Neo Lao Hak Xat**, a political front for the Pathet Lao, won nine of 21 contested seats but was not allowed to take them. The Neo Lao Hak Xat was ideologically opposed to the government's political party, **Rally of the Lao People**, though neither group was strong enough to rule without some type of coalition. The next crisis in Laotian politics occurred in August 1960 when Army Captain **Kong Le** initiated a successful coup d'état and returned Souvanna Phouma to the head of the government. Souvanna Phouma was quickly replaced by General **Phoumi Nosavan**, who had the backing of the **United States**.

Subsequently, the neutralists allied themselves with the communist insurgents and began to receive support from the **Soviet Union** and additional aid from the DRV, while Phoumi Nosavan's rightist regime received support from the U.S. As the Eisenhower administration ended its second term, Laos was considered the most dangerous spot in the Cold War in Southeast Asia. President Dwight D. Eisenhower would call Laos the keystone for all of Southeast Asia as he left office in 1961. Phoumi Nosavan stayed in power until the 1962 **Geneva Accords** on Laos, which brought that country back to neutralism and saw Souvanna Phouma return to head the government. He remained the prime minister until 1975.

During the **Second Indochina War**, Laos continued to proclaim its neutrality even though the North Vietnamese occupied the areas in the east and aided the Pathet Lao in a continuous war across the **Plain of Jars**. The war in Laos was divided into two distinct parts based on the geography of the country in relation to Vietnam. In the northern part of Laos, specifically in Military Region 2, a more traditional land battle ensued based on the weather, while the conflict in the southern part of the country was dictated by the importance of the **Hồ Chí Minh Trail** that ran through that part of the country. The war in Laos became America's secret war because Laotian neutrality prohibited the introduction of U.S. combat troops into the country.

The U.S. supported five major air campaigns in Laos during the war. The first was Operation **Barrel Roll**, begun in 1964, which consisted of air-to-ground support over the entire country but mainly focused on the northern area after 1965. This campaign lasted until 1973. Operation **Steel Tiger**, which started in 1965, was an interdiction campaign against the Hồ Chí Minh Trail, while Operation **Tiger Hound** was a similar operation that was carved out of Steel Tiger but under the command of **Military Assistance Command, Vietnam**. Steel Tiger and Tiger Hound were replaced by Operation **Commando Hunt** in 1968, when **Rolling Thunder sorties** were significantly reduced in March. Commando Hunt lasted until 1972, when the North Vietnamese **Easter Offensive** diverted attention and resources away from Laos. The final air campaign was in support of the February 1971 **Army of the Republic of Vietnam** operation Lam Sơn 719, the failed attempt to cut the Hồ Chí Minh Trail at **Tchepone**.

The majority of the Laotian Armed Forces fought in the Plain of Jars against the **People's Army of Vietnam** (PAVN) and the Pathet Lao. The battles were often determined by weather. During the dry season, the PAVN and Pathet Lao went on the offensive against the overmatched Laotian Armed Forces, with the U.S. providing as much air-to-ground support as possible. During the monsoon season, when the roads were impassable, the government forces used **airmobility** to concentrate their personnel on regaining area lost during the dry season. Also prominent in the battle was control of the **Lima Sites**, tall rock outcroppings that dominated the Plain of Jars, from which one could observe the enemy from a distance and manage the battlefield. It was in this manner that the war was fought until 1973.

In early 1973, the Lao People's Revolutionary Party, the communist party in Laos, entered into a coalition government after the **Paris Peace Accords**. While a ceasefire was put in place, it did not end the shooting war, though that had diminished, and it had no effect on political intrigue in Vientiane. When **Phnom Penh** fell to the **Khmer Rouge** on 17 April 1975 and the **Sài Gòn** government was surrounded two weeks later, the Pathet Lao stepped up their military activities and eventually entered Vientiane in December 1975. On 2 December 1975, the Pathet Lao established the Lao People's Democratic Republic after the king abdicated his throne. The new government allied itself with the Socialist Republic of Vietnam and the Soviet Union. Like Cambodia and the **Republic of Vietnam**, Laos had also been taken by the communists.

LAVELLE, JOHN DANIEL (1916–1979). United States Air Force (USAF) general. Lavelle was born in Cleveland, Ohio, and was educated at

John Carroll University, graduating in 1938. He entered the Army Air Corps in 1939 as an aviation cadet and became a second lieutenant in June 1940. During World War II, he flew with the 412th Fighter Squadron in Europe. After the war, he served as the deputy chief of statistical services at headquarters from 1946 to 1949.

He would serve in a variety of positions before becoming commander of the **7th Air Force** in Vietnam on 29 July 1971, including stints with the North Atlantic Treaty Organization, director of the USAF aerospace program, chief of the Southeast Asia Programs Team, commander of the 17th Air Force, and vice commander-in-chief of the Pacific Air Force. As commander of the 7th Air Force and deputy commander for air operations under the **Military Assistance Command, Vietnam**, Lavelle was critical of the policy that forbade bombing the **Democratic Republic of Vietnam** (DRV) except in situations where an airstrike was retaliation for American **reconnaissance** aircraft that had been targeted or attacked.

Lavelle was forced to retire on 7 April 1972 after it was learned that he had allegedly authorized his pilots to file false claims of attacks against them in order to allow for retaliation bombing **sorties** against North Vietnam. Lavelle believed that the U.S. was allowing the DRV to construct its war-making industry without impediment, which would result in losing the war. Lavelle also allegedly authorized strikes against unauthorized targets. Lavelle was exposed when one of his men wrote a letter to Senator Harold Hughes (D-Iowa) who then informed Air Force Chief of Staff General John Ryan on 8 March 1972.

An Air Force investigation revealed at least 147 sorties that had been illegally authorized, though approximately 1,300 **protective reaction strikes** were recorded during his tenure as commander of the 7th Air Force. While Lavelle initially assumed responsibility for the strikes, he testified in front of the House Armed Services Committee about the situation. In his testimony, Lavelle indicated that General **Creighton W. Abrams**, commander of the Military Assistance Command, Vietnam, was aware of the air strikes, though he conceded that Abrams was not aware of Lavelle's duplicity. Lavelle acknowledged that he liberally interpreted his orders and the rules of engagement, but he suggested in his testimony that his actions were not discouraged by his superiors.

On 4 August 2010, President Barack H. Obama posthumously nominated Lavelle for advancement on the retired rolls to the rank of general to regain the status he had lost as a result of the 1972 alleged action. This came after a 2007 investigation which showed that **President Richard M. Nixon** had in fact authorized the air strikes against the DRV. Declassified documents also suggested that Lavelle had moved to discourage the strikes rather than encourage them. Lavelle had covered for his president in order to avoid embarrassment.

LÊ DUẨN (1907–1986). Democratic Republic of Vietnam (DRV) political leader who was sometimes referred to as Brother Number Three (Anh Ba). Lê Duẩn was born in **Quảng Trị** and was one of the founding members of the Indochinese Communist Party in 1930. He served two long terms in the prison on **Poulo Condore** (Côn Sơn) island between 1931 and 1936 and at Sơn La Prison between 1940 and 1945 because of his anti-French activities. In 1946, he helped to organize the communist insurgency in the southern part of Vietnam and served as the secretary of the Nam Bộ Regional Committee and then the **Central Office for South Vietnam**.

After the 1954 **Geneva Agreements**, Lê Duẩn continued to organize the communist insurgency, and in 1956, when **Republic of Vietnam** (RVN) president **Ngô Đình Diệm** announced his intention not to follow through with a national election to unify the two Vietnams, Lê Duẩn argued for increased conflict, even with the **United States**, in order to achieve independence. Lê Duẩn became one of the principal advocates of large-scale military operations against the RVN and was opposed by **Võ Nguyên Giáp**, though he remained outside of the political conflict that arose due to one of his colleagues and supporters, **Trường Chinh**, who also opposed Võ Nguyên Giáp. As a result, Lê Duẩn took over primary responsibility for running the **Lao Động** Party in 1956.

Lê Duẩn consolidated his power in the late 1950s and helped to push forward his strategy of increased violence in the RVN with the objective of overthrowing Ngô Đình Diệm. These actions led to increased insurgency activity and to the eventual creation of the **National Liberation Front** in 1960. Lê Duẩn was officially named the first secretary of the Vietnamese Communist Party in 1960 and remained in that position until 1986, though the title would change to general secretary in 1976. He worked to bring Soviet and Chinese aid into the DRV in order to offset the gradual escalation of the U.S. in Southeast Asia and established firm preconditions to negotiations that would lead to the end of the war in April 1975 and that included the reunification of the two Vietnams. Lê Duẩn was the most powerful man in Vietnam and worked to diminish the real strength and influence of Prime Minister **Phạm Văn Đồng** and the **People's Army of Vietnam** leader General Võ Nguyên Giáp.

Lê Duẩn took over control of the DRV after the death of **Hồ Chí Minh** in September 1969 and continued to govern the country through its eventual reunification with the RVN and the creation of the Socialist Republic of Vietnam (SRV) in 1976. Lê Duẩn was an advocate of the invasion of **Cambodia** in December 1978, and though a supporter of the **People's Republic of China** (PRC) for most of his life, he moved the SRV toward the **Soviet Union** after the PRC invaded the SRV in 1979.

LÊ ĐỨC ANH (1920–). People's Army of Vietnam (PAVN) general and Socialist Republic of Vietnam (SRV) president. Lê Đức Anh was born in **Huế**. In 1938, he joined the Indochinese Communist Party and served with the PAVN at the beginning of the **First Indochina War**. During the war, he was the chief of staff for **Military Region** 7, Military Region 8, and the **Sài Gòn**-Chợ Lớn Special Region. In 1951, he was promoted to chief of staff for Nam Bộ. After the 1954 **Geneva Conference**, Lê Đức Anh was one of 80,000 to travel from the South to the North. He returned to the **Republic of Vietnam** in 1963 as the deputy chief of the PAVN General Staff. In 1964, he was promoted to chief of staff. In 1968, he served as the deputy commander of the **National Liberation Front** and was involved in the 1968 **Tết Offensive** attack against Sài Gòn. In 1969, Lê Đức Anh commanded Military Region 9 and stayed there until 1974. In 1975, he led the Vietnamese forces from the southwest in the final attack against Sài Gòn.

After the war, Lê Đức Anh commanded the PAVN forces in **Cambodia** from 1981 to 1987. In 1987, he became the defense minister for the SRV, and in September 1992 he served as the president. He remained in that position until September 1997 when he stepped down and was replaced by Trần Đức Lương. He continued as an adviser to the Central Committee of the Vietnamese Communist Party until 2001.

LÊ ĐỨC THỌ (1911–1990). Leader within the **Lao Động** Party. Born Phan Đình Khải in Nam Định province in the northern part of Vietnam, Lê Đức Thọ was a founding member of the Indochinese Communist Party in 1930. He spent a considerable amount of time in French colonial jails, first from 1930 to 1936 and then from 1939 to 1945. Upon his release, Lê Đức Thọ worked with the **Việt Minh** against **France** until the end of World War II. He helped organize resistance to the French in the southern part of Vietnam during the **First Indochina War** when he formed an alliance with **Lê Duẩn** and **Phạm Hùng**. Lê Đức Thọ joined the Politburo of the Lao Động Party in 1955 after the signing of the 1954 **Geneva Agreements** and was involved in organizing the Vietnamese resistance to the government of **Ngô Đình Diệm** after the **Republic of Vietnam** refused to participate in the proposed national elections in 1956.

Lê Đức Thọ continued to rise within the Vietnamese Communist Party and emerged as one of the leaders of the faction that opposed **Võ Nguyên Giáp** for control of the southern insurgency. Between 1969 and 1973, he served as a special adviser to the DRV negotiation team lead by Xuân Thủy at the Paris Peace Talks, though he engaged in secret negotiations with **Henry Kissinger** that eventually led to the January 1973 **Paris Peace Accords**. For his work in Paris, Lê Đức Thọ was awarded, with Kissinger, the Nobel Prize for Peace on 10 December 1973, though he declined the award, arguing that peace had not actually been achieved. Kissinger accepted his award.

After the fall of **Sài Gòn** in April 1975, Lê Đức Thọ remained prominent in the politics and diplomacy of the Socialist Republic of Vietnam. He became the chief adviser to the People's Republic of Kampuchea after the Vietnamese invasion in December 1978 and remained in that position until 1982. In 1982, he served as a member of the Central Committee, and in 1986, after stepping down, he became an adviser to that organization. *See also* CAMBODIA.

LÊ KHẢ PHIÊU (1931–). General secretary of the Vietnamese Communist Party. Lê Khả Phiêu joined the Indochinese Communist Party in 1949 and went to military school. He also earned a degree in political science. Lê Khả Phiêu spent over 40 years in the military or public life serving the **Democratic Republic of Vietnam**. During the war, he commanded at nearly every level, as well as acting as a political commissar and commander of the regiment. He was deputy chief of the Army's Political Department of the 2nd Army Corps, deputy political commissar and chief of the Political Department of the Ninth Military Zone, and chief of the Political Department and political commander of **Front** 719. He also served in a variety of positions in the upper echelon of the **People's Army of Vietnam** and as deputy commander of the Vietnamese occupation force in **Cambodia**, with the final rank of lieutenant general. In 1992, Lê Khả Phiêu was elected to the Central Committee of the Vietnamese Communist Party and served as secretariat of the Central Committee. He also was a standing member of the Secretariat. In 1994, he was elected to the Political Bureau of the Central Committee. In 1997, he became the general secretary of the Central Committee of the Vietnamese Communist Party until his resignation in 2001.

LÊ MINH ĐẢO (1933–). Army of the Republic of Vietnam (ARVN) general. Lê Minh Đảo, trained at Fort Benning, Georgia, in the 1950s, served in a variety of positions in the ARVN and government, including as province chief of **Long An** province in January 1964. After his 30 January 1964 coup d'état, General **Nguyễn Khánh** took away Lê Minh Đảo's control of the military units in his province. In 1967, he also served as province chief in Chương Thiện province. He was most famous for his work with the 18th ARVN Division, which had been considered one of the worst divisions in the ARVN when he assumed command in 1972. During the final 1975 **People's Army of Vietnam** (PAVN) offensive, Lê Minh Đảo participated in the final major battle of the war. His 18th ARVN Division, along with **Regional Forces**, fought at **Xuân Lộc**, north of **Sài Gòn**, for nearly two weeks. The ARVN force was outnumbered and outgunned. The division finally collapsed on 21 April. Lê Minh Đảo was captured by the PAVN and spent 17 years in a reeducation camp. After his release from prison in 1992, he moved to the **United States**.

LÊ NGUYÊN KHANG (1931–1996). Lieutenant general and commander of the **Republic of Vietnam** (RVN) **Marine Corps**. Lê Nguyên Khang was born in **Sơn Tây**, located in the north of Vietnam. He was a graduate of the 1st Class of the Nam Định School for Reserve Officers in 1952. At the end of the **First Indochina War**, and as a result of the 1954 **Geneva Agreements**, Lê Nguyên Khang and his family migrated to the South. He joined the RVN Armed Forces, serving as a first lieutenant and chief G-4 for the Marine Group Command, and was promoted to commander, Headquarters Company of the Marine Group, in 1956.

He received additional training in Advanced Infantry Class at the **United States** Army Infantry School in Fort Benning, Georgia, in 1956, and in the Marine Middle Class at the Marine Corps School in Quantico, Virginia, in 1958, while also serving as the commander of the Marine 2nd Battalion in 1957, the 3rd Battalion in 1959, and the 1st Battalion in 1960. In April 1960, he became the acting commander of the Marine Group and, as a major, the commander of the Marine Brigade in 1962. In 1963, as a lieutenant colonel, he served as the military attaché for the RVN embassy in the **Philippines**, in part because of his close association to **Ngô Đình Diệm**, but he returned to command the Marine Brigade on 26 February 1964 after the January 1964 coup d'état by **Nguyễn Khánh**. He was promoted to brigadier general on 11 August 1964 and to major general on 15 October 1964.

Between June 1965 and June 1966, he commanded the Capital Military District, which included **Sài Gòn** and then III Corps. In November 1967, he was promoted to lieutenant general. In August 1968, Lê Nguyên Khang was removed from the III Corps in a political move by President **Nguyễn Văn Thiệu**, though he did retain control over the Vietnamese Marines. Lê Nguyên Khang had been a close supporter of **Nguyễn Cao Kỳ** and was implicated in later coup d'état plots until 1972. In May 1972, he became the assistant for operations to the RVN Armed Forces chief of the Joint General Staff as a result of his effective command during the **Easter Offensive**. The Nguyễn Cao Kỳ–Nguyễn Văn Thiệu rivalry affected Lê Nguyên Khang, who eventually lost command of the marines and moved to the position of inspector general of the armed forces until the war's end.

LÊ QUANG TUNG (1923–1963). Army of the Republic of Vietnam (ARVN) **Special Forces** commander. Lê Quang Tung served as a security officer for the French during the **First Indochina War** and specialized in counterespionage and **counterinsurgency**. When **Ngô Đình Diệm** came into power and proclaimed the **Republic of Vietnam** (RVN), Lê Quang Tung joined the **Cần Lao Party** and rose in prominence due to his ability to raise money for the organization, though it often allegedly occurred through extortion or bribes. His relationship with Ngô Đình Diệm and **Ngô Đình Nhu** caused many in the military to see him as a rival. In 1960, he was placed in charge of the RVN Special Forces, which was still known as the **First Observation Group** at that time.

Using funds from the **Central Intelligence Agency**, Lê Quang Tung was able to build the Vietnamese Special Forces into a formidable force, though it was underutilized in the counterinsurgency war. Lê Quang Tung answered directly to Ngô Đình Nhu even though the Special Forces were under ARVN control. This caused even further intraservice rivalry. During his tenure, Lê Quang Tung authorized a series of sabotage missions against the **Democratic Republic of Vietnam**, but none were successful. He was most known for his role in organizing the 21 August 1963 raids of pagodas in **Sài Gòn** and **Huế** that resulted in hundreds of deaths and thousands detained. With the encouragement of Ngô Đình Nhu, Lê Quang Tung ordered his Special Forces to dress as ARVN soldiers before raiding the pagodas and arresting all of the **Buddhists**, workers, and students who used the temples as safe havens. Lê Quang Tung would also be implicated in an assassination plot to kill **United States** ambassador **Henry Cabot Lodge Jr.**, who had been very critical of Ngô Đình Diệm and Ngô Đình Nhu.

When Lodge and other Americans who were involved in the RVN began to envisage the possibility of a change in government in Sài Gòn, Lê Quang Tung was considered a liability to stability in the region. Lê Quang Tung attempted to trap the coup d'état planners by exposing them in a fake uprising. Once identified, these leaders would be arrested or killed. His efforts failed, and on 1 November 1963, they invited Lê Quang Tung to a meeting at the Joint General Staff headquarters at **Tân Sơn Nhứt** Air Base. He was detained after refusing to join them and was forced to order his men to surrender. Because of his loyalty to Ngô Đình Diệm and his rivalry with the ARVN, Lê Quang Tung was considered a liability in a post–Ngô Đình Diệm RVN. After failing to convince Ngô Đình Diệm to surrender on the evening of 1 November, Lê Quang Tung and his brother, Major Lê Quang Triệu, were executed near the Tân Sơn Nhứt Air Base.

LÊ VĂN HÙNG. Army of the Republic of Vietnam (ARVN) general and commanding officer during the "miracle at An Lộc" in 1972. Lê Văn Hùng came from a prominent Vietnamese family and graduated from the Thủ Đức Military Academy in 1955. He quickly rose in rank in the ARVN as a competent officer even though he did not always agree with his **United States advisers**. Lê Văn Hùng served as a provincial chief in the Mekong Delta until he was given command of the 5th ARVN Division in III **Corps Tactical Zone** (CTZ) in 1971. During the 1972 **Easter Offensive**, he commanded the forces under siege at An Lộc and helped rally his troops against intensive attacks by the 9th **National Liberation Front** (NLF) Division. Lê Văn Hùng held on to An Lộc for 95 days and helped to push the NLF out of the area after being reinforced. For his action at An Lộc, he was promoted to general. He was then given command of the 21st ARVN Division. He returned to the Mekong Delta in 1974 as the deputy commander of the IV CTZ. When the North Vietnamese overran the **Republic of Vietnam** and **Dương Văn Minh** resigned as president, Lê Văn Hùng committed suicide rather than surrender and live under communist rule.

LÊ VĂN VIỄN (BẢY VIỄN) (1904–1970). Bình Xuyên leader. Bảy Viễn collaborated with the Japanese in their occupation of Indochina during World War II, which set up his organization as one of the most powerful in the **Republic of Vietnam**. He was imprisoned briefly at Côn Sơn, which allowed him to recruit for the Bình Xuyên. He escaped in 1945 and was given a position within the **Sài Gòn** police after the 9 March 1945 coup d'état led by the Japanese against the French. Bảy Viễn allied the Bình Xuyên with the **Việt Minh** in 1945. Through shrewd alliances and ruthless actions, Bảy Viễn built up the Bình Xuyên during the **First Indochina War** and established a safe haven in the Rừng Sác, a swamp and marshland to the south of Sài Gòn.

After a split with the Việt Minh, Bảy Viễn reached a compromise with the French and **Bảo Đại** in 1948 that allowed his organization a relatively free rein in and around Sài Gòn and toward the city of **Vung Tàu** on the coast. The Bình Xuyên engaged in a variety of criminal activities with this newfound power. Bảy Viễn and the Bình Xuyên retained control of this territory until their attempt to oust **Ngô Đình Diệm** from power in late April 1955. Ngô Đình Diệm's forces routed the Bình Xuyên, and Bảy Viễn was forced into exile in **France**, where he remained until his death.

LEAPING LENA. Established on 15 May 1964, Leaping Lena was a **Special Forces** project to train Vietnamese Special Forces and **Civilian Irregular Defense Group** personnel how to conduct **long-range reconnaissance patrols**. The project was under the administrative command of the **Republic of Vietnam** but was sponsored by the **Central Intelligence Agency**. Members of the 1st Special Forces Group and 7th Special Forces Group trained the Vietnamese in long-range reconnaissance strategy and tactics. The project was transferred to the **Military Assistance Command, Vietnam**, in June. On

24 June, five eight-man teams were air-dropped into **Laos** around the city of **Tchepone** to provide **intelligence** on the **Hồ Chí Minh Trail**. The teams failed to evade the enemy, and 35 of the men were killed or captured by the time the mission ended on 1 July. The **United States** learned several lessons from the failure of Leaping Lena, first of which was that long-range reconnaissance patrols into Laos required American personnel to lead them if they were to be successful. Leaping Lena became Project Delta in October 1964, which eventually evolved into the **Recondo School** in September 1966.

LEMAY, CURTIS EMERSON (1906–1990). United States Air Force (USAF) general. LeMay, nicknamed Iron Eagle, was born in Columbus, Ohio, and was educated at Ohio State University. He served with the Reserve Officers Training Corps and received his commission in 1930. Before World War II, he was stationed in Michigan, Hawaii, and Virginia. He was one of the first pilots of the B-17 bomber. In 1942, as a colonel, he commanded the 305th Bombardment Group in the European Theater where he instituted a number of improvements in **bombing** technique. In 1944, he moved to the China-Burma-India Theater as commander of the 20th Bomber Command. He was involved in the March 1945 incendiary bombings against Japanese cities and carried out President Harry S. Truman's order to drop atomic bombs on Hiroshima and Nagasaki to end World War II.

LeMay was known for his aggressive style and competent manner. He commanded the Berlin Airlift from 1948 to 1949 and was appointed commanding general of the Strategic Air Command after the airlift's successful conclusion. He was an advocate of airpower and the use of strategic bombing. LeMay became the vice chief of staff of the USAF from July 1957 until 1961, when he was promoted to chief of staff.

LeMay represented the **Hawk** position in Vietnam. He believed in the value of airpower in determining a successful conclusion to the war in Southeast Asia and often came into conflict with President **Lyndon B. Johnson** and Secretary of Defense **Robert McNamara** over what LeMay believed was too cautious an approach to prosecuting the war. LeMay called for sustained bombing of the **Democratic Republic of Vietnam** (DRV) without the restrictions imposed by the White House and Pentagon. He eventually was forced into retirement on 31 January 1965. In 1965, he published his memoir, *Missions with LeMay*, in which he argued that the U.S. should bomb the DRV back into the Stone Age, and he continued to oppose what he considered to be a weak American response in Vietnam.

In 1968, LeMay joined George C. Wallace as his vice presidential candidate in the American Independent Party. LeMay's aggressive position in relation to Vietnam and Wallace's segregationist policies did not sit well with an American population tired of the war and ready for change. The party only received 13.5 percent of the vote and garnered 46 electoral votes. LeMay returned to private life and became involved in charitable organizations until his death.

LIGHT ANTI-TANK WEAPON. The M72, or Light Anti-Tank Weapon (LAW), was a 66-mm caliber weapon used against armored vehicles, specifically **tanks**, but it could also be used against reinforced bunkers or other fixed targets. The weapon weighed a little more than 2.5 kilograms (5.5 pounds). It fired a 50.8-centimeter (20-inch) **missile** that weighed approximately 1.8 kilograms (4 pounds), which could penetrate at least 30 centimeters (12 inches) of armor or up to 61 centimeters (two feet) of reinforced concrete. The LAW had a maximum range of over 915 meters (3,000 feet), though its effective range was shorter at approximately 206 meters (675 feet). While there were some problems with earlier versions of the LAW missile, it proved effective during the 1972 **Easter Offensive**. The **People's Army of Vietnam** and **National Liberation Front**'s answer to the LAW was the rocket-propelled grenade weapon, the RPG-7, built by the **Soviet Union**.

LIMA SITES. A series of mountaintop strongholds located in northern **Laos** that determined strategic control of the battlefield in the **Plain of Jars**. There were approximately 100 such sites, from which the **United States** could utilize its aircraft to aid the Royal Laotian Army as well as the independent armies fighting against the **People's Army of Vietnam** (PAVN) and the **Pathet Lao**. Because the Lima Sites were often on the highest ground in the area, they also served as **intelligence**-gathering and observation stations against the **Democratic Republic of Vietnam** (DRV). Because these sites dominated the battlefield and were among the most strategic points in the northern Laotian war, fighting for the land often involved fierce hand-to-hand combat. During the dry season, when the Laotian forces defended their position against the numerically superior PAVN and Pathet Lao, U.S. aircraft provided air-to-ground support using information gathered at the sites. During the monsoon season, U.S. aircraft served as troop multipliers and sometimes used the Lima Sites to concentrate troops to regain territory lost during the dry season.

There were many important Lima Sites in Laos. One of the most significant was Lima Site 85, located at Phou Pha Thi, because it overlooked the DRV and was used to coordinate air strikes starting in August 1966 when a tactical air navigation system was built on the site. The site's equipment was upgraded in August–September 1967 with a TSQ-81 bomb control radar. It remained in operation until 1968 when the PAVN sent its 316th Division to overrun the station. The site was lost on 11 May after an intense struggle where 11 of the 19 U.S. personnel perished in the ordeal.

LINEBACKER I, OPERATION. United States and Republic of Vietnam **Air Force** air operation in response to the **Democratic Republic of Vietnam**'s (DRV) 1972 **Easter Offensive**. When the North Vietnamese began their three-pronged invasion of the **Republic of Vietnam** (RVN) on 30 March 1972, President **Richard M. Nixon** ordered the redeployment of aircraft to the Southeast Asian theater to assist the beleaguered **Army of the Republic of Vietnam** (ARVN) forces and recommence the **bombing** of the DRV. The Linebacker Operation began on 9 May 1972 under the code name Rolling Thunder Alpha. It absorbed Operation **Freedom Train** that struck at hard targets in the DRV used to support the invasion. It was officially named Linebacker on 10 May. The opening phase of the operation proved to be very effective as the **mining** of **Hải Phòng** and other minor harbors virtually stopped sea traffic in and out of the DRV. Linebacker **sorties** then turned to railroad lines and bridges between the People's Republic of China and the DRV, without the major restrictions that had hampered Operation **Rolling Thunder**. Linebacker took advantage of the new technologies available in the air war, such as the Walleye I and Paveway I **missiles**, as well as the F-111 fighter-bomber.

These new technologies and fewer restrictions allowed for successful destruction of a number of targets that had eluded the aircraft involved in Rolling Thunder, such as the destruction of the Thanh Hóa Bridge on 13 May, which fell in one day. The new weapons also made it possible to continue attacks in all types of weather conditions, which kept up constant pressure on North Vietnamese logistical operations. Linebacker sorties then focused on making it difficult for North Vietnamese personnel and supplies traveling to the front lines. The F-111 was particularly successful in achieving surprise in armed **reconnaissance** missions attacking truck parks and supply depots.

While the primary mission was hampering the transportation lines, Linebacker sorties also struck at North Vietnamese infrastructure used to support the invasion. Aircraft destroyed or damaged such targets as **Hà Nội**'s electric transformer station, the Bắc Giang electric power plant, and the Dang Chi hydroelectric power plant. Through the operation, the U.S. developed tactics to overcome the DRV's air defense system, such as **Teaball**, while B-52 bombers operated with relative impunity over the DRV.

By the late summer of 1972, the Easter Offensive had run its course and the ARVN forces were on the offensive to regain territory lost at the outset of the invasion. By October, Linebacker sorties were scaled down and new restrictions were put in place in order to move toward negotiations at the Paris Peace

Talks. Nixon stopped air operations north of the 20th parallel on 23 October as a show of good faith, though the U.S. continued to bomb south of the 20th parallel. When the Paris Peace Talks failed to bring about a compromise to end the conflict, Nixon ordered the resumption of bombing in what would become known as **Linebacker II**, which began on 18 December.

There were an estimated 40,000 sorties flown and more than 125,000 tons of bombs dropped during the Linebacker I operation. The operation played a critical role in defending the RVN against the North Vietnamese invasion. With limited restrictions and new technologies at its disposal, the U.S. caused serious damage to North Vietnam's infrastructure and ability to sustain the invasion past the first few months. When combined with intense U.S. naval and **artillery** gunfire and **advisers**, the ARVN forces proved themselves on the battlefield. ARVN forces, under **Vietnamization**, were more than a match for the North Vietnamese when they were properly led, supported, and equipped. *See also* POCKET MONEY, OPERATION.

LINEBACKER II, OPERATION. United States Air Force campaign against the **Democratic Republic of Vietnam** as a result of the failure to resolve differences in the ongoing Paris negotiations to end the war. Linebacker II, also known as the Christmas Bombings, began on 18 December 1972 and lasted until 29 December 1972, with a brief pause in the middle. The 12-day operation was one of the most intense campaigns during the war. The U.S. objective was to destroy all of the major targets around **Hà Nội** and **Hải Phòng**, as well as electric power facilities, radio communications, the air defense system, and strategic logistic points. By doing this, the U.S. intended to force the North Vietnamese back to the negotiating table to deliberate in good faith.

The B-52 bomber flew the majority of the nearly 1,400 **sorties** and delivered most of the 20,000 tons of **bombs**. The U.S. lost 26 aircraft in the operation, 15 of which were B-52s. On 30 December, President **Richard M. Nixon** ordered the suspension of bombing north of the 20th parallel in order to force the North Vietnamese back to the negotiation table. By 8 January 1973, negotiations were resumed in earnest leading to a 15 January order to end all bombing above the **Demilitarized Zone** and the eventual signing of the **Paris Peace Accords** on 27 January.

LODGE, HENRY CABOT, JR. (1902–1985). Republican senator from Massachusetts and ambassador to Vietnam. Lodge received his degree from Harvard University in 1924 and worked in the newspaper industry until he was elected to the **United States** Senate in 1936. He resigned on 3 February 1944 to enter service in the U.S. Army during World War II and rose to the rank of lieutenant colonel. He returned to the Senate in 1946, serving only one term, and then became the U.S. representative to the United Nations from February 1953 to 3 September 1960. He was on the losing side of the 1960 presidential election as **Richard M. Nixon**'s running mate. Lodge replaced **Frederick E. Nolting Jr.** as ambassador to the **Republic of Vietnam** (RVN) on 26 August 1963 when the **Buddhist Crisis** had reached its peak. He was an avowed critic of **Ngô Đình Diệm** and worked to isolate the RVN president from U.S. advice and assistance during the fall of 1963. Lodge's Vietnam policy followed that of **Elbridge Durbrow**, who was ambassador from 1957 to 1961, in that he called for Ngô Đình Diệm to either completely reform his government or be removed from office. He left the embassy on 28 June 1964 after Ngô Đình Diệm had been overthrown and assassinated in November 1963.

Lodge served as ambassador to the RVN for a second time from 31 July 1965 to 25 April 1967, during the period of American escalation of the war. After Vietnam, he became an ambassador-at-large until 7 May 1968 and then ambassador to Germany from 7 May 1968 to January 1969. President Richard M. Nixon then appointed him to head the American delegation to the Paris Peace Talks on Vietnam, where he served until 20 November 1969. Lodge next became a U.S. special envoy to the Vatican from 1970 to 1977 before retiring from public life. Lodge dominated U.S. relations with the RVN at two critical times during the war. The first time resulted in the assassination of Ngô Đình Diệm, while during the second he helped to manage American policy in the RVN as the U.S. military took over primary responsibilities for the war effort.

LON NOL (1913–1985). President of the **Khmer** Republic, prime minister of **Cambodia**, and minister of defense. Lon Nol was a product of a French education and rose within the French colonial system, first as a provincial civil servant and then as the head of the Cambodian police. He was one of the founding members of the Khmer Renovation Party, which had formed a bloc with Prince **Norodom Sihanouk**. After **France** left Indochina, he served as the minister of defense on a number of occasions and as the supreme commander of the military from August 1955 onward. In 1955, when Sihanouk formed the Sangkum, Lon Nol was instrumental in dissolving the Khmer Renovation Party in May 1955. He served as prime minister of Cambodia on two occasions. The first was between 25 October 1966 and May 1967, and the second time was under the Salvation Government from 14 August 1969 to 11 March 1972. Lon Nol was an anticommunist who disagreed with Norodom Sihanouk's position of letting the North Vietnamese and **National Liberation Front** (NLF) use Cambodia's eastern border with the **Republic of Vietnam** (RVN) as a staging area for its war against the RVN.

On 18 March 1970, during his second time as prime minister, Lon Nol and his deputy prime minister, Prince **Sisowath Sirik Matak**, orchestrated a coup d'état against Sihanouk. His new government proclaimed strict neutrality in the war and called for the **People's Army of Vietnam** (PAVN) and NLF to leave Cambodia. It was only a matter of weeks before Lon Nol requested American aid and assistance to defend Cambodia against the PAVN, NLF, and **Khmer Rouge**, which threatened **Phnom Penh**, leading to the 1970 **Cambodian Incursion**. While the incursion was successful in displacing the PAVN and NLF, it ushered in a Cambodian civil war that pitted forces loyal to Sihanouk under the Royal Government of the National Union of Kampuchea and the National United Front of Kampuchea against Lon Nol. It did not help that Lon Nol had abolished the monarchy, which motivated many regions outside the cities to oppose his rule and become recruiting areas for the Khmer Rouge.

The civil war continued until 1975 when the Khmer Rouge eventually overran Phnom Penh. During this time, Lon Nol became the president of the Khmer Republic from 10 March 1972 to 1 April 1975, when he resigned his office and fled the country, knowing that he would be executed if he remained. Lon Nol escaped to Indonesia and then resettled in Hawaii and finally in California where he died in 1985.

LONG AN. A province in III **Corps Tactical Zone** in the **Republic of Vietnam** (RVN). It fell within **Front** B2 for the **National Liberation Front** (NLF). Long An was established in 1957 with the union of Tân An and **Chợ Lớn** provinces, with the city of Tân An as the provincial capital. In 1962, the southern section of the province, known as **Rừng Sác**, was separated from Long An and formed the Rừng Sác Special Zone. In 1963, the northwestern part of the province was absorbed into the new province of Hậu Nghĩa.

Long An was one of the most strategic provinces in the RVN. It was also highly contested throughout the **First Indochina War** and **Second Indochina War**. The NLF used the terrain, including the **Plain of Reeds**, for coverage and eluded many attempts to be rooted out by both the **United States** and the **Army of the Republic of Vietnam**. In the north and northeast part of the province, the hill country made it difficult for the allies to locate the NLF, while the southern area was inundated with many mangroves. The province was traversed from north to south by **Route** 4, which linked the provinces of **Gia Định** and Định Tường, and Route 5a, which joined the provinces of Gia Định and Gò Công. Routes 18 and 24 connected the province from east to west. Long An had three major rivers. From west to east, the Vàm Cỏ Tây, Vàm Cỏ Đông, and Nhà Bè made the seven districts of Long An province inhospitable to allied military operations but very suitable for **guerrilla warfare**.

LONG BIÊN BRIDGE (PAUL DOUMER BRIDGE). Built in 1903 and named after French Indochina governor General Paul Doumer, the bridge was the longest in Indochina and connected different sections of **Hà Nội**. The bridge was strategic during the war because it was the only one that connected Hà Nội to **Hải Phòng**. The bridge was spared during Operation **Rolling Thunder** until 1967 because President **Lyndon B. Johnson** wanted to avoid striking at targets used by civilians. In 1967, the target, because of its significance to the war effort, was deemed acceptable. On 11 August 1967, the 388th and 355th Tactical Fighter Wings conducted air **sorties** against the bridge to disrupt traffic. By this time the bridge had been heavily fortified and defended by **antiaircraft artillery** and surface-to-air **missiles**. The 31 F-105 Thunderchiefs initiated Rolling Thunder strike 57 and destroyed one of the center spans of the bridge with a 3,000-pound MK-118 munitions bomb. The **United States** continued to attack the bridge in October and December 1967. Damage was so severe that the North Vietnamese were not able to fully repair the bridge until 1969, after Operation Rolling Thunder had been suspended.

While the bridge was critical to the North Vietnamese war effort, its destruction did not stop the flow of supplies and personnel across the Red River. The North Vietnamese used a pontoon bridge, constructed each evening and taken apart each morning, as well as ferries, sampan, and other floating craft to move the critical war supplies to their forces fighting in the South. After the North Vietnamese initiated the 1972 **Easter Offensive**, President **Richard M. Nixon** authorized Operation **Linebacker I**. One of the first targets, after the mining of Hải Phòng harbor, was the Long Biên Bridge. It was hit with a new laser-guided AGM-62 Walleye I missile on 10 May and again over the next 48 hours. Damage to the bridge denied its usage to the North Vietnamese. It was struck again on 10 September and was not repaired until after the signing of the 1973 **Paris Peace Accords**.

LONG BÌNH. Located to the northeast of **Sài Gòn** and southeast of **Biên Hòa**, near the Đồng Nai River in Biên Hòa province, Long Bình was a major **United States** base area during the war. It housed an estimated 40,000 to 50,000 soldiers, including the 1st Logistics Command, U.S. Army, Vietnam headquarters, as well as two evacuation hospitals, an aviation brigade, and other personnel. In many ways, Long Bình was like an American city inside the **Republic of Vietnam**. It had restaurants, nightclubs, stores, and opportunities to continue education, as well as tennis, volleyball, and basketball courts. Long Bình was also the home of a major ammunition depot, which was attacked each year from 1966 to 1969. On 4 February 1967, the **National Liberation Front** attacked the ammunition depot and destroyed an estimated 15,000 155-mm **artillery** shells.

Long Bình was also the home of Long Bình Jail (LBJ). It was built to handle 400 prisoners, but by 1968, there were over 700 prisoners in the facility, including men who had committed such crimes as smoking marijuana, being absent without leave, theft, and murder. In August 1968, the prisoners rioted, resulting in one death and approximately 60 wounded. This followed a similar riot at a **marine** prison in **Đà Nẵng** a few weeks earlier. The prisoners did not list any grievances other than poor food, too much discipline, and requests for speedier trials, though the LBJ was notorious for its overcrowded conditions. Ironically, the rioters burned the administration building and its files, which resulted in further delays in the start of many trials until the records could be reconstructed.

LONG-RANGE PATROL (LRP). Also known as the **Long-Range Reconnaissance Patrol**, or Lurp, the LRP consisted of small teams of personnel who were specially trained to evade the enemy while conducting reconnaissance in contested areas through the **Republic of Vietnam**. The teams were usually between four and six men, though occasionally the numbers could be more or less. LRP personnel usually volunteered for the assignment and went into enemy-controlled territory to locate members of the **People's Army of Vietnam** or the **National Liberation Front**. LRP personnel also spotted for **artillery** and air strikes.

Early LRP missions were conducted by a limited number of **advisers**. As the war progressed, it became apparent that more LRP personnel were needed, and there was a need for greater standardization and coordination of the available LRP assets. In 1967, the U.S. Army organized LRP companies with as many as 16 six-man teams. The LRP teams trained at the **Recondo School** in **Nha Trang**. In February 1969, LRPs were incorporated into the 75th Ranger Regiment. LRP teams proved to be very successful during the war. The teams provided much-needed **intelligence**, provided invaluable assistance for artillery and air strikes, and had an extremely high kill ratio. The work was extremely dangerous and placed a high level of stress on those who served.

LONG-RANGE RECONNAISSANCE PATROL. *See* LONG-RANGE PATROL.

LÒNG TÀU RIVER. The Sông (river) Lòng Tàu connected the **Sài Gòn** and Nhà Bè rivers, which were the main water route between Sài Gòn and the South China Sea. The river flowed through the **Rừng Sác Special Zone**, a vast area of swampland that was a traditional safe haven for the **National Liberation Front**. The river handled the heavy sea traffic to Sài Gòn, which made it important to keep it open. The river was constantly **mined**, resulting in continuous minesweeping but also several instances of damage, including the sinking of the SS *Baton Rouge* on 23 August 1967.

LORAN. The **United States Air Force** (USAF) used Long-Range Radio Navigation (LORAN) assisted **bomb** deliveries toward the end of the air war in Vietnam. Deployed during **Proud Deep Alpha** in December 1971, LORAN theoretically allowed for greater tracking of aircraft during their **sorties** over the **Democratic Republic of Vietnam** by measuring the difference in radio signal time between the moving aircraft and three stationary receiving facilities located in Vietnam and **Thailand**. When working, LORAN allowed the USAF to accurately determine the location of its aircraft and guide them to their target. During the American response to the 1972 **Easter Offensive**, LORAN did not work as well as hoped, due in part to poor weather conditions, human and mechanical error, and the sophisticated North Vietnamese air defense system. Aircraft that used LORAN could not deviate from a straight line without loss of signal strength. This was difficult to accomplish when confronted with **antiaircraft artillery**, SAMs, or MiGs. LORAN-directed aircraft also engaged a target only once in order to limit **casualties** resulting from the North Vietnamese air defense. This resulted in decreased accuracy and efficiency. Overall, the new technology did not live up to its promise during the Vietnam War, though the system did offer promise for the future.

LÝ TÒNG BÁ (1931–). Army of the Republic of Vietnam (ARVN) general. Lý Tòng Bá entered the **Vietnamese National Army** in the 1950s during the **First Indochina War**. He was trained in armor and rose in rank, reaching captain by the early 1960s. By 1962, he had earned a reputation as an aggressive and competent officer, though this was called into question during the January 1963 **Battle of Ấp Bắc** when **John Paul Vann** criticized the actions of Lý Tòng Bá's unit. His reputation for honesty and efficiency allowed his continuous rise in rank. By 1968, Lieutenant Colonel Lý Tòng Bá served as the chief of **Bình Định** province. In the days before the 1972 **Easter Offensive**, he took command of the 23rd ARVN Division and was involved in the defense of Kon Tum. During the final **People's Army of Vietnam** (PAVN) offensive in 1975, Lý Tòng Bá, stationed in **Tây Ninh**, commanded the 25th ARVN Division as a brigadier general. His unit was one of the last to resist the PAVN attack before **Sài Gòn** fell. Between 28 and 29 April, elements of the 25th ARVN Division fought near Củ Chi. He and his staff were ambushed after making the decision to retreat to Hóc Môn, near Sài Gòn. After evading the PAVN soldiers for nearly 24 hours, Lý Tòng Bá was captured. He spent 12 years in a reeducation camp after the war. In 1990, he moved to the **United States**.

M

MACHINE GUNS. The **United States** used the M60 as its primary machine gun during the war. It had been in service with the U.S. Army since 1957. It was a crew-served weapon that used the 7.62-mm, or .30 caliber, cartridge. The weapon weighed 8.5 kilograms (18.75 pounds) and was over 1 meter (42 inches) long. It could fire 550 rounds per minute, though sustained fire resulted in burning out the gun barrels. Because the M60 had a high rate of fire, crew members carried between 2,000 and 3,000 rounds of ammunition held in prelinked rounds of 100 shells, and usually spare gun barrels. In some cases, all members of a rifle squad carried multiple prelinked rounds. The M60 could be fired from the shoulder of a single soldier, usually one of the largest and strongest in a squad, or using a bi- or tripod. With the latter, the effective range of the M60 was approximately 1,097 meters (3,600 feet).

The M60 was also used on the different versions of the M113 armored personnel carrier, on naval vessels used by the U.S. Army in operations **Market Time** and **Game Warden**, and mounted on **helicopters**. The M60E2 was mounted on vehicles and electrically fired, and the M60B was used on helicopters. The M60C was mounted on aircraft, such as the UH-1 Huey helicopter and the OV-10 Bronco fixed-winged aircraft, and was electrically fired by the pilot.

Another machine gun used during the war was the Browning M2. The M2 was a .50, or 12.7-mm, caliber weapon developed during World War II. Like the M60, it was a belt-fed weapon that could be used by rifle squadrons or mounted on vehicles, aircraft, or vessels. The M2 weighed 38 kilograms (84 pounds) and was over 1.55 meters (61 inches) long. It had a maximum effective range of approximately 1,829 meters (6,000 feet) when mounted on a tripod. The M2 could fire 550 rounds per minute, but sustained fire resulted in burning out the gun barrels.

MANSFIELD, MICHAEL JOSEPH (1903–2001). Representative and senator from Montana. After his military service, from 1917 to 1922 (he lied about his age and entered service at 14), Mansfield worked as a miner and mining engineer in Butte, Montana, and then as a professor of history and political science at the University of Montana from 1933 to 1942. He was a member of the House of Representatives as a Democrat from 1943 until 1953, serving on the House Foreign Affairs Committee, and was then elected to the Senate. He remained in the Senate until 1977. He was the senate majority leader from 1961 to 1977 and also sat on the Senate Foreign Relations Committee. He then became the ambassador to Japan from 1977 to 1988 and later a senior adviser to Goldman, Sachs, and Company.

Mansfield was instrumental in the passage of the Great Society, witnessed American escalation in Vietnam, and experienced the Watergate scandal. Mansfield advocated U.S. involvement in Vietnam during the **John F. Kennedy** administration, though that support waned after the assassination of **Ngô Đình Diệm** in November 1963. He began to voice his opposition to the Americanization of the war in private and opposed President **Lyndon B. Johnson**'s response to the **Gulf of Tŏn Kĭn Incident** in August 1964, but he remained faithful to the president in the public arena. Mansfield argued that the U.S. could not win the war in Southeast Asia unless the **Sài Gòn** government had the support of the people. He remained unconvinced that this was possible, though he advocated for a negotiated peace rather than opposing Johnson's policies in public.

As the senate majority leader, Mansfield oversaw a **Congress** that became increasingly adamant in its opposition to the war in Vietnam. Mansfield balanced this opposition with the desire to pass the Great Society and worked to keep the Senate operating. He did introduce legislation to end the war through negotiations and to regain congressional authority over significant foreign policy decisions. When **Richard M. Nixon** entered the White House, Mansfield became more vocal in his opposition to the war and finally broke with the administration after the 1970 **Cambodian Incursion**. He was a cosponsor of H. J. Res 542, known as the **War Powers Resolution**, which sought to eliminate the possibility of another **Gulf of Tŏn Kĭn Resolution**. The war shaped the politics and philosophy of Mansfield. Rather than continuing to voice opposition to a foreign policy that relied on violent action, he instead sought reconciliation and compromise as the guiding principles of American diplomacy.

MARBLE MOUNTAIN. One of a series of small, steep mountains located to the southeast of **Đà Nẵng**, known to the Vietnamese as Ngũ Hành Sơn. The **United States Marine Corps** (USMC) operated around Marble Mountain and even developed a smaller airfield to the north of the geological formation to accommodate overflow air traffic from the major airstrip at Đà Nẵng. The airstrip was the scene of confusion in the summer of 1969 when a Seaboard World Airlines plane with over 200 personnel mistakenly landed at the

4,300-foot airstrip designed for USMC **helicopters** rather than at Đà Nẵng's 10,000-foot airstrip. Marble Mountain was also the scene of a bloody battle on 27 and 28 October 1965 when a small **National Liberation Front** raiding force attacked the **marines** and damaged or destroyed over 50 helicopters.

MARINE CORPS, UNITED STATES. The majority of U.S. Marine Corps (USMC) personnel who served in Southeast Asia were volunteers, though approximately 44,000 were drafted into service during the height of USMC involvement in the **Republic of Vietnam** (RVN) in the late 1960s. The USMC was involved in Southeast Asia from the early 1950s. A few USMC personnel participated in Operation **Passage to Freedom**, the U.S. **Navy** effort to move Vietnamese **refugees** from the **Democratic Republic of Vietnam** to the South during a 300-day period following the 1954 **Geneva Agreements**. USMC **advisers**, under Lieutenant Colonel Victor Croizat, helped organize the RVN Marine Corps in the 1950s.

During the **John F. Kennedy** administration, the USMC joined Task Force Shufly, which included a **helicopter** squadron, and engaged in combat operations. The USMC personnel, who arrived in April 1962, were based in Sóc Trăng in the **Mê Kông Delta** but were moved to **Đà Nẵng** in September 1962. The number of **marines** slowly increased during the remainder of the Kennedy presidency. In 1964, the USMC was tasked with guarding U.S. facilities in I **Corps Tactical Zone** (CTZ) and sent a rifle company to Đà Nẵng. As the war escalated, President **Lyndon B. Johnson** increased the role of the USMC.

On 8 March 1965, Battalion Landing Team 3rd Battalion, 9th Marine Regiment landed on the beaches of Đà Nẵng. The 1st Battalion, 3rd Marine Regiment was flown to the Đà Nẵng Air Base the same day. The arrival of these two battalions marked the first official U.S. combat troops in the RVN. On 7 May 1965, the III Marine Expeditionary Force was activated in the RVN and included the 3rd Marine **Division** and the 1st Marine Aircraft Wing, with approximately 40,000 personnel. It was later designated as III Marine Amphibious Force (III MAF). It operated in I CTZ. Because the U.S. Navy dominated the coast of Vietnam, the marines were able to conduct **amphibious operations** with relative ease. Operations such as **Starlite**, **Blue Marlin** I and II, **Double Eagle**, and **Defiant Stand** forced the **People's Army of Vietnam** (PAVN) and the **National Liberation Front** (NLF) to abandon the coast. In 1966, the 1st Marine Division joined the III MAF.

The USMC in I CTZ engaged in major operations against the PAVN and the NLF throughout the war. The early focus of the USMC was on **pacification** and controlling the population. This led to conflict with **Military Assistance Command, Vietnam**, commander **William C. Westmoreland**, who advocated engaging the enemy in a war of attrition using **search-and-destroy** missions. The commander of the Fleet Marine Force, General **Victor Krulak**, was especially critical of the attrition strategy, as was Major General **Lewis W. Walt**, who during his tenure as the commander of the III MAF organized **Combined Action Platoons** in an effort to provide security to the people.

The nature of the war shifted the USMC strategy as the PAVN committed its 324B Division to I CTZ in the summer of 1966. The USMC conducted major search-and-destroy operations, such as operations Hastings and Prairie. General William C. Westmoreland also ordered the USMC to establish a major military base at **Khe Sanh** in order to stop the infiltration of PAVN troops from **Laos** into the RVN. The USMC refocused their attention on **Quảng Trị** and began to establish a series of strongholds just south of the **Demilitarized Zone**. In October 1966, the III MAF moved its headquarters from Đà Nẵng to **Huế**.

In 1967, the USMC continued to focus on operations in I CTZ. It had the responsibility of protecting over one million Vietnamese and an area of operations that included more than 4,500 square kilometers (1,700 square miles). The USMC was increasingly distracted by the fight for the hills around Khe Sanh as its base became the target for the PAVN forces in the area and was eventually besieged in the early days of 1968 before the **Tết Offensive**. The Battle for Khe Sanh became the most significant USMC engagement during the war. During the Tết Offensive, the USMC was also responsible for clearing Huế.

During the period preceding the Tết Offensive, Westmoreland ordered army units to take over for the marines who were engaged with the PAVN and NLF forces around Khe Sanh. As a result, the III MAF became a joint command. In 1969, when President **Richard M. Nixon** authorized **Vietnamization**, the marines were among the first units to be withdrawn. The 3rd Marine Division was removed by the end of 1969, and the 1st Marine Division and the III MAF headquarters left in April 1971. During the period of withdrawal, the USMC focused its attention on **Quảng Nam**. Of the 58,193 killed-in-action (KIA) in the war, the USMC suffered 14,838 KIA. While the army lost more men, the USMC had the greatest percentage of men killed of any branch of the armed forces. *See also* ENCLAVE STRATEGY; HARVEST MOON, OPERATION; NEUTRALIZE, OPERATION; ONTOS; OREGON, TASK FORCE; PEGASUS, OPERATION.

MARINE CORPS, VIETNAMESE. During the **First Indochina War**, the French organized two naval assault divisions for service in the French Union Forces after the creation of the Vietnamese **Navy** in March 1952. The divisions became active in 1953 and increased as the French expanded the Vietnamese Armed Forces. By the time of the 1954 **Geneva Conference**, the divisions included a headquarters, four river companies, and one battalion landing force. It was this force that would serve as the foundation for the Vietnamese Marine Corps when, on 13 October 1954, **Ngô Đình Diệm** issued a decree that formally created that military organization.

Early commanders of marine personnel included Major Lê Quang Mỹ who served from August 1954 to October 1954, Colonel Lê Quang Trọng who commanded until January 1956, Major Phạm Văn Liễu who served from January 1956 to August 1956, Captain Phó Chí who remained in charge until October 1956, and Major Lê Như Hùng who served as the commander through April 1960.

The U.S. sent Lieutenant Colonel Victor Croizat to become the first senior **adviser** to the Vietnamese Marine Corps (Thủy Quân Lục Chiến). Croizat worked to expand the Marine Corps, which stood at a little over 1,000 personnel. Most of these core cadres were from the 1st and 2nd Battaillons de Marche, who had operated in the **Red River Delta** at the end of the First Indochina War. Marine volunteers received training at the Thủ Đức training center or the National Military Academy, while some traveled to the **United States** for additional instruction. Over time, the Marine Corps became one of the elite forces in the **Republic of Vietnam** (RVN) Armed Forces.

The marines were deployed against the communist insurgency in the late 1950s. In 1959, an additional battalion was organized, and each of the three battalions added a fourth rifle company, which brought the strength of the Marine Corps up to over 3,000. The Vietnamese Marine Corps joined with the **Army of the Republic of Vietnam** (ARVN) Airborne Brigade as the general reserve for the RVN military. As a result, the Marine Corps was involved in significant and consistent fighting.

In early May 1960, Major **Lê Nguyên Khang** became the acting commander of the Marine Corps. He was very close to Ngô Đình Diệm and sided with him during the abortive November 1960 coup d'état, opposing other marine units that had been tricked into supporting the attempted overthrow. Under Lê Nguyên Khang, the marines continued to expand. In 1961, an additional battalion with a 75-mm howitzer battery was added, and marine operations targeted **National Liberation Front** (NLF) strongholds that had previously been inaccessible.

Lê Nguyên Khang's association with Ngô Đình Diệm led to his exile after the November 1963 coup d'état, though this did not affect the growth of the marines. Nguyễn Bá Liên replaced Lê Nguyên Khang until his return from exile in the **Philippines** in February 1964. Lê Nguyên Khang remained in command until May 1972 when he was replaced by Colonel Bùi Thế Lân who remained in command until the fall of **Sài Gòn** in April 1975.

At the end of December 1964, a combination of ARVN Rangers and the 4th Marine Battalion retook the town of Bình Giã to the east of Sài Gòn after the NLF had overrun it on 27 December. On 31 December, a company of the 4th Marine Battalion was ambushed while on a recovery mission. The rest of the battalion moved to reinforce the embattled unit only to be ambushed as well. As a result, the battalion was devastated, with over 60 percent **casualties**. While the Battle for **Bình Giã** was a serious setback for the Vietnamese Marines and their operations, the Marine Corps continued to grow in the mid-1960s.

The Vietnamese Marines continued to distinguish themselves through frequent contact with the NLF. In February 1964, the 2nd Battalion received the U.S. Presidential Unit Citation for thwarting a similar ambush in **II Corps Tactical Zone** (CTZ). In 1965, a fifth battalion was added to the Marine Corps.

The Vietnamese Marines coordinated with the **U.S. Marines** in **search-and-destroy** operations in 1966 and were involved in ending the Buddhist uprising early in the year in I CTZ. An additional battalion was added in September 1966. Marines fought almost continuously from 1966 onward, though in 1967 their activities were focused in the Capital Military District around Sài Gòn, in the **Rừng Sác Special Zone** to the south of the capital, and within **Bình Định** province in II CTZ. Vietnamese Marines were also at the forefront of the defense of the RVN during the 1968 **Tết Offensive**, including the major battles in Sài Gòn and **Huế**. By the end of 1968, the Vietnamese Marine Corps had one division of three brigades, the 147th, 258th, and 369th, each with three rifle battalions and one **artillery** battalion.

A marine brigade was involved in the 1970 **Cambodian Incursion** and the 1971 Operation **Lam Sơn 719**, though it suffered severely in the latter operation. After Lam Sơn 719, two of the brigades operated in **Quảng Trị** in I CTZ while the other remained near Sài Gòn. During the 1972 **Easter Offensive**, the 258th Brigade was switched to the north to reinforce the ARVN line, and though it failed to turn back the stronger **People's Army of Vietnam** (PAVN) attack, it fought a series of delaying actions that allowed further reinforcements to arrive at the front. In June, the Marine Division participated in the counteroffensive in I CTZ that eventually regained much of the territory lost in the early days of the offensive. The marines suffered over 3,600 casualties in the seven-week operation, or approximately 25 percent of their total force in their efforts in I CTZ. After the offensive, the Marine Division remained in I CTZ. U.S. advisers to the marines left in March 1973.

A fourth brigade was added in December 1974 as the marines continued to protect the **Demilitarized Zone**. When the PAVN forces launched their final offensive in 1975, the Marine Division was responsible for the defense of **Đà Nẵng**. The marines continued to fight even as the ARVN forces disintegrated. When Đà Nẵng was evacuated, those marines who could escape were redeployed to Sài Gòn, where they put up the final defense of the presidential palace. Few Vietnamese Marines escaped Vietnam immediately after the fall of Sài Gòn, opting to fight rather than flee. This determination was the hallmark of one of Vietnam's most effective forces.

MARKET TIME, OPERATION. Naval operation designed to counter the North Vietnamese ability to supply its personnel and allies in the **Republic of Vietnam** (RVN). Operation Market Time began on 11 March 1965 as part of a larger effort to stop and destroy the ability of the North Vietnamese to supply its forces. Market Time focused on interdiction by sea and complemented Operation **Rolling Thunder**, which focused on striking the inland transportation effort. On 31 July 1965, the **United States Navy** (USN) formed Task Force 115, the Coastal Surveillance Force, which would serve at the center of the interdiction effort. Task Force 115 used naval ships and aircraft in three defined zones to stop the **People's Army of Vietnam** (PAVN) and the **National Liberation Front** (NLF).

The first zone was known as the Coastal Air Space Reconnaissance, where aircraft watched for naval activity from the Gulf of Tŏn Kĭn to the Gulf of **Thailand** at a distance of up to 240 kilometers (150 miles) from the coastline. Any suspicious ship identified would be reported to naval ships for investigation. The second line of defense was covered by the **Blue Water** patrols. The U.S., with **Australian** assistance, patrolled the coastline and ocean to a distance of up to 64 kilometers (40 miles) away from land. The primary ship in this defensive line was the destroyer, though other seagoing craft, including **coast guard** cutters, participated in the operation. The final line of defense was patrolled by the **brown-water navy**. Their area of responsibility was closer to the coastline and in the waterways that joined the ocean. This force consisted of the South Vietnamese Junk Force and U.S. **swift boats**.

Operation Market Time proved to be very successful during the course of the war. The data collected on the interdiction missions suggested that very few large North Vietnamese ships penetrated the three-barrier system and that the USN effectively cut off the sea supply routes. Market Time's success forced the North Vietnamese to find other routes to supply their forces engaged against the Sài Gòn government. This led to the further development of the **Hồ Chí Minh Trail** in **Laos** and **Cambodia**, as well as the co-opting of Cambodian neutrality by establishing the **Hak Ly** Corporation, a front company to move North Vietnamese supplies from the port of **Sihanoukville** to PAVN and NLF bases along the Cambodia-RVN border. Operation Market Time was eventually absorbed into **SEALORDS**. *See also* DAGGER THRUST; GAME WARDEN, OPERATION; SIHANOUK TRAIL.

MARTIN, GRAHAM ANDERSON (1912–1990). Last ambassador to the **Republic of Vietnam** (RVN). Martin served as an army intelligence officer during World War II and entered the public sector in 1947 as a counselor and then deputy chief of mission of the embassy in Paris. He served as the deputy **United States** coordinator for the Alliance for Progress and as U.S. representative to the **United Nations** before becoming ambassador to **Thailand** from May 1963 to 9 September 1967, and then special assistant to the secretary of state for refugee and migration affairs. On 30 October 1969, he became ambassador to Rome and remained in that post until 1973, when he was persuaded to succeed **Ellsworth Bunker** as ambassador to the RVN on 21 June 1973.

Martin oversaw the American effort as the war ended with the defeat of the South Vietnamese. He was a strong advocate for continued U.S. aid and assistance to the RVN and allied himself with President **Nguyễn Văn Thiệu**. Martin believed that the U.S. had committed itself to the security of the RVN after the 1973 **Paris Peace Accords** and, as the war continued into 1974–1975, had failed to live up to its guarantees given to Nguyễn Văn Thiệu. He was one of the last Americans to leave Vietnam, the day before **Sài Gòn** fell on 30 April 1975. After the war, he became a special assistant to Secretary of State **Henry Kissinger** before retiring in 1977.

MASHER/WHITE WING, OPERATION. Search-and-destroy mission conducted by the 1st Cavalry **Division** in **Bình Định** province that began on 24 January 1966. The operation focused on the **Bồng Sơn** Plain and included the 1st Cavalry Division, the 22nd **Army of the Republic of Vietnam** Division and the **Republic of Vietnam** Airborne Brigade, and the 1st Regiment of the **Republic of Korea**'s Capitol Division. These **Free World Forces** faced the 3rd **People's Army of Vietnam** (PAVN) division as well as **National Liberation Front** (NLF) regiments. In one of the absurdities and ironies of the war, the name of the operation was changed to White Wing because Masher was considered too violent. The operation ended on 6 March 1966 with the Free World Forces claiming an estimated 2,150 to 2,389 PAVN and NLF killed at a loss of 288 American soldiers killed-in-action and nearly 1,000 wounded. While the **United States** deemed the operation a success, it failed to permanently clear the area of the PAVN and NLF.

MAYAGUEZ INCIDENT. Launched as SS *White Falcon* in April 1944 and renamed *Santa Eliana, Sea,* and finally the SS *Mayaguez* in 1965, the ship supported **United States** efforts in Southeast Asia. On 7 May 1975, the *Mayaguez* left Hong Kong on a normal voyage. On 12 May, it was approximately 100 kilometers (60 miles) off the coast of **Cambodia** and near the island of Poulo Wai, which was claimed by Cambodia, **Thailand**, and Vietnam. In the afternoon, an American-built **swift boat** that had been captured by the **Khmer Rouge** after the fall of **Phnom Penh** approached the ship and fired its 76-mm gun forcing the *Mayaguez* to stop. The captain and crew were taken into custody for violating Cambodian territorial waters, and the *Mayaguez* was forced to follow its Khmer Rouge captors to the port of Kompong Som (**Sihanoukville**). While the crew remained in Kompong Som, the U.S. military mistakenly believed that the crew had been taken to the Koh Tang island, a small island nearer to the Cambodian coast. The U.S. government maintained that the event was an act of piracy, and President **Gerald R. Ford** ordered a military operation to rescue the crew after diplomatic attempts to resolve the crisis failed.

On the morning of 15 May, U.S. **Marines** assaulted the island in **helicopters** to rescue the crew that was not there while a small volunteer force from the Military Sealift Command made a daring attempt to retake the ship. Shortly after 8:00 a.m., the American flag was raised again on the *Mayaguez*, and the captured sailors were released by the Khmer Rouge, though the two events were not related. The sailors had been housed on Kach island and had boarded onto a Thai fishing boat that delivered them to the U.S.S. *Wilson*, which was assisting in the amphibious assault on Koh Tang. The marines landed on Koh Tang unaware that the prisoners had been released. They attacked an entrenched Khmer Rouge force supported by air **sorties** that targeted the areas around where the U.S. believed the captured sailors were located. When the marines learned of the recapture of the ship and the release of the sailors, the force withdrew. The U.S. lost 15 killed and 50 wounded in the operation. Three marines were missing; it was later confirmed that all three had been captured and executed by the Khmer Rouge. In 1979, the *Mayaguez* was decommissioned and scrapped.

MCCARTHY, EUGENE JOSEPH (1916–2005). United States senator and presidential candidate. McCarthy was educated at St. John's University in Minnesota and at the University of Minnesota. While there, he taught high school in North Dakota and Minnesota. In 1940, he returned to St. John's University as a professor of economics and education. In 1944, McCarthy joined the Military Intelligence Division of the War Department as a civilian technical assistant. After the war, he successfully ran as a Democrat for a seat in the House of Representatives. He served in the House from 3 January 1949 to 3 January 1959. He became one of the U.S. senators for Minnesota in 1958 and remained in the Senate until 1971. In 1968, McCarthy tried to become the Democratic nominee for the presidency as an **antiwar** candidate in opposition to Vice President **Hubert Humphrey**. He would repeat his run in 1972 and 1976 without success, as well as an unsuccessful Senate run in 1982.

It was McCarthy's 1968 candidacy for the Democratic nomination that propelled him into the public eye. McCarthy had been an antiwar advocate during the early period of American escalation, which served as a catalyst for his decision to run against incumbent **Lyndon B. Johnson**. In the New Hampshire primary, McCarthy had a surprisingly good result, though he lost to Johnson. His campaign attracted a number of younger voters and antiwar protestors, who made their first foray into politics with McCarthy. The strong antiwar presence in New Hampshire inspired Senator **Robert Kennedy** to announce his candidacy for the Democratic nomination on 16 March 1968. Two weeks later, Johnson announced that he would neither seek nor accept his party's nomination for the presidency.

As a shocked nation watched Johnson, McCarthy realized that his run for the White House had a real chance. McCarthy won the Wisconsin and Oregon primary, but his campaign was no match for Kennedy's organization. When Humphrey entered the race after Johnson's announcement, his consolidation of the party cadre seriously reduced McCarthy's chances. McCarthy's loss to Kennedy in California and the nation's reaction to Kennedy's assassination on 4 June took the spotlight off McCarthy and allowed Humphrey to regain the initiative leading up to the Democratic National Convention in Chicago. McCarthy had less than 25 percent of the delegates at the convention, and most of Kennedy's delegates gravitated toward Senator **George McGovern** rather than McCarthy, which allowed Humphrey to earn the party's nomination amid the chaos occurring in the streets outside the convention hall. After the campaign, McCarthy finished his term in the Senate but chose not to run again. His 1972 presidential run failed to gain the momentum it had in 1968. McCarthy's influence in national and party affairs subsequently diminished, though he continued to oppose President **Richard M. Nixon**'s actions in Vietnam until the end of the war.

MCCONE, JOHN ALEX (1902–1991). Director of the **Central Intelligence Agency** (CIA). McCone was educated at the University of California, Berkeley, receiving his degree in engineering in 1922. He worked for the Llewellen Iron Works in Los Angeles, rising in the company and eventually starting his own firm of Bechtel-McCone, which designed and manufactured petroleum refineries and power plants. He entered public life in 1947 as a member of President Harry S. Truman's Air Policy Commission. In 1948 McCone served as a special deputy to Secretary of Defense James Forrestal, and in 1950–1951 as the undersecretary of the Air Force; McCone turned down President Dwight D. Eisenhower's offer of becoming the secretary of the Air Force in 1954 but did accept the chairmanship of the Atomic Energy Commission in 1958. On 29 November 1961, McCone became the director for central intelligence and remained in that position until 28 April 1965, after which he returned to private industry.

McCone advocated **United States** support for **Ngô Đình Diệm** and was opposed to the U.S. actions that led to the November 1963 coup d'état. McCone remained in his position as director for central intelligence after **John F. Kennedy**'s assassination, though he increasingly opposed a Vietnam policy that favored gradual escalation without clear strategies for victory. His opposition to the entrenched **Lyndon B. Johnson** administration policy, which he believed was not committed to victory but still increased U.S. troop levels, eventually forced him to resign his position with the warning that the war in Vietnam would divide the American people before it had the opportunity to end the conflict with a U.S. and **Republic of Vietnam** victory.

MCGARR, LIONEL CHARLES (1904–1988). **United States Army** general and chief of the **Military Assistance Advisory Group** (MAAG), Vietnam. McGarr graduated from West Point in 1928 and entered World War II as a colonel commanding the 30th Infantry Regiment, though he served for a brief time as the assistant division commander of the 3rd Infantry Division at the end of 1944. After the war, he returned to the 3rd Infantry Division as the assistant division commander until entering the National War College in 1946. Upon graduation in 1947, McGarr worked in the Intelligence Section of the Army General Staff. He served as a commander of the 350th Infantry Regiment in Austria and then as tactical inspector for the U.S. Tactical Command in Austria before becoming the assistant division commander of the 2nd Infantry Division and commander of the Allied Prisoner of War Command during the Korean War. He served in a variety of positions with increasing responsibility and authority until being promoted to lieutenant general and replacing General **Samuel T. Williams** as the chief of the MAAG, Vietnam, in September 1960. McGarr remained in that position until July 1962, when he was replaced by Major General Charles Timmes. During that time, MAAG, Vietnam, was being absorbed into the **Military Assistance Command, Vietnam** (MACV), headed by General **Paul Harkins**.

McGarr's Vietnam service was marked by good relations with **Republic of Vietnam** (RVN) president **Ngô Đình Diệm** and U.S. ambassador **Frederick E. Nolting Jr.**, though his brief relationship with U.S. ambassador **Elbridge Durbrow** was strained. Weeks after his arrival in Vietnam, an 11 November 1960 failed coup d'état shook the confidence of Ngô Đình Diệm, who began to move away from U.S. advice on how to conduct the war and worked toward creating a more independent Vietnamese policy to counter the growing insurgency. McGarr worked with the Vietnamese president and his close confidants during a time when political intrigue often outweighed military necessity. McGarr recommended increasing American troop levels in the RVN to help offset the growth of the **National Liberation Front**, but his advice was rejected by President **John F. Kennedy**. His departure, along with Nolting's the next year, ended the last high-ranking American representative in the RVN with any confidence in Ngô Đình Diệm. After MAAG, McGarr retired from the military as a highly decorated veteran and returned to California.

MCGOVERN, GEORGE STANLEY (1922–). United States senator and presidential candidate. McGovern received his education at Dakota Wesleyan University. In June 1942, he enlisted in the U.S. Army Air Corps and flew in Europe. After the war, he received his PhD from Northwestern University and returned to Dakota Wesleyan University in 1950 as a professor of history and government. He formally entered politics in 1953 when he served for three years as the executive secretary of the South Dakota Democratic Party, and in 1954 as a member of the Advisory Committee on Political Organization of Democratic National Committee. He won a House of Representatives seat as a Democrat in South Dakota and served in **Congress** from 3 January 1957 to 3 January 1961. He was unsuccessful in obtaining a U.S. Senate seat in 1960 but served as the director of the Food for Peace Program in the **John F. Kennedy** administration until he resigned in July 1962 to run, successfully, for the Senate. He served in the Senate from 3 January 1963 to 3 January 1981. He ran failed campaigns for the Democratic nominee for the presidency in 1968 and 1984 and lost to **Richard M. Nixon** in the 1972 presidential election.

McGovern started his opposition to U.S. involvement in Vietnam as early as 1963, during the **Buddhist Crisis** that had turned many Americans against the **Sài Gòn** government. While he voted for the **Gulf of Tỏn Kĩn Resolution** in August 1964 in a move to support his fellow Democrat, President **Lyndon B. Johnson**, he continued to voice his concern for the increased American military attention in Southeast Asia. Even though McGovern publicly turned against the Americanization of the war, being especially galvanized after a November 1965 visit to the **Republic of Vietnam**, he continued to vote for special military appropriations for Vietnam. McGovern would become one of the leading spokesmen against the war in Congress.

McGovern played a minor role in the drama of the 1968 Democratic Convention, in that he siphoned votes away from **Eugene McCarthy**, which helped to solidify the party nomination for **Hubert Humphrey**. After Nixon's election to the White House, McGovern became one of the leading critics of the war and spoke at many of the major **antiwar** protests in Washington, D.C. He argued that the U.S. should leave Vietnam quicker than the **Vietnamization** policy outlined by Nixon, and he worked within the Senate to hasten the process. McGovern not only criticized Nixon but also blamed his fellow senators for failing to act to end the war, publicly attacking senators who supported Nixon's war.

McGovern's antiwar credentials earned him the Democratic nomination in 1972 against the incumbent Nixon. He ran on a platform that called for immediate withdrawal from Vietnam and a reduction of the U.S. military. While the campaign provided several colorful moments, including a change of vice presidential candidates, Nixon soundly defeated McGovern. He went back to the Senate but failed in his reelection bid in 1980. He returned to teaching in 1981, spending two years at the University of New Orleans. He served as U.S. ambassador to the **United Nations** Food and Agricultural Organization in Rome, Italy, between 1998 and 2001, during which time he received the Presidential Medal of Freedom. In 2001, he was appointed United Nations global ambassador on world hunger. He is the author of several works of history and on events in his personal life.

MCNAMARA LINE. In 1966, the **United States** began to construct a series of outposts and firebases in order to stop the movement of North Vietnamese personnel and supplies to the South. The North Vietnamese had been infiltrating into the **Republic of Vietnam** (RVN) through the **Demilitarized Zone** (DMZ) and **Laos** in increasing numbers since 1959, when they established the **559th Transport Group**. Secretary of Defense Robert McNamara approved of the barrier concept after receiving a plan from the JASON division of the Institute for Defense Analysis, which was tasked with finding a way to end the war other than strategic **bombing**. McNamara's name became attached to the barrier concept as a result.

The McNamara Line was originally conceived as two defensive positions. The first line would run parallel to the DMZ in the RVN and consist of outposts and firebases strategically placed in an area that was defoliated and susceptible to **artillery** and air attack. These static positions would be alerted to infiltration through a series of trip wires, minefields, and other early-warning devices placed along the DMZ in projects Dual Blade, Dye Marker, and Muscle Shoals. The second line would connect with the first and run through Laos. While it would not be manned like the first line, it would include electronic detection devices and a myriad of **mines** to make the passage costly. McNamara ordered the construction to begin on 15 September 1966 in what would become known as Project Practice Nine.

The U.S. constructed a series of firebases that supported outposts in the RVN and dropped tens of thousands of electronic listening devices and millions of **Gravel** and Button mines in an area around the DMZ and in Laos. The line did make infiltration into the RVN more difficult for **People's Army of Vietnam** (PAVN) forces, but it did not stop their usage of the **Hồ Chí**

Minh Trail. After McNamara left office, construction of the barrier slowed, especially when the 1968 **Tết Offensive** exposed the vulnerability of the outpost and firebase system to concentrated PAVN and **National Liberation Front** attack as seen at **Lang Vei** and **Khe Sanh**. Construction of the McNamara Line stopped in October 1968 when General **Creighton W. Abrams**, who had replaced **William C. Westmoreland** as the commander of **Military Assistance Command, Vietnam**, began preparations for **Vietnamization** and the start of the U.S. withdrawal from Southeast Asia.

MCNAMARA, ROBERT STRANGE (1916–2009). Secretary of defense during the **John F. Kennedy** and **Lyndon B. Johnson** administrations and president of the World Bank. McNamara was born in San Francisco. He graduated from the University of California at Berkeley with degrees in economics and philosophy and from Harvard University with a master's degree in business administration. He served in World War II, rising to the rank of lieutenant colonel for his work in strategic bombing assessments for the **United States** Army Air Force. McNamara became secretary of defense on 21 January 1961, leaving the Ford Motor Company after becoming its youngest president, if only for a five-week period. As secretary of defense, McNamara oversaw the Americanization of the war, which he helped to orchestrate, and eventually became disillusioned with it after U.S. troop escalation had reached the hundreds of thousands. McNamara secured a significant increase in the Department of Defense budget as well as an increase in the size of the U.S. Armed Forces due to the war and the introduction of conscription.

Like many American leaders of the time, McNamara struggled with the complexities of what seemed to be a simple war in Southeast Asia. He had risen through the ranks of the military and Ford Motor Company using his advanced skills of quantitative analysis, and he applied his business mind to organize and evaluate the war. As a result, the war fought from the Pentagon point of view was meshed in numbers that seemingly ignored the differences in perspective between the adversaries in culture, history, politics, diplomacy, and, most importantly, war aims and requirements for victory. Even in October 1966, as McNamara appeared to move away from loyally supporting escalation of the war, he couched his opposition in quantitative terms. McNamara justified his opposition to escalation in the cost-benefit model he had learned at Harvard so many years before.

McNamara continued to voice his opposition to the war, which created tension within the Johnson White House. On 29 November 1967, President Lyndon B. Johnson announced that McNamara was resigning to take the presidency of the World Bank; he left office on 29 February 1968 after the politically and psychologically damaging **Tết Offensive** had run its course.

There is no question that McNamara believed the war to be a drain on U.S. resources and a mistake, given the seemingly endless escalation of American troops. His reckoning, however, came too late for tens of thousands of American soldiers who had died or were wounded. McNamara also did not escape the ire of the burgeoning **antiwar** movement who saw his actions as criminal and claimed his resignation as a victory to their cause.

McNamara remained at the World Bank until 1981. He became an opponent of nuclear weapons, urging the Ronald W. Reagan administration to eliminate the weapon from the North Atlantic Treaty Organization's arsenal. In 1995, McNamara published, with the help of historians of the Vietnam War, the book *In Retrospect*, which was greeted with both praise for his mea culpa for his part in the war and scorn by those whose lives were altered irrevocably by the decisions McNamara had made as secretary of defense. The controversy surrounding the former secretary of defense was renewed with the publication of his next book, *Argument without End*, as well as the documentary *The Fog of War*, in which McNamara offered his life lessons. McNamara was at the center of the storm that was the Vietnam War. While his role, responsibility, and impact have yet to be fully assessed, there is no question of the significance of his influence on the times in which he served as secretary of defense.

MÊ KÔNG DELTA. Located in the southeastern section of IV **Corps Tactical Zone** and covering approximately 41,500 square kilometers (16,000 square miles) of highly agricultural land, the Mê Kông Delta is an area created by the **Mê Kông River** and its tributaries. The people of the Mê Kông Delta are primarily Vietnamese with some **Khmer** influence. Because of the nature of the terrain and the abundance of water, the area developed its own culture and way of life that was often at odds with the major urban centers such as **Sài Gòn** and **Huế**. The major cities in the delta were Mỹ Tho and **Cần Thơ**, while most of the fertile land was sparsely inhabited by farmers. Because of the unique terrain in the delta and the isolation of many of its people, it became a prime area for insurgents. During the **First Indochina War**, the French developed the Divisions Navales d'Assaut (Dinassaut) to combat those forces opposing French colonial rule. The **United States** modeled its efforts in the delta along similar lines.

The U.S. participated in few major operations involving ground troops in the Mê Kông Delta, though it did send a large number of **advisers** to the area and conducted a series of operations on the waterways to limit the effectiveness of the **National Liberation Front** (NLF) operating in the area. Operations such as **Game Warden** in 1966 and **SEALORDS** in 1968 were effective in cutting off the water-borne infiltration of the NLF from **Cambodia** into the Mê Kông Delta, while the **Mobile Riverine Force**, using a variety of vessels, including the **patrol boat, river** and **swift boat**, struck at the NLF base areas in the labyrinth of waterways throughout the area.

Most of the major ground operations against the NLF were conducted by the **Army of the Republic of Vietnam** (ARVN) and consisted of a series of endless sweep-and-clear or **search-and-destroy** missions. The ARVN attempted to keep the insurgents away from the villagers as well as to provide some of the benefits of modernity to the rural population. Because of the combined efforts of U.S. and ARVN forces and its geographic distance from the **Demilitarized Zone**, the Mê Kông Delta did not suffer as much from the large-scale North Vietnamese attacks during the 1968 Têt Offensive or the 1972 **Easter Offensive**.

MÊ KÔNG RIVER. The largest river in Southeast Asia, which originates in China and flows between **Thailand** and **Laos** and through **Cambodia** and the **Republic of Vietnam** (RVN). The Mê Kông River divides into two major water flows at **Phnom Penh**: the Mê Kông River and the Bassac River (Sông Hậu). From there, it flows into the South China Sea and forms the Mê Kông Delta. The river was very susceptible to the monsoon rains and often flooded, which created difficulties during the war. The river served as a dividing line between **Sài Gòn** and IV **Corps Tactical Zone** and often resulted in the lower fifth of the RVN being isolated from the rest of the country. In the later stages of the war, the river was **mined** by both the **United States** and the **Khmer Rouge**. The U.S. mined the river in order to stop water infiltration into the RVN, and the Khmer Rouge mined the rivers to put added stress on the Phnom Penh government's ability to receive resupply in the last years of the war in Cambodia.

MEDIA, UNITED STATES. The Vietnam War has often been called the television war, a term that was justified by the appearance of continuous images on the evening news. In the early years of the war, the media reported positively on **United States** operations to root out the **People's Army of Vietnam** (PAVN) and **National Liberation Front** (NLF) as well as to improve the lives of the Vietnamese people. Human interest stories and short biographies of the common soldier marked the depth of investigative reporting, though there were a few exceptions, such as the controversy after the **Battle for Ấp Bắc** in January 1963. Most of the early critical reporting focused on the perceived failures of **Ngô Đình Diệm** and his brother **Ngô Đình Nhu**. It was the inability of the **Sài Gòn** government to get the complete support of its people, rather than the political controversy surrounding American officials who worked to eliminate the Ngo family rule, that guided such reporters as **Malcolm Browne, Neil Sheehan**, and **David Halberstam**.

The **John F. Kennedy** and **Lyndon B. Johnson** administrations used the media to help shape public opinion on the war, as a way of testing how the public would react to military and diplomatic strategies for Southeast Asia, and as a vehicle for putting out peace negotiation feelers to the **Democratic Republic of Vietnam**. The administrations provided the media with access to the military in Vietnam, usually just in Sài Gòn, and the media rewarded this access by reporting the data provided to them, with very few exceptions. President Lyndon B. Johnson introduced a set of voluntary guidelines for preserving military operational integrity but left the rules flexible enough that the media did not feel it was being censored.

With the escalation of American involvement in the war, starting with the March 1965 introduction of **marines** into **Đà Nẵng** and additional ground soldiers that summer, reporters grew more confident of their role in Vietnam and less dependent upon the military for information. As **casualties** rose and the number of combat troops exceeded 100,000 with no end of escalation in sight, the media became more investigatory of U.S. operations as well as critical of the role of the **Army of the Republic of Vietnam** in the war. However, the extent to which reporters could get into the field was limited by a number of factors, the most significant of which was the nature of the war itself. Of the credentialed reporters in Vietnam, a significant proportion of them were not working correspondents. Most had to file stories on a timeline that was dictated in the U.S. This meant that reporters needed to stay close to Sài Gòn in order to file their stories in a timely fashion.

Television coverage until 1968 was largely favorable toward the U.S., though the images of the war, unseen by the American public with such frequency during previous U.S. conflicts, brought home the nature of war. Even if the coverage was positive, it demonstrated the violent nature of war and how it affected those who directly participated in it. Television coverage generally left out the actual violence and showed even less of U.S. casualties, but images of dead PAVN and NLF soldiers had a profound, if not the originally intended, impact on the U.S. public.

By the 1968 **Tết Offensive**, there was a growing war weariness that pervaded the American people and was reflected in the media coverage. The U.S. had been in combat for nearly three years, and despite promises by members of the Johnson administration and General **William C. Westmoreland** that the enemy was on the defensive, the PAVN and NLF were able to mount the Tết Offensive that swept through the entire country. It was clear that the "light at the end of the tunnel" was not a reality and that the war's end was nowhere in sight. Media reporting, including the change of attitude by its leading spokesman, **Walter Cronkite**, began to alter the nature of its stories. This had an impact on the public who relied on the nightly news for its information.

As the American war started to diminish with **Vietnamization** in 1969 and the number of operations declined, the U.S. media began to focus on other stories it believed worthy of their attention, such as soldiers' refusal to fight, drug use, racial tension, and other instances that indicated a decline of morale within the U.S. Armed Forces.

The relationship between the media and the **Richard M. Nixon** administration was even more strained than its relationship with the Johnson administration. President Richard M. Nixon turned against the media as its reporting became more critical and emphasized the **credibility gap**. The media also underwent a change, as Vietnam was the first war reported by many of its newest and youngest members. The new members focused more on investigative reporting, inserting more opinion in their stories instead of balanced analysis. There was some justification for the young reporters' actions, especially when one considered the attempts by the Johnson administration to manipulate it. In the end, the Nixon administration proved to be as manipulative as the Johnson administration.

While some have argued that the media shaped public opinion and forced an early withdrawal of American troops through negative reporting, this argument neglects the nature of the war and the ability of much of the American public to understand what its leadership did not: the war, and the Vietnamese role in it, was much more complex and complicated than the Americans gave it credit for. Nonetheless, the media would not escape unscathed. As the war ended, its own credibility was called into question in the decades following the fall of Sài Gòn in April 1975. *See also* ANTIWAR MOVEMENT; PROPAGANDA.

MENU, OPERATION. Air operation designed to destroy the **People's Army of Vietnam** (PAVN) and **National Liberation Front** (NLF) presence in **Cambodia** along the border with the **Republic of Vietnam**. When **Richard M. Nixon** became president, he acknowledged the PAVN and NLF threat in Cambodia, whose force was estimated at over 40,000, and called for immediate action. At the request of General **Creighton W. Abrams**, commander of the **Military Assistance Command, Vietnam**, Nixon authorized Operation Menu, which was comprised of separate air missions labeled Breakfast, Lunch, Supper, Dessert, and Snack. The operation began on 18 March 1969 in a veil of secrecy until its exposure by a 2 May 1970 *New York Times* article. Menu was successful in that its 120,000 tons of munitions threw off balance the PAVN and NLF timetable for their planned 1969 offensive directed toward Sài Gòn. It also set the stage for further American involvement at the end of April 1970 with the **Cambodian Incursion**. Menu's success was not without controversy, and it further discredited the Nixon administration's policies in

Southeast Asia. The operation ended on 26 May 1970 as the **United States** expanded its air commitment over Cambodia with Operation **Freedom Deal**.

MICHELIN RUBBER PLANTATION. A rubber plantation owned by the French corporation Michelin, located in **Tây Ninh** province, approximately 32 kilometers (20 miles) east of Tây Ninh City and to the northeast of Dầu Tiếng. The plantation continued to operate during the war and was the scene of sporadic but sometimes intense fighting. The plantation was a source of frustration for the **United States** soldier. Some speculated that its owners were making payments to the **National Liberation Front** in order to continue functioning; others believed that the U.S. refrained from using **artillery** or conducting air strikes against the plantation as a result of an agreement between the U.S. and French governments that sought to limit damage to the trees.

MICHIGAN STATE UNIVERSITY GROUP (MSUG). In May 1955, Michigan State University established a technical assistance program for Vietnam made possible in part by the good relationship between political science professor Wesley Fishel and **Ngô Đình Diệm**, both of whom opposed communism and shared similar sociopolitical views. The MSUG provided the expertise needed by the **Republic of Vietnam** (RVN) to begin the process of nation building. During the seven years that the MSUG was involved in Vietnam, it produced studies and reports that examined military, social, economic, political, and administrative issues related to the creation of a stable, viable RVN. Tension increased between the MSUG and Ngô Đình Diệm after members of the group published articles and reports critical of Ngô Đình Diệm's rule as a result of their perception that Ngô Đình Diệm was moving toward authoritarian rule. Ngô Đình Diệm responded poorly to the criticism and attacks and eventually terminated the MSUG relationship in June 1962.

MILITARY ASSISTANCE ADVISORY GROUP (MAAG). Members of MAAG, Indochina, were sent to Vietnam by President Harry S. Truman in 1950 for the purpose of organizing **United States** aid to the French who were engaged in the middle of the **First Indochina War**. MAAG personnel arrived in Vietnam on 17 September 1950 under the command of Brigadier General Francis G. Brink. MAAG was a response, in part, to the North Korean invasion into South Korea in June 1950 and the fear that the communist bloc would target Indochina next. While in Vietnam, the group worked with the French, though not always effectively, to train indigenous soldiers and oversee the disbursement of U.S. funds. There was constant tension between American and French personnel, which culminated in early 1954 with the Battle for **Điện Biên Phủ**. As a result of the 1954 **Geneva Agreements** and the end of active French involvement in Indochina, MAAG began to work directly with the Vietnamese under **Ngô Đình Diệm** to help create and maintain the **Army of the Republic of Vietnam** (ARVN). Major General Thomas J. H. Trapnell replaced Brink in August 1952, who was in turn replaced by Lieutenant General **John W. O'Daniel** in April 1954 to the end of October 1955, when MAAG, Indochina, was split into three organizations: MAAG, Vietnam; MAAG, **Laos**; and MAAG, **Cambodia.**

O'Daniel had a good relationship with Ngô Đình Diệm but had to overcome numerous obstacles associated with the new republic, which operated without experienced leadership and had to recover from the First Indochina War and four years of brutal Japanese occupation during World War II. An additional problem for MAAG was the reluctance of the French to hand over power and control without causing trouble. MAAG also had to adhere to the strict personnel ceiling imposed by the Geneva Agreements while trying to provide much-needed services to the **Republic of Vietnam** (RVN). MAAG continued to function as the primary training and assistance organization for ARVN throughout the 1950s as the U.S. engaged in nation building in the RVN. When **John F. Kennedy** entered the White House in 1961, the U.S. effort in Vietnam intensified. Kennedy created the **Military Assistance Command, Vietnam**, to handle the increased American assistance to Vietnam, which caused MAAG to be placed under it. MAAG was eventually renamed the Field Advisory Element, Vietnam. Other MAAG, Vietnam, commanders included Lieutenant General **Samuel T. Williams** from November 1955 to September 1960, Lieutenant General **Lionel C. McGarr** from September 1960 to July 1962, and Major General Charles J. Timmes from July 1962 to May 1964, when MAAG, Vietnam, ceased to exist.

MILITARY ASSISTANCE COMMAND, VIETNAM (MACV). Toward the end of 1961, the **United States** made the decision to expand U.S. assistance to the **Republic of Vietnam** under a unified command, the MACV, which was eventually established on 8 February 1962. MACV provided a joint headquarters for American personnel in Vietnam. In May 1964, it officially replaced the **Military Assistance Advisory Group, Vietnam** (MAAG), which had been under its authority since 1962. MACV surpassed the MAAG involvement in Vietnam by directing operations of military units. With the Americanization of the war, MACV became the single most powerful U.S. organization in Southeast Asia. It oversaw two Field Forces Headquarters, the Marine Amphibious Force, the **7th Air Force**, and U.S. naval forces in Vietnam. It also assumed responsibility for many other programs related to **counterinsurgency** and the war effort, which included all civilian and military **pacification** efforts after May 1967.

MACV was also the principal liaison with **Third Country** forces involved in the war, including those from **Australia, New Zealand**, the **Republic of Korea, Thailand**, and the **Philippines**. MACV was divided into six departments—J1-Personnel, J2-**Intelligence**, J3-Operations, J4-Logistics, J5-Plans, and J6-Communications-Electronics—though it also supervised the offices that performed duties related to the comptroller, judge advocate, provost marshal, chaplain, surgeon, adjutant general, inspector general, and public information establishment, as well as the **Studies and Observation Group**, which operated against the **Democratic Republic of Vietnam** and along the Hồ Chí Minh Trail.

General Paul D. Harkin served as the first commander of MACV from February 1962 to 20 June 1964. He was replaced by General **William C. Westmoreland**, who remained until July 1968. General **Creighton W. Abrams** took over from Westmoreland and was succeeded by General **Frederick C. Weyand** in June 1972. The organization began with 216 officers and men in February 1962. While it included men and **women** from every branch of the armed forces, the majority of the personnel who worked under MACV served in the U.S. Army. It was disbanded in 1973 as a result of the 1973 **Paris Peace Accords** that ended American involvement in Vietnam.

MILITARY REGION. In order to deal with the post-French colonial military programs, the State of Vietnam was divided into military regions after the 1954 **Geneva Conference**. The purpose of the division was to provide some cohesion for the **Vietnamese National Army**, as it assisted in the regrouping of Vietnamese who had fought against the French during the **First Indochina War** to fighting the **Democratic Republic of Vietnam** (DRV), as well as in the resettling and rehabilitation of Vietnamese who had fled the North for the South. The State of Vietnam was divided into three numbered military regions.

After the proclamation of the **Republic of Vietnam**, President **Ngô Đình Diệm** approved the renumbering of the military districts and added three more regions, including one that encompassed **Sài Gòn**, known as the Capital Military Region. As the **United States** became more involved in the war, the regions were reorganized again and began to be referred to as **Corps Tactical Zones** (CTZ). There were four CTZs in the RVN in the 1960s. (*See* maps 2, 3, 4, and 5.)

The DRV also created a series of military regions for Vietnam. There were 10 regions for Vietnam. Military regions 1 through 4 covered the DRV. Military Region 5 was the largest in the RVN and included the provinces from the **Demilitarized Zone** down to the provinces of Khánh Hòa and Darlac. Military Region 6 included the southernmost area of Trung Bộ. Military Region 7 covered the area of eastern Nam Bộ. Military Region 8 included central Nam Bộ. Military Region 9 covered the area of southern Nam Bộ, and Military Region 10 included the provinces of Bình Long, Phước Long, and Quảng Đức, all of which bordered **Cambodia**. (*See* map 7.)

In February 1961, the DRV and **National Liberation Front** reorganized its regions in the RVN into fronts. **Front** B1 included all of Military Region 5, while Front B2 absorbed military regions 6, 7, 8, 9, and 10. Front B1 was further divided on 1 May 1964 with the creation of Front B3, which included the provinces of Darlac, **Plei Ku**, and **Kon Tum**. In April 1966, the northern section of Front B1, which included the provinces of **Thừa Thiên** and **Quảng Trị**, was divided off to create Front B4. In June 1966, the northern portion of Quảng Trị was further divided to create Front B5. (*See* map 6.)

MINES, LAND. A land mine is generally defined as a type of explosive device buried in the ground and triggered either by pressure, trip wire, or handheld device. All sides of the war used land mines for a variety of purposes. The **United States** developed far more sophisticated land mines during the war than their opposition. The U.S. deployed mines for the purposes of interdiction along known **People's Army of Vietnam** (PAVN) or **National Liberation Front** (NLF) trails, for ambushes, or as the first line of defense for firebases or more permanent military facilities. The majority of U.S. land mines deployed in the **Republic of Vietnam** (RVN), **Laos**, and **Cambodia**, and along the southern end of the **Democratic Republic of Vietnam** (DRV), were antipersonnel devices.

The M18A1, known as the claymore, was used by the U.S. during the war as a directional antipersonnel mine in ambushes, for interdiction missions, and to keep the enemy out of friendly camps. It was inserted into the ground with two pairs of scissor legs and was denoted by an electrical charge that set off **C-4**. The claymore fired approximately 700 small steel balls in an arch of approximately 60 degrees from its center for over 91 meters (300 feet), and up to 228 meters (750 feet), from a plastic convex case, though it was more accurate at less than 46 meters (150 feet). The claymore was a very effective weapon, but it could be disarmed or turned around by troops of the PAVN and NLF who had specially trained sappers for that task. When this occurred, the results could sometimes be devastating.

Another antipersonnel weapon was the Gravel mine, also referred to as the Button mine. It was used by allied forces in the war to contest large areas of land that could not be consistently monitored. They were also rapidly deployed to protect allied personnel under threat from the enemy, such as in the case of **search-and-rescue** operations. The U.S. deployed millions of these mines in Vietnam, Laos, and Cambodia, most notably along the **Hồ**

Chí Minh Trail and around **Khe Sanh** during the 1968 siege of that firebase. Gravei mines came in a variety of sizes and levels of explosive power. The mine itself was relatively small, making it an effective weapon when heavily dispersed in a limited area. It usually had enough explosive power to seriously injure, or sometimes kill, personnel. While the overall effectiveness of the Gravel mine was questioned, it did provide a relatively simple and cost-effective way of denying the PAVN and NLF access to land without the possibility of casualty.

Finally, the U.S. and its allies used Foo Gas, from the French *fougasse*. It was a mine with origins in the 1500s, though the Vietnam-era version was created from a 55-gallon drum filled with **napalm** set off by a small explosive charge. The mine was dug into the ground, usually around American bases, and ignited against the enemy when they tried to penetrate the perimeter. The charge would set off the napalm and spread it over a large area, making it a simple but very effective weapon. Foo Gas was widely used by the U.S. during the war.

The DRV and NLF also used land mines, though their supply was varied. They received mines from the communist bloc and developed a few of their own, though many mines were created from stolen or salvaged U.S. and RVN equipment and failed munitions. The PAVN and NLF use of land mines was very effective in closing roads and railways throughout the RVN. They would often force the Vietnamese people to help lay a minefield on a major roadway during the night, which resulted in the U.S. conducting mine-clearing operations for several hours each day to ensure the safety of travelers. Land mines were an inexpensive way to harass the enemy over a prolonged period without endangering allied forces, though civilian **casualties** would continue to occur decades after the last shots were fired. *See also* MCNAMARA LINE; MINES, NAVAL; TRUSCOTT WHITE, OPERATION.

MINES, NAVAL. Both the **United States** and the **Democratic Republic of Vietnam** (DRV) employed mines in the waterways of Southeast Asia during the war. The U.S. used the Mark-36, which was a 1,000-pound **bomb** with between 258 and 285 kilograms (568–627 pounds) of explosives. It was an improved modification of the Mark-26 bomb. The bomb was detonated acoustically, though there were models that were activated by pressure. The other commonly used mine was the Mark-52. It also was a 1,000-pound bomb that was acoustically fused, though other models could be activated magnetically, by pressure, or by a combination of the three. It had a charge of 284 kilograms (625 pounds). Both mines were dropped in DRV waterways during Operation **Rolling Thunder**, though the primary target of **Hải Phòng** was spared because of the potential repercussions of damage to neutral shipping.

Other ports that serviced only DRV ships were mined. The exception was on 4 January 1968, when an American aircraft accidentally dropped naval mines in Hải Phòng that damaged a Soviet transport.

After the 1972 **Easter Offensive** began, President **Richard M. Nixon** ordered the mining of Hải Phòng harbor. On 9 May 1972, Operation **Pocket Money** began, with the deployment of 36 Mark-52 mines in Hải Phòng harbor. The mines were equipped with a 72-hour delay so that neutral ships could depart the harbor before potentially being destroyed. Nine of the 36 neutral ships in Hải Phòng harbor departed. The others remained until after the signing of the January 1973 **Paris Peace Accords**. On 11 May, additional ports were mined, and over the next eight months, nearly 11,000 Mark-36 and over 100 Mark-52 mines were deployed in the waters of the DRV. The mining of Hải Phòng harbor and the other ports in the DRV effectively cut off the ability of the DRV to resupply by sea. This strategy played an important role in the eventual defeat of the 1972 invasion by the **People's Army of Vietnam** into the **Republic of Vietnam**. As a result of the Paris Peace Accords, the U.S. agreed to clear DRV waters of its mines. Operation **Endsweep**, under Task Force 78, began on 6 February 1973. By 27 July 1973, the operation was officially ended, and the waterways were cleared.

The DRV also deployed thousands of naval mines during the war. Most of these were less sophisticated than what the U.S. was able to deliver, but the threat was no less real. The use of naval mines was an effective counter to the introduction of Operation **Game Warden** and the **Mobile Riverine Force** in 1966. To counter this threat, the U.S. **Navy** created Mine Squadron 11, Detachment Alpha on 20 May 1966. It was reorganized as Mine Division 112 after May 1968. U.S. vessels operated out of Nhà Bè, **Đà Nẵng**, and **Cam Ranh Bay**. While U.S. vessels operated throughout the waterways of the RVN, the most important river for mine clearing operations was the **Lòng Tàu River** that connected **Sài Gòn** with the South China Sea. The DRV and **National Liberation Front** targeted minesweepers with a variety of crew-based weapons to make their job even more difficult, but by 1967 the U.S. and its allies had gained the initiative. The river continued to be threatened, but sea traffic was generally safe from naval mines until the end of the war.

A significant number of naval mines were also used in **Laos** and **Cambodia**. The **Khmer Rouge** used Chinese-built mines to close the **Mê Kông River** in 1975 and help complete the encirclement of **Phnom Penh** before that capital city fell to the communists in April 1975. *See also* MINES, LAND.

MINIGUN. A modern variant of the Gatling gun that fired a 7.62-mm caliber shell at a rate of up to 6,000 rounds per minute. The minigun used six parallel barrels that rotated around a common axis using an electric-powered motor.

During the war, the U.S. military employed the minigun on gunships, including the AC-47, AC-119, and AC-130. It was also mounted onto aircraft such as the A-1 and A-37 and was used as one of the many weapons on **helicopters** such as the AH-1. The high rate of fire made the minigun a most formidable weapon for the **United States** and the armed forces of the **Republic of Vietnam**, **Laos**, and **Cambodia**.

MISSILES. The **United States** used two types of air intercept missiles (AIM) in the **air war** in Vietnam. The AIM-7 Sparrow was a medium-range radar-guided missile. It was extensively used in Vietnam, scoring its first kill on 7 June 1965. While the missile had a greater range than the AIM-9 Sidewinder, enemy aircraft had to be visually targeted until impact, making the weapon less useful. Still, the AIM-7 was involved in more than 50 enemy aircraft shot down during the war.

The AIM-9 Sidewinder was utilized by the **U.S. Air Force** and **Navy** over the **Democratic Republic of Vietnam** (DRV). The missile was a short-range, heat-seeking weapon that recorded 82 air-to-air kills during the war. The U.S. used several variations of the missile. The air force scored its most kills with the AIM-9B/E, while the navy was most successful with the AIM-9D/G. An AIM-9H model was developed at the end of the war, but very few were fired in combat. The AIM-9B carried a 4.5-kilogram (10-pound) blast-fragmentation warhead and was effective between a range of 914 meters (3,000 feet) and 4,877 meters (16,000 feet). The E model replaced the B model with improved tracking. The AIM-9D improved the B model seeking device, while the E model improved the weapon's acquisition potential. The North Vietnamese used the Soviet-built K-13 Atoll air-to-air missile, which was a copy of the AIM-9. The K-13 was 12.7 centimeters (5 inches) in diameter, the same as the AIM-9, and had a similar range, though it carried a slightly heavier warhead.

The U.S. also utilized the tube-launched, optically tracked, wire data link (TOW) guided missile, built by Raytheon Systems Company, which was designated the BGM-71. It was introduced into Vietnam in April 1972 as an antitank guided missile but could also be employed against bunker complexes and other stationary targets. The BGM-71 consisted of a sealed tube attached to a launcher that was fired after a target was sighted and was guided to the target by an optical sensor. The BGM-71 was just short of 1.2 meters (4 feet) long, with a diameter of approximately 15 centimeters (6 inches) and a wingspan of 45.7 centimeters (1.5 feet). It carried a 3.9-kilogram (8.5-pound) warhead, which was approximately 20 percent of its total weight of just over 18.6 kilograms (41 pounds), and had a range of approximately 3,658 meters (12,000 feet) and a speed of over 274 meters (900 feet) per second.

The 1st Combat Aerial TOW Team, consisting of three BGM-71 crews, recorded its first **People's Army of Vietnam** (PAVN) **tank** kill near An Lộc on 2 May 1972 during the **Easter Offensive**. The TOW was fired from a U.S. Army UH-1 Huey **helicopter**. A week later, three additional PAVN tanks were destroyed using TOW missiles. By the end of the month, the TOW was credited with 24 tank kills. The TOW missile proved valuable during the Easter Offensive, which was the last major engagement for U.S. personnel before the January 1973 **Paris Peace Accords**.

In 1967, the U.S. first used the Martin-Marietta air-to-ground missile (AGM)—nicknamed the Walleye—in Vietnam. The AGM-62 was an electro-optically guided bomb. It had no power and was deployed as a glide bomb with a television camera mounted in its front. The bomb was steered to its target by the pilot of the aircraft that delivered it or by a trailing aircraft. It was not employed much during Operation **Rolling Thunder**. During operations **Line-backer I** and **Linebacker II**, the AGM-62 was used against hard targets and proved effective because it could penetrate up to 45 centimeters (18 inches) of steel-reinforced concrete. It had a warhead with 375 kilograms (825 pounds) of high explosives and a range of approximately 25 kilometers (16 miles). The U.S. also employed the Paveway I, a laser-guided missile, using the Mark-117 bomb as a prototype, developed by the U.S. and deployed to Vietnam in August 1968. The Paveway I had limited use before President **Lyndon B. Johnson** ordered a halt to all bombing of the DRV in November 1968. During the 1972 Easter Offensive, the Paveway I proved itself useful with its high accuracy rate and received credit for the destruction of a number of hard targets that had eluded Rolling Thunder **sorties**, including the **Thanh Hóa bridge**.

The PAVN used three major missile systems during the war. In response to the escalation of the American air war with Operation Rolling Thunder, the DRV introduced three SA-2 surface-to-air missile (SAM) sites around **Hà Nội** in May 1965. The SA-2 was a mobile air defense weapon that traveled at near Mach 3 and carried a 136-kilogram (300-pound) warhead. Active SAM sites threatened U.S. aircraft conducting air strikes and reconnaissance flights at high altitude. To avoid the SAMs, aircraft could fly at a lower altitude, but they risked the **antiaircraft artillery** that the North Vietnamese had installed to create a sophisticated and integrated air defense system. The first U.S. aircraft loss due to an SA-2 occurred on 26 July 1965 when an F-4C was hit. As more SAM battalions entered the DRV, they became a priority target.

William C. Westmoreland argued that each SAM site should be targeted until destroyed, which gave rise to such missions as **Iron Hand**. By 1966, the number of SAM sites had increased to over 100 and had been expanded beyond Hà Nội and **Hải Phòng**. Not every site contained SA-2 missiles, but those active sites normally held six missiles in a star pattern, which was typical of artillery emplacements. In terms of quantitative statistics, the SA-2 was not a very effective weapon, but it did force the U.S. to alter its bombing strategy and provided an additional obstacle to a successful bombing **sortie**. It also emboldened the North Vietnamese, who often could not see the aircraft delivering the **bombs**. Aircraft shot down by SA-2, or even aircraft shot down by other means, were displayed before the people so that they could see that the U.S. military was not invincible and was paying a price for its bombing campaigns.

Introduced into the DRV in 1972, the SA-7 was a shoulder-fired, low-altitude surface-to-air missile that was used by People's Army of Vietnam and **National Liberation Front** soldiers in the **Republic of Vietnam**. It had a limited range and was not considered a fast enough missile to threaten jet aircraft, though it could be effective against slow-flying fixed-winged aircraft and helicopters. It was often fired as an aircraft passed the position of the soldier firing the weapon. The SA-7 delivered a 0.9-kilogram (2-pound) warhead that could explode on or after contact. The weapon was approximately 1.5 meters (5 feet) long and weighed approximately 13.6 kilograms (30 pounds) with a missile ready to fire.

The Sagger was a Soviet-built antitank missile, known as the AT-3 Sagger by the U.S. but actually designated the 9M14M Malutka. The missile was wire guided, required a crew of three to operate from a ground mount, and had an effective range of just more than 3,000 meters (10,000 feet), which meant that it would take approximately 25 seconds for the missile to reach its target after it was fired. The Sagger was capable of penetrating approximately 38 centimeters (15 inches) of armor with a high accuracy rate, unless the person guiding the weapon was distracted with counterfire. It was first used by the DRV during the 1972 Easter Offensive and initially proved to be very effective in destroying **Army of the Republic of Vietnam** tank and armored vehicles. *See also* LIGHT ANTI-TANK WEAPON.

MISSING-IN-ACTION (MIA). The term "MIA" referred to **United States** personnel whose fate was unknown. At the time of the signing of the 1973 **Paris Peace Accords**, the U.S. listed 1,392 as MIA and 1,113 as MIA but presumed dead under the category Body Not Recovered. The majority of the names taken off the list were a result of the work of the U.S. government working with the Socialist Republic of Vietnam, though the efforts were often hampered by mistrust and memories of the war.

U.S. interest in recovery efforts began in 1973 with the creation of a Central Identification Laboratory in **Thailand** followed by an additional lab in Hawaii. In 1997, the Department of Defense created the Joint Task Force–Full Accounting (JTFFA) with the mission of learning the fate of as many of the missing U.S. servicemen and civilians in Southeast Asia as possible. JTFFA joined with the two labs in 2002 to better coordinate their efforts. In 2003, the U.S. established the Joint POW/MIA Accounting Command (JPAC) with its detachments in Bangkok, **Hà Nội**, Vientiane, and Hawaii. Through labor-intensive and often difficult conditions, JPAC and its predecessors have been able to close nearly 800 of the original files from 1973. While this means that there are still more than 1,150 personnel not accounted for, it is a number far lower than World War II or the Korean War.

MNONG (M'NÔNG). An ethnic minority tribe that was one of many that made up the **Montagnards** people. The tribe was located in the **Central Highlands**, centered near Ban Mê Thuột and **Đà Lạt**, as well as eastern sections of **Cambodia** and spoke the Mon-**Khmer** language. M'Nông were persecuted by the **Khmer Rouge** as well as the communist insurgents and **Sài Gòn** allies in Vietnam. The M'Nông were also known for the domestication of the elephant.

MOBILE RIVERINE FORCE (MRF). Joint **United States Navy** and **Army** effort to deny the waterways of the **Mê Kông Delta** to the **People's Army of Vietnam** (PAVN) and the **National Liberation Front** (NLF). The MRF, which was established in 1966 and later served as the nucleus for Task Force 117 after the creation of the River Assault Flotilla 1, relied on firepower and the unique combination of ground, sea, and air units to take the battle to the enemy. The MRF included a variety of naval craft, army **artillery** and mortar barges, navy **helicopter** gunships, and the 2nd Brigade, 9th Infantry **Division**. The MRF used not only shore-based facilities but also established floating mobile riverine bases to mount operations in areas traditionally held by the PAVN and NLF. One early example that led to the creation of the MRF was Operation River Raider I between 16 February and 20 March 1967. This operation focused on clearing a part of the **Rừng Sác Special Zone** in the shipping lanes leading into **Sài Gòn**, southeast of the capital. In this first attempt at employing the MRF concept, it was deemed successful. The MRF continued to operate in the Mê Kông Delta until it was incorporated into the **SEALORDS** campaign.

MONTAGNARDS. Name given to the people who lived in the **Central Highlands** in the **Republic of Vietnam** (RVN) and extending westward into **Cambodia**. The term *Montagnard* was French and loosely translated as "of the mountains." The Montagnards were not one people but rather a group of tribes who only shared a geographical location. Included in the group were the **Bahnar, Bru, Cor, Hrê, Jarai, Koho, Ra Glai, Rhadé**, and **Sedang**.

The Montagnard had poor relations with the French and the RVN. The people were often deemed inferior, and their territory was considered available for Vietnamese use. RVN president **Ngô Đình Diệm** sought to resettle many of the **refugees** who had fled North Vietnam in 1954–1955 as a result of the 1954 **Geneva Conference** into the territory held by the Montagnards, which resulted in animosity and increased tensions in the 1950s. This culminated in the 1957 **Bajaraka Movement** as well as the creation of the **Front Unifié de Lutte des Races Opprimées** (FULRO), which resulted from the September 1964 rebellion near **Ban Mê Thuột**.

Both the **National Liberation Front** (NLF) and the **United States** sought Montagnard assistance during the war. While the NLF took advantage of the Montagnards' dissatisfaction with the **Sài Gòn** government, the U.S. was able to cultivate an alliance with the people that resulted in greater participation. It was estimated that approximately 40,000 Montagnards fought under U.S. leadership in the **Civilian Irregular Defense Groups**, as well as in other special operations to monitor the **Hồ Chí Minh Trail** and in the secret war in **Laos**. Because of their general support for the U.S. and the Sài Gòn government in the mid-1960s to the end of the war, the Montagnards faced repression under communist rule. Many escaped to Cambodia only to suffer under the rule of the **Khmer Rouge**. A majority of those who fled eventually made their way to the U.S. *See also* HMONG; MOUNTAIN SCOUTS; REFUGEES; SPECIAL FORCES, VIETNAMESE; TRAIL WATCHERS.

MOORER, THOMAS HINMAN (1912–2004). United States Navy admiral. Moorer was born in Alabama, graduated from the U.S. Naval Academy in 1933, and completed naval aviation training in 1936. During the 7 December 1941 Japanese attack at Pearl Harbor, he was with Patrol Squadron 22. Moorer flew in the Pacific Theater during the war and was shot down off the coast of Australia in February 1942, only to have the Philippine freighter that rescued him sunk by a Japanese dive-bomber soon after he was picked up. After the war, he served on the staff of Commander Carrier Division Four, Atlantic Fleet; he commanded the U.S.S. *Salisbury Sound*; and he served as the assistant chief of naval operations. In 1958, he was promoted to rear admiral, and in 1962 to vice admiral.

Upon the latter promotion, Moorer assumed command of the 7th Fleet. In June 1964, he was promoted to full admiral and became the commander-in-chief of the Pacific Fleet. Moorer was in charge of the fleet during the **Gulf of Tŏn Kĭn Incident**. In 1965, he took over the North Atlantic Treaty Organization's U.S. Atlantic Command as well as the U.S. Atlantic Fleet. In August 1967, Moorer was appointed the chief of naval operations. He served as the chairman of the **Joint Chiefs of Staff** from 2 July 1970 to June 1974. Moorer was considered a **Hawk** on the war. He supported the position of **mining Hải Phòng** harbor as well as the more aggressive strategies that involved going after the Vietnamese in **Cambodia** and **Laos**. He advocated the use of airpower in response to the 1972 **Easter Offensive** that would become known as operations **Linebacker I** and **Linebacker II**. Moorer sometimes came into conflict with Secretary of Defense **Robert McNamara** and President **Lyndon B. Johnson**, though he refrained from publicly criticizing their position until after his retirement.

MORSE, WAYNE LYMAN (1900–1974). United States senator. Morse was educated at the University of Wisconsin at Madison, receiving an undergraduate degree in 1923 and a graduate degree in 1924. He graduated from the law department of the University of Minnesota at Minneapolis in 1928 and Columbia University Law School in 1932. During this time, he also held a reserve commission as second lieutenant, field artillery, in the U.S. Army and taught at the University of Wisconsin and the University of Minnesota. In 1929, he became an assistant professor of law at the University of Oregon and dean and professor of law from 1931 to 1944. He served in a variety of positions in consultation with the U.S. government at the same time. In 1944, Morse was elected as a Republican to the U.S. Senate and was reelected in 1950. In 1952, he switched his party affiliation to Independent. In 1956, he ran as a Democrat and was reelected for another two terms.

Morse was best known for his opposition to the **Gulf of Tŏn Kĭn Resolution**, which passed the U.S. Senate by a vote of 88 to 2. Only Morse and Senator Ernest Gruening of Alaska opposed the resolution. He continued to oppose President **Lyndon B. Johnson**'s handling of the war and publicly supported **antiwar** protestors and demonstrations, calling upon the nation to oppose Johnson. Morse's opposition to the war often crossed party lines, such as his support for antiwar candidate Republican Mark Hatfield in his election for governor of Oregon over his Democratic, and prowar, opponent in 1966. Morse lost his Senate seat in 1968 to Oregon state representative Bob Packwood who criticized the incumbent senator for his failure to support financing the war in progress. He was not successful in his 1972 senatorial bid and died during his final attempt to become a U.S. senator during the 1974 election. *See also* CONGRESS, UNITED STATES.

MORTAR. A mortar was a simple-to-use, smoothbore, muzzle-loading weapon that fired a shell for a short elevated distance. The **United States** used several different types of mortar weapons during the war. The M19 60-mm mortar weighed 20 kilograms (45 pounds), with an 81-centimeter (32-inch) barrel. It could fire a 1.4-kilogram (3-pound), 60-mm diameter mortar shell at an elevation of between 40 and 85 degrees to an effective range of just less than 1,798 meters (5,900 feet). Trained crews could fire 18 rounds per minute for a long duration or up to 30 rounds per minute for a brief time. There were not many M19s in service during the war.

The U.S. also used the M29 81-mm mortar, which replaced the M1 81-mm mortar. It weighed more than the M19 at just over 54.4 kilograms (120 pounds) and had a longer range, at approximately 3,048 meters (10,000 feet). The mortar could be disassembled for easy movement, and it possessed a better tube that allowed it a greater rate of fire. The U.S. also employed a heavy mortar weapon in the M30 107-mm, or 4.2-inch, mortar. It weighed approximately 306 kilograms (675 pounds) and was 1.5 meters (5 feet) long. It fired a 4.2-inch shell at a maximum effective range of over 6,705 meters (22,000 feet), with a sustained rate of fire of 3 rounds per minute or 18 rounds per minute for a short period of time.

The **People's Army of Vietnam** (PAVN) and the **National Liberation Front** (NLF) used a variety of mortars ranging from 60 mm to 120 mm, though the 82 mm was the largest caliber that could be easily transported through the jungles of Southeast Asia. The North Vietnamese received many of their mortar weapons as a result of the surrender of the Japanese at the end of World War II. They also captured a number of mortar weapons from the French during the **First Indochina War**. These older systems were replaced in the 1960s by ones manufactured by the **Soviet Union** and the **People's Republic of China**. While the PAVN and NLF possessed field **artillery**, the mortar was utilized as the primary heavy support weapon in the jungle.

MOUNTAIN SCOUTS. A **Central Intelligence Agency** program designed to organize **Montagnards** to operate in small teams in the jungles of Vietnam, though the original idea derived from a South Vietnamese captain named Ngô Văn Hưng in 1961. The first Mountain Scouts were trained by **United States Special Forces** in I **Corps Tactical Zone** in December 1961 near **Huế**, though future training would occur near **Đà Nẵng**. A second group trained in **Plei Ku** province. The program developed as a result of U.S. frustration over the **Republic of Vietnam**'s efforts to develop their own Special Forces. By May 1963, when the program was handed over to the **Military Assistance Command, Vietnam**, the Mountain Scouts had deployed 5,300 men in the 21 mountain provinces.

MUSTE, ABRAHAM JOHANNE (A. J.) (1885–1967). Pacifist, onetime religious leader, civil rights organizer, **antiwar** activist, and executive secretary of the **Fellowship of Reconciliation**. Muste opposed both world wars and was active against the escalation of the Vietnam War until his death.

Muste served as an ordained minister in the Dutch Reformed Church, a pastor in a Congregational Church, a pacifist, a member of the American Civil Liberties Union in Boston, and an organizer of the American Workers Party in 1933. For a brief time, he was a Marxist-Leninist; then he helped to form the Trotskyist Workers Party of America before becoming the executive secretary of the Fellowship of Reconciliation.

Muste was involved in the early civil rights movement and helped to organize the Congress on Racial Equality. After his 1953 retirement, he became the leader of the antinuclear organization, Committee for Nonviolent Action, and worked with liberation movements in Africa. Muste took a group of pacifists to **Sài Gòn** in 1966 and was arrested and then deported after he attempted to lead an antiwar demonstration. Later in the year, he was welcomed to **Hà Nội** where he met **Hồ Chí Minh**. Muste preached nonviolence until his untimely death in 1967, less than a month after visiting the **Democratic Republic of Vietnam**.

MỸ LAI. Site of the 16 March 1968 massacre which involved personnel from Company C, 1st Battalion, 20th Infantry Regiment, 11th Brigade, 23rd Infantry **Division**, also known as the Americal Division. The massacre took place in Mỹ Lai and My Khe hamlets in the village of Sơn Mỹ and resulted from the unit's frustration arising out of continual operations against **guerrilla** fighters, ambushes, and **casualties** from **booby trap**s. The area of the massacre had been one contested for most of the war and was the home of the 48th **National Liberation Front** (NLF) Battalion.

There were 26 Americans charged with various crimes as a result of the episode, though only one, Lieutenant **William Calley**, was convicted of premeditated murder. The **United States Army** estimated that 347 Vietnamese civilians, the vast majority of whom were not of military age, were killed in the massacre, though the Vietnamese list 504 at the memorial in Mỹ Lai. Not all Americans in the area on that day participated in the massacre, and a few, specifically **helicopter** pilot Hugh Thompson, crew chief Glenn Andreotta, and his gunner Lawrence Colburn, worked actively to stop the killings. However, they were not able to stop the massacre or the brutality of events, which were comparable to the **People's Army of Vietnam** and NLF killings at Dak Son and **Huế**.

The truth of the event at Mỹ Lai was not exposed until November 1969, by journalist Seymour Hersh who had interviewed Calley. News of the event enraged those who had already opposed the war and was received with sadness, shock, and denial by most of the U.S. As a result of Hersh's work, the U.S. Army conducted an official investigation into the events under the direction of General William Peers and published the final Peers Commission report in March 1970, which examined the massacre and the subsequent attempt to cover up the event. In November 1970, the U.S. Army charged 14 officers with various crimes, but only the brigade commander, Colonel Oran K. Henderson, stood trial and was acquitted in December 1971. Lieutenant Calley had already been tried and convicted of premeditated murder on 29 March 1971 and was sentenced to life in prison. He served less than five months after his sentence was adjusted. The Mỹ Lai massacre became a catalyst and a justification for the **antiwar movement**, which had already condemned American personnel in Vietnam. While the event was an aberration in the war, it was for a short time the symbol of the American soldier and the Vietnam veteran as the war ended, and it lasted through the decades following the fall of **Sài Gòn** in April 1975.

Senator Wayne Morse (D-Oregon) and President Lyndon B. Johnson meet in the Oval Office, 18 July 1967. White House Photo Office, Serial Number A4442-8. LBJ Library photo by Yoichi R. Okamoto.

General William C. Westmoreland at a meeting in the Cabinet Room, 14 October 1968. White House Photo Office, Serial Number A6966-27a. LBJ Library photo by Yoichi R. Okamoto.

President Lyndon B. Johnson meets with U.S. soldiers at Cam Ranh Bay, Republic of Vietnam, 23 December 1967. White House Photo Office, Serial Number C8052-20A. LBJ Library photo by Yoichi R. Okamoto.

Marine at Khe Sanh. Photograph courtesy of Robert Houck, Millersville, Pennsylvania.

Aerial view of the marine base at Khe Sanh weeks before the beginning of the 1968 siege. Photograph courtesy of Robert Houck, Millersville, Pennsylvania.

Army of the Republic of Vietnam from the 1st Battalion, 1st Regiment, 1st Division on a mission in Quảng Trị Province. Douglas Pike Collection, The Vietnam Archive, Texas Tech University.

UC-123 conducting an herbicide-spraying sortie during Operation Ranch Hand. Rand Hand Association Collection, The Vietnam Archive, Texas Tech University.

C-7 landing at the marine base at Khe Sanh. Photograph courtesy of Robert Houck, Millersville, Pennsylvania.

B-52 Stratofortress. Douglas Pike Collection, The Vietnam Archive, Texas Tech University.

F-4 Phantom readying for takeoff. Photograph courtesy of Jack Yuska, Millersville, Pennsylvania.

A-1 Skyraider on approach for landing. Photograph courtesy of Jack Yuska, Millersville, Pennsylvania.

UH-1 Iroquois (Huey) and a light observation helicopter. Curtis Knapp Collection, The Vietnam Archive, Texas Tech University.

CH-54 Skycrane lifting a UC-123 Provider aircraft that was involved in Operation Ranch Hand. Rand Hand Association Collection, The Vietnam Archive, Texas Tech University.

C-130 Hercules. Admiral Elmo R. Zumwalt Collection, The Vietnam Archive, Texas Tech University.

People's Army of Vietnam antiaircraft artillery. Douglas Pike Collection, The Vietnam Archive, Texas Tech University.

Vietnam War protestors Pittsburgh Veterans for Peace at the March on the Pentagon cross the Abraham Lincoln Bridge in Washington, D.C., 21 October 1967. White House Photo Office, Serial Number 7052-3. LBJ Library photo by Frank Wolfe.

N

NAPALM. Created during World War II, napalm is a mixture of a flammable liquid, usually gasoline, with a thickening agent to form a gelatin. The name comes from the first two letters of *naphthenic* and the first four of *palmitic acids*, which combined to form the thickening agent, though the **United States** experimented with different agents depending upon its use for napalm. During the war, the U.S. used Napalm-B, which was a mixture of gasoline, benzene, and polystyrene plastic. The mixture burned for a much longer time than the original formula and was more stable before deployment. Napalm was delivered by aircraft in a large, silver cylinder known as the BLU-27, and was dropped from **helicopters** in 55-gallon drums.

The weapon had a devastating effect on an exposed enemy. It injured, usually fatally, by incineration or asphyxiation. Napalm was also used to clear heavily vegetated areas to expose the enemy. At **Khe Sanh**, the U.S. also used napalm to collapse the **tunnel** system that the **People's Army of Vietnam** and the **National Liberation Front** developed to get closer to the base perimeter. The weapon was produced by Dow Corporation, which received significant criticism from the **antiwar movement** and human rights groups for producing it. The effects of napalm and its controversial use were captured in the June 1972 Pulitzer Prize winning image by Nick Ut that showed a young girl, Kim Phúc, badly burned by napalm after a **Republic of Vietnam** Air Force attack.

NASTY BOAT. A 24-meter (81-foot) fast patrol boat built in Norway that was propelled by two turbo blown diesel engines and was capable of a top speed of 45 knots (83 kilometers per hour). It could carry a 40-mm and 20-mm gun as well as four 21-inch torpedoes, though the Nasty boats sent to Vietnam did not carry torpedoes. In 1964, Nasty boats were involved in a Studies and Observation Group mission known as **OPLAN 34A** that involved raids against the **Democratic Republic of Vietnam** and helped to precipitate the **Gulf of Tŏn Kĭn Incident** in August. They were also used to transport navy **SEAL** teams operating out of **Đà Nẵng**. The Nasty was particularly useful in stealth operations because of its low silhouette, its high range of over 1,600 kilometers (1,000 miles), and its ability to carry a heavy load.

The **United States** purchased 14 Nasty boats from Norway and constructed 6 more. The U.S. trained **Republic of Vietnam Navy** personnel to operate the Nasty boats, which were then used during Operation **Market Time** to stop the infiltration of North Vietnamese personnel and supplies by sea. *See also* PATROL BOAT, RIVER; SWIFT BOAT.

NATIONAL COORDINATING COMMITTEE TO END THE WAR IN VIETNAM (NCC). After the **United States** introduced combat troops into Southeast Asia and began to Americanize the war, **antiwar** organizations formed at a significant pace. At a national assembly of antiwar organizations in August 1965 in Washington, D.C., the NCC was established with the primary mission of coordinating the activities of the various groups. It organized the 15–16 October 1965 International Days of Protest, an event that had been initiated by the Berkeley Vietnam Day Committee. The NCC was also tasked with establishing a Thanksgiving convention to create a national organization of antiwar groups.

Because of differing perspectives on ending the war and internal disputes, the NCC never fully coordinated the antiwar groups into one movement. However, it did give rise to new organizations dedicated to educating the American people about the war and its impact, and it assisted in strengthening the antiwar movement through the Second International Days of Protest on 25–26 March 1966, even though this event, which involved more than 100,000 people, was organized more at the local level than through the NCC. As the Vietnam War continued to escalate and more groups were founded to oppose the war as well as in support of other social issues, the NCC's effectiveness as a coordinating organization diminished. The NCC was eclipsed by the Spring Mobilization Committee and was eventually relegated to dealing with antiwar activities around Madison, Wisconsin.

NATIONAL EMERGENCY COMMITTEE OF CLERGY CONCERNED ABOUT VIETNAM. An **antiwar** organization established in October 1965 when approximately 100 clergy members met at a conference in New York City to explore options for how they could oppose American involvement in Vietnam. On 11 January 1966, the group formally organized to create the National Emergency Committee in order to legitimize the antiwar movement that had been labeled too radical. The group eventually formed the Clergy Concerned about Vietnam, whose name was changed in May 1966 to the National Emergency Committee of Clergy and Laymen Concerned about Vietnam when the committee opened its membership to all people regardless of religion.

NATIONAL FRONT FOR THE LIBERATION OF SOUTH VIETNAM. See NATIONAL LIBERATION FRONT.

NATIONAL LIBERATION FRONT (NLF). A term used for the National Front for the Liberation of South Vietnam. It was also referred to as the **Việt Cộng** (Cộng Sản Bắc Việt) by the **United States** and the **Republic of Vietnam** (RVN), or as the People's Liberation Armed Forces (PLAF). The organization was formed on 20 December 1960 in **Tây Ninh** province in South Vietnam. The creation of the NLF was in response to a new direction that the war in Vietnam had taken. The Vietnamese Communist Party had been engaged in a six-year struggle to unify the **Democratic Republic of Vietnam** and the **Republic of Vietnam**. Party general secretary **Lê Duẩn** called for armed confrontation to achieve unification, with the ultimate goal of overthrowing the **Sài Gòn** government.

The significance of the NLF for the U.S. was divided. For those who believed that the North Vietnamese wished to overthrow the South Vietnamese, the NLF was under the control of **Hà Nội** as it sought to achieve its objective. For those who opposed the U.S. involvement in Southeast Asia, the NLF represented a true southern insurgency that was fighting a civil war against an oppressive government. Regardless of perspective, the NLF did represent both communist and noncommunist groups, even if the organization was controlled by the Communist Party, and it served as the primary vehicle for organizing against **Ngô Đình Diệm**. It remained a serious threat to the RVN in the struggle to protect and control the rural population until the 1968 **Tết Offensive**, when a significant majority of the organization was either exposed and forced to flee its area of operation or was killed in the failed attempt to incite a popular uprising. After the Tết Offensive, much of the NLF ranks were filled by North Vietnamese to maintain the organizational structure. The NLF remained strong, but it no longer represented a purely southern insurgency.

NATIONAL MOBILIZATION COMMITTEE TO END THE WAR IN VIETNAM (MOBE). An **antiwar** organization established at the Spring Mobilization conference in Washington, D.C., in May 1967 with the objective of organizing monthly nationwide protests. Mobe organized its first major protest on 21 October 1967 in Washington, D.C., which led to the march on the Pentagon building. It would also play a role in the demonstrations that occurred during the 1968 Chicago National Convention. After the election of **Richard M. Nixon** and Mobe's counterinaugural demonstration, it disbanded, though its membership continued to play an active role in other antiwar organizations, including the New Mobilization Committee to End the War in Vietnam that helped organize the Moratorium Day demonstration on 15 October 1969, which could count its participants in the tens of thousands. The 15 November 1969 National Moratorium Day would number in the hundreds of thousands, while monthly demonstrations continued to attract a significant number of people.

NATIONAL SECURITY ACTION MEMORANDUM (NSAM) 57. Produced on 28 June 1961, NSAM 57 outlined how the **United States** would conduct paramilitary operations to produce the most effective and flexible results. The document called for the U.S. to assist, overtly or covertly, friendly governments or insurgents seeking to overthrow an enemy government, with personnel, equipment, and training of indigenous forces. NSAM 57 created the Special Group (5412 Committee) which acted upon the recommendations of the Strategic Resources Group (SRG) after the approval of the president. The SRG would also assign responsibility for the planning, coordination, and execution of the paramilitary operation. The most important aspect of the document was that all paramilitary operations would fall under the Department of Defense, with the **Central Intelligence Agency** in a supporting role.

NATIONAL SECURITY ACTION MEMORANDUM (NSAM) 288. On 16 March 1964, Secretary of Defense **Robert McNamara** forwarded a report to the **National Security Council** that discussed the implementation of **United States** programs for Vietnam. NSAM 288, approved on 17 March, provided a critical assessment of the situation in Vietnam since September 1963. McNamara provided evidence of involvement in the war by the **People's Republic of China** through the supply of 57-mm and 75-mm **recoilless** rifles, heavy **machine guns**, 90-mm rocket launchers and **mortars**, rocket-propelled grenades (**RPG-2**), and a version of the AK-47 rifle. McNamara also revealed the extent to which the communist insurgency had gained ground in the **Republic of Vietnam** (RVN). He reported that 40 percent of the countryside was under **National Liberation Front** control, including more than 50 percent of the land in 23 of 43 provinces. McNamara argued that the government of **Nguyễn Khánh** was weakening and the population was showing signs of apathy. NSAM 288 described an RVN in turmoil and would play a significant role in increased American involvement in the country within the year.

NATIONAL SECURITY ACTION MEMORANDUM (NSAM) 328. NSAM 328, drafted by **McGeorge Bundy,** was based on a series of meetings of the **National Security Council** on 1–2 April 1965. The document provided authorization for **United States** combat troops in Vietnam to move from the secured enclaves established to protect air bases to the offensive against the enemy in support of South Vietnamese troops. When NSAM 328 was issued on 6 April, it escalated the air war over the **Democratic Republic of Viet-**

nam, added air units to Southeast Asia, increased U.S. **Marine Corps** and support troops in the **Republic of Vietnam**, and began the process of what would eventually become the "**Show the Flag**" program to gather **Third Country** support in the war. This document became the marching orders for the Americanization of the war.

NATIONAL SECURITY COUNCIL (NSC). Formed as part of the National Security Act of 1947, the NSC was responsible for providing the White House with national security and foreign policy alternatives to the more significant diplomatic issues of the day. The NSC also coordinated the implementation of these policies for the president.

NATIONAL SECURITY COUNCIL (NSC) 64. After formal recognition of Vietnam, **Laos**, and **Cambodia** on 7 February 1950, Harry S. Truman instructed the **National Security Council** to develop a memorandum that outlined the American position with regard to French Indochina. Approved in March 1950, NSC 64 inserted Indochina into the Cold War strategy of the **United States** as it sought to contain Soviet communism around the world. NSC 64 recommended that the departments of State and Defense develop a strategy for protecting U.S. security interests in the region. It also approved giving aid and assistance in the defense of Indochina against communist rule, which led to the formation of the **Military Assistance Advisory Group**, Indochina, that arrived in **Sài Gòn** in September 1950.

NAVAL GUNFIRE SUPPORT. Starting in 1965, the **United States Navy** (USN) began to provide naval gunfire support to U.S. and Republic of Vietnam armed forces in the war. In addition, naval gunfire was also utilized against coastal installations and facilities in the **Democratic Republic of Vietnam** (DRV). One of the most significant sea campaigns involving intense bombardment and harassment of **People's Army of Vietnam** (PAVN) and **National Liberation Front** forces operating north of the **Demilitarized Zone** (DMZ) was Operation **Sea Dragon**.

Starting on 25 October 1966, the USN's 7th Fleet began raiding DRV coastal positions from the DMZ to the 20th parallel. This form of naval gunfire complemented the U.S. air campaign, Operation **Rolling Thunder**. Sea Dragon missions were designed to harass the PAVN forces and achieved some success, though they did not force the DRV to abandon its coastal positions, and they did not interdict international supplies from reaching it. This form of naval gunfire support also failed to stop the infiltration of personnel and supplies to the South, though it did noticeably reduce the flow. The DRV responded with its own coastal guns but never seriously threatened U.S. naval gunfire support.

Sea Dragon ended on 31 October 1968. Another major naval gunfire support operation occurred during the U.S. response to the 1972 **Easter Offensive**. U.S. naval gunfire played a significant role in assisting **Army of the Republic of Vietnam** forces in repelling PAVN forces in I and II **Corps Tactical Zones** as well as destroying PAVN armor, **artillery**, and war-related material.

The primary weapons used by the U.S. to conduct naval gunfire support were the destroyer, the cruiser, and a single battleship, the U.S.S. *New Jersey*. The destroyer possessed an older 5-inch, 38 caliber gun that fired a 24.5-kilogram (54-pound), 5-inch shell, though only about 30 percent of that was explosive, at a distance of over 15.5 kilometers (51,000 feet). A newer 5-inch, 54 caliber gun fired a heavier shell of 32 kilograms (70 pounds), containing 8.3 kilograms (18.25 pounds) of explosive, with a range of over 23.6 kilometers (77,500 feet). The U.S.S. *New Jersey* had a variety of weapons, including larger 16-inch guns that fired a 1,250-kilogram (2,750-pound) projectile up to 38 kilometers (24 miles) in distance. Because the U.S. had overwhelming superiority in the water and air, U.S. ships were able to direct naval gunfire at any target within range at any time.

NAVARRE, HENRI EUGÈNE (1898–1983). French Army officer in World War I and World War II and commander of the French Union Forces during the **First Indochina War**. Navarre arrived in Indochina in May 1953 to replace General Raoul Salan. He inherited a French Union Force that had been continually frustrated by the Vietnamese, who refused to conduct the war in the style of the Europeans. Navarre was charged with seizing the initiative from the Vietnamese and forcing action, not only to appease the French but also the **United States**, which had become increasingly concerned with the lack of progress in a war that it was helping to fund. Under these dual pressures, Navarre formulated a plan to consolidate his forces in the Tŏn Kĭn region and strike at the enemy in force. Before the plan unfolded, the French were thwarted by **Võ Nguyên Giáp** and his Vietnamese Army.

Navarre altered his original plan and focused on creating a stronghold near the village of **Điện Biên Phủ**, in the northwest part of Vietnam, along strategic **Route** 19 into **Laos**, thereby forcing the Vietnamese to attack. The Battle for Điện Biên Phủ did not turn out as Navarre had anticipated, as the French were surrounded and defeated after a prolonged battle that captured the attention of **France** and the world. The defeat at Điện Biên Phủ effectively ended the military career of Navarre, who retired in 1956 and published his perspective of the war in *Agonie de l'Indochine*. Navarre was highly critical of the French civilian authorities and their management of the war. He remained embittered by his Indochina experience until his death in 1983. *See also* NAVARRE PLAN.

NAVARRE PLAN. Named after the commander of the French Union Forces in Indochina, General **Henri Navarre**, the Navarre Plan was an attempt by **France** in 1953 to reenergize the war against the Vietnamese opposed to French colonial rule. Navarre, with some pressure from the **United States** for action, ordered a consolidation of his forces in the **Red River Delta** in order to strike at the enemy in force and seize the initiative in the **First Indochina War** that had been raging since 1945. Before Navarre could complete the initial concentration, Vietnamese general **Võ Nguyên Giáp** disrupted his plans by launching a series of ambushes and attacks on French positions throughout northern Indochina. Navarre altered his original strategy and decided to establish a fortress near the village of **Điện Biên Phủ** in the northwestern section of Vietnam near strategic **Route** 19, which was the only major road between **Laos** and the **Democratic Republic of Vietnam**. The revised strategy led to the failed Battle of Điện Biên Phủ and the end of the French colonial experience in Indochina.

NAVY, REPUBLIC OF VIETNAM. The first Vietnamese Navy was formed as part of the French effort to fight those attempting to thwart their efforts at colonialism in Indochina. The naval force, originating in 1952, was small, with its vessels transferred to the navy by the French Divisions Navales d'Assaut (Dinassaut). At the end of the **First Indochina War**, the **Republic of Vietnam** (RVN) formed its own navy with the assistance of the **United States**. The RVN Navy consisted of only 4,500 men in August 1961, though that number would increase nearly tenfold by 1972, especially after the initiation of **Vietnamization** in 1969. By the end of the war, the RVN Navy ranked among the top of the world's naval forces, with over 43,000 servicemen and **women** and over 1,400 ships, vessels, crafts, junks, and sampans. Its most significant vessels were the **patrol boat, river**; the **swift boat**; and the **coast guard** cutter. The majority of RVN operations consisted of **brown-water navy** activities.

NAVY, UNITED STATES (USN). The USN had a significant advantage over the **Democratic Republic of Vietnam** (DRV) in the quality and quantity of its fighting ships. As a result, it was able to accomplish nearly every one of its objectives during the war. The USN had four major missions during the war. The most significant was interdiction. The USN was involved in interdicting personnel and supplies coming through the Gulf of Tŏn Kĭn and inland waterways. The USN was successful in its interdiction efforts, though the DRV was able to discover alternatives by moving supplies by sea to **Sihanoukville** in neutral **Cambodia** and by developing the **Hồ Chí Minh Trail**. On 18 October 1968, the commander of naval forces, Vietnam, Vice Admiral **Elmo R. Zumwalt Jr.**, established the Southeast Asia Lake Ocean River Delta Strategy (**SEAL-**

ORDS), which coordinated previous naval activities. SEALORDS turned out to be one of the most successful actions of the U.S. during the war.

The second significant mission of the USN was providing fire support for troops engaged against the enemy, as well as harassment against DRV coastal facilities. The third mission involved **amphibious operations** along the coast and within the waterways to areas that had previously been inaccessible. The USN dominated the sea with its **blue-water navy** and was able to engage the enemy along the coast anywhere and at any time it wished. The final mission for the USN involved it in the **air war** over the DRV and in support of **Free World Forces**. USN aircraft operated at **Yankee Station** in the Gulf of Tŏn Kĭn and, for a brief period of time, at **Dixie Station** in the South China Sea.

During the war, the USN was commanded by the chief of naval operations (CNO). There were six CNOs during the American involvement in Vietnam: Admiral Robert B. Carney (1953–1955), Admiral Arleigh A. Burke (1955–1961), Admiral George W. Anderson Jr. (1961–1963), Admiral David L. McDonald (1963–1967), Admiral **Thomas H. Moorer** (1967–1970), and Admiral Elmo R. Zumwalt Jr. (1970–1974). *See also* BARRIER REEF, OP-ERATION; FOUL DECK, OPERATION; GAME WARDEN, OPERATION; GIANT SLINGSHOT, OPERATION; MARKET TIME, OPERATION; MO-BILE RIVERINE FORCE; SEALORDS; SEARCH TURN, OPERATION.

NEAK LUONG. City located on the **Mê Kông River** in Prey Veng prov-ince in **Cambodia** approximately 65 kilometers (40 miles) to the southeast of **Phnom Penh**. Neak Luong is situated near **Route** 1, which was the road between **Sài Gòn** and Phnom Penh, and housed the ferry that made passage across the river possible. During the **Cambodian Incursion**, Neak Luong was an **Army of the Republic of Vietnam** base area, but it was best known for the 6 August 1973 B-52 incident, when one of those aircraft accidently dropped its **bombs**, an estimated 20 tons of munitions, in the crowded city. The error resulted in 137 killed and over 260 wounded. Reporters on the scene witnessed the effects of the 30 craters that ran nearly one mile along the main road of the city that devastated the city market as well as the houses of nearly 3,000 soldiers and their families. The incident occurred nine days before the 15 August 1973 deadline imposed by the **Case-Church Amend-ment**. The city fell to the **Khmer Rouge** on 1 April 1975, and like Phnom Penh it suffered from the genocide that followed the end of the war.

NEO LAO HAK XAT (LAO PATRIOTIC FRONT). Political front for the **Pathet Lao** that was created to contest the Laotian National Assembly elec-tion in May 1958. The Neo Lao Hak Xat won 9 of the 21 seats decided in the election from a total of 59 seats in the National Assembly. The Neo Lao

Hak Xat joined with the neutralist Santiphab faction, who had four seats, but it was not enough to control the assembly that was dominated by the **Rally of the Lao People**, a political party formed of nationalists and independents that were anticommunist. The Neo Lao Hak Xat continued to advocate the Pathet Lao position, which called for no Western interference, specifically from the **United States**, in the internal affairs of **Laos**.

As a result, the leader of the party, Prince **Souphanouvong**, and his fellow Neo Lao Hak Xat assembly members were placed under arrest. As the conditions continued to deteriorate in Laos, the Neo Lao Hak Xat found it harder to voice political opposition in the assembly, a matter made more difficult when its opposition, the **Committee for the Defense of National Interests**, won a landslide victory in the April 1960 national elections. In August 1960, **Kong Le** orchestrated a coup d'état against the newly elected government that left the Neo Lao Hak Xat out of the political arena until **Souvanna Phouma** formed a new government on 11 June 1962. Followers of the Neo Lao Hak Xat held four posts.

The Pathet Lao protested the 1965 National Assembly elections, and the political interaction between the Neo Lao Hak Xat and other politicians deteriorated as the decade concluded. As the war in Vietnam ended for the U.S. and it appeared that the Americans might not honor their agreements to sustain their commitments to the governments in **Sài Gòn, Phnom Penh**, and Vientiane, the Laotians agreed to a coalition government, which included the Neo Lao Hak Xat, in April 1974. By this time, the National Assembly had ceased to be a productive unit of government and was dissolved on 13 April 1975 by King Savang Vatthana. The Neo Lao Hak Xat was replaced by the formation of the Communist Lao People's Revolutionary Party (Phak Pasason Pativat Lao) after the establishment of the Lao People's Democratic Republic in December 1975.

NEUTRALIZE, OPERATION. With the ongoing siege of the firebase at Con Thien—five kilometers (three miles) south of the **Demilitarized Zone**—intensifying in September 1967, the **United States** diverted aircraft employed in air operations over the **Democratic Republic of Vietnam** to come to the aid of the embattled **marines**. On 12 September 1967, aircraft from the **U.S. Air Force**, **Navy**, and Marine Corps began flying artillery-suppression missions under Operation Neutralize to eliminate the North Vietnamese howitzers, **mortars**, and rockets. The operation lasted until 1 November, the day after the siege was lifted.

NEW LIFE VILLAGES. A variation in the **pacification** effort to secure villages against **People's Army of Vietnam** (PAVN) and **National Libera-**

tion Front (NLF) interference. The first variations, the **Agroville Program** and the **Strategic Hamlet Program**, failed to achieve the desired security. The New Life Village was an attempt to reestablish this component of the pacification effort. The program worked in conjunction with other programs under the **Civil Operations and Revolutionary Development Support**. New Life Villages construction was the responsibility of the villagers, though the **Army of the Republic of Vietnam** often assisted in delivering supplies and sometimes provided the manual labor. New Life Villages were supposed to have schools, markets, medical facilities, and other structures designed to make the lives of the villagers more comfortable and safe.

In theory, those within the New Life Village received an education and were safe from PAVN and NLF soldiers, though the success of the program was dependent on other factors outside of villagers' control. Like the Strategic Hamlet Program, the New Life Village was also supposed to mobilize the people to support the republic and eliminate the insurgency. **Propaganda** about the benefits of the New Life Villages was also disseminated in leaflets, booklets, posters, and even a comic book that was published in May 1968. New Life Villages also were a part of the land reform effort initiated by the **Sài Gòn** government, though the war severely disrupted the process.

NEW ZEALAND. New Zealand's participation in the war paralleled that of **Australia**, though its experience was on a much smaller scale. As part of the ANZUS Treaty with Australia and the **United States**, New Zealand had a vested interested in ensuring an American presence in Southeast Asia as a bulwark against the growing communist movement behind post–World War II nationalism. The first personnel, 25 military engineers, arrived in June 1964, though New Zealand had contributed civilian assistance from the 1950s. This number remained somewhat constant until May 1965, after Australia had committed a battalion to the war effort, when New Zealand offered a field **artillery** battery for service. The 120-man force arrived in July and supported the **173rd Airborne Brigade** in its operations. When Australia added a second infantry battalion and established a task force in Phước Tuy province, the New Zealand contingent moved its base of operations to support the Australian Task Force.

Two companies of infantry entered the war after a third Australian battalion joined the task force in 1967. Personnel from the Royal Navy and Air Force also contributed to the New Zealand effort. With the beginning of **Vietnamization** in July 1969, New Zealand troops began the process of withdrawing. The first troops left in November 1970, with the final troops departing in 1972. An estimated 3,900 soldiers served during the war, though the peak strength never exceed 550. New Zealand lost 37 killed-in-action and 187 wounded. New Zealand also experienced turmoil at home as a result of the war. A small but dedicated **antiwar movement** began soon after the first troops arrived in Vietnam and grew proportionally with New Zealand's commitment.

NGÔ ĐÌNH CẨN (1911–1964). Fifth son of Ngô Đình Khâ and younger brother to **Ngô Đình Diệm** who served as the de facto ruler of central Vietnam from 1955 to 1963. Ngô Đình Cẩn was instrumental in seeing to his brother's return to Vietnam in 1954 and his rise to power over the next year. He also oversaw the **counterinsurgency** effort in the area under his control, from Phat Thiết to the **Demilitarized Zone**, which was very successful, with the creation of his Popular Forces militia that consisted of volunteers who underwent intensive training and operated at the village level to insert anticommunist influence on the people. His effectiveness against the **National Liberation Front** came with a price as he maintained his own army, ruled with what many considered an oppressive air, and was linked to corruption and abusive practices that had the potential to destabilize his effectiveness as a leader.

Ngô Đình Cẩn's questionable practices had significant consequences in 1963 when his actions served as a catalyst for the **Buddhist Crisis** that contributed to the overthrow of Ngô Đình Diệm on 1 November 1963. With the change in leadership, Ngô Đình Cẩn was no longer safe in Vietnam. He brokered a deal with the military junta who had assumed leadership of the country and the **United States** embassy for his departure from Vietnam. Instead, on his journey to **Sài Gòn**, he was turned over to the new government with the approval of U.S. ambassador **Henry Cabot Lodge Jr.**, who argued that Ngô Đình Cẩn did not need asylum because he would be safe in Vietnam. He was promptly arrested and condemned to death for his oppressive actions over the previous nine years, including accusations of mass killings and the use of torture against his enemies. He was executed by firing squad on 9 May 1964.

NGÔ ĐÌNH DIỆM (1901–1963). President of the **Republic of Vietnam** (RVN). Born the third son of Ngô Đình Khâ, **Ngô Đình Diệm** was influenced by his father, who had served as the minister of rites and counselor to the Nguyễn Dynasty emperor Thành Thái. Ngô Đình Khâ resisted French colonial rule by resigning from his position in the government and as a result embedded in his sons a nationalist spirit that would influence them throughout their lives. Ngô Đình Diệm's father also made sure his sons received a Western education that allowed Ngô Đình Diệm to rise in rank in the civil service, reaching the position of minister of the interior in 1933 under Emperor **Bảo Đại**. He resigned from that position in protest against the French influence on the emperor's rule.

Ngô Đình Diệm also resisted French colonial rule, like his father, which brought him into contact with many of the leading Vietnamese nationalists of the time, though he managed to escape the notice of the French Sûreté. Ngô Đình Diệm remained out of Vietnamese government during World War II, though Emperor Bảo Đại called on him to form a government on more than one occasion. Ngô Đình Diệm, however, was not interested in legitimizing the Japanese occupational force or the Vichy form of French colonialism. He also refused to join the **Việt Minh** at the end of the war and turned down an offer from **Hồ Chí Minh** to participate in the new government in January 1946. In 1946, Ngô Đình Diệm maintained that Bảo Đại should be given the opportunity to lead his people against the French while he argued that the Việt Minh had no authority to take that role.

Though Ngô Đình Diệm was not as active as other Vietnamese during the **First Indochina War**, he never wavered from his nationalist objectives, nor would he compromise with Bảo Đại and **France**. He rejected the 8 March 1949 agreement between the French and Bảo Đại that resulted in French recognition of Vietnamese independence, with Bảo Đại as the head of state. He would also decline another Bảo Đại offer to assume the role of premier in May 1949. If he agreed to Bảo Đại's request, Ngô Đình Diệm maintained, he would be acquiescing to French colonial rule. Ngô Đình Diệm's continual refusals to join Bảo Đại or the Việt Minh earned him enemies. He fled Vietnam, fearing for his life, and traveled to several countries, including the **United States** and Belgium. During this time, Ngô Đình Diệm met a number of Americans who would play an influential role in U.S.-Vietnamese relations, including Senator **John F. Kennedy**. While in Belgium, the First Indochina War was winding down with the culminating Battle at **Điện Biên Phủ**. Bảo Đại would again ask Ngô Đình Diệm to form a government, which he eventually consented to do.

Returning from exile on 16 June 1954, Ngô Đình Diệm formed his government on 7 July 1954, serving as the president of the Council of Ministers for the State of Vietnam. The first few months of his new government were fraught with challenges and obstacles that made governing a country that had experienced nearly 100 years of French colonialism an almost impossible undertaking. Among the tasks were disarming the Vietnamese who had fought the French; working with, cajoling, or threatening the various organizations such as the **Cao Đài**, **Hòa Hảo**, and **Bình Xuyên**, who had worked within the French system for their own personal benefit; and the beginning of the influx of 810,000 Vietnamese from the North, some of whom were Catholic and supported Ngô Đình Diệm but others who had been tied to the French and were not fully supportive of their new premier's policies. Ngô Đình Diệm survived these early challenges and consolidated his control over the country.

In the process of doing this, Ngô Đình Diệm became disillusioned with Bảo Đại, who he maintained no longer had the best interests of the Vietnamese people in mind. On 15 May 1955, after successfully defeating the Bình Xuyên and elements of the Cao Đài and Hòa Hảo that still opposed him in the Battle of **Sài Gòn**, Ngô Đình Diệm abolished Bảo Đại's Imperial Guard. In a national referendum on 23 October 1955, Ngô Đình Diệm defeated Bảo Đại and officially became the head of state. Three days later, he would proclaim himself president of the newly formed RVN.

Ngô Đình Diệm's Vietnam was in turmoil from its first days as northern **refugees** began to arrive in the South. His government was hampered by a lack of experienced administrators and military officers, as well as a communist insurgency, even though that insurgency was relatively inactive until Ngô Đình Diệm announced that the RVN would not participate in the planned July 1956 elections. His decision not to participate in the elections as outlined in Article 7 of the 1954 **Geneva Agreements** was a controversial, calculated risk, as was his justification that the communists would not allow for free elections and that no representative of his government had signed the document. His refusal to engage in the elections assured a more active communist insurgency against the Sài Gòn government that pressured the people to turn against Ngô Đình Diệm. In the years that followed, Ngô Đình Diệm focused on building up the infrastructure of his country while fighting off the insurgents. He was helped in this process by the **Michigan State University Group**, headed by Wesley Fishel, and the **Military Assistance Advisory Group**, Vietnam, under the command of generals **John W. O'Daniel** and **Samuel T. Williams**. Ngô Đình Diệm was thwarted in his attempts to build his nation by the insurgents' policy of **Trụ Giãn** (extermination of traitors), which targeted loyal and efficient RVN officials as well as village leaders who supported the Sài Gòn government.

Ngô Đình Diệm's response to this policy of assassination was not popular with Sài Gòn intellectuals or with some within the U.S. embassy. He consolidated power over the villagers who had not been able to protect themselves and were not aided by the inefficient civil service. He orchestrated a sometimes effective anticommunist denunciation campaign that identified communists but also noncommunists who were caught up in the campaign because of personality or ideological clashes. In mid-1959, Ngô Đình Diệm introduced the **Agroville Program** campaign to combat insurgent violence in the countryside. The program failed to eliminate the communist threat and did not fulfill its promise of improving the lives of all of the villages that it affected or disrupted. While Ngô Đình Diệm focused on **pacification** in the countryside, he also had to deal with internal dissent as well as growing apprehension of his unwillingness to follow American advice within the U.S. embassy.

In April 1960, 18 members of the Bloc for Liberty and Progress issued a proclamation, known later as the **Caravelle Manifesto**, which called for reforms. This group influenced American thinking, including U.S. ambassador **Elbridge Durbrow**, who would begin to orchestrate a move to replace Ngô Đình Diệm. Ngô Đình Diệm continued to shy away from the U.S. embassy after a failed 11 November 1960 coup d'état attempted by some dissatisfied Vietnamese paratroopers and other **Army of the Republic of Vietnam** (ARVN) personnel. Durbrow refused to fully back the Vietnamese president and made some remarks in Sài Gòn and with Washington suggesting that he lamented the fact that the coup d'état had not been successful.

Over the last three years of his life and rule in the RVN, Ngô Đình Diệm continued to distrust American personnel, especially within the embassy, with the exception of a few who had a longer history with him. Men like General **Edward Lansdale**, who had been involved in Vietnam since his Saigon Military Mission days in 1954–1955, had influence with Ngô Đình Diệm, but they did not have the political power base in Washington to counter critics like Ambassador-at-Large **W. Averill Harriman**. The deteriorating nature of the special relationship forged between Ngô Đình Diệm and the U.S. forced the Vietnamese president to rely more and more on his family and resulted in some poor decisions authorized by Ngô Đình Diệm that led to his increased unpopularity in Washington and in the RVN. Events such as the failed 1962–1964 **Strategic Hamlet Program** run by **Ngô Đình Nhu** and the 1963 **Buddhist Crisis**, inflamed in part by **Ngô Đình Cẩn**, made Ngô Đình Diệm a liability to the U.S. in its Cold War struggle with communism and its commitment of containment in Southeast Asia. Ngô Đình Diệm also opposed the Kennedy administration's attempt to neutralize **Laos** via the 1962 **Geneva Accords**, which, when coupled with the Strategic Hamlet Program and preceding the Buddhist Crisis, brought him the reputation of being obstinate and out of touch with the realities of Cold War diplomacy.

Internal dissent and friction with U.S. personnel in Sài Gòn was worsened by an increase in activity of the **National Liberation Front**, which was directly supported by the **People's Army of Vietnam**. ARVN soldiers fared poorly during this period, culminating in the debacle at the **Battle of Ấp Bắc** in January 1963. For many Americans, these events led to the conclusion that Ngô Đình Diệm no longer represented the best interests of the U.S. in the region. By the late summer and early fall of 1963, rumors of coup d'état plots circulated throughout Sài Gòn, making Ngô Đình Diệm more paranoid about his Vietnamese and American colleagues. On 1 November 1963, with the tacit approval of the U.S. ambassador to the RVN, **Henry Cabot Lodge Jr.**, major generals **Dương Văn Minh**, **Tôn Thất Đình**, and Trần Van Đôn launched a coup d'état against Ngô Đình Diệm that resulted in his assassination, along with that of his brother Ngô Đình Nhu, on 2 November.

NGÔ ĐÌNH LUYỆN (1914–1990). Sixth son of Ngô Đình Khả and younger brother to **Ngô Đình Diệm** who served as **Republic of Vietnam** ambassador to Great Britain. He was also a representative of the Vietnamese delegation that helped to conclude the 1954 **Geneva Conference**. He remained a diplomat until 2 November 1963, the day after the coup d'état that ended his brother's rule in Vietnam. Ngô Đình Luyện escaped execution because he was in London at the time and moved to Paris.

NGÔ ĐÌNH NHU (1910–1963). Fourth son of Ngô Đình Khả and younger brother to **Ngô Đình Diệm**, adviser to the president, and head of the **Cần Lao Party**. Ngô Đình Nhu received his education in **France**, graduating from the l'École Nationale des Chartes, where he trained as an archivist. He returned to Vietnam during World War II and worked in the National Library in **Hà Nội** and then in Đà Lat. Ngô Đình Nhu fought for Vietnamese independence, though his efforts were mainly intellectual. When Ngô Đình Diệm was appointed president of the Council of Ministers to the State of Vietnam in July 1954, Ngô Đình Nhu joined his brother in **Sài Gòn** to help with the construction of a Vietnamese state. He was largely responsible for the introduction of personalism (Nhân Vị) into Vietnam, which helped to serve as a counter ideology to communism and to mobilize the peasantry toward support for the republic.

Ngô Đình Nhu would also head the Cần Lao Party, established to serve as a political organization to maintain Ngô Đình Diệm's rule in Vietnam. He used the party to consolidate power and support for his brother, often at the cost of attacks or perceived attacks on the very ideals the republic was supposed to safeguard. This earned him the ire of many Vietnamese, as well as Americans who aided the republic during its formative years. Ngô Đình Nhu continued to serve as the military and political enforcer for the republic and even had nominal control over the **Army of the Republic of Vietnam Special Forces**. He ordered the capture of members and suspected members of the **National Liberation Front** (NLF), sometimes finding the latter in organizations that were not completely in support of Ngô Đình Diệm, which allowed many to level charges that Ngô Đình Nhu was abusing his power. Ngô Đình Nhu became the target of many Americans in Vietnam, including ambassadors **Elbridge Durbrow** and **Henry Cabot Lodge Jr.**, both of whom called for his removal from the country. Ngô Đình Nhu, however, continued to serve the republic in the best way he saw fit. He acted as presidential counselor and headed the Interministerial Committee for **Strategic**

Hamlets in an effort to mobilize the population against the insurgency that was gaining momentum in 1962.

In 1963, Ngô Đình Nhu helped to quell the **Buddhist Crisis** by authorizing a preemptive strike against several pagodas in Sài Gòn and **Huế**, including a raid against the **Xá Lợi Pagoda** in Sài Gòn. The 21 August 1963 action resulted in hundreds of Vietnamese casualties. It also brought about direct interdiction by the **United States** embassy, under Lodge, which harbored two monks who had escaped the raids. Lodge also openly condemned the Sài Gòn government for its actions. The family of Ngô Đình Nhu became a focal point of criticism, especially after **Madame Nhu**'s callous and demeaning comments about the Buddhist protests and the self-immolation of **Thích Quảng Đức** and other monks. While Ngô Đình Nhu became the symbol of what was wrong in Vietnam for the U.S., his brother and president was also increasingly relying on Ngô Đình Nhu's advice, as Ngô Đình Diệm saw the Americans as adversaries rather than allies. Lodge insisted that Ngô Đình Nhu be removed from Vietnam, and when Ngô Đình Diệm refused, both became expendable in his eyes. Ngô Đình Nhu was assassinated on 2 November 1963, along with his brother Ngô Đình Diệm, after the 1 November coup d'état that removed them from power.

NGÔ ĐÌNH NHU, MADAME (1924–). Born Trần Lệ Xuân in **Hà Nội**, Madame Ngô Đình Nhu, often referred to as Madame Nhu, was the wife of **Ngô Đình Nhu** and acted as the first lady of the **Republic of Vietnam** for President **Ngô Đình Diệm**, who was a bachelor. Madame Nhu came from a prominent Vietnamese family. Her father, **Trần Văn Chương**, served as the ambassador to the **United States**, and her mother was a granddaughter of Emperor Đồng Khánh and was related to **Bảo Đại**. She dropped out of the Lycée Albert Sarraut before graduation. She married Ngô Đình Nhu in 1943, even though he was significantly older than she was. She ran afoul of the **Việt Minh** after World War II, in part because of the actions of the Ngô Đình brothers, and was exiled for a brief time. Her family moved to Đà Lạt, where they remained until the end of the **First Indochina War**. When Ngô Đình Diệm became president of the Council of Ministers to the State of Vietnam in July 1954, Madame Nhu and her husband went to **Sài Gòn**, where he served as a political counselor and she acted as a hostess at government functions.

Madame Nhu would become the first lady of the republic when Ngô Đình Diệm won the 23 October 1955 referendum against Bảo Đại. While Madame Nhu was a controversial figure during the Ngô Đình Diệm regime, she did try to improve the lives of the Vietnamese people and expand opportunities for Vietnamese **women**. She created the Women's Solidarity Movement that organized women into a militia, and she also worked on a variety of humanitarian projects designed to help those affected by the war or by natural disaster or who were simply in need. The organization provided millions of dollars toward these projects, though Madame Nhu was not remembered for this work but rather for her no-nonsense, often callous remarks against the Buddhists during the 1963 **Buddhist Crisis** and for her moves to improve morality in the cities, which were often not appreciated by the urban population, who saw a double standard between her words and her actions.

Madame Nhu was never one to back down from controversy. When the Buddhist Monk **Thích Quảng Đức** committed self-immolation on 11 June 1963, Madame Nhu called the event a Buddhist barbecue and commented that the monk and those that followed were being influenced by foreigners and had even used foreign gasoline. Madame Nhu would also become a vocal critic of the U.S. when it failed to support Ngô Đình Diệm during the crisis. When the 1 November 1963 coup d'état occurred that resulted in the assassinations of Ngô Đình Diệm and Ngô Đình Nhu, Madame Nhu was traveling in the U.S. and was spared a similar fate. She lost access to her family fortune and later moved to the Holy See within Rome, and then to **France** where she lived on the French Riviera.

NGÔ ĐÌNH THỤC (1897–1984). Roman Catholic archbishop of **Huế** and the younger brother of **Ngô Đình Diệm**. Ngô Đình Thục was born in Huế and entered seminary at the age of 12. He was ordained into the priesthood in 1925, after which he traveled to Paris and taught at the Sorbonne. Before returning to Vietnam in 1927, he earned doctorates in philosophy, theology, and canon law at the Pontifical Gregorian University in Rome, Italy. Ngô Đình Thục returned to Huế to teach. On 4 May 1938, he became the third Vietnamese priest to reach the rank of bishop when he was chosen to oversee the Apostolic Vicariate at Vĩnh Long. One of his most notable achievements was the establishment of **Đà Lạt** University in 1957. Ngô Đình Thục represented the interests of his brother, Ngô Đình Diệm, who was president of the **Republic of Vietnam** (RVN). On 24 November 1960, Ngô Đình Thục became the archbishop of Huế.

Ngô Đình Thục played an important role in Central Vietnam both as a representative of the Roman Catholic Church and of the **Sài Gòn** government. He was accused of using his position to demand bribes and to greatly enhance his wealth through questionable business practices and monopolies of desired products in Central Vietnam. In 1963, he was involved in one of the most significant controversies in the Ngô Đình Diệm presidency when he flew the Catholic flag over the flag of the RVN during his jubilee. He then supported the Sài Gòn government's decision to enforce a decree that restricted such a practice when **Buddhists** wished to fly their flag in honor of Buddha's birthday. On 8 May 1963, the **Buddhist Crisis** erupted, resulting in the deaths of nine Vietnamese protestors.

When the controversy did not abate, Ngô Đình Thục was forced into an extended trip to Rome in September 1963 to attend the Second Vatican Council. After the coup d'état and assassination of Ngô Đình Diệm, Ngô Đình Thục remained in Italy in exile. In 1978, he moved to Toulon, **France**. While he ceased to play a role in Vietnamese politics during the war, he earned the wrath of the Vatican at the end of 1975 when he ordained two men into the priesthood and consecrated them and three others to the episcopate on 1 January 1976. Pope Paul VI excommunicated Ngô Đình Thục for this action, though he received absolution after distancing himself from the men. He continued to run afoul of the Roman Catholic Church for the remainder of his life.

NGÔ QUANG TRƯỞNG (1929–2007). Army of the Republic of Vietnam (ARVN) general and a prolific author of military studies of strategy and tactics. Ngô Quang Trưởng's military service began in 1954 after he graduated from the Thủ Đức Officer Candidate School and the Command and Staff School at Đà Lat. He served with the 5th Airborne Battalion, eventually rising to command the unit in 1963. In 1965, he became the chief of staff of the Airborne Division. He commanded the 1st ARVN Division from 1966 to 1970, at which time he took over as commander of IV **Corps Tactical Zone** (CTZ).

Ngô Quang Trưởng demonstrated the effectiveness of ARVN leadership during the 1972 **Easter Offensive** after he replaced Lieutenant General Hoàng Xuân Lãm who had failed to rally his troops in I CTZ and had nearly lost **Huế**. Ngô Quang Trưởng ordered the counteroffensive that allowed the ARVN to regain much of the territory lost during the operation, which highlighted how successful President **Richard M. Nixon**'s **Vietnamization** program had been when given proper support and leadership. Ngô Quang Trưởng was considered one of the best ARVN generals and had superior leadership skills, integrity, and dedication to the survival of the republic. He faithfully served his country until 1975 during the final offensive of the war. Ngô Quang Trưởng was forced to evacuate much of I CTZ to the communist forces and eventually fled to the **United States** after his country fell in April 1975.

NGUYỄN CAO KỲ (1930–). Air marshal, member of the Armed Forces Council, prime minister and vice president of the **Republic of Vietnam** (RVN). Nguyễn Cao Kỳ started his service in the Republic of Vietnam **Air Force** in 1954, reaching the rank of air marshal after his support for the November 1963 coup d'état against **Ngô Đình Diệm**. He supported the government of **Nguyễn Khánh** in 1964 and served as the spokesman for the Armed Forces Council after 18 December 1964. Usually dressed in a military uniform with a purple scarf and armed with an ivory-handled John Wayne Commemorative Colt .45 revolver, he became the RVN prime minister on 19 June 1965 under the presidency of **Nguyễn Văn Thiệu** and oversaw the Americanization of the war. He also served as the chairman of the National Executive Committee. Nguyễn Cao Kỳ was considered an effective prime minister even though he initially lacked professional political training. He worked to end corruption in the RVN, though he found it difficult given the widespread nature of the corruption in the 1960s, and he tried to foster better relations among the Vietnamese generals, who had been feuding with one another instead of fighting the **People's Army of Vietnam** and the **National Liberation Front** after the coup d'état against Ngô Đình Diệm.

In 1967, Nguyễn Cao Kỳ was slated to run for the presidential election, but he instead backed Nguyễn Văn Thiệu and became his vice president on 31 October 1967. The Thiệu-Kỳ ticket was less than harmonious, with both strong personalities vying for power and influence. Their rivalry helped to fracture an already divided Vietnam. In 1971, Nguyễn Cao Kỳ intended to run for president again, but as in 1967 he was a victim of Vietnamese politics. He retired that year only to return to military service in the final weeks of the **Sài Gòn** government in 1975. Nguyễn Cao Kỳ had hoped to rally the **Army of the Republic of Vietnam** against the North Vietnamese offensive, but the longtime enmity between Nguyễn Văn Thiệu and Nguyễn Cao Kỳ negated that possibility. He fled the RVN on 30 April 1975 and lives in the **United States**.

NGUYỄN CHÁNH THI (1923–2007). Army of the Republic of Vietnam (ARVN) general. Nguyễn Chánh Thi was born in **Huế**. He joined the French Army in 1940 and was loyal to the French until they left following the 1954 **Geneva Conference**. Nguyễn Chánh Thi remained in the army, joining the newly organized Army of the Republic of Vietnam as an officer. He supported **Ngô Đình Diệm** in his 1955 fight against the **Bình Xuyên**, for which he was promoted to colonel and given command of the Vietnamese Airborne Brigade. As commander of that unit, he helped stage a coup d'état against Ngô Đình Diệm on 11 November 1960 but failed to rally the military to his side. He argued that Ngô Đình Diệm was not vigorously pursuing the war against the **National Liberation Front**, but he had also been passed over for promotion, which was probably a major reason for his decision. He went into self-exile in **Cambodia** until after the assassination of Ngô Đình Diệm in November 1963. He joined in the coup d'état that brought **Nguyễn Khánh** into power on 30 January 1964, and he helped Nguyễn Khánh stay in power until he was replaced in February 1965. Nguyễn Chánh Thi earned a negative reputation through his involvement in **Sài Gòn** politics and coup d'état planning.

He commanded I Corps until 10 March 1966, he served as a member of the National Leadership Committee, and he was one of the principal causes of the 1966 Buddhist uprising in **Đà Nẵng** and Huế after his dismissal from military service by **Nguyễn Cao Kỳ**. After he was fired, Buddhists, students, and others who were unhappy with the Sài Gòn government took to the streets to protest his removal. Đà Nẵng was shut down, and troops loyal to the general rather than the republic threatened to start another war, which would have ravaged the five northern provinces that made up I **Corps Tactical Zone**. After Nguyễn Cao Kỳ sent troops to quell the uprising, Nguyễn Chánh Thi was ordered to the **United States** for medical treatment, even though he was not sick. He lived a very modest life until his death. He did try to return to the **Republic of Vietnam** during the 1972 **Easter Offensive**, but he was not allowed to leave his airplane and was forced to return to the U.S.

NGUYỄN CHÍ THANH (1914–1967). People's Army of Vietnam (PAVN) general. Born Nguyễn Chí Vịnh, Nguyễn Chí Thanh was raised in **Thừa Thiên** province in Central Vietnam. In 1938, Nguyễn Chí Thanh became the secretary of the Thừa Thiên province committee of the Indochinese Communist Party. He spent most of his youth in French prisons and was released at the end of World War II. He fought the French during the **First Indochina War**, which earned him a Politburo position in 1951. He served as a general in the PAVN for the remainder of the war and headed the General Political Directorate of the PAVN until 1961. He then became an officer in the **Central Office for South Vietnam** (Văn Phòng Trung Ương Cục Miền Nam/ COSVN) until his death in July 1967 while visiting **Hà Nội**.

Nguyễn Chí Thanh was responsible for the origins of what would become known as the 1968 **Tết Offensive**. He was committed to the total conquest of the **Republic of Vietnam** and the complete social and economic transformation of that country. Nguyễn Chí Thanh opposed negotiations and aligned with those within the Politburo who argued for a long protracted war.

NGUYỄN HỮU HẠNH (1923–). Army of the Republic of Vietnam (ARVN) general. Born in Mỹ Tho province in the **Mê Kông Delta**, Nguyễn Hữu Hạnh joined the military in 1946 and worked under **Dương Văn Minh**. He supported **Ngô Đình Diệm** during his 1955 fight against the **Bình Xuyên** and **Cao Đài**, serving as the chief of staff for Colonel Dương Văn Minh in Operation Hoang Dieu. Nguyễn Hữu Hạnh turned against Ngô Đình Diệm when the **Republic of Vietnam** (RVN) president began to mistreat Dương Văn Minh. Nguyễn Hữu Hạnh supported the 1 November 1963 coup d'état against the RVN president by keeping loyal troops in IV **Corps Tactical**

Zone (CTZ) isolated from **Sài Gòn**. Nguyễn Hữu Hạnh was tied to General Dương Văn Minh and rose and fell with the general.

In 1967, Colonel Nguyễn Hữu Hạnh of the 21st ARVN Division served as head of the 44th Special Tactical Zone and was responsible for the interdiction of **People's Army of Vietnam** (PAVN) and **National Liberation Front** personnel and supplies from **Cambodia** into the IV CTZ. He, however, had begun to work with the enemy and used his position to aid in sustaining the war in the South.

In May 1974, Nguyễn Hữu Hạnh was retired from the ARVN as a result of internal discord that involved RVN President **Nguyễn Văn Thiệu** and General Dương Văn Minh. In the final days of the RVN, Nguyễn Hữu Hạnh returned to Sài Gòn. He briefly served as president, and, as the senior ARVN officer at the Joint General Staff Headquarters, he issued the order to surrender to the PAVN on 30 April 1975. After the war, he joined the Fatherland Front for Hồ Chí Minh City, the new name for the former capital of the RVN.

NGUYỄN HỮU THỌ (1910–1996). Chairman of the **National Liberation Front** (NLF). Nguyễn Hữu Thọ was born in **Chợ Lớn** and educated in **France** where he received a law degree. He practiced law in Cochin China and was involved in anti-French demonstrations but did not join the Indochinese Communist Party until 1949. He was arrested in 1950 and spent two years in jail for his part in demonstrations against the French. Nguyễn Hữu Thọ supported the 1954 **Geneva Agreements** but ran afoul of **Ngô Đình Diệm**. In August 1954, he founded the Committee in Defense of Peace and the Geneva Agreements, which was banned by Ngô Đình Diệm in November 1954. He was jailed by the **Sài Gòn** government until his 1961 escape.

After his escape, Nguyễn Hữu Thọ became chairman of the Central Committee of the NLF and worked toward the elimination of the Sài Gòn government and American support for the **Republic of Vietnam**. He continued his work and was rewarded for his loyalty in 1969 when he became the chairman of the Consultative Council of the **Provisional Revolutionary Government of the Republic of South Vietnam**. He remained in that position until 1976 when the two parts of Vietnam were united into the Socialist Republic of Vietnam (SRV). He served as a vice president of the SRV and became acting president on 30 March 1980 when Tôn Đức Thắng died. He was succeeded on 4 July 1981 by **Trường Chinh**. Nguyễn Hữu Thọ became vice chairman of the Council of State in 1981 and remained in that position until 1992.

NGUYỄN KHÁNH (1927–). General, commander-in-chief, chief of state, and prime minister. Nguyễn Khánh first saw military service with the **Việt Minh** but quickly became disillusioned with their objectives. He graduated from the l'Écoles de Saint-Cyr Coëtquidan in 1946 and was commissioned as a lieutenant in 1947 after graduating from the Viễn Đông Military Academy and Saint Saumur Military Academy. He commanded the parachute company in Vietnam from 1949 to 1952 and, after promotion to captain, the 1st Parachute Battalion. As a major, he commanded the 13th Division from 1953 to 1955 and the 1st **Army of the Republic of Vietnam** (ARVN) from 1956 to 1957 as a colonel. Nguyễn Khánh was loyal to **Ngô Đình Diệm** and proved himself a capable leader. Ngô Đình Diệm appointed him secretary general of the Defense Ministry in 1959, and as a result of his support during the failed November 1960 coup d'état, Nguyễn Khánh was promoted to major general.

As a trusted supporter of the republic, he commanded the II **Corps Tactical Zone** (CTZ) in 1962, but Nguyễn Khánh joined in the November 1963 coup d'état that led to the assassination of Ngô Đình Diệm. For his role, he was promoted to lieutenant general in 1963 with responsibility for I CTZ. Nguyễn Khánh led a bloodless coup d'état against **Dương Văn Minh**'s rule on 30 January 1964. He ruled as prime minister from 4 February to 30 October 1964 and as commander-in-chief of the ARVN and chairman of the Armed Forces Council from 18 December 1964 to 21 February 1965, when **Nguyễn Cao Kỳ** and **Nguyễn Văn Thiệu** led a coup against him. In order to get him out of the country, he was appointed ambassador to **France** on 25 February 1965, a position he retained until the fall of **Sài Gòn** on 30 April 1975. He left France in 1977 and moved to the **United States**. He maintained an interest in Vietnamese politics and was selected as the head of state of the Government of Free Vietnam, whose purpose was the overthrow of the Socialist Republic of Vietnam and a return to a noncommunist Vietnam.

NGUYỄN KHOA NAM (1927–1975). Army of the Republic of Vietnam (ARVN) general. Nguyễn Khoa Nam joined the Vietnam National Army during the **First Indochina War** and graduated from the Thủ Đức Military Academy in 1953. In 1955, he joined the ARVN as a lieutenant in the airborne and received promotions to company commander in the 7th Airborne Battalion and commander of the 5th Airborne Battalion and the 3rd Airborne Brigade. As a brigadier general, he commanded the 7th ARVN Division and was promoted to major general in command of IV **Corps Tactical Zone**, where he remained until the fall of **Sài Gòn**. Nguyễn Khoa Nam committed suicide on 30 April 1975 rather than surrender or flee Vietnam.

NGUYỄN NGỌC LOAN (1930–1998). Brigadier general and chief of the national police for the **Republic of Vietnam** (RVN). Nguyễn Ngọc Loan served in the RVN **Air Force** and was a supporter of **Nguyễn Cao Kỳ**, to whom he owed much of his advancement in the armed forces. Nguyễn Ngọc

Loan was allegedly tied to corruption in **Sài Gòn**, though his methods as chief of the national police earned him praise from the **United States**. Nguyễn Ngọc Loan became a symbol of U.S. war weariness when he was filmed executing a **National Liberation Front** (NLF) prisoner on 1 February 1968 during the **Tết Offensive**. The photograph of the event, taken by Eddie Adams, won the 1969 Pulitzer Prize for Spot News Photography and shocked the American people for its callous nature.

The entire story behind Nguyễn Ngọc Loan's execution of the prisoner, who had been involved in the targeted assassination of Sài Gòn residents, was not made available at the time. The image had as much impact on American public opinion of the failure of the Sài Gòn government as the **Malcolm Browne** photograph of the self-immolation of **Thích Quảng Đức** on 11 June 1963 during the **Buddhist Crisis**. Nguyễn Ngọc Loan resigned his position after a 5 May 1968 wound taken while confronting NLF soldiers in Sài Gòn. He fled Vietnam before the fall of Sài Gòn in April 1975 and moved to the U.S. where he opened a pizza restaurant. He was forced into retirement in 1991 when his identity became known and threats against his life were made, mostly as a result of the memory of the Adams image.

NGUYỄN NGỌC THƠ (1908–). Republic of Vietnam vice president under **Ngô Đình Diệm** and briefly prime minister in 1963–1964. Nguyễn Ngọc Thơ was a career politician who first entered public office in 1930, during the period of French rule, rising to the position of provincial chief before World War II. After the war, he served as the minister of the interior. Nguyễn Ngọc Thơ supported Ngô Đình Diệm in his early consolidation of power against the **Cao Đài** and **Hòa Hảo**, for which Ngô Đình Diệm rewarded him with the vice presidency of the republic.

Nguyễn Ngọc Thơ also held the position of secretary of state for economic development, during which time he oversaw the expropriation of over 4,250 square kilometers (1,640 square miles) of land from nearly 1,400 landowners which were redistributed to approximately 125,000 farmers. The program, however, was not viewed as a success by the **United States** embassy and Ambassador **Elbridge Durbrow**, who had grown disenchanted with the rule of Ngô Đình Diệm. Nguyễn Ngọc Thơ vied with other members of the cabinet and with the president's family for the support of Ngô Đình Diệm, which often led to conflict and a high level of tension in **Sài Gòn**, especially as Nguyễn Ngọc Thơ clashed with **Ngô Đình Nhu**, who was an individual already targeted for removal by the U.S. embassy.

Nguyễn Ngọc Thơ was not considered the most effective politician by most Americans, but in a country whose political tradition had only begun after the removal of the French colonial system, Nguyễn Ngọc Thơ was more than competent among his peers. After the 1 November 1963 coup d'état that removed Ngô Đình Diệm, Nguyễn Ngọc Thơ served as prime minister, though his degree of power and control of the government was severely limited by the Military Revolutionary Council. He also headed the Ministry of Finance and National Economy in the provisional government. His rule was made ineffectual by the carryover of infighting, competition, and distrust resulting from the turbulent events of 1963, which included the coup d'état and the **Buddhist Crisis**. Nguyễn Ngọc Thơ was also plagued by his association with Ngô Đình Diệm, as well as his involvement in the planning of the coup d'état. As a result, he became an easy individual to vilify in a post–Ngô Đình Diệm country that lacked stability and strong leadership and that saw an increase in American involvement. He was eventually ousted from power when **Nguyễn Khánh** successfully completed a bloodless coup d'état on 30 January 1964. Nguyễn Ngọc Thơ retired from politics, though he lived to see the fall of Sài Gòn and the destruction of the republic that he had worked to preserve.

NGUYỄN THỊ BÌNH (1927–). National Liberation Front (NLF) leader. Nguyễn Thị Bình was born in Sa Đéc province in the **Mê Kông Delta** and was educated at the Lycée Sisowath in **Cambodia**. She worked as a teacher in the 1940s and joined the Indochinese Communist Party in 1948. In 1950, she protested against **United States** support for French colonial rule in Vietnam as a member of the Association of Progressive Women and worked with **Nguyễn Hữu Thọ**, who later headed the NLF. As a result of her activities, Nguyễn Thị Bình was arrested in 1951 and was jailed at the Chí Hòa prison until 1954.

During the American phase of the war, she served on the Central Committee of the NLF and was the vice chairperson of the South Vietnamese Women's Liberation Association. Nguyễn Thị Bình served as a diplomat for the NLF, traveling to the **Soviet Union**, the **People's Republic of China**, Indonesia, North Korea, and Egypt. When she was in the **Republic of Vietnam**, she made her headquarters in **Tây Ninh** province. She headed the NLF delegation at the **Paris Peace Talks**, arriving on 4 November 1968. In 1969, she was promoted to the position of foreign minister for the **Provisional Revolutionary Government of the Republic of South Vietnam**. Nguyễn Thị Bình served as the minister of education for the Socialist Republic of Vietnam (SRV) from 1976 to 1987. In 1982, she joined the Central Committee of the Vietnam Communist Party and served as the vice president of the SRV from 1992 to 2002.

NGUYỄN THỊ ĐỊNH (1920–1992). Founding member of the **National Liberation Front** (NLF). Nguyễn Thị Định was born in Kiến Hòa province. She joined the Indochinese Communist Party sometime around 1938 and fought against the French. In 1940, she was arrested and imprisoned until 1943. Toward the end of World War II, she led an uprising in **Bến Tre**. She would lead another uprising in 1960 in Bến Tre that signaled the beginning of the NLF, and she was one of the few senior **women** in that organization, serving as its deputy commander. In 1965, she became the chairwoman of the South Vietnam Women's Liberation Association, and after the war she served on the Central Committee of the Vietnamese Communist Party and as president of the Vietnam Women's Association. She also was the first major general in the **People's Army of Vietnam**. In 1976, she published her memoir, *No Other Road to Take: Memoir of Mrs. Nguyen Thi Dinh.*

NGUYỄN VĂN HIẾU (1929–1975). Army of the Republic of Vietnam (ARVN) general and deputy commander of III **Corps Tactical Zone** (CTZ). Nguyễn Văn Hiếu graduated from the Đà Lat Military School in 1951, after which, commissioned as a lieutenant, he was put in charge of operations and plans (G3) for the Joint General Staff of Colonel **Trần Văn Đôn**, rising to the rank of major in 1957 as G3 for the 1st Corps. He became the chief of staff for the 1st ARVN Division in 1963 and was promoted to lieutenant colonel and then colonel after the assassination of **Ngô Đình Diệm**. He commanded the 22nd ARVN Division for much of his career, reaching the rank of brigadier general on 1 November 1967 and major general the following November.

During his military career, he also served as deputy commander of I and III CTZ, commander of the 5th ARVN Division, and minister of anticorruption. As commander of the 22nd ARVN Division, Nguyễn Văn Hiếu initiated a number of major operations against the **People's Army of Vietnam** and the **National Liberation Front**. He participated in the **Cambodian Incursion** as the 5th ARVN Division commander, taking part in operations in the **Fishhook**. Nguyễn Văn Hiếu had a reputation as an aggressive and honest military leader. After the North Vietnamese launched their final offensive in 1975, he was found dead in his office on 8 April. While it was reported that he had committed suicide, there was strong suspicion that he was assassinated on the orders of General Nguyen Van Toàn, the III Corps commander, who may have been the object of controversial speculations while Nguyễn Văn Hiếu was minister of anticorruption.

NGUYỄN VĂN LINH (1915–1998). General secretary of the Indochinese Community Party. Born Nguyễn Văn Cúc in Hưng Yên province in the Tŏn Kĭn region of Vietnam, Nguyễn Văn Linh became involved in anti-French activities at an early age. He joined the Revolutionary Youth League and in 1930 was arrested by the French. Nguyễn Văn Linh remained in jail until

1936. He joined the Indochinese Communist Party after his release from jail and traveled to **Sài Gòn** to help with the resistance movemert. During World War II, he was again put in jail and was not released until 1945. Nguyễn Văn Linh continued to work against **France** during the **First Indochina War**, serving under **Lê Duẩn**. In 1957, he replaced Lê Duẩn as head of the Nam Bộ Regional Committee and continued in that position when the committee was transformed into the **Central Office for South Vietnam** (Văn Phòng Trung Ương Cục Miền Nam/COSVN) in 1961. He remained in that position until 1964 when he was transferred to be deputy head of the COSVN under **Nguyễn Chí Thanh** until 1967 and under **Phạm Hùng** until the end of the war. He also rose within the **Lao Động** Party, becoming a member of its Central Committee in 1960. Nguyễn Văn Linh helped to organize the Sài Gòn phase of the 1968 **Tết Offensive**.

After the war, Nguyễn Văn Linh became a member of the Politburo and chief of the Party Committee for **Hồ Chí Minh City**, which had been Sài Gòn, the former capital of the **Republic of Vietnam**. He was removed from his position in Hồ Chí Minh City in 1978 and from the Politburo in 1982 because of his disagreements with Lê Duẩn on how to transform southern society. Nguyễn Văn Linh cautioned that a slower approach was preferable to social and economic revolution. In 1985, he was reinstated to the Politburo and became the general secretary of the party in 1986. Nguyễn Văn Linh advocated the economic policy of Đổi Mới (openness or innovation). He supported private industry and dismantled collectives that had proven to be a disaster for the Vietnamese people. In 1989, he ordered the Vietnamese occupation force in **Cambodia** to return to the Socialist Republic of Vietnam. Despite his understanding of the need for change, Nguyễn Văn Linh remained committed to the socialist model until his retirement in 1991 because of poor health. He advised the Central Committee from 1991 to 1997, and toward the end of his life he denounced the Western exploitation of Đổi Mới, which had harmed the socialist experiment in Vietnam.

NGUYỄN VĂN THIỆU (1923–2001). Army of the Republic of Vietnam (ARVN) general and president of the **Republic of Vietnam**. Nguyễn Văn Thiệu entered the National Military Academy at Đà Lạt in 1949 after a brief time with the **Việt Minh** and at the Merchant Marine Academy. He graduated in 1951 and was commissioned as a second lieutenant in the Vietnam National Army. At the end of the **First Indochina War**, Nguyễn Văn Thiệu rose to the rank of lieutenant colonel. He became a colonel after the 1 November 1963 coup d'état against **Ngô Đình Diệm**, commanding the 5th ARVN Division. On 4 February 1964, as a brigadier general, he was promoted to chief of staff of the Joint General Staff and commander of the ARVN. Nguyễn

Văn Thiệu was made a member of the Armed Forces Council and a cabinet member of the **Phan Huy Quát** government on 16 February 1965. He then served as chairman of the National Leadership Committee and as head of state in June 1965.

Nguyễn Văn Thiệu became the head of state under **Nguyễn Cao Kỳ** until he was elected RVN president on 3 September 1967 and was sworn in on 1 November. Nguyễn Văn Thiệu's presidency was marred by conflict with Nguyễn Cao Kỳ and by the continued escalation of American troops in Vietnam until the beginning of **Vietnamization** in 1969. His presidency was often criticized by Americans and by supporters of Nguyễn Cao Kỳ for its corruption and for its centralization of power. The 1971 presidential election did little to assuage this criticism when none of his opponents agreed to run against him because they believed the election would be fixed. Nguyễn Văn Thiệu's relationship with the **United States** continued to deteriorate with Vietnamization and the January 1973 **Paris Peace Accords**, which he opposed but was forced into accepting by President **Richard M. Nixon** and Secretary of State **Henry Kissinger**. Nguyễn Văn Thiệu remained in office until 21 April 1975, less than two weeks before the fall of **Sài Gòn** and the end of the war. He was exiled to England and then moved to the U.S. where he died in 2001.

NGUYỄN VIẾT THANH (1931–1970). Army of the Republic of Vietnam (ARVN) general. Nguyễn Viết Thanh was born in **Đà Lạt** and was educated at the Lycée Chasseloup-Laubet in **Sài Gòn**. He received his military training at the military academy in Đà Lạt and rose in the ranks of the **Vietnamese National Army** during the **First Indochina War**. He served as an officer in the ARVN and as the province chief for **Long An** province in the early 1960s. He was fired from this position in 1963 for disagreeing with the Sài Gòn government. After the coup d'état against **Ngô Đình Diệm**, he regained his earlier influence. Nguyễn Viết Thanh supported **Nguyễn Văn Thiệu** and rose within the ARVN under his patronage. He commanded the 7th ARVN Division in IV **Corps Tactical Zone** (CTZ) between 1965 and 1968.

During the **Tết Offensive**, Nguyễn Viết Thanh and his family were taken hostage by the **National Liberation Front**. He refused to negotiate with the enemy, and his troops continued to fight. He and his family were released unharmed. After the Tết Offensive, he was named commander of IV CTZ. In part, this promotion was a result of his alliance with Nguyễn Văn Thiệu, but it was also because General **William C. Westmoreland** had rated him as one of the best ARVN generals in the IV CTZ, despite inconsistent results during military operations. Nguyễn Viết Thanh was a popular leader within the military but also among the people of the **Mê Kông Delta**. As a lieutenant general, Nguyễn Viết Thanh was involved in the organization and execution of the May 1970 **Cambodian Incursion** in support of General **Đỗ Cao Trí**, who commanded the ARVN forces in that operation. He died on 2 May when his **helicopter** collided with an AH-1 Cobra helicopter.

NGUYỄN XUÂN OÁNH (1921–2003). Republic of Vietnam prime minister, sometimes referred to as "Jack Owens" by the Americans. Nguyễn Xuân Oánh was born in Phủ Lạng Thương in North Vietnam. He was educated at the Lycée Albert Sarraut in **Hà Nội** and earned an undergraduate degree from Kyoto Imperial University. He received further education at Harvard University where he earned a PhD in economics in 1954. Nguyễn Xuân Oánh taught economics in the **United States** until accepting a job with the International Monetary Fund in 1960. In 1963, he returned to Vietnam as the head of the National Bank of Vietnam. He remained in that position until August 1965. He also served as the minister of finance and the vice minister for economy from 4 February to 4 November 1964, and as deputy premier after the coup d'état against **Ngô Đình Diệm**.

He had two brief stints as the acting premier. The first was between 29 August and 3 September 1964, and the second lasted from 28 January to mid-February 1965, when he replaced **Trần Văn Hương** and was succeeded by **Phan Huy Quát**. After his time as acting premier, Nguyễn Xuân Oánh became the president of the National Institute of Economic Development in **Sài Gòn**. His name continued to be mentioned for various government positions, but he attempted to remain outside the political intrigue that ran rampant in Sài Gòn. After the war, he was put under house arrest for a time, but he became an economic adviser to the Socialist Republic of Vietnam (SRV) after his release. He then served in the National Assembly and was involved in the Vietnamese economic plan of Đổi Mới (openness or innovation). He worked to increase U.S. economic relations with the SRV and became an economic adviser to **Nguyễn Văn Linh**, the general secretary of the Vietnamese Communist Party, and **Võ Văn Kiệt**, who was the SRV prime minister from 1991 to 1992.

NHA TRANG. Located on the coast of the South China Sea in Khánh Hòa province in II **Corps Tactical Zone**, Nha Trang was the home of a major **United States Air Force** base and the **Army of the Republic of Vietnam**'s (ARVN) Non-commissioned Officers School. In 1949, the French established an air base near Nha Trang for use during the **First Indochina War**, with the first Vietnamese trained at the facility in 1951. Nha Trang became a major training center for Vietnamese pilots in the Vietnam Air Force under French control. In 1955, the **Republic of Vietnam Air Force** (RVNAF) established Tactical Base No. 1 on the same ground and flew T-28 aircraft in support of

ARVN operations. It was used by the RVNAF throughout the war, and the U.S. Armed Forces began using the facility in 1957. The air base also housed a Communications and Electronics School and was home to the RVNAF 62nd Wing. In 1974, it would become the headquarters for the RVNAF 2nd Air Division.

When the U.S. initiated Operation **Rolling Thunder** and U.S. aircraft increased air-to-ground support in the **Republic of Vietnam** (RVN) in 1965, Nha Trang grew dramatically. The air base was the home, at one point, for the 14th Air Commando Wing and the headquarters for the 5th **Special Forces** Group. During the final **People's Army of Vietnam** offensive in 1975, Nha Trang was abandoned by ARVN forces around 1 April. Most of the RVNAF aircraft stationed at the base were removed before its fall, but some were captured and were used against **Sài Gòn** in the final days of the RVN.

NIAGARA, OPERATION. During the siege of **Khe Sanh**, the **United States Air Force** (USAF) formulated a plan to provide close air support to the beleaguered **marines** defending the base. The first air **sortie** of Operation Niagara was launched on 21 January. It provided an intense bombardment around **Khe Sanh** that severely hampered the **People's Army of Vietnam**'s ability to threaten the base. The USAF flew nearly 10,000 sorties and dropped over 14,000 tons of munitions, while the marines flew over 7,000 sorties and delivered over 17,000 tons of munitions. **Navy** air assets flew over 5,000 sorties and dropped nearly 8,000 tons of munitions. The combined number of sorties and tonnage dropped around Khe Sanh made the operation one of the most intense during the war. The operation ended in March with the beginning of Operation **Pegasus**, which relieved Khe Sanh in mid-April.

NIXON DOCTRINE. On 25 July 1969, President **Richard M. Nixon** held a press conference at **Guam**, during which he outlined what would become known as the Nixon Doctrine. Nixon argued that the **United States** would continue to maintain its treaty commitments and to provide an appropriate response if any American allies were threatened by a nuclear power that was vital to U.S. national security. However, he announced that while the U.S. would continue to furnish military and economic assistance to threatened allies around the world, the U.S. expected any threatened ally to provide its own manpower in its defense. The doctrine was a direct response to the war in Vietnam. It marked the beginning of the policy of **Vietnamization**, or handing over American military hardware to the **Republic of Vietnam**, so that U.S. forces could withdraw from the region.

NIXON, RICHARD MILHOUS (1913–1994). 37th president of the **United States**. Richard M. Nixon was born in California and educated at

Whittier College in 1934 and Duke University Law School in 1937. He was a navy lieutenant commander in World War II with service in the Pacific Theater. Nixon entered public life in 1946 after he was elected as one of California's members in the U.S. House of Representatives. He had a number of assignments, including the Education and Labor Committee and the Herter Committee, which helped to create the Marshall Plan. Nixon's most famous position as a member of the House was his appointment to the House Un-American Activities Committee (HUAC) in 1948. Nixon made a name for himself by leading the investigation of Alger Hiss, a former State Department official who was accused of espionage. He was reelected in 1948, and in 1950 he won an election as one of California's U.S. senators by using a combination of his popularity from his participation in the HUAC and by engaging in anticommunist **propaganda**. He accused his opponent, Democratic congresswoman Helen Gahagan Douglas, of being pink right down to her underwear. It was in this campaign that Nixon earned the nickname "Tricky Dick."

Nixon was an outspoken critic of President Harry S. Truman and his administration of the Korean War. Nixon's reputation for and position related to anticommunist advocacy in both domestic and foreign policy issues earned him the nomination as the vice presidential candidate during the 1952 presidential election with Dwight D. Eisenhower. The two won the election despite a scandal that involved Nixon and some prominent businessmen who had donated a sum of money to aid the vice presidential candidate in his campaign expenses. The scandal was squashed when Nixon went before a nationally televised audience, explained his actions, and discussed another gift his family had received, a cocker spaniel dog, whom his daughter Tricia had named Checkers. The "Checkers" speech saved Nixon's political career and also showed how adept he was at using the new **media** of television to support and enhance his reputation.

Nixon served as vice president for all eight years of the Eisenhower administration. He was involved in a number of important domestic and foreign policy issues and often represented the U.S. on foreign trips around the world, including a July 1959 visit to the **Soviet Union** where he engaged the Soviet leader Nikita Khrushchev in the famous "kitchen debate" in front of a display of modern American kitchen appliances at the American National Exhibit in Moscow. Nixon's public role as vice president earned him the Republican Party's nomination for the presidential election in 1960, where he faced off against **John F. Kennedy**. Nixon lost that election in part because of the contrast between the two candidates when viewed on television, and because of Kennedy's insistence that a missile gap existed between the U.S. and the Soviet Union after the Soviets launched their Sputnik satellites into space.

Returning to California after the defeat, Nixon practiced law and wrote his first memoir, *Six Crises*. He ran against Edmund G. Brown Sr. in the 1962 gubernatorial election in California but lost by almost 300,000 votes. After the failed gubernatorial election, Nixon moved to New York City to practice law. He continued to play a role in Republican politics and enhanced his foreign policy credentials with a series of articles relating to American diplomacy. In the presidential election of 1968, Nixon decided to run one final election for office. He won the Republican nomination, defeating California governor Ronald W. Reagan who also voiced a pro-Vietnam policy, by calling for a return to traditional American values. Nixon sought to represent stability during a time of dissension and confusion as a result of the **antiwar movement** and the civil rights struggle. He won the election with his running mate **Spiro T. Agnew**, the Maryland governor, against a divided Democratic Party, still reeling from the assassination of **Robert Kennedy** and the debacle at the Democratic National Convention. The Democrats split their vote between Vice President **Hubert Humphrey** and third-party candidate George Wallace, who claimed nearly 10 million votes in the South.

When Nixon entered the White House, the U.S. had also completed its fourth year in Vietnam with combat troops, but with no real end in sight. The antiwar movement numbered in the hundreds of thousands, and the fabric of American society seemed to be unraveling before the eyes of the American people. Nixon had campaigned with the notion of winning the peace in Vietnam. But this implied a major change in American policy as initially expressed in the **Nixon Doctrine**, for he then implemented a plan of what he termed **Vietnamization**, a procedure by which the U.S. would begin to withdraw its combat troops from Vietnam while strengthening the fighting capacity of the **Army of the Republic of Vietnam** (ARVN). The ARVN would assume the burden of the war as the U.S. disengaged from Southeast Asia. The first American troops to withdraw without replacement left Vietnam in June 1969.

With Americans leaving the country, Nixon and his military needed to ensure that the South Vietnamese could handle the war. As a result, Nixon authorized a series of actions in Vietnam to allow the ARVN time to strengthen. He ordered the secret bombing of **Cambodia** via Operation **Menu** to destroy the established **People's Army of Vietnam** and **National Liberation Front** (NLF) base camps along the Cambodia-**Republic of Vietnam** (RVN) border, he supported the anticommunist Cambodian government under **Lon Nol**, and he authorized the 1970 **Cambodian Incursion** and the 1971 Laotian operation **Lam Sơn 719**. Each of these acts, which the antiwar movement considered escalatory, lost Nixon political support from portions of the U.S.

population who were tired of the war. Yet these military operations were necessary in order to allow Vietnamization to succeed.

While Nixon pushed Vietnamization, he authorized negotiations with the North Vietnamese in Paris. These talks never progressed far until after the failed 1972 **Easter Offensive** and Nixon's response with the air campaigns **Linebacker I** and **Linebacker II**. In January 1973, the North Vietnamese, South Vietnamese, U.S., and NLF reached an agreement to end the war in Vietnam. The **Paris Peace Accords** could have been Nixon's greatest achievement had the North Vietnamese not decided to violate the agreements in the following year and launch a final attack against the RVN in 1975. Nixon's ability to fulfill his pledge to South Vietnamese president **Nguyễn Văn Thiệu** to come to his aid if the North Vietnamese violated the treaty was hampered by a series of congressional acts that included the repeal of the **Gulf of Tŏn Kĭn Resolution** on 24 June 1970; the 5 January 1971 **Cooper-Church Amendment** that limited U.S. options for combat operations in **Laos** and Cambodia; the 19 June 1973 **Case-Church Amendment** that prohibited American operations in the **Democratic Republic of Vietnam**, RVN, Laos, and Cambodia; and the 7 November 1973 **War Powers Resolution** that severely limited the ability of the president to conduct armed diplomacy. Nixon's involvement in the Watergate scandal also diminished his ability to rally the American people behind the RVN's cause.

When Nixon decided to run for reelection in 1972, he covered up his knowledge of a break-in at the Democratic National Committee offices in the Watergate office complex in Washington, D.C. The scandal grew as more revelations were brought to the American people that outlined the extent to which Nixon and his administration had interfered with the electoral process as well as his handling of **Daniel Ellsberg**, who had leaked the **Pentagon Papers** to the *New York Times*. Before **Congress** could impeach the president, Nixon announced that he would resign the presidency on 9 August 1974. Less than a month later, President **Gerald R. Ford**, who had been Nixon's vice president after Spiro Agnew had been forced to resign earlier, pardoned Nixon for any and all offenses against the U.S.

Nixon and his family returned to California. In 1981, they moved back to New York City and then to New Jersey. Nixon partially regained his public status and focused on foreign policy in his post-presidency years. His work in reopening U.S. and Chinese relations in 1972 and his visit to Moscow later that year allowed him to retain his reputation as a diplomatic expert after Watergate. He wrote several books, including one, *No More Vietnams*, in which he argued that the U.S. had won the war but Congress had lost the peace. He continued to be an elder statesman and foreign policy specialist until his death in 1994.

NOLTING, FREDERICK ERNEST, JR. (1911–1989). United States ambassador to the **Republic of Vietnam** between 10 May 1961 and 15 August 1963. Nolting received degrees from the University of Virginia and Harvard University before joining the navy during World War II. He entered service in the State Department in 1946 and worked as an assistant to Secretary of State **John Foster Dulles**. In 1955, he was appointed to the U.S. mission to the North Atlantic Treaty Organization and was named permanent representative in 1957. He also served as U.S. representative to the Organization of American States. Nolting took over the Vietnam ambassadorship from **Elbridge Durbrow** on 10 May 1961 and had to do much to regain the trust and respect of **Ngô Đình Diệm**, whose confidence had been severely shaken by Durbrow's failure to provide active support for him during the abortive November 1960 coup d'état.

Ngô Đình Diệm and Nolting established a solid relationship and did restore some of the old rapport enjoyed between the U.S. and the Republic of Vietnam, but Nolting was continually being undermined by the State Department and by members of the U.S. **media**. Unlike Durbrow and Nolting's successor, **Henry Cabot Lodge Jr.**, Nolting did not have the political capital in Washington to push for a more positive Vietnamese policy. Meanwhile, individuals like **W. Averell Harriman** and Joseph Mendenhall, who had served as Durbrow's number two in the U.S. embassy and then in positions of increasing influence within the State Department, worked to undermine U.S. support for Ngô Đình Diệm, which eventually led to the Vietnamese president's demise.

Nolting lauded Ngô Đình Diệm's efforts to improve the Vietnamese economy, he was supportive of the **Strategic Hamlet Program**, and he opposed the actions of the media when they reported on the **Battle of Ấp Bắc**. His position on these issues and events earned him wide criticism from the anti–Ngô Đình Diệm factions in Vietnam and the U.S., but he never wavered. Nolting left Vietnam for a planned vacation that preceded the end of his ambassador's tour of duty just before the **Buddhist Crisis** erupted in May 1963. For not being at his post or returning to Vietnam, he was intensely criticized. When he asked to return, he was not given the option, as Henry Cabot Lodge Jr. had already been selected to replace him, and the U.S. policy for Vietnam was already irrevocably different from Nolting's position. After Nolting left Vietnam for the last time on 15 August, he continued to advocate the pro–Ngô Đình Diệm position, but he remained somewhat quiet on the American war in Vietnam over the next 10 years. He wrote his memoirs, *From Trust to Tragedy*, in 1988, lamenting the 1 November 1963 coup d'état that resulted in the assassinations of Ngô Đình Diệm and **Ngô Đình Nhu.**

NORTH VIETNAM. A more common name for the **Democratic Republic of Vietnam** used by the **United States** during the war. North Vietnam was established as a result of the 1954 **Geneva Agreements** that temporarily divided the country near the 17th parallel until a national election could be conducted within two years. Vietnamese also referred to North Vietnam as **Bắc Bộ**, though the area in Bắc Bộ was greater than the nearly 100,000 kilometers (62,000 square miles) that made up North Vietnam. North Vietnam also included the French administrative territory of Tŏn Kĭn and part of An Nam. North Vietnam was eventually united with the **Republic of Vietnam**, also known as South Vietnam, in 1975 and was renamed the Socialist Republic of Vietnam in 1976.

NÚI BÀ ĐEN. Located in **Tây Ninh** province, 10 kilometers (6 miles) from Tây Ninh City and 29 kilometers (18 miles) from the Cambodian border, Núi Bà Đen, or the Black Virgin Mountain, was a large cone-shaped granite outcropping that was approximately 975 meters (3,200 feet) high. The mountain was surrounded by flat ground and rice fields, with rocks and boulders at its base. The **United States** established a reconnaissance base at the top of Núi Bà Đen after a May 1964 operation secured the mountain. The base was outfitted with radar equipment and a radio retransmitting station. While U.S. troops controlled the top of the mountain, the **National Liberation Front** operated around the bottom of it throughout the war and dug into the slope, making their base area difficult to locate and destroy. In addition to its strategic importance in the war, Núi Bà Đen also held religious and political significance for the Vietnamese people. It was the site of many Vietnamese **Buddhist** legends and several Buddhist temples. The **Republic of Vietnam** held on to Núi Bà Đen until 6 January 1975, when it was overrun by the **People's Army of Vietnam**.

NÙNG. One of the many ethnic minority groups in Vietnam who practiced farming and lived very simple lives. The Nùng originated along the Vietnamese-Chinese border but migrated into the northern part of Vietnam after the 1500s in the provinces of Cao Bằng and Lạng Sơn. The Nùng belong to the Tai language group. A group estimated at nearly 40,000 fled North Vietnam, after the 1954 **Geneva Conference**, on U.S. ships conducting Operation **Passage to Freedom** and the South Vietnamese equivalent, Operation Exodus. The Nùng were considered anticommunist and were seen as supporters of the **Republic of Vietnam**. They constituted the majority of the **Army of the Republic of Vietnam**'s (ARVN) 5th Division until the early 1960s. They were also involved in local militia and clandestine operations against the **National Liberation Front**.

One of the early Nùng leaders and notables in modern Vietnamese history was Nông Văn Dền, known as Kim Đồng, who lived from 1928 to 1943. Kim Đồng worked with the anti-French movement in Indochina during World War II, carrying messages and, in one instance, helping the escape of a prisoner arrested by the French. He was killed at the age of 14 by the French while delivering messages and became a martyr to the nationalist cause. Nùng fighters were involved in the 6 July 1964 Battle of Nam Đông, which resulted in the first U.S. Medal of Honor recipient, **Roger H. C. Donlan.** The Nùng earned a reputation as very competent military men who were dedicated to the crusade against communism. Several Nùng rose to important military rank, including a commander of the ARVN Airborne Division from 1964 to 1972, **Dư Quốc Đống**, who later became the commander of the Capital Military District.

O

O'DANIEL, JOHN WILSON (1894–1975). United States general. O'Daniel was born in Delaware and educated at Delaware College. He joined the Delaware National Guard in 1913 and was involved in the Mexican campaign preceding the U.S. entry into World War I. He finished school in 1917 and was commissioned as a second lieutenant in the infantry reserve on 15 August 1917 and received a regular commission on 26 October. He joined the 11th Infantry and participated in battles at St. Mihiel and Neuse during the Argonne offensives toward the end of the war, where he was wounded.

O'Daniel remained in the military after the war and served in a variety of positions. He was promoted to colonel when the U.S. entered World War II and served as the assistant chief of staff for operations of the 3rd Army. He joined the Allied Force Headquarters in Europe as commander of the American Invasion Training School in the British Isles in July 1942 and, in September, commanded the 168th Infantry through North Africa. He was promoted to general on 20 November and continued to organize operations and lead army units through North Africa, Italy, and into the southern part of France. He was involved in the invasion of Germany and the capture of Nuremburg at the end of the war.

After the war, O'Daniel served as the commandant and then commanding general of the Infantry School at Fort Benning. In June 1948, he became the military attaché to the U.S. embassy in the **Soviet Union** and later, in August 1950, served as the infantry inspector in the Office of the Chief of Army Field Forces at Fort Monroe, Virginia. During the Korean War, O'Daniel commanded the 1st Corps of the 8th Army until becoming commanding general of U.S. Army Forces Pacific at Fort Schafter, Hawaii, on 1 September 1952.

In April 1954, O'Daniel became the first chief of the **Military Assistance Advisory Group** (MAAG), Indochina. O'Daniel was involved in the military and civilian efforts to help build the State of Vietnam during the 1954 **Geneva Conference** and in the months that followed. He also helped to coordinate Operation **Passage to Freedom**, the U.S. naval operation that lasted from August 1954 to May 1955, which moved approximately 310,000 Vietnamese

from the North to the South. He also assisted in helping to resettle and rehabilitate the 810,000 Vietnamese who fled the North during this same period.

O'Daniel led the 342 men of the MAAG who were charged with helping the Vietnamese military organize to confront the communist insurgency in the South and the expected threat from the North. He advocated
increased American involvement in Vietnam during this period until the
end of his tour in October 1954. O'Daniel was a strong supporter of **Ngô
Đình Diệm** and remained so until the president of the **Republic of Vietnam**'s assassination in November 1963. He retired from active service on
31 December 1955. After his military career, O'Daniel remained involved
in Vietnamese affairs by chairing the **American Friends of Vietnam**
(AFVN), a civilian organization designed to aid the Vietnamese people
and to educate the American people on the plight of the Vietnamese. He
resigned from the AFVN in September 1963, disillusioned with the organization's change of focus away from support for Ngô Đình Diệm. He
remained outside of the political and military public debate surrounding
America's escalation in Vietnam.

OFFICE OF CIVIL OPERATIONS (OCO). Organized in November 1966
in an effort to improve the efficiency of **pacification** programs, the OCO recognized the need to bring together the various civilian efforts to improve the
security of, and bring the benefits of American aid to, the Vietnamese people.
While the OCO was supposed to be under the control of Deputy Ambassador
William Porter as an independent organization, Ambassador **Henry Cabot
Lodge Jr.**'s absence from the **Republic of Vietnam** (RVN) meant that Porter
could not devote the necessary time and attention to the new organization.
Porter selected L. Wade Lathram, who was the deputy director of the **Sài
Gòn** office of the Agency for International Development to oversee the OCO,
but Lathram took a leave of absence from his post soon after being made the
director. The lack of a cadre of leadership at the top of the organization negatively affected the program.

The OCO directed all civilian efforts related to pacification in the RVN. It
was designed to coordinate the activities of the various agencies. The OCO's
organizational responsibility was divided into six responsibilities, which included **refugees**; psychological operations; **New Life Villages**; revolutionary
development cadres; the **Chiêu Hồi**, or "Open Arms," program; and public
safety. Nearly 1,000 U.S. personnel were involved in OCO programs, though
there were nearly 1,500 positions available. The total cost of the programs
equaled approximately $128 million. Most of the personnel and funding for
the OCO came from the Agency for International Development and the **Central Intelligence Agency**.

The OCO proved beneficial in U.S. efforts toward pacification even though it caused tension as rival agencies and organizations competed for its resources. For the RVN, the OCO consolidated and improved the quantity of advice it was given. The OCO was eventually absorbed into a new organization, **Civil Operations and Revolutionary Development Support** (CORDS), which was created on 10 May 1967 and was designed to coordinate both civil and military pacification efforts. **Robert Komer**, who had been involved in the creation of the OCO organization and objectives, became the first director of CORDS with the rank of ambassador and the military equivalent of a three-star general. Komer reported directly to General **William C. Westmoreland**, the commander of the **Military Assistance Command, Vietnam**. CORDS reflected the lessons learned from the OCO experience and proved to be a much more effective and efficient organization. *See also* PROPAGANDA.

ONTOS. The M50 Ontos was a light-armored tracked antitank weapon. Because of the limited number of North Vietnamese **tanks**, the Ontos was used by the **United States Marine Corps** during the war as a direct fire support weapon. It was equipped with six M40 **recoilless** rifles that proved to be very accurate, and it included one .30 caliber **machine gun** and four .50 caliber spotting **rifles**. Its armor was approximately 13 mm (.51 inches) thick, and it carried a crew of three. It had a maximum speed of 48 kilometers (30 miles) per hour and a range of approximately 240 kilometers (150 miles). The Ontos allowed mobile **artillery** to dominate the battlefield; this was especially true during the Battle for **Huế** during the 1968 **Tết Offensive**. It was generally approved of as a weapon, though it was vulnerable to land **mines**. The marines stopped using the Ontos in May 1969, and the last of the vehicles were returned to the U.S. in 1970.

OPLAN 34A. In the fall of 1963, President **John F. Kennedy** authorized a program that used American personnel to gather **intelligence** on North Vietnamese coastal defenses. The Americans would also support South Vietnamese missions designed to harass North Vietnamese villages and offshore naval facilities. The **United States** and the **Republic of Vietnam** argued that OPLAN 34A, as it was designated, was no different than what **Hà Nội** had authorized a few years earlier, while the North Vietnamese declared that the U.S.-supported actions were overt acts of aggression that would result in a declaration of war and international condemnation. Both arguments had merits. While the actual raids were conducted by the South Vietnamese, the personnel involved were transported by U.S. naval craft that were sometimes piloted by Americans.

The raids did have a positive psychological effect for the South Vietnamese, who had limited ability to take the war to the North. They succeeded in destroying or damaging coastal defenses and facilities that supported the war against the South, and they killed or kidnapped a number of North Vietnamese personnel who were associated with the war. American involvement in the operation, however, was very close to an undeclared war, and its actions would eventually lead to an escalation of hostilities. On 30–31 July 1964, an OPLAN 34A mission intersected with a **DeSoto** mission conducted by the U.S.S. *Maddox* (DD-731), which was collecting electronic intelligence on North Vietnamese coastal defenses. The two separate operations heightened North Vietnamese attention to the area and culminated in the 2 August **Gulf of Tŏn Kĭn Incident** and the alleged action on 4 August, which resulted in the **Gulf of Tŏn Kĭn Resolution** and an escalation of U.S. involvement in the war.

ORDER OF BATTLE DISPUTE. The number of **People's Army of Vietnam** (PAVN) and **National Liberation Front** (NLF) personnel in the **Republic of Vietnam** (RVN) had always been estimated by the **United States**. This was due primarily to the fact that the U.S. intelligence agencies involved in determining that number were undermanned early in the war and then disagreed about the actual number later in the war.

Starting in 1962, the **Military Assistance Command, Vietnam** (MACV), began to compile statistics related to communist forces that were operating in the RVN. The difficulty in maintaining these statistics resulted from the fact that the PAVN forces infiltrated into the RVN through neutral **Laos** and **Cambodia** via the **Hồ Chí Minh Trail**, while the NLF were either hidden in the jungles or inaccessible areas of the countryside or they blended into the general population. Before the Americanization of the war in 1965, MACV never committed enough personnel to the PAVN or NLF order of battle. After 1965, more personnel were devoted to gathering the information, but a dispute arose between MACV and the **Central Intelligence Agency** (CIA).

MACV had maintained a lower number of enemy personnel in the field, essentially controlling the statistics in order to manage perceptions of the war within the U.S. The CIA also began to gather information on the enemy order of battle and in 1967 began to dispute the lower MACV statistics. The difference in numbers was significant because the **Lyndon B. Johnson** administration had begun a significant public relations campaign in which it argued that the war was being won. The CIA numbers directly countered that claim. The two sides agreed to a compromise on how to count the enemy, by keeping the CIA method but dropping a few of the lesser categories from the total count in order to maintain the MACV numbers.

The dispute between the **intelligence** officers continued, and it became public after a 19 March 1968 *New York Times* article written by **Neil Sheehan** who had received documents from **Daniel Ellsberg**. In 1975, the House of Representatives Select Committee on Intelligence held hearings related to the order of battle dispute, which then became the basis for a 23 January 1982 CBS documentary titled *The Uncounted Enemy: A Vietnam Deception*, which claimed that **William C. Westmoreland** had deceived the American people and government by purposefully underestimating the number of PAVN and NLF soldiers in the RVN. This led to the 1984 *Westmoreland v. CBS* libel lawsuit, which kept the insidious nature of the war on the front pages of the newspapers and exposed Westmoreland to additional criticism. Westmoreland eventually withdrew the lawsuit after a few senior MACV officers in intelligence testified for the defense. *See also* MEDIA, UNITED STATES.

OREGON, TASK FORCE. Military Assistance Command, Vietnam, commander **William C. Westmoreland** created the task force in February 1967 to fill a gap created in I **Corps Tactical Zone** (CTZ) when the **United States Marines** were shifted toward the **Demilitarized Zone**. Because no divisions were available to replace the marines in the southern part of the CTZ, Westmoreland brought together a multibrigade task force under the name Oregon. It included the 1st Brigade, 101st Airborne **Division**; the 3rd Brigade, 25th Infantry Division; and the 196th Light Infantry Brigade.

The Task Force was based out of **Chu Lai** and conducted operations in Quảng Ngãi province after it became operational on 20 April 1967. The task force was under the command of Major General Richard T. Knowles who was replaced by Brigadier General Samuel W. Koster on 22 September 1967. On 25 September 1967, the task force became the basis for the 23rd Infantry Division, known as the Americal Division. The task force was not without controversy. It was featured in two *New Yorker* magazine articles in March 1968 that highlighted the more destructive nature of its **search-and-destroy** operations.

P

PACIFICATION. The attempt by the **Republic of Vietnam** (RVN) and the **United States** to secure the villages in Vietnam. Pacification not only provided for security but also worked toward improving economic, social, and cultural opportunities for the Vietnamese. The first informal attempts at pacification occurred during the 1954–1955 period, when approximately 810,000 Vietnamese relocated from north of the **Demilitarized Zone** to the South after the 1954 **Geneva Conference**. The U.S. spearheaded the attempt at pacification through its U.S. Overseas Missions and the Special Technical and Economic Missions. The main focus of the pacification effort was on the rehabilitation and resettlement of the **refugees** in areas not under the control or influence of the communist insurgency.

The next attempt occurred in 1959 when RVN president **Ngô Đình Diệm** introduced the **Agroville Program** in an effort to pacify the countryside and deny the insurgency access to the people. When this program failed, the **Sài Gòn** government organized the **Strategic Hamlet Program** in 1962. Like the Agroville Program, it focused more on security and was never able to achieve the positive results necessary to bring about pacification. The Vietnamese people never realized the benefits of pacification, as their loyalty was consistently being tested by both the **National Liberation Front** (NLF) and the RVN.

After the November 1963 coup d'état against Ngô Đình Diệm, the U.S. was more focused on regaining control of the situation. In 1964, the **Central Intelligence Agency** (CIA) authorized the establishment of People's Action Teams, which worked with villagers in similar ways to the NLF. The People's Action Teams evolved into the **Revolutionary Development Cadres** by February 1966. These mobile 59-man teams emulated the NLF strategy in their efforts to improve the lives of the Vietnamese people by working, eating, and staying with the people in their villages. The Revolutionary Development Cadres strategy was the first real effort to integrate rather than impose pacification on the countryside.

The program, however, was not very well organized and proved to be inefficient. Pacification involved both civilian and military organizations, and they vied with one another for limited resources. In November 1966, the U.S. established the **Office of Civil Operations**, which oversaw the civilian pacification efforts. The Revolutionary Development Program controlled the military efforts, which included the Revolutionary Development Cadres and U.S. military Civic Action Programs. The Vietnamese side of the operation was headed by Major General Nguyễn Đức Thắng. While separate organizations helped to improve pacification coordination, it was not until the civilian and military side were joined that pacification had a real chance to be successful.

On 10 May 1967, the U.S. created the **Civil Operations and Revolutionary Development Support** (CORDS). It was headed by **Robert Komer** who held the rank of ambassador and reported directly to the **Military Assistance Command, Vietnam**, commander General **William C. Westmoreland**. Under CORDS, pacification efforts intensified as Komer and Westmoreland were able to better coordinate military operations with civic action. CORDS helped to improve the **Chiêu Hồi** program to rally defectors to the RVN, it enhanced refugee relief and rehabilitation programs, it continued other psychological efforts to improve safety and security, and it developed the **New Life Villages**. CORDS also established the **Phoenix Program** (Phụng Hoàng), which had the objective of destroying the infrastructure of the NLF.

The pacification effort was disrupted by the 1968 **Tết Offensive**, and Komer became increasingly frustrated with RVN president **Nguyễn Văn Thiệu** who moved too slowly to fill the vacuum left by the NLF's military disaster as a result of the offensive. Pacification did receive renewed interested when Komer's successor, **William Colby**, persuaded Nguyễn Văn Thiệu to authorize an Accelerated Pacification Campaign. Colby worked with Westmoreland's successor, General **Creighton W. Abrams**, to press the remaining NLF in the countryside.

Colby's pacification philosophy included all of the CORDS efforts but also focused on extending existing security in the countryside to villages that had been previously contested. Colby worked to improve the **Regional Forces** and **Popular Forces** by upgrading their weapons to the M16 **rifle** and by increasing the number of U.S. army **advisers** in the units. Colby also helped to establish the **People's Self-Defense Force**, which received less training, equipment, and advisement but offered a military presence in nearly every village.

Pacification efforts were the strongest between 1969 and 1971 as the U.S. began to withdraw. The U.S. worked with the RVN to leave behind a big enough force to combat the NLF and the **Democratic Republic of Vietnam**. Pacification efforts ended with the 1972 **Easter Offensive**, when all available RVN Armed Forces were committed to the defense of the RVN after the **People's Army of Vietnam** launched a three-pronged attack that sought to militarily overwhelm the RVN. Without U.S. assistance after the 1973 **Paris**

Peace Accords, pacification efforts were never able to recover and were eventually abandoned. *See also* HAMLET EVALUATION SYSTEM.

PARIS PEACE ACCORDS. Signed in Paris on 27 January 1973, the *Agreement on Ending the War and Restoring Peace in Vietnam*, as it was officially known, or the Paris Peace Accords, was the document that served as the outline to end the war in Vietnam. **United States** secretary of state William P. Rogers, **Republic of Vietnam** (RVN) minister for foreign affairs Trần Văn Lắm, **Democratic Republic of Vietnam** (DRV) minister for foreign affairs Nguyễn Duy Trinh, and **Provisional Revolutionary Government of the Republic of South Vietnam** minister for foreign affairs **Nguyễn Thị Bình** signed the accords. The Paris Peace Accords also had four protocol agreements: a 14-article "Protocol to the Agreement on Ending the War and Restoring Peace in Vietnam Concerning the Return of Captured Military Personnel and Foreign Civilians and Captured and Detained Vietnamese Civilian Personnel"; an 18-article "Protocol to the Agreement on Ending the War and Restoring Peace in Vietnam Concerning the **International Commission of Control and Supervision** (ICCS)"; a 19-article "Protocol to the Agreement on Ending the War and Restoring Peace in Vietnam Concerning the Cease-Fire in South Vietnam and the Joint Military Commissions"; and an 8-article "Protocol to the Agreement on Ending the War and Restoring Peace in Vietnam Concerning the Removal, Permanent Deactivation, or Destruction of Mines in the Territorial Waters, Ports, Harbors, and Waterways of the **Democratic Republic of Vietnam**."

The Paris Peace Accords were not strongly endorsed by the RVN, as it left tens of thousands of **People's Army of Vietnam** (PAVN) troops below the **Demilitarized Zone**. President **Nguyễn Văn Thiệu** only reluctantly agreed to the accords after President **Richard M. Nixon** promised that the U.S. would respond to any violations by the DRV with strong force. After Nixon's political future became troubled and **Congress** exerted its authority in foreign policy, President **Gerald R. Ford** was not able to keep this promise. The 23 articles in the final agreement called for a number of things, including a return to the spirit of the 1954 Geneva Agreements, the withdrawal of U.S. troops and an end to U.S. military activities in support of the RVN, and the suspension of all fighting and movement of troops except in the case of removal from the forward lines. The U.S. was to end its involvement within 60 days. Article 8 was particularly important for the U.S., as it called for the return of captured personnel and the sharing of information about men who were captured or **missing-in-action**. Article 9 called for the right of the RVN to self-determination, though that right would be eliminated in less than three years. Article 15 called for the reunification of the DRV and RVN through peaceful means at a time to be decided by both sides. This article also proved to be useless, as PAVN forces continued to attack **Army of the Republic of Vietnam** personnel until the end of the final 1975 offensive.

The accords created the ICCS, which replaced the defunct **International Control Commission** created after the 1954 **Geneva Conference and Agreements**. The ICCS oversaw the accords and the protocols and investigated alleged violations. The ICCS included personnel from Hungary, Poland, **Canada**, and Indonesia, though the Canadian delegation withdrew after a few of its members were held captive and one of the ICCS **helicopters** was shot down. Personnel from Iran replaced the Canadians.

The Paris Peace Accords also referred to the 1954 Geneva Agreements on **Cambodia** and the 1962 **Geneva Accords** on **Laos** as a basis for establishing peace in the rest of Southeast Asia, though the accord failed to stop the **Khmer Rouge** from defeating the **Phnom Penh** government and initiating genocide, or the political victory by the **Pathet Lao** in December 1975 which saw that country fall to communism. Another controversial article called for the U.S. to contribute to healing the wounds of war and to postwar reconstruction of the DRV. The DRV interpreted this as war reparations, and when the U.S. refused to follow through on Article 21 because of numerous violations between January 1973 and April 1975, the DRV failed to follow through on the articles related to missing-in-action and **prisoners of war**. *See also* KISSINGER, HENRY ALFRED; LÊ ĐỨC THỌ.

PARROT'S BEAK. Area located in Svay Rieng province, **Cambodia**, along the border with the **Republic of Vietnam** (RVN) that received its name based on its shape. The area was a long, thin salient that divided III **Corps Tactical Zone** (CTZ) and IV CTZ and pointed east-southeast toward **Sài Gòn**. Base 367, a facility used by the **People's Army of Vietnam** and the **National Liberation Front** for attacks into the RVN, was located in the Parrot's Beak, making it a high-priority target for an 8,700-man-strong **Army of the Republic of Vietnam** task force and elements of the **United States** 25th **Division** during the 1970 **Cambodian Incursion**.

PASSAGE TO FREEDOM, OPERATION. For a 10-month period between August 1954 and May 1955, the **United States Navy** accomplished one of the greatest humanitarian operations in modern history when it participated in the evacuation of Vietnamese from North to South Vietnam as a result of articles 8, 14, and 15 of the 1954 **Geneva Agreements**. The U.S. initiated Operation Passage to Freedom on 8 August at the request of **Ngô Đình Diệm**—who had already organized Operation Exodus to help those wishing to leave the North—with the hope of accomplishing three major goals: to assist in the movement of Vietnamese away from the communists, to provide transportation for Vietnamese who had voiced opposition to communism by their flight, and to take advantage of the **propaganda** value of the large movement of people.

For the tens of thousands of U.S. sailors and officers involved in the operation, it was a very emotional, difficult, and rewarding experience. U.S. sailors became the first contact between the American and Vietnamese cultures. Sailors went beyond the call of duty to see to the comfort and care of the **refugee** population while overcoming obstacles related to culture, food preference, and language, as well as communist propaganda that warned of American atrocities at sea and French obstinacy designed to thwart the American effort. Under the command of Vice Admiral Lorenzo Sabin, Task Force 90 moved approximately 310,000 of the 810,000 Vietnamese and ethnic minorities who fled the DRV, as well as transporting 69,000 tons of equipment and 8,135 vehicles. During the operation, there were 184 Vietnamese births aboard U.S. ships and 66 Vietnamese deaths, all from preexisting conditions. There were also approximately 80,000 Vietnamese who chose to go from the South to the North. Their movement was mostly done on Polish ships that were not associated with Passage to Freedom.

PATHET LAO. The Pathet Lao (Land of the Lao) was established as early as 1950 as a group of **Lao** soldiers led by Prince **Souphanouvong** in support of the Vietnamese fighting the French during the **First Indochina War**. Pathet Lao troops joined the **Việt Minh** during the war in a series of operations in northern Indochina and even established a Laotian government at Viengxay. The Pathet Lao, with Việt Minh assistance, were able to hold much of the Laotian territory by the time of the 1954 **Geneva Conference**. With the end of French rule as a result of the agreements reached at the conference, the Pathet Lao, working closely with the North Vietnamese, sought to install communist rule in **Laos**. The group created a political organization, the **Neo Lao Hak Xat**, or Lao Patriotic Front, and joined a coalition government in 1957. In the May 1958 national elections, it legally gained 9 of 21 seats in the National Assembly, but the political gain of the Pathet Lao was thwarted when the anticommunist Phoui Sananikone became prime minister in August 1958. In the ensuing months, one of the two Pathet Lao battalions was forced to surrender, and Prince Souphanouvong and many of the Neo Lao Hak Xat leaders were arrested. For the next four years, the Pathet Lao fought the forces loyal to the Royal Laotian Government until a political compromise was brokered at the 1962 Geneva Conference.

The agreements from the Geneva Conference promised neutrality for Laos, but that hope was quickly dashed by the North Vietnamese, who were becoming reliant on transit through Laotian territory to support their war in the **Republic of Vietnam** and the Pathet Lao, who held the upper hand against the Royal Laotian Government. The Pathet Lao continued to grow in the 1960s, with the aid and assistance of the **People's Army of Vietnam**, but it was faced with new threats as the **United States** and **Thailand** began to support the Royal Laotian Army. Pathet Lao forces were numerically superior to their enemy and had the advantage during the dry season in northern Laos when they went on the offensive and would capture much of the area between the Laos–North Vietnamese border and the capital of Vientiane in west-central Laos, known as the **Plain of Jars**. While Pathet Lao involvement in this war was significant for the Laotian people, the North Vietnamese commanded much of the action and provided the majority of personnel and weapons to sustain the conflict. The Pathet Lao fought until 1973, when it signed a cease-fire agreement with the government on 21 February, shortly after the signing of the **Paris Peace Accords**. Like the agreement signed in Paris, the Vientiane Treaty did not hold, and the Pathet Lao continued its fight until the government conceded defeat.

The Pathet Lao established the Lao People's Democratic Republic in December 1975, eliminating the Laotian monarchy. It signed a formal alliance with the new Socialist Republic of Vietnam and ruled the country, albeit with strong Vietnamese influence, carrying out a genocide against the **Hmong** people that was on a much smaller scale than the atrocities committed by the **Khmer Rouge** in **Cambodia** but still devastating to the Laotian people and country. *See also* HOTFOOT, PROJECT; HOTSPOT; LAO THEUNG; SAM NEUA.

PATIO, OPERATION. Aerial operation in **Cambodia** that preceded the 1970 **Cambodian Incursion**. Operation Patio began on 24 April 1970 and was scheduled to last for 30 days, though the most intense missions occurred in the six days before **United States** forces and **Army of the Republic of Vietnam** forces crossed the Cambodian border to destroy **People's Army of Vietnam** (PAVN) and **National Liberation Front** (NLF) base areas located along the border between the **Republic of Vietnam** and Cambodia. Operation Patio supplemented Operation **Menu**, which had begun on 18 March 1969. The operation was requested as a result of increased pressure placed on the **Phnom Penh** government headed by **Lon Nol** after he ordered the PAVN and NLF forces out of Cambodia.

Because of Cambodia's neutrality, Patio missions were kept secret, and the **sorties** were falsely assigned targets in the Republic of Vietnam in order to account for the expenditure of munitions and other resources. The majority of the Patio missions were conducted in the northeastern section of Cambodia where the **Khmer Rouge** had established a strong presence. Initial air strikes focused on a zone within 12.8 kilometers (8 miles) of the border, but the target area was expanded to 29 kilometers (18 miles) by the second day. Operation Patio was terminated on 4 May, more than two weeks earlier than expected, after the U.S. decided to initiate Operation **Freedom Deal**, which concentrated a more intense air attack in roughly the same area. All in all, 156 sorties were flown during Patio, with an estimated 260 tons of munitions dropped.

PATROL AIR CUSHION VEHICLE (PACV). Built by Bell, the SRN-5 PACV was the military version of the civilian hovercraft. It was slightly under 11.9 meters (39 feet) long and just less than 7.3 meters (24 feet) wide. It carried a complement of four and could travel over land or water at up to 110 kilometers (70 miles) per hour, with a cruising speed of 80 kilometers (50 miles) per hour. It had a range of approximately 300 kilometers (190 miles). The PACV was armed with a .50 caliber M2 **machine gun** and two M60 machine guns. The **United States Navy** purchased three PACVs from the British in 1965 for use in the **Mê Kông Delta**. After training, the PACVs and their crew arrived in Vietnam in 1966. The weapon was used in operations **Market Time** and **Game Warden**, but the cost to operate it outweighed its benefits. The U.S. Army developed its own version of the PACV, the Air Cushioned Vehicle (ACV). Three of these were used during the war in the **Plain of Reeds** near the Cambodian border in IV **Corps Tactical Zone** (CTZ).

The PACV proved to be an effective weapon in traversing the water-dominated area of IV CTZ. It could travel in areas that had been previously prohibited and so was able to engage the enemy on his own terrain. This was demonstrated in the November 1966 operation called Quái Vật (Monster), as the **National Liberation Front** (NLF) had labeled the weapon. The PACV was loud and thus not effective in surprise, but it used the advantage of speed and firepower to disrupt the NLF along the **Republic of Vietnam**–Cambodian border, striking at NLF bases before they could react. The program was eventually suspended after the implementation of **Vietnamization**. *See also* PATROL BOAT, RIVER.

PATROL BOAT, RIVER (PBR). A small, highly maneuverable fiberglass-hulled boat that was introduced into the war in 1966 and served as one of the principal weapons for the **brown-water navy**. The PBR was used primarily to patrol those waterways that were less accessible to allied forces. It was powered by a water-jet drive that allowed it to operate in shallow water. It was also not affected by water-borne debris such as river weeds. The first PBRs arrived in March 1966 and were deployed under Task Force 116. These

PBRs inspected Vietnamese watercraft in an effort to interdict **National Liberation Front** personnel and supplies. The majority of PBRs worked in the waterways of IV **Corps Tactical Zone** (CTZ) where the **Mê Kông Delta** dominated the terrain, though a few were deployed in I CTZ.

In addition to interdiction missions, PBRs provided fire support for troops engaged with the enemy and were involved in personnel insertion into contested areas. The Mark I model of the PBR was 9.4 meters (31 feet) long, while the Mark II model, introduced at the end of the year, was 9.8 meters (32 feet) long. Both models had a cruising speed just short of 29 knots (54 kilometers per hour) and were armed with twin 12.7-mm **machine guns** forward and a single 12.7-mm machine gun in the rear. It also mounted side weapons that included a 7.62-mm machine gun, a **grenade launcher**, or a 20-mm cannon. The PBR was a very effective weapon during the war and was feared by the enemy. *See also* PATROL AIR CUSHION VEHICLE (PACV); RIVER PATROL FORCE.

PAVEWAY I. *See* MISSILES.

PEGASUS, OPERATION. Operation designed to relieve the base at **Khe Sanh** that had been under siege since January 1968. Planning for the operation began soon after the **People's Army of Vietnam** (PAVN) initiated its attack at Khe Sanh, but it was not implemented until 1 April. The operation included a combination of **marine** battalions, the 1st Air Cavalry, and the 3rd **Army of the Republic of Vietnam** (ARVN) Airborne Task Force supported by air and **artillery** firepower. As the marines began the overland phase of the operation, followed by the 11th Engineer Battalion which cleared **Route** 9 from its base at Ca Lu near the **Rockpile**, the 1st Air Cavalry used its **helicopters** to secure key positions in advance of the marines. There was little opposition from the PAVN except for a few intense battles on 6 April and near Khe Sanh village. The 2nd Battalion, 7th Cavalry entered Khe Sanh on 8 April, and the engineers officially opened the road on 11 April.

Operation Pegasus ended on 15 April, with the **United States** losing 92 killed-in-action and 667 wounded. The ARVN lost 33 killed-in-action with 187 wounded. PAVN **casualties** were estimated at over 1,000. While the operation was successful, it was not without controversy, both in Vietnam and the U.S. Many marines insisted that the operation was not necessary, as Khe Sanh was not really under siege, while others were resentful of being put in harm's way at Khe Sanh and dismissed the entire affair. When Khe Sanh was abandoned that July, many in the U.S. began to question the risks placed upon American servicemen both within Khe Sanh and as part of Operation Pegasus, seeking justification for actions taken that did not seem necessary.

PENTAGON PAPERS. In 1967, Secretary of Defense **Robert McNamara** authorized a study of **United States** involvement in Vietnam since the end of World War II. The study, *United States-Vietnam Relations, 1945–1967: A Study Prepared by the Department of Defense*, was completed the next year. Commonly referred to as the Pentagon Papers, it exposed several areas of duplicity in U.S. actions leading up to the Americanization of the war. The study remained classified and out of public circulation until one of its contributors, **Daniel Ellsberg**, began to give copies of the documents and texts used in the study to **Neil Sheehan**, who worked for the *New York Times*. In June 1971, the *New York Times* began publishing articles based on the Pentagon Papers.

There were several attempts by the **Richard M. Nixon** administration to force the *New York Times* to cease publication and to target Ellsberg for conviction under the Espionage Act of 1917, but after Senator Mike Gravel (D-Alaska) entered a portion of the document into the Congressional Record, enough damage had been done to discredit President **Lyndon B. Johnson** and to hamper any actions proposed by President Richard M. Nixon to win the war. The Pentagon Papers confirmed to those opposed to the war that the Johnson administration had tricked and deceived the American public into the conflict. The study justified past **antiwar** activities and provided credibility to the more active antiwar activists like the **Vietnam Veterans Against the War** to pursue more intense means to criticize the war effort.

PEOPLE'S ARMY OF VIETNAM (PAVN). The PAVN or North Vietnamese Army (Quân Đội Nhân Dân Việt Nam) was the main military organization used by the North Vietnamese in its war against the **Republic of Vietnam** (RVN). The organization was preceded by the Armed Propaganda Unit for National Liberation, organized in December 1944, which evolved into the Vietnam Liberation Army in May 1945. After the end of World War II, it was renamed the Vietnam National Defense Army, with **Võ Nguyên Giáp** as its first commander. Through its various iterations, the organization remained small, with only a few hundred soldiers. As the **First Indochina War** began, it grew to division-size strength. The Vietnamese were at a disadvantage against the French Union Forces in open warfare but achieved success in frustrating the French through ambush and guerrilla-style tactics. By 1954, with the Battle of **Điện Biên Phủ**, the Vietnamese Army of six divisions had transformed into an experienced fighting force that was more than a match for **France**'s troops.

The PAVN continued to support the insurgency in the South after the 1954 **Geneva Agreements** but did not actively participate in open conflict until the late 1950s, when the future of the insurgency was in question as a result of the success of the government of **Ngô Đình Diệm**. By the mid-1960s, the PAVN

356 • PEOPLE'S SELF-DEFENSE FORCES

had helped to develop the **Hồ Chí Minh Trail** from a series of footpaths and disconnected roads and waterways of the 1950s to one of the most sophisticated networks of trails, roadways, and waterways in Southeast Asia. PAVN forces used the Hồ Chí Minh Trail to infiltrate into the RVN in the 1960s to fight against the **Sài Gòn** government and its **United States** allies who escalated their commitment to a total of 543,000 troops by June 1969. While the PAVN fought few major engagements against the U.S. or the **Army of the Republic of Vietnam** after its first encounter at the Battle for the Ia Đrăng Valley in November 1965, it continually put pressure on the U.S. and South Vietnamese militaries and threatened the civilian population.

The major exceptions to this strategy were the 1968 **Tết Offensive** and the 1972 **Easter Offensive**, both of which ended in military defeat for the PAVN. PAVN forces also aided the **Pathet Lao** in **Laos** and the **Khmer Rouge** in **Cambodia** in their insurgencies to overthrow the two royal governments. The **Soviet Union** aided the PAVN in its military ventures in the RVN, Laos, and Cambodia by supplying the majority of its **tanks** and tracked vehicles, **artillery**, and air assets. The **People's Republic of China** and Eastern Bloc countries also supplied military hardware and munitions to fight the war. While the Vietnam War was never considered a conflict like World War II or Korea, it ended with a major, overt assault led by PAVN forces in 1975 that did not conclude until the fall of Sài Gòn on 30 April 1975.

PEOPLE'S SELF-DEFENSE FORCES (PSDF). When the **United States** introduced **Vietnamization** and the first group of U.S. soldiers was withdrawn without replacement in June 1969, the **Republic of Vietnam** (RVN) began the process of reorganizing the responsibilities for its armed forces. **Army of the Republic of Vietnam** soldiers assumed more of the burden of offensive operations with the support of **Regional Forces** and **Popular Forces**. Anticipating Vietnamization, and as a result of the 1968 **Tết Offensive**, which proved that no area was safe from the **People's Army of Vietnam** (PAVN) and the **National Liberation Front** (NLF), the RVN created the PSDF in the June 1968 General Mobilization Law. The PSDF took over the static role of village defense.

Any South Vietnamese males outside of the age recruited by the South Vietnamese Armed Forces were mandated to contribute to the PSDF, if able. Those too young or old or with some type of disability that prohibited active military service were expected to join another type of organization that supported the war effort. Training for members of the PSDF was limited, while the leadership cadre received a short, four-week training course. Eleven-person teams of the PSDF, with three teams equaling one section, conducted guerrilla-style operations, though they were discouraged from confronting the enemy when he held the advantage. The PSDF supplemented the armed forces, Regional Forces, and Popular Forces and had grown to more than 3.5 million by the end of 1970, though the combat branch of the organization numbered closer to one million.

While the PSDF was neither well trained nor well armed, it served a valuable purpose. In the words of Civilian Operations and Revolutionary Development Support director **William Colby**, the PSDF meant that the NLF could no longer enter a village without opposition. It served as the first line of defense for the people and provided them with a sense of hope where disillusionment had previously existed. Unfortunately, the PSDF was no match for the PAVN troops, as they invaded in 1972 and again in 1974–1975. *See also* PACIFICATION.

PHẠM HÙNG (1912–1988). Born Phạm Văn Thiện and also known as Bảy Cường, Phạm Hùng joined the Indochinese Communist Party in 1930 after being expelled from school for his radical activities two years earlier. In 1931, he was arrested by the French and was sentenced to death, but that decision was commuted. Phạm Hùng spent the next 14 years in jail, mostly at the prison on **Poulo Condore** (Côn Sơn) island. When **Hồ Chí Minh** proclaimed Vietnamese independence in September 1945, he was released from prison and returned to the **Việt Minh**. In 1946, he was selected as the secretary of the Nam Bộ Provisional Regional Committee and as a member of the **Lao Động** Party in 1951. In 1952, he became the deputy secretary of the **Central Office for South Vietnam** (COSVN).

After the 1954 **Geneva Agreements**, Phạm Hùng became the North Vietnamese representative to the **International Control Commission**. He joined the Politburo in 1956 and was made deputy prime minister in 1958. Phạm Hùng supported the position of **Lê Duẩn** and **Lê Đức Thọ** who called for a more intense conflict in the **Republic of Vietnam**. In 1967, he became the secretary of the COSVN, replacing **Nguyễn Chí Thanh** after he died, and the political commissar of the southern insurgency during the final offensive to end the war in 1975.

After the war, Phạm Hùng served as deputy prime minister in 1976, and in 1980 he became the minister of the interior. He remained influential in the Socialist Republic of Vietnam, eventually reaching the second highest position in the Politburo in December 1986. In 1987, he was replaced as the interior minister in a political shake-up, but in June he was named prime minister, replacing **Phạm Văn Đồng**. He remained prime minister until his death.

PHẠM NGỌC THẢO (1922–1965). Republic of Vietnam (RVN) provincial chief, **Army of the Republic of Vietnam** (ARVN) colonel, and communist spy. Born Phạm Ngọc Thuần, Phạm Ngọc Thảo grew up in the northern part of Indochina in a family that was anti-French, though his family was Catholic. While attending school in **Sài Gòn**, Phạm Ngọc Thảo became acquainted with members of the **Việt Minh**. At the end of World War II, Phạm Ngọc Thảo joined other Vietnamese intent upon overthrowing French colonialism. He fought in the **Mê Kông Delta** during the **First Indochina War**. After the 1954 **Geneva Agreements**, Phạm Ngọc Thảo helped to reorganize the remnants of the Việt Minh who did not relocate north of the 17th parallel. He remained in the south working with the local cadre in the event the RVN did not adhere to the national election scheduled to take place before July 1956.

He became a teacher and renounced communism in an attempt to put himself in a position of trust within the republic. When **Ngô Đình Diệm** announced that he would no longer adhere to the agreements because the RVN had not signed them and then initiated an anticommunist campaign to root out the insurgents who had stayed behind, Phạm Ngọc Thảo remained visible but used his Catholic background to avoid arrest. His friendship with Ngô Đình Diệm's brother, **Ngô Đình Thục**, who was also the bishop of Vĩnh Long, helped him gain entry into the Sài Gòn government's inner ranks. He worked for the National Bank in 1956, commanded the police in Vĩnh Long and Bình Dương provinces, and assisted in the activities of the **Cần Lao Party**.

Phạm Ngọc Thảo rose within the ranks of the ARVN by training the **Civil Guard**, and he even helped crush the abortive November 1960 coup d'état attempt against Ngô Đình Diệm. He eventually became the province chief of Kiến Hoa in 1962. In Kiến Hoa, Phạm Ngọc Thảo received praise for his work from the Sài Gòn government and the **United States**, even while he was active in recruiting for the **National Liberation Front** (NLF) and was working to create instability in the **Strategic Hamlet Program**. Phạm Ngọc Thảo was so successful in his duplicity that he was selected as a special inspector for the program in late 1962.

In 1963, Phạm Ngọc Thảo plotted with those disaffected by Ngô Đình Diệm to overthrow the RVN president, using the **Buddhist Crisis** and the success of the NLF in the countryside as justification. His actions helped to sow discontent within the Sài Gòn government and instability in the countryside. He was involved in the November 1963 coup d'état and assisted in the attack on the presidential palace on 2 November. After the coup d'état, Phạm Ngọc Thảo helped to organize the Council of Notables, a group of prominent Sài Gòn intellectuals. The group spent most of its time debating rather than offering any substantial suggestions for improving the RVN in the post–Ngô Đình Diệm era. When **Nguyễn Khánh** overthrew the military junta, Phạm Ngọc Thảo was made press officer.

Nguyễn Khánh sent him to Washington as the press attaché to **Trần Thiện Khiêm**, who served as the new ambassador to the U.S. He was recalled in December 1964 and went underground, fearing execution because of his anti–Nguyễn Khánh rhetoric. On 19 February, he attempted a failed coup d'état against Nguyễn Khánh. He was able to escape arrest and offered to surrender if he and other officers involved in the event were given amnesty. Instead, he was sentenced to death in absentia in May 1965. On 20 and 21 May, he was involved in another coup d'état attempt that failed before it even began when the plotters were arrested.

It was later reported that he died in July 1965, though the circumstances surrounding his death remained confused. One report had him dying in a **helicopter** crash, while **Nguyễn Cao Kỳ** reported that he had been jailed and beaten to death. Others suggested that it was **Nguyễn Văn Thiệu** who orchestrated the capture and execution. Phạm Ngọc Thảo was honored for his role in the ARVN during the war, he was promoted posthumously to the rank of general, and after the war he was also honored for his work for the NLF. He became a symbol of the extent to which the Vietnamese would go for independence and an example of how difficult it was for the U.S., and even the South Vietnamese, to identify the enemy.

PHẠM VĂN ĐỒNG (1906–2000). Phạm Văn Đồng was born in Quảng Ngãi province into a family of privilege. His father was a mandarin and worked as a private secretary to a Vietnamese emperor. He was educated at the Lycée Quốc Học, as were **Hồ Chí Minh** and **Ngô Đình Diệm**. His first foray into protest against French rule occurred during a 1925 student strike in **Hà Nội**, after which he was forced to flee to China to escape arrest by the French Sûreté. He soon joined the Vietnamese Revolutionary Youth Association and returned to Vietnam in 1929 to organize communist resistance cells in **Sài Gòn**. He was arrested by the French in 1930 and was imprisoned on **Poulo Condore** (Côn Sơn) island for seven years.

In 1939, Phạm Văn Đồng fled again to China after another strike failed. He joined Hồ Chí Minh and with him began the process of recruiting and training Vietnamese to fight the French. In 1941, Phạm Văn Đồng, along with Hồ Chí Minh, helped to create the **Việt Minh**. The two would establish the **Democratic Republic of Vietnam** (DRV) during the August 1945 revolution, toward the end of World War II. Phạm Văn Đồng served as the minister of finance while Hồ Chí Minh became its first president. Phạm Văn Đồng traveled with Hồ Chí Minh to Paris in 1946 to negotiate a peaceable end of the fighting between the Vietnamese and **France**, but they failed. Their return to Vietnam signaled the beginning of the **First Indochina War**.

After the Battle of Điện Biên Phủ, Phạm Văn Đồng headed the Vietnamese delegation to the May–July 1954 **Geneva Conference**, which led to the signing of the 1954 Geneva Agreements. Though Phạm Văn Đồng believed that the **People's Republic of China** had sacrificed Vietnam's interest for its own Cold War agenda, he did bring the potential for peace to Vietnam. In 1955, during the first National Conference in Hà Nội, Phạm Văn Đồng became the prime minister of the DRV. He was instrumental in the 1950s in transforming the DRV into a communist state as well as resisting attempts by the **Republic of Vietnam** or the **United States** to interfere in the North's communist revolution.

During the war, Phạm Văn Đồng never wavered from a strong position for the DRV, even against the continued escalation of the U.S. On 8 April 1965, he outlined the four conditions for the DRV to negotiate an end to the war with the South Vietnamese and Americans. He required independence for all Vietnamese, nonintervention in Vietnam by foreign powers, a political settlement of all issues, and reunification of the country. These four points remained fixed as the communists' nonnegotiable conditions for peace. This conviction would frustrate two U.S. presidents and a generation of Americans. He would also serve as prime minister of the Socialist Republic of Vietnam from 1976 to 1987. After his retirement from public life, Phạm Văn Đồng acted as an elder statesman and adviser to the government. He opposed Đổi Mới, though his influence within the Communist Party ebbed as he aged and suffered from illness. He died one day short of the 25th anniversary of the fall of Sài Gòn.

PHAN HUY QUÁT (1911–1979). Medical doctor and prime minister of the **Republic of Vietnam** (RVN). Phan Huy Quát was a leading member of the Nationalist Party of Greater Vietnam (Đại Việt Quốc Dân Đảng) and served first as minister of education to **Bảo Đại** and then as minister of defense to the emperor, during which time he oversaw the formation of the **Vietnamese National Army**. He was appointed prime minister of the RVN by the Armed Forces Council on 16 February 1965 under Head of State **Phan Khắc Sửu** after **Nguyễn Khánh** was deposed. Even though Phan Huy Quát oversaw the Americanization of the war, he was opposed to it. As a result of this resistance, both he and Phan Khắc Sửu resigned on 11 June 1965 rather than face the consequences, and they were replaced by **Nguyễn Văn Thiệu** and **Nguyễn Cao Kỳ**.

PHAN KHẮC SỬU (1893–1970). Member of the **Cao Đài** and head of state of the **Republic of Vietnam** (RVN). Phan Khắc Sửu was trained as an agricultural engineer and was involved in Vietnamese politics as a member of

Bảo Đại's government. He opposed **Ngô Đình Diệm** and was mentioned in **United States** embassy reports as a possible replacement for him if a successful coup d'état occurred in 1959. He was known to have the support of many **Buddhists** and the Cao Đài. Phan Khắc Sửu was a member of the group that penned the 26 April 1960 **Caravelle Manifesto**; as a result of his participation he was arrested, though he was later released.

On 5 November 1960, he was one of three national assemblymen who submitted three drafts concerning freedom and the status of the press to the National Assembly Inter-committee for Information, Justice, and Internal Affairs for consideration and debate, and he was again considered by some in **Sài Gòn** as a possible replacement for Ngô Đình Diệm during the failed 11 November 1960 coup d'état. As a result, Phan Khắc Sửu was under some form of arrest or in hiding until after the November 1963 assassination of Ngô Đình Diệm. He became the chairman of the Vietnamese High National Council on 26 September 1964 and then head of state of the RVN from 26 October 1964 until his voluntary resignation on 11 June 1965. His role in politics was diminished in his final years.

PHILIPPINES. The Philippines took a leading role in assisting the **Republic of Vietnam** (RVN) in both civilian and military projects. The first Filipinos arrived in Indochina to participate in a humanitarian mission known as Operation **Brotherhood**. Starting in 1953, this operation focused on providing aid, such as health services, to Vietnamese families. While Operation Brotherhood was largely a civilian operation, the Philippines government provided economic assistance to the RVN through the 1950s and 1960s. The first military presence arrived in August 1964 when 16 army officers joined **Military Assistance Command, Vietnam**, to help with psychological warfare and civil affairs. They followed a government-sponsored program that sent 34 medical personnel to the RVN as a result of action taken by the Philippines Congress. The success of the Filipino officers resulted in further requests by the Vietnamese for assistance.

The introduction of the Filipinos into the RVN corresponded with President **Lyndon B. Johnson**'s "**Show the Flag**" program, which was initiated in April 1964. When Philippine president Diosdada Macapagal visited the **United States** in late 1964, Johnson and Secretary of Defense **Robert Mc-Namara** requested an additional presence by the Philippines, including military personnel if possible. For his part, Macapagal bargained for additional aid under the Military Assistance Program to help better protect the Philippines from the growing threat of Sukarno's Indonesia. Thus the Philippines participating in the RVN became tied to American assistance to that country under the Military Assistance Program. While the U.S. desired an additional

Filipino presence in the RVN for political and diplomatic reasons, General **William C. Westmoreland** objected to a larger contingent because of logistical problems associated with different countries' needs and requirements.

After a series of meetings in late 1964 and early 1965 that defined the Filipino force for Vietnam, the two sides came to an agreement in which the U.S. would fund the force. The Filipinos focused on civil action missions rather than offensive operations. The recommendation was for a task force of approximately 2,500 infantry, engineers, and civic action personnel as well as a small number of navy and air force personnel. During the course of discussions, Ferdinand E. Marcos won election to the Philippines presidency. Though Marcos had opposed sending troops to the RVN, he modified this position in early 1965, but the final disposition of the task force included more engineers, medical workers, and civil action personnel than combat troops.

It was not until 18 June 1966 that Marcos signed a congressional bill that allowed for the dispatch of a 2,000-strong task force to Vietnam to work on civil action projects. While Marcos made it a point to stress the importance of the Philippines providing assistance to the RVN in order for that country to have a chance at independence, the U.S. did increase its Military Assistance Program funds and covered the expenses of the task force while in Vietnam. An advanced team, including Chief of Staff of the Armed Forces of the Philippines General Ernesto S. Mata, arrived in **Sài Gòn** on 20 July 1966 for three days. The meetings resulted in agreements signed between the Philippines and the U.S. and between the Philippines and the RVN. An advanced contingent of the Philippine Civil Action Group (PHILCAG) arrived on 28 July 1966, and the first large number of personnel arrived on 16 August. The PHILCAG was situated in **Tây Ninh** because of the low number of **National Liberation Front** (NLF) incidents in that area. By the end of September, PHILCAG had established its base camp, and most of its essential personnel had arrived in the RVN. The remainder of the group would arrive in October, bringing the total to 2,068.

PHILCAG began its civic action campaign in the Thanh Điền forest, building roads, clearing vegetation for farmers, and disposing of NLF **mines** and **booby traps**. While it had to overcome heavy rains and occasional sniper fire, PHILCAG was able to complete its mission. This occurred despite increased NLF armed attacks and a more intense **propaganda** effort to discredit the Filipinos. There was also increased opposition in the Philippines by individuals who believed that the money and resources expended in the RVN could be better used at home. Through 1967, the Philippines was concerned about replacing members of PHILCAG whose two-year tours were ending and about continuing to fund the force's involvement in civic action. Marcos found it more difficult to deflect criticism over Philippines involved in the

RVN, and the presence of Americans in the Philippines continued to serve as a lightning rod for **antiwar** sentiment and anti-American demonstrations. Toward the end of 1967, it became clear that the Philippines would need to reduce its presence in the RVN for financial reasons. Members of PHILCAG were no longer replaced upon departure, and the total number of personnel decreased to approximately 1,800 by July 1968.

Within the Philippines, the Nacionalista Party, which had consistently resisted any assistance other than humanitarian aid for the RVN, called for the replacement of the civic action group with medical personnel, while Marcos' party wanted the U.S. to pay the entire amount of PHILCAG or withdraw the unit from the RVN. The calls by the Philippines for greater American aid prompted a study on how effective the Filipino projects were to the South Vietnamese. The study concluded that the Philippines was making a positive contribution to the war effort but that the U.S. could probably provide the same services at reduced cost. However, the Philippines contribution, while effective and welcome, served a diplomatic purpose for the U.S. as it tried to garner the support of the Free World for the South Vietnamese cause and to demonstrate to the North Vietnamese and its allies that attempts at subversion in the South would be met by a united force.

On 14 November 1969, the Philippine government informed the U.S. embassy in Manila that it would begin to withdraw the PHILCAG. The majority of the unit redeployed back to the Philippines by the middle of December, while the remaining Filipino force exited Vietnam on 15 February 1970, after returning its equipment to the U.S. and finishing its remaining tasks. But the end of PHILCAG did not mean the end of Filipino participation in the RVN. A small force of approximately 130 remained under the Philippine Contingent, Vietnam. One half of this group was composed of medical personnel in the tradition of Operation Brotherhood, while the rest supported the medical mission.

PHILCAG provided the RVN with many successful projects, including the building of roads, bridges, and **refugee** centers. Filipino engineers cleared over 70 square kilometers (27 square miles) of land and helped to relocate over 1,000 families. Its major contribution was medical. It is estimated that the unit was involved in nearly 725,000 medical visits and almost 220,000 dental visits, and its doctors performed over 35,800 surgeries. More importantly, PHILCAG showed the RVN that it was not alone, and the Philippines helped to justify the U.S. effort as part of a larger Free World effort to help the South Vietnamese people in their struggle against the communists and toward a better way of life.

PHNOM PENH. Capital of **Cambodia** located on the confluence of the **Mê Kông** and Tonlé Sap rivers. The city escaped damage caused by the war with the **Khmer Rouge** in the 1960s. It was affected by the escalation of the war in Cambodia in 1970 when **refugees** fled to the city to escape the Khmer Rouge and the results of the incursion by **United States** and **Army of the Republic of Vietnam** forces. There were an estimated three million Cambodians in the capital at the war's end. After the war, the Khmer Rouge systemically cleared the city of its inhabitants, singling out for execution any individual who had been influenced by the West. The genocide in the city stretched throughout the country, with an estimated 1.7 to 3 million killed before the **Socialist Republic of Vietnam** invaded the country and took over the city in 1979.

PHOENIX PROGRAM. On 10 May 1967, the **Civil Operations and Revolutionary Development Support** (CORDS) group was established to coordinate the military and civilian **pacification** efforts in the **Republic of Vietnam**. CORDS created the Intelligence Coordination and Exploitation Program to manage the activities of civilian and military intelligence agencies that gathered information on **National Liberation Front** (NLF) personnel. It was renamed later in the year as the Phụng Hoàng program after the mythical Chinese bird who appeared before peace and prosperity. The closest approximation for the **United States** was the Egyptian bird the Phoenix.

The Phoenix Program's main purpose was to eliminate or neutralize the **Việt Cộng** Infrastructure (VCI), including the leaders and significant cadres of the NLF. This population was estimated at up to 100,000 in 1967 and had penetrated down to the village level. The program became controversial when the means by which it achieved its goals were publicized. The Phoenix Program gathered its information and indentified the VCI leadership through infiltration and then neutralized this force through kidnapping and assassination, though there were also attempts to encourage desertion through the **Chiêu Hồi** program. The program was designed to eliminate the leadership of the VCI in order to make the rest of the NLF ineffective. While the Phoenix Program operated under the same strategy and tactics as the communist insurgency in the late 1950s and the NLF in the 1960s, it was heavily criticized by opponents of the war.

These critics voiced outrage at the assassinations and also expressed concern about the seemingly indiscriminate use of firepower against the Vietnamese, the detention of civilians with less than probable cause, and the randomness of the incarceration of individuals. Ironically, the main purpose of the Phoenix Program was not to assassinate. It was more effective in turning NLF to the RVN or in capturing the enemy to gather further information about the VCI.

In 1971, **William Colby**, the director of CORDS, testified before **Congress** about the program. Colby claimed that 20,587 persons had been killed, though estimated numbers have been as high as 26,300, and 28,978 VCI leaders had been captured, of which 17,717 had accepted the benefits of the Chiêu Hồi program. When the **Democratic Republic of Vietnam** launched its 1972 **Easter Offensive**, resources designated to the Phoenix Program were reassigned in order to deal with the communist offensive.

The Phoenix Program continued to be controversial after the end of the U.S. presence in Southeast Asia. Critics of the program argued that it ultimately did not end the VCI threat or the ability of the VCI to operate in the countryside. They argued that the program instead discredited the American justifications for being in Southeast Asia and diminished the moral credibility of the U.S. William Colby, however, argued that the program, along with the other CORDS projects, was designed to deny the NLF entry into the villages, to create instability within the VCI, and to offer the people of the **Republic of Vietnam** the opportunity to work and live in a secure environment. *See also* CENTRAL INTELLIGENCE AGENCY; INTELLIGENCE; KOMER, ROBERT WILLIAM; TRỤ GIẢN.

PHONG SALY. Northernmost province in **Laos** and the scene of intense fighting between the **Pathet Lao** and forces loyal to the Royal Laotian Government. The province bordered the **People's Republic of China** to its north and west and the **Democratic Republic of Vietnam** (DRV) on its east. Phong Saly, which was heavily forested, was approximately 16,250 square kilometers (6,275 square miles). After the signing of the 1954 **Geneva Agreements**, the province served as the staging area for the Pathet Lao and was separated from the rest of the country. In 1958, it was reintegrated back into Laos, but the Pathet Lao completed their control over the region by 1961 with the capture of the provincial capital at Phong Saly. Because of the proximity of the province to China and the DRV, it remained in Pathet Lao hands for the remainder of the war.

PHOUMI NOSAVAN (1920–1985). Laotian general and political leader. Phoumi Nosavan served in the French colonial administration but also became a leader of the Lao Issara, which organized against French rule in Indochina and allied with the **Việt Minh**. In 1950, he joined the French-backed Lao National Army and became chief of staff of the Royal Lao Army in 1955. After the 4 May 1958 supplementary election in **Laos** in which the newly formed **Pathet Lao** political organization **Neo Lao Hak Xat** won 9 of the 21 seats contested, Phoumi Nosavan helped to organize and became the leader of the **Committee for the Defense of National Interests** (CDNI). On 25 December 1959, he and the CDNI carried out a bloodless coup d'état against Premier Phoui Sananikone. After the April 1960 national elections,

Phoumi Nosavan formed a new political party, the Paxa Sangkhom (Social Democrats), which eventually replaced the CDNI.

Phoumi Nosavan, supported by the **Central Intelligence Agency**, represented the right wing of the political spectrum in Laos. In August 1960, his government was overthrown by the neutralist **Kong Le**, who had received assistance from the **Soviet Union**. Phoumi Nosavan attempted to regain the capital of Vientiane in September 1960 but failed. A second attempt in December 1960 was successful. He served as the deputy premier and minister of defense of the Royal Laotian Government. When President **John F. Kennedy** entered the White House in January 1961, he pressured Phoumi Nosavan to join with **Souvanna Phouma** who had replaced Kong Le as the neutralist leader. When Phoumi Nosavan refused, the **United States** began to withdraw resources and assistance from him, and he allegedly turned to drug trafficking to recover the lost American aid.

In June 1962, Phoumi Nosavan finally agreed to merge with Souvanna Phouma and served as the deputy premier and minister of finance. In April 1964, his government was overthrown by a group of Laotian military generals, though he was retained as the vice premier. In February 1965, he tried to regain power but failed and was exiled to **Thailand**. After the Pathet Lao formed a coalition government in December 1975, Phoumi Nosavan helped the Kou Xat, an anticommunist organization, in its opposition against the Vientiane government. He established a government in exile from Bangkok, Thailand, but failed to gain any sustained legitimacy before his death.

PHÚ BÀI. Located in **Thừa Thiên** province south of **Huế** in I **Corps Tactical Zone** (CTZ), Phú Bài served as a base area for the **United States Marine Corps** (USMC). The first American personnel arrived in the city in 1964 to establish a listening outpost for **Democratic Republic of Vietnam** radio broadcasts. By the end of 1965, the USMC operated a **helicopter** squadron from the city, and a reinforced battalion conducted **Combined Action Platoon** missions in the area. In October 1966, Phú Bài became the headquarters of the 3rd Marine **Division**, and in February 1968 it served as the headquarters for U.S. personnel operating in I CTZ. Phú Bài was also the center for military operations during the 1968 **Tết Offensive**.

PIERCE ARROW, OPERATION. An operation conducted on 5 August 1964 in response to the alleged North Vietnamese attack on the U.S.S. *Maddox* (DD-731) and the U.S.S. *Turner Joy* (DD-951). The operation consisted of 64 **sorties**. Aircraft from the U.S.S. *Ticonderoga* (CV-14) attacked the North Vietnamese motor torpedo boat facilities at Quảng Khê and Phúc Lợi, which were believed to be the origin of the alleged 4 August attack, and the oil storage facility at Vinh. Meanwhile, aircraft from the U.S.S. *Constellation* (CV-64) attacked the motor torpedo boat facilities at Hòn Gay and Lộc Cháo. The operation was considered a success even though the North Vietnamese refused to heed the warning of the retaliatory attack and continued to mount pressure on the American forces in the **Republic of Vietnam**. During the operation, one pilot, Richard Sather, was killed, and another, Everett Alvarez, was shot down and captured. Alvarez became the first **United States Navy** prisoner of war and spent the next eight years in the **Democratic Republic of Vietnam**. *See also* GULF OF TǑN KǏN INCIDENT.

PIPE STEM, PROJECT. The **United States** used an October 1961 air show in **Sài Gòn** organized by the **Republic of Vietnam** to send four RF-101 aircraft to conduct air **reconnaissance** missions using sophisticated camera equipment that enabled aerial photography from as high as 15.2 kilometers (50,000 feet). The RF-101 was less vulnerable to **People's Army of Vietnam** and **National Liberation Front** air defenses than other aircraft used in air reconnaissance and proved itself a valuable tool. When the South Vietnamese canceled the air show, the four RF-101s remained in Sài Gòn and, under Project Pipe Stem, began photographing evidence of Soviet assistance to the **Pathet Lao** in northern **Laos**. The RF-101s left on 21 November, though the Project Pipe Stem personnel and equipment remained in Sài Gòn. *See also* INTELLIGENCE.

PIRANHA, OPERATION. A **search-and-destroy** operation conducted by a joint **United States Marine Corps, Republic of Vietnam** Marine Corps, and **Army of the Republic of Vietnam** (ARVN) force approximately 40 kilometers (25 miles) to the south of **Chu Lai** that began on 7 September 1965. The operation was designed to maximize the amphibious and **airmobility** advantage of the U.S. and South Vietnamese against the **National Liberation Front** (NLF), whose 1st Battalion was thought to be on the Batangan Peninsula. The 1st Battalion, 7th Marines made a beach landing on the northern part of the Batangan Peninsula and moved southward along the Chau Me Dong River, while the 3rd Vietnamese Marine Battalion moved up the An Ky Peninsula to the south of the marine landing and separated from the Batangan Peninsula by the Sa Ky River. As these units were put into place, the 3rd Battalion, 7th Marines and the 2nd Battalion, 4th ARVN Regiment were airlifted into blocking positions to the west and south. The three-day operation yielded few positive results, though an NLF field hospital was uncovered. The U.S. and ARVN forces claimed 178 killed but only 20 weapons captured. Two U.S. and five ARVN personnel were killed-in-action, while the U.S. suffered 14 wounded, and the ARVN 33.

PLAIN OF JARS. Located in the northern part of **Laos**, the Plain of Jars was a plateau situated to the northeast of the Laotian capital of Vientiane in an area known as the Xieng Khouang plain. Its name derived from a series of large, 2,000-year-old clay jars that littered the area. There are approximately 400 sites that contain these jars which range from 1 meter (3 feet) to 3 meters (10 feet) high, with some containing hundreds of artifacts.

During the war, there was continuous conflict across the Plain of Jars and centered around bases, known as **Lima Sites,** placed at the top of large rock outcroppings. During the dry season from November to April, the **Pathet Lao** and the **People's Army of Vietnam** (PAVN) used their numerical superiority to go on the offensive, while the Royal Laotian Army (RLA) relied on U.S. air **sorties** from Operation **Barrel Roll** to provide air-to-ground support for the defensively minded RLA. During the wet season from April to November, the RLA took advantage of the poor weather and impassible roads by utilizing U.S. aircraft for airlift and tactical air support to regain ground lost in the previous PAVN and Pathet Lao offensive. This ebb and flow of the battle meant continuous combat over the same terrain for nearly a decade.

While the U.S. was restricted in the targets it could strike in the Plain of Jars, it did increase air sorties in the area after 1969. The U.S. initiated Operation Raindance in March 1969, and on 17 February 1970 it began to use B-52 bombers to support the RLA under Operation Good Look. In the end, American support for the RLA before the U.S. withdrew from Southeast Asia was not enough, and the Plain of Jars was secured by the Pathet Lao before it brokered an agreement with the Vientiane government that resulted in a communist government in Laos in December 1975.

PLAIN OF REEDS. Known in the **Republic of Vietnam** as Đồng Tháp Mười, the Plain of Reeds was located west of **Sài Gòn** and covered most of the provinces of Kiện Tường, **Long An**, Đình Tường, and Hậu Nghĩa. It spread into **Cambodia** and was an area that was heavily and constantly contested by the **National Liberation Front**. It was prone to flooding during the monsoon season, which made **search-and-destroy** operations difficult, and the thick vegetation allowed for easy concealment.

PLEI KU. Capital city of a province of the same name located in the **Central Highlands** of the **Republic of Vietnam** (RVN). Plei Ku was inhabited by the **Montagnard** tribes known as the **Bahnar** and **Jarai**. The province, which included strategic **routes** 14 and 19, was significant to the war because of its centralized position in relation to Buôn Mê Thuột, **Kon Tum**, and **Cambodia**. Plei Ku represented the military center of the **United States** and RVN defense for the Central Highland. It was also known for the 7 February 1965 attack by

National Liberation Front personnel who penetrated Camp Holloway and killed nine Americans, wounded over 100 personnel, and destroyed 11 aircraft. This attack led to Operation **Flaming Dart** and Operation **Rolling Thunder**.

In addition to serving as a base for U.S. and RVN personnel, Plei Ku was also the home of an air base for the RVN Air Force (RVNAF) and **U.S. Air Force**. The airfield was built in 1962 and housed RVNAF A-1 aircraft under the 62nd Tactical Wing until the U.S. began to utilize it. Later the air base would serve as the headquarters for the RVNAF 6th Air Division, which included both fixed-winged and **helicopter** aircraft. In 1965, the U.S. expanded the runway and stationed a number of units there until the American withdrawal in the 1970s. American units included the 6th Air Commando Squadron from February 1968 to November 1969, the 9th Air Commando Squadron from January 1967 to October 1969, and the 362nd Tactical Electronic Warfare Squadron for a brief time during the 1972 **Easter Offensive**. In 1975, RVN president **Nguyễn Văn Thiệu** ordered the evacuation of Plei Ku because he believed it to be indefensible. This resulted in the abandonment of the Central Highlands and the loss of I **Corps Tactical Zone** with little resistance.

POCKET MONEY, OPERATION. When the **Democratic Republic of Vietnam** (DRV) launched its 1972 **Easter Offensive**, President **Richard M. Nixon** authorized the mining of **Hải Phòng** harbor as well as other DRV ports in order to cut off sea resupply. The operation, known as Pocket Money, began on 9 May 1972 and was part of the larger air campaign known as Operation **Linebacker I**. Three A-6A and six A-7E aircraft took off from the U.S.S. *Coral Sea* in the morning and dropped 36 Mark-52 naval **mines** in Hải Phòng harbor. The mines were equipped with a delay fuse of 72 hours so that neutral ships would have an opportunity to leave the DRV without risk of destruction. There were 36 ships in Hải Phòng harbor when Nixon announced the mining operation. Nine of the ships departed, but the other 27 remained until after the signing of the January 1973 **Paris Peace Accords**.

On 11 May, naval mines were dropped on other DRV ports as well as on the approaches to Hải Phòng harbor in what was once known as Henrietta Pass. The operation lasted for nearly eight months and deployed 108 Mark-52 and over 11,000 Mark-36 mines. Operation Pocket Money proved to be very successful in prohibiting DRV resupply by sea and was a factor in forcing the DRV to abandon the Easter Offensive by the summer of 1972. With the signing of the January 1973 Paris Peace Accords, Operation Pocket Money ended, and Operation **Endsweep**, the clearing of the naval mines, commenced.

POL POT (1928–1998). Born Saloth Sar, but better known as Pol Pot after April 1975, he led the **Khmer Rouge** during the war and served as the prime minister of **Cambodia** during the genocide that claimed between 1.7 and 3 million lives. Pol Pot became interested in communist ideology while studying in **France** after the French Communist Party began to advocate for Vietnamese independence along with its support for the **Việt Minh** during the **First Indochina War**. He joined the French Communist Party before his return to Cambodia in January 1954, having failed to successfully complete his studies. He worked with various groups who were resisting the French, and after the 1954 **Geneva Agreements**, he tried to link the political parties sympathetic to the left with Cambodia's emerging communist party. He was not very active during the late 1950s, but when the leader of the Pracheachon—the political party to which Pol Pot was attached—was arrested and executed in early 1962, he took over the leadership of the organization. The next year, he fled to Vietnam to escape imprisonment after his name appeared on a police list for questioning. As the Vietnam War escalated, Pol Pot worked toward making the Cambodian communist insurgency more effective and meaningful. He traveled to **Hà Nội** and gained support for his organization, which would become known as the Khmer Rouge, and worked against Prince **Norodom Sihanouk**, recruiting peasants in the countryside and intellectuals in the cities. As Sihanouk aligned Cambodia closer to the **Democratic Republic of Vietnam** while maintaining a public image of neutrality, Pol Pot worked to undermine the Cambodian government, often without North Vietnamese approval.

By 1968, the Khmer Rouge was an established and dangerous organization, and Pol Pot was the undisputed leader. He continued to rally the Cambodian people to his cause with anti-Sihanouk **propaganda** but also targeted the **United States** and its support for pro-government and right-wing organizations. When Prime Minister **Lon Nol** orchestrated a coup d'état that removed Sihanouk from power in March 1970, Pol Pot led the most powerful organization on the left. Sihanouk, who had been out of the country, was forced into allying himself with the Khmer Rouge to regain power. This provided credibility to Pol Pot while the North Vietnamese moved to cement their alliance with the Khmer Rouge against a new Cambodian government that was anticommunist.

Pol Pot used **People's Army of Vietnam** (PAVN) and **National Liberation Front** forces to fight the Cambodian government but was always wary of their intentions when the Vietnam War ended. He accepted aid but also issued statements that were decidedly anti-DRV. This duplicity did not go unnoticed, but the DRV's focus was on **Sài Gòn**, and support for the Khmer Rouge against **Phnom Penh** added to the instability in the region, which benefited the DRV.

After the 1973 **Paris Peace Agreements**, there were few PAVN units in Cambodia, and the Khmer Rouge had control of a large part of the country.

Pol Pot authorized the beginning of a land reform program and issued anti-Western decrees that would become the hallmark of Khmer Rouge rule during the genocide that lasted from 1975 to 1979. The Khmer Rouge continued to battle the Cambodian Royal Army, isolating Phnom Penh toward the end of 1973, and consolidated control in the countryside where it began to purge the educated from military and civilian leadership. As the war continued into 1974, Pol Pot removed individuals from the Khmer Rouge who might oppose his policies when the conflict was over. By this time, Pol Pot was committed to a complete social and economic revolution in Cambodia more extreme than that envisioned in Vietnam.

Phnom Penh was overrun in April 1975, and the remnants of the Lon Nol government surrendered on 17 April. Pol Pot worked toward creating a new government that focused on a return to agrarian practice. The monarchy was abolished on 5 January 1976 with the passage of a new constitution that elected Pol Pot as the head of government, and Cambodia was renamed the Democratic Republic of Kampuchea. With his political legitimacy established, Pol Pot began the genocide that targeted intellectuals, including all those who supported or had experienced Western ideas, were educated, or were ethnic minorities. Anyone who would not, or could not, contribute to the new agrarian state was eliminated in the Killing Fields outside the major cities.

While Pol Pot orchestrated the genocide, he also intensified the ongoing conflict between Cambodia and Vietnam. Border raids and retaliatory attacks between the two countries culminated in the December 1978 Vietnam invasion into Kampuchea which overthrew the Khmer Rouge and forced Pol Pot to flee to **Thailand** where he continued to exercise his leadership over the Khmer Rouge. In 1985, he was forced into exile in Thailand when the Vietnamese initiated an offensive into Khmer Rouge territory. He stayed in Thailand, only moving to the **People's Republic of China** in 1986 to receive medical treatment for cancer. He returned to Thailand in 1988, and when the Vietnamese left Cambodia in 1989, he returned to his home where he rallied the Khmer Rouge and disrupted attempts to broker peace for the country and the region. In 1995, Pol Pot suffered a severe stroke that paralyzed the left side of his body. With his health failing, he oversaw the dissolution of the Khmer Rouge as soldiers began to desert. He died on 15 April 1998, just before it was announced that he would be turned over to an international tribunal to make him account for his crimes during the genocide.

POPEYE, PROJECT. Project designed to create favorable conditions for an early and prolonged monsoon season in order to hamper North Vietnamese use of the **Hồ Chí Minh Trail** in **Laos**. Project Popeye sought to seed clouds over Laos to increase the likelihood of intense and prolonged rain. On

1 September 1966, the **Joint Chiefs of Staff** authorized the project over the Se Kong watershed. The project began on 29 September and lasted until 28 October. The **United States Air Force** monitored the progress of the project and tested the affected air. Eighty-five percent of the 56-case sample showed positive results, though the project failed to stop the flow of personnel and supplies down the trail. Project Popeye was one of many attempts to influence the weather, though none achieved the success desired by the U.S. *See also* CLIMATE, SOUTHEAST ASIA.

POPULAR FORCES. The Popular Forces was a group of militia that served as the first line of defense for South Vietnamese villages against **People's Army of Vietnam** (PAVN) and **National Liberation Front** incursion. The Popular Forces originated from the **Civil Guard** and **Self-Defense Corps** created during the **Ngô Đình Diệm** period. In 1964, Popular Forces were absorbed into the **Army of the Republic of Vietnam** (ARVN), where they were considered by ARVN soldiers to be more of a liability than an ally against a common enemy. Though Popular Forces were less trained and were equipped with poorer-quality weapons, they did retain a spirit of defense when protecting their own homes. After 1965, when **United States** and ARVN troops engaged in **search-and-destroy** missions away from the Popular Forces villages, the militias performed poorly.

The Popular Forces needed better training and equipment than what the ARVN or U.S. provided. With **Vietnamization**, the Popular Forces returned to joint operations with the ARVN and left village defense to the People's Self-Defense Forces. This allowed it to regain some of its initial value. Popular Forces became better equipped through Vietnamization, and the U.S. created mobile advisory teams to assist in the training of the Popular Forces. The units became much more effective and actually began to conduct offensive operations of their own in addition to providing most of the Vietnamese contributions toward **pacification**. **Regional Forces** and Popular Forces suffered a casualty rate that was almost double that of the ARVN between the 1968 **Tết Offensive** and the 1972 **Easter Offensive**, though neither was a match for the final PAVN attacks that ultimately overwhelmed the country in 1975. *See also* COMBINED ACTION PLATOON.

POULO CONDORE (CÔN SƠN). A 10-mile-long island in the Côn Đảo archipelago, located approximately 80 kilometers (50 miles) to the southeast of the entrance to the **Mê Kông River** in IV **Corps Tactical Zone**. The island, referred to by the Vietnamese as Côn Sơn island, was best known for its housing of a prison during the war, though the facility was established in the mid-19th century. The prison held many communist leaders at some point in their early careers as resisters to French colonial rule. After the 1954 **Geneva Agreements**, the **Sài Gòn** government took over the facility and continued to use it as a prison. Rumors of torture, sometimes leading to death, were often heard during the 1960s, but it was not until a July 1970 visit by two **congressmen** and three other Americans that the rumors were confirmed as truth. The Côn Sơn prison used **tiger cages**, where prisoners were shackled within a restrictive space and denied basic necessities, and various forms of torture to extract confessions and gather **intelligence**. The treatment of the prisoners on Côn Sơn island, coupled with revelations of such events as the **Mỹ Lai** massacre, helped to justify the **antiwar movement**'s contention that the U.S. was involved in an immoral war. *See also* PRISONERS OF WAR.

PRAIRIE FIRE. The **Studies and Observation Group**, which had been conducting missions in **Laos** under Operation **Shining Brass**, renamed this activity when the mission name was compromised. Under the new name, Prairie Fire, the operation began in 1967 and was combined with Operation **Daniel Boone**, a similar type of mission in **Cambodia**. Prairie Fire missions involved American personnel teamed with **Montagnard** or **Nùng** who provided reconnaissance along the **Hồ Chí Minh Trail**. When these small reconnaissance teams located **People's Army of Vietnam**, **National Liberation Front**, or **Pathet Lao** forces, they sometimes called in **hatchet teams** to confront them. Prairie Fire missions were conducted in secret, without the knowledge of the Vientiane government, which led to a confrontation between the **Military Assistance Command, Vietnam**, commander **William C. Westmoreland** and the **United States** ambassador to Laos, **William Sullivan**. In 1971, U.S. personnel involved in Prairie Fire stopped operations into Laos, and the missions were taken over by the **Republic of Vietnam** in Operation Phù Đổng.

PRISONERS OF WAR (POW). Term used for individuals who were captured during the war. The status and rights of POWs were protected under the 1949 Geneva Convention. During the war in Southeast Asia, the treatment of POWs sometimes violated the convention agreements. All sides to the conflict tortured or killed POWs and often abused their rights in order to extract information.

People's Army of Vietnam and National Liberation Front troops captured by the **United States** or **Third Country** forces were handed over to the **Republic of Vietnam** (RVN). The most famous prison in the RVN was the one located on **Poulo Condore** (Côn Sơn) island. It was used first by the French to imprison members of the **Việt Minh** or other Vietnamese nationalists. During the Vietnam War, the prison facility became a source of controversy when it became public knowledge that prisoners were being kept in **tiger cages**. The **Democratic Republic of Vietnam** (DRV) had several prisons, the most famous of which was the Hỏa Lò facility in **Hà Nội**, known as the "Hanoi Hilton." It had also served as a French prison before 1954.

As a result of the 27 January 1973 **Paris Peace Accords**, POWs were to be released within 60 days. Under Operation Homecoming, the U.S. received 591 POWs from the DRV, most of whom had been shot down as a result of the **air war**. The longest-held U.S. prisoner, Everett Alvarez Jr., was shot down on 5 August 1964 during Operation **Pierce Arrow**. He spent more than eight years in prison. The RVN released approximately 27,000 POWs, while the DRV returned over 5,300 from its prison, though these numbers vary by sources. The Vietnamese exchange extended beyond the 60-day period as stipulated in the Paris Peace Accords.

The POW issue was controversial after the war as there were approximately 1,350 American POW or **missing-in-action** (MIA) and 1,200 U.S. personnel killed-in-action for which the bodies had not been recovered and still needed to be accounted for. Accusations that the Socialist Republic of Vietnam (SRV) had held back prisoners as well as poor relations between the SRV and the West kept the issue at the forefront in the U.S. Such organizations as the National League of Families of American Prisoners and Missing in Southeast Asia helped to publicize the POW issue during and after the war, while the National Alliance of Families for the Return of America's Missing Servicemen and such government organizations as the Joint Task Force–Full Accounting and Joint POW/MIA Accounting Command worked to recover Americans who remained missing. *See also* CASUALTIES.

PROPAGANDA. Both sides of the war engaged in a propaganda war to win people over to their side. For the **Democratic Republic of Vietnam** (DRV), propaganda efforts were directed toward its own people, the people within the **Republic of Vietnam** (RVN), the **United States**, and the international community. The DRV maintained a steady stream of propaganda for its own people to continue the fight against the RVN and the U.S. This became critical as more and more North Vietnamese left to fight in the South and the casualties of war mounted. After March 1965, when the U.S. initiated Operation **Rolling Thunder**, propaganda served to embolden the people against the air war. Images of antiaircraft artillery units defending the DRV were issued at frequent intervals with captions that suggested a much greater loss of American aircraft and pilots than had actually occurred. Individuals in the DRV were also recognized for acts of heroism or sacrifice to the socialist cause.

The DRV also flooded the RVN with propaganda that focused on what it labeled the corrupt and authoritarian government of **Ngô Đình Diệm** and, after the coup d'état, the military regimes and the presidency of Nguyễn Văn Thiệu. This propaganda effort was directed toward the objective of an uprising against the Sài Gòn government. Within the U.S., the DRV directed a propaganda campaign to reinforce the antiwar movement and often provided the words and statistics used by that movement in their efforts to end the American war in Vietnam, while the DRV also directed propaganda to the international community to drive a wedge between it and the U.S. and to call into question the American commitment to developing a free and independent Vietnam. These efforts were often well received, in part because of the effectiveness of the propaganda and the willingness of individuals within the American and international **media** to accept and disseminate it.

The RVN also engaged in a propaganda effort, though it paled in comparison to the efforts of the DRV and the **National Liberation Front** (NLF). The RVN focused on justifying its actions during the war, exposing the brutality of **People's Army of Vietnam** (PAVN) and NLF activity, and winning over those individuals in the RVN who had not taken a position. The RVN was hampered in its propaganda campaign by accusations that it was no more than an American puppet, which resulted in a major portion of its efforts being used to counter DRV and NLF propaganda. In the war for winning the hearts and minds of the Vietnamese people, the DRV held the initiative, which forced the RVN to respond to its accusations rather than focusing on issues it held to be significant.

The U.S. engaged in propaganda at many different levels during the war. Like the DRV, it directed its efforts internally, within Southeast Asia, and internationally. At home, the U.S. used propaganda to rally the nation for war against the DRV and NLF while it countered antiwar activists who offered an alternative, and sometimes effective, argument against the war. As the war progressed, these efforts were not helped by the development of a **credibility gap** that emerged as official accounts of actions in Vietnam were questioned by the media.

In Vietnam, the U.S. directed efforts toward shoring up the South Vietnamese people's support for the Sài Gòn government, which was often countered by DRV and NLF propaganda or RVN action, and worked toward turning PAVN and NLF personnel against the DRV. Propaganda was effective in gaining individuals who defected (**Hồi Chánh**) under the Open Arms (**Chiêu Hồi**) program. The U.S. worked to win the hearts and minds of the South Vietnamese people through propaganda, but also through action with **pacification** programs and other forms of humanitarian assistance.

Internationally, the U.S. worked to counter DRV claims that its actions were imperialist. The U.S. garnered **Third Country** support for its efforts to defend the RVN in order to show the international community that the U.S. had no intention of replacing **France** as a colonial power in Vietnam. The

U.S. also developed propaganda that showed how the DRV had invaded the RVN and committed acts of brutality.

The propaganda battle during the war was as contested as the ground war and as intense as the air war. In the end, the DRV proved to be more effective in its propaganda as it projected criticism and forced the U.S. and RVN to respond to its accusations, thus giving it the initiative in this phase of the conflict. It was much easier to point out the appearance of inconsistency than to explain the complexities of the war to the Vietnamese, the Americans, and the international community.

PROTECTIVE REACTION STRIKES. On 1 November 1968, President **Lyndon B. Johnson** ended Operation **Rolling Thunder** after three and a half years of sustained **bombing** of the **Democratic Republic of Vietnam** (DRV). The **United States** did not resume bombing the DRV in an organized air campaign until Operation **Proud Deep Alpha** in December 1971 on a limited scale and Operations **Freedom Train** and **Linebacker I** in response to the 1972 **Easter Offensive**. Between November 1968 and December 1971, the U.S. continued to send **reconnaissance** aircraft over the DRV. These aircraft were to avoid combat but could fire on targets in the DRV if they were fired upon or tracked by enemy radar in an aggressive manner. If either of these events occurred, the U.S. aircraft were allowed to conduct protective reaction strikes. At first, the number of protective reaction strikes was limited, but it increased from 1970 and 1971.

When General **John Lavelle** assumed command of the **7th Air Force** in July 1971, he liberally interpreted the rules of engagement that allowed for protective reaction strikes, which eventually led to his forced resignation in April 1972 after it was learned that he had allowed pilots to falsify aggressive enemy action in order to carry out protective reaction strikes. The need for protective reaction strikes ended with Operation Proud Deep Alpha. In 2007, documents that were declassified revealed that Lavelle, rather than acting as a maverick, had been ordered by President **Richard M. Nixon** to conduct the air strikes.

PROUD DEEP ALPHA. From 26 December to 30 December 1971, the **United States Air Force** conducted a preemptive strike against war material stockpiled by the North Vietnamese near the **Demilitarized Zone** in preparation for their 1972 offensive. Code-named Proud Deep Alpha, the 1,000-sortie operation targeted the area south of the 20th parallel but was not as effective as planned due to poor weather conditions.

PROVISIONAL REVOLUTIONARY GOVERNMENT OF THE RE-PUBLIC OF SOUTH VIETNAM (PRG). Established in 1969, the PRG served as a shadow of the **Republic of Vietnam**'s (RVN) government. It was needed, in part, due to the significant military defeat of the **National Liberation Front** (NLF) during the 1968 **Tết Offensive**. The PRG was made up primarily of representatives from the NLF, though it did have support from outside of that organization. The PRG became the political organization for the NLF and was recognized as the legitimate government of the RVN by communist states around the world. It was also recognized as a legitimate government by many Third World countries that had remained neutral in the Cold War.

On 8 June 1969, representatives from the NLF; the People's Revolutionary Party; the Alliance of National, Democratic, and Peace Forces; and others established the PRG. **Huỳnh Tấn Phát** became the first chairman of the PRG with five vice chairmen serving concurrently under him. **Nguyễn Thị Bình** became the minister of foreign affairs and would negotiate for the PRG at the Paris Peace Conference, which led to the 1973 **Paris Peace Accords**. **Trần Nam Trung** served as the minister of defense.

The PRG was situated in **Tây Ninh** province, near the Cambodian border, though it was displaced during the 1970 **Cambodian Incursion**. It reestablished itself in the region and in 1972 was involved in the southern prong of the **Easter Offensive** that focused on An Lộc with the objective of inciting the Vietnamese people to rise up against the **Sài Gòn** government. When this failed, the PRG waited until the signing of the 1973 Paris Peace Accords, of which it was a signatory, before reasserting its influence throughout the Republic of Vietnam. When Sài Gòn fell on 30 April 1975, the PRG took over control of the South. The PRG led the South in its reunification with the North and the formation of the Socialist Republic of Vietnam on 2 July 1976.

Q

QUẢNG NAM. A province located in the middle of I **Corps Tactical Zone**, with borders on **Laos** and the South China Sea. Quảng Nam was home to the **United States Marine Corps** (USMC) headquarters. In French Indochina, Quảng Nam originally included the area recognized in the **Republic of Vietnam** as Quảng Tín province. The **Democratic Republic of Vietnam** continued to recognize the larger province of Quảng Nam, as it was identified by the French, during the war. The province, which linked **Route** 1 between **Thừa Thiên** province toward the **Demilitarized Zone** and Quảng Tín in the direction of **Sài Gòn**, was the scene of several significant events during the war, including the introduction of the first USMC combat troops to **Đà Nẵng** on 8 March 1965.

The province was contested throughout the war, with heavy fighting after 1965, and included the infamous **Arizona Territory** located to the southwest of Đà Nẵng. During the 1968 **Tết Offensive**, Quảng Nam was the scene of early attacks by the **National Liberation Front**. There were several major operations in Quảng Nam, including **Blue Marlin** and **Harvest Moon**. Quảng Nam was also the home to a major air base near Đà Nẵng. In addition to Đà Nẵng, other important locations included **Chu Lai** and the **Quế Sơn Valley**.

QUẢNG TRỊ. A province in the **Republic of Vietnam** that bordered the **Demilitarized Zone** to the north, **Thừa Thiên** province to the south, **Laos** to the west, and the South China Sea to the east. During the period of French colonization, Quảng Trị was a part of Annam. After the 1954 **Geneva Agreements**, Quảng Trị became the RVN's northernmost province, with its capital at Quảng Trị City. The province was part of the **People's Army of Vietnam**'s (PAVN) **Front** B4 after April 1966. The province had two strategic routes. The first, **Route** 1, was the major north–south road in the RVN, while Route 9 was the major east–west road that linked Route 1 at **Đông Hà** to Laos and along which the **United States** established a series of firebases to withstand an expected PAVN attack. These bases included Camp Carroll, Cam Lộ, the **Rockpile**, and **Khe Sanh**. Quảng Trị was one of the most strategic areas for the RVN during the war.

Quảng Trị saw intense fighting during the war, including the 1968 **Tết Offensive** and the 1972 **Easter Offensive**. Much of the American attention during the 1968 Tết Offensive was centered on the **U.S. Marine Corps** (USMC) firebase at Khe Sanh, which was besieged. During the Easter Offensive, Quảng Trị City was destroyed in an **Army of the Republic of Vietnam** counterattack that regained control of the capital after it had earlier been abandoned. The province was also the scene of several major military actions, including such operations as Operation **Starlite** from 18 August to 24 August 1965, which was the first USMC **search-and-destroy** operation of the war; Operation Hastings from 16 July to 30 July 1966, during which time the Sông Ngàn Valley earned the nickname **Helicopter Valley**; and the search-and-destroy Operation **Apache Snow** from 10 May and 7 June 1969. The province finally succumbed to the PAVN during the final 1975 campaign that ended with the fall of **Sài Gòn**.

QUÉ SƠN VALLEY. Also known as the Núi Lộc Sơn, the name of the dominant mountain in the area, the Quế Sơn Valley was situated between **Quảng Nam** and Quảng Tín provinces in the southernmost part of I **Corps Tactical Zone**. The area was heavily populated and was a food-producing region. It was contested by the **People's Army of Vietnam** (PAVN), which included the arrival of the 2nd PAVN Division in 1967. The **United States** and the **Army of the Republic of Vietnam** (ARVN) conducted a number of operations to clear the area, including Operation **Harvest Moon** in December 1965 and Beaver Cage and Union I and II in 1967. The U.S. and the ARVN wanted to eliminate the enemy from the region to deny them food supplies and the opportunity to recruit, but the enemy remained elusive and the valley was contested for most of the war.

QUI NHƠN. Located on the coast in **Bình Định** province in II **Corps Tactical Zone** (CTZ), Qui Nhơn was the capital of the province and served as the logistical center for the **United States** Armed Forces in the northern part of II CTZ. It was the eastern terminus of **Route** 19 which cut across the provinces of Bình Định and **Plei Ku** to **Laos**. Qui Nhơn was also the headquarters for the Republic of Korea's Capital Division (Tiger Division) when it arrived in the **Republic of Vietnam** between September and November 1965. The **coast guard** operated out of Qui Nhơn as part of Task Force 115, the Coastal Surveillance Force, and the city was home to the headquarters of the Patrol Craft Force.

On 10 February 1965, the **National Liberation Front** attacked an American billet in Qui Nhơn, killing 23 and wounding 21, which resulted in a second round of **sorties** in Operation **Flaming Dart** and justified the sustained

bombing campaign of the **Democratic Republic of Vietnam** with Operation **Rolling Thunder**.

QUICK REACTION FORCE. B-52 Stratofortresses employed in **Arc Light** missions were located at Andersen Air Force Base on **Guam** and took nearly six hours to reach targets in Southeast Asia. This meant that 24 hours passed between the time a target was identified and when it was struck, which often resulted in lost opportunities. To cut down the turnaround time, the **United States Air Force** created a Quick Reaction Force, which placed B-52s and **aerial refueling** KC-135 aircraft on standby alert status. This cut down the turnaround time to an average of nine hours. *See also* AIRCRAFT (BOMBERS), UNITED STATES.

QUỲNH LƯU UPRISING. Between 2 and 14 November 1956, residents in the **Democratic Republic of Vietnam**'s (DRV) Nghệ An province revolted against the **Hà Nội** government's land redistribution policy. Those involved in the revolt, which centered in the Quỳnh Lưu district of the province, were mostly Catholics who had been denied an opportunity to participate in Operation Exodus after the 1954 **Geneva Agreements**, which saw the movement of over 810,000 people from the North to the South. The people here had been discriminated against because of their opposition to the communist reforms, and they revolted against the local communist officials in the district. The uprising was crushed before it had a chance to gain momentum and served as a precedent for the people of the DRV who were critical of **Hồ Chí Minh**'s policies. It became clear that opposition to social and economic transformation in the DRV would not be tolerated, and those opposed to it would be severely punished. There would be few attempts to resist the Hà Nội government after this incident.

R

RA GLAI. Also known as the Rai, Trong Giai, or La Vang, the Ra Glai were a **Montagnard** group who spoke a dialect within the Malayo-Polynesian language. The group lived primarily to the west of **Nha Trang** and to the south of **Đà Lạt**. The Ra Glai opposed the practices of the Vietnamese communists and supported efforts by both **France** and the **United States** to defend the **Republic of Vietnam**.

RABORN, WILLIAM FRANCIS (1905–1990). Vice admiral in the **United States Navy** and director of the **Central Intelligence Agency** (CIA). Raborn was born in Texas and educated at the U.S. Naval Academy, graduating in 1928. He spent over 35 years in the navy serving in a variety of positions, such as the executive officer for the aircraft carrier U.S.S. *Hancock* during World War II. After the war, he commanded the aircraft carriers U.S.S. *Bairoko* and U.S.S. *Bennington*. On 8 November 1955, with the rank of rear admiral, he became the director of special projects at the Bureau of Weapons with the mission of developing submarine-launched ballistic missile technology. In 1960, he was appointed vice admiral for his successful work in this position.

In 1962, Raborn became deputy chief of naval operations for development. He retired from the navy in 1963 and became a vice president of the Aerojet-General Corporation. On 28 April 1965, Raborn became the director of the CIA, replacing **John McCone**. He was an advocate of expanding the air war but also supported the carrot-and-stick approach of **bombing pauses** to encourage the **Democratic Republic of Vietnam** to agree to negotiations. He resigned from office on 30 June 1966 with a mixed record and was succeeded by **Richard Helms**. He returned to Aerojet-General Corporation and in 1970 became head of the W. F. Raborn Company in Virginia.

RALLY OF THE LAO PEOPLE (RLP). A conservative political party formed after the 4 May 1958 supplementary election in **Laos** in which the **Neo Lao Hak Xat**, the newly formed **Pathet Lao** political organization, won 9 of the 21 seats contested. Leaders in the Nationalist and Independent parties agreed to merge into one party, the RLP (Lao Hom Lao), to confront the left-wing threat that the Pathet Lao now offered. The RLP held a majority of the seats in the National Assembly, 36 of 59, and elected **Souvanna Phouma** as president. The RLP's central tenet was to organize the Laotian people against political ideologies that threatened the very existence of Laotian culture and society. Because the group was conservative, this threat actually emanated from the left and the Neo Lao Hak Xat. The RLP was often in conflict with the other conservative organization in Laos, the **Committee for the Defense of National Interests** (CDNI). The CDNI received the political support of the **United States** and the financial support of the **Central Intelligence Agency**.

The RLP called for a reduction of the Laotian military and lessening ties with the U.S. The CDNI dominated the April 1960 elections, which many believed should have been won by the RLP if they had been fairly conducted. Souvanna Phouma's organization of the Neutralist Party (Lao Pen Kang) sapped the energy of the RLP, though it did win eight seats in the 18 July 1965 election, the third most behind the Neutralists and the Social Democrats, the newer version of the CDNI. The infighting between the CDNI and the RLP was frustrating for the U.S. which continually tried to unite the two anticommunist groups to fight against the Pathet Lao and the North Vietnamese who used Laos in their war against the **Republic of Vietnam**.

RANCH HAND, OPERATION. An air campaign with the objective of spraying herbicides in Southeast Asia in order to deny the enemy the advantages of the dense and plentiful foliage. Operation Ranch Hand had two main objectives: to clear the jungle and vegetation area used by the **People's Army of Vietnam** (PAVN) and the **National Liberation Front** (NLF), thus denying them coverage, and the destruction of potential food sources. Strategically, Ranch Hand had the potential for taking the advantage of the jungle away from the PAVN and NLF, especially when **topography** was used by the enemy to great effect. PAVN and NLF troops often hid under a double and triple canopy, which made reconnaissance nearly impossible. They also used the jungle coverage for ambushes.

Ranch Hand also had the advantage of destroying the food crops of the NLF. Herbicides were first considered in July 1961 to destroy the vegetation near major highways and roads. After a series of tests later in the year to determine the type of herbicide to use and the method of delivery, Ranch Hand missions began. The first was on 12 January along **Route** 15 to the northwest of **Sài Gòn**. The next year, the mission area was expanded to include areas that had been under NLF control, such as the **Cà Mau** Peninsula. Under the command of the 315th Air Commando Wing, **sorties** increased during the **Lyndon B. Johnson** administration to include areas of the **Hồ Chí Minh Trail** that flowed into the **Republic of Vietnam**.

While the **United States** tested several different types of herbicides, the three most deployed were agents Orange, Blue, and White. Ranch Hand sorties continued until 1971, though they peaked in 1967 when over 1.5 million acres were sprayed with herbicides. Between 12 January 1962 and 7 January 1971, Operation Ranch Hand sprayed over 19 million gallons of herbicides. The results were striking, though most areas required multiple applications. The U.S. also experimented with herbicides in operations such as **Sherwood Forest**, which attempted to use herbicides to kill vegetation and then ignite it to create a firestorm.

The U.S. also used herbicides in the **Democratic Republic of Vietnam**, **Cambodia**, and **Laos** to uncover PAVN, NLF, **Pathet Lao**, and **Khmer Rouge** forces, all of whom used the plant life to support their war aims. While it is difficult to determine how much of the NLF food crops were destroyed or how many lives were saved from ambushes averted because of vegetation destruction, it is clear that Ranch Hand sorties provided a positive benefit for the **Free World Forces**. In the postwar years, controversy surrounded **Agent Orange** as a factor that contributed to medical complications for those exposed to the herbicide. This controversy continues to be debated among veterans, scholars, scientists, and international governments, with compelling evidence on both sides of the argument.

RAVEN. A group of **forward air controllers** (FACs) who operated over **Laos** during the war under the call sign "Raven." In 1964, the **United States** increased its activities in Laos after it was clear that one of the July 1962 Geneva Accords, the International Agreement on the Neutrality of Laos, had failed to stop the Laotian insurgents, the **Pathet Lao**, or stem the advance of the **People's Army of Vietnam** into Laos as it developed what would become known as the **Hồ Chí Minh Trail**.

In 1966, the U.S. initiated a project that involved FACs, known as Raven, to fly unarmed **reconnaissance** missions to mark likely targets with smoke and direct air strikes against them. The O-1 and T-28 were the most common aircraft flown by the group. Raven FACs were almost always located at the Udorn Royal Thai Air Force Base in **Thailand** and were given identification that marked them as employees of civilian agencies, usually the U.S. Agency for International Development. The group was under the administrative control of the **U.S. Air Force**, but the relationship was strained, resulting in Raven FACs being passed over for promotion or receiving poor ratings.

RECOILLESS RIFLE. The most commonly used recoilless rifle during the war was the M40. It was a breech-loaded rifle that fired a single shell from a rifled barrel. When loaded, it was aimed and fired at a target, usually with devastating effectiveness. The M40 fired a 105-mm shell. It was lightweight, at approximately 200 kilograms (460 pounds) when ready to fire, and was easily transportable. It was a little more than 3.4 meters (11 feet) long and had a maximum range of over 7,620 meters (25,000 feet), though its effective range was approximately 2,743 meters (9,000 feet). It was originally designed as an antitank weapon but was also used for antipersonnel missions, including the firing of **flechettes** and direct fire support, especially by the U.S. **Marine Corps**, which placed six M40 rifles on their M50 **Ontos**. The M40 proved to be highly accurate, while the M50 offered much-needed maneuverability. It could also be fixed to a jeep or truck, though usually as a single gun.

RECONDO SCHOOL. Established officially by **Military Assistance Command, Vietnam** (MACV), commander General **William C. Westmoreland** in September 1966, the MACV Recondo School was charged with training **United States** and allied personnel in **long-range patrol** and reconnaissance. This type of training actually began earlier, in 1964, with Project **Leaping Lena** and then Project Delta. The Recondo School was physically and mentally demanding as individuals were instructed on how to operate in contested territory in small groups. Training at the Recondo School lasted 20 days and had a success rate of approximately 67 percent. It graduated over 3,000 U.S. and 300 allied personnel before it was disbanded by General **Creighton W. Abrams**, who replaced Westmoreland. The school officially closed on 19 December 1970.

RECONNAISSANCE, AIR. As a result of the unique topographical and climatic environment of Southeast Asia, air reconnaissance played a major role in the war. For the **United States**, the use of aircraft in reconnaissance missions provided valuable information on enemy troop location and disposition. The U.S. began reconnaissance **sorties** in January 1961 with the introduction of a modified version of the C-47. Early missions concentrated on northern **Laos** but soon expanded to the **Republic of Vietnam** (RVN) by the end of the year. Under projects **Pipe Stem** and **Able Marble**, the U.S. intensified its reconnaissance missions in the RVN and increased the number and type of aircraft committed to reconnaissance. By the time of the **Gulf of Tŏn Kĭn Incident** and the introduction of American combat troops into the RVN, reconnaissance missions were a daily occurrence. The **United States Air Force** (USAF), U.S. **Navy** (USN), and U.S. **Marine Corps** shared reconnaissance duties in Southeast Asia. For missions over the **Democratic Republic of Vietnam**, the division of responsibilities was determined by **Route Package**. The Strategic Air Command conducted missions above the 19th parallel, while the 7th Air Force flew reconnaissance sorties in Route

Package 1. The USN had responsibility for route packages 2 and 3 to the 19th parallel. The USAF flew the majority of sorties over the RVN, though the **Republic of Vietnam Air Force** (RVNAF) also shared in the burden. Typical reconnaissance missions included identifying and photographing fixed and moving targets, providing **bombing** damage assessment, collecting other **intelligence**, and photographing **topography** to better understand the conditions on the battlefield.

In 1970, reconnaissance aircraft strength reached its peak. With **Vietnamization**, the RVNAF began to take over aerial reconnaissance duties, though the missions suffered from a lack of skilled technicians with command of the English language who could successfully complete the necessary training courses. This problem meant less than satisfactory maintenance of equipment and aircraft as well as slower photograph development and analysis. South Vietnamese aerial reconnaissance also focused on missions south of the **Demilitarized Zone**, but they were never able to fully coordinate air and ground power to react effectively to the intelligence gathered. *See also* AIRCRAFT (FIGHTER), UNITED STATES; CLIMATE, SOUTHEAST ASIA; DRONES; FORWARD AIR CONTROLLER; RAVEN.

RED RIVER DELTA. An area of approximately 15,000 square kilometers (5,800 square miles) that is formed by the Red River and its many tributaries. The Red River Delta (Đồng Bằng Sông Hồng) is located in the **Democratic Republic of Vietnam** (DRV) and includes the cities of **Hà Nội** and **Hải Phòng**. It was a heavily populated area and a producer of much of the DRV's rice. It was **bombed** during the war, though much of it was under some type of restriction during Operation **Rolling Thunder**. During the 1972 **Linebacker I** and **Linebacker II** operations, the delta's **dikes**, which were used by the North Vietnamese to house **antiaircraft artillery**, were bombed, causing international condemnation of the **United States**.

REFUGEES. The war in Southeast Asia produced a number of refugees who fled, or were forced away, from the fighting or who chose to remove themselves from their homes in search of new opportunities or a chance at prosperity. There were three major refugee periods during war. The first major refugee movement occurred as a result of the 1954 **Geneva Agreements**, when Vietnam was temporarily divided near the 17th parallel. The Vietnamese were given the opportunity to move north to south or south to north within a 300-day period. Approximately 810,000 Vietnamese and Chinese **Nùng** left the **Democratic Republic of Vietnam** for the State of Vietnam under operations Exodus and **Passage to Freedom**. **United States** estimates suggested that approximately 80,000 Vietnamese moved northward. Not much is known about the refugee population that moved north. The refugees who made their way south experienced a variety of obstacles in their attempt at a new life.

These refugees left the DRV for different reasons. American officials assumed that the majority of the refugees were Catholic and therefore supported **Ngô Đình Diệm** who was also a Catholic. This was not the case. Some were Catholics who worried about communist persecution of their religious beliefs, while most left because they feared retribution for their support of **France**'s colonial administration. The refugees placed an enormous strain on the State of Vietnam, which did not have the infrastructure to absorb the new population. The U.S. assisted the **Sài Gòn** government in the resettlement and rehabilitation of the refugee population. This process was problematic because refugees were often placed in areas in which they could not pursue their livelihood, or they displaced **Montagnard** groups in the **Central Highlands** as the Sài Gòn government attempted to find them homes. The refugee population was slowly assimilated into the **Republic of Vietnam** (RVN) by the end of the 1950s.

The next wave of refugees occurred during the 1960s and early 1970s after the war escalated. Vietnamese were often displaced as a result of the conflict in the Republic of Vietnam. In most cases, Vietnamese living in the countryside sought refuge in the urban centers. The populations of Sài Gòn and **Huế** dramatically increased during the war as a result, especially during the 1968 **Tết Offensive** and the 1972 **Easter Offensive**. The number of refugees strained the limited resources of the RVN, which helped to discredit the Sài Gòn government, and served as a pool from which potential recruits were sought for the **National Liberation Front**.

The final wave of refugees occurred after the fall of Sài Gòn on 30 April 1975. Over the next several years, Vietnamese fled Vietnam and resettled in overseas communities in the U.S., Canada, Australia, and Europe. There were approximately 130,000 refugees who came to the U.S. during this first wave of immigration. They were processed in refugee camps at Camp Pendleton, California; Fort Chaffee, Arkansas; Eglin Air Force Base, Florida; and Fort Indiantown Gap, Pennsylvania. In the subsequent waves of immigration out of Southeast Asia, over one million additional Vietnamese fled the Socialist Republic of Vietnam, with the majority resettling in the U.S. in either California or along the Gulf Coast between Louisiana and Texas.

REGIONAL FORCES. A unit that was a form of militia used by the **United States** and the **Army of the Republic of Vietnam** (ARVN) to perform static duty in order to free more troops for operations. Regional Forces guarded outposts and transportation choke points such as bridges and river crossings. The majority of the Regional Forces served in IV **Corps Tactical Zone**. In

1964, the ARVN absorbed the Regional Forces into its organization. Regional Forces performed in a supporting role, leaving the majority of the static duty to the **People's Self-Defense Force**. After the implementation of **Vietnamization** in 1969, Regional Forces conducted more operations in support of the ARVN, often outside of their own district and sometimes outside of their province. ARVN and U.S. soldiers did not respect the Regional Forces during the war. They were poorly armed and not very well trained, but some units did perform well when defending their home territory. *See also* POPULAR FORCES.

REPUBLIC OF KOREA (ROK). Since the 1950–1953 Korean War, the ROK had always had a vested interest in protecting Asian countries against the encroachment of communism. Toward the end of the **First Indochina War**, Korea offered to send a contingent to aid the **Vietnamese National Army** and French Union Forces. The request was rejected even though the **United States** would solicit allied assistance a few months later through their **United Action** effort in the weeks before the fall of **Điện Biên Phủ** on 7 May 1954. The ROK continued to provide technical aid and assistance to the **Republic of Vietnam** (RVN) through the 1950s and 1960s.

As the war escalated and President **Lyndon B. Johnson** initiated his **Show the Flag** program in 1964, the U.S. targeted Korea as a potential contributor. On 5 September 1964, the ROK and the RVN signed an agreement, funded under the Military Assistance Program, that would send an army mobile hospital unit of 34 officers, 96 enlisted men, and 10 Tae Kwon Do instructors. The troops arrived on 13 September. The Koreans added an engineer construction support group in December 1964 and an additional army construction support group, a Korean Marine Corps engineer company, Korean Navy LSTs (landing ships, tank) and LSMs (landing ships medium), and a Korean Army security company by June 1965. These personnel were commonly referred to as the Dove Unit and officially as the Republic of Korea Military Assistance Group, Vietnam. The Dove Unit had its base camp at **Biên Hòa**. There were 2,416 Korean personnel that supported the RVN by the middle of 1965.

The ROK's contribution increased in 1965 after it agreed to send an army division to Vietnam at the request of the U.S. The Koreans were motivated to escalate their involvement for several reasons. First and foremost, the Koreans understood what it was like to be threatened and occupied by a communist force and empathized with the South Vietnamese. The ROK also depended upon the U.S. to maintain a presence along its border with North Korea to deter a future invasion. Sending Korean troops to Vietnam meant that U.S. troops could remain in South Korea. Finally, the U.S. funded and equipped the Korean expeditionary force and made arrangements for a variety of economic and military assistance initiatives for the ROK, which provided a significant economic boost for the country.

Between September and November 1965, most of the ROK's Capital Infantry Division (Tiger Division), the 2nd Marine Gores Brigade (Blue Dragon Brigade), and supporting elements arrived in Vietnam. The Capital Division was under the command of General Lew Byong Hion. Overall command of the Korean force fell to General Chae Myung Shin. By the end of the year, the total number of Koreans in Vietnam had risen to over 20,000. The Tiger Division deployed near **Qui Nhơn**, while the Blue Dragon Brigade was eventually deployed to Tuy Hòa. With a further request by the U.S., the ROK added a second division in 1966. When the 9th ROK Division (White Horse Division) was completely deployed to Vietnam on 8 October, the total number of Koreans serving in Vietnam neared 45,000. The division was deployed to Ninh Hòa, Tuy Hòa, and **Cam Ranh Bay**. In 1967, an additional Korean Marine battalion and support forces of nearly 3,000 were added, bringing the total number of troops to nearly 48,000. The Koreans reached a peak of just over 50,000 troops in 1968.

The Korean troops operated semiautonomously from U.S. troops and quickly gained a reputation as a fierce fighting force. Their reputation was such that the forces of the **People's Army of Vietnam** (PAVN) and the **National Liberation Front** (NLF) would often refuse to engage the Koreans. Instead, the North Vietnamese worked to discredit the value of the ROK's contribution by making claims that it was no more than a mercenary force whose brutality was unprecedented and that often committed violations of international law. It was true that the Koreans were funded by the U.S., which made the former accusation hard to deny. The Koreans were brutal in their conduct of the war, but no different from the PAVN and NLF, who were involved in numerous incidents that would have been considered violations of international law.

The Korean forces conducted a number of joint operations with U.S. and **Army of the Republic of Vietnam** troops. The Tiger and White Horse divisions were involved in **search-and-destroy** missions with the U.S. **Marines** and the 101st Airborne **Division**. They participated in such joint operations as Flying Tiger, Jefferson, **Defiant Stand**, and **Irving**, as well as many of their own. The Koreans obtained a very high kill ratio, exceeding, on average, 10 to 1. In addition to search-and-destroy operations, the Koreans participated in civil action and **pacification** operations, though they preferred small-unit operations. Korean troops were considered very well prepared and committed to fighting the insurgency war. The military personnel were deliberate in their operations and were better at relating to the Vietnamese people than the U.S.

However, pacified villages were expected to provide **intelligence** on the enemy and to resist NLF attempts to infiltrate them. Failure to do so sometimes resulted in Korean troops punishing villagers for their failure to fight back and resulted in the conclusion that the villagers were sympathetic to the insurgents' cause and were therefore enemy combatants. Overall, the Korean contribution was seen as positive, though a few U.S. military officers argued that the Koreans were too excessive in their demands for **helicopters** and air support and were not worth the expense, financially, logistically, or militarily. By the time the Koreans withdrew from Vietnam, over 300,000 had served in the war, with approximately 5,000 killed and over 11,000 wounded. *See also* ADVISERS; AMPHIBIOUS OPERATIONS, UNITED STATES; MASHER/WHITE WING, OPERATION; THIRD COUNTRY FORCES.

REPUBLIC OF VIETNAM (RVN). Established in October 1955, the RVN was carved out of the State of Vietnam, which existed between 1949 and 1955, and included the territory from the **Demilitarized Zone** along the 17th parallel to the **Cà Mau** Peninsula. The RVN was often referred to as **South Vietnam**. Prime Minister **Ngô Đình Diệm** proclaimed himself the first president of the RVN after a referendum between himself and **Bảo Đại** that most believed had been questionably conducted. Ngô Đình Diệm was replaced in a 1 November 1963 military coup d'état led by **Dương Văn Minh**, who was in turn overthrown by **Nguyễn Khánh** in January 1964. There were several governments over the next 20 months, the two most significant led by **Trần Văn Hương** and **Phan Huy Quát**. Political stability returned with the rise of **Nguyễn Văn Thiệu** as president and **Nguyễn Cao Kỳ** as prime minister, though the two men led factions that would continue to divide the civilian and military leadership throughout the war. On 21 April 1975, Trần Văn Hương became the new president when Nguyễn Văn Thiệu resigned. Trần Văn Hương resigned a week later after he failed to end the fighting through negotiations. Dương Văn Minh returned to power to oversee the final collapse of the RVN.

While it existed, the RVN served as the bulwark against communism in Southeast Asia, and its experimentations as a republic served as a model for emerging Third World countries. In 1967, the RVN constitution created a bicameral National Assembly with a Senate and House of Representatives, though similar forms of republic government had existed during the tenure of Ngô Đình Diệm. Because of the nature and intensity of the war, the political experiment in the RVN was never able to take hold, while the political rivalry between Nguyễn Văn Thiệu and Nguyễn Cao Kỳ kept the political environment in **Sài Gòn** unstable.

The RVN would continue to exist until 30 April 1975, when the **People's Army of Vietnam** overran its capital of Sài Gòn. Sài Gòn was renamed **Hồ**

Chí Minh City on 1 May 1975, and the RVN merged with the DRV to form the Socialist Republic of Vietnam the next year.

REVOLUTIONARY DEVELOPMENT CADRES. These mobile 59-man teams were created in February 1966 with the mission of improving the lives of the villagers in the countryside in what was considered one of the first attempts at focused **pacification** after the Americanization of the war. The Revolutionary Development Cadres conducted themselves in similar fashion to the **National Liberation Front** (NLF) by eating, sleeping, and working with the rural Vietnamese. It was believed that this type of mission would allow for greater exposure of government forces in the villages and would provide an alternative to the ever-present NLF. The program had the potential to be very effective in deterring village participation in the NLF cause, but internal dissent and resistance by both political and military figures in the **Republic of Vietnam** plagued the program from the onset.

RHADÉ. One of the **Montagnard** tribes that lived in the **Central Highlands** in Darlac province and **Cambodia**. The Rhadé are also known as the Ê Đê. The Ê Đê language is a part of the **Cham** group of the Malayo-Polynesian language. The Rhadé were among the first to participate with the **United States** in the fight against the communist insurgency. In 1961, they joined what would become known as the **Civilian Irregular Defense Group**. *See also* Y-BIH ALEO.

RIFLES. The **United States** and the **Army of the Republic of Vietnam** (ARVN) had two rifles during the war. The M14 rifle was used early in the war until it was replaced with the M16 assault rifle. The M14 could be utilized as either a semi- or fully automatic rifle and used a 7.62-mm bullet. It had a muzzle velocity of nearly 853 meters (2,800 feet) per second and a maximum capability of firing approximately 700 to 750 rounds per minute. During the war, the M14 proved to be a reliable weapon, though it was much heavier than the M16.

The M16 assault rifle was a modified version of the AR15, which was designed to replace the semiautomatic M1 and select-fire M14. During its testing period, the AR15 was considered a very reliable weapon. The M16 assault rifle was a very accurate weapon that was easy to handle and effective during combat, though early versions of the M16A1, which entered Vietnam in 1966, had some jamming problems. The bullet was different from the munitions used when the weapon went through its testing period. The M16 fired a 5.56-mm bullet, which was also smaller than the 7.62-mm bullet used by the **People's Army of Vietnam** (PAVN) and the **National Liberation Front**

(NLF). It had a muzzle velocity of over 991 meters (3,250 feet) per second but had a tendency to deflect on jungle foliage at a distance. The conditions in Vietnam made it difficult to keep the weapon clean, which also resulted in jamming issues.

Future versions of the weapon improved its reliability by making the rifle more compatible with the ammunition, and a cleaning kit was integrated into the butt of the weapon. The M16 fired between 750 and 900 rounds per minute depending on the model and had an effective range of approximately 609 meters (2,000 feet). The weapon was lighter than the M14, weighing 3.5 kilograms (7.8 pounds) unloaded.

In addition to captured rifles, the PAVN and NLF used the AK-47 assault rifle, which was a semiautomatic weapon designed in the **Soviet Union** by Mikhail Kalashnikov. The AK-47 was a gas-operated, rotating-bolt weapon that used a 7.62-mm cartridge, which was slightly larger than the caliber of the U.S. M16 assault rifle. It was adopted into the Soviet Army in 1949. In Vietnam, the majority of PAVN and NLF personnel used the Type 56 rifle, manufactured by the People's Republic of China. It was an exact copy of the AK-47, which began production in 1956. As a result, it was often confused for the Soviet-made AK-47. It weighed a little over 3.6 kilograms (8 pounds) and was .87 meters (34.4 inches) long. The AK-47 could fire between 600 and 650 rounds per minute, with a muzzle velocity of 731 meters (2,400 feet) per second and an effective range of up to 721 meters (2,400 feet), though the weapon was not as accurate as the M16. *See also* NSAM 288.

RIPCORD, FIRE SUPPORT BASE (FSB). Located in **Thừa Thiên** province, FSB Ripcord was rebuilt in March 1970 to serve as a supporting facility for Operation Texas Star. In the operation, the 101st Airborne **Division** and **Army of the Republic of Vietnam** (ARVN) troops targeted **People's Army of Vietnam** (PAVN) forces located in the A Shau and Đa Krông valleys. U.S. troops moved to FSB Ripcord in June 1970 as U.S. and ARVN forces initiated the **Cambodian Incursion**. On 1 July 1970, PAVN forces attacked the FSB in what became a 23-day siege. PAVN forces fired 60-mm and 82-mm mortar fire and 75-mm recoilless rifle fire into the FSB. On 18 July, a CH-47 **helicopter** was shot down by small arms fire and crashed into a 105-mm ammunition storage area, which caused extensive damage and the destruction of the six 105-mm howitzers in B Battery, 2nd Battalion, 319th Artillery. A second CH-47 carrying 105-mm ammunition was shot down on 23 July and crashed into another 105-mm ammunition storage area, destroying a counter-mortar radar, two 105-mm **artillery** guns, and a radio set. On 23 July 1970, the U.S. abandoned the FSB, having lost 250 men killed-in-action while inflicting an untold number of PAVN **casualties**.

RIVER PATROL FORCE. Established on 18 December 1965, the River Patrol Force, also known as Task Force 116 or Operation **Game Warden**, was designed to engage the **People's Army of Vietnam** and **National Liberation Front** forces who were using the inland waterways to transport personnel and supplies into the **Republic of Vietnam** in support of the effort to overthrow the **Sài Gòn** government. The River Patrol Force used the **patrol boat, river**, to watch the waterways, rivers, and canals. The operation faced many obstacles, including the large area of operation, the remoteness of the more than 3,000 nautical miles (5,556 kilometers) of water routes, and the jungle terrain that often grew all the way to the waterline.

ROADRUNNERS. The **United States Special Forces** helped to established small reconnaissance teams, typically made up of **Montagnards**, who provided **intelligence** on **People's Army of Vietnam** and **National Liberation Front** movements along known infiltration routes into the **Republic of Vietnam**. These units, referred to as Roadrunners, were involved in the Special Forces projects starting with Delta in May 1964 and continued in August 1966 with Omega in II **Corps Tactical Zone** (CTZ) and Sigma in III CTZ.

ROCKET RIDGE. Located between **Kon Tum** and **Đắk Tô** in Kon Tum province in III **Corps Tactical Zone**, Rocket Ridge was a series of ridges between the Krông Pôkôto River and **Route** 14 on which the **United States** built firebases. The U.S. presence resulted in the **People's Army of Vietnam** (PAVN) firing a significant number of 122-mm rockets into the ridgeline. During the 1972 **Easter Offensive**, the ridge, which had been handed over to the **Army of the Republic of Vietnam** (ARVN), was attacked. The ARVN forces abandoned it on 25 April, which allowed the PAVN to move against Kon Tum and nearly cut the **Republic of Vietnam** in two along Route 19 at **Plei Ku**.

ROCKPILE. The nickname for an 800-foot rock outcropping near the **Demilitarized Zone** (DMZ) used by the **United States Army** and **Marines** as an observation post and **artillery** base. The Rockpile was situated along **Route** 9 and served as one of the many military stations in the northern section of I **Corps Tactical Zone** designed to thwart a North Vietnamese attack across the DMZ.

ROLLING THUNDER, OPERATION. Originally conceived as a limited air campaign designed to stop the infiltration of North Vietnamese personnel and supplies into the **Republic of Vietnam**, Operation Rolling Thunder would become one of the largest, and longest, air campaigns in **United States** history. On 12 February 1965, the **Joint Chiefs of Staff** forwarded to Secretary of Defense **Robert McNamara** an eight-week plan for air strikes that would be connected to overt North Vietnamese and Việt Cộng attacks. Begun on 2 March, Rolling Thunder missions soon became closely connected with U.S. troop escalation as its mission expanded and transformed.

As one of its missions, Rolling Thunder targeted transportation choke points such as the **Thanh Hóa bridge**, which was struck multiple times. The North Vietnamese, while hampered by the sustained **bombing** campaign, were able to adjust to the hardships created by Rolling Thunder and continued the flow of personnel and supplies to support the war in the South. As Rolling Thunder escalated into its second phase, other targets of opportunity, such as radar installations, barracks, and ammunition and supply depots, were identified and destroyed. By 23 April 1965, air **sorties** were authorized above the 20th parallel to demonstrate to the North Vietnamese that there would be no sanctuary if they continued to pursue the war.

As the air campaign continued, Washington adopted a policy of gradually reducing its publicity in order to limit the reaction from the **Soviet Union** and the **People's Republic of China** (PRC). Concern for international reactions would also result in a series of restrictions placed on the air campaign that limited its potential. The areas around **Hà Nội** and **Hải Phòng**, as well as the border between the PRC and the **Democratic Republic of Vietnam** (DRV), remained off limits, while each attack was planned to reduce civilian **casualties** even though it was inevitable that civilians would suffer.

Rolling Thunder did achieve some initial success, but it did not do enough to alter the North Vietnamese strategy. The DRV continued to support the southern insurgency with both personnel and supplies in an attempt to match American escalation. Admittedly, Rolling Thunder forced the North Vietnamese to divert significant resources to repair damage done during the air strikes and to increase its air defense system, but it also increased the North's spirit of resistance and added to its strategy of total war, where every citizen was expected to contribute to the war effort.

At the January 1966 Honolulu Conference, Rolling Thunder was reevaluated. The main objective of the air campaign remained the same, disrupting the North's ability to supply its allies in the South by using three tactics: reducing the military support received from other countries, destroying northern military and industrial infrastructure, and interdiction of personnel and supplies used to support the war. The U.S. retained its restrictions on where it could bomb, which continued to hamper the air campaign.

By 1968, Rolling Thunder had resulted in significant destruction of military targets in the DRV. A **U.S. Air Force** (USAF) report highlighted noteworthy damage or disruption in power; industry; petroleum, oil, and lubricant facilities; and transportation, while 106 of the 144 targeted military facilities were no longer in service. These statistics and the 1968 **Tết Offensive** did not belie the fact that the air campaign had failed to achieve its primary objective. On 31 March 1968, President **Lyndon B. Johnson** declared that he would not seek or accept his party's nomination for a second term as president. He also announced that Rolling Thunder would be curtailed as a sign of good faith toward the resumption of peace negotiations. On 1 April, Johnson ended all air strikes north of the 20th parallel. Two days later, Johnson ordered the end of air strikes north of the 19th parallel. This did not end Rolling Thunder. In fact, air sorties increased with a concentration of force against **Route Package** 1. Between April and June, the USAF flew 27,406 sorties over the DRV, nearly doubling the number from the first three months of the year.

On 1 November, Johnson ended Rolling Thunder. While this was done in part to aid **Herbert Humphrey**'s chances in the presidential election against **Richard M. Nixon**, it was also an admission of Rolling Thunder's failure, which would become linked to Johnson's failure in Vietnam. *See also* AIRCRAFT (BOMBERS), UNITED STATES; AIRCRAFT (FIGHTER), UNITED STATES; BLUE TREE; BOLO, OPERATION; BOMBING PAUSES; COMBAT SKYSPOT; FACT SHEET, OPERATION; GATE GUARD; IRON HAND; LONG BIÊN BRIDGE (PAUL DOUMER BRIDGE); SEA DRAGON, OPERATION; STEEL TIGER, OPERATION.

ROSTOW, WALT WHITMAN (1916–2003). Adviser to presidents **John F. Kennedy** and **Lyndon B. Johnson**. Rostow was born in New York City and was educated at Yale University, Balliol College at Oxford on a Rhodes Scholarship, and Columbia University, where he earned a PhD in economics. During World War II, he worked for the Office of Strategic Services and was involved in bombing assessment and target selection in Western Europe. He taught economics at the Massachusetts Institute of Technology from 1950 to 1961 where he gained a reputation as a scholar of economics and world affairs. In 1960, Rostow published *The Stages of Economic Growth: A Non-Communist Manifesto*, which argued that the **United States** needed to support Southeast Asia economically in order to win influence in that region away from the communists. Rostow also coined the Kennedy phrase "New Frontier" used in the 1960 campaign.

Because of his academic reputation and connection with the Kennedy vision for the U.S., Rostow was sought out by members of the Kennedy administration. He was among those considered the "Best and the Brightest" the nation had to offer. He worked as a deputy to National Security Assistant **McGeorge Bundy** and was an early proponent of Kennedy's escalatory moves in 1961. From April to May 1961, Rostow was one of the members of the Presidential Task Force on Vietnam. He also made a very influential trip to the **Republic of Vietnam** with General **Maxwell D. Taylor** in October 1961 that helped formulate Kennedy's Vietnam policy in 1962 and 1963.

As a result of these services, he would help to guide American policy in Southeast Asia for most of the 1960s. He served as a deputy special assistant to the president for national security affairs until 4 December 1961, after which he became the counselor of the Department of State and chairman of the Policy Planning Council in the Department of State. In this capacity, Rostow advocated a stronger military posture in Vietnam and believed that the U.S. could have won the war if it had been fully committed. Rostow was considered one of the leading war **Hawks** and frequently urged increased American bombing and additional military personnel to fight the war.

He remained chairman of the Policy Planning Council until 31 March 1966 when he became a special assistant to President Johnson. He served as Johnson's closest adviser on foreign policy issues. On 14 October 1966, Rostow became the undersecretary of state for political affairs. He left public life at the end of the Johnson administration and returned to academia. He taught at the University of Texas and had a close connection with the Johnson Presidential Library, which was located on the campus. He continued to maintain his position on, and defend his decision in, Vietnam throughout his life while others changed their views or offered a mea culpa for their actions. Rostow continued to write and was involved in charitable organizations until his death.

ROUTE PACKAGES. Name used to delineate areas of responsibility for the **United States Air Force** (USAF), U.S. **Navy** (USN), U.S. **Marine Corps**, and **Military Assistance Command, Vietnam**, in overseeing air **sorties** for **Rolling Thunder.** At the end of 1965, the **Democratic Republic of Vietnam** was divided into six different areas; the sixth area around **Hà Nội** was further subdivided into two parts, known as route packages. The USAF managed inland targets while the USN oversaw targets nearer the coast.

ROUTES (ROADS), REPUBLIC OF VIETNAM. The road system in the **Republic of Vietnam** (RVN) was slow to develop during the war. There were several major routes that were paved, but these roads could not handle the capacity of an interstate in the **United States** nor were they easily defended against the **guerrilla warfare** tactics used by the **National Liberation Front**. Route 1 was the north-south road that connected **Hà Nội** and **Sài Gòn**. From Sài Gòn, Route 1 continued to **Phnom Penh** in **Cambodia**. It connected all of the major coastal or urban cities in the RVN, including **Quảng Trị**, **Huế**, **Đà Nẵng**, **Qui Nhơn**, Cam Ranh, **Biên Hòa**, and Sài Gòn. Route 1 was strategically significant during the war and was the focus of several operations on both sides. The United States, South Vietnamese, and **Free World Forces**

worked to protect the road and keep it open while the North Vietnamese and **National Liberation Front** staged ambushes, planted **mines**, and worked to close the road.

The other major routes, from south to north, included routes 4, 13, 19, 14, and 9. Route 4 connected Sài Gòn with the **Mê Kông Delta** and served as the only major road between III and IV **Corps Tactical Zones** (CTZ). The route traversed **Cần Thơ**, Sóc Trăng, and Bạc Liêu; it terminated at **Cà Mau**.

To the north of Sài Gòn, Route 13 ran through the provinces of **Gia Định**, Bình Dương, and Bình Long. It connected Sài Gòn via Route 1 with such significant towns as Gia Định, Phú Cường, Bến Cát, An Lộc, and Lộc Ninh before entering Cambodia. Route 13 also connected the provinces of **Tây Ninh** and Phước Long through the southern end of Bình Long province.

Route 19 was a major road that ran east to west across II CTZ. Route 19 originated on the coast at Qui Nhơn in **Bình Định** province, intersected Route 1 just south of An Nhơn, passed through An Khê which was the one-time home of the 1st Cavalry **Division**, and terminated in **Plei Ku** province at Plei Ku City. Route 19 held a strategic position during the war; it was argued that control of the road meant control of the RVN. During the 1972 **Easter Offensive**, the **People's Army of Vietnam** unsuccessfully attempted to cut the road and deny the **Army of the Republic of Vietnam** the ability to move reinforcements and supplies by land between I CTZ and III CTZ.

Route 14 was a major route through the **Central Highlands** that ran from I CTZ to III CTZ. It intersected Route 1 south of Đà Nẵng and north of Hội An and traveled west and south through **Quảng Nam**. It continued south through II CTZ, nearing the border of Cambodia in Quảng Đức province. It terminated at Chơn Thành in Bình Long province, though the road continued into Tây Ninh province as Route 13.

Route 9 was the northernmost route in the RVN. It ran east to west in Quảng Trị, originating at an intersection with Route 1 at **Đông Hà** between the cities of Gio Linh and Quảng Trị. It traveled westward through Cam Lộ and then took a southerly turn toward the city of Ca Lu where it resumes a westerly direction near **Khe Sanh**, through Lang Vei, and into **Laos** toward **Tchepone**. Route 9 continued westward to Savannakhet on the **Mê Kông River**. Route 9 was the focus of Operation **Pegasus**, the overland relief campaign of Khe Sanh during the 1968 battle of the marine base and was the main axis of the 1971 South Vietnamese incursion into Laos known as Operation **Lam Sơn 719**. (*See* map 2.)

RPG-2. A rocket-propelled grenade (RPG) designed by the **Soviet Union** and used by the **People's Army of Vietnam** (PAVN) and the **National Liberation Front** (NLF) during the war. In Vietnam, the weapon was referred to as a B-40. The RPG-2 was an inexpensive, easy-to-use weapon. When ready to fire, it weighed slightly over 4.5 kilograms (10 pounds) and measured just less than 66 centimeters (26 inches). The RPG-2 fired an 82-mm warhead from a 40-mm (1.57 inches) tube that weighed less than 1.8 kilograms (4 pounds) with an effective range of 100 to 150 meters (300–480 feet) and a maximum range of nearly 185 meters (600 feet). A properly trained crew of two could fire between three and four rounds per minute. Most of the PAVN and NLF RPG-2s were provided by the Soviet Union or the **People's Republic of China**.

RỪNG SÁC SPECIAL ZONE. Located approximately 32 kilometers (20 miles) south-southeast of **Sài Gòn**, the Rừng Sác Special Zone was an area of approximately 1,250 square kilometers (485 square miles) with nearly 4,800 kilometers (3,000 miles) of interlocking waterways. It was situated between Phước Tuy province to the east and **Long An** province to the west. During the French colonial period, new inhabitants to the area generally consisted of individuals who were forced to migrate there because of their resistance to **France**'s rule. As such, the area became a safe haven for bandits and those who opposed colonial rule. During the **First Indochina War**, the French used a river assault group to control the area, in addition to building numerous forts and outposts to control the waterways leading to Sài Gòn. The area also became a refuge for the **Bình Xuyên** after the 1955 Sect War.

The **National Liberation Front** (NLF) operated in the area during the 1960s and threatened the territory around Sài Gòn and points south. The terrain was conducive to concealed bunkers and base areas while the ability of the **United States** and the **Republic of Vietnam** to move personnel and supplies was limited by the inhospitable **topography**. Both the **Việt Minh** and the NLF received support from the inhabitants of the Rừng Sác Special Zone. In April 1966, the Central Office of South Vietnam, the NLF government parallel to Sài Gòn, established a special military region (Doan-10 or D-10) in the Rừng Sác. Despite several attempts by the U.S. and the **Army of the Republic of Vietnam** (ARVN) to clear the area of NLF supporters, the area remained a safe haven for the NLF. The U.S. and ARVN conducted the 1966 operations Baton Rouge, Jack Stay, and Lexington and the 1967 operations Palm Beach, River Raider, and Tiger Coronado in the Rừng Sác Special Zone. It was not until the implementation of the 1968 **SEALORDS** program that the Rừng Sác Special Zone was mostly pacified, but even that remained temporary as the war progressed into the early 1970s.

RUSK, DAVID DEAN (1909–1994). United States secretary of state during the **John F. Kennedy** and **Lyndon B. Johnson** administrations. Rusk was educated at Davidson College, attended St. John's College at Oxford University on a Rhodes Scholarship, and earned his undergraduate and graduate degrees there in 1933 and 1934. He taught at Mills College in California from 1934 to 1940 and then studied law at the University of California, Berkeley, though he never finished the program. Rusk joined the army in 1940 and served with the 3rd Infantry Division and the Military Intelligence Service. Between 1943 and 1945, he was involved in the China-Burma-India Theater, reaching the rank of colonel by the end of the war. Rusk served on the General Staff in the War Department in Washington, D.C., where he worked under General George C. Marshall. Marshall assigned Rusk to head the Office of Special Political Affairs within the Department of State in 1947. In 1950, Secretary of State **Dean Acheson** appointed Rusk as the assistant secretary of state for far eastern affairs where he practiced his containment and anticommunist philosophy. In 1952, Rusk became the president of the Rockefeller Foundation, where he remained until being tasked to head the Department of State under Kennedy in 1961.

The war in Southeast Asia dominated much of Rusk's time toward the latter years of the Kennedy administration and through his tenure as secretary of state during the Johnson administration. Rusk believed that communism needed to be contained in Southeast Asia and that the U.S. had an obligation to support the **Republic of Vietnam** in its efforts against the insurgency and the North. He advocated escalation and as a result became a target for **antiwar** protests and demonstrations. He left public life with the defeat of the Democrats in 1968. Rusk returned to academia in 1969, teaching international law at the University of Georgia, where he remained until his death.

RUSSELL, RICHARD BREVARD, JR. (1897–1971). Democratic governor and **United States** senator from Georgia. Russell was in the U.S. Senate from 1932 to 1971. He served on the Appropriations Committee his entire career, chaired it from 1969 to 1971, and was the chairman of the Senate Armed Services Committee from 1951 to 1969. Russell began his opposition to U.S. involvement in Vietnam in the early 1950s when he argued against supporting the French in the **First Indochina War**. As the Americanization of the war took place, Russell again stood on the opposite side of President **Lyndon B. Johnson**. He warned the president that the U.S. had to either commit enough force to win the war or get out. Russell's influence did not sway Johnson who butted heads with the Georgian senator over civil rights and the Great Society. When Johnson committed U.S. combat troops, Russell supported the effort publicly, ensuring that the troops received the financial support they needed to fight the war, though he continued to privately advise Johnson against the decision. He died on 21 January 1971 in Washington, D.C.

S

SA-2. *See* MISSILES.

SA-7. *See* MISSILES.

SAGGER. *See* MISSILES.

SÀI GÒN. Capital of the **Republic of Vietnam** (RVN) and renamed **Hồ Chí Minh City** after the collapse of the RVN in April 1975 though it continues to be referred to as Sài Gòn. Sài Gòn was the capital of the French colony of Cochin China during the French colonial period, though the name was not adopted until 1861. Previously, the area was settled by Vietnamese in the 17th century. Before the Vietnamese, **Khmer** fishermen inhabited the area. Sài Gòn is located on the Sài Gòn River which winds its way from the capital city nearly 55 kilometers (35 miles) to the South China Sea. Its architecture was heavily influenced by the French, with imposing colonial structures and wide boulevards. Sài Gòn was often referred to as the Paris of the Orient. The city was located within the III **Corps Tactical Zone** area, though it was identified as its own military region. It has a tropical **climate** with monsoon rains from May to November and a dry season from December to April. Its average temperature is within a few degrees of 90 degrees Fahrenheit throughout the year.

In 1949, Emperor **Bảo Đại** made Sài Gòn the capital of the State of Vietnam. It remained the capital after **Ngô Đình Diệm** proclaimed the RVN in October 1955. Sài Gòn was considered the most significant sea port in the RVN. It was the principal point of disembarkation for Vietnamese **refugees** during Operation **Passage to Freedom** in 1954–1955 when over 810,000 Vietnamese fled the North after the 1954 **Geneva Agreements**. Sài Gòn was the center of political life during the Vietnam War. Sài Gòn intellectuals formed the cadre of critics against Ngô Đình Diệm that eventually assisted in the November 1963 coup d'état against him. They remained politically active throughout the 1960s and 1970s. Control of the city was contested throughout the war. The **National Liberation Front** (NLF) conducted many operations in the city, including the famous 1968 **Tết Offensive**, during which the NLF attacked the U.S. embassy, the Sài Gòn radio station, **Tân Sơn Nhứt**, and other significant institutions.

As a result of the war, Sài Gòn's population grew as people who were displaced by the war sought shelter and safety. By 1968, it housed more than four million people—many of whom were refugees from the war—which was well beyond the city's capacity. This led to widespread poverty, crime, and easy recruitment for the NLF. The fall of the city on 30 April 1975 marked the end of the Vietnam War.

SÀI GÒN EVACUATION, 1975. *See* FREQUENT WIND, OPERATION.

SALISBURY, HARRISON EVANS (1908–1993). Pulitzer Prize–winning journalist. Salisbury was born in Minnesota and educated at the University of Minnesota, graduating in 1930. His first job was with United Press (UP), where he spent 18 years and reported from London and Moscow during World War II. He served as the foreign editor for UP from 1944 to 1948. Salisbury joined the *New York Times* in 1949 and became its bureau chief in Moscow. In 1955, he won the Pulitzer Prize for international reporting for 14 articles related to his observations while in the **Soviet Union**. Between 1962 and 1964, he served as the chief of the *New York Times* correspondents in the **United States** and then became an assistant managing editor from 1964 to 1972 and associate editor from 1972 to 1973. In 1970, Salisbury became the first editor of the Op-Ed page and remained in that position until he retired in 1973.

On 23 December 1966, Salisbury arrived in **Hà Nội** for a brief visit to the capital of the **Democratic Republic of Vietnam** (DRV) to report on the war. He remained until early January 1967 and wrote a series of articles on the impact of Operation **Rolling Thunder** in the DRV. These war dispatches drew heavy criticism from those who supported the air campaign against the North. Salisbury argued that U.S. aircraft had bombed nonmilitary targets in the DRV which directly contradicted American military and government officials' claims that these civilian areas had not been impacted. His first dispatch directly called into question the U.S. government assertion that civilians had remained unharmed, stating that he had seen considerable damage. Salisbury's critics argued that he had simply repeated Hà Nội **propaganda** and that he served as a willing spokesperson for the communist government.

Salisbury was considered for a second Pulitzer Prize for his reporting from the DRV, but the Pulitzer Prize advisory board rejected the prize jury's decision by a vote of five to four. Those who supported Salisbury argued that the decision was based on politics rather than journalistic accomplishment. After Salisbury retired from the *New York Times*, he continued to write and remained involved in politics, though his focus had moved away from Vietnam and toward the **People's Republic of China**. He served as president of the American Academy and Institute of Arts and Letters between 1975 and 1976 and of the Authors League between 1980 and 1985. Salisbury also wrote 29 books on a variety of topics, but with a focus on Russian and Chinese history.

SAM NEUA. Northeastern province in **Laos** bordering the **Democratic Republic of Vietnam** (DRV) whose capital shared the same name. During the cease-fire that followed the 1954 **Geneva Agreements**, the provinces of Sam Neua and Phong Saly became areas for the **Pathet Lao**, the communist insurgents, to regroup. It was also the location of a fixed inspection team of the **International Control Commission**. Sam Neua was integrated back into Laos in 1958 but was the scene of intense fighting in July 1959 as the Pathet Lao regained control of the province. As the war progressed, the Pathet Lao used Sam Nuea province and its caves as headquarters to attack the forces loyal to the Vientiane government through the **Plain of Jars**. Sam Neua's proximity to the DRV, from which the Pathet Lao received assistance, also made it a logical location for its headquarters.

SAPPERS. Sappers are traditionally combat engineers who are specially trained to construct structures, such as bridges, or to clear minefields under combat conditions. During the war, the **People's Army of Vietnam** and the **National Liberation Front** used sappers in a different function. These personnel, known as Đặc Công, were highly trained commandos who infiltrated **United States** and **Republic of Vietnam** armed forces facilities, such as **fire support bases**, to cause as much damage as possible. Vietnamese sappers used **bombs**, grenades, and **mines** to kill personnel and destroy important structures. Đặc Công teams usually consisted of three-to-five-man teams in order to maintain secrecy and increase the likelihood of infiltration. These sappers operated mostly on land but were also successful in the water as seen in the 2 May 1964 attack on the converted helicopter-carrying ship the U.S.S. *Card*, which was docked in **Sài Gòn** harbor.

SEA DRAGON, OPERATION. Naval operation that focused on intense bombardment and harassment fire against North Vietnamese personnel and facilities, designed to complement Operation **Rolling Thunder**. From 25 October 1966 to 31 October 1968, the 7th Fleet raided coastal positions from the **Demilitarized Zone** to the 20th parallel and provided fire support for allied troops that engaged suspected **People's Army of Vietnam** and **National Liberation Front** positions operating in I **Corps Tactical Zone**. Sea Dragon raids against the North Vietnamese sought to wreak havoc and sow confusion. This was aided by their ability to attack anywhere and at any time. Sea Dragon targets in the **Democratic Republic of Vietnam** (DRV) usually included radar stations, shore guns, maintenance facilities, and supply depots.

Like Rolling Thunder, Sea Dragon caused discomfort and created a diversion of resources for the DRV, but it did not stop the infiltration of personnel and supplies to the South. It also failed to force the North Vietnamese to abandon their coastal facilities for safer havens inland. The DRV responded to the operation by placing more shore guns in areas that were heavily targeted, though these emplacements represented a minimal threat to the **United States Navy**. There were five naval personnel killed during the course of Sea Dragon missions. *See also* COAST GUARD, UNITED STATES; NAVAL GUNFIRE SUPPORT.

SEA, AIR, AND LAND (SEAL) TEAMS. Highly trained and motivated teams organized into platoons of 14 men who conducted day and night ambushes, raids against enemy positions, reconnaissance patrols, salvage operations, and personnel extraction. Created in 1961 as a result of the need for a **United States Navy** equivalent to the **Army's Special Forces**, the SEAL teams sought to fulfill that role. The men of the first two teams came from personnel of the Underwater Demolition Teams. Members of the SEAL teams arrived in the **Republic of Vietnam** in March 1962 as **advisers** to the **Army of the Republic of Vietnam** Special Forces, though the men were ordered to expand their responsibilities the next year to include reconnaissance and counter-**guerrilla** operations. Though the SEALs operated throughout Southeast Asia, they concentrated on operations in the **Rừng Sác Special Zone** to the south of **Sài Gòn**, which had been a haven for the **National Liberation Front** during the war, and in IV **Corps Tactical Zone** where various waterways dominated the **topography** of the region. SEAL teams engaged in unconventional warfare, often penetrating enemy positions for reconnaissance, ambush, or personnel extraction, and they also worked within the **Democratic Republic of Vietnam**, **Laos**, and **Cambodia** when the situation became suitable. The teams conducted formal operations during the war until 1973.

SEALORDS. On 18 October 1968, Vice Admiral **Elmo R. Zumwalt Jr.**, the commander of Naval Forces, Vietnam, created the Southeast Asia Lake Ocean River Delta Strategy (SEALORDS). The primary mission of this strategy was the reorganization of the existing naval efforts into one unified force in order to eliminate waste and improve the coordination of assets fighting the naval battle, with special emphasis on **pacification** in the **Mê Kông Delta**. SEALORDS combined operations **Market Time** and **Game Warden** as well as the **Mobile Riverine Force**. Zumwalt used SEALORDS to prevent the **People's Army of Vietnam** (PAVN) and the **National Liberation Front** (NLF) from using the waterways and to completely interdict supply routes by sea.

SEALORDS proved to be a very effective strategy in denying the PAVN and NLF transportation routes. It also eliminated areas accessible by water that had been safe havens for the PAVN and NLF. Within SEALORDS, there were several missions that used existing canals and rivers to block off access to the **Republic of Vietnam** (RVN) from **Cambodia**. This barrier strategy began with Operation **Search Turn** on 2 November 1968, which was a five-day operation that concentrated river patrols between the Gulf of **Thailand** at Rạch Giá and the Bassac River at Long Xuyên. Search Turn was followed by Operation **Foul Deck**, later renamed Trần Hưng Đạo in November 1968, which expanded the barrier to the Giang Thành–Vĩnh Tế canal system. Another barrier began with Operation **Giant Slingshot**, which focused on the Vàm Cỏ Đông and Vàm Cỏ Tây rivers to the west of **Sài Gòn** and near the famous **Parrot's Beak** region on the RVN border with Cambodia in December 1968. Operation **Barrier Reef** linked Giant Slingshot and Trần Hưng Đạo when it started on 2 January 1969. The final barrier created a continuous line of patrols for 400 kilometers (250 miles), from the Gulf of Thailand to the mouth of the Sài Gòn River. SEALORDS ended in April 1971 with the transfer of operations to the South Vietnamese through the **Vietnamization** program.

SEARCH TURN, OPERATION. First naval operation that made up the attempt under the **SEALORDS** strategy to interdict the **People's Army of Vietnam** and **National Liberation Front** infiltration of the waterways between **Cambodia** and the **Republic of Vietnam** by establishing a barrier between the two countries using the existing canal system. The five-day operation began on 2 November 1968, with a combination of **United States** and **Army of the Republic of Vietnam** soldiers and naval assets establishing a line between Rạch Giá on the Gulf of **Thailand** to Long Xuyên on the Bassac (Sông Hậu) River in IV **Corps Tactical Zone**. The success of the operation led to a subsequent operation known as **Foul Deck**, which expanded the barrier farther to the north.

SEARCH-AND-DESTROY. Term given to the **United States** tactic employed during the war to help with the strategy of attrition warfare. Search-and-destroy missions sought to uncover **People's Army of Vietnam** (PAVN) and **National Liberation Front** (NLF) soldiers who used the **topography** of Southeast Asia to their advantage and to engage them with overwhelming firepower, resulting in their elimination. The tactic was used in Vietnam to help offset the nature of the war in which the PAVN and NLF soldiers refused to engage in direct confrontation with the allied forces, preferring instead ambushes, raids, and hit-and-run operations. The use of the search-and-destroy tactic did result in a significant number of PAVN and NLF **casualties**, but it did not result in the security of the Vietnamese people, which was a necessary requirement for victory in the war. Search-and-destroy missions relied on mobility and firepower. The former meant that areas controlled were often not retained, while the latter sometimes resulted in unintended casualties that brought new recruits to the PAVN and NLF.

One of the first search-and-destroy operations was Operation **Starlite**, conducted by the U.S. Marines against the 1st Battalion of the **National Liberation Front** (NLF). The operation concentrated on an area approximately 16 kilometers (10 miles) to the south of **Chu Lai** in I **Corps Tactical Zone**. The six-day operation in August 1965 yielded some positive results but also exposed the problems of search-and-destroy operations, which focused on body counts rather than tactical control of an area. Similar operations occurred in 1966 with operations **Masher/White Wing**, **Thayer**, and **Irving**. In 1967, operations **Junction City** and **Cedar Falls** attempted to remove the PAVN and NLF from **War Zone C** and **War Zone D**. Though all of these operations resulted in significant PAVN and NLF casualties, they did not result in the operational area becoming secure against PAVN and NLF threats. Search-and-destroy operations would continue throughout the war with mixed success. *See also* ABILENE, OPERATION; APACHE SNOW, OPERATION; ATTLEBORO, OPERATION; BLUE MARLIN, OPERATION; BỒNG SƠN PLAIN; DEWEY CANYON I, OPERATION; DEWEY CANYON II, OPERATION; DOUBLE EAGLE I, OPERATION; DOUBLE EAGLE II, OPERATION; ENCLAVE STRATEGY; HARVEST MOON, OPERATION; KING, MARTIN LUTHER, JR.; MÊ KÔNG DELTA; PIRANHA, OPERATION; PLAIN OF REEDS; POPULAR FORCES; REPUBLIC OF KOREA; SPEEDY EXPRESS, OPERATION; STARLITE, OPERATION; WESTMORELAND, WILLIAM CHILDS.

SEARCH-AND-RESCUE (SAR). The search and rescue of downed pilots during the war began with the creation of the Pacific Air Rescue Center at Hickam Air Force Base, Hawaii, on 8 October 1961. With it, Detachment 3 was organized at **Tân Sơn Nhứt** Air Base in **Sài Gòn** on 1 April 1962. The mission of the detachment was to coordinate SAR operations. Until American combat troops entered the war, SAR missions depended on **Army of the Republic of Vietnam** (ARVN) troops using **United States Army** or U.S. **Marine Corps helicopters**. Between January 1962 and June 1964, only two of 240 aircraft losses were not located. This success rate was significant when considering that ARVN support and coordination proved challenging as it often insisted that regimental strength be deployed to crash sites while South Vietnamese SAR **helicopters** sometimes failed to arrive in a timely manner.

As American involvement in the war increased, a **U.S. Air Force** (USAF) SAR force was created in May 1964 under the direction of the 3rd Aerospace Rescue and Recovery Group. Nonmilitary units in Southeast Asia such as **Air America** also assisted in SAR missions. Air America rescued 22 pilots in **Laos** between June 1964 and June 1965 compared to four SAR recoveries by USAF helicopters, though Air America work remained classified during the war.

Each SAR mission during the war was unique and had its own challenges. As a result, unifying the missions was difficult, but the USAF did attempt it with a basic SAR Task Force (SARTF) that included two HH-3 helicopters, four A-1 escorts, and one HC-130. When word of a mission reached the SARTF, two A-1s and the HC-130 traveled directly to the site to assess the situation and locate the aircrew. The other A-1 and HH-3 followed to extract the pilots after the area was secure. The A-1 was extremely effective in providing cover fire to protect the downed pilots and secure the area as the extraction took place.

Through 1971, there were 2,348 combat and 1,133 noncombat rescues in the **Democratic Republic of Vietnam** or Laos. SAR missions in the **Republic of Vietnam** (RVN) posed fewer problems than those in the other theaters of Southeast Asia. Crash sites were nearer the SAR base camps, which meant less time to the rescue site. By the war's end, SAR personnel had successfully rescued over 2,800 soldiers in the RVN.

SECOND INDOCHINA WAR. More commonly referred to as the Vietnam War by the **United States** and the West, and as the American War by the **Democratic Republic of Vietnam** (DRV) and the East, the Second Indochina War started after the 1954 **Geneva Agreements**. The actual start date is controversial. The U.S. and the **Republic of Vietnam** (RVN), founded in 1955, argued that the **First Indochina War** never really ended, as the insurgents, who would become known as the **National Liberation Front** (NLF) in 1960, simply worked to undermine the **Sài Gòn** government while the **People's Army of Vietnam** became more active after 1959. The DRV maintained that the war really did not get started until after the U.S. and the RVN failed to adhere to the 1954 Geneva Agreements. The DRV was forced to increase assistance to the NLF against a repressive **Ngô Đình Diệm**, who was considered a lackey of the U.S.

While the U.S. supported the RVN from its inception, it was during the **John F. Kennedy** administration that the gradual escalation of **advisers** began. The U.S. continued to increase its number of advisers and introduced combat troops and a sustained air campaign against the DRV during the **Lyndon B. Johnson** administration in March 1965. The war ended for the U.S. with the 1973 **Paris Peace Accords** and in 1975 for the RVN with the fall of Sài Gòn. As the victor, the DRV consolidated its power in the South and renamed the country the Socialist Republic of Vietnam in 1976.

SEDANG. Ethnic **Montagnards** who speak a language within the Mon-**Khmer** group. The Sedang were situated primarily in **Kon Tum** province, northwest of the city of Kon Tum and in eastern **Laos**. The group's identity originated in 1888 as a result of the intrigue of Charles-Marie David de Mayréna who was tasked with creating treaties with the Sedang people to serve as a buffer between French Indochina and the Kingdom of Siam but instead formed his own kingdom. De Mayréna united the **Bahnar**, Rengao, and Sedang tribes into his kingdom, but after failing to strike a bargain with the French colonial officials or to pit the Prussians and British against **France** for control of his kingdom, his influence ebbed. He died mysteriously in 1890. The Sedang continued to live in the area but were under **People's Army of Vietnam** or **National Liberation Front** control for most of the war.

SELECTIVE SERVICE SYSTEM. On 18 May 1917, the **United States Congress** passed the Selective Service Act in order to gather information on men between the ages of 18 and 25, to make these men eligible for 12 months of military service, and to give the president the authority to draft men into military service. This draft was ended in 1920, well after the end of World War I and the need for a large standing army in the U.S. Prior to World War II, the U.S. initiated a similar act as the nation prepared for war. This act expired in 1947, only to be replaced with the Selective Service Act of 1948, which reintroduced conscription. The Korean War resulted in a revision to this act to meet the demands of that conflict. Under this set of rules, students who attended college or were in a full-time training program were eligible for exemption. In 1963, President **John F. Kennedy** issued an executive order that extended exemptions to married men, though President **Lyndon B. Johnson** would rescind that executive order in 1965 with his own. It was this system that was in place, with a few minor adjustments, as the war in Southeast Asia escalated for the U.S. The selective service process would remain relatively untouched until 1967. During that time, between 1960 and 1966, approximately one million men were inducted into the U.S. Armed Forces, with the most significant increase occurring in 1966 when the number more than tripled from the previous year to over 340,000 inductees.

In 1967, Congress passed the Military Selective Service Act of 1967, which increased the range of potential inductees to 18 to 35 years of age. Student deferments were retained, but this exemption terminated at the end of the four-year degree or when the individual turned 24. This effectively ended student deferments for many who had sought refuge on the college campus rather than running the risk of being drafted and sent to Southeast Asia. Nearly 300,000 were inducted in 1967 and over 340,000 entered service in 1968.

On 26 November 1969, President **Richard M. Nixon** amended the Military Selective Service Act of 1967 by establishing a lottery that randomly determined induction. On 1 December 1969, the first lottery for the draft was held since 1942 during World War II. Men between the ages of 18 to 26, or born between 1 January 1944 and 31 December 1950, were eligible. New York Republican representative Alexander Pirnie, who served on the House Armed Services Committee, selected the first of 366 small round blue plastic capsules, each of which contained a different date within a calendar year. The capsule listed 14 September as the first number in the lottery. Men were inducted into the U.S. Armed Forces through the first 195 dates (24 September) drawn in this first lottery. Additional lotteries occurred on 1 July 1970, 5 August 1971, and 2 February 1972. Nixon further amended the Selective Service Act in 1971 by making registration compulsory. There were three more lotteries before the fall of **Sài Gòn** in April 1975, but these men would not have been sent to the **Republic of Vietnam** because of the January 1973 **Paris Peace Accords**.

While all males between the ages of 18 and 35 were eligible for the draft during the height of the war in Southeast Asia, there were still many ways to avoid the various Selective Service Acts. Potential draftees could be classified as conscientious objectors available for noncombatant military service (1-AO) or conscientious objectors available for alternate community service (1-O) with the appropriate paperwork and history of religious affiliation, though this decision was determined by the local draft boards established in communities around the country.

These local draft boards also determined all other classifications, which ranged from available for unrestricted military service (1-A) to registrant not acceptable for military service (4-F), though the ranking system went as low as a registrant who was over the age of liability or was previously deferred (5-A). There was a total of 31 different rankings to cover the many varieties of individuals eligible for the draft. The Selective Service System was under the directorship of Lewis Blaine Hershey from July 1941 to 15 February 1970, before Dee Ingold replaced him as acting director because of the controversy surrounding selective service and the **antiwar movement**. Curtis W. Tarr assumed the position on 6 April 1970 and remained until 1 May 1972, to be replaced by Byron V. Pepitone who held the position until after the war was over.

SELF-DEFENSE CORPS (SDC). Established after the formation of the **Republic of Vietnam** (RVN) in 1955, the SDC was a paramilitary force that operated at the village level. It was loosely connected with the **Civil Guard**, which operated at the district level, though neither organization was originally a part of the RVN Armed Forces. It was under the authority of the Ministry of the Interior. The SDC was ill-equipped and trained. Unlike the Civil Guard, the SDC did not receive funding from the **United States** Military Aid Program, which rendered it almost ineffective when confronted with organized resistance. On 13 May 1961, in the first few weeks of the presidency of **John F. Kennedy**, the U.S. transformed its relationship with the RVN Armed Forces, Civil Guard, and SDC. Kennedy approved a $41 million **counterinsurgency** plan developed by the **Military Assistance Advisory Group** and the U.S. embassy in **Sài Gòn**. The plan called for an increase in the **Army of the Republic of Vietnam** (ARVN), the Civil Guard, and American **advisers**, as well as for expanding the level of advisory support for the SDC.

On 4 December 1961, Kennedy authorized the increased training of the SDC so that it could relieve the ARVN from static missions. The U.S. also created training centers for the Civil Guard and SDC. SDC forces continued providing for village defense but also started to conduct civil action programs. By 1962, the SDC had increased in strength to nearly 100,000, while MAP funds authorized the strength for 1963 at slightly over 100,000. With MAP funds, the SDC was reorganized into squads and platoons and received a six-week, American-led training program. The U.S. established 26 training centers in the RVN in 1962. Despite the training and equipping of the new SDC, the **National Liberation Front** continued to overrun SDC posts, which were often isolated and were seldom reinforced by other RVN units. The SDC was never considered a priority and was not equipped at the level of the Civil Guard or ARVN. In 1964, the SDC was transformed into the **Popular Forces**.

SHARP, ULYSSES SIMPSON GRANT (1906–2001). United States Navy admiral. Born in Montana and educated at the U.S. Naval Academy, Sharp graduated in 1927. He served aboard a minesweeper and destroyer during World War II in the European Theater. He also served in the Pacific Theater from 1943 to the end of the war. Sharp continued his career in the navy and, after graduating from the Naval War College in 1950, he was the fleet planning officer for the Inchon landing during the Korean War. He would become the deputy chief of naval operations for policy and planning in the early 1960s and, in September 1963, the commander-in-chief of the Pacific, succeeding Admiral John H. Sides. He was advanced to commander-in-chief of all military forces in the Pacific Theater on 30 June 1964.

SHEEP DIPPING • 411

Sharp advocated a stronger U.S. military response than President **Lyndon B. Johnson** allowed. He called for aggressive tactics and a quicker buildup of U.S. assets to prosecute the war in Southeast Asia, while Johnson adopted a gradual approach to buildup in order to keep domestic attention away from the growing crisis in Southeast Asia. Sharp was a proponent of significant **bombing** of the **Democratic Republic of Vietnam** and joined others, like General **Curtis E. LeMay**, in asserting that the U.S. needed to conduct unrestricted and massive bombing on the DRV in order to force the **Hà Nội** government into submission. He was opposed by Secretary of Defense **Robert McNamara**, who continued to advocate a gradual approach and eventually called for stabilization of the bombing campaign in order to negotiate an end to the conflict. On 31 July 1968, Sharp retired from the U.S. Navy. He continued to protest the way Johnson had handled the war, writing a *Reader's Digest* article in 1969 titled "We Could Have Won in Vietnam Long Ago" and a 1978 book, *Strategy for Defeat: Vietnam in Retrospect*, which highlighted the shortcomings of Johnson's Vietnam policy. *See also* HAWK.

SHEEHAN, NEIL (1936–). Journalist. Born Cornelius Mahoney Sheehan in Massachusetts, Sheehan was educated at Harvard University and graduated in 1958. He served in the **United States Army** from 1959 to 1962, after which he joined the United Press International and covered the **Republic of Vietnam** (RVN) from 1962 to 1964. Sheehan was very critical of RVN president **Ngô Đình Diệm** and worked to discredit the **Sài Gòn** government's efforts to fight the **National Liberation Front**. He often directly contradicted the commander of the **Military Assistance Command, Vietnam**, General **Paul Harkins**, especially over the controversial **Battle for Ấp Bắc**.

Sheehan moved to the *New York Times* in 1964, reporting in Indonesia and Vietnam before returning to the U.S. to serve as the correspondent to the Pentagon and the White House. While with the *New York Times*, Sheehan was involved in the publishing of the **Pentagon Papers** after **Daniel Ellsberg** released portions of the Department of Defense study on U.S. involvement in Vietnam from 1954 to 1967 to the newspaper. In 1989, Sheehan won a Pulitzer Prize and National Book Award for his biography of **John Paul Vann** titled *A Bright Shining Lie*. *See also* CREDIBILITY GAP; MEDIA, UNITED STATES; ORDER OF BATTLE DISPUTE.

SHEEP DIPPING. A term that denoted the practice of obscuring the national identities of individuals so that they could be inserted into another country without detection or accusations that they were violating international law or agreements. Sheep Dipping was used primarily during the war in **Laos** because that country was neutral. The **United States**, often through the **Central Intelligence Agency,** created new, fraudulent identities for its personnel so that they could operate as civilians in Southeast Asia without being directly tied to the U.S. or with the military. The practice was also used with Filipino and Thai personnel who supported the Royal Laotian Government against the **Pathet Lao** and the **People's Army of Vietnam**. *See also* PHILIPPINES; THAILAND.

SHERWOOD FOREST, OPERATION. The **United States** experimented with the use of herbicides to destroy **National Liberation Front** (NLF) food supplies and to defoliate areas known to hide **People's Army of Vietnam** (PAVN) and NLF troops. Sherwood Forest, conceived in December 1964, also had as its objective the burning out of enemy strongholds. Using Operation **Ranch Hand sorties**, the 2nd Air Commando Squadron sprayed 78,800 gallons of defoliant on a 125 square kilometer (48 square mile) section of the **Bời Lời** woods to the north-northwest of **Sài Gòn**, near the Cambodian border. The PAVN and NLF had built up this area and had used it as a base of operations to threaten III Corps. Spraying began on 22 January and lasted until 18 February 1965. After waiting for a few weeks for the herbicide to take effect, the **U.S. Air Force** then dropped incendiary munitions in an effort to create a firestorm and burn out the area.

The dead vegetation quickly caught fire while secondary explosions confirmed the destruction of PAVN and NLF facilities and supplies. An unforeseen result of the firestorm was that the combination of intense heat and debris from the fires served as a catalyst to produce rain clouds in the very moist sky. The heavy rains that followed put out all of the fires by the next day. Sherwood Forest failed to achieve its objective even if part of the Bời Lời woods was destroyed. Despite its failure, the U.S. continued to use herbicides in similar types of operations throughout the war, specifically in projects Hot Tip I and II in the Chư Pơng mountains and Project Pink Rose in **War Zone C** and **War Zone D** to the north of Sài Gòn.

SHINING BRASS, OPERATION. As the **United States** escalated its involvement in Vietnam in 1965, it became apparent that the **Democratic Republic of Vietnam** (DRV) was using the neutral countries of **Laos** and **Cambodia** to transport personnel and supplies down the **Hồ Chí Minh Trail**. This was especially critical after the initial success of Operation **Market Time**, which effectively cut off the sea as a supply route for the DRV. In November 1965, the **Studies and Observation Group** (SOG) began to conduct reconnaissance operations into Laos in order to monitor activities down the trail. Earlier attempts to conduct similar missions using South Vietnamese personnel had been less than successful. Operation Shining Brass was made secret because of Laotian neutrality, which meant that teams inserted into Laos were left on their own in most cases. Because of the politically sensitive nature of the operation, there was also considerable jockeying for position as to who would control the actual mission targets. SOG leaders and U.S. ambassador to Laos **William Sullivan** each believed that they should control the events, while the U.S. government had to appease Laotian concerns about violations of its neutrality.

Operation Shining Brass missions were kept small in order to avoid detection by the **Pathet Lao,** the armed insurgents who wished to overthrow the Vientiane government, and **People's Army of Vietnam** (PAVN) troops. Teams began their missions from firebases near the Laotian border within the **Republic of Vietnam**. Once the team arrived at its location, it would conduct reconnaissance and then forward any targets of opportunity to a **Forward Air Control** aircraft, which then guided air **sorties** into the target area. Operations continued throughout the war, though the name was changed from Shining Brass to **Prairie Fire** in March 1967. While the missions were successful in identifying targets and confirming the extent to which the PAVN and **National Liberation Front** had infiltrated into Laos, they were not able to stop the North Vietnamese use of the Hồ Chí Minh Trail.

SHOW THE FLAG PROGRAM. President **Lyndon B. Johnson** sent Secretary of State **Dean Rusk** to Sài Gòn between 17 and 20 April 1964 in order to assess what **United States** action could be employed to convince the **Democratic Republic of Vietnam** (DRV) that the U.S. was committed to the **Republic of Vietnam** (RVN) and that future DRV action would never result in victory. Rusk recommended that the U.S. engage more flags in the RVN. On 23 April, Johnson held a press conference during which he proposed a plan that evolved into the Many Flags or Show the Flag program. Johnson called for other flags in the RVN to help stop the spread of communism in Southeast Asia, but more importantly he announced that the U.S. was committed to the defense of the RVN and that he did not want the U.S. to become involved in that region of the world without **Third Country** support.

Throughout the Show the Flag program, the U.S. insisted that the concerned countries become more involved in the Southeast Asian struggle; they would have to contribute their fair share. On 1 May 1964, Rusk sent a circular to the U.S. embassies of allies that might contribute, instructing his ambassadors to request assistance from their host countries. Rusk informed the American officials that the angle they were to take was that the U.S. was fully committed to Vietnam and expected its allies to share in the burden.

While the program was successful in the sense that more, and a greater percentage of, Third Country forces participated in Southeast Asia than during the Korean War, the program failed to accomplish its other objective of uniting the Free World against the communist threat in Southeast Asia. Among the concerned countries were Australia, New Zealand, the Philippines, the Republic of Korea, and Thailand. *See also* FREE WORLD FORCES.

SIHANOUK TRAIL. Name given to the network of roads, paths, and walkways in **Cambodia** used by the North Vietnamese to supply their forces. The Sihanouk Trail was very similar to the **Hồ Chí Minh Trail**, which ran through southeastern **Laos**. North Vietnamese land supply routes became significant after the implementation of Operation **Market Time** in March 1965, which effectively cut off the North Vietnamese ability to resupply by sea. The **United States** provided the name for the trail after discovering a new road leading from Cambodia into Laos. **Route** 110 went from Siem Pang into Laos and connected with Route 16, which ran east into the **Republic of Vietnam** (RVN), just north of **Kon Tum**.

Even though the U.S. knew that this new route was supporting the **People's Army of Vietnam** and **National Liberation Front** forces fighting in the RVN, it failed to close the road for fear of how **Norodom Sihanouk** would react. There were attempts to disrupt the trail, however, starting with carefully planned B-52 air strikes in December 1965 and Operation **Daniel Boone** in April 1967. In 1969, President **Richard M. Nixon** authorized Operation **Menu**, which struck at the Sihanouk Trail, among other targets. After the March 1970 coup d'état against Sihanouk by General **Lon Nol**, the U.S. initiated the **Cambodian Incursion** followed by an air campaign known as Operation **Freedom Deal**. These efforts did help to disrupt the trail, but they also served as recruiting tools for the **Khmer Rouge**.

After the Cambodian Incursion and the loss of the port at **Sihanoukville**, the North Vietnamese placed greater emphasis on keeping the trail open in Cambodia. They created the 470th Transportation Group to coordinate Cambodian logistical operations. The Sihanouk Trail was extended southward along the **Mê Kông River** toward Stung Treng. It would eventually have the capacity to supply Khmer Rouge forces fighting around **Phnom Penh** in 1975.

SIHANOUK, PRINCE NORODOM (1922–). King and prince of **Cambodia**. Sihanouk, the son of King Norodom Suramarit and Queen Sisowath Kossamak, became king in September 1941 after the death of his maternal grandfather, Sisowath Monivong, on 23 April 1941. Sihanouk advocated an end to French colonialism in Indochina even though the crown had a connection to the French for much of the 20th century. At one point in 1953, Sihanouk fled from the French Sûreté to **Thailand** for fear of his life, though Cambodia would receive its independence from **France** on 9 November 1953. On 2 March 1955, Sihanouk abdicated the throne to his father, Norodom Suramarit and took the position of prime minister. When King Norodom Suramarit died in 1960, Sihanouk became the head of state, a position he would hold until March 1970 even though he had orchestrated a move to make his position one for life.

Sihanouk frequently engaged in duplicity during the war. He publicly advocated Cambodian neutrality but privately worked with the **Democratic Republic of Vietnam** to allow **People's Army of Vietnam** (PAVN) and **National Liberation Front** (NLF) personnel to travel through his country to fight the war against the **Republic of Vietnam** (RVN), especially after the effectiveness of Operation **Market Time** in 1965. Sihanouk opened the port of **Sihanoukville** (Kompong Som) to neutral ships that carried personnel and supplies for the North Vietnamese; he allowed the creation of the **Hak Ly** Company, which served as a communist front for these unneutral activities; and he tolerated the presence of PAVN and NLF soldiers along Cambodia's border with the RVN. These Vietnamese soldiers had established a sophisticated network of bases to fight the war against **Sài Gòn**. While Sihanouk's policies were far from neutral, he justified his actions by the very real concern that the war could still be won by either side, and he needed to accommodate both in order to secure Cambodian independence when the conflict was over.

Sihanouk's pro–North Vietnamese and Chinese policies earned him a number of adversaries. When he was forced to create the Salvation Government in August 1969, he acknowledged the North Vietnamese and NLF presence in his country, called for their removal, and tolerated an American **bombing** campaign named Operation **Menu** to target the foreigners. Sihanouk agreed to allow **Lon Nol** to become prime minister and Prince **Sisowath Sirik Matak** to become deputy prime minister. Both were anticommunist and opposed Sihanouk's old policies; Sihanouk announced a return to neutrality with the creation of the new government. When the North Vietnamese rearranged their agreements with Sihanouk and brought him back to his earlier procommunist policies, Lon Nol and Matak orchestrated a coup d'état on 18 March 1970 that deposed Sihanouk, who was in France at the time. Sihanouk called for the removal of Lon Nol and Matak, but without effect. He created the National United Front of Kampuchea (Front Uni National du Kampuchéa/ FUNK) from his new place of exile in Beijing, **People's Republic of China**, and began to work with the Cambodian communist insurgency, the **Khmer Rouge**, to oust the new government.

Sihanouk's support for the Khmer Rouge allowed that organization to flourish despite the 1970 **Cambodian Incursion** and increased American support for the Cambodian Royal Armed Forces. For the remainder of the war, he had influence in Cambodia but wielded little power. The Khmer Rouge, under **Pol Pot**, continued the war to its conclusion when it overran **Phnom Penh** in early April 1975. Sihanouk was forced out of office within a year, though he remained in the country during the genocide that took between 1.7 and 3 million Cambodian lives. He fought a political battle against the Socialist Republic of Vietnam when it invaded his country in December 1978. As a result of the invasion, he was exiled and did not return to Cambodia until 14 November 1991. In 1993, he once again became the king, but this time in a constitutional monarchy. He abdicated the throne on 7 October 2004 after suffering from a variety of illnesses, including prostate and stomach cancer.

SIHANOUKVILLE. Sihanoukville was the major port in **Cambodia**, approximately 185 kilometers (115 miles) to the southwest of **Phnom Penh**. It was built by the French before they left Indochina and was officially established as a port city in 1960. It was named after King **Norodom Sihanouk**. Sihanoukville became important during the war after the **United States** initiated Operation **Market Time**, which effectively shut down the ability of the North Vietnamese to move supplies by sea to support their troops in the **Republic of Vietnam** (RVN). Instead, the North Vietnamese sent their supplies to Sihanoukville, beyond the 150 mile barrier imposed by Market Time. These supplies were offloaded at Sihanoukville and moved by land to Phnom Penh and then to the **People's Army of Vietnam** (PAVN) and **National Liberation Front** (NLF) forces who operated along the Cambodian-RVN border. After **Lon Nol**'s 18 March 1970 coup d'état against Sihanouk, the port continued to be busy. U.S. ships replaced those that had supported the PAVN and NLF to equip the Cambodian Royal Army in its fight against the **Khmer Rouge**, PAVN, and NLF.

At the end of the war, Sihanoukville was one of the last places from which the Americans evacuated Cambodians who wished to flee Khmer Rouge rule. In May 1975, the U.S. fought the Khmer Rouge in Sihanoukville after the SS *Mayaguez* had been seized earlier in international waters. When the Khmer Rouge fell to the Socialist Republic of Vietnam forces in 1979, Sihanoukville revived as a port city, was renamed Kompong Som, and became a significant resource in Cambodia's recovery after the Khmer Rouge genocide that claimed between 1.7 and 3 million lives.

SISOWATH SIRIK MATAK, PRINCE (1914–1975). Member of the Cambodian Royal family and fierce anticommunist who became a victim of the **Khmer Rouge** during the Cambodian genocide. Though a cousin of Prince **Norodom Sihanouk**, Sirik Matak was one of his main critics during Sihanouk's rule in **Cambodia**. Sirik Matak had served in a variety of positions of leadership from 1954, including as minister of national defense and chief of staff to the Royal Cambodian Armed Forces (1954–1955); as minister of defense and minister of the interior (1956); as first deputy prime minister of

Cambodia in charge of interior, order, security, education, and religious affairs (1969–1970); and as first deputy prime minister under **Lon Nol** after the creation of the Salvation Government in August 1969. Sirik Matak opposed the presence of the **People's Army of Vietnam** (PAVN) and the **National Liberation Front** (NLF) in his country and resisted Khmer Rouge efforts to destabilize the **Phnom Penh** government.

On 18 March 1970, Sirik Matak and Lon Nol orchestrated a coup d'état against Sihanouk, which was approved by the Cambodian National Assembly in a secret vote. He supported the **United States bombing** of the PAVN and NLF bases along the Cambodian-**Republic of Vietnam** border in Operation **Menu** as well as the continued air campaigns of Operations **Freedom Deal** and **Freedom Action** after the May 1970 **Cambodian Incursion**. Sirik Matak continued to serve his country, even becoming prime minister from 6 May 1971 to 18 March 1972. When Lon Nol resigned the Cambodian presidency on 1 April 1975 and fled Cambodia days before the Khmer Rouge overran Phnom Penh, Sirik Matak chose to stay. He refused to flee before the enemy and rejected the offer of asylum from the U.S. He was captured by the Khmer Rouge in Phnom Penh and executed on 21 April 1975.

SMITH, WALTER BEDELL (1895–1961). U.S. Army general. Smith was with the 4th Division during World War I and was chief of staff for Dwight D. Eisenhower, the Supreme Allied Commander, during World War II. He negotiated the surrender of both Italy and Germany. After the war, he served as the American ambassador to the **Soviet Union** from 3 April 1946 to 25 December 1948 and as the director of the **Central Intelligence Agency** from 7 October 1950 to 9 February 1953. As undersecretary of state in 1954, Smith represented the **United States** at the **Geneva Conference**. Secretary of State **John Foster Dulles** instructed him to refuse to sign the final agreement and instead issue an American statement that reaffirmed the U.S. position to respect the document.

SƠN NGỌC THÀNH (1908–1977). Cambodian politician and leader of the **Khmer Serei**. Sơn Ngọc Thành was born in southern Vietnam in an area that was inhabited by Cambodians. He received his education in **Sài Gòn** and Paris, where he studied law, and returned to **Cambodia** to become a librarian at the Buddhist Institute in **Phnom Penh** in 1933. In 1936, he was one of the founders of *Nagarvatta*, the first Cambodian-language newspaper. During World War II, he helped to organize anti-French demonstrations and barely escaped imprisonment for his actions. He was exiled to Japan until the end of the war. After Japan staged a takeover of Indochina on 9 March 1945 and King **Norodom Sihanouk** established Cambodian independence two days later, Sơn Ngọc Thành returned to Cambodia and served as the prime minister from 14 August to 16 October 1945. He was arrested by the French in October and was replaced as prime minister by Prince Sisowath Monireth. He was sent to **France** where he lived under house arrest until 1951.

Sơn Ngọc Thành's return was hailed by the people, though he refused to enter active politics. Instead he founded a newspaper, *Khmer Krauk*, which the French banned within a month. Sơn Ngọc Thành traveled to join the Khmer Issarak rebels, who opposed the French, in Siem Reap. After failing to gain control over the Khmer Issarak, he established the Khmer Serei (Free Khmer) movement and worked against Sihanouk, the North Vietnamese, the **National Liberation Front**, and the **Khmer Rouge**. He moved between Cambodia and the **Republic of Vietnam** during the war, recruiting from the **Khmer Krom**. He organized the Khmer Serei on the premise that Sihanouk had allied with the communists and as a result no longer deserved to lead Cambodia. When Sihanouk was replaced by **Lon Nol** in a March 1970 coup d'état, Sơn Ngọc Thành was appointed a senior adviser and later became the prime minister for a second time on 18 March 1972, replacing Prince **Sisowath Sirik Matak**. He remained the prime minister until 15 October 1972 when Lon Nol dismissed him from office. Sơn Ngọc Thành fled to Vietnam for the remainder of the war and was arrested by the North Vietnamese after the fall of Sài Gòn. He died in prison.

SƠN TÂY. Located approximately 37 kilometers (23 miles) to the northwest of **Hà Nội**, Sơn Tây was the capital of Sơn Tây province. It was the home of the Vietnamese People's Army Infantry Academy as well as a prison made famous as a result of a 21 November 1970 attempt, known as Operation **Kingpin**, to raid the facility and free its prisoners. Operation Kingpin failed in its objective as the **United States Special Forces** discovered that there were no prisoners located in the prison.

SORTIE. Term used to denote one aircraft that flew one mission. During the war, the **United States** flew millions of combat and noncombat sorties, including bombing missions, **Combat Air Patrol**, **reconnaissance**, **search-and-rescue**, **medevac**, training, psychological operations, transportation, and other related missions over the **Democratic Republic of Vietnam**, the **Republic of Vietnam**, **Laos**, and **Cambodia**.

SOUPHANOUVONG, PRINCE (1909–1995). President of the Lao People's Democratic Republic, half brother to Prince **Souvanna** and ally of the **Democratic Republic of Vietnam** (DRV). Prince Souphanouvong was educated at the École Nationale des Ponts et Chaussées in **France** and French

Indochina. He joined the communists who resisted the French and supported **Hồ Chí Minh** in Vietnam. Prince Souphanouvong organized the First Congress of the Lao Freedom Front (Neo Lao Issara) which evolved into the **Pathet Lao**, the military arm of the communist insurgency in **Laos**.

He held a number of positions within the Laotian government, including deputy prime minister and minister of economics, and he represented the Pathet Lao at the 1962 **Geneva Conference** on Laos sponsored in part by the **United States**. Prince Souphanouvong allied with the DRV against the Royal Laotian Government, and when Laos was taken over by the communists in 1975, he became the first president of the Lao People's Democratic Republic, though he served in more of a ceremonial role. In 1991, he was removed from that position, though he continued to maintain a position as adviser of the Party's Central Committee.

SOUTH EAST ASIAN TREATY ORGANIZATION (SEATO). Formed on 8 September 1954, SEATO included the **United States**, **France**, **Great Britain**, **New Zealand**, **Australia**, the **Philippines**, **Thailand**, and Pakistan, with the intent to create a regional collective security arrangement to confront the growing communist threat in Southeast Asia. Though not included as members, the **Republic of Vietnam**, **Laos**, and **Cambodia** were offered protection by the organization should any one of them be threatened by external communist forces. While SEATO provided a possible justification for U.S. escalation into the Vietnam War, the treaty was never invoked and really only functioned as a means for limited collective military training and information sharing.

As the war ended for the U.S. in 1973, the need for SEATO diminished. Members had already become disillusioned with the concept of SEATO and with earlier U.S. involvement in Vietnam. Pakistan left in 1973 when its interests were not met in its war against **India**, while France had been critical of the U.S. experience in Vietnam since the 1960s. After **Phnom Penh** and **Sài Gòn** fell in April 1975 and Vientiane succumbed to the communists later in the year, the need for SEATO ceased. It was disbanded on 30 June 1977.

SOUTH VIETNAM. Area known as Cochin China and part of An Nam during the period of French colonialism. In July 1954, the **Geneva Agreements** divided the State of Vietnam into two regions that would be united after national elections occurred within two years. The northern region was known as the **Democratic Republic of Vietnam**, or North Vietnam, while the southern region maintained the name of the State of Vietnam, or South Vietnam. South Vietnam included approximately 173,500 square kilometers (67,000 square miles). On 26 October 1955, the **Republic of Vietnam** (RVN) was established, which consisted of the area known as South Vietnam. The RVN ceased to exist after the fall of **Sài Gòn** on 30 April 1975.

SOUVANNA PHOUMA (1901–1984). Laotian prince and prime minister. Souvanna Phouma was the son of Luang Prabang, a Laotian vice king and the nephew of King Sisavan Vong. He was educated in **Hà Nội** and **France**, where he received a degree in engineering. In 1931, he returned to **Laos** to work in the French colonial government. He did not become politically active as a nationalist until after World War II when France sought to regain Indochina. Souvanna Phouma joined the Neo Lao Issara, dedicated to Laotian independence. He spent a few years in exile in **Thailand** but returned in 1949. Souvanna Phouma was elected prime minister in 1951, for the first of four times. He worked hard to keep Laos neutral during the **First Indochina War**. He left office in 1954 but returned in 1956 for two more years, during which time he strived to bring the communists into his more conservative government. The coalition failed in 1958. He returned as prime minister, briefly, for a third time in 1960 and again in July 1962, where he remained until 1975.

Souvanna Phouma continually sought reconciliation with his half brother and head of the **Pathet Lao,** Prince **Souphanouvong**, but he refused to surrender control to the communists. As the war was ending in Vietnam and **Cambodia**, Souvanna Phouma recognized his tenuous position and formed a coalition government with the Pathet Lao in April 1974. He remained prime minister until his resignation in December 1975 and served as an adviser to the new government until his death. Souvanna Phouma's political career was one of limited compromise and reconciliation. He sought to keep Laos neutral in the wars that ravaged Southeast Asia but failed, as his country was pivotal to the **Democratic Republic of Vietnam**'s success against the **Republic of Vietnam**.

SOVIET UNION. The Union of Soviet Socialist Republics (USSR) became aware of the Vietnamese nationalist movement in the 1920s when **Hồ Chí Minh** traveled to Moscow. The Soviets supported Hồ Chí Minh's efforts to organize a Vietnamese communist party with advice and financial assistance around 1925. The Indochinese Communist Party was founded in 1930. The Soviet-Vietnamese relationship was strained during the 1930s as Hồ Chí Minh and his military leader, **Võ Nguyên Giáp**, moved away from the Soviet model and focused on Vietnamese nationalism in its struggle against **France**'s colonial rule.

Indochina became less of a focus during World War II as the Soviet Union fought for its survival against the Germans. The Soviets were also more concerned with internal recovery from the war's destruction and the emerging

Cold War confrontation with the **United States** in the late 1940s. After the Korean War began in 1950 and the U.S. recognized the French-controlled State of Vietnam in that same year, the Soviet Union began to supply some aid to the Vietnamese engaged in the **First Indochina War**. The amount of assistance was small, in part to avoid the attention of the Americans who were engaged in the Korean War. Most of the Soviet aid was filtered through the **People's Republic of China**.

As the First Indochina War concluded after the **Battle of Điện Biên Phủ** and the convening of the 1954 **Geneva Conference**, the Soviet Union and China encouraged the leaders of the **Democratic Republic of Vietnam** (DRV) to reach an accommodation with the French and the West. The Soviets were concerned that the U.S., after it ended its war in Korea with an armistice, would concentrate its attention in Indochina and escalate that conflict. Hồ Chí Minh reluctantly agreed, even though Võ Nguyên Giáp's forces had control over much of the region. The Geneva Agreements divided Vietnam near the 17th parallel, with a promise for national elections to reunify the country within two years.

Because of this stipulation, the Soviets advocated a political solution to the crisis in Vietnam rather than military action. Even after **Republic of Vietnam** (RVN) President **Ngô Đình Diệm**, with U.S. consent, refused to hold elections, the Soviets preached peaceful coexistence with the West and pressured the DRV to follow that model. When, in 1957, the U.S. attempted to gain RVN membership in the **United Nations**, the Soviet Union vetoed the application. The U.S. hoped that UN recognition of the RVN would help that country gain legitimacy within the international community. The Soviet Union offered a proposal to accept both the RVN and the DRV, but the U.S. refused to acknowledge the authority and legitimacy of the communist state. By the end of the 1950s, it was clear that Ngô Đình Diệm had created a viable RVN. Many Vietnamese, with Chinese backing, called for increased warfare. The Soviets eventually consented to this change of strategy in 1959 but continued to call for limited armed aggression to keep Western attention away from the region.

The Soviets followed a similar pattern in **Laos**. In August 1960, a coup d'état by army captain **Kong Le** returned **Souvanna Phouma** to power. Because of his neutralist position, the U.S. supported General **Phoumi Nosavan** in his successful attempt to take over. This caused the neutralists to ally themselves with the communist insurgents and begin receiving support from the Soviet Union. The U.S. countered with **Project Pipe Stem** in which it used RF-101 **reconnaissance** aircraft to monitor Soviet assistance to the **Pathet Lao** in northern Laos. Laos became the next real threat in Southeast Asia. The Soviet Union was anxious not to intensify conflict in the region and, with the U.S., called for another Geneva Conference in late 1961. The conference led to the **1962 Geneva Accords** in which all sides agreed to maintain Laotian neutrality. As a result, the Soviet Union decreased aid to the Pathet Lao, though the DRV continued to operate in the country in order to develop and maintain the **Hồ Chí Minh Trail**.

A consequence of the 1962 Geneva Accords and the Soviet reluctance to support overt aggression was a lessening of Soviet influence and an increase in Chinese advice and military assistance. The period between 1963 and 1964 was the nadir of Soviet-Vietnamese relations. Vietnamese who continued to support the Soviet position, such as Võ Nguyên Giáp, were labeled revisionists, were eased from power, or were imprisoned. Because Võ Nguyên Giáp enjoyed the confidence of Hồ Chí Minh, he remained in his position, but his influence ebbed. By the time of the **Gulf of Tŏn Kĭn Incident** in August 1964, the Soviets had reevaluated their Vietnam policy.

Although the majority of military hardware was provided by China during this period, the Soviets were more willing to provide assistance. While Soviet Premier Alexi Kosygin visited **Hà Nội** in February 1965, the U.S. decided to retaliate against attacks to Americans in the RVN. The U.S. bombing of the DRV, under Operation **Flaming Dart**, while Kosygin was engaged in a state visit helped to prod the Soviets into providing additional aid. The most significant contribution was the delivery of the SA-2, a surface-to-air **missile** that offered a real threat to the U.S. air campaign against the DRV. Along with Soviet air defense weapons, Soviet technicians entered the DRV. This caused the **Lyndon B. Johnson** administration to limit when and where it struck, for fear of killing or wounding Soviet citizens and escalating the war. The Soviets also supplied a variety of aircraft and **antiaircraft artillery** to offset the U.S. advantage in the air.

Vietnamese pilots had long received training in China and the Soviet Union and flew MiG-15, MiG-17, MiG-19, and MiG-21 fighter aircraft. A Vietnamese MiG-17 earned its first confirmed kill on 3 April 1965 when it downed an F-105 Freedom Fighter. The MiG-21 was the most sophisticated Soviet-built aircraft used in the war. It was donated to the DRV, as a gift to the people, and saw its first action in the war in April 1966. The Soviets also delivered the K-13 Atoll air-to-air missile, which was a copy of the U.S.-built AIM-9.

As the air campaign Operation **Rolling Thunder** increased, the U.S. adopted a policy of gradually reducing the publicity of air strikes in order to minimize reactions from the Soviet Union and China. Concern for international reactions would also result in a series of restrictions placed on the air campaign that limited its potential. The areas around Hà Nội and **Hải Phòng**, as well as the border between China and the DRV, remained off limits, while each attack was planned to reduce civilian **casualties** even though it was inevitable that civilians would suffer.

While the Chinese continued to supply the bulk of the weapons used by the **People's Army of Vietnam** (PAVN) and the **National Liberation Front** (NLF), Soviet weapons did make their way into Southeast Asia. The Soviet-built rocket-propelled grenade (**RPG-2**) was an inexpensive, easy-to-use weapon. It fired an 82-mm warhead that weighed less than 1.8 kilograms (4 pounds), with an effective range of 100 to 150 meters (330–480 feet) and a maximum range of nearly 185 meters (600 feet). It was effective against armor and stationery objects.

The Soviet-built, Mikhail Kalashnikov–designed AK-47 **rifle** was also a significant weapon of the war, though the majority of the PAVN and NLF personnel used the Chinese-made Type 56 rifle, an exact copy of the AK-47, which began production in 1956. PAVN forces did employ several types of Soviet-built **artillery**, including the 85-mm artillery field gun, the 122-mm M1938 field howitzer, the 130-mm M1954 field gun, and the 152-mm M1955 howitzer. There were Chinese designs of the same weapon that flowed into the DRV. The Vietnamese also used Soviet- and Chinese-built **mortars**.

PAVN **tanks** included the Soviet-built T-54 and PT-76, though they did not arrive on the battlefield in great numbers until the late 1960s. In the one engagement between the Soviet-built tank and U.S. armor, on 3 and 4 March 1969 at **Bến Hét**, the U.S. tanks proved to be superior. The PAVN did use Soviet tanks during its 1972 **Easter Offensive** but lost an estimated 50 percent of them, many to the TOW guided **missile**. The Soviets sent their own antitank missile, the 9M14M Malutka, known by the U.S. as the AT-3 Sagger. It was used successfully in the 1972 Easter Offensive against **Army of the Republic of Vietnam** tank and armored vehicles.

Soviet weapons played a role in the DRV war against the RVN and the U.S. But like the Chinese, it was the Soviet threat of escalation that served as the main deterrent to an American expansion of the war during the Johnson administration. In reality, the Soviet Union did not want to escalate the war, and as its border skirmishes with China increased in the late 1960s, it was eager to deescalate the Vietnam War even if a stalemate ensued.

SPECIAL FORCES, UNITED STATES. After some experimentation with the concept during World War II, the first U.S. Special Forces group formed on 20 June 1952 at Fort Bragg, North Carolina. It was not until 1957 that Special Forces personnel became involved in Southeast Asia. The 1st Special Forces Group was established on 24 June 1957 on Okinawa and started to train volunteers from the **Army of the Republic of Vietnam** (ARVN) at the Commando Training Center in **Nha Trang**. U.S. Special Forces also trained Vietnamese personnel in what would become known as the **First Observation Group**.

U.S. Special Forces also became involved in **Laos** in 1959. In July 1959, under Project **Hotfoot**, the 77th Special Forces Group, whose members were **sheep dipped**, began to train Royal Laotian Army personnel. In 1961, the project was renamed Monkhood, and it was again changed in April 1961 to project **White Star**, after which U.S. personnel began to wear military uniforms. As a result of the 1962 **Geneva Accords** on Laos, Special Forces personnel were removed from that country only to refocus their attention on the **Republic of Vietnam** (RVN).

On 21 September 1961, as President **John F. Kennedy** increased American assistance to the RVN, the 5th Special Forces Group, 1st Special Forces was activated at Fort Bragg. This group took over all Special Forces activities, including the training of the **Civilian Irregular Defense Group** (CIDG) program, which began in the fall of 1961. The CIDG's objective was to train ethnic minorities in **counterinsurgency** and reconnaissance missions. The CIDG program fell within the responsibility of the Vietnamese, but rivalry between the ethnic groups, especially with the **Rhadé**, resulted in American personnel moving beyond their advisory role to become involved in combat operations.

U.S. Special Forces also organized **Montagnards** to operate in small teams in the Vietnamese jungles based on a plan conceived by Captain Ngô Văn Hưng in 1961. This effort was motivated in part by American frustration with the inability of the South Vietnamese to organize their own Special Forces. Under the auspices of the **Central Intelligence Agency** (CIA), the **Mountain Scouts** trained and operated in I **Corps Tactical Zone** (CTZ) starting in December 1961. The program expanded to II and III CTZ, and by May 1963, when the program was handed over to the **Military Assistance Command, Vietnam** (MACV), the Mountain Scouts had deployed 5,300 men in the 21 mountain provinces.

Another project sponsored by the CIA was the creation of the **Trail Watchers**. The Special Forces helped to train Montagnards to observe North Vietnamese movement down the **Hồ Chí Minh Trail**. Trail Watchers were tasked with trying to stop the infiltration or, if confronted by a much larger force, directing ARVN forces to the infiltrators. In November 1963, the Trail Watchers and other CIDG projects came under the operational control of the MACV through Operation **Switchback**. Trail Watchers were eventually absorbed into the Special Forces–authorized Border Surveillance–Control Operating concept. The teams recruited and trained new personnel to serve as observers, created an **intelligence** network, conducted psychological operations and civic action programs, and helped with **pacification** efforts.

Operation Switchback was completed on 1 July 1963. It also resulted in the creation of the U.S. Army Special Forces (Provisional), Vietnam, under the MACV. In January 1964, the CIA handed over covert operations, which led to the creation of the **Studies and Observation Group**, and on 1 October 1964, the 5th Special Forces (Airborne) was officially assigned to the RVN.

The Special Forces units were organized into A detachments or A-Teams, which usually consisted of about a dozen men, with two officers and the rest noncommissioned officers. In the organizational chart for Special Forces, four A-Teams were overseen by a B detachment, while a C detachment controlled three B detachments. Because of the nature of the Special Forces missions, this structure was often modified in order to better suit the conditions of the war.

U.S. Special Forces continued to work with RVN Special Forces personnel and the Montagnards throughout the rest of the war in a variety of operations and projects. On 15 May 1964, the Special Forces established **Leaping Lena**, a project to train Vietnamese Special Forces and Civilian Irregular Defense Group personnel on **long-range patrols** (LRPs). Members of the 1st Special Forces Group and 7th Special Forces Group trained the Vietnamese in LRP strategy and tactics. In October 1964, Leaping Lena became **Project Delta** and then the **Recondo School** in September 1966.

Also established in October 1964, the **Mobile Strike Force**, which was also referred to as the MIKE Force or Eagle Flight, was involved in operations in II CTZ. It involved specialized training for members of the CIDG who acted as a **quick reaction force**, though they were also involved in raids, ambushes, and armed reconnaissance. A Mobile Strike Force company was led by an A-Team and usually consisted of a headquarters element, three rifle platoons, a weapons platoon, and a reconnaissance platoon.

In the fall of 1966, the U.S. Special Forces also helped to develop the Mobile Guerrilla Forces, who were organized in a similar fashion to the Mobile Strike Force except that a reconnaissance platoon replaced the weapons platoon. These units operated in contested territory and conducted missions that involved interdiction, reconnaissance, and surveillance. The Mobile Guerrilla Force operated like the **National Liberation Front** (NLF). It stayed in the field for up to two months and lived off the land. It worked to control its area of operation and made it difficult for the **People's Army of Vietnam** (PAVN) or the NLF to move freely in its area. The Mobile Guerrilla Force was led by a U.S. Special Forces A-Team and operated without support, reinforcement, or commitment to other military operations in its area.

Like Project Delta, projects Omega and Sigma involved long-range reconnaissance and intelligence-gathering missions. Project Omega, under the control of Detachment B-50, operated from Nha Trang and was involved in operations in II CTZ. Project Sigma was under the control of Detachment B-56 and operated in III CTZ. Both projects used **Roadrunner** teams that operated along known PAVN and NLF pathways to discover the enemy and

direct Mobile Strike Forces against them when possible. *See also* SPECIAL
FORCES, VIETNAMESE; SPIKE TEAMS.

SPECIAL FORCES, VIETNAMESE. The Lực Lượng Đặc Biệt Quân Lực
Việt Nam Cộng Hòa (LLDB), or Vietnamese Special Forces, was established
in February 1956 when the **United States** started to train South Vietnamese
in the **First Observation Group** program. Training began in **Nha Trang** with
a special emphasis on psychological warfare, reconnaissance, **intelligence**
gathering, and sabotage missions. While the LLDB was organizationally
under the **Army of the Republic of Vietnam** (ARVN) when that organization was created in October 1956, it really answered to **Ngô Đình Nhu**, the
brother of RVN president **Ngô Đình Diệm**. LLDB personnel were highly
trained and equipped but were used in limited military operations. Colonel
Lê Quang Tung commanded the LLDB and assured that the LLDB was most
loyal to Ngô Đình Diệm. It was kept near **Sài Gòn** in case of an attempted
coup d'état and was often used to suppress domestic dissent. The Vietnamese
Special Forces expanded in September 1962 when its counterpart **U.S. Special Forces** assumed responsibility for anti-infiltration and reconnaissance
missions along the border between the **Democratic Republic of Vietnam**
(DRV), **Laos**, and the **Republic of Vietnam** (RVN).

Also in 1962, the U.S. Special Forces tried to integrate the LLDB with the
Civilian Irregular Defense Group (CIDG) program in order to increase the
efficiency of both organizations in **counterinsurgency** warfare. The CIDG,
however, was made up mostly of **Montagnards** who did not get along very
well with the LLDB. The Vietnamese Special Forces did not achieve success
in its operations against the DRV, but its reputation and negative perception
came not from that failure but from its actions during the 1963 **Buddhist
Crisis**. By August 1963, **Buddhist** demonstrations had expanded to all of
the major urban centers in the RVN after an incident in May 1963 resulted
in the deaths of nine demonstrators in **Huế**. Fearing a coup d'état, Ngô Đình
Nhu orchestrated a countercoup action using Vietnamese Special Forces personnel who were dressed like regular ARVN soldiers. The 21 August action
furthered the serious rift that had already developed between the RVN and
the U.S. American officials demanded that the Vietnamese Special Forces be
used in counterinsurgency operations, but Ngô Đình Diệm, who feared a coup
d'état, refused. This led to the U.S. cutting off its funding for the organization.
Lê Quang Tung was also executed during the 1 November coup d'état that
ended with the assassination of Ngô Đình Diệm.

In the post–Ngô Đình Diệm period, the U.S. Special Forces initiated Project
Leaping Lena to train the Vietnamese Special Forces and Civilian Irregular
Defense Group in long-range reconnaissance patrols. This experiment also

ended in disaster as nearly all of the men in the five eight-man teams air-dropped into Laos around the city of **Tchepone** to provide intelligence on the **Hồ Chí Minh Trail** were killed or captured before the mission ended. Despite this failure, and with the aid of the U.S. Army's 5th Special Forces Group, the Vietnamese Special Forces slowly improved in quality and increased in quantity. By 1967, LLDB officers commanded CIDG units and camps without incident. With the advent of **Vietnamization** and the beginning of the withdrawal of U.S. Special Forces from Southeast Asia, the CIDG and Vietnamese Special Forces were absorbed into the ARVN as the organization was disbanded. Many former Special Forces personnel entered into the ARVN Rangers.

SPEEDY EXPRESS, OPERATION. **Search-and-destroy** operation involving the **United States** 9th **Division** and the **Army of the Republic of Vietnam** (ARVN) 7th Division, supported by the **Mobile Riverine Force** around Định Tường and Kiến Hoa provinces in IV **Corps Tactical Zone**. The operation began on 1 December 1968 and lasted until the end of May 1969. The main objective of the operation was to support **pacification** in the area and disrupt the **National Liberation Front** (NLF) from operating south of **Sài Gòn**. The operation became controversial because of the high number, approaching 11,000, of NLF claimed killed by the U.S. compared to the low number of U.S. and ARVN killed. Members of the **media** claimed that the operation's body count was based in part on indiscriminate killing of civilians who happen to be in the wrong place at the wrong time as well as on the overuse of airpower, which caused civilian deaths.

SPIKE TEAMS. Small groups of South Vietnamese, usually consisting of ethnic minorities, under **United States Special Forces** leadership. Spike teams were within the operational control of the **Studies and Observation Group** and carried out reconnaissance missions in **Laos** and **Cambodia**, only striking at the enemy if it was appropriate or necessary. Normally the teams consisted of around a dozen men, with two or three Americans. They provided valuable **intelligence** for the U.S. and the **Republic of Vietnam** in their fighting of the secret wars in Laos and Cambodia.

SPRING MOBILIZATION TO END THE WAR IN VIETNAM. An **anti-war** group, which was established in 1967, that coordinated mass demonstrations against the war. It organized a 25 April 1967 protest that experienced support across the country, including approximately 130,000 protestors in New York City and half that number in San Francisco. In May 1967, the name of the organization was changed to the **National Mobilization Committee to End the War in Vietnam**, which was shortened to Mobe for convenience.

STALEY MISSION. On 16 June 1961, President **John F. Kennedy** sent a group of experts in the field of economics to the **Republic of Vietnam** (RVN) headed by the president of the Stanford Research Institute, Dr. Eugene Staley. The Staley Mission was to work with their Vietnamese counterparts to assess Vietnam economic policy. The team was also tasked with the mission of determining if the RVN could finance an expansion of its army. RVN president **Ngô Đình Diệm** had requested an increase in the number of personnel in order to counter the more aggressive actions of the **National Liberation Front**. Based on the recommendations of the Staley Mission provided on 4 August 1961, Kennedy agreed to fund the increase of an additional 30,000 troops. The report also suggested that the **Sài Gòn** government needed to initiate political, social, and economic reforms.

STARLITE, OPERATION. **Search-and-destroy** operation designed to take the battle to the enemy rather than wait for attacks. Operation Starlite was the first major **United States Marine Corps** (USMC) offensive during the war and targeted the 1st Battalion of the **National Liberation Front** (NLF). The operation concentrated on an area approximately 16 kilometers (10 miles) to the south of **Chu Lai** in I **Corps Tactical Zone**. Early in the morning on 18 August 1965, the 3rd Battalion, 3rd Marines made an amphibious landing near the hamlet of An Cường to the south of the suspected headquarters of the 1st Battalion at Vạn Tường. The landing was supported by a battery of USMC **artillery** and 20 USMC A-4s and F-4s. After the marines landed and secured An Cường hamlet, other USMC units from the 4th Marine Regiment were airlifted into blocking positions to the west and northwest of the amphibious landing.

Most of the marines experienced light contact with the NLF forces in the area, though a group of approximately 100 were spotted in the afternoon when a force disembarked at **Landing Zone** (LZ) Blue, the southernmost point of the operation. The NLF practiced strict fire discipline and allowed the first wave of **helicopters** to land at the LZ before opening fire on the exposed marines. After the marines regrouped, they began to move toward the objective—phase line Banana—to the northeast, only to discover a series of NLF firing positions in their way. Once phase line Banana was achieved, the marines could push the NLF into the sea.

On 18 August, more marines landed and took up positions to the south and west of the known NLF location and moved to engage the enemy on 19 August, only to find that the NLF had escaped through the **United States** line. The marines continued to move from phase line Banana to the coast, including the short Phước Thuận Peninsula, which was completed by the end of the day. The operation was extended an additional five days, though only a few enemy soldiers were killed. The marines claimed 614 NLF soldiers killed, with 9 prisoners and 42 suspects detained. They also captured 109 weapons. There were 45 marines killed-in-action and 203 wounded.

While the marines caused a significant amount of damage to the NLF, they did not eliminate the 1st Battalion, which continued to operate south of Chu Lai for much of the war. The marines were also criticized by the South Vietnamese, though much of that had to do with the fact that the operation received a great deal of press coverage. As a result, General **William C. Westmoreland** ordered more combined actions involving U.S. and Vietnamese troops in order to better publicize the Vietnamese involvement. Operation Starlite would be the first of many search-and-destroy operations that would be deemed successful even though the enemy retained enough strength to maintain a presence and threaten the stability of the area.

STEEL TIGER, OPERATION. An air interdiction operation that focused on the southern region of **Laos**. On 3 April 1965, the **United States** initiated Operation Steel Tiger to stop the flow of personnel and supplies down the **Hồ Chí Minh Trail**. The operation was designed to complement Operation **Rolling Thunder**. Even though approximately 1,000 **sorties** per month were sent against targets of opportunity, Steel Tiger suffered from command and control issues between the U.S. embassy in Vientiane, which demanded final authorization over target selection, and the **U.S. Air Force** and **Military Assistance Command, Vietnam** (MACV). Political indecision coupled with concern for civilian **casualties** and cultural and religious landmarks also hindered the operation. In December 1965, **William C. Westmoreland** carved out a portion of the Steel Tiger area that bordered the **Republic of Vietnam** (RVN) and assumed responsibility in what became known as Operation **Tiger Hound**. While this created tension between the MACV and the U.S. embassy in Vientiane, the military necessity of coordinating air operations in southern Laos with ground troops in the northern part of the RVN won out. Steel Tiger continued until December 1968, albeit in a smaller area.

Steel Tiger used day-and-night **bombing** to apply constant pressure on the enemy, employing a number of different types of aircraft, from the WW II–era B-57 and A-26 to the more modern F-4, F-100, and F-105 fighter-bombers during the day and the AC-47, AC-119, and AC-130 gunships coordinating with O-1 and OV-10 **reconnaissance** aircraft to strike at night. One of the outgrowths of the operation was the development of more sophisticated night-vision equipment. The Starlight Scope made night vision possible by capturing all available light. This allowed forces on the ground to better identify and direct Steel Tiger sorties to the most efficient targets. While Steel Tiger did not shut down the Hồ Chí Minh Trail in southern Laos, it did force the North Vietnamese to devote additional resources to keep the flow of personnel and supplies moving down the trail.

STENNIS, JOHN CORNELIUS (1901–1995). United States Democratic senator. Stennis was born in Mississippi and educated at Mississippi State College, graduating in 1923. He also graduated from the University of Virginia Law School in 1928. He served in the Mississippi House of Representatives from 1928 to 1932 and then became the district prosecuting attorney until 1937. From 1937 to 1947, he served as a circuit judge before being elected as a senator representing Mississippi to fill a vacancy resulting from death on 5 November 1947.

Stennis remained in the Senate until 3 January 1989. He chaired the Select Committee on Standards and Conduct and was a member of the Committee on Armed Services and the Committee on Appropriations. In his last two years in the Senate, Stennis was elected president pro tempore. He was initially against the escalation of the war but supported President **Lyndon B. Johnson** once American troops arrived in Vietnam. Stennis was considered a friend of the military and used his influence in the Senate to allow military leaders to use their testimony to criticize the restrictions placed upon the military, especially in terms of the air war, that hampered the war effort. *See also* HAWK.

STRATA. The Short-Term Roadwatch and Target Acquisition (STRATA) program was organized in September 1967 to infiltrate into the **Democratic Republic of Vietnam** (DRV). STRATA teams, consisting of **Republic of Vietnam** (RVN) volunteers who were trained in survival and evasion skills, were inserted by **helicopter** south of the 20th parallel near the Laotian border and remained in the DRV for between two and four weeks. The RVN troops were clothed in **People's Army of Vietnam** uniforms (PAVN) and were equipped with PAVN weapons. The STRATA teams were not very effective, and approximately 25 percent of the personnel were killed or captured.

STRATEGIC HAMLET PROGRAM. A program designed to provide security for the people living in the countryside against the threat of **National Liberation Front** (NLF) activities. On the heels of the failed **Agroville Program**, **Ngô Đình Diệm** and his brother, **Ngô Đình Nhu**, originally designed the Strategic Hamlet Program to mobilize the Vietnamese people by having them claim a stake in their future peace and prosperity, with the government's assistance, and encouraging them to resist the communist insurgency. Where the Agroville Program called for the mass relocation of peasants to often less-than-ideal sites, the 1962 Strategic Hamlet Program was designed to limit the inconvenience of relocation as much as possible.

A strategic hamlet was deemed complete when some type of protective barrier, which often included a mud wall, ditch, sharpened bamboo sticks, or concertina wire, surrounded a village and the village had a militia and means to communicate with an **Army of the Republic of Vietnam** (ARVN) unit or other strategic hamlets in the area.

The plan was originally conceived by the Vietnamese but was soon transformed into an American plan when the **United States** called in the British **counterinsurgency** expert Sir **Robert Thompson**, who had successfully defeated the communist insurgency in Malaya in the 1950s. Thompson imprinted his mark on the Strategic Hamlet Program, which incorporated some of the Vietnamese objectives but not all. As a result, the Vietnamese and the U.S. disagreed on the best approach for implementation. Ngô Đinh Nhu wanted to take a holistic approach to the problem and establish as many strategic hamlets in as short a time as possible, while Thompson called for an inkblot strategy, where strategic hamlets were created in a slow and methodical manner. Additional controversy for the plan existed within the U.S., as the State Department and U.S. embassy personnel in Vietnam pushed for the Thompson plan while military leaders criticized it because it would result in static duty for the ARVN soldiers who, it was argued, would be better suited for large-scale military operations.

While the Strategic Hamlet Program had the potential to neutralize the NLF threat in the **Republic of Vietnam** (RVN), the tension created by disagreement within the U.S. and between the U.S. and the RVN contributed to its ultimate failure. The program was also plagued by corruption at the lower levels and by unrealistic goals set by Ngô Đinh Nhu who wanted to impress upon the people the ability of the **Sài Gòn** government to protect them and to show the Americans that the Vietnamese could establish and maintain their own internal security.

STUDENTS FOR A DEMOCRATIC SOCIETY (SDS). Originally known as the Student League for Industrial Democracy, the organization reformed as the SDS in January 1960 in Ann Arbor, Michigan. The SDS emerged as one of the early organizations that assumed the leadership of the **antiwar movement**, building upon its history and techniques developed during its involvement in the civil rights movement. After Operation **Pierce Arrow** in 1964, the air strike reprisals for the **Gulf of Tŏn Kĭn Incident**, the SDS focused on college and university campuses to organize demonstrations against American military action. In 1965, it was also active in sponsoring **teach-ins** and coordinating the signing of "We Won't Go" petitions for men who were eligible for the draft. The SDS organized a major antiwar demonstration in Washington, D.C., on 17 April 1965, which numbered approximately 20,000.

The active opposition to the war caused a spiraling in SDS membership, whose total reached 30,000 in 1966, but the organization was also fraught with tension and differing views on how to proceed. As the war continued to escalate, members of the SDS intensified their opposition, passing resolutions at their 1967 national convention that called for draft resistance, encouragement of conflict within the military, and an immediate withdrawal from Vietnam. The SDS was involved in the controversial demonstration-turned-melee against Dow Chemical at the University of Wisconsin in Madison on 17 October 1967 and in the 21 October 1967 March on the Pentagon during which half of the 100,000 participants moved to the Department of Defense building to protest the war and, in a few cases, to attempt to levitate the building.

In 1968, the SDS organized the "Ten Days of Resistance" and worked with the Student Mobilization Committee to coordinate antiwar demonstrations, including the 26 April 1968 national strike. At the height of the SDS influence in the **United States**, it began to fracture as some participants in the organization chose to turn to more militant means to get their antiwar message heard. Other factions, while still focused on the antiwar movement, introduced new social messages into the organization that helped to further weaken its cohesion. Marxists, Maoists, and feminists, among many others, vied for a voice in the SDS during the 1968 national Democratic convention in Chicago, while other members formed such groups as the Revolutionary Youth Movement and the Weather Underground Organization. By the fall of 1969, this internal tension resulted in the disbanding of a number of SDS chapters. While the SDS continued to work toward the goal of ending the war, its position as a leader in the antiwar movement diminished after 1969, though the organization continued to influence Democratic politics and antiwar protests through 1972.

STUDIES AND OBSERVATION GROUP (SOG). The **Military Assistance Command, Vietnam**–Studies and Observation Group (MACV-SOG), often referred to as SOG, was a secretive organization that engaged in covert, unconventional warfare during the Vietnam War. It was established on 24 January 1964. It operated inside the **Democratic Republic of Vietnam** (DRV), **Laos**, and **Cambodia** in missions not normally associated with **United States** personnel. The SOG assisted in **reconnaissance**, **search-and-rescue** missions, and the rescue of prisoners of war.

SOG membership included personnel from all branches of the U.S. Armed Forces, including such specially trained personnel as members of the Army **Special Forces**, Marine Corps Force Reconnaissance units, and the U.S. Navy **SEALs**. There were also **Central Intelligence Agency** personnel as well as individuals whose special training or expertise lent itself to unconventional warfare operations. SOG was involved in such operations as **OPLAN 34A**, which helped to precipitate the August 1964 **Gulf of Tŏn Kĭn Incident** and the first American air strikes against the DRV. SOG personnel and equipment continued to provide support for **Republic of Vietnam** (RVN) commandos and Special Forces in a variety of missions directed against the DRV.

SOG was also involved in missions into Laos in order to monitor the **Hồ Chí Minh Trail**. Operation **Shining Brass**, begun in November 1965, was an operation in which small teams were inserted into Laos to provide reconnaissance and disrupt trail operations if possible. Operations continued throughout the war, though the name was changed from Shining Brass to **Prairie Fire** in March 1967 after its missions were exposed by the U.S. **media**.

SOG also had control over Operation **Daniel Boone**, which began in September 1967 and targeted **People's Army of Vietnam** (PAVN) and **National Liberation Front** (NLF) troops in Cambodia. Small teams of 12 men conducted reconnaissance missions that paralleled Shining Brass operations in Laos. Daniel Boone missions into Cambodia also involved deploying antipersonnel devices to disrupt the Hồ Chí Minh Trail and the **Sihanouk Trail**. In 1969, the operation was renamed Salem House. After the **Cambodian Incursion**, RVN personnel took over the responsibilities, and in April 1971 the operation was renamed Thốt Nốt. SOG also developed a program to support RVN personnel who operated in the DRV. The Short-Term Roadwatch and Target Acquisition (**STRATA**) teams worked above the **Demilitarized Zone** (DMZ) to gather **intelligence** and harass the PAVN when it was possible.

SOG operations changed dramatically with the 1968 **Tết Offensive**. Its missions against the DRV, Laos, and Cambodia became secondary to operations within the RVN. At first the focus was on recovery, but it switched to exploiting the military defeat of the PAVN and NLF. SOG operations remained in the RVN as President **Lyndon B. Johnson** ordered the end of covert operations north of the DMZ and in neutral Laos and Cambodia. Johnson attempted to move the DRV toward negotiations by decreasing some of the more provocative U.S. operations against the DRV, including Operation **Rolling Thunder**. The end of Operation Rolling Thunder and the concentration of U.S. air assets against the Hồ Chí Minh Trail in Laos in Operation **Commando Hunt** provided SOG with a new opportunity to satisfy its mission.

While these missions were successful to some degree, the PAVN was able to organize local militias to counter the effectiveness of SOG personnel by laying ambushes at known points of debarkation by **helicopter**. As a result, SOG personnel found themselves increasingly harassed by the enemy and found their time on the actual mission decreased as the Vietnamese concentrated on negating their effectiveness. SOG continued to participate in high-

434 • SULLIVAN, WILLIAM HEALY

profile, if not secret, operations including support for the 1970 Cambodian Incursion and the **Sơn Tây** raid to rescue U.S. personnel in the DRV.

SOG was deactivated on 1 May 1972 and was replaced by Strategic Technical Directorate Assistance Team 158. Personnel from SOG were absorbed into other organizations and focused on providing support for Vietnamese special operations. SOG ceased to play an active role in Southeast Asia in the summer of 1973. *See also* FOOTBOY; HATCHET TEAMS; SPIKE TEAMS; SWITCHBACK, OPERATION.

SULLIVAN, WILLIAM HEALY (1922–). **United States** ambassador to **Laos**, the Philippines, and Iran. Sullivan was born in Rhode Island and educated at Brown University. He served in the U.S. Navy during World War II and after the war entered the Foreign Service. He remained in the Foreign Service and eventually became the assistant to Assistant Secretary of State for Far Eastern Affairs **W. Averell Harriman** starting in December 1961. Sullivan became Harriman's special assistant when the latter was promoted to undersecretary of state for political affairs in April 1963. He served as the **United Nations** adviser to the Bureau of Far Eastern Affairs in the Department of State until 28 April 1963, after which he became the assistant to the undersecretary of state. In March 1964, Sullivan was promoted to the position of the secretary of state's special assistant for Vietnamese affairs and head of the interagency Vietnam Coordinating Committee. In July 1964, he went to the **Republic of Vietnam** to become the assistant to U.S. ambassador **Maxwell D. Taylor**.

On 23 December 1964, Sullivan replaced Leonard S. Unger as U.S. ambassador to Laos. He remained in that position until 18 March 1969. As ambassador, Sullivan struggled for control over U.S. operations in Laos. He was often in conflict with **Military Assistance Command, Vietnam**, commander General **William C. Westmoreland** and members of the **U.S. Air Force** over the air campaign in Laos, including operations **Barrel Roll** and **Steel Tiger**. Sullivan was concerned with the political ramifications of the military operations and worked to control international reactions to the American war in Southeast Asia. He limited U.S. ground operations in Laos, such as **Prairie Fire** and **Shining Brass**, in order to avoid attention.

In April 1969, Sullivan became the deputy assistant secretary of state for East Asian and Pacific affairs. He worked with National Security Adviser **Henry Kissinger** during the Paris Peace negotiations and in 1973 became the ambassador to the Philippines. In 1977, he was transferred to Iran where he served as the last U.S. ambassador to that country before the Islamic Revolution in 1979, though he was replaced by the chargé d'affaires before the embassy was overrun and its inhabitants held hostage. In 1984, he published his memoir, *Obbligato: Notes on a Foreign Service Career.*

SWIFT BOAT. The Patrol Craft Fast, known more commonly as the swift boat, was a 24.3-meter (50-foot) long aluminum vessel with a shallow draft that was used by the **United States Navy** during the war. The first version introduced into Vietnam, the Mark I, had a range of up to 1,360 kilometers (850 miles) depending on its speed, it carried a crew of six, and it was armed with two .50 caliber **machine guns** and a combination .50 caliber machine gun and 81-mm **mortar**. The first Mark I swift boats arrived in Vietnam in August 1965. The boats were used in Operation **Market Time** and played a significant role in Task Force 115, the Coastal Surveillance Force. Swift boats were also used in Operation **Game Warden**, the **Mobile Riverine Force**, and **SEALORDS** in 1968, organized by Admiral **Elmo R. Zumwalt Jr.** As the war was winding down, the swift boats were transferred to the **Republic of Vietnam** Navy, and the last of the swift boat personnel left Southeast Asia in 1973.

SWITCHBACK, OPERATION. Under **National Security Action Memorandum** (NSAM) 57, approved on 28 June 1961, President **John F. Kennedy** authorized the Department of Defense to take over **Central Intelligence Agency** (CIA) projects if they became too large. NSAM 57 was a direct response to the failure of the CIA with the Bay of Pigs operation in Cuba earlier in 1961. In July 1962, Secretary of Defense **Robert McNamara** decided that the **Civilian Irregular Defense Group** (CIDG) had grown beyond the scope of the CIA. He ordered the **Military Assistance Command, Vietnam**, to take over responsibility for the program. This transfer was accomplished with Operation Switchback, which was completed on 1 July 1963. One of the more significant programs was the **Trail Watchers** teams. These teams established CIDG camps near the **Republic of Vietnam** border with **Laos** and **Cambodia**. In January 1964, the CIA handed over covert operations, which resulted in the creation of the **Studies and Observation Group**.

T

TACTICAL AIRLIFT. Because of the difficult challenges presented by the terrain in Southeast Asia, the **United States** and the **Army of the Republic of Vietnam** depended on tactical airlift to support the war against the **People's Army of Vietnam** and the **National Liberation Front**. Transport aircraft moved personnel and materials needed for operations, often delivering its cargo in areas that were inaccessible by land. The tactical airlift began in 1953 with the insertion of aircraft from the 315th Air Division to support the French in the **First Indochina War**. Operations such as Iron Age and **Wounded Warrior** transported French Union Forces and supplies using C-119 transports. On 7 December 1961, at the request of **Ngô Đình Diệm**, the 315th Air Division sent C-123 aircraft to assist in military operations as part of Project Mule Train under Operation **Farm Gate**.

On 3 July 1963, the 315th Troop Carrier Group (Assault) was formed with 51 C-123B aircraft to handle the supply needs of the increased American presence in the **Republic of Vietnam** (RVN). With the introduction of U.S. combat troops, tactical airlift expanded with the inclusion of the 2nd Aerial Port Group. It was responsible for loading and offloading supplies. During the first year of U.S. combat troop activity in Vietnam, **Tân Sơn Nhứt** airfield surpassed the activity of the busiest airport in the U.S., O'Hare Airport in Chicago, while the U.S. introduced new aircraft into the theater, such as the C-7, which was more suitable for operational responsibilities. By 1966, U.S. involvement in the war exceeded the capacity of the 315th Air Division. The 834th Air Division, the largest air division in the world, replaced it in October 1966.

The 834th Air Division conducted many different missions, including the transport of materials and personnel, **aeromedical evacuation** of stable but seriously wounded soldiers out of Vietnam, and the training of **RVN Air Force** pilots and crew. It was also involved in missions related to the spraying of herbicides under Operation **Ranch Hand** and the creation of **landing zones** under **Commando Vault**. The 834th Air Division airlifted **Thai** and **Korean** troops, relocated civilians when necessary, and dropped flyers and pamphlets over the **Democratic Republic of Vietnam**. Between 1961 and 1971, tactical airlift was responsible for moving over 16 million individuals and 3 million tons of cargo. *See also* AIR WAR; AIRCRAFT (CARGO TRANSPORT), UNITED STATES.

TAILWIND, OPERATION. Operation conducted by **United States Air Force** Pathfinder Teams and three companies of **Montagnard hatchet teams**. The operation was authorized by the **Studies and Observation Group**. The operation placed 16 Americans and 110 Montagnards into the southern part of **Laos**, in one of the deepest penetrations into that country at the time. The two-day operation, which began on 11 September 1970, had the objective of diverting **People's Army of Vietnam** (PAVN) resources away from attacks against **Hmong** forces fighting nearby. The Tailwind mission was constantly harassed by the PAVN and relied on movement and airpower to survive the ordeal. Three Montagnards were killed during the operation, while the combined force included 49 wounded, including all of the Americans.

The operation would have gone unnoticed save for a 1998 broadcast by Cable News Network (CNN) titled "The Valley of Death," in which the narrator of the piece, Peter Arnett, claimed that sarin gas was used in the operation and that it had been targeted against men, women, and children. The 7 June broadcast was followed by a 15 June *Time* magazine article that reinforced the claims. After an extensive investigation, the claims were proven to be inaccurate, though the producers of the broadcast continued to support their allegations. In July 1998, the president of CNN announced that an internal investigation by the company found that the accusations in the stories could not be supported.

TALLY HO, OPERATION. United States Air Force interdiction operation that served as an extension of **Tiger Hound** and was designed to stop the infiltration of personnel and supplies reaching the **Republic of Vietnam** (RVN) from the North. Tally Ho began on 18 July 1966 and concentrated on the **Democratic Republic of Vietnam** from the **Demilitarized Zone** (DMZ) to the area around Đồng Hới, supplementing Tiger Hound operations in **Laos**. The operation was conceived to counter the logistical buildup of the 324B **People's Army of Vietnam** (PAVN) Division that was responsible for transportation in the area. All four major branches of the U.S. Armed Forces participated in the operation, which sometimes included Tiger Hound **sorties** when necessary. Tally Ho missions proved successful in obstructing North Vietnamese supply lines across the DMZ, but not enough to stop the ability of resupply to the PAVN and **National Liberation Front** fighting in the RVN.

TÂN SƠN NHỨT. Located to the north-northwest of the center of **Sài Gòn**, Tân Sơn Nhứt served as the main airport for the capital as well as a major base for the **United States** Armed Forces during the war. The original airfield was constructed by the French in the 1920s for air transport to and from their colony. It was expanded and improved during the Japanese occupation during World War II and the **First Indochina War** when **France** used it for military operations. In 1955, the **Republic of Vietnam Air Force** (RVNAF) came into existence and used Tân Sơn Nhứt as a base of operations. The next year, the **U.S. Air Force** began training and assisting the RVNAF, which started continuous growth and improvement of Tân Sơn Nhứt so that by 1968 it had become one of the busiest airfields in the world. The runway was expanded to accommodate jet aircraft, while the facilities increased many fold to handle the influx of American, South Vietnamese, and allied aircraft. In addition to the numerous air wings, squadrons, and groups assigned to the Tân Sơn Nhứt Air Base, other organizations used the facilities as their headquarters, including the **Military Assistance Advisory Group** and **Military Assistance Command, Vietnam**. The Tân Sơn Nhứt airfield also accommodated Continental airlines, which flew approximately 700 flights per week, as well as Air Vietnam. The last U.S. unit left Tân Sơn Nhứt on 23 March 1973, and the air base and field fell to the communists on 30 April 1975. Tân Sơn Nhứt continues to function as an airfield.

TANKS. The **United States**, the **Army of the Republic of Vietnam** (ARVN), and the **People's Army of Vietnam** (PAVN) employed tanks during the war, though the weapon was not used with as great a frequency as in previous wars, largely due to the **climate** and **topography**. Early in the war, the U.S. introduced the M48A3 Patton tank. It possessed one 90-mm cannon, a 7.62-mm **machine gun**, and a .50 caliber machine gun that could be used in air defense. The Patton had a range of just over 480 kilometers (300 miles), with a maximum speed of 48 kilometers (30 miles) per hour. It had a crew of four and weighed approximately 47,000 kilograms (52 tons) fully loaded.

In 1969, the U.S. brought the M551 Sheridan to Vietnam. The Sheridan was a light tank weighing 15,422 kilograms (17 tons) fully loaded. The Sheridan carried a 152-mm gun or **missile** launcher and also had one 7.62-mm machine gun and a .50 caliber machine gun that could be used in air defense. It had a range of over 435 kilometers (270 miles), with a maximum speed of 72 kilometers (45 miles) per hour. Like the Patton, it carried a crew of four. The Sheridan was built as an air-droppable lightweight assault vehicle, which meant that its armor was thin, with a hull made of welded aluminum and a molded steel turret. Its light weight and questionable armor made it prone to land **mines** in Vietnam.

The majority of ARVN tanks were supplied by the United States. In January 1965, the M41A3 Walker Bulldog arrived. It had one 76-mm cannon, one 7.62-mm machine gun, and one 12.7-mm machine gun used for air defense. The Walker Bulldog had a range of 158 kilometers (99 miles) and a maximum speed of 72 kilometers (45 miles) per hour. It carried a crew of four and had a fully loaded weight of 23,586 kilograms (26 tons). As the U.S. continued its withdrawal from Southeast Asia in 1971, it began to transfer M48A3 tanks to the ARVN. Many arrived in 1972 under **Project Enhance** and **Project Enhance Plus**.

PAVN tanks included the Soviet-built T-54 and PT-76 and the Chinese-built Type 63 and T-59. The former was similar to the PT-76, while the latter was a near duplicate of the T-54. The T-54 used a 100-mm rifled cannon and two 7.62-mm machine guns. It had a range of approximately 600 kilometers (375 miles) and a maximum speed of 55 kilometers (34 miles) per hour; it carried a crew of four and weighed just less than 36,287 kilograms (40 tons). The PT-76 was a lightweight amphibious tank that weighed 12,700 kilograms (14 tons). It had a 76-mm gun and a 7.62-mm machine gun. It had a range of 258 kilometers (160 miles), a maximum speed of nearly 45 kilometers (28 miles) per hour, and housed a crew of three.

North Vietnamese tanks did not arrive on the battlefield in great numbers until the late 1960s. U.S. and PAVN tanks encountered one another only once during the war. During a PAVN attack at **Bến Hét** on 3 and 4 March 1969, the U.S. tanks proved to be superior. PAVN tanks were utilized during the 1972 **Easter Offensive** and the final offensive in 1975. During the Easter Offensive, it was estimated that 50 percent of the tanks used had been destroyed or damaged beyond repair by the end of the campaign. But the lasting image of the PAVN tank was the one that involved the destruction of the presidential palace front gate on 30 April 1975 that signaled the end of the war. *See also* LAM SƠN 719; LANG VEI; LIGHT ANTI-TANK WEAPON; MISSILE; SOVIET UNION.

TÂY NINH. A province located to the northwest of **Sài Gòn** and bordering **Cambodia**. The capital of the province was Tây Ninh City, which was situated at the intersection of **Routes** 13 and 22 and approximately 88 kilometers (55 miles) from the capital of the **Republic of Vietnam** (RVN). Tây Ninh province was the home of the **Cao Đài** religious sect, which, when coupled with its strategic location next to Cambodia, made it one of the more important and contested provinces in III **Corps Tactical Zone** (CTZ) during the war. Tây Ninh province also included the area known as **Angel's Wing**, located to the south of Tây Ninh City and north of the formation known as the **Parrot's Beak**, which was within Cambodia and was used by the **National Liberation Front** (NLF) as a staging area to apply pressure upon Sài Gòn and the other major urban populations in III CTZ.

There were several well-known formations located in Tây Ninh province, including the Black Virgin Mountain (**Núi Bà Đen**), which was a large cone-shaped granite outcropping that was approximately 975 meters (3,200 feet) high. Núi Bà Đen held religious and political significance for the Vietnamese people and was the site of many Vietnamese **Buddhist** legends and several Buddhist temples. It also contained the **Bời Lời** woods, a forest area used by the NLF and the **Michelin Rubber Plantation**. This plantation was a French-controlled industry that was the scene of sporadic but sometimes intense fighting that served as a source of frustration for the **United States** soldier. Because it was a working plantation, but also known NLF territory, there were restrictions imposed on the military operating in the area.

On 20 December 1960, the NLF was formed in Tây Ninh province as a response to a new direction that the war in Vietnam had taken. Tây Ninh province was the scene of heavy fighting when, on 26 January 1961, four companies of NFL soldiers attacked a camp of the 32nd **Army of the Republic of Vietnam** regiment, killing or wounding 66 soldiers. **Front B2**, which included the southern section of the RVN, was headquartered north of Tây Ninh City in **War Zone C**. This organization was also referred to as the **Central Office for South Vietnam**.

Later in the war, the **Philippine** Civil Action Group used Tây Ninh as its headquarters as it conducted its civic action campaign in the Thanh Điền forest. After 1966, the fighting in Tây Ninh province intensified, and the **casualties** surpassed all provinces outside of I CTZ.

TAYLOR, MAXWELL DAVENPORT (1901–1987). A graduate of the **United States** Military Academy in 1922, Taylor served in the 82nd Airborne **Division** during the Italian Campaign of World War II. He commanded the 101st Airborne Division from 1944 to the end of the war, when he was appointed the superintendent of West Point. In 1949, he commanded the contingent of allied troops in Berlin until 1951, he served as commander of the 8th Army in Korea in 1953, and he was the army chief of staff between 1955 and 1959. He retired from active duty in July 1959. Taylor became involved in the **John F. Kennedy** administration with his participation in the Cuba Study Group, which examined the failure of Operation Zapata, the attempt to support the invasion to overthrow Fidel Castro in Cuba at the Bay of Pigs.

After his work with the Cuba Study Group, Taylor accepted the position of military representative to the president on 1 July 1961. President John F. Kennedy asked him to review the Vietnam strategy and provide his views on **Ngô Đình Diệm**'s request for a significant increase in the **Army of the Republic of Vietnam**. Taylor visited Vietnam with **Walter W. Rostow** in October 1961 in what became known as the **Taylor-Rostow Mission**. He later became the chairman of the **Joint Chiefs of Staff**, the only individual recalled from retired status to serve in that capacity, from 1 October 1962 to 30 June 1964, and then became ambassador to the **Republic of Vietnam** from 14 July 1964 to 30 July

1965. He remained a special consultant to President **Lyndon B. Johnson** and chairman of the Foreign Intelligence Advisory Board until 1969.

TAYLOR-ROSTOW MISSION. Between 18 and 24 October 1961, the military representative to the president, General **Maxwell D. Taylor**, and the deputy special assistant to the president for national security affairs, **Walter W. Rostow**, visited Vietnam at the request of President **John F. Kennedy**. Taylor and Rostow were tasked with finding answers on how the **United States** should respond to the **National Liberation Front**'s (NLF) buildup and increased activities, how the **Sài Gòn** government could better relate to the people, and whether the **Army of the Republic of Vietnam** (RVN) could effectively fight the NLF without U.S. assistance. Finally, they were to determine whether **Ngô Đình Diệm** was the RVN's best solution for future stability and independence.

The Taylor-Rostow Mission recommended a series of escalatory moves, including the introduction of **helicopters** and fixed-winged aircraft operated by uniformed American personnel, increased air **reconnaissance**, and air-to-ground support. The two advisers also called for U.S. training of the **Civil Guard** and **Self-Defense Corps**, additional economic assistance, and an 8,000-soldier Task Force to assist the South Vietnamese under the guise of helping with the damage caused by flooding in the **Mê Kông Delta** as a result of heavy monsoon rains. In order to organize the increased activity, Taylor and Rostow recommended changing the **Military Assistance Advisory Group** to a larger Military Advisory Command. The Taylor-Rostow Mission confirmed Kennedy's decision to escalate the war in Vietnam, moving it from an experiment in nation building as attempted by the Eisenhower administration to a full-fledged fight against communism, with America's prestige and honor at stake.

TCHEPONE. Also known as Xepon or Sepon, Tchepone was located in the southeast of **Laos**, near the border with the **Republic of Vietnam** (RVN), just south of the **Demilitarized Zone**. It was situated just south of **Route** 9 near its junction with Route 92, which made up the **Hồ Chí Minh Trail**. As a result, Tchepone became a strategic logistics center for **People's Army of Vietnam** (PAVN) forces in the early 1960s and was very important as the Hồ Chí Minh Trail became the main source of supporting PAVN and **National Liberation Front** forces after the implementation of Operation **Market Time** in March 1965. The town and surrounding area were repeatedly bombed in the 1960s, and it earned a reputation as one of the more strongly defended towns with **antiaircraft artillery**. In 1971, the **Army of the Republic of Vietnam** (ARVN) launched an offensive, **Lam Sơn 719**, with the objective of seizing Tchepone. While the South Vietnamese achieved their objective after the

PAVN abandoned the town, the operation ended in disaster when the ARVN forces were ambushed on their return to the RVN.

TEABALL. An early-warning system developed during the Korean War and reinvented in Vietnam to provide better protection for American aircraft engaged in operations over the **Democratic Republic of Vietnam** (DRV). Created in 1972, Teaball allowed for the centralization of data collection at Nakhon Phanom Airbase in **Thailand** from early-warning systems and MiG activities in order to better coordinate and prepare **United States** aircraft for their missions over the DRV. Teaball was established in July and was put into effect in September. During the early phases of **Linebacker I**, before the implementation of Teaball, the U.S. suffered a loss ratio of .47 to 1. After Teaball was activated, the ratio reversed to 3.8 to 1. Use of the new tactic also resulted in the first U.S. fighting ace during the Vietnam War.

TEACH-INS. As the **United States** escalated the war in 1965, **antiwar** activists on university and college campuses began to organize. One form of antiwar protest was the teach-in, modeled on the nonviolent civil rights sit-in activities of the early 1960s. The first teach-in occurred on the campus of the University of Michigan in Ann Arbor on 24 March 1965. The two-day event was attended by approximately 2,500 participants. Nearly 30,000 people attended the 21–23 May 1965 teach-in at the University of California, Berkeley, following the first national teach-in on 15 May, which occurred on 122 campuses around the country. Teach-ins focused on educating the participants about the war and Southeast Asia.

In most instances, both sides of the argument were given equal access, though the teach-ins quickly became a source for antiwar information and calls for action against U.S. escalation in Vietnam. The teach-in movement waned as the summer vacation began on college campuses in 1965, and the antiwar movement took on a more active, less conciliatory approach as it demonstrated against the Americanization of the war in the fall of 1965 and beyond.

TEMPORARY EQUIPMENT RECOVERY MISSION (TERM). On 9 February 1956, Secretary of State **John Foster Dulles** announced that the **Military Assistance Advisory Group** (MAAG) would be temporarily increased by up to an additional 350 personnel with the creation of TERM. In June 1956, TERM personnel began to arrive in Vietnam with two major objectives. It supervised the recovery and removal of Mutual Defense Assistance Program equipment provided to the French during the **First Indochina War**, and it improved the logistical capabilities of the newly created **Army of the Republic of Vietnam** (ARVN).

The **United States** also initiated TERM in order to increase the number of U.S. personnel in Vietnam from 342 to 692. While the mission was tasked with equipment recovery, it actually provided additional training and assistance to the newly created ARVN. TERM personnel were assigned to ARVN military units and focused on logistics, medical, quartermaster, transportation, ordnance, engineer, and signal units. The **International Control Commission** never agreed to TERM, and in December 1958 it passed a resolution that called for the mission to leave by 30 June 1959. In May 1960, TERM was absorbed into the MAAG, making the temporary mission permanent.

TẾT. Tết Nguyên Đán, usually referred to as just Tết, was the most significant **Buddhist** festival in Vietnam. Tết marked the beginning of spring and was based on the lunar calendar. It often occurred in January or February and almost always coincided with the Chinese New Year. There is no single Western holiday that encompasses the important elements of Tết, when the Vietnamese visit relatives, friends, and ancestral burial areas. The Tết holiday was often used for cease-fires between the **United States**, the **Republic of Vietnam** (RVN), the **Democratic Republic of Vietnam** (DRV), and the **National Liberation Front** (NLF). For the U.S., the Tết truces were a time for the Americans to scale back or stop bombing the DRV, and Vietnamese troops often took a break from fighting to celebrate the holiday. The major exceptions were the 1965 and 1968 **Tết Offensives**, when the DRV and NLF initiated attacks against U.S. and Army of the Republic facilities and, in the case of 1968, staged attacks throughout the RVN.

TẾT OFFENSIVE, 1968. Offensive begun on 31 January 1968, the start of the Tết holiday, with the objective of causing as much damage as possible to **United States** and **Army of the Republic of Vietnam** forces in the **Republic of Vietnam** (RVN) and of encouraging a general uprising of the people against the **Sài Gòn** government. As a preliminary to the offensive, the **Democratic Republic of Vietnam** focused its attention on the **marine** base at **Khe Sanh**, in the northwestern part of the RVN, hoping to divert American attention away from the urban centers in the South. The marines at Khe Sanh had been stationed at the base to monitor and interdict personnel and supplies coming into the RVN via the **Hồ Chí Minh Trail** in **Laos**. An estimated 20,000 to 40,000 **People's Army of Vietnam** (PAVN) and **National Liberation Front** (NLF) forces surrounded the 6,000 marines and finally attacked on 21 January, 10 days before the start of the actual Tết Offensive. The PAVN and NLF were defeated in the initial assaults and turned to **artillery** and mortar barrages to keep the marines pinned down and the attention focused on Khe Sanh.

While the Battle for Khe Sanh occupied American attention, the PAVN and NLF infiltrated into the RVN's urban centers in preparation for the offensive. Early attacks near **Plei Ku**, **Quảng Nam**, and Darlac did not give away the surprise of the coordinated attacks that began the offensive on 31 January. The PAVN and NLF attacked every significant urban center, including nearly all of the provincial capitals. The major thrust of the offensive centered in Sài Gòn and **Huế**. In Sài Gòn, PAVN and NLF forces attempted to penetrate the U.S. embassy but only succeeded in getting onto the grounds before being decimated. Other attacks occurred at the presidential palace; the radio station; the **Military Assistance Command, Vietnam**, compound; and the **Tân Sơn Nhứt** airfield. While these attacks were quickly repulsed, fighting continued in Sài Gòn in the suburb of **Chợ Lớn** until the end of February. In Huế, the PAVN and NLF attacked and occupied most of the citadel until it was recaptured at the end of February after an intense fight. The PAVN and NLF also overran the University of Huế. After forcing the PAVN and NLF out of the city, American and Vietnamese troops discovered the bodies of over 3,000 Vietnamese in mass graves who had been tortured and killed by the PAVN and NLF during their occupation.

The Tết Offensive was a military failure for the PAVN and NLF, with their **casualties** at approximately 45,000. American and South Vietnamese casualties numbered approximately 4,300 killed and 16,000 wounded. An important outcome of the offensive was the decimation of the NLF, which had exposed itself during the offensive, with dire consequences. The NLF, which had significant control of the countryside leading into the Tết Offensive, found themselves without a safe haven and diminished in numbers. While the offensive was clearly a military success for the U.S. and the RVN, whose forces not only absorbed the attack but defeated it with relative ease, the political and psychological consequences of the offensive were less than ideal for the U.S. The **Lyndon B. Johnson** administration had pushed a public relations campaign in the late fall of 1967, bringing in **William C. Westmoreland** for support, claiming that the PAVN and NLF no longer held the initiative and could not mount a major offensive in the RVN. The Tết Offensive proved these statements wrong. As a result, President Johnson was forced to defend himself and his Vietnam policy against a growing **antiwar movement** that included **congressmen** and politicians from his own party.

Upon the recommendation of Secretary of Defense **Clark Clifford** and the president's personal advisers, Johnson refused Westmoreland's request for an additional 206,000 troops to take advantage of the political vacuum created in the countryside as a result of the destruction of the NLF. On 31 March 1968, Johnson announced that he would not seek or accept his party's nomination for the presidency in the 1968 election and ordered a **bombing pause** north of the 19th parallel. These actions, on the heels of the U.S. military victory during the Tết Offensive, demoralized members of the armed forces and emboldened the North Vietnamese and NLF to continue their struggle despite the significant loss of men and materials from their failed offensive.

The PAVN and NLF attempted two additional offensives in 1968, commonly known as mini-Tết offensives. The second offensive began in May with the objective of inflicting as many casualties as possible. The PAVN and NLF focused on Sài Gòn and Chợ Lớn but failed in their attempt as U.S. air strikes forced them to flee. The third and final offensive occurred in August, targeting **Đà Nẵng** and **Tây Ninh**. It failed to gain any momentum, as U.S. airpower destroyed or dispersed the concentration of PAVN and NLF troops before they started to attack. *See also* TẾT.

THAILAND. Situated to the west of **Cambodia** and **Laos**, Thailand played a significant role in the war as a participant in the conflicts in Laos and the **Republic of Vietnam** (RVN) and serving as a base area for the **United States air war** against the **Democratic Republic of Vietnam**. The country, with its capital in Bangkok, is just less than 520,000 square kilometers (200,000 square miles), with a tropical monsoon **climate.** Other major cities include Nakhon Ratchasima and Chiang Mai. Its population is made up of mostly Thai, with a vast majority practicing Theravada **Buddhism**. It was ruled under a constitutional monarchy.

Thailand sided with the U.S. during the Cold War and was a staunch ally of the coalition of anticommunist nations battling the insurgent movements in the RVN, Laos, and Cambodia. It was one of the original signatories of the **South East Asian Treaty Organization** and reinforced its alliance in a 1962 joint communiqué between Secretary of State **Dean Rusk** and Foreign Minister Thanat Khoman. Thailand initiated a series of civic action programs in Laos and the RVN, and in July 1965 the Thai government agreed to contribute combat troops to the war. It would be more than two years before the first Thai troops arrived. On 21 September 1967, the Queen's Cobra Regiment arrived in the RVN working with the 9th **Division**. Thai forces were augmented the following year in response to President **Lyndon B. Johnson**'s **Show the Flag** program, which called for additional allied efforts in the war. The Black Panthers Division arrived in August 1968.

By 1970, the total number of Thai troops in the RVN exceeded 11,500, and they remained there until their withdrawal in 1971. Thailand suffered 350 killed-in-action and over 1,000 wounded. Thai troops also served in the war in Laos, though their contribution there was not as heavily publicized as their participation in the RVN. It is estimated that 22,000 Thais served in the Police

Aerial Reconnaissance Units and worked with U.S. assets to impede movement down the **Hồ Chí Minh Trail**. Thailand also served as a major area for U.S. air bases. U.S. aircraft were located at Don Muang, Korat, Nam Thong, Nakhon Phanom, Takhli, U Tapao, Ubon, and Udorn. As many as 49,000 U.S. military personnel served in Thailand, with the first American servicemen arriving in 1961 to support air operations and the last leaving in 1976 when the Thai government requested that the U.S. leave its country. *See also* AIR WAR; FIREFLY, PROJECT.

THANH HÓA BRIDGE. Also known as the Dragon's Jaw (Hàm Rồng), the Thanh Hóa bridge traversed the Sông (River) Mã and was located approximately five kilometers (three miles) to the northeast of Thanh Hóa, the capital of Thanh Hóa province. The bridge was built during the French colonial period and was the objective of several sabotage attacks by anti-French Vietnamese nationalists. After the end of the **First Indochina War**, the **Democratic Republic of Vietnam** (DRV) rebuilt the bridge, which was nearly 167 meters (550 feet) long. The bridge was the target of several **Rolling Thunder sorties** designed to destroy it. As a result, and because of its significance in moving personnel and supplies south, it was one of the most heavily protected sites in the DRV. Between 1965 and 1968, the bridge was never permanently put out of commission. The **United States** made several attempts, including the dropping of magnetic **mines** in the river that were to explode upon contact. Eventually, it was severely damaged on 27 April 1972 during Operation **Linebacker I** by a combination of 2,000-pound Paveway I and Walleye I laser-guided **missiles**. Another attack on 6 October 1972 on the bridge rendered it unusable. Until its destruction after nearly eight years of bombing, the Thanh Hóa bridge was a symbol of resistance for the North Vietnamese and a source of frustration for the U.S.

THAYER, OPERATIONS. **Search-and-destroy** operations conducted in 1966 in **Bình Định** province. The operation involved the 1st Cavalry **Division**, the 3rd **Army of the Republic of Vietnam** (ARVN) Airborne Brigade, and the 41st ARVN Regiment. The initial stages of the operation began on 7 September 1966 with OPLAN 23-66. The operation plan called for **United States** and allied forces to sweep through the Kim Sơn Valley. This first phase of OPLAN 23-66 became Operation Thayer, which officially began on 13 September. The second and third phases would become Operation **Irving** and Operation Thayer II. The operation was deemed successful by the military because of its effectiveness in destroying enemy enclaves in the western part of the province. Operation Thayer II was a continuation of Thayer I and involved not only the 1st Air Cavalry but also the 25th Division and battalions for the Vietnamese **Marines**. The allied forces claimed over 1,750 killed-in-action as a result of the operation.

THÍCH. Honorific given to **Buddhist** monks.

THÍCH QUẢNG ĐỨC (1897–1963). Buddhist monk who committed self-immolation during the **Buddhist Crisis** in protest of the **Ngô Đình Diệm** government. He was born Lâm Văn Túc and became a Mahayana Buddhist monk in **Sài Gòn** under the name Thích Quảng Đức. When the Buddhists began to protest against Ngô Đình Diệm and his family's treatment of the Buddhists in **Huế** in May 1963, Thích Quảng Đức joined in the protests. On 11 June 1963, he committed self-immolation in Sài Gòn to highlight the oppressive nature of the Sài Gòn government. The act shocked Americans and forced President **John F. Kennedy** to reexamine the role of the **United States** in Vietnam as well as its continued support for Ngô Đình Diệm. The Sài Gòn government dismissed the act as one isolated incident inspired by communists who had infiltrated the movement. **Madame Ngô Đình Nhu** made matters worse by a series of callous remarks that stood out in contrast to the images of Thích Quảng Đức on fire. Those images were captured by **Malcolm Browne**, who was tipped off about the event beforehand, as well as by the words of **David Halberstam**, who authored the article describing the event. Both journalists won Pulitzer Prizes. Many point to the self-immolation as the single event that turned the U.S. government against Ngô Đình Diệm, though a series of events and personality clashes made the situation inevitable.

THÍCH TRÍ QUANG (1924–). Born in Quảng Bình province in the central part of Vietnam, Thích Trí Quang traveled to the South and settled in the **Huế** area after participating in anti-French activities and traveling to Ceylon to study **Buddhist** philosophy. He became a Buddhist monk following the teaching of Mahayana Buddhism and was best known for his agitation during the 1963 **Buddhist Crisis** and the 1966 Buddhist uprising. Thích Trí Quang helped organize the Buddhist demonstration in Huế, starting in May 1963. On 7 May 1963, Buddhists in Huế, as part of a celebration marking the 2,507th anniversary of the birth of Buddha, wanted to fly the Buddhist flag. The **Sài Gòn** government refused the request. Thích Trí Quang argued that this policy was inconsistent, as **Ngô Đình Diệm** had allowed his brother, the archbishop of Huế, Ngô Đình Thục, to fly the white-and-gold Catholic flag during his Episcopal silver jubilee.

As a result, Thích Trí Quang organized a demonstration for the next day that resulted in the deaths of nine of the protestors. Both the Buddhist leaders and the Ngô Đình Diệm government claimed that the deaths were the responsibility of the other side. Both sides were unwilling to reconcile their differences, and as a result, tensions mounted. Thích Trí Quang traveled to Sài Gòn to continue agitation against the government, and when on 21 August 1963 **Ngô Đình Nhu** ordered raids on the pagodas in Sài Gòn and Huế, he received refuge at the **United States** embassy. Thích Trí Quang remained in the embassy until after the November 1963 coup d'état that ousted Ngô Đình Diệm from power.

Thích Trí Quang continued to serve as a leader of the Buddhist community in the 1960s. He opposed the coup d'état by **Nguyễn Khánh** that occurred on 30 January 1964, believing that he planned to restore the type of government that existed before the assassination of Ngô Đình Diệm. In April 1966, Thích Trí Quang protested the removal of General **Nguyễn Chánh Thi** as the commander of I **Corps Tactical Zone** and led the Buddhist Struggle Movement. After Prime Minister **Nguyễn Cao Kỳ** sent troops to quell the uprising, Nguyễn Chánh Thi was sent to the U.S. for medical treatment even though he was not sick, and Thích Trí Quang was arrested. He was released later in the year but again fell out of favor with the government during the 1968 **Tết Offensive** and was put under house arrest from February to June 1968.

During the war, he served as an official of the General Association of Buddhists and as secretary general of the High Council of the United Buddhist Association. Toward the end of the war, Thích Trí Quang organized demonstrations against **Republic of Vietnam** president **Nguyễn Văn Thiệu**. He continued to urge Buddhists to protest communist rule after the fall of Sài Gòn in April 1975 and was again imprisoned for over a year. Thích Trí Quang continued to be involved in Buddhist affairs, including serving as the vice president of the Vietnamese Buddhist Sangha and helping to organize the 2008 Fifth International United Nations Day of Vesak in the Socialist Republic of Vietnam.

THIRD COUNTRY FORCES. Name provided by the **United States** for allied involvement during the war and interchangeable with the term **Free World Forces**. The U.S. was motivated by several factors to include other nations in the fight against communism in Southeast Asia. Significant Third Country forces would counter accusations that the U.S.' motives were imperialist as well as answer domestic critics who feared that the U.S. would bear the brunt of the military responsibility as it had in the Korean War, especially when the **South East Asian Treaty Organization** had not been evoked. A united front against communist aggression would also demonstrate solidarity against the **Democratic Republic of Vietnam** (DRV) and improve international relations with neutral countries. The U.S. became involved in the Vietnam War in part because of the Cold War mentality that had developed since the end of World War II. Pitting the Free World against the Communist Bloc provided the appropriate political jargon to underscore the necessity of their inclusion for

propaganda and military purposes. For the South Vietnamese, Third Country forces were desired, in part, to appease the U.S., but also because such involvement would reinforce the legitimacy of the **Republic of Vietnam** (RVN) as a viable member of the international community. The search for allies began on 17 November 1961 when the State Department informed the ambassadors or chargés to **Australia, New Zealand, Thailand,** Pakistan, the **Philippines,** and **Canada** that it intended to increase assistance to the RVN in the form of equipment, transport, training, and **advisers**. While the initial responses were less than expected, the **John F. Kennedy** administration continued to apply pressure on its allies. By the summer of 1963, only Australia and the **Republic of Korea** had made significant contributions to Southeast Asia.

During the **Lyndon B. Johnson** administration, the need for Third Country forces increased as the U.S. became more committed to the defeat of the communist insurgency. After an April 1964 trip to the RVN, Secretary of State **Dean Rusk** drew up a list of steps he believed were necessary for the survival of the **Sài Gòn** government. The first requirement was to engage more flags. This requirement evolved into the Many Flags or **Show the Flag** program, during which the U.S. applied significant pressure on its allies who had a regional interest in the preservation of the RVN's independence. For the remainder of 1964, the results were disappointing, with only Australia, New Zealand, and the Republic of Korea providing any tangible military assistance. The first Third Country combat troops arrived in 1965 with the insertion of an Australian battalion. This was soon followed by a much larger Republic of Korea contingent.

By the end of 1965, there were an estimated 22,500 Third Country forces. This number increased to 63,500 in 1966 and reached its peak in 1968 at 65,800, with representatives from Australia, New Zealand, the Republic of Korea, the Philippines, and Thailand. There were also smaller contingents from Spain and the **Republic of China**. Third Country forces represented approximately 12 percent of the total non–South Vietnamese forces in Vietnam. While it was easily dwarfed by the American commitment, it exceeded the total number of allied forces when compared to the U.S. during the Korean War.

Despite these statistics, Third Country forces in Southeast Asia did not fully satisfy all of the original hopes of the U.S. While the troops fought with uncommon valor, the movement to garner international support was plagued with difficulties and misperceptions that were easily exploited by the DRV. Only the Australians and New Zealanders paid for their own expenses. The Korean soldiers were accused not only of being mercenary troops but of engaging the enemy with tactics, sometimes considered brutal, that allowed the North Vietnamese a propaganda advantage in the public relations battle for the support of the international community.

Finally, the overall effort fell short of American expectations. By the end of 1968, the U.S. listed 43 countries that had responded to the appeal for contributions to the war, with a total amount of $94 million in aid over a four-and-a-half-year period. On paper this seemed impressive, until the countries and type of aid were examined. Only nine of the 43 countries contributed more than $1 million to the RVN, while 19 of the 43 countries contributed less than $25,000. Many of these contributions were one-time events, including a contribution by Morocco of 10,000 cans of sardines valued at $2,000 and Austria's $50 contribution in cholera vaccine. **France** and Sweden were listed as allies, though both nations were opposed to the U.S. presence in Southeast Asia. The U.S. push to include allies in the fight for the RVN failed to elicit the quality and quantity expected, though for those countries that did become truly involved, such as Australia, New Zealand, the Republic of Korea, and Thailand, their contribution was substantial and much appreciated. *See also* FREE WORLD FORCES.

THOMPSON, SIR ROBERT GRAINGER KER (1916–1992). British counterinsurgency expert. Thompson received his commission in the Royal Air Force in 1936 and fought in Burma during World War II. His experience in jungle warfare was tested in the Malayan Emergency of the 1950s, where he served as the permanent secretary of defense. Thompson helped to suppress the communist insurgency in Malaya and, as a result, was selected to help the **United States** deal with the **National Liberation Front** (NLF). In September 1961, Thompson arrived in the **Republic of Vietnam** (RVN) to head the British Advisory Mission. In this position, he influenced U.S. efforts to take over the **Strategic Hamlet Program**, which had been conceived by **Ngô Đình Diệm** and **Ngô Đình Nhu** in order to mobilize the civilian population against the NLF. Thompson sought to apply the lessons learned in Malaya toward the RVN, even though the two situations had marked differences.

The Strategic Hamlet Program failed to isolate the NLF and fell short of providing the promised benefits offered by the **Sài Gòn** government. This failure led to increased tension between U.S. officials dealing with Southeast Asia and Ngô Đình Diệm's government. Thompson would blame Ngô Đình Nhu for attempting to quell the communist insurrection by applying a top-down approach rather than winning the hearts and minds of the people. He argued that Ngô Đình Nhu had attempted to use the Strategic Hamlet Program to solve all of Vietnam's problems at once rather than applying a gradual pressure on the NLF by establishing strategic hamlets and spreading the program after it had been successfully administered and maintained. He criticized the American use of firepower and its support for training the **Army of the Republic of Vietnam** to rely on technology and firepower rather than working with the Vietnamese people to identify and isolate the enemy.

Thompson left the British Advisory Mission in 1965. He returned to Vietnam during the **Richard M. Nixon** administration as a special adviser to the president. Between his two postings to Vietnam, Thompson wrote two influential works that outlined his thinking on the situation in Vietnam: *Defeating Communist Insurgency: Experiences in Malaya and Vietnam* (1966) and *No Exit from Vietnam* (1969). In 1989, he published his autobiography, *Make for the Hills*.

THỪA THIÊN. A province located in I **Corps Tactical Zone**. It was directly south of **Quảng Trị**, which was the northernmost province in the **Republic of Vietnam**, and stretched from the South China Sea to **Laos**. The province was very diverse in **topography**, with significant mountains, jungles, coastal territory, lagoons, and sand dunes. The most significant city in Thừa Thiên was **Huế**, and **Route** 1 traversed the entire province from north to south. Thừa Thiên province was the scene of heavy fighting throughout the war, but significantly from the year preceding the 1968 **Tết Offensive** until the 1972 **Easter Offensive**. The province accounted for the most U.S. personnel killed in combat during the war at just less than 2,900. Thừa Thiên fell under **Front B1** for the North Vietnamese but was absorbed into Front B4 in 1966.

TIGER CAGES. Form of imprisonment used by the **Republic of Vietnam** (RVN) for individuals accused of crimes against the state. It was a box-shaped, usually iron-wrought cage that held dedicated **National Liberation Front** operatives but also individuals who had run afoul of South Vietnamese officials. In July 1970, President **Richard M. Nixon** sent a delegation of 10 **congressmen** to Vietnam to investigate **pacification** and to visit a typical prison. Two congressmen with their aides, including future senator Tom Harkin and interpreter Don Luce, visited the prison on Côn Sơn island. Using a map drawn by former prisoners, the group visited a building where prisoners were being held in tiger cages. The deplorable conditions of the prisoners, and photographs by Harkin, caused considerable embarrassment for the **Sài Gòn** government and further eroded American support for the RVN.

TIGER HOUND, OPERATION. An air interdiction operation in southern **Laos**. On 6 December 1965, **William C. Westmoreland** initiated Tiger Hound in direct response to the growing infiltration of enemy personnel and supplies coming down the **Hồ Chí Minh Trail** and the inability of the **Military Assistance Command, Vietnam**, and the **United States Air Force** (USAF) to coordinate with the U.S. embassy in Vientiane. The area for Tiger Hound was carved out of Operation **Steel Tiger**, an air interdiction campaign started in April 1965. The objectives of the air operation were to stop infiltration when possible and create bottleneck situations along the trail to increase target opportunities. Westmoreland argued that Tiger Hound, which would be under his control, afforded better coordination with the interdiction campaign along the **Demilitarized Zone** and ground operations in I **Corps Tactical Zone**. Target selection and authorization was not as restrictive as it had been in Steel Tiger, though striking villages or using **napalm** still required approval by the U.S. embassy in Vientiane.

Working with the 2nd Air Division to conduct armed **reconnaissance sorties** and the 309th Air Commando Squadron's Special Aerial Spray Flight in Operation **Ranch Hand** missions, the early effects of Tiger Hound missions were disappointing. It was not until the defoliation took effect in 1966 and **Forward Air Controller** pilots learned the **topography** of the Tiger Hound area that the operation began to make an impact. The USAF flew the majority of the sorties during the operation, followed by the U.S. **Marine Corps** and the U.S. **Navy**. **Arc Light** missions were also incorporated into the operation when rich targets of opportunity occurred. Also included in Tiger Hound was the experimental project **Popeye**, which attempted to start the monsoon season early by seeding the clouds, and Operation **Tally Ho**, which extended the area of operation for Tiger Hound into the southern part of the **Democratic Republic of Vietnam**. Tiger Hound continued through 1968, but while it forced the North Vietnamese to commit more resources to keep the Hồ Chí Minh Trail open, it did not stop the infiltration of personnel and supplies from reaching the **Republic of Vietnam** in support of the communist insurgency.

TOÀN THẮNG, OPERATIONS. A series of operations in III **Corps Tactical Zone** in response to the 1968 **Tết Offensive**. Toàn Thắng (Complete or Total Victory) began on 8 April 1968 and continued through to the end of the war. The operation was divided by numbers. Toàn Thắng 1 was conducted to the north of **Sài Gòn** and lasted to 31 May 1968. Operations Toàn Thắng 43 through 46 were the **Army of the Republic of Vietnam**'s contribution to the 1970 **Cambodian Incursion**.

TÔN THẤT ĐÍNH (1926–). Army of the Republic of Vietnam general. Born in **Huế** and a graduate of the National Military Academy in 1948, Tôn Thất Đính rose through the ranks of the Vietnamese Army as a paratrooper during the **First Indochina War**. He served as commander of the 2nd Infantry Division between 1951 and 1953 and the 1st Infantry Division between 1953 and 1954. In August 1958, he became the commander of II **Corps Tactical Zone** (CTZ) and, in December 1962, was switched to III CTZ, where he remained until 30 January 1964. Tôn Thất Đính was a supporter of **Ngô Đình Diệm** and enjoyed the backing of the **Sài Gòn** government. When the **Buddhist Crisis** erupted in May 1963 and lingered into the summer, he was selected as the military governor of Sài Gòn from 21 August to the 1 November 1963 coup d'état. **Ngô Đình Nhu** believed that Tôn Thất Đính could expose the military personnel involved in the coup d'état planning of 1963. He was trusted by the Sài Gòn government even after he had joined those intent upon ousting Ngô Đình Diệm.

After the coup d'état, Tôn Thất Đính remained commander of III CTZ, but he also served as the second deputy chairman of the Executive Committee of the Military Revolutionary Council and as the minister of public security in the provisional government. He also was the minister of interior. On 30 January 1964, **Nguyễn Khánh** initiated his own coup d'état and removed Tôn Thất Đính from power and arrested him. He was not convicted of any crimes and resumed his military career as the chief of the Central Military Training Center and as the inspector general of the **Republic of Vietnam** Armed Forces. In April 1966, he was made the commander of I CTZ and helped to suppress the Buddhist uprising in that sector. Tôn Thất Đính's actions during the crisis caused Prime Minister **Nguyễn Cao Kỳ** to arrest him because he was considered too lenient with the **Buddhists**. He was released after only a brief time in jail and ran for the Senate in the 1967 elections. Tôn Thất Đính won his race and became the chairman of the Senate Defense Committee from 1967 to 1968 and again from 1970 to 1972, when he also headed the Social Democrat Bloc. He also served as the publisher and editor of a daily newspaper, *Công Luận* (Public Opinion), and headed the Vietnamese Publishers Association. When Sài Gòn fell to the communists in April 1975, Tôn Thất Đính fled to the **United States**.

TOPOGRAPHY, VIETNAM. Vietnamese topography determined many of the strategies and tactics employed during the war. Rice paddies, interspersed with mangroves, dominated the landscape in the **Mê Kông** and **Red River deltas**, while the Annamite Chain towered over the interior landscape of Vietnam from the Chinese border to just north of **Sài Gòn** and divided the two Vietnams from **Laos** and **Cambodia**. While the coastline contained sandy beaches in some places, triple canopy and dense humid jungle dominated most of the interior outside of the deltas, with the exception of the high plains area near the center of the **Republic of Vietnam**. This diverse topography made it difficult to conduct and coordinate ground and air operations and challenged the tacticians of the war. *See also* CLIMATE, SOUTHEAST ASIA.

TOUR OF DUTY. In the war, members of the **United States** Armed Forces would have a tour of duty in Vietnam. For the **army**, **navy**, and **air force**, this time was generally limited to 12 months in Vietnam, while the **marines** served for 13 months. The tour of duty was designed to lessen any hardships for U.S. military personnel. This became especially important with the increase in the draft through the **Selective Service System**. While the tour of duty system strived for equality, there were also negative consequences. As those involved in a tour reached their end date, known as the Date Eligible to Return from Overseas (DEROS), there was a reluctance among such "short-timers" to take risks that might endanger their lives. This became more of a concern as **Vietnamization** was initiated in July 1969 and the U.S. disengaged from Southeast Asia.

The tour of duty also limited the time that military personnel could operate in Vietnam after learning about the country, its people, and its threat. This was especially true for **intelligence** personnel and military **advisers**. It took time to learn the nuances of Vietnam for the intelligence officers, while advisers needed their full time in the field to learn the situation and gain the trust of their Vietnamese counterparts. Officers usually spent six months in the field with combat troops and six months in the rear area before being rotated out.

Tours of duty also affected unit cohesion, especially when **casualty** levels increased, which resulted in higher numbers of new troops rotated into units as replacements. The tour of duty systems also diminished unit and command knowledge as military personnel had to relearn what their predecessors had acquired in their year of service. As a result, after the 12 or 13 month process, soldiers who had gained the knowledge to fight for and defend the people of the **Republic of Vietnam** were leaving the country only to be replaced by individuals who knew very little about how to fight in Southeast Asia.

TRAIL WATCHERS. A **Central Intelligence Agency** program initiated in April 1962 designed to train **Montagnards** to observe North Vietnamese movement down the **Hồ Chí Minh Trail** and infiltrate into the **Republic of Vietnam**. The Trail Watchers team was one of the many projects within the **Civilian Irregular Defense Group** (CIDG) program. The Trail Watchers were tasked with trying to stop the infiltration or, if confronted by a much larger force, to direct **Army of the Republic of Vietnam** forces to the infiltrators. In November 1963, the Trail Watchers and other CIDG projects came under the operational control of the **Military Assistance Command, Vietnam**, through Operation **Switchback**. After Operation Switchback, Trail Watchers were absorbed into the **Special Forces**–authorized Border Surveillance–Control Operating concept. The teams were responsible for recruiting and training new personnel to serve as observers, create an **intelligence** network, conduct psychological operations and civic action programs, and help with **pacification** efforts.

TRẦN NAM TRUNG (1912–2009). Born in Quảng Ngãi province, Trần Nam Trung joined the Vietnamese resisting French colonialism in Nghệ An at an early age. In 1931, he became a member of the Indochinese Communist Party and was in and out of jail as a result of his anti-French activities. He returned to Quảng Ngãi in 1944 where he took the alias name of Trần Lương and helped to establish the Athletic National Salvation Committee. In 1945, he was involved in Vietnamese efforts against the Japanese and French in Ba Tơ district, Quảng Ngãi province. His group joined in the August 1945 revolution near the end of World War II. During the **First Indochina War**, he served in a number of leadership positions, and during the Battle for **Điện Biên Phủ** he was involved in logistical support for the **People's Army of Vietnam**.

In 1955, Trần Nam Trung became the secretary of **Military Region** 5, which included the northern provinces of the **Republic of Vietnam**, for the **Lao Động** Party. He was made a lieutenant general in 1961 and continued to work with the newly formed **National Liberation Front** as the vice president of its Presidium and head of the Military Commission. He served as the chief of staff for the headquarters of the **Central Office for South Vietnam** and eventually became the minister of national defense of the **Provisional Revolutionary Government of the Republic of South Vietnam**, which served as a shadow of the **Sài Gòn** government. Trần Nam Trung remained in that position from 1969 to 1976. In 1976, he became the chairman of the Committee of the Government Inspectorate until his retirement in 1982. Trần Nam Trung was sometimes confused with **Trần Văn Trà**, who at one time used as his own alias the name Trần Nam Trung. *See also* FRANCE.

TRẦN THIỆN KHIÊM (1925–). Army of the Republic of Vietnam (ARVN) general and prime minister of the **Republic of Vietnam** (RVN). Trần Thiện Khiêm was born in **Sài Gòn** and received formal military training at the National Military Academy in **Đà Lạt**, graduating in July 1947. He served in the **Vietnamese National Army**. In July 1948, he was promoted to first lieutenant in the Militia Guards. In July 1951, he became a captain, and in March 1955 he joined the Joint General Staff. In March 1957, he served as deputy chief of the General Staff with a specific responsibility for logistical operations until October 1957, when he was promoted to acting chief of the Joint General Staff as a colonel. In January 1958, he became the commander of the 4th Field Division, and in September 1960 he commanded Military Region 5 until January 1961, when he was given command of the ARVN 21st Division. Between December 1962, when he was promoted to major general, and November 1963, when he was promoted to lieutenant general, Trần Thiện Khiêm served as chief of the Joint Staff for the Republic of Vietnam Armed Forces. He was instrumental in the coup d'état against **Ngô Đình Diệm**.

After the coup d'état, he was given command of III **Corps Tactical Zone**, where he remained until **Nguyễn Khánh** initiated his coup d'état in January

1964. Trần Thiện Khiêm was promoted to general in July 1964 and became the minister of defense and chairman of the Joint General Staff until September 1964. In October 1964, after Nguyễn Khánh had lost faith in him, Trần Thiện Khiêm was appointed ambassador to the **United States**. He served as the ambassador to the **Republic of China** from October 1965 to May 1968 when he became the minister for the interior. During this time, he also took the position of deputy prime minister for Pacification and Reconstruction, which he assumed on 12 March 1969. Trần Thiện Khiêm succeeded **Trần Văn Hương** as prime minister in September 1969. He remained prime minister until 4 April 1975 and was replaced by Nguyễn Bá Cẩn.

TRẦN VĂN CHƠN (1920–). Born in Vũng Tàu, Trần Văn Chơn received his certificate of graduation from the Vietnamese Naval Academy in 1952. He served as the vice commanding officer of the 23rd Assaulting River Group in 1953 and was promoted to the vice navy commander in 1956. He added the position of director of **United States** Naval Dockyards in 1957. In 1960, Trần Văn Chơn completed the Foreign Officer's course at the U.S. Naval War College, where he became closely tied to U.S. naval strategy and tactics. Upon his return to the **Republic of Vietnam**, he commanded the Security River Force in 1961 and became the deputy commander of the **Regional Forces** and **Popular Forces** from 1962 until 1966, when on 1 November 1966 he was promoted to chief of naval operations (CNO) for the Vietnamese **Navy**. Trần Văn Chơn was considered a fighting officer who was pro-American and a strong liaison to the U.S. naval officers who participated in the war. He remained the CNO until he was replaced by Chung Tấn Cang in early April 1975. He was imprisoned after the fall of **Sài Gòn** on 30 April 1975 and spent 13 years in a reeducation camp. After his release, he and his family moved to the U.S. where he was sponsored by, and lived with, the family of Admiral **Elmo R. Zumwalt Jr.**, the former U.S. CNO.

TRẦN VĂN CHƯƠNG (1898–1986). Father of **Madame Ngô Đình Nhu** and **Republic of Vietnam** (RVN) ambassador to the **United States**. Trần Văn Chương married into the Vietnamese royal family and, because of this, was able to rise in rank during the rule of **Bảo Đại** to the position of first foreign secretary. In July 1954, Trần Văn Chương became the minister of state in **Ngô Đình Diệm**'s first government but quickly was sent to Washington as the Vietnamese ambassador to replace Trần Văn Kha. He remained the RVN ambassador until his resignation on 22 August 1963 amid the **Buddhist Crisis** and immediately after the **Xá Lợi Pagoda** Raids. During the 1 November 1963 coup d'état, Trần Văn Chương and his wife were out of the country and did not suffer the same fate as his son-in-law and RVN president. He lived in the U.S. until he was murdered by his son, supposedly for changing his will which would have disinherited his son.

TRẦN VĂN ĐÔN (1917–1999). Army of the Republic of Vietnam general and government leader after the coup d'état against **Ngô Đình Diệm** in November 1963. Trần Văn Đôn was born in **France** but returned to Vietnam before World War II. He served as a French Army officer during World War II, having received his training at the École Spéciale Militaire de Saint-Cyr. When the French created the **Vietnamese National Army**, Trần Văn Đôn served as an officer in that army. After the **First Indochina War**, he was promoted to colonel and supported Ngô Đình Diệm as he consolidated his power in 1955. For his support, he became a general. He served as Ngô Đình Diệm's chief of staff and as a major general commanding I Corps until December 1962.

Trần Văn Đôn was moved out of the position after coming into conflict with Ngô Đình Cẩn, Ngô Đình Diệm's brother and de facto ruler of Central Vietnam. In order to avoid conflict between the two, he was promoted to commander of the **Army of the Republic of Vietnam** (ARVN) and then acting chief of the Joint General Staff after August 1963. Trần Văn Đôn had become disillusioned with Ngô Đình Diệm by then and began organizing plans for a coup d'état to remove Ngô Đình Diệm from power.

Trần Văn Đôn was successful in his planning and helped to orchestrate the event on 1 November 1963. After the coup d'état, Trần Văn Đôn became the first deputy chairman of the Executive Committee of the Military Revolutionary Council and then minister of national defense after 4 November 1963. He was removed from office after the bloodless coup d'état by **Nguyễn Khánh** on 30 January 1964. Trần Văn Đôn was placed under house arrest for 18 months and retired in 1965. He was elected to the RVN Senate in 1967 and then served as the minister of defense toward the end of the war. He left **Sài Gòn** for the **United States** on 29 April 1975, a day before the city fell to the North Vietnamese. He wrote a book on his Vietnam experiences titled *Our Endless War*, which was published in 1978.

TRẦN VĂN HƯƠNG (1902–1982). Sài Gòn mayor, prime minister, vice president, and second to last president of the **Republic of Vietnam** (RVN). Trần Văn Hương spent most of his early life as a teacher. He first served as the mayor of Sài Gòn in 1954–1955 and spent time in jail on charges of conspiracy against **Ngô Đình Diệm**. He returned to the mayor's office in September 1964. Trần Văn Hương was involved in the removal of **Nguyễn Khánh** from power during his first round as prime minister from 4 November 1964 to 27 January 1965. He also served as prime minister from 18 May 1968 to August 1969 and was even considered the best civilian candidate to run against **Nguyễn Văn Thiệu** in the 1967 presidential elections. Trần Văn Hương eventually served as Nguyễn Văn Thiệu's vice president, and when the latter resigned on 21 April 1975, he became the president of the RVN. Trần Văn Hương would resign a week later after his failed attempts to end the fighting through negotiations. Trần Văn Hương spent the next two years under house arrest and remained in Vietnam until his death.

TRẦN VĂN MINH (1923–). Often referred to as Little Minh to avoid confusion with General **Dương Văn Minh,** who in turn was known as Big Minh. Trần Văn Minh served as the chief of staff for the Republic of Vietnam **Air Force** between 1953 and 1955 and as commander of the **Army of the Republic of Vietnam** for the southwest during the sect troubles from 1955 until 1957, when he was transferred to the military academy to serve as its commander. Trần Văn Minh became the inspector general for the armed forces from 1959 until 1960, when he left public life. He returned to military service after the coup d'état against **Ngô Đình Diệm** in November 1963, an event that he supported. He became the chief of the Joint Staff until May 1965 and acting commander-in-chief of the Vietnamese Armed Forces on 21 February 1965, as well as minister of defense after another change of government. In November 1967, Trần Văn Minh took over as commander of the air force, succeeding **Nguyễn Cao Kỳ** when he became vice president after the national elections. Trần Văn Minh also served as ambassador to Tunisia.

TRẦN VĂN QUANG (1917–). Born in Nghệ An province in the central part of the **Democratic Republic of Vietnam**, Trần Văn Quang, also known as Trần Thúc Kính, joined the Indochinese Communist Party in 1936 and operated in the **Sài Gòn**–**Chợ Lớn** area in the late 1930s. He escaped arrest by the French in 1939 and fled back to Nghệ An province only to be arrested in 1941 and sentenced to life imprisonment. He was released in 1945 at the end of World War II and was involved in the 1945 Nghệ An uprising. He worked under the General Staff of the **People's Army of Vietnam** (PAVN) and was involved in the organization of the victory at **Điện Biên Phủ** in May 1954.

In 1959, he became the deputy chief of staff to the PAVN, and in 1961 he went south as the commissioner of the **Central Office for South Vietnam**. Trần Văn Quang also served as an alternate member to the Central Community of the Vietnamese Communist Party from 1960 to 1976. In 1965, he went back to the North and commanded **Military Region** 4, and in 1966 he returned to the **Republic of Vietnam** as the commander of the Trị-Thiên Military Region, which included the provinces of **Quảng Trị** and **Thừa Thiên**. Trần Văn Quang was familiar with the region, having served as the commander of forces there between 1948 and 1949. He was involved in the 1968 **Tết Offensive** and was implicated in the **Huế Massacre**.

In 1974, Trần Văn Quang was promoted to lieutenant general and returned to his old position as deputy general chief of staff. In 1978, he commanded the Vietnamese personnel in **Laos**, where he remained until 1981, when he became the deputy minister of defense. Between 1992 and 2002, he served as the president of the Vietnam War Veterans' Association.

Trần Văn Quang was widely known for his connection to the "1205 Document" discovered in April 1993 by the *New York Times* in the archives of the Communist Party in Moscow. The Soviet document, allegedly a translation of a 1972 report by Trần Văn Quang, suggested that the DRV held 1,205 Americans as **prisoners of war**. This was significantly more than the 386 that the DRV claimed it held. Trần Văn Quang denied his authorship of the original document, and U.S. government officials involved in POW issues agreed that the document contained too many inconsistencies to be considered authentic. *See also* FRANCE.

TRẦN VĂN TRÀ (1918–1996). National Liberation Front (NLF) officer and general in the **People's Army of Vietnam** (PAVN). Trần Văn Trà was also known as Nguyễn Chấn, Tư Chi, and Tư Nguyễn. He was born in Quảng Ngãi province and became a member of the Indochinese Communist Party in 1938. Because of his anti-French activities, he was imprisoned during World War II. After the war, he was released and fought against **France** during the **First Indochina War**. Trần Văn Trà was one of the estimated 80,000 Vietnamese who chose to go north after the 1954 **Geneva Agreements**, where he became a deputy chief of staff in the PAVN. He commanded the 330th PAVN Division and rose to the rank of major general in 1958. He was promoted to the rank of lieutenant general in 1961. In 1964, Trần Văn Trà became the military commander of **Front** B2, which included the southern section of the **Republic of Vietnam**, and was headquartered north of **Tây Ninh** City in **War Zone C**. This organization was also referred to as the **Central Office for South Vietnam** (COSVN). The objective of the units under Trần Văn Trà's command was to destroy the best **Army of the Republic of Vietnam** (ARVN) units available in **Sài Gòn**. When the **United States** entered the war, Front B2 changed its tactics, though Trần Văn Trà continued to advocate big unit engagements rather than smaller hit-and-run tactics. Between July and October 1966, he also served as the acting political commander for Front B2 until **Phạm Hùng** assumed command.

Trần Văn Trà was one of the generals responsible for the attack on Sài Gòn during the 1968 **Tết Offensive**, which he helped to direct from his forward command post at Hóc Môn. He returned to Front B2 and was involved in the southernmost prong of the 1972 **Easter Offensive**. In February 1973, he became the chief representative of the **Provisional Revolutionary Government of the Republic of South Vietnam** on the Four-Party Joint Military Commission created as a result of the **Paris Peace Accords**, whose mission was to oversee the terms of the agreements. Trần Văn Trà soon returned to Front B2 and continued in that position until the end of the war. During the last years of the war, Trần Văn Trà was known for his aggressive operations against the ARVN.

In 1976, he joined the Central Committee of the Vietnamese Communist Party, and in 1978 he served as the vice minister of defense. He held both positions until 1982, when he published a book, *Vietnam: History of the Bulwark B-2 Theater, Vol. 5: Concluding the 30-Year War*. In the book, Trần Văn Trà argued that the 1968 Tết Offensive had failed to achieve its objectives, and he blamed the **Hà Nội** government for underestimating the U.S. and overrating the abilities of the NLF and PAVN. His criticism forced him into retirement, and he was placed under house arrest until 1985, after which he devoted the remainder of his life to veteran's issues.

TRỊ THIÊN MILITARY REGION. The **Democratic Republic of Vietnam** created this region in April 1966, which comprised the two northernmost provinces, **Quảng Trị** and **Thừa Thiên**, of I **Corps Tactical Zone** (CTZ) in the **Republic of Vietnam**. These provinces had been a part of Military Region 5 before the change. The military region was established in response to the new military strategy that called for increased conflict with **United States** personnel in order to inflict more **casualties** and refocus attention away from the other CTZs. The strategy worked, in that nearly 25 percent of the U.S. casualties between 1966 and 1972 occurred in the newly formed region. Trị Thiên Military Region was under the command of General **Trần Văn Quang** until 1973.

TRỤ GIÃN. Term used to describe the political assassinations conducted by communist insurgents toward the end of the 1950s. The communist insurgents targeted honest and efficient officials who worked with the peasants while leaving alone those who were corrupt or inefficient. The insurgents also concentrated on attacking members of the Công An (Secret Police), educators, and civil action cadres. Between 1958 and 1959, the insurgents killed over 400 individuals who supported the government, and they kidnapped an estimated 575 people. The increased intensity of the insurgent attacks forced **Ngô Đình Diệm** to enact severe countermeasures such as the **Agroville Program** and his promulgation of Law 10/59, which called for severe penalties for antigovernment activity.

TRƯỜNG CHINH (1907–1988). Born Đặng Xuân Khu in Nam Định province, which was situated in the southern section of the **Red River Delta** on the Gulf of Tốn Kĩn. He was educated at the Lycée Albert Sarraut in **Hà Nội** and joined the Indochinese Communist Party sometime in the 1930s. He changed his name to Trường Chinh (Long March) in honor of Mao Zedong, of whom he was a great admirer. Trường Chinh became the general secretary of the Indochinese Communist Party in 1941 and continued in that position when the **Lao Động** Party replaced it in 1951.

He fell out of favor in the 1950s when he became the principal architect for the failed land reforms after the 1954 **Geneva Agreements**, which ultimately caused the deaths of tens of thousands of Vietnamese. He was forced out of office in 1956. While Trường Chinh advocated the Chinese model of revolution, he moderated his stance in the 1960s and sided with those who were influenced by the **Soviet Union**. Trường Chinh opposed the more overt military offensive policies of **Nguyễn Chí Thanh**, **Lê Duẩn**, and **Lê Đức Thọ**. He remained influential in the **Democratic Republic of Vietnam** as a member of the Politburo and, in 1960, as the chairman of the National Assembly's Standing Committee. He remained chairman until 1981.

After the war, Trường Chinh became the president of the Socialist Republic of Vietnam in 1981, succeeding **Nguyễn Hữu Thọ**. He also served as the general secretary of the Communist Party of Vietnam in 1986 after the death of Lê Duẩn. While in that position, he helped initiate the policy of Đổi Mới. He left office before the end of the year at the Sixth Party Congress in December as a result of reformers within the party who were seeking more aggressive action. He also resigned from the Politburo. He resigned as president because of illness in 1987 and was replaced by **Võ Chí Công**. *See also* CHINA, PEOPLE'S REPUBLIC OF.

TRƯƠNG ĐÌNH DZŨ (1917–). 1967 presidential candidate and lawyer. Trương Đình Dzũ was born in **Qui Nhơn** and was educated as a lawyer. In his school years at the University of **Hà Nội**, he was involved in resistance against the French colonial administration. He moved to **Sài Gòn** and practiced law, though he was mired in controversy over alleged corruption and the solicitation of bribes from Americans to clear them of criminal charges. As a Sài Gòn lawyer and director of the Rotary Club of Southeast Asia, he opposed **Ngô Đình Diệm** in the April 1961 election but decided not to contest the incumbent when the election laws were released. Trương Đình Dzũ argued that the laws were designed to ensure that Ngô Đình Diệm would win, but other factors, including charges of corruption, were probably as significant a factor in his decision.

He ran as a **Dove** candidate, with his running mate Trần Văn Chiều, former president of the Sài Gòn Chamber of Commerce, in the 3 September 1967 presidential election despite election laws that were even more favorable to the incumbent than in 1961. His ticket won 800,000 votes, or approximately 17 percent of the vote. He was arrested on 1 May 1968 for advocating a neutral government and peace negotiations with the **National Liberation Front** during the election. On 26 July 1968, a Special Military Court sentenced him to five years imprisonment on Côn Sơn island. Trương Đình Dzũ was among the few whose sentence was not reduced the next year by **Republic of Vietnam** (RVN) president **Nguyễn Văn Thiệu**. In 1971, his sentence was reduced to four years, and he was released on 1 May 1972. On the day of his release, he was placed under temporary detention and was not freed until 26 March 1973. Trương Đình Dzũ remained in seclusion for the remainder of the war. He was sent to a reeducation camp after the fall of Sài Gòn and died sometime in the 1980s.

TRUSCOTT WHITE, OPERATION. A joint **United States Army** and **U.S. Air Force** (USAF) operation begun in April 1968 to interdict North Vietnamese supplies and personnel moving along the **Hồ Chí Minh Trail** in the area where the **Democratic Republic of Vietnam**, **Laos**, and **Cambodia** meet. In order to identify enemy movement, the army inserted **long-range reconnaissance patrols** and used O-1 aircraft with side-looking airborne radar and infrared to locate the enemy, while USAF **forward air controllers** patrolled the air to direct tactical air strikes. In the first and third phases of the operation, B-52 **Arc Light** missions as well as other available aircraft struck the target once it was identified. While Arc Light missions saturated the target with **bombs**, other aircraft suppressed **antiaircraft artillery** and dropped XM-41 gravel **mines** and CS-1 gas, which had the positive effect of keeping repair crews away from the damaged target.

In phase two, heavy **artillery** and other airpower assumed the firepower role. From 7 April 1968 to 29 June 1968, when the monsoon rains began, there were approximately 1,420 **sorties** in Truscott White. Reconnaissance of the area of operation suggested that the interdiction efforts were successful in stopping or severely hampering North Vietnamese transit through the area. But they did not eliminate the North Vietnamese presence, nor did they dissuade the enemy from continuing to use the roads and bridges during the next dry season.

TUBE-LAUNCHED, OPTICALLY TRACKED, WIRE DATA LINK (TOW) GUIDED MISSILE. *See* MISSILES.

TUNNEL RATS. Name given to allied soldiers who went into **People's Army of Vietnam** and **National Liberation Front tunnel** complexes to root out or kill the enemy. These soldiers would enter the tunnel head first, normally armed only with a pistol and flashlight. The tunnel rat job was very dangerous, as the men who performed the duty faced not only the tunnel's human inhabitants but also **booby traps**, snakes, scorpions, and other man-made or natural obstacles. Tunnel rats were among the bravest of those who served in Vietnam because they faced the enemy alone, in the enemy's own territory, and with the enemy fully aware of their presence.

TUNNELS. The **Việt Minh**, **National Liberation Front** (NLF), and **People's Army of Vietnam** (PAVN) used tunnels throughout the **First Indochina War** and **Second Indochina War**. Tunnels provided a modicum of protection from **artillery** and air strikes but were especially valuable for concealment against **United States** and **Republic of Vietnam** air **reconnaissance** and ground missions. The type of tunnel varied depending upon the needs and conditions of the battlefield. In **guerrilla warfare**, the tunnel could be a small hole, often known as a spider hole, which concealed one man who worked as part of a larger ambush mission or as a sniper. These existed throughout the RVN and were particularly troublesome in harassing U.S. and allied troops.

The Việt Minh, NLF, and PAVN also developed more extensive tunnel complexes that sometimes stretched for miles underground. The largest, and most famous, was the tunnel complex system in **Củ Chi** district in Hậu Nghĩa province, which was used to conduct operations against **Sài Gòn** and the Capital Military Region. Tunnel systems like those at Củ Chi contained all of the requirements for conducting war. This included hospitals, supply depots, training facilities, sleeping and eating quarters, and operations and logistical centers.

The U.S. and its allies continually searched the tunnel systems and used airpower to identify and destroy them. Operation **Ranch Hand** sprayed herbicides in contested areas to kill the vegetation that was used to conceal tunnel entrances, while U.S. and RVN aircraft used **bombs** and **napalm** to collapse tunnels near allied military facilities. When tunnels were discovered, the U.S. brought in personnel who were specially trained to deal with the situation. These men, known as **tunnel rats**, entered tunnel systems with a pistol and flashlight and often operated alone to investigate and clear tunnels. Despite the use of specialized training and superior firepower, the U.S. and its allies were never able to negate the advantages of the tunnel system strategy employed by the NLF and PAVN. *See also* DOGS.

U

U MINH FOREST. An area located between the borders of Kiên Giang and An Xuyên provinces in the **Cà Mau**, in the southernmost part of IV **Corps Tactical Zone**. The forest mixed with swamplands made it almost inaccessible. During the **First Indochina War**, the U Minh Forest served as a safe haven for groups that resisted the French. The forest remained a contested area through the war in the 1960s and 1970s despite **United States** and South Vietnamese attempts to pacify the region. From the forest, the **National Liberation Front** could harass U.S. and **Army of the Republic of Vietnam** personnel through sniper fire, **booby traps**, and the **mining** of roads. **Republic of Vietnam** officials in the region were never able to effectively control the area because of a general apathy of the civilian population and a lack of effective leadership for its troops operating in the area.

UNION, OPERATION (I AND II). A series of operations, known by the Vietnamese as Liên Kết 102, conducted in 1967 in the **Quế Sơn Valley**. The operations were also known as Núi Lộc Sơn, the name of the dominant mountain in the area, which was situated between **Quảng Nam** and Quảng Tín provinces in the southernmost part of I **Corps Tactical Zone**. Operation Union I began on 21 April 1967 and lasted until 16 May. It involved the 1st Marine Regiment facing the 2nd **People's Army of Vietnam** (PAVN) Division. The Quế Sơn Valley had always been considered a strategic area during the war because of its agricultural land and large population. Union I was a large-scale clearing operation. It succeeded in driving the PAVN force out of the valley. On 26 May, the 5th Marine Regiment continued working the valley in what had become known as Operation Union II. This second operation lasted until 5 June. It was estimated that the PAVN force lost approximately 700 personnel, with 23 captured. The **United States** lost 110 killed and had over 240 wounded. The Union operations were successful but limited, in that the Quế Sơn Valley continued to be contested until the end of the war.

UNITED ACTION. A plan formulated as a result of a meeting between Secretary of State **John Foster Dulles** and French Foreign Minister Georges

Bidault during the 1954 **Điện Biên Phủ** crisis. In the proposed plan, the **United States** would lead an allied intervention into Indochina to relieve pressure on the beleaguered French fortress. The U.S. approached allies who had a special interest in preserving the stability of Indochina and thwarting communist advancement in the region. One requirement for the plan to go forward was the active cooperation of Great Britain so that the U.S. would not act alone as had been the perception during the Korean War. When London refused, **Australia** and **New Zealand** also balked, and without British agreement, Dulles and President Dwight D. Eisenhower conceded that **Congress** would never approve the plan. The concept of United Action would serve as the basis for the **South East Asian Treaty Organization** that was established in September 1954.

UNITED NATIONS (UN). During the Vietnam War, the UN failed to play a significant role in either the military or diplomatic arena. In the 1950s, the central issue on which the UN focused was the question of admitting the **Republic of Vietnam** (RVN) and the **Democratic Republic of Vietnam** (DRV) to its General Assembly. When in 1957 the **United States** attempted to gain RVN membership to the UN, the **Soviet Union** vetoed the application. The U.S. hoped that UN recognition of the RVN would help that country gain legitimacy within the international community. The Soviet Union offered a proposal to accept both the RVN and the DRV, but this was not acceptable to the U.S., which refused to acknowledge the authority of the communist state.

During the **John F. Kennedy** administration, the UN was never considered a viable option, especially after the failure to neutralize **Laos** during the 1962 **Geneva Conference**. It was clear that the UN would not play a role in Southeast Asia as it had on the Korean Peninsula in the early 1950s. Neither Moscow nor Washington would allow the other to manipulate the UN for its own military or diplomatic gain. During the presidency of **Lyndon B. Johnson**, the UN was relegated to a minor role and was replaced by the **Show the Flag** program, which was initiated in April 1964 and was aimed at garnering **Third Country** support for the defense of the RVN.

After the U.S. began to escalate its involvement in Vietnam in 1965 with the introduction of combat troops and the sustained bombing of the DRV, the UN secretary general, U Thant, who had been a supporter of the U.S., started to express his misgivings about U.S. action. American escalation was done without the consent of the UN, and its overwhelming use of firepower, despite attempts to limit civilian **casualties**, resulted in more intense international condemnation. On 10 January 1967, U Thant openly criticized the U.S. in a press conference after he was appointed for a second term as general secretary on 2 December 1966. U Thant argued that the U.S. bombing of the DRV needed to end before negotiations to end the war could commence. The U.S. had attempted to tie **bombing pauses** to peace talks since 1965 with no success. U Thant also argued that the **National Liberation Front** was a legitimate and independent force in the RVN that had to be included in any negotiations.

After U Thant's break with the U.S., the UN's potential influence in helping to solve the problem in Vietnam diminished. He was succeeded by Kurt Waldheim who failed to wield any influence as the American war ended with the January 1973 **Paris Peace Accords** and the Vietnamese war ended with the fall of **Sài Gòn** in April 1975.

UNITED STATES. When the United States recognized the Associated States of Vietnam, **Laos**, and **Cambodia** on 7 February 1950, it began a 25-year relationship that ended in failure. The U.S. experience in Vietnam was marked by good intentions, dedicated individuals, and, at times, a sound strategy. It was also marred by a narrow vision of the world, individuals who could not look past their belief system that relegated the Vietnamese to a secondary position, and a strategy that focused, at times, on what the U.S. wanted rather than what the Vietnamese needed. It is this complementary, yet conflicting, relationship that typifies U.S.-Vietnamese relations from 1950 to 1975.

Between 1950 and 1954, a period that covers the administrations of Harry S. Truman and Dwight D. Eisenhower, the U.S. supported **France**'s effort during the **First Indochina War**. The U.S. aided the French not so much to help that country regain its colonial empire as to serve as a bulwark against the perceived communist encroachment in Asia that had begun with the loss of **China** to the communists in 1949 and the outbreak of the Korean War in 1950. While the U.S. increasingly supported the French war with material and money, its military leaders warned against an American escalation that included combat troops. During this troubled time in the Cold War, the U.S. military argued that it did not have the resources to commit to peripheral areas of concern without weakening other commitments of greater significance. As the French effort stumbled, the U.S. continued to increase its assistance and place pressure on the French government to produce results. By 1954, the situation in Indochina was tenuous. The U.S. supplied approximately 75 percent of the money and demanded some positive results for its contribution.

As a result, the French Union Forces, under the command of General **Henri Navarre**, launched a 1954 operation designed to maximize its strengths against the Vietnamese insurgents. When the plan failed to proceed because of the military countermoves orchestrated by Vietnamese general **Võ Nguyên Giáp**, Navarre reorganized his strategy and settled on a plan to force the Vietnamese to confront his troops, with their overwhelming firepower, at **Điện Biên Phủ.** As the situation deteriorated there, the U.S. had to decide whether to escalate in Indochina against the wishes of its military and

Congress or allow the French to fail and achieve the best possible peace it could at the upcoming Geneva Conference. The U.S. resisted the French plan, Operation Vulture, to saturation bomb the Vietnamese position around Điện Biên Phủ and failed to garner international support for its **United Action** program to insert a **Free World Force** to rescue the French at the fortress. The inability, or unwillingness, of the U.S. to act and the failure of the French to continue the fight resulted in a French defeat at Điện Biên Phủ and the 1954 **Geneva Agreements**.

After the Geneva Agreements, the U.S. took a greater interest in Vietnam. It supported the exodus of Vietnamese from the northern section of the country to the South with Operation **Passage to Freedom** and began to assume the role that the French had played in advising the Vietnamese. The Eisenhower administration supported **Ngô Đình Diệm** after he had proven himself capable of surviving the political intrigues of Sài Gòn during the 1955 Sect Crisis and began to give aid to the newly formed **Republic of Vietnam** (RVN) in a nation-building effort. The American commitment, which was more than just material but included a moral dimension as a result of the Passage to Freedom experience, went beyond military aid. **Michigan State University** contracted with the U.S. and Sài Gòn governments to help construct the country, while organizations and individuals such as the **American Friends of Vietnam** and Dr. Thomas A. Dooley worked to educate the American public about Southeast Asia and to coordinate humanitarian relief efforts.

By the end of the 1950s, the U.S. was committed to the defense of the RVN, but evidence of strains in the relationship began to emerge. The U.S. ambassador to the RVN, Elbridge Durbrow, cautioned Washington on the obstinacy of Ngô Đình Diệm and warned the RVN president that he had to either reform his government and practices or suffer the consequences. Ngô Đình Diệm was not as easy to manipulate as Durbrow thought, nor was he willing to be told how to govern his country. Durbrow, and a growing number of American officials, began to argue that Ngô Đình Diệm was the cause of the failure to rid the RVN of the communist insurgency and called for his removal. Durbrow personified one of the problems in America's Vietnam experience. He consistently blamed the RVN leadership for the failures in Vietnam rather than acknowledging that the U.S. had different goals and procedures to attain those objectives. He also failed to understand how the enemy fought or its requirements for victory. This would have a detrimental consequence for Ngô Đình Diệm, but it was also a dangerous precedent for future U.S. activities in Southeast Asia.

When **John F. Kennedy** entered the White House in January 1961, Laos represented a more serious threat to Southeast Asia than the RVN. That country had just experienced a coup d'état, and infighting among the more conservative elements of the government threatened to give the communist insurgency, the **Pathet Lao**, an opening to gain power. The Kennedy administration settled on a policy of neutralization for Laos with the International Conference on the Settlement of the Laotian Question. The U.S. was satisfied with the July 1962 **Geneva Accords**, but Ngô Đình Diệm opposed the American plan, which earned him further condemnation. In the RVN, the Kennedy administration decided on a policy of escalation rather than neutrality. The U.S. increased its advisory role, introduced more sophisticated weapons, and transformed the **Military Assistance Advisory Group** into the **Military Assistance Command, Vietnam**. Kennedy considered only escalatory options during his first 18 months in office as the situation in the region continued to deteriorate.

When the Sài Gòn government introduced the **Strategic Hamlet Program** to replace the failed **Agroville Program**, many U.S. officials were skeptical, including holdouts from the Durbrow embassy. U.S.-RVN relations continued to deteriorate even after **Frederick E. Nolting Jr.** replaced Durbrow in May 1961. Ngô Đình Diệm's distrust of American advice not only earned him denunciation but also quietly initiated the process of some within Washington discussing how to replace him. In 1963, the situation reached an impasse. The January 1963 **Battle of Ấp Bắc** confirmed to many Americans that the **Army of the Republic of Vietnam** (ARVN) was incapable of fighting the war on its own, while the **Buddhist Crisis** that began in May 1963 highlighted a Ngô Đình Diệm who appeared to be increasingly brutal and oppressive.

In August 1963, **Henry Cabot Lodge Jr.** replaced Nolting, and with him a stricter anti–Ngô Đình Diệm position followed. The U.S. openly sided with the Buddhist leaders, even providing shelter in the U.S. embassy for two of the more outspoken bonzes after the 21 August **Xá Lợi Pagoda** raids. By October, Lodge and his representatives were holding discussions with ARVN generals who were plotting to overthrow Ngô Đình Diệm. On 1 November, a coup d'état occurred, and while Lodge, Kennedy, and the U.S. government could claim that they had not orchestrated the event, Americans in Sài Gòn allowed the change in government to occur, which resulted in the deaths of Ngô Đình Diệm and his brother **Ngô Đình Nhu**. Three weeks later, Kennedy was assassinated in Dallas, Texas.

Lyndon B. Johnson inherited a country mourning for the loss of its president and a Vietnam policy in disarray. As Vietnamese generals and intellectuals vied for power and intensified the already rampant political intrigue in Sài Gòn, the U.S. reassessed its Vietnam policy. Johnson concluded that he needed to continue the Kennedy legacy, which included his domestic agenda but also his commitment to helping defend the RVN against the communist threat. While Johnson's Vietnam policy was tempered with domestic concerns, including his proposed Great Society legislation and his 1964 presidential election campaign against **Barry Goldwater**, he continued to commit American prestige and power to Southeast Asia.

The U.S. military presence in Laos and the RVN increased in 1964 with the introduction of Operation **Barrel Roll** in the former and Operation **Pierce Arrow** in the latter after the August **Gulf of Tŏn Kĭn Incident**. After continued **National Liberation Front** (NLF) attacks against U.S. personnel and the destruction of U.S. material, Johnson changed U.S. policy in March 1965 with the introduction of two **marine** battalions to **Đà Nẵng** and the authorization for Operation **Rolling Thunder**.

Combat troops and the sustained air campaign irreversibly changed America's Vietnam policy. With U.S. military prestige committed not only to the defense of the RVN but to the defeat of the NLF and submission of the **Democratic Republic of Vietnam**, the Johnson administration undertook a gradual escalation of the war that ushered in a further commitment of personnel and the launching of major **search-and-destroy** missions. Between 1965 and 1968, the U.S. fought a war of attrition against an enemy that followed a different set of rules and requisites for victory. As a result, the U.S. achieved what it considered success on the battlefield but was frustrated by its inability to defeat the enemy. While its military strategy seemed to be successful, the U.S. was slowly losing the political battle at home and abroad as **antiwar** organizations and protests against the war steadily increased. By 1968, the U.S. was at a crossroads that proved to be detrimental to the success of its Vietnam experience.

The January 1968 **Tết Offensive** marked a major turning point in the war. Three years of fighting and tens of thousands of casualties proved not to be enough, as the **People's Army of Vietnam** (PAVN) and the NLF launched a nationwide attack against U.S. and ARVN forces. While the offensive was a military failure, it did score a political and psychological victory as the U.S. military was discredited and Johnson scaled back U.S. activities against the Democratic Republic of Vietnam. The Tết Offensive galvanized the antiwar movement and the **media**, which was more intent on using its power and influence to guide American foreign policy than to report it. As a result, the nation reeled from what should have been a major victory for the U.S. and RVN. By the end of the year, the U.S. was not able to take advantage of the military victory, and Johnson had been replaced by **Richard M. Nixon**.

The Nixon administration was tasked with recovering from a Vietnam policy that had failed to achieve its desired results in a timely manner and without a significant loss of life. In order to salvage the situation, Nixon authorized the policy of **Vietnamization**, in which the U.S. slowly handed the war back to the South Vietnamese by supplying the necessary firepower and training to strengthen the ARVN. Ironically, Nixon provided in 1969 what

Ngô Đình Diệm had requested a decade earlier: the means to fight the war without American conditions attached to the aid and assistance. Nixon's Vietnamization was guardedly welcomed, but his future actions fueled antiwar sentiment and failed to achieve the desired results.

As part of Vietnamization, Nixon authorized the secret bombing of **Cambodia**. The objective of Operation **Menu** was to deny the border sanctuaries between Cambodia and the RVN that were enjoyed by the PAVN and NLF during the Johnson administration. He then authorized a limited incursion into Cambodia in 1970 that was militarily successful but aroused the antiwar movement, and he supported a 1971 insertion into Laos by the ARVN. Nixon's actions, along with revelations of such events as the **Mỹ Lai** massacre and the release of the **Pentagon Papers**, resulted in a congressional move to limit the power of the president to act in Southeast Asia and conduct foreign policy. While Nixon fought with **Congress**, the U.S. continued to disengage from Southeast Asia. This confluence of events led to the 1972 **Easter Offensive** in which PAVN forces launched an overt offensive against the South. The offensive failed, in part because of a stubborn ARVN defense and U.S. firepower, but it did not give Nixon any leeway. The U.S. was committed to ending its participation in the war and leaving Southeast Asia.

On 27 January 1973, the U.S. satisfied these objectives with the signing of the **Paris Peace Accords**. The documents ended the U.S. war, though the fighting in Vietnam was far from over. Many in the U.S. who had supported the RVN from its inception watched helplessly as America refused to come to the aid of the Vietnamese even as the DRV violated the agreements and Nixon's involvement in the Watergate scandal forced President **Gerald Ford** into an impossible situation. Days before the fall of Sài Gòn on 30 April 1975, and after the earlier loss of Phnom Penh to the Khmer Rouge, Ford pronounced the end of the Vietnam nightmare to an enthusiastically applauding audience at Tulane University. While the military war was over, the Vietnam experience continued.

The U.S. military spent several decades recovering from its Vietnam experience as the lessons learned in Southeast Asia were evaluated and applied to modern strategy. Many American servicemen suffered from their experience. Some underwent posttraumatic stress disorder or felt the effects of **Agent Orange**, while others simply needed a prolonged period to readjust from their time in Vietnam. The U.S. public failed to honor its veterans, while veterans of earlier wars delayed in accepting the newest members into their elite society. **Women** who served in Vietnam suffered from even greater alienation, as their service was not considered to be in a combat zone. The credibility of the media, which had strived to improve its position in the U.S., also suffered. In a poll in late 1972, more Americans failed to believe media reports of Operation **Linebacker II** bombing damage in **Hà Nội** than condemned Nixon for authorizing the air campaign in the first place.

As the nation grappled with its first military experience that did not end in victory, it also dealt with the **prisoner-of-war** (POW) and **missing-in-action** situation. Internationally, the U.S. lost the prestige that Johnson had tried so hard to maintain as it was criticized for both its actions in Vietnam and its failure to support its 25-year ally in the final days of the war. The U.S. also was reminded of its failure with the influx of hundreds of thousands of Vietnamese **refugees** who fled Vietnam rather than live under communist rule. In one of the numerous ironies of the war, many who fled in 1975 as a result of the U.S. failure to live up to its promises came from the same families who had left the DRV in 1954–1955 aboard American ships to travel south with a promise that the U.S. would help to provide them with a safer and more prosperous home. The U.S. continues to apply, or misapply, the lessons of Vietnam in the early 21st century, though the two adversaries now have normalized relations, and Americans in Hà Nội are tourists and businessmen rather than POWs. The wounds of the war will most likely never heal for the generation that experienced it, but for the U.S., the memory of the war has started to fade from reality into history.

V

VĂN TIẾN DŨNG (1917–2002). People's Army of Vietnam (PAVN) general. Văn Tiến Dũng was born in the **Hà Nội** area into a peasant family. He worked in a textile mill, which helped to shape his early views of **France**'s colonial rule. He assumed a leadership position in the Fraternal Association of Textile Workers, and in 1937 he joined the Indochinese Communist Party and was jailed repeatedly between 1939 and 1944. He fought against both the French and the Japanese at the end of World War II. In 1945, he became the secretary of the Northern Party Organization and a member of the Northern Revolutionary Army Committee. During the latter stages of the **First Indochina War**, Văn Tiến Dũng commanded the PAVN 320th Division and was promoted to PAVN chief of staff in November 1953. He was involved in planning the victory at **Điện Biên Phủ** in 1954.

He continued to serve as chief of staff until 1978 and maintained a solid reputation as a military leader. In 1951, he served as an alternate member of the **Lao Động** Party, and in 1960 he became a full member of the Central Committee and an alternate member of the Politburo. Văn Tiến Dũng allied himself with the **Lê Duẩn-Lê Đức Thọ** faction that opposed the strategy of **Võ Nguyên Giáp**. Meanwhile, his military reputation made him one of the more popular generals in the **Democratic Republic of Vietnam**.

Văn Tiến Dũng directed PAVN troops in the **Republic of Vietnam, Laos**, and **Cambodia** and was involved in the planning of the 1972 **Easter Offensive**. He commanded the PAVN forces engaged in I **Corps Tactical Zone**, known as the **Trị-Thiên Military Front**. In 1974, he became the PAVN commander-in-chief and oversaw the final offensive against **Sài Gòn** in 1975. After the war, Văn Tiến Dũng was involved in the December 1978 Socialist Republic of Vietnam's invasion of Democratic Kampuchea (Cambodia). In February 1980, he was elected to the Politburo and was appointed minister of defense, replacing his longtime colleague and rival, Võ Nguyên Giáp. He remained in these positions until 1986 when the Vietnamese Communist Party underwent significant internal change and he was gradually eclipsed, although he did remain a member of the Central Committee until 1991. He was the author of several books on military strategy and the war.

VANG PAO (1931–). Major general in the Royal Lao government's Royal Lao Army. Vang Pao began his military career when he joined the French Union Forces and led **Hmong** militia against the Japanese occupation during World War II. During the **First Indochina War**, he fought the **Việt Minh** and remained in the military after the 1954 **Geneva Agreements**, rising to the rank of general. He was the only ethnic Hmong to do so at the time. Vang Pao led a large private army that continued to battle the **People's Army of Vietnam**, the **National Liberation Front**, and the **Pathet Lao** during the war with the support of the Royal Laotian Government and the **United States** through the **Central Intelligence Agency**. The U.S. aided Vang Pao's army by providing air support during the dry seasons when his army was outnumbered and air transport during the wet season when American airpower served as a troop multiplier, accessing areas cut off by the monsoons and allowing for more mobility in his offensive. Vang Pao was loyal to the crown and was an anticommunist, though his legacy in the Laotian resistance was marred by accusations of drug trafficking. He fled **Laos** in 1975 when the communists took over, and he eventually immigrated to the U.S.

VANN, JOHN PAUL (1924–1972). **United States Army** colonel and adviser to the **Army of the Republic of Vietnam** (ARVN). Vann was born in Virginia and entered the Army Air Corps in 1943 during World War II. He did not see combat during the war, and in 1947 he decided to stay in the army rather than join the newly formed **U.S. Air Force**. As a result, Vann fought with the 25th Infantry Division during the Korean War. He left that assignment with the rank of captain.

Vann continued in the army through the 1950s and was stationed in Germany and in the U.S. In April 1962, he arrived in the **Republic of Vietnam** (RVN) and was assigned as an adviser to the ARVN 7th Division, which was under the command of Colonel **Huỳnh Văn Cao**. Vann became disenchanted with the ARVN leadership, especially during the January 1963 **Battle of Ấp Bắc**. In the aftermath of the battle, Vann became the anonymous military official who criticized the ARVN performance in interviews with American newsmen. He directly confronted and contradicted **Military Assistance Command, Vietnam** (MACV), commander General **Paul Harkins** who had claimed victory in the battle even though the ARVN troops had been bloodied and had only achieved their objective of seizing the areas of Ấp Bắc and Ấp Tân Thôi after the **National Liberation Front** had abandoned its positions. Vann's confrontation with Harkins, who had objected to Vann going public with his criticisms of the ARVN and directly contradicting the official MACV position, resulted in him being forced out of Vietnam in March 1963 and leaving the army that summer.

In March 1965, Vann returned to Vietnam as a member of the Agency for International Development (AID). He was involved in the training of the People's Action Teams and supervised AID **counterinsurgency** programs in 1966. He was assigned as the senior **adviser** of Hậu Nghĩa province for **Civil Operations and Revolutionary Development Support** (CORDS) in III **Corps Tactical Zone** (CTZ) in 1967. Vann remained in that role until November 1968, when he was moved to IV CTZ. During his time in Vietnam, Vann earned a reputation as a very competent adviser and one who was committed to the ARVN. He had been pessimistic about the chances of the RVN until the 1968 **Tết Offensive**, but the military victory in that offensive changed his outlook, as did the U.S. effort that led to the **Accelerated Pacification Program**.

In May 1971, Vann left IV CTZ to become the director of the 2nd Regional Assistance Group in II CTZ. In this position, he helped to coordinate the civilian and military aid programs. Though a civilian, Vann was given de facto command of the U.S. forces in II CTZ and served as the principal adviser to the ARVN commander in the region, General Ngô Dzu. Vann was instrumental in the defense of **Kon Tum** during the 1972 **Easter Offensive**. He was killed in a **helicopter** crash on 9 June 1972 while directing U.S. action as it related to the American response to the offensive. President **Richard M. Nixon** awarded him posthumously the Medal of Freedom on 18 June. He was also awarded posthumously the Distinguished Service Cross, which was unique because of his civilian status.

VIỆT CỘNG. Shortened version of Vietnamese communist (Cộng Sản Việt Nam), which was the term used by **Ngô Đình Diệm** to describe the communist insurgency operating in the **Republic of Vietnam** from the mid-1950s until the end of the war. The **United States** often called the Việt Cộng Victor Charlie. The insurgents called themselves the National Front for the Liberation of South Vietnam (Mặt Trận Dân Tộc Giải Phóng Miền Nam Việt Nam/ NLF), which has been westernized to the **National Liberation Front**.

VIỆT MINH (VIỆT NAM ĐỘC LẬP ĐỒNG MINH HÔI, LEAGUE FOR THE INDEPENDENCE OF VIETNAM). Formed at the Eighth Plenum of the Indochinese Communist Party Central Committee meeting at Pác Bó in Tŏn Kĭn on 9 May 1941, the Việt Minh served as the coordinating agency for groups opposed to French colonialism, and then Japanese occupation, in Indochina. While the organization included communists, it also had in its ranks socialists and democrats who were united in support of the nationalist cause. Communist organizers of the Việt Minh, including **Hồ Chí Minh**, **Phạm Văn Đồng**, and **Võ Nguyên Giáp**, focused on national liberation rather than class revolution in order to bring together as broad a coalition as possible. The Việt Minh led the August Revolution in 1945, which established the **Democratic Republic of Vietnam** and served as the primary organization of opposition to **France**'s efforts to reinstate colonialism during the **First Indochina War**.

After Hồ Chí Minh's 2 September 1945 declaration of independence speech, based loosely on the American Declaration of Independence, the Indochinese Communist Party dissolved itself, which left the Việt Minh as the only official Vietnamese party. The Việt Minh were absorbed into a new version of the communist party, the Vietnam Workers Party (Đang Lao Động Việt Nam), in 1951, while the structure of the Việt Minh resurfaced in the form of the Hội Liên Hiệp Quốc Dân Việt Minh (Liên Việt Front) after the 1954 **Geneva Conference**.

VIETNAM MORATORIUM COMMITTEE. Group established to help organize the Moratorium Day demonstrations of 15 October 1969. The original plan had been for a general strike, but the committee, guided by David Hawk, Sam Brown, David Mixner, Marge Sklenkar, and John Gage, took a more moderate path and simply called for a national protest of the war. The 15 October 1969 Moratorium counted its participants in the tens of thousands. The 15 November 1969 National Moratorium Day would number in the hundreds of thousands, while monthly demonstrations continued to attracted a significant number of people through 1971. A similar committee was organized in **Australia** to protest that country's involvement in the war.

VIETNAM VETERANS AGAINST THE WAR (VVAW). The VVAW was founded in 1967 by six Vietnam veterans who met during an **antiwar** protest in New York City. The group of veterans worked toward ending the war in Vietnam as well as exposing what they believed to be war crimes committed by the **United States**. The group sponsored the 31 January–2 February 1971 **Winter Soldier investigation** in Detroit, Michigan, during which time veterans and others made claims against U.S. action in Vietnam. The organization also coordinated the 19–23 April 1971 protest in Washington, D.C., known as **Dewey Canyon** III. Over 1,000 veterans joined in the protests that took place in front of the White House, **Congress**, the Pentagon, the Supreme Court, and the gates of Arlington Cemetery. The group also organized a march from Concord, Massachusetts, to Boston on Memorial Day 1971, but the approximately 440 protesters were arrested before the march began. Members of the VVAW also barricaded themselves in the Statue of Liberty on 26 December 1971 and held out for two days in an effort to attract public attention to the war. The group continued to protest until the last of the American troops were out of Vietnam.

VIETNAMESE NATIONAL ARMY (VNA). Created in 1949 for the State of Vietnam, the VNA (Quân Đội Quốc Gia Việt Nam) was the product of French general Jean Joseph Marie Gabriel de Lattre de Tassigny with the approval of Vietnamese emperor **Bảo Đại**. The VNA was organized along the French military model with Nguyễn Văn Hinh serving as its chief of staff. The VNA fought on the side and under the leadership of the French during the **First Indochina War**, though it was not well equipped or trained by its French allies. Most of its officers were trained at the Preparatory Military School in **Đà Lạt**, though a few of the future leaders of the army would receive training in **France**. When the State of Vietnam was replaced by the **Republic of Vietnam** in October 1955, the VNA was transformed into the **Army of the Republic of Vietnam**.

VIETNAMIZATION. In 1968, the **United States** began to consider the possibility of withdrawing from the war and handing over the fighting to the **Republic of Vietnam**. The Republican presidential candidate in 1968, **Richard M. Nixon**, campaigned on a platform of ending the war, while the new **Military Assistance Command, Vietnam**, commander **Creighton W. Abrams**, who had replaced **William C. Westmoreland**, began consolidating his forces in areas that had been abandoned by the **People's Army of Vietnam** (PAVN) and the **National Liberation Front** (NLF) after the failed 1968 **Tết Offensive**. After Nixon's presidential election victory, he authorized a program to disengage from Southeast Asia. In what became known as the **Nixon Doctrine**, which he announced during a 25 July 1969 press conference in **Guam**, Nixon authorized the policy of Vietnamization. It called for increased training and equipping of the **Army of the Republic of Vietnam** (ARVN) and its **air force, navy**, and **marines** as the U.S. slowly withdrew. The previous month, Nixon had authorized the withdrawal of 25,000 soldiers and would remove an additional 150,000 by the end of the year.

Even though Vietnamization would end the American war, it was not without controversy. It called for U.S. and ARVN offensive operations in neutral **Cambodia** in 1970, known as the **Cambodian Incursion**, to eliminate that country's use as a base for the PAVN and NLF, and an operation in **Laos**, called **Lam Sơn 719**, designed to cut off the **Hồ Chí Minh Trail** near the city of **Tchepone**. Thus Nixon felt he had to escalate the war in order to withdraw from Vietnam. The **antiwar movement** saw the actions as contradictory and united in its opposition to Nixon. The slow nature of Vietnamization also affected U.S. morale as American personnel had difficulty fighting and dying for a country that the U.S. was abandoning. Few were willing to be the last American combat soldier to die in Vietnam.

VÕ CHÍ CÔNG (1912–). Founding member of the **National Liberation Front** (NLF). Võ Chí Công was born in **Quảng Nam** and began his anti-French activities at the age of 18. In 1935, he joined the Indochinese Communist Party and continued his nationalist activities during World War II. In 1942, he was arrested by the French. Võ Chí Công resurfaced in 1960 when he became a member of the Central Committee of the **Lao Động** Party and in 1961 was elected the vice chairman of the NLF.

In 1964, Võ Chí Công headed the Regional Committee for **Military Region 5** and remained in that position until the end of the Second Indochina War. In 1976, he was given a seat in the Politburo and served as a deputy prime minister until 1982. He also served as the minister of agriculture between 1977 and 1978. In 1987, he succeeded **Trường Chinh** as president of the Socialist Republic of Vietnam and remained in that position until replaced by **Lê Đức Anh** in 1992. He continued to serve as an adviser to the Central Committee of the Communist Party until 1997.

VÕ NGUYÊN GIÁP (1911–). People's Army of Vietnam (PAVN) general. Võ Nguyên Giáp was born in Quảng Bình province in the northern part of French Indochina. He spent his early years in protest against the French, though these nationalist activities did not become serious until his entry into the Quốc Học in the late 1920s. Võ Nguyên Giáp was expelled from the school because of his anti-French activities. He joined the Indochinese Communist Party in 1930 and was sentenced to jail for two years for his involvement in demonstrations. In 1933, he enrolled in **Hà Nội** University to study political economy and law and also assisted in founding the Democratic Front. After graduation in 1936, Võ Nguyên Giáp taught history and spent time in Paris, during which he established two newspapers. It was during this work that Võ Nguyên Giáp came into contact with a number of Vietnamese leaders within the Communist Party. In 1939, Võ Nguyên Giáp went to China to escape the French police who were arresting communists in **France**.

While in China, Võ Nguyên Giáp joined with **Phạm Văn Đồng** and **Hồ Chí Minh** who had organized the **Việt Minh**. He would return to Vietnam in 1944 and organize military forces to resist the Japanese at the end of World War II. His forces would later serve as the foundation for the PAVN. When the Việt Minh took over Hà Nội and **Sài Gòn** in August 1945, Võ Nguyên Giáp became the minister of the interior. He would lead the PAVN after the Việt Minh failed to reach a compromise with the French over the fate of French Indochina. He served as the main military tactician and minister of defense for the **Democratic Republic of Vietnam** during the **First Indochina War** and was the commanding officer of such military victories as the 1950 battles of Lạng Sơn and Cao Bằng and the 1954 Battle of **Điện Biên Phủ**. During the seven years of war, Võ Nguyên Giáp fought a people's war against the French that denied the French Union Forces the initiative by setting the pace and intensity of the attack. This allowed the Vietnamese to dictate **casualty** rates and draw the war out long enough to cause French war weariness that forced an end to the conflict in July 1954.

Võ Nguyên Giáp continued to lead the PAVN forces after the **Geneva Conference**, though his strategy of protracted warfare came under challenge by **Lê Duẩn** and **Lê Đức Thọ**, who called for more large-scale military operations. When the **United States** entered the war in the 1960s, Võ Nguyên Giáp was also confronted by **Nguyễn Chí Thanh** who wanted to move away from the concept of a people's war to overt aggression. Võ Nguyên Giáp was constantly under scrutiny by these opposing factions, while those who supported him had their loyalty called into question. Võ Nguyên Giáp always had the support of Hồ Chí Minh, and attempts to discredit him were never effective.

Võ Nguyên Giáp opposed the 1968 **Tết Offensive**, which had been conceived by Nguyễn Chí Thanh, though he was held responsible for its failures. The 1972 **Easter Offensive** was also imposed on Võ Nguyên Giáp and served as a desperate gamble to defeat the **Republic of Vietnam** Armed Forces and the remaining American troops during the 1972 U.S. presidential election. After the failed offensive, Võ Nguyên Giáp was slowly eased out of power and replaced by his deputy, General **Văn Tiến Dũng**, who helped to orchestrate the final offensive in 1975. Võ Nguyên Giáp, however, still held significant military influence at the end of the war.

After the war, in July 1976, Võ Nguyên Giáp became the deputy prime minister of the Socialist Republic of Vietnam and retained the minister of defense portfolio. He continued to be confronted by Lê Duẩn and his faction for being too closely aligned with the **Soviet Union**. Without the patronage of Hồ Chí Minh, his position and influence waned. In 1980, he was removed as minister of defense and was forced out of the Politburo in 1982, of which he had been a member since 1951. He retained the deputy prime minister position and was a member of the Central Committee until 1991. Võ Nguyên Giáp wrote several books on military and political strategy and has been the subject of a number of important historical works.

VÕ VĂN KIỆT (1922–2008). Socialist Republic of Vietnam (SRV) prime minister. Born Phan Văn Hòa, he chose the name Võ Văn Kiệt after joining the Indochinese Communist Party in 1939 but also went under the name Sáu Dân. Võ Văn Kiệt was born in southern Vietnam in what was known as Cochin China. He joined the nationalist movement, the Anti-imperialist Youth Movement, and was involved in anti-French activities through the **First Indochina War** as a member of the **Việt Minh**. He served as an alternate member of the Communist Party Central Committee from 1960 to 1972 and then as a full member. After the defeat of the **Republic of Vietnam** in 1975, Võ Văn Kiệt assumed the position of **Sài Gòn** party secretary, formally known as the chairman of the People's Committee of **Hồ Chí Minh City**. He earned a reputation in this position as one who was less inclined to impose the harsh rule of **Hà Nội** on the South or to incorporate southern industry into the new socialist state. He was one of the leaders of the 1986 policy of Đổi Mới that led to a lessening of the state's strict control over the economy.

In 1982, he became the vice premier and chairman of the State Planning Commission and the first deputy prime minister of the SRV in 1987. When Prime Minister **Phạm Hùng** died in 1988, Võ Văn Kiệt served as acting prime minister from March to June 1988. He also served as the SRV prime minster from 8 August 1991 to 25 September 1997. In December, he was awarded the Gold Star. In the last decade of his life, he was an outspoken advocate of greater reconciliation between the overseas Vietnamese population and the SRV.

VULCAN CANNON. The M61A1 (Vulcan Cannon) was a six-barreled, rotary-action Gatling gun that fired up to 6,000 rounds per minute, or 1,000 rounds per barrel per minute. It was used on the F-104 Starfighter, F-105 Thunderchief, F-4 Phantom, F-111 Aardvark, and A-7 Corsair. It was also mounted on the AC-119 and AC-130 gunships. The M61 usually fired armor-piercing or high-explosive incendiary rounds and was used primarily in air combat at close range, where air-to-air **missiles** had limited effectiveness.

VULTURE, OPERATION. During the Battle of **Điện Biên Phủ**, the French requested **United States** military assistance to stave off defeat. On 23 March 1954, French chief of staff General Paul Ely asked for American aircraft to help relieve the increasingly critical situation at the French fortress. Operation Vulture (Vautour) evolved from that request in which the U.S. would use B-29 bombers to destroy the Vietnamese in the hills surrounding the French at Điện Biên Phủ. Most within the Dwight D. Eisenhower administration believed that the air campaign would not decide the battle and were reluctant to expose American pilots to the intense **antiaircraft artillery** employed by the Vietnamese besieging the French position.

Another American concern with Operation Vulture was the need for fighter escorts for the B-29 bombers, as they were vulnerable to the threat of Chinese interceptors. Operation Vulture would have significantly increased the size of the American commitment to Vietnam and drawn the U.S. further into the conflict. President Eisenhower argued that the U.S. would not escalate its involvement in the battle without active allied support. When this did not happen, Operation Vulture ceased to be a viable alternative to saving the French Union Forces at Điện Biên Phủ. *See also* CHINA, PEOPLE'S REPUBLIC OF; FRANCE.

VUNG TÀU. Resort city and port of entry to the **Republic of Vietnam**, which served as a rest and relaxation center for Vietnamese, American, and allied troops during the war. The city is located approximately 124 kilometers (77 miles) to the south-southeast of **Sài Gòn** in the province of Phước Tuy, resting at the end of a 16-kilometer (10-mile) long and 4.8-kilometer (3-mile) wide peninsula that creates a natural harbor. Vung Tàu had a long naval history, formally settled by the Vietnamese after Emperor Ming Mang granted the lands to generals who defeated Malay pirates in the area in the early 19th century.

During France's occupation, the city was referred to as Cap Saint Jacques and was used to protect entry into the Sài Gòn River and served as a resort town for the French colonials. Between 1954 and 1955, Cap Saint Jacques was one of the largest ports to received **refugees** from the North during Operation **Passage to Freedom**. During the war, the **National Liberation Front**, which also used the beaches as a rest and relaxation center, constantly challenged the **United States** and allied troops for control of the area surrounding the city. In 1966, the 1st **Australian** Task Force established its base of operations in Phước Tuy province, conducting operations around Vung Tàu to secure the use of it. During the entire war, there was an unwritten truce in the city and on its beaches.

W

WALLEYE I. See MISSILES.

WALT, LEWIS WILLIAM (1913–1989). United States Marine general and assistant commandant of the U.S. **Marine Corps** (USMC). Walt was educated at Colorado State University, where he was the student class president, captain of the football team, and a cadet colonel of the Reserved Officers Training Corp. He received his commission as a second lieutenant in the Army Field Artillery Reserve. He resigned the commission to become a second lieutenant in the marines in 1936. After training, he was deployed to China in 1937 and **Guam** in 1939. As a captain at the beginning of World War II, Walt served as a company commander in the Officer Candidates' Class, USMC Schools, in Quantico, Virginia. He volunteered for the 1st Marine Raider Battalion and fought in the Pacific Theater with distinction. In November 1944, Lieutenant Colonel Walt became the chief of the Officer Candidates' School Tactics Section at the USMC Schools in Quantico, Virginia. He was promoted to colonel in November 1951 and fought in the Korean War, serving with the 5th Marines. He continued in service through the 1950s and 1960s in a variety of training positions, and in June 1965, as a major general, he took command of the III Marine Amphibious Force and 3rd Marine **Division** in Vietnam. He also served as the chief of naval forces, Vietnam, and senior adviser, I Corps, and I Corps coordinator in the **Republic of Vietnam** (RVN). He was promoted to lieutenant general on 7 March 1966.

Walt oversaw the Americanization of the war for the USMC and commanded such major operations as **Starlite**, **Blue Marlin**, **Piranha**, and **Double Eagle** I and II. He organized the Combined Action Company that sent marines into the villages to work with the Vietnamese people to defend themselves against the **People's Army of Vietnam** and the **National Liberation Front**. Walt believed in lasting **pacification** and in assisting the Vietnamese in the defense of their own country. He left Vietnam in June 1967 to become the deputy chief of staff of manpower and the director of personnel at the headquarters of the USMC. On 1 January 1968, he became the assistant commandant of the USMC. Walt was promoted to four stars on 2 June 1969 and retired on 1 February 1971. He published three books on military strategy.

WAR POWERS RESOLUTION. In July 1973, **Congress** formulated the House Joint Resolution 542, known as the War Powers Resolution. The resolution was Congress's attempt to curb the power of the presidency to introduce, for a prolonged period, American troops in a foreign country without congressional approval. The resolution reaffirmed the role of Congress in foreign policy decisions that had been perceived to have been lost with the **Gulf of Tŏn Kĭn Resolution** and the Americanization of the war. The resolution required the president to report to Congress within 48 hours if he committed **United States** troops to a foreign conflict or if he "substantially" increased the number of combat troops in a foreign country. These troops were required to be withdrawn unless Congress approved the president's action within 60 days. Both the House of Representatives and the Senate passed the resolution on 7 November 1973 by a two-thirds majority after President **Richard M. Nixon** had vetoed it. The resolution hampered the ability of President **Gerald R. Ford** to aid the South Vietnamese in 1974 and 1975.

WAR RESISTERS LEAGUE (WRL). The WRL had been active against all forms of war since its establishment in 1923. During the Vietnam War, the WRL, headed by David Dellinger, was one of the first organizations to call for an end to American involvement in Vietnam. It protested the **John F. Kennedy** administration's escalation of **advisers**, and on 16 May 1964, it sponsored a demonstration in New York City during which 12 men burned their draft cards. The WRL was involved in the planning of **antiwar** demonstrations throughout the war and organized **teach-ins** and draft resistance seminars.

WAR ZONE C. An area to the northwest of **Sài Gòn** near **Tây Ninh** province, bordering **Cambodia**, which was the center of intense **National Liberation Front** (NLF) activity during the war. War Zone C was home to the provisional government of the NLF and included the western part of the **Iron Triangle**, which was an area of significant combat operations during the war. *See also* WAR ZONE D.

WAR ZONE D. An area of heavy concentration of **National Liberation Front** soldiers to the north and northeast of **Sài Gòn**. The borders for War Zone D ran to the east of **Route** 13, south of Route 14, and north of Route 1. Its eastern border ran roughly parallel to Sông Đồng Nai. It was located in III **Corps Tactical Zone** to the east of **War Zone C** and the **Iron Triangle**.

WASHINGTON GREEN, OPERATION. Search-and-clear operation designed to improve **pacification** efforts in the An Lão Valley in **Bình Định** province. The operation, which involved the **173rd Airborne Brigade**, began on 15 April 1969 and ended on 1 January 1971. Through the course of this long operation, the **United States** lost 64 killed compared to an estimated 1,957 **People's Army of Vietnam** personnel killed. The valley had long been a stronghold for the **National Liberation Front** and a source of frustration for U.S., **Army of the Republic of Vietnam**, and allied troops who worked the area. While the operation did provide a framework for potential success, **Vietnamization** of the war and the failure of **Lam Sơn 719** after the operation's end refocused attention away from the province.

WATERPUMP, PROJECT. With increased hostilities in **Laos** after the 1962 **Geneva Accords**, the **United States** began to take a more active interest in supporting the Laotians against the communist insurgents, the **Pathet Lao**, who were assisted by the **Democratic Republic of Vietnam**. Project Waterpump focused on training and equipping the Royal Laotian Air Force (RLAF) under Operation **Barrel Roll**. The **U.S. Air Force** sent Detachment 6, 1st Air Combat Wing to Udorn, **Thailand**, in 1964 to train Laotian pilots and crew on the T-28 aircraft. While the U.S. trained the RLAF, Thai pilots replaced them in missions in Laos under Project **Firefly**. The U.S. experienced much frustration in working with the RLAF, from aircraft declared as not operational because its crew believed it to be possessed of evil spirits to issues of corruption. It was not until May 1968 that the RLAF conducted its first missions without a U.S. presence. By 1969 and 1970, the RLAF was active in Barrel Roll **sorties**, but contrary to the project's objective, it never became fully self-sufficient.

WESTMORELAND, WILLIAM CHILDS (1914–2005). Commander of **Military Assistance Command, Vietnam** (MACV), and **United States Army** chief of staff. Westmoreland graduated from West Point in 1936 with the highest rank possible, first captain, and was recognized as the most able cadet with his award of the Pershing Sword. He served in the artillery and participated in the American advance through North Africa, Italy, France, and Germany during World War II. He left the war as a colonel, having served in support of the 82nd Airborne Division and as chief of staff of the 9th Division. After the war, he served with the 82nd Airborne Division and commanded the 187th Regimental Combat Team during the Korean War. In 1953, he was promoted to brigadier general and rose to major general in 1956.

In 1958, Westmoreland commanded the 101st Airborne Division until he assumed the position of superintendent of West Point in 1960. In 1963, he commanded the XVIII Airborne Corps until asked to go to Vietnam in January 1964. He served under MACV commander General **Paul Harkins** as his deputy and took over Harkin's duties on 20 June 1964. Westmoreland held his position until 2 July 1968 when he was promoted to U.S. Army chief of staff, a position he retained until June 1972. Westmoreland oversaw the escalation of U.S. combat troops during the war and served as the focal point for critics of the war who argued that he was mismanaging the war through a policy of attrition that focused on body counts, **search-and-destroy** missions, and large unit actions. Westmoreland was also criticized for not being forthright with the **media**. He was charged with deceiving the American public by inflating the enemy killed-in-action and the **order of battle**.

Even with the constant criticism of his strategy and tactics during the war as well as opponents of the war who questioned his integrity, Westmoreland was able to keep the U.S. military functioning and active in its combat against the enemy. The U.S. military made important gains during the war that staved off defeat for the U.S. and the **Republic of Vietnam** (RVN). This often occurred in the midst of political and diplomatic intrigue that made it difficult to conduct operations in Southeast Asia that would cause the maximum damage or inconvenience to the **People's Army of Vietnam** (PAVN) and **National Liberation Front** (NLF) forces. Westmoreland was roundly criticized during the 1968 **Tết Offensive** for reporting, in 1967, that the PAVN and NLF forces fighting in the RVN had been pushed to the defensive and no longer held the initiative in the war. The 1968 Tết Offensive destroyed Westmoreland's credibility with many within the U.S., even though the PAVN and NLF forces were defeated in what was the most significant loss for the **Democratic Republic of Vietnam** in the war to that point.

The war continued to absorb most of Westmoreland's attention after he left Vietnam in July 1968. As U.S. Army chief of staff, Westmoreland had to deal with an army that was becoming unraveled by its Vietnam experience, the process of **Vietnamization**, and events such as the **Mỹ Lai** massacre, the **Cambodian Incursion**, and **Lam Sơn 719** that put added pressure on an already stressful job. In 1972, Westmoreland retired from the U.S. Army and wrote his memoir, *A Soldier's Report*. Vietnam, however, continued to haunt him. A 23 January 1982 CBS documentary titled *The Uncounted Enemy: A Vietnam Deception* claimed that Westmoreland had deceived the American people and government by purposely underestimating the number of PAVN and NLF soldiers in the Republic of Vietnam. This led to the 1984 *Westmoreland v. CBS* libel lawsuit, which kept the insidious nature of the war on the front pages of the newspapers and exposed Westmoreland to additional criticisms. The fact that Westmoreland lost the libel case did not help to revive his reputation. Westmoreland remained guarded in his public appearances related to the war, though he continued to defend himself and worked with others to explain his role in the war.

WEYAND, FREDERICK CARLTON (1916–2010). United States Army general and commander of the **Military Assistance Command, Vietnam**. Weyand was commissioned as a second lieutenant in 1938 and rose through the ranks in the year preceding U.S. involvement in World War II. When the U.S. entered the war, he was serving with the 6th Artillery until he became adjutant of the Harbor Defense Command, San Francisco, reaching the rank of major. In 1942, he worked in the Office of the Chief of Intelligence, War Department General Staff, until he was assigned as the assistant chief of staff for Intelligence, China-Burma-India Theater, in 1944. After the war, he served in a number of offices, such as the Military Intelligence Service, chief of staff for Intelligence; U.S. Army Forces, Middle Pacific; and battalion commander in the 7th Infantry Division. When the Korean War began, he became the assistant chief of staff (G3) for the 3rd Infantry Division until he took a position on the faculty of the Infantry School in 1952. Weyand continued to advance in the U.S. Armed Forces through the 1950s and into the 1960s. He entered the Vietnam War as a temporary major general in command of the 25th Infantry Division in 1966. In September 1966, he served as the deputy of **II Field Force, Vietnam**, until March 1967, then as its commander from July 1967 until August 1968. II Field Force had responsibility for III **Corps Tactical Zone** and the provinces surrounding **Sài Gòn**.

Weyand was a proponent of **pacification** and disagreed with the attrition strategy employed by General **William C. Westmoreland** to bring the enemy to its knees. Weyand also correctly assessed the **People's Army of Vietnam** and **National Liberation Front** strategy for the 1968 **Tết Offensive**. His actions before the offensive reduced the severity of it after the initial surprise was lost. After II Field Force, Weyand became the chief of the Office of Reserve Components. He was also promoted to permanent brigadier and major general and temporary lieutenant general. In 1969, he served as the military adviser at the Paris Peace Talks but returned to Vietnam to become the deputy commander of the Military Assistance Command, Vietnam, in April 1970. He succeeded **Creighton W. Abrams** as commander of the Military Assistance Command, Vietnam, in April 1972 until it was dissolved in March 1973. Some of his postwar positions included commander-in-chief of the U.S. Army, Pacific; vice chief of staff of the U.S. Army; and chief of staff of the U.S. Army, again succeeding Abrams, all of which occurred in the 1973–1976 period during which the U.S. Army was reeling from its Vietnam experience and was undergoing severe criticism from both civilian and military personnel. He retired from the U.S. Army in October 1976.

WHEELER, EARLE GILMORE (1908–1970). United States Army general, army chief of staff and chairman of the **Joint Chiefs of Staff**. Wheeler graduated from West Point in 1932 and, after spending some time at Fort Benning, went to Tientsin, China, in 1936 with the 15th Infantry Regiment. He returned to the U.S. with the unit in 1938 and was involved in the training of infantry during most of World War II. In 1944, he went to Europe as chief of staff for the 63rd Infantry Division. He served in a variety of assignments after the war, including instructor at Fort Sill and member of the U.S. Constabulary in Germany, the North Atlantic Treaty Organization staff, and the General Staff at the Pentagon. In 1958, he assumed command of the 2nd Armored Division and the III Corps in 1959.

In 1960, Wheeler was promoted to director of the Joint Staff until 1962, when he briefly served as deputy commander of U.S. forces in Europe. By the end of the year, he was chief of staff of the U.S. Army. He remained in this position until July 1964 when he took over as chairman of the Joint Chiefs of Staff. He served as chairman until 2 July 1970. At this point, he retired from active service. Wheeler often disagreed with the war decisions of President **Lyndon B. Johnson** and Secretary of Defense **Robert McNamara**. He had advocated the call-up of military reserves to contend with the growing escalation of the war and opposed the self-imposed restriction not to violate **Cambodia**'s neutrality when it became clear that the **National Liberation Front** (NLF) was using the border area to stage attacks into the **Republic of Vietnam**. Wheeler backed General **William C. Westmoreland**'s continued calls for more troops and, after the 1968 **Tết Offensive**, pushed for an additional 206,000 men to take advantage of the **People's Army of Vietnam** and NLF military failure.

When **Richard M. Nixon** entered the White House, Wheeler voiced his opposition to **Vietnamization** but followed through on his commander-in-chief's orders. He strongly supported the 1970 Cambodia Incursion. Wheeler suffered a heart attack in 1968 that limited his activity, but he remained in office until his retirement. He has been roundly criticized by historians and others for not taking a more active stance in winning the war in Southeast Asia and for not forcefully opposing the restrictions imposed by Johnson and McNamara. But he was also constrained in his opposition by his sense of duty to the secretary and president, and he worked within these constraints to guide the Joint Chiefs of Staff and influence Vietnam policy.

WHITE PHOSPHORUS. White phosphorus (Willy Pete) was a chemical agent employed as a flare, smoke marker, or incendiary. It was first used in combat during World War I. In Vietnam, it was utilized in a variety of ways. During **search-and-rescue** missions, white phosphorus created a smoke wall to separate the individual being rescued from his would-be capturers. It could also be applied by infantry to create a smokescreen or fired from a rocket to mark a target for air strikes. Because white phosphorus burned very hot, it could also be used as an incendiary.

WHITE STAR, PROJECT. Name given to the project that oversaw the use of American **advisers** in **Laos**. The project was originally conceived in 1959 under Project **Hotfoot** but was renamed in 1961 as part of the larger recognition by the **United States** of its advising role in Laos. Under White Star, American personnel wore U.S. uniforms as they helped to train the Royal Laotian Army and the irregular forces made up of **Hmong** and **Lao Theung** that were funded, in part, by the **Central Intelligence Agency**. Until White Star, U.S. personnel did not wear uniforms because an official American presence in Laos would constitute a violation of the 1954 **Geneva Agreements**. The operation ended as a result of the 23 July 1962 **Geneva Accords** on Laos, and the troops were withdrawn by October 1962. American involvement continued in Laos, though secrecy once again became the order of the day as the U.S. worked to avoid being caught violating the agreements.

WILD WEASEL, PROJECT. An air mission designed to identify and destroy North Vietnamese air defense systems such as radar and surface-to-air **missiles** (SAM). The predecessor of the Wild Weasel was a project called **Iron Hand** begun in August 1965. The first Wild Weasel aircraft was the F-100. A volunteer crew of two flew the aircraft, usually in groups of four, over known North Vietnamese SAM sites. When the SAMs were launched at one of the aircraft, the others would target the site to destroy the radar guidance system, remaining missiles, personnel, and any other air defense equipment nearby. The F-105 replaced the F-100 as the predominant Wild Weasel aircraft in 1966. The F-105 possessed superior electronic equipment and weapons that allowed it to perform the mission more efficiently and with a greater chance of survival. As the F-105 was rotated out of service, the F-4 became the aircraft of choice for Wild Weasel missions. Rather than avoiding the SAM site and all that it protected from Operation **Rolling Thunder sorties**, the Wild Weasel aircraft provided the **United States** with an opportunity to strike at the primary weapon in the North Vietnamese air defense system and allowed the U.S. to retain control over the skies of Vietnam.

WILLIAMS, SAMUEL TANKERSLEY (1897–1984). Williams was commissioned as a second lieutenant in August 1917 and fought with the 359th Infantry Regiment in France during World War I. Between the World Wars, he rose in rank. In February 1943, as a brigadier general, he commanded the

378th Infantry Regiment and served as the assistant division commander of the 90th Division. On 6 June 1944, D-Day, he landed on Utah Beach. In September 1944 until the end of the war, he served as the assistant chief of staff (G3) of the XXII Corps, European Theater of Operations. During the Korean War, Williams commanded the 25th Division from 1952 to August 1953.

Williams arrived in Vietnam as a lieutenant general on 24 October 1955 when he assumed command from General **John W. O'Daniel** of the **Military Assistance Advisory Group** (MAAG), Indochina. The command was renamed MAAG, Vietnam, the next week. He remained the commander until August 1960. Williams was responsible for helping to organize the **Army of the Republic of Vietnam** (ARVN) into a large conventional force that could resist an overt invasion from the North. Williams also favored a greater role for the **Civil Guard** to supplement ARVN operations in the field. He had good relations with **Ngô Đình Diệm**, the president of the **Republic of Vietnam**, but he was often at odds with Ambassador **Elbridge Durbrow**.

WINTER SOLDIER INVESTIGATION. Organized by the **Vietnam Veterans Against the War** (VVAW), the Winter Soldier Investigation occurred between 31 January 1971 and 2 February 1971 in Detroit, Michigan. The event featured testimony from 109 veterans and 16 civilians. The veterans and civilians told of war atrocities that they had been involved in, had witnessed, or had heard of in Vietnam. The VVAW wanted the Winter Soldier Investigation to reenergize the **antiwar movement** that had slowed after the May 1970 **Cambodian Incursion** and the events at **Kent State University** and **Jackson State University**. It did result in Senator **J. William Fulbright** convening Senate hearings in April and May 1971, and like the **Mỹ Lai** court martial, it kept the objectives of the antiwar movement fresh in the minds of American citizens. *See also* CONGRESS, UNITED STATES.

WOMEN, UNITED STATES. American women who served in Vietnam did so in a variety of ways from as early as 1964 until the last Americans left the country. Women served in the Women in the Air Force (WAF), Women Accepted for Voluntary Emergency Service (WAVES), and the Women's Army Corps (WAC). These women primarily worked in the field of administration, replacing their male counterparts. The exception to this rule was nurses, most of whom served in the U.S. Army.

The WAC was founded on 16 May 1942, as the **United States** mobilized after the start of World War II. Its purpose was to utilize the skills and knowledge of women in the U.S. to add to the military effort against the Axis powers. Approximately 700 WACs, both officers and enlisted, served in Vietnam between November 1964 and March 1973, with the greatest number,

20 officers and 139 enlisted women, in January 1970. They were the first women's military organization to serve in Vietnam. The WACs had a number of responsibilities, including stenography, personnel and administrative support, public information, **intelligence**, logistics, and military justice. The majority of WACs served in **Sài Gòn**, with others in **Long Bình**, **Qui Nhơn**, and **Cam Ranh Bay**. WACs were also known for humanitarian work with the Vietnamese on their own time.

The primary WAC mission was to aid in the organization of the Women's Armed Forces Corps for the **Republic of Vietnam**. The first WAC **advisers**, Major Kathleen I. Wilkes and Sergeant Betty L. Adams, arrived in Sài Gòn on 15 January 1965. No WACs were killed or received serious injury during the war, though there were some minor injuries during the 1968 **Tết Offensive**. One WAC received the Purple Heart and was the first WAC to receive this medal since World War II. Vietnam would be the last war during which women served in a separate organization from men in the U.S. Army.

The WAVES were formed as part of the **United States Navy** in August 1942 during World War II. The nine WAVES who served in Vietnam, all of whom were officers, performed mostly clerical work. They were assigned to either the **Military Assistance Command, Vietnam**, in Sài Gòn or at Cam Ranh Bay with the Naval Support Activity unit. In 1972–1973, Commander Elizabeth Barrett served as the highest-ranking woman line officer for 450 enlisted men in the naval advisory group in Sài Gòn and was the only woman to command in a combat zone.

Organized in 1948, WAF members worked within the **Air Force** in a variety of noncombat positions. Between 1967 and 1973, there were more than 500 WAF personnel in Southeast Asia assigned to either the **7th Air Force** in Vietnam or the 13th Air Force in Thailand. They served under the command of Jeanne M. Holm, who later became the first female United States Air Force one-star general and retired as a two-star general, the first in any branch of the armed forces. Noncommissioned WAFs generally were involved in clerical jobs, while officers worked in communications, logistics, and information services.

Of the approximately 7,500 nurses who served in the armed forces in Vietnam, 6,250 were in the army. The nurses, all of whom were commissioned officers, volunteered to serve one-year tours. These women joined the army for many of the same reasons as men, though many were recruited from student nursing programs. Most nurses had very little experience in their profession and were not properly prepared for the nature of the war in Vietnam. In addition to the physical and mental challenges associated with the war effort, many nurses also underwent severe emotional strain, as they were expected to perform all of their required duties as well as substituting for the emotional needs of the men who were far away from their mothers, wives, sisters, and girlfriends. After the war, women shared in the alienation of the Vietnam veteran but were denied proper treatment in Veteran Administration hospitals and membership in veteran's organizations. It was not until 11 November 1993, when Glenna Goodacre's bronze statue was unveiled at the Vietnam Memorial in Washington, D.C., that the nation began to recognize the role of women during the war.

WOMEN, VIETNAMESE. The **Democratic Republic of Vietnam** (DRV) fought a total war, utilizing all of its citizens and resources toward the defeat of the **United States** and the **Republic of Vietnam** and a complete social and economic transformation of southern society based on the northern model. To this end, North Vietnamese women played a significant role in the war effort. Women were charged with caring for their families, tending to families that had lost parents in the war, and replacing men in agriculture and industry. While these pursuits paralleled the efforts of the South Vietnamese, the **Hà Nội** government also encouraged the active involvement of women in the military. Women soldiers helped to maintain the DRV's sophisticated air defense system and worked to repair damage and maintain war-related systems such as the **Hồ Chí Minh Trail**, and they also filled the traditional role of nurse and administrator. North Vietnamese women benefited from the communist system that provided for relative equality in responsibility and benefit. In the South, women served in the **Việt Minh** and **National Liberation Front** units, fighting alongside men as well as serving in a variety of other roles such as spy, informant, propagandist, and organizer of southern peasants.

South Vietnamese women who supported the **Sài Gòn** government engaged in similar activities, save active combat duty. There were several women's organizations in the South that supported the republic, such as the **Women's Solidarity Movement**, organized by **Madame Ngô Đình Nhu** to garner support for **Ngô Đình Diệm**'s role. These women formed a paramilitary organization, though their influence rarely moved beyond Sài Gòn. They were also involved in a major humanitarian effort to help those who had suffered during the war. Vietnamese women had always played an active role in the defense of their country, starting with the fabled Trưng sisters (Hai Bà Trưng) who led the 1st-century rebellion against the Han Dynasty. While both the North and the South encouraged similar behavior, the DRV was more effective in mobilizing women toward their war objectives.

WOMEN'S SOLIDARITY MOVEMENT. The Women's Solidarity Movement was the **Republic of Vietnam**'s (RVN) response to the **People's Army of Vietnam** and **National Liberation Front** (NLF) use of **women** in their war effort. The organization, formed by **Madame Ngô Đình Nhu**, played a minimal role in the war, though it was very active in charity for those who were affected by the war. Members of the Women's Solidarity Movement were involved in **intelligence** work, official demonstrations that supported the **Sài Gòn** government policy, and work toward mobilizing the population against the NLF. The Women's Solidarity Movement helped to organize the Women's Paramilitary Training Center (Trung Tâm Huấn Luyện Bạn Quân Sự Phụ Nữ), which was designed to become a 360,000-member women's military corps that would perform static duty in the villages and civil action work for the government. The first class of 1,500 women between the ages of 18 and 35 began their training on 29 November 1961. The organization failed to become the force that Madame Nhu or **Ngô Đình Diệm** expected after his assassination on 2 November 1963 and her exile from the RVN.

WOUNDED WARRIOR, OPERATION. Operation Wounded Warrior involved the **United States** 6481st Medical Air Evacuation Group and the 315th Air Division in the transportation of 502 wounded French soldiers from French Indochina to **France** between May 1953 and July 1954. The airmen of the 315th Air Division also conducted maintenance on C-119 transports involved in support of the French in the **First Indochina War** and trained French personnel on how to operate the aircraft.

XÁ LỢI PAGODA RAID. Buddhist unrest, which had begun as a result of a clash between Buddhist protestors and **Huế** police on 8 May 1963, served as a backdrop to the 21 August 1963 raids against pagodas around the **Republic of Vietnam**, including **Sài Gòn**'s Xá Lợi Pagoda, by which the series of raids was commonly known. **Ngô Đình Nhu** ordered the raids as a counter coup d'état against forces he believed were conspiring to use the **Buddhist Crisis** to overthrow his brother, **Ngô Đình Diệm**. In the early morning of 21 August, police and **Special Forces** units dressed in **Army of the Republic of Vietnam** uniforms to disguise their true identity raided the pagodas and arrested hundreds of protestors in and around the targeted pagodas. While the Sài Gòn government called the incident an internal issue, it became international when two Buddhist monks received entry into the **United States** embassy to avoid arrest. Forces involved in the Xá Lợi raid surrounded the compound, threatening the diplomatic status of the American personnel inside. The issue was resolved peacefully but severely damaged U.S.-Vietnamese relations, as did the overwhelming international condemnation of the raids. After the raids, Ngô Đình Diệm declared martial law, with orders to shoot violators of the curfew. The Xá Lợi Pagoda raids convinced many within the U.S. that Ngô Đình Diệm had served his purpose for the U.S. and that it was time to replace him, an event that occurred on 1 November 1963.

XUÂN LỘC, BATTLE OF. One of the last major battles of the Vietnam War. By 9 April 1975, **People's Army of Vietnam** (PAVN) forces had moved without too much serious opposition across the **Demilitarized Zone** and toward **Sài Gòn**. Near Xuân Lộc, north of Sài Gòn in Long Khánh province, the 18th **Army of the Republic of Vietnam** (ARVN) Division stood its ground and held off three PAVN divisions, the 341st, 6th, and 7th, for 18 days, prompting many in the **Republic of Vietnam** to label the battle the miracle of Xuân Lộc. The ARVN troops were led by Major General **Lê Minh Đảo**. While the 18th ARVN Division, and the reinforcements brought north to help the beleaguered division, was eventually forced to retire, the battle contradicted **media** reports which claimed that ARVN soldiers were refusing to defend their country and people against the North. The South Vietnamese also showed an adept ability at aerial resupply and reinforcement as well as coordinated air-to-ground support. Throughout the battle, the ARVN forces were outnumbered and outgunned, but they continued to fight for every inch of ground and inflicted significant **casualties** on the PAVN forces. After the battle was over, it took less than two weeks for Sài Gòn to fall, signaling the end of the war.

XUÂN THUỶ (1912–1985). Democratic Republic of Vietnam (DRV) foreign minister and chief negotiator during the Paris Peace Talks. Born Nguyễn Trọng Nhâm, Xuân Thuỷ was educated in **Hà Nội** under the French colonial system and joined **Hồ Chí Minh**'s Revolutionary Youth League in 1926. His nationalist tendencies caused him trouble with the French, including jail time spent on five separate occasions through World War II. After the war, he edited the newspaper *Cứu Quốc*, which represented the **Việt Minh**, and served in the National Assembly for the DRV. He served as a diplomat for the new country, representing its interests at the 1962 **Geneva Conference** on **Laos** and as foreign minister from 1963 to 1965.

In 1968, Xuân Thuỷ returned to public life as the chief of the North Vietnamese Delegation to the Paris Peace Talks and remained in that position until the January 1973 **Paris Peace Accords**. He also served as the chief of the Central Party Committee's External Relations Commission and led the Central Commission for Mass Mobilization and Front. After the war, he served as a vice president of the Council of State and was vice chairman of the Socialist Republic of Vietnam's (SRV) National Assembly. In 2005, the SRV conferred upon him posthumously the Gold Star Order, the highest award in the country.

YANKEE STATION. Yankee Station was an area in the Gulf of Tŏn Kĭn in which aircraft carriers from Task Force 77 launched air strikes against the **Democratic Republic of Vietnam** (DRV) and **Laos**. Starting in April 1964, the **United States Navy** stationed at least one aircraft carrier at Yankee Station during Operation **Rolling Thunder** and the two **Linebacker** operations, though there were usually three aircraft carriers present. Because the U.S. had complete naval superiority against the North Vietnamese, U.S. ships operating from Yankee Station could perform their missions without fear of reprisal. This allowed the U.S. to provide quick air support when needed in the **Republic of Vietnam** and to adopt a flexible approach to its **bombing** campaigns against the DRV throughout the war. The last aircraft carrier left Yankee Station on 15 August 1973. *See also* YANKEE TEAM.

YANKEE TEAM. On 19 May 1964, the **United States** began low- and medium-level **reconnaissance** flights over the southern portion of **Laos** conducted by RF-101s stationed at **Tân Sơn Nhứt**. The **sorties** were designed to aid the Royal Laotian Armed Forces in their struggle against the **Pathet Lao, People's Army of Vietnam**, and **National Liberation Front** forces operating in the area that would become known as the **Hồ Chí Minh Trail**. On 21 May, **Navy** RF-8As and RA-3Bs launched from **Yankee Station** conducted similar sorties in the northern section of Laos. The Yankee Team flights were under the command authority of the 2nd Air Division. The objectives of the campaign were to provide **intelligence** for the Laotians on the enemies' disposition, offer encouragement to the beleaguered Laotian forces, and demonstrate American determination in the fight against communism in the region. After two Yankee Team aircraft were lost to **antiaircraft artillery** in November 1964, the **Joint Chiefs of Staff** recommended changing the role of Yankee Team. In December, Yankee Team aircraft conducted air strikes against infiltration points and Pathet Lao and Vietnamese facilities. This new mission evolved into Operation **Barrel Roll**.

Y-BIH ALEO (1901–). Member of the **Rhadé** tribe, leader in the **Bajaraka Movement**, and member of the **National Liberation Front** (NLF). Y-Bih Aleo served as an interpreter for the French before becoming disillusioned with French colonial rule. He joined the **Việt Minh** in 1945, though his objective was the independence of the **Montagnard** people in conjunction with a free Vietnam. He was a leading member of the Bajaraka Movement in 1958. In 1960, in parallel with the formation of the NLF, the southern insurgency created the Front for the Liberation of the Highlands (Mặt Trận Giải Phóng Tây Nguyên), for which Y-Bih Aleo served as the chairman. Y-Bih Aleo was lured into the organization by **Hồ Chí Minh**'s promise of liberation for the Montagnard people after the war.

The group organized the Montagnard people to resist the **Sài Gòn** government and defy increased American attempts to organize the people against the communists. Y-Bih Aleo continued to work with the NLF as the chairman of the minorities committee in 1962 and as a member of the Advisory Council of the **Provisional Revolutionary Government of the Republic of Vietnam** in 1969. With the fall of Sài Gòn, Y-Bih Aleo joined the Presidium of the Vietnam Fatherland Front (Mặt Trận Tổ Quốc Việt Nam).

YOUNG TURKS. A group of **Republic of Vietnam** (RVN) officers who opposed the rule of triumvirate generals **Trần Thiện Khiêm**, **Dương Văn Minh**, and **Nguyễn Khánh** who had taken over the **Sài Gòn** government after the coup d'état against **Ngô Đình Diệm** in November 1963. The group organized in 1964, believing that there needed to be a change of government. Its spokesperson, though not necessarily its leader, was Air Marshall **Nguyễn Cao Kỳ**. The group included Airborne Brigade commander Colonel **Dư Quốc Đống**, Marine Brigade commander General **Lê Nguyên Khang**, 7th **Army of the Republic of Vietnam** (ARVN) commander Colonel Nguyễn Bảo Trị, I Corps commander General Tôn Thất Xứng, 1st ARVN commander General **Nguyễn Chánh Thi**, 2nd Infantry commander Nguyễn Thanh Sằng, 9th ARVN commander General Vĩnh Lộc, and 21 ARVN commander General Đặng Văn Quang. The group controlled much of the ARVN operational command in the summer of 1964 and eventually forced Nguyễn Khánh into exile in February 1965. It then splintered into two major factions: those who followed Nguyễn Cao Kỳ and others who favored **Nguyễn Văn Thiệu**. Even if the Young Turks had the best interests of the RVN in mind, their actions allowed for continued instability at a critical time during the war and provided ideal conditions for the insurgency to survive and grow.

Z

ZUMWALT, ELMO RUSSELL, JR. (1920–2000). Admiral in the **United States Navy**; commander of Naval Forces, Vietnam; and chief of naval operations (CNO). Zumwalt graduated with distinction from the U.S. Naval Academy in 1942, the National War College in 1952, and the Naval War College in 1953. During World War II, he distinguished himself at the Battle of Leyte Gulf and through his capture of the Japanese gunboat *Ataka* on the Yangtze River. He continued to advance within the navy due to his actions and skills. He served as a navigator on the battleship U.S.S. *Wisconsin* during the Korean War and commanded the U.S.S. *Dewey* (DLG-14), a guided-missile frigate, from 1959 to 1961. In 1964, he rose to the rank of rear admiral. Before he entered the war, Zumwalt commanded Cruiser-Destroyer Flotilla 7 from July 1965 to July 1966. He then served as the director of the CNO Systems Analysis Group from August 1966 to August 1968.

In September, Zumwalt assumed command of the U.S. Naval Forces, Vietnam, and became chief of the Naval Advisory Group within the **Military Assistance Command, Vietnam**, from 1 October 1968 to 15 May 1970. In Vietnam, Zumwalt created the Southeast Asia Lake Ocean River Delta Strategy (**SEALORDS**), which sought to interdict the **People's Army of Vietnam** (PAVN) and **National Liberation Front** (NLF) supply routes by sea, to harass the PAVN and NLF in their traditional safe havens, and to apply **pacification** to the **Mê Kông Delta**. President **Richard M. Nixon** nominated Zumwalt as the chief of naval operations on 14 April 1970, a position he obtained with the rank of admiral on 1 July 1970. He remained in that position until his retirement on 1 July 1974. Zumwalt was the youngest rear admiral in U.S. Navy history and the youngest four-star admiral to serve as the CNO. While CNO, Zumwalt oversaw the transformation of a U.S. Navy that was still reeling from the American experience in Vietnam and from increased racial tension that reflected the times. Through a series of orders, known as Z-grams, Zumwalt modernized the U.S. Navy.

In the postwar period, Zumwalt ran unsuccessfully as the Democratic candidate for a Virginia U.S. Senate seat. He continued to be active in veteran's affairs and worked to secure medical benefits for personnel exposed to **Agent**

Orange during the war. Zumwalt was the recipient of numerous medals for valor and service, including the highest U.S. civilian award, the Medal of Freedom, and the Distinguished Service Medal with two Gold Stars. Zumwalt published two books. In 1976, *On Watch: A Memoir* was published. He also wrote another book in 1986, *My Father, My Son*, which told, in part, the story of his son's battle with cancer, which Zumwalt believed was due to his exposure to Agent Orange.

Bibliography

CONTENTS

INTRODUCTION

The Vietnam War has attracted, and continues to attract, historical interest as scholars and participants analyze its origins, events, personalities, escalation, and consequences. There have been thousands of books written about the war that explore every aspect of it. It is not possible to examine all of the significant works written on the war in such a short space, especially given the sophistication in the ever-evolving historiography. Like the American Civil War and World War II, the Vietnam War has captured the attention and imagination of the professional and amateur historian, while those in the public arena with an interest in history have gravitated toward the stories and histories of this time period. The Vietnam War continues to this day to set the tone of our historical understanding and has even been linked to the foundation for understanding events in the post–September 11, 2001, world. This essay simply offers an introduction to the complexities and subtleties that the war has inspired in the written word.

There are a number of reference works that provide basic knowledge about the war. These books generally avoid providing interpretation and instead provide encyclopedic information similar to this edition of *The Historical Dictionary of the Vietnam War*, which aids readers when they are reading more specific and specialized accounts of the war. The previous edition of this historical dictionary, written by Edwin Moïse, is a good starting point and includes a number of entries not in this edition. Spencer Tucker, *Encyclopedia of the Vietnam War* (2000), is as complete an encyclopedia as is available and even attempts to use Vietnamese diacritical marks, though not always correctly. A basic overview of the war is available with Ronald B. Frankum Jr. and Stephen F. Maxner, *The Vietnam War for Dummies* (2003), and David L. Anderson, *The Vietnam War* (2005). The most valuable reference work on U.S. military units is Shelby L. Stanton, *Vietnam Order of Battle* (1981).

While there is no single work that satisfies the professional or amateur historian when it comes to explaining the Vietnam War, there have been several legitimate attempts to do so. For a good, general overview, all of the following are helpful: A. J. Langguth, *Our Vietnam: The War, 1954–1975*

(2000); Arthur J. Dommen, *The Indochinese Experience of the French and the Americans: Nationalism and Communism in Cambodia, Laos, and Vietnam* (2001); Mitchell K. Hall, *The Vietnam War* (2007); James M. Carter, *Inventing Vietnam: The United States and State Building, 1954–1968* (2008); Mark Atwood Lawrence, *The Vietnam War: A Concise International History* (2008); Mark Philip Bradley, *Vietnam at War* (2009); Gary R. Hess, *Vietnam: Explaining America's Lost War* (2009); and John Prados, *Vietnam: The History of an Unwinnable War, 1945–1975* (2009). Each of these works offers a broad overview of the major events, and while the interpretations may vary, the basic history of the war is covered.

There are several significant wartime studies that offer insight into the complexities of the war. Among the best are Jeffrey Race, *War Comes to Long An* (1972), and Arthur Schlesinger, *Bitter Heritage: Vietnam and American Democracy, 1941–1966* (1967). Race concludes that the military defeat of the United States and its Sài Gòn allies resulted from a misguided policy that ignored the realities in Vietnam and underestimated the enemy's ability to react to U.S. escalation. Schlesinger, writing from a liberal progressive perspective, argues that the U.S. commitment to Vietnam was self-created, and thus any attempt to withdraw without a successful conclusion would have destroyed the prestige the U.S. enjoyed at the end of World War II as the protector of democracy. In outlining this quagmire thesis, Schlesinger criticizes the American position in Vietnam, but he excuses the presidents because they relied on faulty data.

Other significant works from wartime include Gerald C. Hickey, *Village in Vietnam* (1964); Ellen Hammer, *The Struggle for Indochina* (1966); J. William Fulbright, *The Arrogance of Power* (1966); Richard H. Rovere, *Waist Deep in the Big Muddy: Personal Reflections on 1968* (1968); Robert W. Tucker, *Nation or Empire? The Debate over American Foreign Policy* (1968); Henry F. Graff, *The Tuesday Cabinet: Deliberation and Decision on Peace and War under Lyndon B. Johnson* (1970); and David Halberstam, *The Best and the Brightest* (1972). There were few important books in the immediate postwar period that offered exceptional or varied analysis of the war. The American population was still recovering from the Vietnam experience while historians had yet to tap into the extensive documents that would become available later. Exceptions to this are Guenter Lewy, *America in Vietnam* (1978); George C. Herring Jr., *America's Longest War: The United States and Vietnam, 1950–1975* (1979); and Leslie H. Gelb and Richard K. Betts, *The Irony of Vietnam: The System Worked* (1979).

Unlike Race who concludes that the U.S. effort in Vietnam was negative, Lewy argues the opposite. Lewy's work is considered one of the first of the revisionists in the post-Vietnam period that contemplates two of the important questions about the war: its morality, and whether it could have been won. The intertwining answers to these questions produce a rather compelling defense of U.S. action during the war as well as explain why the United States did not win the contest. Herring offers the first real synthesis of early Vietnam War historiography. While his work was still based in part on the Pentagon Papers and the limited number of documents available, he constructs a provocative interpretation of how U.S. foreign policy sank into the Vietnamese quagmire. He concludes that U.S. involvement in Southeast Asia was a result of the failed policy of containment.

Gelb and Betts offer an alternative to the quagmire thesis, which they acknowledge, by arguing that the American presidents knowingly followed a course that achieved stalemate. Gelb and Betts suggest that the war in Vietnam was a "secret hot potato" for the United States. Each president believed he could handle the potato and toss it to the next without getting burned or burning his successor. For Gelb and Betts, the system—that is, the domestic decision-making process—worked in Vietnam, and as a result the early presidents need to acknowledge their share of the blame for America's Vietnam experience.

In the 1980s, a series of revisionist works appeared that were authored by military personnel who had served in the war. These books also grappled with the question of whether the war could have been won and who shared the most responsibility for its defeat. Several important works appeared at this time including Harry Summers, *On Strategy: The Vietnam War in Context* (1982), and Bruce Palmer Jr., *The 25-Year War: America's Military Role in Vietnam* (1984). Summers attempts to understand the complexities of a war in which the United States succeeded in everything it set out to do, won almost all engagements with the enemy, and yet still lost the war. Summers, like many of the military officers who wrote at the time, argued that failures such as not mobilizing the American public for the war, avoiding a declaration of war, and the inability of the military, especially the Joint Chiefs of Staff, to communicate to the civilian leaders led to the U.S. defeat.

The air war also received special attention during this time as military officials and historians asked the question of how the Democratic Republic of Vietnam (DRV) was able to overcome the series of air campaigns that should have destroyed the country. One theory was that the failure of the air war in the DRV was not a military one; rather, it was a result of an overzealous civilian and political sector of the U.S. government that hampered the ability of those involved in the air war to exert maximum force to achieve their results. Admiral U.S.G. Sharp's *Strategy for Defeat: Vietnam in Retrospect* (1978) argues that the Johnson administration, rather than letting the Air Force destroy the industrial, economic, and political infrastructure of the DRV, used Operation Rolling Thunder to persuade the North Vietnamese to cease their support for the war by taking the war directly to the North. American politicians, and Johnson specifically, believed that the DRV would falter with the prospects of a prolonged air war. This thesis has found numerous supporters including James Clay Thompson, *Rolling Thunder: Understanding Policy and Program Failure* (1980); Zalin Grant, *Over the Beach: The Air War in Vietnam* (1986); and John Schlight, *The War in South Vietnam: The Years of the Offensive, 1965–1968* (1988).

Mark Clodfelter, *The Limits of Air Power: The American Bombing of North Vietnam* (1989), however, reassesses this claim and concludes that the Air Force strategy of undertaking a strategic bombing campaign similar to the one conducted during World War II did not suit the wartime realities of Vietnam. Even if the civilian leaders had restrained the air campaigns, the military strategy was far from sound. Clodfelter's work reinforces the earlier thesis developed by J. William Gibson, *The Perfect War: Technowar in Vietnam* (1986), while Earl H. Tilford Jr., *Crosswinds: The Air Force's Setup in Vietnam* (1991), offers a similar but much more critical assessment of the Air Force.

Other revisionism occurred in the 1980s, as well, some of which was politically charged, while other works tended to incorporate new perspectives. Two good examples are Gabriel Kolko, *Anatomy of a War: Vietnam, the United States, and the Modern Historical Experience* (1985), and Timothy Lomperis, *The War Everyone Lost—and Won: America's Intervention in Viet Nam's Twin Struggles* (1984). Like Herring, Kolko argues that U.S. intervention in Vietnam was a result of a failed containment policy. However, Kolko maintains that this policy was designed to preserve economic hegemony over the world community. Unlike the military revisionists of the time, he suggests that the United States did not lose the Vietnam War because of its faulty strategy; rather, it resulted from the North Vietnamese and NLF determination to win. Lomperis concedes that the United States did lose the war, but he maintains that it did force the North Vietnamese to install a government in Vietnam without national legitimacy. Lomperis asserts that while the North Vietnamese won the war, they lost their national and revolutionary legitimacy when they switched from a people's war to a conventional war during the 1968 Tết Offensive.

These books, and other important works such as Larry Berman, *Planning a Tragedy: The Americanization of the War in Vietnam* (1982), who examines the relationship of the members in the Johnson administration during the critical year 1965, and Ralph B. Smith, *An International History of the Vietnam War* (1983), who offers a solid analysis of non-American and Asian factors that played a role in shaping the war, set the tone for scholarship into the 1990s. Several factors contributed to the explosion of academic books on the war in that decade, including the near completion of the State Department's Foreign Relations of the United States series on Vietnam as well as the release of hundreds of reels of microfilm from government and non-government sources, including the presidential libraries. These documents allowed for more sophisticated analysis of the war than what the Pentagon Papers had provided.

While memoirs had been published before the 1990s, there were several significant works published during the decade including Dean Rusk, *As I Saw It* (1990); Joseph A. Califano Jr., *The Triumph and Tragedy of Lyndon Johnson: The White House Years* (1991); Clark Clifford, *Counsel to the President: A Memoir* (1991); and Robert S. McNamara, *In Retrospect: The Tragedy and Lessons of Vietnam* (1995). Unquestionably, McNamara's work attracted the most attention and was heavily scrutinized to the point that the Vietnam Center at Texas Tech University sponsored one of its first major conferences around the book. The controversy surrounding the book confirmed the intensity and emotion that the war continued to provoke.

The 1990s also experienced a surge in topical works that helped fill in some of the gaps or add to the impressive standard works within the historiography. On the First Indochina War, two works on Điện Biên Phủ, Howard R. Simpson, *Dien Bien Phu: The Epic Battle America Forgot* (1994), and Võ Nguyên Giáp, *Dien Bien Phu* (1998), offered valuable insight into that most important battle that ended the French colonial experiment, while Edwin E. Moïse, *Tonkin Gulf and the Escalation of the Vietnam War* (1996), and Erza Y. Siff, *Why the Senate Slept: The Gulf of Tonkin Resolution and the Beginning of America's Vietnam War* (1999), helped to clarify the mystery and intrigue of the Gulf of Tŏn Kĭn incident.

Other controversial events such as the 1968 Mỹ Lai massacre also received academic attention, specifically with the edited work by David L. Anderson, *Facing My Lai: Moving Beyond the Massacre* (1998), and Trent Angers, *The Forgotten Hero of My Lai: The Hugh Thompson Story* (1999), whose study helped provide perspective on this tragic event. A reexamination of the year 1968 was also noticeable during the 1990s, as seen in John Prados and Ray W. Stubbe, *Valley of Decision: The Siege of Khe Sanh* (1991); Richard A. Hunt, *Pacification: The American Struggle for Vietnam's Hearts and Minds* (1995); and James J. Wirtz, *The Tet Offensive: Intelligence Failure in War* (1991).

Other specialized topics covered during the decade include the missing in action controversy as examined in Malcolm McConnell, *Inside Hanoi's Secret Archives: Solving the MIA Mystery* (1995), while Christian G. Appy, *Working Class War: American Combat Soldiers and Vietnam* (1993), offers an interesting interpretation of the American soldiers who fought in the war. The role of women, on all sides of the conflict, also received special attention in the 1990s, using the foundation of Kathryn Marshall, *In the Combat Zone: An Oral History of American Women in Vietnam, 1966–1975* (1987), from the previous decade. Of note are the edited works of Betty Merrell and Priscilla

Tunnell, *Stories That Won't Go Away: Women in Vietnam, 1959–1975* (1995); Karen Gottschang Turner and Phan Thanh Hào, *Even the Women Must Fight: Memories of War from North Vietnam* (1998); and Sandra C. Taylor, *Vietnamese Women at War: Fighting for Ho Chi Minh and the Revolution* (1999).

The antiwar movement has always been a popular topic among historians, and the 1990s was no exception. Charles DeBenedetti, *An American Ordeal: The Antiwar Movement of the Vietnam Era* (1990); Mitchell K. Hall, *Because of their Faith: CALCAV and Religious Opposition to the Vietnam War* (1990); Melvin Small, *Covering Dissent: The Media and the Anti-Vietnam War Movement* (1994); and the edited work by Mary Susannah Robbins, *Against the Vietnam War: Writings by Activists* (1999), are among the best.

B. G. Burkett, *Stolen Valor: How the Vietnam Generation Was Robbed of Its Heroes and Its History* (1998), marked a turning point for the Vietnam veteran who had been negatively typecast since the end of the war. Burkett went on the offensive against those who had claimed veteran status and called into question the stereotypes so commonly applied to the Vietnam veteran. While his work was not the first to reexamine the veteran, it did cause the most controversy. As veterans entered the 21st century, hundreds of their personal experiences appeared in press. This was reinforced in part by the abundance of vanity and Internet presses available, but also by the fact that the generation of men and women who had experienced the war in Southeast Asia had reached a point in their lives when the frustration of the war no longer outweighed the need to tell the story from their perspective.

Such well-constructed works as Harold G. Moore and Joseph L. Galloway, *We Were Soldiers Once . . . and Young: Ia Drang, the Battle that Changed the War in Vietnam* (1992); Chuck Carlock, *Firebirds: The Best First-person account of Helicopter Combat in Vietnam Ever Written* (1995); Fred Leo Brown, *Vietnam War Diary* (1998); and Joe P. Dunn, *Desk Warrior: Memoirs of a Combat REMF* (1999), lead the way, though there are many others written in the 1980s and 2000s that deserve attention.

The 21st century has not seen a lack of works that vie for their place in the historiography of the Vietnam War. New materials and different perspectives have broadened the understanding of the complexities and nuances that surrounded Southeast Asia. Of the several significant trends within Vietnam War studies, two stand out: the move to internationalize the war started by Ralph B. Smith in the 1980s, and the effort to provide the Vietnamese a voice. While international scholars often led the way in providing the international perspective, such as Gregory Pemberton, *All the Way: Australia's Road to Vietnam* (1987), whose work on Australia's role in Vietnam set the tone for Australian scholars, a number of works by American historians have also offered a fresh approach. Of particular interest are the edited works of Lloyd C.

Gardner and Ted Gittinger, *International Perspectives on Vietnam* (2000), and William Schoenl, *New Perspectives on the Vietnam War: Our Allies' Views* (2002), as well as Ronald B. Frankum Jr., *The United States and Australia in Vietnam, 1954–1968: Silent Partners* (2001); Greg Donaghy, *Tolerant Allies: Canada and the United States, 1963–1968* (2002); Peter Busch, *All the Way with JFK? Britain and Kennedy's War in Vietnam* (2003); Mark Atwood Lawrence, *Assuming the Burden: Europe and the American Commitment to War in Vietnam* (2005); Greg Lockhart, *The Minefield: An Australian Tragedy in Vietnam* (2007); and Billy Barnz, *Voices from Vietnam: The Stories of New Zealanders Who Served Their Country in Vietnam* (2008).

The 2000s have also witnessed a significant move to examine South Vietnamese documents that might shed new light on the war. Such studies as Philip E. Catton, *Diem's Final Failure: Prelude to America's War in Vietnam* (2002), and Andrew Wiest, *Vietnam's Forgotten Army: Heroism and Betrayal in the ARVN* (2008), have done much to force a reexamination of the long-held beliefs of historians who had relied on the Pentagon Papers. Other books have continued to add to the historiography by focusing on specific events that have been neglected by earlier historians.

Books that provide a specialized study within the RVN include Robert J. Topmiller, *The Lotus Unleashed: The Buddhist Peace Movement in South Vietnam, 1964–1966* (2002), who examines the Buddhist uprising that occurred during the period of early American escalation that almost lost South Vietnam to the communists. Robert K. Brigham, *ARVN: Life and Death in the South Vietnamese Army* (2006), offered one of the earliest attempts by a U.S. scholar to examine America's ally. Ronald B. Frankum Jr.'s *Operation Passage to Freedom: The United States Navy in Vietnam, 1954–1955* (2007) was the first book to explore the most significant event to occur after the 1954 Geneva Conference, which helped to establish American foreign policy for the 1950s. Other books, such as Larry Berman's *Perfect Spy: The Incredible Double Life of Pham Xuan An, Time Magazine Reporter and Vietnamese Communist Agent* (2007), explore the world of espionage and highlight how difficult it was for the United States to determine who was an ally and who was an enemy. Mark Moyar, *Phoenix and the Birds of Prey: The CIA's Secret Campaign to Destroy the Viet Cong* (2007), also explored this theme.

A number of works focus on expanding the war beyond the borders of the RVN. Christopher E. Goscha and Soren Ivarsson, *Contesting Visions of the Lao Past: Lao Historiography at the Crossroads* (2003), offer an excellent assessment of Laos, while John M. Shaw's *The Cambodian Campaign: The 1970 Offensive and America's Vietnam War* (2005) provides an in-depth analysis of the Cambodian incursion. Michael Lumbers, *Piercing the Bamboo Curtain: Tentative Bridge-Building to China during the Johnson Years*

(2008), examines the China question that plagued the Johnson administration during the war, while Rufus Phillips, *Why Vietnam Matters: An Eyewitness Account of Lessons Not Learned* (2008), relies on his life experiences in Vietnam and Laos to offer an insightful study on the significance of the war.

Other focused studies offer a variety of significant perspectives that had not been readily accessible by earlier historians. These works are testament to the controversial and contentious issues that still remain with the war. Evelyn Grubb and Carol Jose, *You Are Not Forgotten: A Family's Quest for Truth and the Founding of the National League of Families* (2008), explore the issues surrounding the missing in action and how Americans responded to the soldiers who did not return to the United States. Thomas H. Keith and J. Terry Riebling, *SEAL Warrior: Death in the Dark: Vietnam 1968–1972* (2009), offer an analysis of the more secretive side of the war, while Ang Cheng Guan's *Ending the Vietnam War: The Vietnamese Communists' Perspective* (2004) challenges the reader to explore the other face of Vietnam that has been so long neglected by American historians.

There are a number of organizations that have dedicated themselves to the collection and preservation of material related to the Vietnam War. The Vietnam Center at Texas Tech University is among the most important. In addition to a collection of information related to the war regardless of perspective and an active oral history project that seeks to preserve the memories of those who made the history, it is also involved in an extensive digitization project to make its collections available through the Virtual Vietnam Archive. Other digitization collections of note include the National Security Archives at George Washington University and the Foreign Relations of the United States Digitization Project at the University of Wisconsin. All of these resources are open to anyone interested in learning more about the war. The National Archive and Records Administration at College Park, Maryland, is the largest holder of materials related to the Vietnam War. Record Group 472: Records of the U.S. Forces in Southeast Asia, 1950–1975 consists of thousands of linear feet of materials. Documents related to the Vietnam War are also available in Record Group 59: General Records of the State Department; Record Group 84: Foreign Service Post Files; Record Group 330: Records of the Office of the Secretary of Defense; and Group 469: Records of the U.S. Foreign Assistance Agencies, among many others.

The Internet has played a major role in disseminating information about the war as well. Vietnam veterans have developed websites to educate the public on their role during the war. There are hundreds of Vietnam veteran associations. A few of the noteworthy are B Troop, 2/17th Cavalry Association; the Counterparts Association; and the Mobile Riverine Forces Association, though there are many more with websites that provide a unique perspective of the war. In addition to Texas Tech University, organizations such as the Vietnam Veterans Memorial Fund (VVMF) have created websites to teach schoolchildren about the war and have offered lesson plans for high school and university-level teachers. The VVMF has also developed a virtual Vietnam Memorial Wall to provide access to that national landmark for when traveling to Washington, D.C., is not possible. The Public Broadcasting Service website, The American Experience, also offers a host of educational material for teachers and students, as well as its own archive. The Internet continues to be a source for information on the war and offers a variety of perspectives not found in the traditional classroom or book.

Even after the last helicopter left Sài Gòn and the guns fell silent in the RVN capital, the Vietnam experience continued to shape how historians, politicians, and the interested American public viewed the world. After the tragic events of September 11, 2001, many within the United States were quick to make parallels between Vietnam and the war in Iraq. While several of the parallels were no better than the 1968 comparison between Khe Sanh and Điện Biên Phủ, a few works offer interesting insight, such as Robert Brigham, *Iraq, Vietnam, and the Limits of American Power* (2008). The war in Afghanistan has also attracted similar interest, even to the point that several Vietnam War scholars have abandoned their specialty to draw links to this newest conflict. Whether the parallels deserve serious attention is yet to be determined.

Although the Vietnam War has been over for several decades, our understanding of it is still far from complete. Historians and veterans will continue to contribute to the historiography, in some cases repeating the words and errors of the past. However, with each new offering, fresh insight, or novel interpretation, the war that consumed nations and generations comes more into focus as time passes.

HISTORICAL OVERVIEW

Reference Works and Bibliographies

Anderson, David L. *The Columbia Guide to the Vietnam War*. New York: Columbia University Press, 2002.

———. *The Vietnam War*. New York: Palgrave Macmillan, 2005.

Bowman, John S., ed. *The Vietnam War: An Almanac*. Cleveland, Ohio: World Almanac Publications, 1985.

Clark, Gregory R. *Words of the Vietnam War: The Slang, Jargon, Abbreviations, Acronyms, Nomenclature, Nicknames, Pseudonyms, Slogans, Specs, Euphemisms, Double-talk, Chants, and Names and Places of the Era of United States Involvement in Vietnam*. Jefferson, N.C.: McFarland, 1990.

Clodfelter, Michael. *Vietnam in Military Statistics: A History of the Indochina Wars, 1772–1991*. Jefferson, N.C.: McFarland, 1995.

Corfield, Justin, and Laura Summers. *Historical Dictionary of Cambodia*. Lanham, Md.: Scarecrow Press, 2003.

Frankum, Ronald B., Jr., and Stephen F. Maxner. *The Vietnam War for Dummies*. New York: Wiley, 2003.

Kelly, Michael P. *Where We Were in Vietnam: A Comprehensive Guide to the Firebases, Military Installations and Naval Vessels of the Vietnam War, 1945–1975*. Central Point, Ore.: Hellgate, 2002.

Kutler, Stanley I. *Encyclopedia of the Vietnam War*. New York: Scribner, 1996.

Langer, Howard. *The Vietnam War: An Encyclopedia of Quotations*. Westport, Conn.: Greenwood, 2005.

Lockhard, Bruce, and William Duiker. *Historical Dictionary of Vietnam*. Lanham, Md.: Scarecrow Press, 2006.

Olson, James S., ed. *Dictionary of the Vietnam War*. New York: Greenwood, 1988.

Stanton, Shelby L. *Vietnam Order of Battle*. Washington, D.C.: U.S. News Books, 1981.

Summers, Harry G., Jr. *The Vietnam War Almanac*. New York: Facts on File, 1985.

———. *Historical Atlas of the Vietnam War*. Boston: Houghton Mifflin, 1995.

Tucker, Spencer, ed. *Encyclopedia of the Vietnam War: A Political, Social, and Military History*. New York: Oxford University Press, 2000.

General

Addington, Larry. *America's War in Vietnam: A Short Narrative History*. Bloomington, Ind.: Indiana University Press, 2000.

Allen, Joe. *Vietnam: The (Last) War the U.S. Lost*. Chicago: Haymarket Books, 2008.

Ang Cheng Guan. *The Vietnam War from the Other Side: The Vietnamese Communists' Perspective*. New York: RoutledgeCurzon, 2002.

Baritz, Loren. *Backfire: A History of How American Culture Led Us into Vietnam and Made Us Fight the Way We Did*. New York: Morrow, 1985.

Berman, Larry. *Planning a Tragedy: The Americanization of the War in Vietnam*. New York: Norton, 1982.

Bradley, Mark Philip. *Vietnam at War*. New York: Oxford University Press, 2009.

Buttinger, Joseph. *The Smaller Dragon: A Political History of Vietnam*. New York: Praeger, 1958.

———. *Vietnam: A Dragon Embattled*. New York: Praeger, 1967.

———. *Vietnam: A Political History*. New York: Praeger, 1968.

———. *A Dragon Defiant: A Short History of Vietnam*. New York: Praeger, 1972.

———. *Vietnam: The Unforgettable Tragedy*. New York: Horizon Books, 1977.

Cairns, James Ford. *The Eagle and the Lotus: Western Intervention in Vietnam, 1847–1971*. Melbourne, Australia: Lansdowne Press, 1971.

Carter, James M. *Inventing Vietnam: The United States and State Building, 1954–1968*. New York: Cambridge University Press, 2008.

Colby, William, with James McCargar. *Lost Victory*. Chicago: Contemporary Books, 1989.

Davidson, Phillip B. *Vietnam at War: The History, 1946–1975*. Novato, Calif.: Presidio Press, 1988.

———. *Secrets of the Vietnam War*. Novato, Calif.: Presidio Press, 1990.

DeGroot, Gerald J. *A Noble Cause? America and the Vietnam War*. London: Longman, 1999.

Dommen, Arthur J. *The Indochinese Experience of the French and the Americans: Nationalism and Communism in Cambodia, Laos, and Vietnam*. Bloomington, Ind.: Indiana University Press, 2001.

Duiker, William J. *U.S. Containment Policy and the Conflict in Indochina*. Stanford, Calif.: Stanford University Press, 1994.

———. *Sacred War: Nationalism and Revolution in a Divided Vietnam*. New York: McGraw-Hill, 1995.

Elliott, David. *The Vietnamese War: Revolution and Social Change in the Mekong Delta, 1930–1975*. Armonk, N.Y.: M. E. Sharpe, 2003.

Fall, Bernard. *The Two Viet-Nams*. New York: Praeger, 1964.

———. *Viet-Nam Witness, 1953–1966*. New York: Praeger, 1966.

Fitzgerald, Frances. *Fire in the Lake: The Vietnamese and the Americans in Vietnam*. New York: Random House, 1972.

Gelb, Leslie H., with Richard K. Betts. *The Irony of Vietnam: The System Worked*. Washington, D.C.: Brookings Institution, 1979.

Gilbert, Marc Jason, ed. *Why the North Won the Vietnam War*. New York: Palgrave, 2002.

Hall, Mitchell K. *The Vietnam War*. New York: Longman, 2007.

Haycraft, William Russell. *Unraveling Vietnam: How American Arms and Diplomacy Failed in Southeast Asia*. Jefferson, N.C.: McFarland, 2006.

Hearden, Patrick J. *The Tragedy of Vietnam*. New York: HarperCollins, 2008.

Hess, Gary R. *Vietnam and the United States: Origins and Legacy of War*. Boston: Twayne, 1990.

———. *Vietnam: Explaining America's Lost War*. Malden and Oxford: Blackwell Publishing, 2009.

Jamieson, Neil L. *Understanding Vietnam*. Berkeley, Calif.: University of California Press, 1993.

Kahin, George McT. *Intervention: How America became Involved in Vietnam*. New York: Knopf, 1986.

Kahin, George McT., and John Lewis, *The United States in Vietnam*. New York: Dial Press, 1969.

Karnow, Stanley. *Vietnam: A History*. New York: Viking, 1983.

Kolko, Gabriel. *Anatomy of a War: Vietnam, the United States, and the Modern Historical Experience*. New York: Pantheon, 1985.

Krepinevich, Andrew F., Jr. *The Army in Vietnam*. Baltimore, Md.: Johns Hopkins University Press, 1986.

Langguth, A. J. *Our Vietnam: The War, 1954–1975*. New York: Simon & Schuster, 2000.

Lawrence, Mark Atwood. *The Vietnam War: A Concise International History*. New York: Oxford University Press, 2008.

Levine, Alan J. *The United States and the Struggle for Southeast Asia, 1945–1975*. Westport, Conn.: Praeger, 1995.

Lewy, Guenter. *America in Vietnam*. New York: Oxford University Press, 1978.

Lind, Michael. *Vietnam the Necessary War: A Reinterpretation of America's Most Disastrous Military Conflict*. New York: Free Press, 1999.

Logevall, Fredrik. *Choosing War: The Lost Chance for Peace and the Escalation of War in Vietnam*. Berkeley, Calif.: University of California Press, 1999.

Lomperis, Timothy J. *The War Everyone Lost—and Won: America's Intervention in Viet Nam's Twin Struggles*. Baton Rouge, La.: Louisiana State University Press, 1984.

———. *From People's War to People's Rule: Insurgency, Intervention, and the Lessons of Vietnam*. Chapel Hill, N.C.: University of North Carolina Press, 1996.

Maclear, Michael. *The Ten Thousand Day War: Vietnam: 1945–1975*. New York: St. Martin's Press, 1981.

Mann, Robert. *A Grand Delusion: America's Descent into Vietnam*. New York: Basic Books, 2001.

Michon, Michel M. *Indochina Memoir: Rubber, Politics, and War in Vietnam and Cambodia, 1955–1972*. Tempe, Ariz.: Arizona State University, 2001.

Morrison, Wilbur H. *The Elephant and the Tiger: The Full Story of the Vietnam War*. New York: Hippocrene, 1990.

Moss, George D. *Vietnam: An American Ordeal*. Englewood Cliffs, N.J.: Prentice Hall, 1990, 2010.

Neale, Jonathan. *The American War: Vietnam, 1960–1975*. London: Bookmarks, 2001.

Neu, Charles E. *America's Lost War: Vietnam 1945–1975*. Wheeling, Ill.: Harlan Davidson, 2005.

Olson, James S., and Randy Roberts. *Where the Domino Fell: America and Vietnam, 1945–1990*. New York: St. Martin's Press, 1991.

Palmer, Bruce, Jr. *The 25-Year War: America's Military Role in Vietnam*. Lexington, Ky.: University Press of Kentucky, 1984.

Palmer, Dave Richard. *The Summons of the Trumpet*. San Rafael, Calif.: Presidio Press, 1984.

Podhoretz, Norman. *Why We Were in Vietnam*. New York: Simon & Schuster, 1982.

Prados, John. *Vietnam: The History of an Unwinnable War, 1945–1975*. Lawrence, Kans.: University Press of Kansas, 2009.

Record, Jeffrey. *The Wrong War: Why We Lost in Vietnam*. Annapolis, Md.: Naval Institute Press, 1998.

Schandler, Herbert Y. *America in Vietnam: The War That Couldn't Be Won*. Lanham, Md.: Rowman & Littlefield, 2009.

Schulzinger, Robert D. *A Time for War: The United States and Vietnam, 1941–1975*. New York: Oxford University Press, 1997.

Shaplen, Robert. *The Lost Revolution: The U.S. in Vietnam, 1946–1966*. New York: Harper & Row, 1965.

———. *Time Out of Hand: Revolution and Reaction in Southeast Asia*. New York: Harper & Row, 1969.

———. *The Road From War: Vietnam, 1965–1971*. New York: Harper & Row, 1970.

Sheehan, Neil. *A Bright Shining Lie: John Paul Vann and America in Vietnam*. New York: Random House, 1988.

Short, Anthony. *The Origins of the Vietnam War*. New York: Longman, 1989.

Smith, Ralph B. *An International History of the Vietnam War*. New York: St. Martin's Press, 1983.

———. *Revolution versus Containment, 1955–61*. New York: St. Martin's Press, 1985.

———. *The Making of a Limited War, 1965–66*. New York: St. Martin's Press, 1990.

———. *Communist Indochina*. New York: Routledge, 2008.

Summers, Harry. *On Strategy: The Vietnam War in Context*. Novato, Calif.: Presidio Press, 1982.

Thayer, Thomas C. *War without Fronts: The American Experience in Vietnam*. Boulder, Colo.: Westview, 1985.

Tucker, Spencer. *Vietnam*. Lexington, Ky.: University Press of Kentucky, 1999.

Turley, William S. *The Second Indochina War: A Short Political and Military History, 1954–1975*. Boulder, Colo.: Westview, 1986.

Walton, C. Dale. *The Myth of Inevitable US Defeat in Vietnam*. London: Frank Cass, 2002.

Westheider, James E. *The Vietnam War*. Westport, Conn.: Greenwood, 2007.

Wintler, Justin. *The Viet Nam Wars*. New York: St. Martin's Press, 1991.

Woodruff, Mark R. *Unheralded Victory: The Defeat of the Viet Cong and the North Vietnamese Army, 1961–1973*. Arlington, Va.: Vandamere Press, 1999.

Young, Marilyn B. *The Vietnam Wars, 1945–1990*. New York: HarperCollins, 1991.

World War II and the First Indochina War

Allen, Louis. *The End of the War in Asia*. London: Hart-Davis, MacGibbon, 1976.

Arnold, James R. *The First Domino: Eisenhower, the Military, and America's Intervention in Vietnam*. New York: Morrow, 1991.

Bartholomew-Feis, Dixee. *The OSS and Ho Chi Minh: Unexpected Allies in the War against Japan*. Lawrence, Kans.: University Press of Kansas, 2006.

Bayly, Christopher, and Tim Harper. *Forgotten Wars: Freedom and Revolution in Southeast Asia*. Cambridge, Mass.: Harvard University Press, 2007.

Billings-Yun, Melanie. *Decision against War*. New York: Columbia University Press, 1988.

Bodard, Lucien. *The Quicksand War*. Boston: Little, Brown, 1967.

Dalloz, Jacques. *The War in Indochina, 1945–1954*. New York: Barnes & Noble, 1990.

Drachman, Edward R. *United States Policy toward Vietnam, 1940–1945*. Rutherford, N.J.: Farleigh Dickinson University Press, 1970.

Dunn, Peter M. *The First Vietnam War*. London: C. Hurst, 1985.

Eisenhower, Dwight D. *The White House Years: Mandate for Change, 1953–1956*. New York: Doubleday, 1963.

Fall, Bernard. *Street without Joy: Indochina at War, 1946–1954*. Harrisburg, Penn.: Stackpole Books, 1961.

Fenn, Charles. *At the Dragon's Gate: With the OSS in the Far East.* Annapolis, Md.: Naval Institute Press, 2004.

Galambos, Louis, and Daun Van Ee, ed. *The Papers of Dwight David Eisenhower.* Baltimore, Md.: Johns Hopkins University Press, 1970–2001.

Gardner, Lloyd C. *Approaching Vietnam: From World War II through Dienbienphu.* New York: Norton, 1988.

Hammer, Ellen. *The Struggle for Indochina.* Stanford, Calif.: Stanford University Press, 1966.

Hess, Gary R. *The United States' Emergence as a Southeast Asian Power, 1940–1950.* New York: Columbia University Press, 1987.

Honaker, Keith. *The Eagle Weeps.* Knoxville, Tenn.: K & W Publishers, 1994.

Irving, R. E. M. *The First Indochina War: French and American Policy, 1945–1954.* London: Croom Helm, 1975.

Kelly, George A. *Lost Soldiers: The French Army and Empire in Crisis, 1947–1962.* Cambridge, Mass.: MIT Press, 1965.

Koburger, Charles W., Jr. *The French Navy in Indochina: Riverine and Coastal Forces, 1945–1954.* New York: Praeger, 1991.

———. *Naval Expeditions: The French Return to Indochina, 1945–1946.* New York: Praeger, 1997.

Lacouture, Jean. *De Gaulle.* New York: Norton, 1990.

Lancaster, Donald. *The Emancipation of French Indochina.* London: Oxford University Press, 1961.

Lankford, Nelson D. *The Last American Aristocrat: The Biography of Ambassador David K. E. Bruce.* Boston: Little, Brown, 1996.

Lawrence, Mark Atwood. *Assuming the Burden: Europe and the American Commitment to War in Vietnam.* Berkeley, Calif.: University of California Press, 2005.

Lawrence, Mark Atwood, and Fredrik Logevall, ed. *The First Vietnam War: Colonial Conflict and Cold War Crisis.* Cambridge, Mass.: Harvard University Press, 2007.

Lê Mạnh Hùng, *The Impact of World War II on the Economy of Vietnam, 1939–1945.* Singapore: Eastern Universities Press, 2004.

Leffler, Melvyn P. *A Preponderance of Power: National Security, the Truman Administration and the Cold War.* Stanford, Calif.: Stanford University Press, 1992.

Marr, David G. *Vietnam 1945: The Quest for Power.* Berkeley, Calif.: University of California Press, 1995.

Neville, Peter. *Britain in Vietnam: Prelude to Disaster, 1945–1946.* London: Routledge, 2007.

Patti, Archimedes. *Why Vietnam?* Berkeley, Calif.: University of California Press, 1980.

Raffin, Anne. *Youth Mobilization in Vichy Indochina and Its Legacies, 1940 to 1970.* Lanham, Md.: Lexington Books, 2005.

Rice-Maximin, Edward. *Accommodation and Resistance: The French Left, Indochina and the Cold War, 1944–1954.* Westport, Conn.: Greenwood, 1986.

Rotter, Andrew J. *The Path to Vietnam.* Ithaca, N.Y.: Cornell University Press, 1987.

Shipway, Martin. *The Road to War: France and Vietnam, 1944–1947.* Oxford: Berghahn Books, 1996.

Smith, Timothy O. *Britain and the Origins of the Vietnam War: UK Policy in Indo-China, 1943–1950.* New York: Palgrave Macmillan, 2007.

Spector, Ronald H. *In the Ruins of Empire: The Japanese Surrender and the Battle for Postwar Asia.* New York: Random House, 2007.

Statler, Kathryn C. *Replacing France: The Origins of American Intervention in Vietnam.* Lexington, Ky.: University Press of Kentucky, 2007.

Tanham, George K. *Communist Revolutionary Warfare: The Vietminh in Indochina.* New York: Praeger, 1961.

Tarling, Nicholas. *Britain, Southeast Asia and the Onset of the Cold War, 1945–50.* Cambridge, Mass.: Cambridge University Press, 1998.

Tonnesson, Stein. *The Vietnamese Revolution of 1945: Roosevelt, Ho Chi Minh, and de Gaulle in a World at War.* Newbury Park, Calif.: Sage, 1991.

———. *Vietnam 1946: How the War Began.* Berkeley, Calif.: University of California Press, 2009.

Trường Chinh. *The August Revolution.* Hanoi: Foreign Languages Publishing House, 1958.

Võ Nguyên Giáp. *Unforgettable Days.* Hanoi: Foreign Languages Publishing House, 1975.

Worthing, Peter. *Occupation and Revolution: China and the Vietnamese August Revolution of 1945.* Berkeley, Calif.: Institute of East Asian Studies, 2001.

Zervoudakis, Alexander. *French Operational Strategy and Tactics in Indochina, 1951–1952.* London: Frank Cass, 2002.

Era of Ngô Đình Diệm

Anderson, David L. *Trapped by Success: The Eisenhower Administration and Vietnam, 1953–1961.* New York: Columbia University Press, 1991.

Bayless, Robert M. *Vietnam: Victory Was Never an Option.* Victoria, B.C., Canada: Trafford, 2005.

Blagov, Sergei. *Honest Mistakes: The Life and Death of Trinh Minh The (1922–1955): South Vietnam's Alternative Leader.* Huntington, N.Y.: Nova Science Publishers, 2001.

Blight, James G., Janet M. Lang, and David A. Welch. *Vietnam if Kennedy Had Lived: Virtual JFK.* Lanham, Md.: Rowman & Littlefield, 2009.

Bouscaren, Anthony T. *Last of the Mandarins: Diem of Vietnam.* Pittsburgh, Penn.: Duquesne University Press, 1965.

Browne, Malcolm. *The New Face of War.* Indianapolis, Ind.: Bobbs-Merrill, 1965.

Catton, Philip E. *Diem's Final Failure: Prelude to America's War in Vietnam.* Lawrence, Kans.: University Press of Kansas, 2002.

Chomsky, Noam. *Rethinking Camelot: JFK, the Vietnam War, and U.S. Political Culture.* Boston: South End Press, 1993.

Dallek, Robert. *An Unfinished Life: John F. Kennedy, 1917–1963.* Boston: Little, Brown, 2003.

Dockery, Martin J. *Lost in Translation: Vietnam; A Combat Advisor's Story.* New York: Presidio Press, 2003.

Dooley, Thomas A. *Deliver Us from Evil: The Story of Viet Nam's Flight to Freedom*. New York: Farrar, Straus & Cudahy, 1956.

———. *The Edge of Tomorrow*. New York: Farrar, Straus & Cudahy, 1958.

———. *The Night They Burned the Mountain*. New York: Farrar, Straus & Cudahy, 1958.

Ernst, John P. *Forging a Fateful Alliance: Michigan State University and the Vietnam War*. East Lansing, Mich.: Michigan State University Press, 1998.

Fay, Paul B., Jr. *The Pleasure of His Company*. New York: Harper & Row, 1966.

Fisher, James T. *Dr. America: The Lives of Thomas A. Dooley, 1927–1961*. Amherst, Mass.: University of Massachusetts Press, 1997.

Frankum, Ronald B., Jr. *Operation Passage to Freedom: The United States Navy in Vietnam, 1954–1955*. Lubbock, Tex.: Texas Tech University Press, 2007.

Freedman, Lawrence. *Kennedy's Wars: Berlin, Cuba, Laos, and Vietnam*. New York: Oxford University Press, 2000.

Gardner, Lloyd C., and Tet Gittinger, eds. *Vietnam: The Early Decisions*. Austin, Tex.: University of Texas Press, 1997.

Givhan, John B. *Rice and Cotton: South Vietnam and South Alabama*. Philadelphia: Xlibris, 2000.

Halberstam, David. *The Making of a Quagmire*. New York: Random House, 1965.

Hammer, Ellen J. *A Death in November: America in Vietnam, 1963*. New York: E. P. Dutton, 1987.

Higgins, Marguerite. *Our Vietnam Nightmare*. New York: Harper & Row, 1965.

Hilsman, Roger. *To Move a Nation*. New York: Doubleday, 1967.

Hoang Ngoc Thanh and Than Thi Nhan Duc. *President Ngo Dinh Diem and the US: His Overthrow and Assassination*. San Jose, Calif.: Tuan-Yen & Quan-Viet Mai-Nam Publishers, 2001.

Hoàng Văn Chí. *From Colonialism to Communism: A Case History of North Vietnam*. New York: Praeger, 1964.

Jacobs, Seth. *America's Miracle Man in Vietnam: Ngo Dinh Diem, Religion, Race, and U.S. Intervention in Southeast Asia, 1950–1957*. Durham, N.C.: Duke University Press, 2004.

———. *Cold War Mandarin: Ngo Dinh Diem and the Origins of America's War in Vietnam, 1950–1963*. Lanham, Md.: Rowman & Littlefield, 2006.

Jones, Howard. *Death of a Generation: How the Assassinations of Diem and John F. Kennedy Prevented the Withdrawal of American Troops from Vietnam*. New York: Oxford University Press, 2003.

Labin, Suzanne. *Vietnam: An Eye-Witness Account*. Springfield, Va.: Crestwood, 1965.

Lacouture, Jean. *Vietnam: Between Two Truces*. New York: Vintage Books, 1966.

Lindholm, Richard W., ed. *Vietnam, the First Five Years: An International Symposium*. East Lansing, Mich.: Michigan State University Press, 1959.

Logevall, Fredrik. *The Origins of the Vietnam War*. New York: Longman, 2001.

Maneli, Mieczyslaw. *War of the Vanquished*. New York: Harper & Row, 1971.

Mecklin, John. *Mission in Torment*. New York: Doubleday, 1965.

Meyer, Harold J. *Hanging Sam: A Military Biography of General Samuel T. Williams from Pancho Villa to Vietnam*. Denton, Tex.: University of North Texas Press, 1990.

Moyar, Mark. *Triumph Forsaken: The Vietnam War, 1954–1965*. New York: Cambridge University Press, 2006.

Murti, B. S. N. *Vietnam Divided: The Unfinished Struggle*. New York: Asia Publishing House, 1964.

Neese, Harvey, and John O'Donnell, eds. *Prelude to Tragedy: Vietnam, 1960–1965*. Annapolis, Md.: Naval Institute Press, 2001.

Newman, John M. *JFK and Vietnam: Deception, Intrigue, and the Struggle for Power*. New York: Warner, 1992.

O'Leary, Bradley S., and Edward Lee, *The Deaths of the Cold War Kings: The Assassinations of Diem & JFK*. Baltimore, Md.: Cemetery Dance, 2000.

Parmet, Herbert S. *JFK: The Presidency of John F. Kennedy*. New York: Dial, 1983.

Pike, Douglas. *Viet Cong: The Organization and Techniques of the National Liberation Front of South Vietnam*. Cambridge, Mass.: MIT Press, 1966.

Porter, D. Gareth. *The Perils of Dominance: Imbalance of Power and the Road to War in Vietnam*. Berkeley, Calif.: University of California Press, 2005.

Prouty, L. Fletcher. *JFK: The CIA, Vietnam and the Plot to Assassinate John F. Kennedy*. New York: Carol, 1992.

Race, Jeffrey. *War Comes to Long An*. Berkeley, Calif.: University of California Press, 1972.

Rosenau, William. *US Internal Security Assistance to South Vietnam: Insurgency, Subversion and Public Order*. London: Routledge, 2005.

Rust, William J. *Kennedy in Vietnam*. New York: Scribner, 1985.

Schlesinger, Arthur, Jr. *A Thousand Days: John F. Kennedy in the White House*. Boston: Houghton Mifflin, 1965.

Scigliano, Robert. *South Vietnam: Nation under Stress*. Boston: Houghton Mifflin, 1963.

Sorensen, Theodore. *Kennedy*. New York: Harper & Row, 1965.

———. *Counselor: A Life at the Edge of History*. New York: HarperCollins, 2008.

Statler, Kathryn C. *Replacing France: The Origins of American Intervention in Vietnam*. Lexington, Ky.: University Press of Kentucky, 2007.

Strober, Gerald S., and Deborah Hart Strober. *Let Us Begin Anew: An Oral History of the Kennedy Presidency*. New York: HarperCollins, 2003.

Thayer, Carlyle. *War by Other Means: National Liberation and Revolution in Viet-Nam, 1954–1960*. Cambridge, Mass.: Unwin Hyman, 1989.

Toczek, David M. *The Battle of Ap Bac, Vietnam: They Did Everything but Learn from It*. Annapolis, Md.: Naval Institute Press, 2008.

Tregaskis, Richard. *Vietnam Diary*. New York: Holt, Rinehart & Winston, 1963.

Warner, Denis. *The Last Confucian*. Baltimore, Md.: Penguin, 1964.

Winters, Francis X. *The Year of the Hare: America in Vietnam, January 25, 1963–February 15, 1964*. Athens: University of Georgia Press, 1997.

Johnson Administration

Cable, Larry. *Unholy Grail: The US and the Wars in Vietnam, 1965–1968*. New York: Routledge, 1991.

Gardner, Lloyd C. *Pay Any Price: Lyndon Johnson and the Wars for Vietnam*. Chicago: Ivan R. Dee, 1995.

Gardner, Lloyd C., and Tet Gittinger, eds. *The Search for Peace in Vietnam, 1964–1968*. College Station, Tex.: Texas A&M University Press, 2004.

Gibson, James. *The Perfect War: Technowar in Vietnam*. Boston: Atlantic Monthly Press, 1986.

Hennessy, Michael A. *Strategy in Vietnam: The Marines and Revolutionary Warfare in I Corps, 1965–1972*. Westport, Conn.: Praeger, 1997.

Herring, George C. *LBJ and Vietnam: A Different Kind of War*. Austin, Tex.: University of Texas Press, 1994.

———. *America's Longest War: The United States and Vietnam, 1950–1975*. New York: McGraw-Hill, 2002.

Knoebl, Kuno. *Victor Charlie: The Face of War in Viet-Nam*. New York: Praeger, 1967.

Mangold, Tom, and John Penycate. *The Tunnels of Cu Chi: The Untold Story of Vietnam*. New York: Random House, 1985.

Meyerson, Harvey. *Vinh Long*. Boston: Houghton Mifflin, 1970.

Mortensen, K. G. *The Battle of An Loc, 1972*. Parkville, Victoria, Australia: Gerald Griffin Press, 1996.

Schell, Jonathan. *The Military Half: An Account of Destruction in Quang Ngai and Quang Tin*. New York: Knopf, 1968.

Sigler, David B. *Vietnam Battle Chronology: U.S. Army and Marine Corps Combat Operations, 1965–1973*. Jefferson, N.C.: McFarland, 1992.

Sorley, Lewis. *A Better War: The Unexamined Victories and the Final Tragedy of America's Last Years in Vietnam*. New York: Harcourt, Brace, 1999.

———, ed. *Vietnam Chronicles: The Abrams Tapes, 1968–1972*. Lubbock, Tex.: Texas Tech University Press, 2004.

Spector, Ronald H. *After Tet: The Bloodiest Year in Vietnam*. New York: Free Press, 1993.

Stanton, Shelby L. *The Rise and Fall of an American Army: U.S. Ground Forces in Vietnam, 1965–1973*. Novato, Calif.: Presidio Press, 1985.

Thies, Wallace. *When Governments Collide: Coercion and Diplomacy in the Vietnam Conflict, 1964–1968*. Berkeley, Calif.: University of California Press, 1980.

Zaffiri, Samuel. *Hamburger Hill: May 11–20, 1969*. Novato, Calif.: Presidio Press, 1988.

Nixon and Ford Administrations

Ambrose, Stephen. *Nixon: The Triumph of a Politician, 1962–1972*. New York: Simon & Schuster, 1989.

———. *Nixon: Ruin and Recovery, 1973–1990*. New York: Simon & Schuster, 1991.

Andradé, Dale. *Trial by Fire: The 1972 Easter Offensive, America's Last Vietnam Battle*. New York: Hippocrene, 1995.

Botkin, Richard. *Ride the Thunder: A Vietnam War Story of Honor and Triumph*. Los Angeles: WND Books, 2009.

Brodine, Virginia, Mark Selden, Keith M. Buchanan, and John W. Dower. *Open Secret: The Kissinger-Nixon Doctrine in Asia*. New York: Harper & Row, 1972.

Bundy, William. *A Tangled Web: The Making of Foreign Policy in the Nixon Presidency*. New York: Hill & Wang, 1998.

Cannon, James M. *Time and Chance: Gerald Ford's Appointment with History*. New York: HarperCollins, 1994.

Crowley, Monica. *Nixon in Winter*. New York: Random House, 1998.

Dallek, Robert. *Nixon and Kissinger: Partners in Power*. New York: HarperCollins, 2007.

DeFrank, Thomas M. *Write It When I'm Gone: Remarkable Off-the-Record Conversations with Gerald R. Ford*. New York: Putnam, 2007.

Hanhimaki, Jussi N. *The Flawed Architect: Henry Kissinger and American Foreign Policy*. New York: Oxford University Press, 2004.

Hersh, Seymour. *The Price of Power: Kissinger in the Nixon White House*. New York: Summit Books, 1983.

Hoff, Joan. *Nixon Reconsidered*. New York: Basic Books, 1994.

Horne, Alistair. *Kissinger: 1973, the Crucial Year*. New York: Simon & Schuster, 2009.

Isaacson, Walter. *Kissinger: A Biography*. New York: Simon & Schuster, 1992.

Korb, Lawrence J. *The Fall and Rise of the Pentagon: American Defense Policies in the 1970s*. Westport, Conn.: Greenwood, 1979.

Lâm Quang Thi. *Hell in An Loc: The 1972 Easter Offensive and the Battle That Saved South Viet Nam*. Denton, Tex.: University of North Texas Press, 2009.

Mieczkowski, Yanek. *Gerald Ford and the Challenges of the 1970s*. Lexington, Ky.: University Press of Kentucky, 2005.

Morris, Roger. *Uncertain Greatness: Henry Kissinger and American Foreign Policy*. New York: Harper & Row, 1977.

Perlstein, Rick. *Nixonland: The Rise of a President and the Fracturing of America*. New York: Scribner, 2008.

———, ed. *Richard Nixon: Speeches, Writings, Documents*. Princeton, N.J.: Princeton University Press, 2008.

Randolph, Stephen P. *Powerful and Brutal Weapons: Nixon, Kissinger, and the Easter Offensive*. Cambridge, Mass.: Harvard University Press, 2007.

Rodman, Peter W. *More Precious Than Peace: The Cold War and the Struggle for the Third World*. New York: Scribner, 1994.

Safire, William. *Before the Fall: An Inside View of the Pre-Watergate White House*. Garden City, N.Y.: Doubleday, 1975.

Schell, Jonathan. *The Time of Illusion*. New York: Knopf, 1976.

Siniver, Asaf. *Nixon, Kissinger, and U.S. Foreign Policy Making: The Machinery of Crisis*. Cambridge, Mass.: Cambridge University Press, 2008.

Small, Melvin. *The Presidency of Richard Nixon*. Lawrence, Kans.: University Press of Kansas, 1999.

Strober, Deborah Hart, and Gerald S. Strober. *The Nixon Presidency: An Oral History of the Era*. Dulles, Va.: Brassey's, 2003.

Suri, Jeremy. *Henry Kissinger and the American Century*. Cambridge, Mass.: Harvard University Press, 2007.

Szulc, Tad. *The Illusion of Peace: Foreign Policy in the Nixon Years*. New York: Viking, 1978.

Van Atta, Dale. *With Honor: Melvin Laird in War, Peace, and Politics*. Madison, Wisc.: University of Wisconsin Press, 2008.

The Ground War

Amchan, Arthur J. *Killed in Action: The Life and Times of SP4 Stephen H. Warner, Draftee, Journalist, and Anti-war Activist*. McLean, Va.: Amchan Publications, 2003.

Anderson, Charles. *The Grunts*. Novato, Calif.: Presidio Press, 1976.

Berens, Charlyne. *Chuck Hagel: Moving Forward*. Lincoln, Nebr.: University of Nebraska Press, 2006.

Bergerud, Eric M. *Red Thunder, Tropic Lightning: The World of a Combat Division in Vietnam*. Boulder, Colo.: Westview, 1993.

Bird, Annette, and Tim Prouty. *So Proudly He Served: The Sam Bird Story*. Wichita, Kans.: Okarche Books, 1993.

Bissell, Tom. *The Father of All Things: A Marine, His Son, and the Legacy of Vietnam*. New York: Pantheon, 2007.

Brant, Toby L. *Journal of a Combat Tanker: Vietnam, 1969*. New York: Vantage Press, 1988.

Brennan, Matthew, ed. *Headhunters: Stories from the 1st Squadron, 9th Cavalry, in Vietnam, 1965–1971*. Novato, Calif.: Presidio Press, 1987.

———, ed. *Hunter Killer Squadron: Aero-weapons, Aero-scouts, Aero-Rifles, Vietnam, 1965–1972*. Novato, Calif.: Presidio Press, 1990.

Bryan, Courtlandt D. B. *Friendly Fire*. New York: Putnam, 1976.

Ebert, James R. *A Life in a Year: The American Infantryman in Vietnam, 1965–1972*. Novato, Calif.: Presidio Press, 1993.

Edelman, Bernard, ed. *Dear America: Letters Home from Vietnam*. New York: Norton, 1985.

Garland, Albert N., ed. *Infantry in Vietnam: Small Unit Actions in the Early Days, 1965–1966*. Nashville, Tenn.: Battery Press, 1967.

———, ed. *A Distant Challenge: The US Infantryman in Vietnam, 1967–1972*. Nashville, Tenn.: Battery Press, 1983.

Gilbert, Oscar. *Marine Corps Tank Battles in Vietnam*. Havertown, Penn.: Casemate, 2007.

Glenn, Russell W. *Reading Athena's Dance Card: Men against Fire in Vietnam*. Annapolis, Md.: Naval Institute Press, 2000.

Hemingway, Al. *Our War Was Different: Marine Combined Action Platoons in Vietnam*. Annapolis, Md.: Naval Institute Press, 1994.

Henderson, Charles. *Marshalling the Faithful: The Marines' First Year in Vietnam*. New York: Berkeley Caliber, 1993.

Hymoff, Edward. *The First Air Cavalry Division, Vietnam*. New York: Lads, 1967.

———. *First Marine Division, Vietnam*. New York: Lads, 1967.

Jablon, Howard. *David M. Shoup: A Warrior against War*. Lanham, Md.: Rowman & Littlefield, 2005.

Johnson III, Lawrence H. *Winged Sabers: The Air Cavalry in Vietnam, 1965–1973*. Harrisburg, Penn.: Stackpole Books, 1990.

Lanning, Michael Lee. *Inside the Crosshairs: Snipers in Vietnam*. New York: Ivy Books, 1998.

Lee, Alex. *Utter's Battalion: 2/7 Marines in Vietnam, 1965–1966*. New York: Ballantine, 2000.

Lehrack, Otto J. *The First Battle: Operation Starlite and the Beginning of the Blood Debt in Vietnam*. Havertown, Penn.: Casemate, 2004.

Leshikar, Chuck, ed. *Delta Raiders: D Company, 2/501 Infantry, 101st Airborne (AMBL)*. St. Petersburg, Fla.: Southern Heritage Press, 1998.

Longley, Kyle. *Grunts: The American Combat Soldier in Vietnam*. Armonk, N.Y.: M. E. Sharpe, 2008.

Marshall, Samuel Lyman Atwood. *Battles in the Monsoon*. New York: William Morrow, 1967.

———. *West to Cambodia and the Fields of Bamboo*. Garden City, N.Y.: Nelson Doubleday, 1968.

———. *Ambush and Bird*. Garden City, N.Y.: Nelson Doubleday, 1969.

Miller, John Grider. *The Bridge at Dong Ha*. Annapolis, Md.: Naval Institute Press, 1989.

———. *The Co-Vans: U.S. Marine Advisors in Vietnam*. Annapolis, Md.: Naval Institute Press, 2000.

Murphy, Edward F. *Dak To: The 173d Airborne Brigade in South Vietnam's Central Highlands, June–November 1967*. Novato, Calif.: Presidio Press, 1993.

———. *Semper Fi—Vietnam: From Da Nang to the DMZ, Marine Corps Campaigns, 1965–1975*. Novato, Calif.: Presidio Press, 1997.

———. *The Hill Fights: The First Battle of Khe Sanh*. Novato, Calif.: Presidio Press, 2003.

Myers, William L. *Honor the Warrior: The United States Marine Corps in Vietnam*. Lafayette, La.: Redoubt, 2000.

Nolan, Keith W. *Death Valley: The Summer Offensive, I Corps, August 1969*. Novato, Calif.: Presidio Press, 1987.

———. *Into Cambodia: Spring Campaign, Summer Offensive, 1970*. Novato, Calif.: Presidio Press, 1990.

———. *Operation Buffalo: USMC Fight for the DMZ*. Novato, Calif.: Presidio Press, 1991.

———. *The Magnificent Bastards: The Joint Army-Marine Defense of Dong Ha, 1968*. Novato, Calif.: Presidio Press, 1994.

———. *Sappers in the Wire: The Life and Death of Firebase Mary Ann*. College Station, Tex.: Texas A&M University Press, 1995.

———. *Ripcord: Screaming Eagles under Siege, Vietnam, 1970*. Novato, Calif.: Presidio Press, 2000.

O'Donnell, John E. *None Came Home: The War Dogs of Vietnam*. Bloomington, Ind.: 1st Books Library, 2001.

Prashker, Ivan. *Duty, Honor, Vietnam: Twelve Men of West Point Tell Their Stories*. New York: Warner, 1990.

Reed, David. *Upfront in Vietnam*. New York: Funk & Wagnalls, 1967.

Senich, Peter R. *The Long-Range War: Sniping in Vietnam*. Boulder, Colo.: Paladin, 1994.

———. *The One-Round War: USMC Scout-Snipers in Vietnam*. Boulder, Colo.: Paladin, 1996.

Silver, Benjamin S. *Ride at a Gallop*. Waco, Tex.: Davis Brothers Publishing, 1990.

Simonsen, Robert A. *Every Marine: 1968 Vietnam: A Battle for Go Noi Island*. Westminster, Md.: Heritage Books, 2005.

Squires, Bill. *Find the Bastards . . . Then Pile On*. Paducah, Ky.: Turner Publishing, 1997.

Stanton, Shelby L. *Anatomy of a Division: The 1st Cav in Vietnam*. Novato, Calif.: Presidio Press, 1987.

Stroud, Carsten. *Iron Bravo: Hearts, Minds, and Sergeants in the U.S. Army*. New York: Bantam, 1995.

Walter, Peter L., ed. *The Blackhorse Regiment in Vietnam, 1966–1972*. Dubuque, Iowa: Kendall Hunt Publishing, 1997.

Wilson, James R. *Landing Zones: Southern Veterans Remember Vietnam*. Durham, N.C.: Duke University Press, 1990.

The Naval War

Bryant, Jimmy R. *Man of the River: Memoir of a Brown Water Sailor in Vietnam, 1968–1969*. Fredericksburg, Va.: Sergeant Kirkland's Press, 1998.

Carlin, Mike. *Trial: Ordeal of the USS Enterprise*. West Grove, Penn.: Tuscarora, 1993.

Croizat, Victor J. *The Brown Water Navy: The River and Coastal War in Indo-China and Vietnam, 1948–1972*. Dorset, UK: Blandford Press, 1984.

Cutler, Thomas J. *Brown Water, Black Berets: Coastal and Riverine Warfare in Vietnam*. Annapolis, Md.: Naval Institute Press, 1988.

Dunnavent, R. Blake. *Brown Water Warfare: The U.S. Navy in Riverine Warfare and the Emergence of a Tactical Doctrine, 1775–1970*. Gainesville, Fla.: University Press of Florida, 2003.

Ferguson, Bill. *Laughter on the Rivers of Death: One Sailor's Humorous Experiences in Vietnam*. Bloomington, Ind.: AuthorHouse, 2007.

Forbes, John, and Robert Williams. *Riverine Force: Illustrated History of the Vietnam War*. New York: Bantam, 1987.

Fordham, Bruce. *Cherry Snow Cone*. Bloomington, Ind.: AuthorHouse, 2004.

Foster, Wynn F. *Fire on the Hangar Deck: Ordeal of the Oriskany*. Annapolis, Md.: Naval Institute Press, 2002.

Francillon, Rene. *Tonkin Gulf Yacht Club: U.S. Carrier Operations off Vietnam*. Annapolis, Md.: Naval Institute Press, 1988.

———. *Sailors to the End: The Deadly Fire on the USS Forrestal and the Heroes who Fought It*. New York: William Morrow, 2002.

Freeman, Gregory A. *Troubled Water: Race, Mutiny, and Bravery on the USS Kitty Hawk*. New York: Palgrave Macmillan, 2009.

Goldsmith, Wynn. *Papa Bravo Romeo: U.S. Navy Patrol Boats at War in Vietnam.* New York: Ballantine, 2001.

Gregory, Barry. *Vietnam Coastal and Riverine Forces Handbook.* New York: Sterling, 1988.

Larzelere, Alex. *The Coast Guard at War: Vietnam, 1965–1975.* Annapolis, Md.: Naval Institute Press, 1997.

Marolda, Edward J., and Dean C. Allard. *The U.S. Navy in the Vietnam War: An Illustrated History.* Dulles, Va.: Brassey's, 2002.

Schreadley, R. L. *From the Rivers to the Sea: The U.S. Navy in Vietnam.* Annapolis, Md.: Naval Institute Press, 1992.

Scotti, Paul C. *Coast Guard Action in Vietnam: Stories of Those Who Served.* Central Point, Ore.: Hellgate Press, 2000.

Sheppard, Don. *Riverine: A Brown-Water Sailor in the Delta, 1967.* Novato, Calif.: Presidio Press, 1992.

Sherwood, John Darrell. *Black Sailor, White Navy: Racial Unrest in the Fleet during the Vietnam War Era.* New York: New York University Press, 2007.

Symmes, Weymouth D. *War on the Rivers: A Swift Boat Sailor's Chronicle of the Battle for the Mekong Delta.* Missoula, Mont.: Pictorial Histories, 2004.

Tulich, Eugene N. *USCG, The United States Coast Guard in South East Asia during the Vietnam Conflict.* Washington, D.C.: Public Affairs Division, United States Coast Guard, 1975.

Uhlig, Frank, Jr., ed. *Vietnam: The Naval Story.* Annapolis, Md.: Naval Institute Press, 1986.

Zumwalt, Elmo. *On Watch.* New York: New York Times Books, 1976.

FIRSTHAND ACCOUNTS

General

Adler, Bill, ed. *Letters from Vietnam.* New York: Presidio Press, 2003.

Beesley, Stanley W. *Vietnam: The Heartland Remembers.* Norman, Okla.: University of Oklahoma Press, 1987.

Berry, John Stevens. *Those Gallant Men: On Trial in Vietnam.* Novato, Calif.: Presidio Press, 1984.

Cross, Charles T. *Born a Foreigner: A Memoir of the American Presence in Asia.* Lanham, Md.: Rowman & Littlefield, 1999.

Freeman, James M. *Hearts of Sorrow: Vietnamese-American Lives.* Stanford, Calif.: Stanford University Press, 1989.

Hargrove, Thomas R. *A Dragon Lives Forever: War and Rice in Vietnam's Mekong Delta, 1969–1991 and Beyond.* New York: Ivy Books, 1994.

Huchthausen, Peter A., and Nguyen Thi Lung. *Echoes of the Mekong.* Baltimore, Md.: Nautical & Aviation Publishing, 1996.

Lee, Eric. *Saigon to Jerusalem.* Jefferson, N.C.: McFarland, 1992.

Maurer, Harry. *Strange Ground: Americans in Vietnam, 1945–1975; An Oral History.* New York: Henry Holt, 1989.

Morrison, Joan, and Robert K. Morrison, eds. *From Camelot to Kent State: The Sixties Experience in the Words of Those Who Lived It*. New York: Oxford University Press, 2001.

Reilly, Thomas. *Next of Kin: A Brother's Journey to Wartime Vietnam*. Dulles, Va.: Brassey's, 2003.

Santoli, Al. *Everything We Had: An Oral History of the Vietnam War by Thirty-three American Soldiers Who Fought It*. New York: Random House, 1981.

———. *To Bear Any Burden: The Vietnam War and Its Aftermath in the Words of Americans and Southeast Asians*. New York: Dutton, 1985.

Steinman, Ron. *The Soldiers' Story: Vietnam in Their Own Words*. New York: TV Books, 1999.

Strober, Gerald S., and Deborah Hart Strober. *Let Us Begin Anew: An Oral History of the Kennedy Presidency*. New York: HarperCollins, 1993.

Takiff, Michael. *Brave Men, Gentle Heroes: American Fathers and Sons in World War II and Vietnam*. New York: Morrow, 2003.

Taylor, Thomas. *Where the Orange Blooms: One Man's War and Escape in Vietnam*. New York: McGraw-Hill, 1989.

Thatcher, Dennis. *Cut on Six Sides*. Quincy, Ohio: Thatcher Farms Publishing, 1999.

Willenson, Kim, et al. *The Bad War: An Oral History of the Vietnam War*. New York: New American Library, 1987.

Politicians

Acheson, Dean. *Present at the Creation: My Years in the State Department*. New York: Norton, 1969.

Albert, Carl B. *Little Giant: The Life and Times of Speaker Carl Albert*. Norman, Okla.: University of Oklahoma Press, 1990.

Ball, George. *The Past Has Another Pattern*. New York: Norton, 1982.

Bowles, Chester. *Promises to Keep: My Years in Public Life, 1941–1969*. New York: Harper & Row, 1971.

Califano, Joseph A., Jr. *The Triumph and Tragedy of Lyndon Johnson: The White House Years*. New York: Simon & Schuster, 1991.

Christian, George. *The President Steps Down: A Personal Memoir of the Transfer of Power*. New York: Macmillan, 1970.

Clifford, Clark, with Richard Holbrooke. *Counsel to the President: A Memoir*. New York: Random House, 1991.

Cooper, Chester L. *The Lost Crusade: America in Vietnam*. New York: Dodd, Mead, 1970.

Dirksen, Everett McKinley. *The Education of a Senator*. Champaign, Ill.: University of Illinois Press, 1998.

Enthoven, Alain C., and K. Wayne Smith. *How Much Is Enough? Shaping the Defense Program, 1961–1969*. New York: Harper & Row, 1971.

Ford, Gerald R. *A Time to Heal: The Autobiography of Gerald R. Ford*. New York: Harper & Row, 1979.

Fulbright, J. William. *The Arrogance of Power*. New York: Random House, 1966.

————. *The Pentagon Propaganda Machine*. New York: Liveright, 1970.

————. *The Crippled Giant: American Foreign Policy and Its Domestic Consequences*. New York: Vintage Books, 1972.

Goldwater, Barry M. *With No Apologies: The Personal and Political Memoirs of United States Senator Barry M. Goldwater*. New York: Morrow, 1979.

Goldwater, Barry M., with Jack Casserly. *Goldwater*. New York: Doubleday, 1988.

Goodwin, Richard N. *Triumph or Tragedy: Reflections on Vietnam*. New York: Random House, 1966.

————. *Remembering America: A Voice from the Sixties*. Boston: Little, Brown, 1988.

Gore, Albert A. *The Eye of the Storm: A People's Politics for the Seventies*. New York, 1970.

————. *Let the Glory Out: My South and Its Politics*. New York: Viking, 1972.

Gruening, Ernest. *Many Battles: The Autobiography of Ernest Gruening*. New York: Liveright, 1973.

Gruening, Ernest, and Herbert W. Beaser. *Vietnam Folly*. Washington, D.C.: National Press, 1968.

Gulley, Bill, with Mary Ellen Reese. *Breaking Cover*. New York: Simon & Schuster, 1980.

Haig, Alexander M., Jr., with Charles McCarry. *Inner Circles: How America Changed the World*. New York: Warner, 1992.

Haldeman, Harry Robbins. *The Haldeman Diaries: Inside the Nixon White House*. New York: Putnam, 1994.

Harriman, W. Averell. *America and Russia in a Changing World*. New York: Doubleday, 1971.

Humphrey, Hubert H. *The Education of a Public Man: My Life and Politics*. Garden City, N.Y.: Doubleday, 1976.

Johnson, Lyndon Baines. *The Vantage Point*. New York: Popular Library, 1971.

Johnson, U. Alexis, with Jef Olivarius McAllister. *The Right Hand of Power: The Memoirs of an American Diplomat*. Englewood Cliffs, N.J.: Prentice-Hall, 1984.

Kennedy, Edward M. *True Compass: A Memoir*. New York: Twelve, 2009.

Kennedy, Robert F. *To Seek a Newer World*. Garden City, N.Y.: Doubleday, 1967.

Kissinger, Henry. *White House Years and Years of Upheaval*. Boston: Little, Brown, 1982.

————. *Diplomacy*. New York: Simon & Schuster, 1994.

————. *Years of Renewal*. New York: Simon & Schuster, 1999.

————. *Crisis: The Anatomy of Two Major Foreign Policy Crises*. New York: Simon & Schuster, 2003.

————. *Ending the Vietnam War: A History of America's Involvement in and Extrication from the Vietnam War*. New York: Simon & Schuster, 2003.

Klein, Herbert G. *Making It Perfectly Clear: An Inside Account of Nixon's Love-Hate Relationship with the Media*. Garden City, N.Y.: Doubleday, 1980.

McGovern, George S. *Grassroots: The Autobiography of George McGovern*. New York: Random House, 1977.

McNamara, Robert S., with Brian VanDeMark. *In Retrospect: The Tragedy and Lessons of Vietnam*. New York: Random House, 1995.

Monagan, John S. *A Pleasant Institution: Key—C Major*. Lanham, Md.: University Press of America, 2002.

Nixon, Richard. *RN: The Memoirs of Richard Nixon*. New York: Grosset & Dunlap, 1978.

———. *No More Vietnams*. New York: Arbor House, 1985.

Nolting, Frederick, Jr. *From Trust to Tragedy*. New York: Praeger, 1989.

Rostow, Walt W. *The Diffusion of Power: An Essay in Recent History*. New York: Macmillan, 1972.

———. *The United States and the Regional Organization of Asia and the Pacific, 1965–1985*. Austin, Tex.: University of Texas Press, 1986.

———. *Concept and Controversy: Sixty Years of Taking Ideas to Market*. Austin, Tex.: University of Texas Press, 2003.

Rusk, Dean, with Richard Rusk. *As I Saw It*. New York: Norton, 1990.

Sullivan, William H. *Obbligato: Notes on a Foreign Service Career*. New York: Norton, 1984.

Taylor, Maxwell D. *Swords and Plowshares*. New York: Norton, 1972.

Whalen, Richard J. *Catch the Falling Flag: A Republican's Challenge to His Party*. Boston: Houghton Mifflin, 1972.

Nonmilitary General

Ashmore, Harry S., and William C. Baggs. *Mission to Hanoi: A Chronicle of Double-Dealing in High Places*. New York: Berkley, 1968.

Balaban, John. *Remembering Heaven's Face: A Moral Witness in Vietnam*. New York: Poseidon, 1991.

Brandon, Henry. *Anatomy of Error: The Inside Story of the Asian War on the Potomac, 1954–1969*. Boston: Gambit, 1969.

Carroll, James. *An American Requiem: God, My Father, and the War That Came between Us*. Boston: Houghton Mifflin, 1996.

Coward, Russell H. *A Voice from the Vietnam War*. Westport, Conn.: Greenwood, 2004.

Dawson, Alan. *55 Days: The Fall of South Vietnam*. Englewood Cliffs, N.J.: Prentice Hall, 1977.

Frankel, Max. *The Times of My Life and My Life with the Times*. New York: Random House, 1999.

Greene, Bob. *Homecoming: When the Soldiers Returned from Vietnam*. New York: Putnam, 1989.

Hefley, James C. *By Life or by Death*. Grand Rapids, Mich.: Zonderman, 1969.

Hickey, Gerald C. *Window on a War: An Anthropologist in the Vietnam Conflict*. Lubbock, Tex.: Texas Tech University Press, 2002.

James, Sam. *Servant on the Edge of History: Risking All for the Gospel in War-Ravaged Vietnam*. Garland, Tex.: Hannibal Books, 2005.

Martin, Earl S. *Reaching the Other Side*. New York: Crown Publishers, 1978.

McNamara, Francis Terry, with Adrian Hill. *Escape with Honor: My Last Hours in Vietnam*. Dulles, Va.: Brassey's, 1997.

Miller, Carolyn P. *Captured*. Chappaqua, N.Y.: Christian Herald Books, 1977.

Miller, Robert Hopkins. *Vietnam and Beyond: A Diplomat's Cold War Education*. Lubbock, Tex.: Texas Tech University Press, 2002.

Noel, Chris, with Bill Treadwell. *Matter of Survival: The "War" Jane Never Saw*. Boston: Branden, 1987.

Noel, Reuben, and Nancy Noel. *Saigon for a Song: The True Story of a Vietnam Gig to Remember*. Phoenix, Ariz.: UCS Press, 1987.

Patterson, Robert. *While They Died: A Memoir*. Emmett, Idaho: Patterson Press, 1993.

Roberts, Charles. *LBJ's Inner Circle*. New York: Delacorte, 1965.

Scalapino, Robert A. *From Leavenworth to Lhasa: Living in a Revolutionary Era*. Berkeley, Calif.: Institute for East Asian Studies, 2008.

Schwarz, George W., Jr. *April Fools: An American Remembers South Viet Nam's Final Days*. Baltimore, Md.: PublishAmerica, 2001.

Simpson, Howard R. *Tiger in the Barbed Wire: An American in Vietnam, 1952–1991*. Dulles, Va.: Brassey's, 1992.

Snepp, Frank. *Decent Interval: An Insider's Account of Saigon's Indecent End Told by the CIA's Chief Strategy Analyst in Vietnam*. Lawrence, Kans.: University Press of Kansas, 2002.

Taylor, Liz. *Dust of Life: Children of the Saigon Streets*. London: Hamish Hamilton, 1977.

Army

Adams, Carl S. *Remember the Alamo: A Sentry Dog Handler's View of Vietnam from the Perimeter of Phan Rang Air Base*. Fort Bragg, Calif.: Lost Coast Press, 2003.

Archer, Michael. *A Patch of Ground: Khe Sanh Remembered*. Central Point, Ore.: Hellgate Press, 2004.

Arthurs, Ted G. *Land with No Sun: A Year in Vietnam with the 173rd Airborne*. Mechanicsburg, Penn.: Stackpole Books, 2006.

Atkins, Stephen E. *Writing the War: My Ten Months in the Jungles, Streets and Paddies of South Vietnam, 1968*. Jefferson, N.C.: McFarland, 2009.

Bahnsen, John C., Jr. *American Warrior: A Combat Memoir of Vietnam*. Charleston, S.C.: Citadel, 2007.

Black, Robert W. *A Ranger Born: A Memoir of Combat and Valor from Korea to Vietnam*. New York: Ballantine, 2002.

Bordenkircher, Donald E., as told to Shirley A. Bordenkircher. *Tiger Cage: An Untold Story*. Cameron, W.Va.: Abby, 1998.

Bradfield, Carl W. *The Blue Spaders—Vietnam: A Private's Account*. Lakeland, Fla.: ASDA Publishing, 1992.

Bradford, Alfred S. *Some Even Volunteered: The First Wolfhounds Pacify Vietnam*. Westport, Conn.: Praeger, 1994.

Brelis, Dean. *The Face of South Vietnam*. Boston: Houghton Mifflin, 1968.

Brennan, Matthew. *Brennan's War: Vietnam, 1965–1969*. Novato, Calif.: Presidio Press, 1985.

Briscoe, Bobby. *The Jungle Warriors: A True Story*. Castroville, Tex.: J. T. Advertising and Graphics, 2000.

Brown, F. C. *Delta Advisor: The War at the Rice Roots Level; Chau Doc, Vietnam, 1969–1970*. Bennington, Vt.: Merriam Press, 1990.

Brown, Fred Leo. *Vietnam War Diary*. Palos Heights, Ill.: Combat Ready Publishing, 1998.

Brown, John M. G. *Rice Paddy Grunt: Unfading Memories of the Vietnam Generation*. Lake Bluff, Ill.: Regnery, 1986.

Brown, Richard L. *Palace Gate: Under Siege in Hue City, Tet, January 1968*. Atglen, Penn.: Schiffer Military History, 1995.

Burnam, John C. *Dog Tags of Courage: The Turmoil of War and the Rewards of Companionship*. Fort Bragg, Calif.: Lost Coast Press, 1999.

Burns, Richard R. *Pathfinder: First In, Last Out*. New York: Ballantine, 2002.

Callaway, Joseph W., Jr. *Mekong First Light*. New York: Presidio, 2004.

Calley, William L., and John Sack. *Lieutenant Calley: His Own Story*. New York: Viking, 1971.

Christopher, Ronald Lee. *A Troop 9th Cavalry*. Baltimore, Md.: PublishAmerica, 2006.

Clarke, Bruce B. G. *Expendable Warriors: The Battle of Khe Sanh and the Vietnam War*. Westport, Conn.: Praeger, 2007.

Cleland, Max. *Strong at the Broken Places: A Personal Story*. Atlanta, Ga.: Longstreet Press, 2000.

Cleland, Max, with Ben Raines. *Heart of a Patriot: How I Found the Courage to Survive Vietnam, Walter Reed and Karl Rove*. New York: Simon & Schuster, 2009.

Clodfelter, Michael. *Mad Minutes and Vietnam Months*. Jefferson, N.C.: McFarland, 1988.

Coleman, J. D. *Pleiku: The Dawn of Helicopter Warfare in Vietnam*. New York: St. Martin's Press, 1988.

Corbett, John. *West Dickens Avenue: A Marine at Khe Sanh*. Novato, Calif.: Presidio Press, 2003.

Dancy, Tyrone T. *Serving under Adverse Conditions: Wars and the Aftermath*. Bloomington, Ind.: AuthorHouse, 2005.

Downs, Frederick, Jr. *The Killing Zone: My Life in the Vietnam War*. New York: Norton, 1978.

———. *Aftermath*. New York: Norton, 1984.

Dunn, Joe P. *Desk Warrior: Memoirs of a Combat REMF*. Needham Heights, Mass.: Pearson Custom Publishing, 1999.

Eby, Omar. *A House in Hue*. Scottdale, Penn.: Herald Press, 1968.

Estep, James L. *Comanche Six: Company Commander, Vietnam*. Novato, Calif.: Presidio Press, 1991.

Fitz-Enz, David G. *Why a Soldier? A Signal Corpsman's Tour from Vietnam to the Moscow Hot Line*. New York: Ballantine, 2000.

Flood, Charles Bracelen. *The War of the Innocents*. New York: McGraw-Hill, 1970.

Gadd, Charles. *Line Doggie: Foot Soldier in Vietnam*. Novato, Calif.: Presidio Press, 1987.

Glasser, Ronald J. *365 Days*. New York: George Braziller, 1971.

Grady, Bernard E. *On the Tiger's Back*. Brunswick, Maine: Biddle, 1994.

Gwin, Larry. *Baptism: A Vietnam Memoir*. New York: Ivy Books, 1999.

Hackworth, David H., and Eilhys England. *Steel My Soldiers' Hearts: The Hopeless to Hardcore Transformation of 4th Battalion, 39th Infantry, United States Army, Vietnam.* New York: Rugged Land, 2002.

Hackworth, David H., and Julie Sherman. *About Face: The Odyssey of an American Warrior.* New York: Simon & Schuster, 1989.

Hall, Ed Y. *Valley of the Shadow.* Spartanburg, S.C.: Honoribus Press, 1986.

Harrison, Benjamin L. *Hell on a Hill Top: America's Last Major Battle in Vietnam.* Lincoln, Nebr.: iUniverse, 2004.

Hartline, David L. *Vietnam: What a Soldier Gives.* Summerville, Ga.: Espy, 1984.

Haworth, Larry. *Tales of Thunder Run: The Convoys, the Noise, the Ambushes . . . Stories of QL 13, the Route 66 of Viet Nam.* Eugene, Ore.: ACW Press, 2004.

Hayes, Roger. *On Point: A Rifleman's Year in the Boonies; Vietnam, 1967–1968.* Novato, Calif.: Presidio Press, 2000.

Hemphill, Robert. *Platoon: Bravo Company.* Pittsburgh: RoseDog Books, 2006.

Henderson, Charles. *Goodnight Saigon: The True Story of the U.S. Marines' Last Days in Vietnam.* New York: Berkley Caliber, 2005.

Herbert, Anthony. *Soldier.* New York: Holt, Rinehart & Winston, 1973.

Herr, Michael. *Dispatches.* New York: Knopf, 1977.

Herrgesell, Margaret, ed. *Dear Margaret, Today I Died . . . Letters from Vietnam by LTC Oscar Herrgesell.* San Antonio, Tex.: Naylor, 1974.

Herrington, Stuart. *Peace with Honor? An American Reports on Vietnam, 1973–1975.* Novato, Calif.: Presidio Press, 1983.

Herrod, Randy. *Blue's Bastards.* Washington, D.C.: Regnery Gateway, 1989.

Hogue, Richard. *We Were the Third Herd.* Morrison, Colo.: Richlyn Publishing, 2003.

Hovde, Jon, and Maureen Anderson. *Left for Dead: A Second Life after Vietnam.* Minneapolis, Minn.: University of Minnesota Press, 2005.

Hughes, Larry. *You Can See a Lot Standing under a Flare in the Republic of Vietnam.* New York: Morrow, 1969.

Humphries, James F. *Through the Valley: Vietnam, 1967–1968.* Boulder, Colo.: Lynne Rienner, 1999.

Irzyk, Albin F. *Unsung Heroes, Saving Saigon.* Raleigh, N.C.: Ivy House, 2008.

Jacobs, Jack, and Douglas Century. *If Not Now, When? Duty and Sacrifice in America's Time of Need.* New York: Berkley, 2008.

James, L. D. *Unfortunate Sons: A True Story of Young Men and War.* Washington, Del.: Cambridge Dent, 2005.

Jorgenson, Kregg P. J. *Acceptable Loss.* New York: Ivy Books, 1991.

Jury, Mark. *The Vietnam Photo Book.* New York: Grossman, 1971.

Kane, Rod. *Veteran's Day: A Combat Oddyssey.* New York: Crown, 1990.

Kinnard, Douglas. *The War Managers: American Generals Reflect on Vietnam.* Annapolis, Md.: Naval Institute Press, 2007.

Kitchin, Dennis. *War in Aquarius: Memoir of an American Infantryman in Action along the Cambodian Border during the Vietnam War.* Jefferson, N.C.: McFarland, 1994.

Kukler, Michael A. *Operation Barooom.* Gastonia, N.C.: TPC, 1980.

Lacombe, Tom. *Light Ruck: Vietnam, 1969.* Fort Valley, Va.: Loft Press, 2002.

Lanning, Michael Lee. *The Only War We Had.* New York: Ivy Books, 1987.
———. *Vietnam, 1969–1970: A Company Commander's Journal.* New York: Ivy Books, 1988.
Larson, Mike. *Heroes: A Year in Vietnam with the First Air Cavalry Division.* Bloomington, Ind.: iUniverse, 2008.
Lawrence, A. T. *Crucible Vietnam: Memoir of an Infantry Lieutenant.* Jefferson, N.C.: McFarland, 2009.
Leninger, Jack. *Time Heals No Wounds.* New York: Ivy Books, 1993.
Leppelman, John. *Blood on the Risers: An Airborne Soldier's Thirty-five Months in Vietnam.* New York: Ivy Books, 1991.
Lewis, Jack, ed. *Dateline: Vietnam.* North Hollywood, Calif.: Challenge Publications, 1966.
Maberry, John. *Waiting for Westmoreland.* Alexandria, Va.: Eagle Peak Press, 2007.
Mack, Richard E. *Memoir of a Cold War Soldier.* Kent, Ohio: Kent State University Press, 2001.
Maguire, Steve. *Jungle in Black.* New York: Bantam, 1992.
Mahler, Michael D. *Ringed in Steel: Armored Cavalry, Vietnam, 1967–1968.* Novato, Calif.: Presidio Press, 1986.
Maslowski, Peter, and Don Winslow. *Looking for a Hero: Staff Sergeant Joe Ronnie Hooper and the Vietnam War.* Lincoln, Nebr.: University of Nebraska Press, 2005.
McDonald, Cherokee Paul. *Into the Green: A Reconnaissance by Fire.* New York: Plum, 2001.
McDonough, James. *Platoon Leader.* Novato, Calif.: Presidio Press, 1985.
Menzel, Sewall. *Battle Captain: Cold War Campaigning with the U.S. Army in Vietnam, Cambodia, and Laos, 1967–1971.* Bloomington, Ind.: AuthorHouse, 2007.
Merritt, William E. *Where the Rivers Ran Backward.* Athens, Ga.: University of Georgia Press, 1989.
Mertel, Kenneth D. *Year of the Horse: Vietnam.* New York: Exposition Press, 1968.
Montgomery, George. *Till We All Die.* New York: Carlton, 1991.
Moore, Harold G., and Joseph L. Galloway. *We Were Soldiers Once . . . and Young: Ia Drang, the Battle That Changed the War in Vietnam.* New York: Random House, 1992.
Morgan, Paul B. *K-9 Soldiers: Vietnam and After.* Central Point, Ore.: Hellgate Press, 1999.
Murphy, Ed, and Zoeann Murphy. *Vietnam: Our Father Daughter Journey.* New York: Philmark Press, 2006.
Nesser, John A. *The Ghosts of Thua Thien: An American Soldier's Memoir of Vietnam.* Jefferson, N.C.: McFarland, 2008.
Nylen, Robert. *Guts: Combat, Hell-raising, Cancer, Business Start-ups, and Undying Love; One American Guy's Reckless, Lucky Life.* New York: Random House, 2009.
Olsen, Howard. *Issues of the Heart: Memoirs of an Artilleryman in Vietnam.* Jefferson, N.C.: McFarland, 1990.
O'Meara, Andrew P., Jr. *Accidental Warrior: The Forging of an American Soldier.* Oakland, Ore.: Elderberry Press, 2003.
———. *Only the Dead Came Home: Vietnam's Hidden Casualties.* Oakland, Ore.: Elderberry Press, 2003.

Oplinger, Jon. *Quang Tri Cadence: Memoir of a Rifle Platoon Leader in the Mountains of Vietnam*. Jefferson, N.C.: McFarland, 1993.

Pakis, Vic. *Immigrant Soldier: From the Baltics to Vietnam*. Central Point, Ore.: Hellgate Press, 1999.

Parker, James E., Jr. *Last Man Out*. Camden, S.C.: John Culler & Sons, 1996.

Parrish, Robert D. *Combat Recon: My Year with the ARVN*. New York: St. Martin's Press, 1991.

Peterson, Robert. *Rites of Passage: Odyssey of a Grunt*. Middleton, Wisc.: Badger Books, 1997.

Pezzoli, Ray, Jr. *A Year in Hell: Memoir of an Army Foot Soldier Turned Reporter in Vietnam, 1965–1966*. Jefferson, N.C.: McFarland, 2006.

Phillips, Rufus. *Why Vietnam Matters: An Eyewitness Account of Lessons Not Learned*. Annapolis, Md.: Naval Institute Press, 2008.

Puckett, David. *Memories*. New York: Vantage, 1987.

Rast, Franklin D. *Don's Nam*. Universal Publishers, 1999.

Reich, Dale Everett. *Rockets Like Rain: A Year in Vietnam*. Central Point, Ore.: Hellgate Press, 2001.

Ronnau, Christopher. *Blood Trails: The Combat Diary of a Foot Soldier in Vietnam*. New York: Presidio, 2006.

Russell, Norman L. *Suicide Charlie: A Vietnam War Story*. Westport, Conn.: Praeger, 1993.

Schild, James J. *For Garry Owen in Glory: The True Account of an Airmobile Platoon Leader in Vietnam, 1968–1969*. Florissant, Mo.: Auto Review, 1989.

Schneider, Ches. *From Classrooms to Claymores: A Teacher at War in Vietnam*. New York: Ivy Books, 1999.

Schwarzkopf, H. Norman, with Peter Petrie. *It Doesn't Take a Hero*. New York: Bantam, 1992.

Sefton, G. William. *It Was My War: I'll Remember It the Way I Want To*. Manhattan, Kans.: Sunflower University Press, 1994.

Senka, John T. *Wounded Body, Healing Spirit: An Arkport Soldier's Inspirational Journey as a Vietnam Combat Veteran*. Binghamton, N.Y.: Brundage, 2004.

Shelton, James E. *The Beast Was Out There: The 28th Infantry Black Lions and the Battle of Ong Thanh, Vietnam, October 1967*. Chicago: Cantigny First Division Foundation, 2002.

Smith, George W. *The Siege at Hue*. New York: Ballantine, 2000.

Solis, Gary D. *Son Thang: An American War Crime*. Annapolis, Md.: Naval Institute Press, 1997.

Starry, Donn A. *Armored Combat in Vietnam*. Indianapolis, Ind.: Bobbs-Merrill, 1980.

Steinbeck, John, IV. *In Touch*. New York: Dell, 1970.

Swauger, Ed. *Earning the CIB: The Making of a Soldier in Vietnam*. Yellville, Alaska: Whitehall Publishing, 2005.

Tauber, Peter. *The Sunshine Soldiers*. New York: Simon & Schuster, 1971.

Teel, Joe, Jr. *Welcome Home, Joe*. Parker, Colo.: Outskirts Press, 2007.

Thomas, Jack Lyndon. *Coyote Jack: Drawing Meaning from Life and Vietnam; A Memoir*. Houston, Tex.: Lyndonjacks, 2006.

Tonsetic, Robert L. *Warriors: An Infantryman's Memoir of Vietnam*. New York: Presidio, 2004.

———. *Days of Valor: An Inside Account of the Bloodiest Six Months of the Vietnam War*. Philadelphia: Casemate, 2007.

———. *Forsaken Warriors: The Story of an American Advisor with the South Vietnamese Rangers and Airborne, 1970–1971*. Philadelphia: Casemate, 2009.

Topmiller, Robert J. *Red Clay on My Boots: Encounters with Khe Sanh, 1968 to 2005*. Minneapolis, Minn.: Kirk House, 2007.

Tripp, Nathaniel. *Father, Soldier, Son: Memoir of a Platoon Leader in Vietnam*. Hanover, N.H.: Steerforth, 1997.

Turley, Gerald H. *The Easter Offensive*. Novato, Calif.: Presidio Press, 1985.

Wager, John. *Quiet Year at War*. Lanham, Md.: Hamilton Books, 2008.

Walker, Paul D. *Jungle Dragoon: The Memoir of an Armored Cav Platoon Leader in Vietnam*. Novato, Calif.: Presidio Press, 1999.

Warr, Nicholas. *Phase Line Green: The Battle for Hue, 1968*. Annapolis, Md.: Naval Institute Press, 1997.

Watson, George M. *Voices from the Rear: Vietnam, 1969–1970*. Bloomington, Ind.: Xlibris, 2001.

Webster, Daniel C. *The Pucker Factor: One Noncombatant's Vietnam Memoirs*. Bloomington, Ind.: 1stBooks, 2003.

Westmoreland, William. *A Soldier Reports: Memoirs of the Man Who Commanded U.S. Forces in Vietnam from 1964 to 1968*. New York: Doubleday, 1976.

White, Joseph J. *Ebony and White: The Story of the K-9 Corps*. Wilsonville, Ore.: Doral, 1996.

Wiknik, Arthur, Jr. *Nam Sense: Surviving Vietnam with the 101st Airborne Division*. Havertown, Penn.: Casemate, 2005.

Willbanks, James H. *The Battle of An Loc*. Bloomington, Ind.: Indiana University Press, 2005.

Wilson, Jim. *The Sons of Bardstown: 25 Years of Vietnam in an American Town*. New York: Crown, 1994.

Wise, E. Tayloe. *Eleven Bravo: A Skytrooper's Memoir of War in Vietnam*. Jefferson, N.C.: McFarland, 2004.

Wolff, Tobias. *In Pharaoh's Army: Memories of the Lost War*. New York: Knopf, 1994.

Young, Rick. *Combat Police: U.S. Army Military Police in Vietnam*. Farmingdale, N.J.: Sendraak's Writings, 1997.

Zumbro, Ralph. *Tank Sergeant*. Novato, Calif.: Presidio Press, 1986.

Helicopter Pilots

Ballentine, David A. *Gunbird Driver: A Marine Huey Pilot's War in Vietnam*. Annapolis, Md.: Naval Institute Press, 2008.

Beamon, Samuel K. *Flying Death: The Vietnam Experience*. Bloomington, Ind.: AuthorHouse, 2007.

Boyle, Jerome M. *Apache Sunrise*. New York: Ivy Books, 1994.

Brandt, Robert J. *Thunderbird Lounge*. Victoria, British Columbia: Trafford, 2001.

Brown, N. Glenn. *Blue Max: Missions and Memories*. Parker, Colo.: Outskirts Press, 2006.

Carey, Ronald. *The War above the Trees*. Victoria, British Columbia: Trafford Publishing, 2004.

Carlock, Chuck. *Firebirds: The Best First-person Account of Helicopter Combat in Vietnam Ever Written*. New York: Summit Books, 1995.

Childers, Jerry W. *Without Parachutes: How I Survived 1,000 Attack Helicopter Combat Missions in Vietnam*. Bloomington, Ind.: AuthorHouse, 2006.

Eastman, David L. *Outlaws in Vietnam: 1966–1967 in the Delta*. Portsmouth, N.H.: Peter E. Randall, 2001.

Fino, Dominic. *The Making of a Falcon*. New York: Vantage, 1995.

Gebhart, John J. *LBJ's Hired Gun: A Marine Corps Helicopter Gunner and the War in Vietnam*. Havertown, Penn.: Casemate, 2007.

Grant, William T. *Wings of the Eagle: A Kingsmen's Story*. New York: Ivy Books, 1994.

Gross, Chuck. *Rattler One-Seven: A Vietnam Helicopter Pilot's War Story*. Denton, Tex.: University of North Texas Press, 2004.

Johnson, Tom A. *To the Limit: An Air Cav Huey Pilot in Vietnam*. Dulles, Va.: Potomac Books, 2006.

Joyce, James. *Pucker Factor 10: Memoir of a U.S. Army Helicopter Pilot in Vietnam*. Jefferson, N.C.: McFarland, 2003.

Kelly, Daniel E. *Seawolves: First Choice*. New York: Ivy Books, 1998.

Knott, Richard. *Fire from the Sky: Seawolf Gunships in the Mekong Delta*. Annapolis, Md.: Naval Institute Press, 2005.

Lake, Bruce. *Fifteen Hundred Feet over Vietnam: A Marine Helicopter Pilot's Diary*. Haverhill, N.H.: Almine Library, 1990.

Lazzarini, Tony. *Highest Traditions*. Larkspur, Calif.: Voyager Publications, 2003.

Mains, Randolph P. *Dear Mom, I'm Alive: Letters Home from Blackwidow 25*. New York: Avon, 1992.

Marshall, Tom. *The Price of Exit*. New York: Ivy Books, 1998.

Mason, Robert. *Chickenhawk*. New York: Viking, 1983.

Meacham, William C. *Lest We Forget: The Kingsmen, 101st Aviation Battalion, 1968*. New York: Ivy Books, 1999.

Miller, Bob. *Kill Me If You Can, You SOB*. Tucson, Ariz.: Wheatmark, 2007.

Mills, Hugh L., Jr., with Robert A. Anderson. *Low Level Hell: A Scout Pilot in the Big Red One*. Novato, Calif.: Presidio Press, 1992.

Novosel, Michael J. *Dustoff: The Memoir of an Army Aviator*. Novato, Calif.: Presidio Press, 1999.

Robinson, Robert W. *Scarface 42: United States Marine Corps Helicopter Air/Ground Support, Vietnam "In Close."* Bismarck, N.Dak.: Tailwind Publications, 2008.

Schatz, James F. *Shotgunner: The Story of a Helicopter Door Gunner in Vietnam*. New York: Vantage, 2000.

Sever, Al. *Xin Loi, Viet Nam: Memoir of the War over Viet Nam*. Martinsburg, W.Va.: Quiet Storm, 2002.

Sinsigalli, R. J. *Chopper Pilot: Not All of Us Were Heroes.* Paducah, Ky.: Turner Publishing, 2002.

Sisk, Robert W. *Wings for the Valiant.* New York: Warner, 1991.

Smith, Tom. *Easy Target: The Long, Strange Trip of a Scout Pilot in Vietnam.* Novato, Calif.: Presidio Press, 1996.

Spalding, Richard D. *Centaur Flights.* New York: Ivy Books, 1997.

Stoffey, Bob. *Cleared Hot: A Marine Combat Pilot's Vietnam.* New York: St. Martin's Press, 1992.

Sturkey, Marion F. *Bonnie-Sue: A Marine Corps Helicopter Squadron in Vietnam.* Plum Branch, S.C.: Heritage, 1996.

Winter, Ronald E. *Masters of the Art: A Fighting Marine's Memoir of Vietnam.* New York: Carlton Press, 1989.

Zahn, Randy R. *Snake Pilot: Flying the Cobra Attack Helicopter in Vietnam.* Dulles, Va.: Potomac Books, 2003.

Marines

Akins, John. *Nam Au Go Go: Falling for the Vietnamese Goddess of War.* Port Jefferson, N.Y.: Vineyard Press, 2005.

Ball, Phil. *Ghosts and Shadows: A Marine in Vietnam, 1968–1969.* Jefferson, N.C.: McFarland, 1998.

Barker, Dan A. *Warrior of the Heart.* Chevy Chase, Md.: Burning Cities, 1992.

Brown, Jim. *Impact Zone: The Battle of the DMZ in Vietnam, 1967–1968.* Tuscaloosa, Ala.: University of Alabama Press, 2004.

Camp, Richard D., Jr., with Eric Hammel. *Lima-6: A Marine Company Commander in Vietnam.* Pacifica, Calif.: Pacifica Press, 1999.

Caputo, Philip. *A Rumor of War.* New York: Holt, Rinehart & Winston, 1977.

Clark, Clair William, II. *Land, Sea and Foreign Shore: A Missileer's Story.* Bloomington, Ind.: Xlibris, 2002.

Clark, Johnnie M. *Guns Up!* New York: Ballantine, 1988.

Coan, James P. *Con Thien: The Hill of Angels.* Tuscaloosa, Ala.: University of Alabama Press, 2004.

Conroy, Michael R. *Don't Tell America.* Red Bluff, Calif.: Eagle Publishing, 1994.

Cooper, Charles G., with Richard E. Goodspeed. *Cheers and Tears: A Marine's Story of Combat in Peace and War.* Victoria, British Columbia: Trafford Press, 2002.

Cox, Franklin. *Lullabies for Lieutenants: Memoir of a Marine Forward Observer in Vietnam, 1965–1966.* Jefferson, N.C.: McFarland, 2010.

Croizat, Victor J. *Journey among Warriors: The Memoirs of a Marine.* Shippensburg, Penn.: White Mane Publishing, 1996.

Culbertson, John J. *Operation Tuscaloosa: 2nd Battalion, 5th Marines, at An Hoa, 1967.* New York: Ivy Books, 1997.

———. *A Sniper in the Arizona: 2d Battalion, 5th Marines, in the Arizona Territory, 1967.* New York: Ivy Books, 1999.

———. *13 Cent Killers: The 5th Marine Snipers in Vietnam.* New York: Ballantine, 2003.

Dark, Gene R. *The Brutality of War: A Memoir of Vietnam*. Lincoln, Nebr.: iUniverse, 2007.

Doherty, Jerome. *A Civilian in Green Clothes*. Raleigh, N.C.: Ivy House, 2007.

Ehrhart, William Daniel. *Vietnam-Perkasie: A Combat Marine's Memoir*. New York: Zebra, 1985.

———. *Going Back: An Ex-Marine Returns to Vietnam*. Jefferson, N.C.: McFarland, 1987.

———. *Passing Time: Memoir of a Vietnam Veteran against the War*. Jefferson, N.C.: McFarland, 1989.

———. *In the Shadow of Vietnam: Essays, 1977–1991*. Jefferson, N.C.: McFarland, 1991.

———. *Ordinary Lives: Platoon 1005 and the Vietnam War*. Philadelphia: Temple University Press, 1999.

Estes, Jack. *A Field of Innocence*. New York: Warner, 1990.

Farrington, Arthur C. *Pacific Odyssey: Connections*. Manhattan, Kans.: Sunflower University Press, 2003.

Flynn, Robert. *A Personal War in Vietnam*. College Station, Tex.: Texas A&M University Press, 1989.

Flynn, Thomas. *A Voice of Hope*. Baltimore, Md.: American Literary Press, 1994.

Fox, Wesley L. *Marine Rifleman: Forty-three Years in the Corps*. Dulles, Va.: Brassey's, 2002.

Gems, Gerald R. *Viet Nam Vignettes: Tales of the Magnificent Bastards*. Haworth, N.J.: St. Johann Press, 2006.

Glass, Doyle D. *Lions of Medina: An Epic Account of Marine Valor during the Vietnam War*. Louisville, Ky.: Coleche Press, 2007.

Goodson, Barry L. *CAP Môt: The Story of a Marine Special Forces Unit in Vietnam, 1968–1969*. Denton, Tex.: University of North Texas Press, 1997.

Griffis, Don W. *Eagle Days: A Marine Legal/Infantry Officer in Vietnam*. Tuscaloosa, Ala.: University of Alabama Press, 2007.

Hammel, Eric. *Ambush Valley: I Corps, Vietnam; The Story of a Marine Infantry Battalion's Battle for Survival*. Novato, Calif.: Presidio Press, 1990.

Hardwick, William H. *Down South: One Tour in Vietnam*. New York: Ballantine, 2004.

Helms, E. Michael. *The Proud Bastards*. New York: Zebra, 1990.

Hodgins, Michael C. *Reluctant Warrior: A True Story of Duty and Heroism in Vietnam*. New York: Fawcett, 1997.

Jackson, Richard D. *Yesterdays Are Forever: A Rite of Passage through the Marine Corps and Vietnam War*. Norcross, Ga.: Protea, 2000.

Jaunal, Jack W. *Vietnam '68: Jack's Journal*. San Francisco: Denson Press, 1981.

Jensen, Ronald John. *Tail End Charlie: Memoir of a United States Marine in the Vietnam War*. Jefferson, N.C.: McFarland, 2004.

Jordan, Kenneth N., Sr. *Marines under Fire: Alpha 1/1 in Vietnam; From Con Thien to Hue and Khe Sanh*. Frederick, Md.: Publish America, 2008.

Kelly, Jeff. *DMZ Diary: A Combat Marine's Vietnam Memoir*. Jefferson, N.C.: McFarland, 1992.

Kirschke, James J. *Not Going Home Alone: A Marine's Story*. New York: Ballantine, 2001.

Kovic, Ron. *Born on the Fourth of July*. New York: McGraw-Hill, 1976.

Krulak, Victor H. *First to Fight: An Inside View of the U.S. Marine Corps*. Annapolis, Md.: Naval Institute Press, 1984.

Kugler, Ed. *Dead Center: A Marine Sniper's Two-Year Odyssey in the Vietnam War*. New York: Ivy Books, 1999.

Kurth, Gerald F. *Walk with Me: A Vietnam Experience*. Leawood, Kans.: Leathers Publishing, 2000.

Lisi, Patrick J. *My Time in Hell*. Port Washington, N.Y.: Ashley Books, 1977.

Maffioli, Len, with Bruce H. Norton. *Grown Gray in War*. Annapolis, Md.: Naval Institute Press, 1996.

McGarrah, Jim. *A Temporary Sort of Peace: A Memoir of Vietnam*. Indianapolis, Ind.: Indiana Historical Society, 2007.

McLean, Jack. *Loon: A Marine Story*. Novato, Calif.: Presidio Press, 2009.

McNally, Paul A. *The Best of the Best: The Fighting 5th Marines Vietnam: Dying Delta*. Parker, Colo.: Outskirts Press, 2008.

Merson, John. *War Lessons: How I Fought to be a Hero and Learned That War is Terror*. Berkeley, Calif.: North Atlantic Books, 2008.

Mulldune, David W. *The Mailman Went UA: A Vietnam Memoir*. Bennington, Vt.: Merriam Press, 2009.

Myers, Donald F. *Your War, My War: A Marine in Vietnam*. Raleigh, N.C.: Pentland Press, 2000.

Peavey, Robert E. *Praying for Slack: A Marine Corps Tank Commander in Vietnam*. St. Paul, Minn.: Zenith Press, 2004.

Peterson, Michael E. *The Combined Action Platoons: The U.S. Marines' Other War in Vietnam*. New York: Praeger, 1989.

Puller, Lewis B., Jr. *Fortunate Son: The Autobiography of Lewis B. Puller, Jr.* New York: Bantam, 1993.

Roberts, Craig, and Charles W. Sasser. *The Walking Dead: A Marine's Story of Vietnam*. New York: Pocket Books, 1989.

Shellenbarger, Jean. *The 9th Engineer Battalion, First Marine Division, in Vietnam: 35 Personal Accounts*. Jefferson, N.C.: McFarland, 2000.

Spiller, Harry. *Death Angel: A Vietnam Memoir of a Bearer of Death Messages to Families*. Jefferson, N.C.: McFarland, 1992.

———. *Scars of Vietnam: Personal Accounts by Veterans and Their Families*. Jefferson, N.C.: McFarland, 1994.

Sympson, Kenneth P. *Images from the Otherland: Memoir of a United States Marine Corps Artillery Officer in Vietnam*. Jefferson, N.C.: McFarland, 1995.

Truitt, W. Charles. *Pop a Yellow Smoke and Other Memories! From a Combat Veteran Marine, Vietnam, 1969–1970*. Ozark, Ala.: ACW Press, 2005.

Walt, Lewis W. *Strange War, Strange Strategy: A General's Report on Vietnam*. New York: Funk & Wagnalls, 1970.

Ward, Joseph T. *Dear Mom: A Sniper's Vietnam*. New York: Ivy Books, 1991.

West, Francis J., Jr. *The Village*. New York: Harper & Row, 1972.

Woodruff, Mark W. *Fox Trot Ridge: A Battle Remembered*. St. Petersburg, Fla.: Vandamere Press, 2002.

Air Force

Barry, Bill. *A Trash Hauler in Vietnam: Memoir of Four Tactical Airlift Tours, 1965–1968*. Jefferson, N.C.: McFarland, 2008.

Basel, Gene I. *Pak Six: A Story of the War in the Skies of North Vietnam*. New York: Jove, 1987.

Bell, Kenneth H. *100 Missions North: A Fighter Pilot's Story of the Vietnam War*. Dulles, Va.: Brassey's, 1993.

Blesse, Frederick C. *Check Six: A Fighter Pilot Looks Back*. New York: Ballantine, 1992.

Bottomly, Heath. *Dishonored Glory: Colonel Bo's Vietnam War Journal*. Bloomington, Ind.: AuthorHouse, 2008.

Brantley, Samuel. *Zero Dark Thirty*. Central Point, Ore.: Hellgate Press, 2002.

Broughton, Jacksel. *Thud Ridge*. Philadelphia: Lippincott, 1969.

———. *Going Downtown: The War against Hanoi and Washington*. New York: Orion, 1988.

———. *Rupert Red Two: A Fighter Pilot's Life from Thunderbolts to Thunderchiefs*. Minneapolis, Minn.: Zenith Press, 2008.

Busch, Dennis. *Psywarrior: The Misadventures of an Insolent Warrior*. Parker, Colo.: Outskirts Press, 2009.

Capozzella, Vincent. *Headhunter One One: The Vietnamese Memoir of a Recon-Observation Pilot*. Westminster, Md.: Heritage Books, 2007.

Chinnery, Philip D. *Life on the Line*. New York: St. Martin's Press, 1988.

Cook, Jerry W. *Once a Fighter Pilot*. New York: McGraw-Hill, 1997.

Eubank, Taylor. *Alone, Unarmed, and Unafraid: Tales of Reconnaissance in Vietnam*. Jefferson, N.C.: McFarland, 1992.

Flanagan, John F. *Vietnam above the Treetops: A Forward Air Controller Reports*. New York: Praeger, 1992.

George, Ronnie Ridley. *Airspeed, Altitude, and a Sense of Humor: The Adventures of a Jet Tanker Pilot*. Austin, Tex.: Eakin Press, 2001.

Grimes, Keith R. *Special Operations Weatherman: An Oral Autobiography*. Scott AFB, Ill.: Military Airlift Command, United States Air Force, 1978.

Harrison, Marshall. *A Lonely Kind of War: Forward Air Controller, Vietnam*. Novato, Calif.: Presidio Press, 1989.

Hathorn, Reginald. *Here There Are Tigers: The Secret Air War in Laos and North Vietnam, 1968–1969*. Harrisburg, Penn.: Stackpole Books, 2008.

Hoopes, Townsend. *The Limits of Intervention*. New York: McKay, 1969.

Jackson, Mike, and Tara Dixon-Engel. *Naked in Da Nang: A Forward Air Controller in Vietnam*. St. Paul, Minn.: Zenith Press, 2004.

Johnson, Howard C., and Ian A. O'Connor. *Scrappy: Memoir of a U.S. Fighter Pilot in Korea and Vietnam*. Jefferson, N.C.: McFarland, 2007.

LeMay, Curtis E., with Dale O. Smith. *America Is in Danger*. New York: Funk & Wagnalls, 1968.

Lenski, Al. *Magic 100: The Story of an F-105, 100 Combat Mission Tour, NVN '67*. Paducah, Ky.: Turner, 1995.

Luckett, Perry D., and Charles L. Byler. *Tempered Steel: The Three Wars of Triple Air Force Cross Winner Jim Kasler*. Dulles, Va.: Potomac Books, 2005.

McCarthy, Mike. *Phantom Reflections: The Education of an American Fighter Pilot in Vietnam*. Westport, Conn.: Praeger, 2006.

Moriarty, J. Michael. *Ground Attack Vietnam: The Marines Who Controlled the Skies*. New York: Ivy Books, 1993.

Myers, Richard B., with Malcolm McConnell. *Eyes on the Horizon: Serving on the Front Lines of National Security*. New York: Threshold Editions, 2009.

Rasimus, Ed. *When Thunder Rolled: An F-105 Pilot over North Vietnam*. Washington, D.C.: Smithsonian Institution Press, 2003.

———. *Palace Cobra: A Fighter Pilot in the Vietnam Air War*. New York: St. Martin's Press, 2006.

Rock, Edward T., ed. *First In, Last Out: Stories by the Wild Weasels*. Bloomington, Ind.: AuthorHouse, 2005.

Ross, Bob. *The Warriors: Reflections of a Fighter Pilot, Test Pilot, and Veteran of the Air Wars over Vietnam*. Las Cruces, N.Mex.: Yucca Tree, 2002.

Samuel, Wolfgang W. E. *Glory Days: The Untold Story of the Men Who Flew the B-66 Destroyer into the Face of Fear*. Atglen, Penn.: Schiffer Military History, 2008.

Shepperd, Don, ed. *Misty: First Person Stories of the F-100 Misty FACs in the Vietnam War*. Bloomington, Ind.: 1stBooks, 2002.

Trotti, John. *Phantom over Vietnam*. Novato, Calif.: Presidio Press, 1984.

Vaughan, David K. *Runway Visions: An American C-130 Pilot's Memoir of Combat Airlift Operations in Southeast Asia, 1967–1968*. Jefferson, N.C.: McFarland, 1998.

Yarborough, Tom. *Danang Diary: A Forward Air Controller's Year of Combat over Vietnam*. New York: St. Martin's Press, 1990.

Naval Air War

Cunningham, Randy, with Jeff Ethell. *Fox Two: The Story of America's First Ace in Vietnam*. Mesa, Ariz.: Champlin Fighter Museum, 1984.

Elkins, Frank C. *The Heart of a Man: A Naval Pilot's Vietnam Diary*. Annapolis, Md.: Naval Institute Press, 1991.

Fields, Kenny Wayne. *The Rescue of Streetcar 304: A Navy Pilot's Forty Hours on the Run in Laos*. Annapolis, Md.: Naval Institute Press, 2007.

Foster, Wynn F. *Captain Hook: A Pilot's Tragedy and Triumph in the Vietnam War*. Annapolis, Md.: Naval Institute Press, 1992.

Gillcrist, Paul T. *Feet Wet: Reflections of a Carrier Pilot*. Novato, Calif.: Presidio Press, 1990.

Gray, Stephen R. *Rampant Raider: An A-4 Skyhawk Pilot in Vietnam*. Annapolis, Md.: Naval Institute Press, 2007.

Lavell, Kit. *Flying Black Ponies: The Navy's Close Air Support Squadron in Vietnam*. Annapolis, Md.: Naval Institute Press, 2000.

McCain, John, with Mark Salter. *Faith of My Fathers: A Family Memoir*. New York: Random House, 1999.

Rausa, Rosario. *Gold Wings, Blue Sea: A Naval Aviator's Story*. Annapolis, Md.: Naval Institute Press, 1980.

Vietnamese

Appy, Christian G. *Patriots: The Vietnam War Remembered from All Sides*. New York: Viking, 2003.

Bong-Wright, Jackie. *Autumn Cloud: From Vietnamese War Widow to American Activist*. Sterling, Va.: Capital Books, 2001.

Cao Ngọc Phương. *Learning True Love: How I Learned and Practiced Social Change in Vietnam*. Berkeley, Calif.: Parallax Press, 1993.

David Lan Pham. *Two Hamlets in Nam Bo: Memoirs of Life in Vietnam through Japanese Occupation, the French and American Wars, and Communist Rule, 1940–1986*. Jefferson, N.C.: McFarland, 2000.

Elliott, Duong Van Mai. *The Sacred Willow: Four Generations in the Life of a Vietnamese Family*. New York: Oxford University Press, 1999.

Hess, Martha. *Then the Americans Came: Voices from Vietnam*. New York: Four Walls Eight Windows, 1993.

Krall, Yung. *A Thousand Tears Falling: The True Story of a Vietnamese Family Torn Apart by War, Communism, and the CIA*. Atlanta, Ga.: Longstreet, 1995.

Le Huu Tri. *Prisoner of the Word: A Memoir of the Vietnamese Reeducation Camps*. Seattle, Wash.: Black Heron Press, 2001.

Lữ Văn Thanh. *The Inviting Call of Wandering Souls: Memoir of an ARVN Liaison Officer to United States Forces in Vietnam Who Was Imprisoned in Communist Re-Education Camps and Then Escaped*. Jefferson, N.C.: McFarland, 1997.

Nguyễn Đình Hoà. *From the City Inside the Red River: A Cultural Memoir of Mid-Century Vietnam*. Jefferson, N.C.: McFarland, 1999.

Nguyễn Ngoc Ngan, with E. E. Richey. *The Will of Heaven*. New York: E. P. Dutton, 1982.

Nguyễn Qúi Đức. *Where the Ashes Are: The Odyssey of a Vietnamese Family*. Reading, Mass.: Addison-Wesley, 1994.

Nguyễn Thị Thu Lâm, with Edith Kreisler and Sandra Christenson. *Fallen Leaves: Memoirs of a Vietnamese Woman from 1940 to 1975*. New Haven, Conn.: Yale Center for International and Area Studies, 1989.

Nguyễn Thị Tuyết Mai. *The Rubber Tree: Memoir of a Vietnamese Woman Who Was an Anti-French Guerrilla, an Aide to the First President of the Republic of Vietnam, a Publisher and a Peace Activist*. Edited by Monique Senderowicz. Jefferson, N.C.: McFarland, 1994.

Thích Nhất Hạnh. *Fragrant Palm Leaves: Journals 1962–1966*. Translated by Mobi Warren. Berkeley, Calif.: Parallax, 1998.

AIR WAR

General

Boniface, Roger. *Aces of North Vietnam: Pilots—Units—Operations—Aircraft—Statistics, 1965–1975*. Altgen, Penn.: Schiffer Military History, 2001.

Churchill, Jan. *Hit My Smoke: Forward Air Controllers in Southeast Asia*. Manhattan, Kans.: Sunflower University Press, 1997.

Clodfelter, Mark. *The Limits of Air Power: The American Bombing of North Vietnam*. New York: Free Press, 1989.

Cook, John L. *Rescue under Fire: The Story of Dust Off in Vietnam*. Atglen, Penn.: Schiffer Military History, 1998.

Coulthard-Clark, Chris. *The RAAF in Vietnam: Australian Air Involvement in the Vietnam War, 1962–1975*. St. Leonards, NSW, Australia: Allen & Unwin, 1995.

Davis, Larry. *Wild Weasel: The SAM Suppression Story*. Carrollton, Tex.: Squadron/Signal Publications, 1986.

Dorr, Robert F. *Air War Hanoi*. London: Blandford Press, 1988.

———. *Air War South Vietnam*. London: Arms & Armour, 1991.

Eschmann, Karl J. *Linebacker: The Untold Story of the Air Raids over North Vietnam*. New York: Ivy Books, 1989.

Ethell, Jeffrey, and Alfred Price. *One Day in a Long War*. New York: Random House, 1989.

Francillon, Rene. *Vietnam: The War in the Air*. New York: Arch Cape Press, 1987.

Frankum, Ronald B., Jr. *Like Rolling Thunder: The Air War in Vietnam, 1964–1975*. Lanham, Md.: Rowman & Littlefield, 2005.

Glasser, Jeffrey D. *The Secret Vietnam War: The United States Air Force in Thailand, 1961–1975*. Jefferson, N.C.: McFarland, 1995.

Gunston, Bill. *Aircraft of the Vietnam War*. San Bernardino, Calif.: Borgo Press, 1989.

Hannah, Craig C. *Striving for Air Superiority: The Tactical Air Command in Vietnam*. College Station, Tex.: Texas A&M University Press, 2002.

Harder, Robert O. *Flying from the Black Hole: The B-52 Navigator-Bombardiers of Vietnam*. Annapolis, Md.: Naval Institute Press, 2009.

Harvey, Frank. *Air War: Vietnam*. New York: Bantam, 1967.

Head, William. *Shadow and Stinger: Development of the AC-119G/K Gunships in the Vietnam War*. College Station, Tex.: Texas A&M University Press, 2007.

Herz, Martin F., with Leslie Rider. *The Prestige Press and the Christmas Bombing, 1972: Images and Reality in Vietnam*. Lanham, Md.: University Press of America, 1985.

Hooper, Jim. *A Hundred Feet over Hell: Flying with the Men of the 220th Recon Airplane Company over I Corps and the DMZ, 1968–1969*. Minneapolis, Minn.: Zenith Press, 2009.

Horwood, Ian. *Interservice Rivalry and Airpower in the Vietnam War*. Ft. Leavenworth, Kans.: Combat Studies Institute Press, 2006.

Jackson, George R. *Linebacker II: An Examination of Strategic Use of Air Power*. Maxwell AFB, Ala.: Air University, 1989.

Jenkins, Dennis R. *F-105 Thunderchief: Workhorse of the Vietnam War*. New York: McGraw-Hill, 2000.

Littauer, Raphael, and Norman Uphoff, eds. *The Air War in Indochina*. Boston: Beacon Press, 1972.

Marrett, George J. *Cheating Death: Combat Air Rescues in Vietnam and Laos*. Washington, D.C.: Smithsonian Institution Press, 2003.

McCarthy, James R., and Robert E. Rayfield. *Linebacker II: A View from the Rock*. Maxwell AFB: Air War College, 1979.

———. *B-52s over Hanoi: A Linebacker II Story*. Fullerton, Calif.: California State Fullerton Press, 1995.

Mesko, Jim. *VNAF: South Vietnamese Air Force: 1945–1975*. Carrollton, Tex.: Squadron/Signal Publications, 1987.

Michel, Marshall L., III. *Clashes: Air Combat over North Vietnam, 1965–1972*. Annapolis, Md.: Naval Institute Press, 1997.

———. *The Eleven Days of Christmas: America's Last Vietnam Battle*. San Francisco: Encounter Books, 2002.

Mikesh, Robert C. *B-57 Canberra at War, 1964–1972*. New York: Scribner, 1980.

———. *Flying Dragons: The South Vietnamese Air Force*. Atglen, Penn.: Schiffer Military History, 2005.

Mutza, Wayne. *The A-1 Skyraider in Vietnam: The Spad's Last War*. Atglen, Penn.: Schiffer Military History, 2003.

Nalty, Bernard C., Jacob Neufeld, and George M. Watson. *An Illustrated Guide to the Air War over Vietnam: Aircraft of the Southeast Asia Conflict*. New York: Arco, 1981.

Peterson, Lowell. *The Birds Were Silver Then: Stories of the Vietnam Air War*. Appleton, Wisc.: Peterson House, 2006.

Reardon, Carol. *Launch the Intruders! A Naval Attack Squadron in the Vietnam War, 1972*. Lawrence, Kans.: University Press of Kansas, 2005.

Scutts, Jerry. *Wrecking Crew: The 388th Tactical Fighter Wing in Vietnam*. New York: Warner, 1990.

Sherwood, John Darrell. *Fast Movers: Jet Pilots and the Vietnam Experience*. New York: Free Press, 1999.

Sikora, Jack, and Larry Westin. *Batcats: The United States Air Force 553rd Reconnaissance Wing in Southeast Asia*. Lincoln, Nebr.: iUniverse, 2003.

Smith, John T. *Rolling Thunder: The Strategic Bombing Campaign, North Vietnam, 1965–1968*. Walton on Thames, UK: Air Research Publications, 1994.

———. *The Linebacker Raids: The Bombing of North Vietnam, 1972*. London: Arms & Armour, 1998.

Thompson, James Clay. *Rolling Thunder: Understanding Policy and Program Failure*. Chapel Hill, N.C.: University of North Carolina Press, 1980.

Thompson, Wayne. *To Hanoi and Back: The U.S. Air Force and North Vietnam, 1966–1973*. Washington, D.C.: Smithsonian Institution Press, 2000.

Tilford, Earl H. *Crosswinds: The Air Force's Setup in Vietnam*. Texas A&M Press, 1993.

Toperczer, Istvan. *Air War over North Vietnam: The Vietnamese People's Air Force, 1949–1977*. Carrollton, Tex.: Squadron/Signal, 1998.

Wagner, William. *Lightning Bugs and Other Reconnaissance Drones*. Fallbrook, Calif.: Armed Forces Journal International and Aero Publishers, 1982.

Whitcomb, Darrel D. *The Rescue of Bat 21*. Annapolis, Md.: Naval Institute Press, 1998.

Winnefeld, James A., and Dana J. Johnson. *Joint Air Operations: Pursuit of Unity in Command and Control, 1942–1991*. Annapolis, Md.: Naval Institute Press, 1993.

Helicopters

Alexander, Ron, and Charles W. Sasser. *Taking Fire: The True Story of a Decorated Chopper Pilot*. New York: St. Martin's Press, 2001.

Carlock, Chuck, and Ron Seabolt, eds. *Rattlers and Firebirds: Combat Action with an Assault Helicopter Company in Vietnam*. North Richland Hills, Tex.: Smithfield Press, 2004.

Chinnery, Philip D. *Vietnam: The Helicopter War*. Annapolis, Md.: Naval Institute Press, 1991.

Kirkland, Richard C. *Tales of a Helicopter Pilot*. Washington, D.C.: Smithsonian Institution Press, 2002.

Mutza, Wayne. *CH-47 Chinook in Action*. Carrollton, Tex.: Squadron/Signal Publications, 1989.

———. *LOACH! The Story of the H-6/Model 500 Helicopter*. Atglen, Penn.: Schiffer Military History, 2005.

———. *Green Hornets: The History of the U.S. Air Force 20th Special Operations Squadron*. Atglen, Penn.: Schiffer Military History, 2007.

Rosenburgh, Bob. *Snake Driver*. New York: Ivy Books, 1993.

Williams, Glenn M. *So Others Might Live*. Mukilteo, Wash.: WinePress, 1998.

Naval

Grant, Zalin. *Over the Beach: The Air War in Vietnam*. New York: Norton, 1986.

Levinson, Jeffrey L. *Alpha Strike Vietnam: The Navy's Air War, 1964 to 1973*. Novato, Calif.: Presidio Press, 1989.

Mersky, Peter B., and Norman Polmar. *The Naval Air War in Vietnam*. Annapolis, Md.: Nautical & Aviation Publishing, 1981.

Nichols, John B., and Barrett Tillman. *On Yankee Station: The Naval Air War over Vietnam*. Annapolis, Md.: Naval Institute Press, 1987.

O'Connor, Mike. *MiG Killers of Yankee Station*. Friendship, Wisc.: New Past Press, 2003.

Sherwood, John Darrell. *Afterburner: Naval Aviators and the Vietnam War*. New York: New York University Press, 2004.

Stoffey, Robert E. *Fighting to Leave: The Final Years of America's War in Vietnam, 1972–1973*. Minneapolis, Minn.: Zenith Press, 2008.

Wilcox, Robert K. *Scream of Eagles: The Creation of Top Gun and the U.S. Air Victory in Vietnam*. New York: Wiley, 1990.

THIRD COUNTRY AND INTERNATIONAL

General

Blackburn, Robert M. *Mercenaries and Lyndon Johnson's "More Flags": The Hiring of Korean, Filipino and Thai Soldiers in the Vietnam War*. Jefferson, N.C.: McFarland, 1994.

Colvin, John. *Twice Around the World: Some Memoirs of Diplomatic Life in North Vietnam and Outer Mongolia*. London: Leo Cooper, 1991.

Daum, Andreas W., Lloyd C. Gardner, and Wilfried Mausbach, eds. *America, the Vietnam War, and the World*. New York: Cambridge University Press, 2003.

Fielding, Leslie. *Before the Killing Fields: Witness to Cambodia and the Vietnam War*. London: I. B. Tauris, 2007.

Gardner, Lloyd C., and Ted Gittinger, eds. *International Perspectives on Vietnam*. College Station, Tex.: Texas A&M University Press, 2000.

Glyn, Alan. *Witness to Vietnam: The Containment of Communism in Southeast Asia*. London: Johnson, 1968.

Hastings, Max. *Going to the Wars*. London: Pan Books, 2001.

Schoenl, William, ed. *New Perspectives on the Vietnam War: Our Allies' Views*. Lanham, Md.: University Press of America, 2002.

Australia

Albinski, Henry Stephen. *Politics and Foreign Policy in Australia: The Impact of Vietnam and Conscription*. Durham, N.C.: Duke University Press, 1970.

Anderson, Paul. *When the Scorpion Stings: The History of the 3rd Cavalry Regiment, South Vietnam, 1965–1972*. Crow's Nest, NSW, Australia: Allen & Unwin, 2002.

Barclay, Glen St. J. *A Very Small Insurance Policy: The Politics of Australian Involvement in Vietnam, 1954–1967*. St Lucia, Australia: University of Queensland Press, 1988.

Barr, Marshall. *Surgery, Sand and Saigon Tea: An Australian Army Doctor in Viet Nam*. Crow's Nest, NSW, Australia: Allen & Unwin, 2001.

Barwick, Garfield. *A Radical Tory: Garfield Barwick's Reflections and Recollections*. Leichhardt, NSW, Australia: Federation Press, 1995.

Biedermann, Narelle. *Tears on My Pillow: Australian Nurses in Vietnam*. Milsons Point, NSW, Australia: Random House Australia, 2004.

Blair, Anne. *There to the Bitter End: Ted Serong in Vietnam*. Crow's Nest, NSW, Australia: Allen & Unwin, 2001.

———. *Ted Serong: The Life of an Australian Counter-Insurgency Expert*. New York: Oxford University Press, 2004.

Brass, Alister. *Bleeding Earth: A Doctor Looks at Vietnam*. Melbourne, Australia: Heinemann, 1968.

Breen, Bob. *First to Fight: Australian Diggers, N.Z. Kiwis and U.S. Paratroopers in Vietnam, 1965–66*. Sydney, NSW, Australia: Allen & Unwin, 1988.

Brodie, Scott. *Tilting at Dominoes: Australia and the Vietnam War*. Brookvale, NSW, Australia: Child & Associates, 1987.

Buick, Bob, with Gary McKay. *All Guts and No Glory: The Story of a Long Tan Warrior*. St. Leonards, NSW, Australia: Allen & Unwin, 2000.

Burstall, Terry. *The Soldiers' Story: The Battle at Xa Long Tan, Vietnam, 18 August 1966*. Brisbane, Australia: University of Queensland Press, 1986.

———. *A Soldier Returns: A Long Tan Veteran Discovers the Other Side of Vietnam*. Brisbane, Australia: University of Queensland Press, 1990.

———. *Vietnam: The Australian Dilemma*. St Lucia, Australia: University of Queensland Press, 1993.

Cable, Ross W. *An Independent Command: Command and Control of the 1st Australian Task Force in Vietnam*. Canberra, ACT, Australia: Australian National University, 2000.

Clarke, Colin John, ed. *Yours Faithfully: A Record of Service of the 3d Battalion, the Royal Australian Regiment in Australia and South Vietnam, 16 February 1969–16 October 1971*. Brookvale, NSW, Australia: Print Craft Press, 1972.

Coe, John J., ed. *Desperate Praise: The Australians in Vietnam*. Perth, Western Australia: Artlook Books, 1982.

Colman, Mike. *Payne VC: The Story of Australia's Most Decorated Soldier of the Vietnam War*. Sydney, NSW, Australia: ABC Books, 2009.

Cooper, Garry, and Robert Hillier. *Sock It to 'Em Baby: Forward Air Controller in Vietnam*. Crow's Nest, NSW, Australia: Allen & Unwin, 2006.

Coulthard-Clark, Chris. *The RAAF in Vietnam: Australian Air Involvement in the Vietnam War, 1962–1975*. St. Leonards, NSW, Australia: Allen & Unwin, 1995.

———. *Hit My Smoke: Targeting the Enemy in Vietnam*. St. Leonards, NSW, Australia: Allen & Unwin, 1997.

Crowley, Barrie. *View from a Low Bough*. St. Leonards, NSW, Australia: Allen & Unwin, 1997.

Davies, Bruce. *Battle at Ngok Tavak: A Bloody Defeat in South Vietnam, 1968*. Crow's Nest, NSW, Australia: Allen & Unwin, 2008.

Davies, Bruce, and Gary McKay. *The Men Who Persevered: The AATTV—The Most Highly Decorated Australian Unit of the Viet Nam War*. Crow's Nest, NSW, Australia: Allen & Unwin, 2005.

Dennis, Donald James. *One Day at a Time: A Vietnam Diary*. St. Lucia, Australia: University of Queensland Press, 1992.

Doyle, Jeff, Jeffrey Gray, and Peter Pierce. *Australia's Vietnam War*. College Station, Tex.: Texas A&M University Press, 2002.

Eather, Steve. *Target Charlie*. Weston Creek, ACT, Australia: Aerospace Publications, 1993.

———. *Get the Bloody Job Done: The Royal Australian Navy Helicopter Flight-Vietnam and the 135th Assault Helicopter Company, 1967–1971*. St. Leonards, NSW, Australia: Allen & Unwin, 1998.

Edwards, Peter. *A Nation at War: Australian Politics, Society and Diplomacy during the Vietnam War, 1965–1975*. St. Leonards, NSW, Australia: Allen & Unwin, 1997.

Edwards, Peter, with Gregory Pemberton. *Crises and Commitments: The Politics and Diplomacy of Australia's Involvement in South-East Asian Conflicts, 1948–1965*. North Sydney, NSW, Australia: Allen & Unwin, 1992.

English, Michael C. *The Riflemen: The Unit History of 3 RAR in Vietnam, 1971*. Loftus, NSW, Australia: Australian Military History Publications, 1999.

Fairfax, Denis. *Navy in Vietnam: A Record of the Royal Australian Navy in the Vietnam War, 1962–1972*. Canberra, ACT, Australia: Australian Government Publishing Service, 1980.

Frankum, Ronald B., Jr. *The United States and Australia in Vietnam, 1954–1968: Silent Partners*. Lewiston, N.Y.: Edwin Mellen Press, 2001.

Frost, Frank. *Australia's War in Vietnam*. Sydney, NSW, Australia: Allen & Unwin, 1987.

Grandin, Robert. *The Battle of Long Tan, as Told by the Commanders to Bob Grandin*. Sydney, NSW, Australia: Allen & Unwin, 2004.

Grey, Jeffrey. *Up Top: The Royal Australian Navy and Southeast Asian Conflicts, 1955–1972*. St. Leonards, NSW, Australia: Allen & Unwin, 1998.

Grey, Jeffrey, and Jeffrey Doyle, eds. *Vietnam: War, Myth, and Memory; Comparative Perspectives on Australia's War in Vietnam*. St. Leonards, NSW, Australia: Allen & Unwin, 1992.

Hall, Robert A. *Combat Battalion: The Eighth Battalion in Vietnam*. Crow's Nest, NSW, Australia: Allen & Unwin, 2000.

Haran, Peter. *Trackers: The Untold Story of the Australian Dogs of War*. Sydney, NSW, Australia: New Holland Publishers, 2000.

Haran, Peter, and Robert Kearney. *Crossfire: An Australian Reconnaissance Unit in Vietnam*. Sydney, NSW, Australia: New Holland Publishers, 2001.

Hasluck, Paul. *Mucking About: An Autobiography*. Carlton, Victoria, Australia: Melbourne University Press, 1977.

Horner, David. *Strategic Command: General Sir John Wilton and Australia's Asian Wars*. New York: Oxford University Press, 2005.

King, Peter, ed. *Australia's Vietnam*. Sydney, NSW, Australia: Allen & Unwin, 1983.

Krasnoff, Stan. *Krazy Hor: A Soldier's Story*. Sydney, NSW, Australia: Allen & Unwin, 2004.

Lamensdorf, Jean Debelle. *Write Home for Me: A Red Cross Woman in Vietnam*. Milsons Point, NSW, Australia: Random House Australia, 2006.

Langley, Greg. *A Decade of Dissent: Vietnam and the Conflict on the Australian Home Front*. Sydney, NSW, Australia: Allen & Unwin, 1992.

Lockhart, Greg. *The Minefield: An Australian Tragedy in Vietnam*. Sydney, NSW, Australia: Allen & Unwin, 2007.

Mackay, Ian. *Australians in Vietnam*. Sydney, NSW, Australia: Rigby, 1968.

Maddock, Kenneth, ed. *Memories of Vietnam*. Milsons Point, NSW, Australia: Random House, 1991.

Maddock, Kenneth, and Barry Wright, eds. *War: Australia and Vietnam*. Sydney, NSW, Australia: Harper & Row, 1987.

Marr, David. *Barwick*. North Sydney, NSW, Australia: Allen & Unwin, 1992.

McAulay, Lex. *The Battle of Long Tan*. Hawthorn, Australia: Hutchinson, 1986.

———. *The Battle of Coral*. Hawthorn, Australia: Hutchinson, 1988.

———. *Contact: Australians in Vietnam*. Milson's Point, NSW, Australia: Hutchinson Australia, 1989.

McCulloch, Jock. *The Politics of Agent Orange: The Australian Experience*. Melbourne, Australia: Heinemann, 1984.

McHugh, Siobhan. *Minefields & Miniskirts: Australian Women and the Vietnam War*. Sydney, NSW, Australia: Doubleday, 1993.

McKay, Gary. *Vietnam Fragments: An Oral History of Australians at War*. Sydney, NSW, Australia: Allen & Unwin, 1992.

———. *Delta Four: Australian Riflemen in Vietnam*. St. Leonards, NSW, Australia: Allen & Unwin, 1996.

———. *In Good Company: One Man's War in Vietnam*. St. Leonards, NSW, Australia: Allen & Unwin, 1998.

McKay, Gary, and Graeme Nicholas. *Jungle Tracks: Australian Armour in Viet Nam*. Crow's Nest, NSW, Australia: Allen & Unwin, 2001.

McNeill, Ian. *The Team: Australian Army Advisors in Vietnam, 1962–1972*. St. Lucia, Australia: University of Queensland Press, 1984.

———. *To Long Tan: The Australian Army and the Vietnam War, 1950–1966*. St. Leonards, NSW, Australia: Allen & Unwin, 1993.

McNeill, Ian, and Ashley Ekins. *On the Offensive: The Australian Army in the Vietnam War, January 1967–June 1968*. Crow's Nest, NSW, Australia: Allen & Unwin, 2003.

Mollison, Charles S. *Long Tan and Beyond: Alpha Company 6 RAR in Vietnam, 1966–1967*. Woombye, Queensland, Australia: Cobb's Crossing Publications, 2005.

Murphy, John. *Harvest of Fear: A History of Australia's Vietnam War*. Boulder, Colo.: Westview, 1993.

Newman, D. S. *Vietnam Gunners: 161 Battery RNZA, South Vietnam, 1965–1971*. Wellington, New Zealand: Moana Press, 1988.

Newman, K. E., ed. *The Anzac Battalion: A Record of the Tour of 2nd Battalion, the Royal Australian Regiment, 1st Battalion, the Royal New Zealand Infantry Regiment (the Anzac Battalion), in South Vietnam, 1967–1968*. Brookvale, NSW, Australia: Printcraft Press, 1968.

Nolan, Peter. *Possums & Bird Dogs: Australian Army Aviation's 161 Reconnaissance Flight in South Vietnam*. Crow's Nest, NSW, Australia: Allen & Unwin, 2006.

Nott, Rodney, and Noel Payne. *The Vung Tau Ferry: HMAS Sydney and Escort Ships: Vietnam, 1965–1972*. Kenthurst, NSW, Australia: Rosenberg Publishing, 2008.

O'Brien, Michael. *Conscripts and Regulars: With the Seventh Battalion in Vietnam*. Sydney, NSW, Australia: Allen & Unwin, 1995.

Odgers, George. *Mission Vietnam: Royal Australian Air Force Operations, 1964–1972*. Canberra, ACT, Australia: Australian Government Publication Service, 1974.

O'Farrell, Terry. *Behind Enemy Lines: An Australian SAS Soldier in Vietnam*. St. Leonard's, NSW, Australia: Allen & Unwin, 2002.

O'Keefe, Brendan, with F. B. Smith. *Medicine at War: Medical Aspects of Australia's Involvement in Southeast Asia, 1950–1972*. St. Leonards, NSW, Australia: Allen & Unwin, 1994.

O'Neill, Robert J. *Vietnam Task: The 5th Battalion, the Royal Australian Regiment, 1966–1967*. Melbourne, Australia: Cassell, 1968.

Palazzo, Albert. *Australian Military Operations in Vietnam*. Canberra, ACT, Australia: Army History Unit, 2006.

Pemberton, Gregory. *All the Way: Australia's Road to Vietnam*. Sydney, NSW, Australia: Allen & Unwin, 1987.

———, ed. *Vietnam Remembered*. Sydney, NSW, Australia: Weldon, 1990.

Petersen, Barry. *Tiger Men: An Australian Soldier's Secret War in Vietnam*. South Melbourne, Australia: Macmillan, 1988.

Pierce, Peter, Jeffrey Grey, and Jeff Doyle, eds. *Vietnam Days: Australia and the Impact of Vietnam*. New York and London: Penguin, 1991.

Roberts, A. R., ed. *The Anzac Battalion, 1970–1971*. Sydney, NSW, Australia: Printcraft Press for the Royal Australian Regiment, 2nd Battalion, 1972.

Roser, Iris Mary. *Ba Rose: My Years in Vietnam, 1968–1971*. Sydney, NSW, Australia: Pan, 1991.

Rowe, Maree, ed. *Vietnam Veterans: Sons of the Hunter; The Stories of 104 Vietnam Veterans*. Loftus, NWS, Australia: Australian Military History Publications, 2002.

Savage, David. *Through the Wire: Action with the SAS in Borneo and the Special Forces in Vietnam*. St. Leonards, NSW, Australia: Allen & Unwin, 1999.

Sexton, Michael. *War for the Asking: Australia's Vietnam Secrets*. Ringwood, Victoria, Australia: Penguin, 1981.

Steinbrook, Gordon L. *Allies & Mates: An American Soldier with the Australians and New Zealanders in Vietnam, 1966–1967*. Lincoln, Nebr.: University of Nebraska Press, 1995.

Tate, Don. *The War Within*. Sydney, NSW, Australia: Murdoch Books, 2008.

Taylor, Jerry. *Last Out: 4RAR/NZ (ANZAC) Battalion's Second Tour in Vietnam*. Crow's Nest, NSW, Australia: Allen & Unwin, 2001.

Terry, Susan. *House of Love: Life in a Vietnamese Hospital*. Melbourne, Australia: Lansdowne Press, 1967.

Torney-Parlicki, Prue. *Somewhere in Asia: War, Journalism and Australia's Neighbors, 1941–1975*. Sydney, NSW, Australia: University of New South Wales Press, 2000.

Towers, Mike. *A Jungle Circus: Memories of Vietnam*. St. Leonards, NSW, Australia: Allen & Unwin, 1999.

Whitlam, Gough. *The Whitlam Government, 1972–1975*. Ringwood, Victoria, Australia: Penguin, 1985.

Woodard, Garry. *Asian Alternatives: Australia's Vietnam Decision and Lessons on Going to War*. Melbourne, Australia: Melbourne University Publishing, 2004.

Canada

Arial, Tracey. *I Volunteered: Canadians in Vietnam*. Winnipeg, Canada: Watson & Dwyer, 1997.

Blanchette, Arthur E., ed. *Canadian Peacekeepers in Indochina, 1954–1973*. Ottawa, Canada: Golden Dog Press, 2002.

Brown, Les D. *There It Is: A Canadian in the Vietnam War*. Toronto: McClelland & Stewart, 2000.

Culhane, Claire. *Why Is Canada in Vietnam? The Truth about our Foreign Aid*. Toronto: NC Press, 1972.

Donaghy, Greg. *Tolerant Allies: Canada and the United States, 1963–1968*. Montreal: McGill-Queen's University Press, 2002.

Gaffen, Fred. *Unknown Warriors: Canadians in Vietnam*. Toronto: Dundurn Press, 1990.

———. *Cross Border Warriors*. Toronto: Dundurn Press, 1995.

Ross, Douglas A. *In the Interests of Peace: Canada and Vietnam, 1954–1973*. Toronto: University of Toronto Press, 1984.

New Zealand

Barnz, Billy. *Voices from Vietnam: The Stories of New Zealanders Who Served Their Country in Vietnam*. Christchurch, New Zealand: Willson Scott Publishing, 2008.

Challinor, Deborah. *Grey Ghosts: New Zealand Vietnam Vets Talk about Their War*. Auckland, New Zealand: Hodder Moa Beckett, 1998.

Gustafson, Barry. *Kiwi Keith: A Biography of Keith Holyoake*. Auckland, New Zealand: Auckland University Press, 2007.

Rabel, Roberto. *New Zealand and the Vietnam War: Politics and Diplomacy*. Auckland: Auckland University Press, 2005.

Shackleton, Michael. *Operation Vietnam: A New Zealand Surgical First*. Dunedin, New Zealand: University of Otago Press, 2004.

Sisson, Colin P. *Wounded Warriors: The True Story of a Soldier in the Vietnam War and of the Emotional Wounds Inflicted*. Auckland, New Zealand: Total Press, 1993.

Subritzky, Mike, ed. *The Vietnam Scrapbook: The Second Anzac Adventure*. Papakura, New Zealand: Three Feathers, 1995.

Wilkie, Dave. *Year of the Dove: Diaries of a Medico in Vietnam*. Christchurch, New Zealand: Quoin, 1998.

Europe and the World

Busch, Peter. *All the Way with JFK? Britain and Kennedy's War in Vietnam*. New York: Oxford University Press, 2003.

Buszynski, Leszek. *S.E.A.T.O.: The Failure of an Alliance Strategy*. Singapore: Singapore University Press, 1983.

Burdeos, Ray L. *Filipinos in the U.S. Navy & Coast Guard during the Vietnam War*. Bloomington, Ind.: AuthorHouse, 2008.

Cross, J. P. *OBE, First in Last Out: An Unconventional British Officer in Indo-China, 1945–1976*. Dulles, Va.: Brassey's, 1992.

Das, Parimal Kumar. *India and the Vietnam War*. New Delhi: Young Asia Publications, 1972.

Ellis, Sylvia. *Britain, America, and the Vietnam War*. Westport, Conn.: Praeger, 2004.

Kalam, Abdul. *Peacemaking in Indochina, 1954–1975*. Dhaka, Bangladesh: University of Dhaka, 1983.

Kemp, Ian. *British G.I. in Vietnam*. London: Hale, 1969.

SarDesai, Damodar R. *Indian Foreign Policy in Cambodia, Laos, and Vietnam, 1947–1964*. Berkeley, Calif.: University of California Press, 1968.

Schwartz, Thomas A. *Lyndon Johnson and Europe: In the Shadow of Vietnam*. Cambridge, Mass.: Harvard University Press, 2003.

Thompson, Robert G. K. *No Exit from Vietnam*. New York: McKay, 1970.

———. *Peace Is Not at Hand*. London: Chatto & Windus, 1974.

———. *Make for the Hills*. London: Leo Cooper, 1989.

Wilson, Harold. *The Labour Government, 1964–1970: A Personal Record*. London: Weidenfeld & Nicolson, 1971.

SOUTHEAST ASIA

ARVN and RVN

Brigham, Robert K. *ARVN: Life and Death in the South Vietnamese Army*. Lawrence, Kans.: University Press of Kansas, 2006.

Bùi Diễm, with David Chanoff. *In the Jaws of History*. Boston: Houghton Mifflin, 1987.

Cao Văn Viên. *Leadership*. McLean, Va.: General Research Corporation, 1978.

Critchfield, Richard. *The Long Charade: Political Subversion in the Vietnam War*. New York: Harcourt, Brace & World, 1968.

Dacy, Douglas C. *Foreign Aid, War, and Economic Development: South Vietnam, 1955–1975*. New York: Cambridge University Press, 1986.

Donnell, John C., and Charles A. Joiner, eds. *Electoral Politics in South Vietnam*. Lexington, Mass.: Lexington Books, 1974.

Fontaine, Ray. *The Dawn of Free Vietnam: A Biographical Sketch of Doctor Phan Quang Dan*. Brownsville, Tex.: Pan American Business Services, 1992.

Goodman, Allan E. *Politics in War: The Bases of Political Community in South Vietnam*. Cambridge, Mass.: Harvard University Press, 1973.

Hà Mai Việt. *Steel and Blood: South Vietnamese Armor and the War for Southeast Asia*. Annapolis, Md.: Naval Institute Press, 2008.

Haines, David W. *The Limits of Kinship: South Vietnamese Households, 1954–1975*. DeKalb, Ill.: Northern Illinois University Press, 2006.

Hosmer, Stephen T., Konrad Kellen, and Brian M. Jenkins. *The Fall of South Vietnam: Statements by Vietnamese Military and Civilian Leaders*. New York: Crane, Russak, 1980.

Joiner, Charles A. *The Politics of Massacre: Political Processes in South Vietnam*. Philadelphia: Temple University Press, 1974.

Kiểm Dò, and Julie Kane. *Counterpart: A South Vietnamese Naval Officer's War*. Annapolis, Md.: Naval Institute Press, 1998.

Lâm Quang Thi. *Autopsy: The Death of South Vietnam*. Phoenix, Ariz.: Sphinx Publishing, 1986.

———. *The Twenty-five Year Century: A South Vietnamese General Remembers the Indochina War to the Fall of Saigon*. Denton, Tex.: University of North Texas Press, 2001.

Martin, Michael N., ed. *Angels in Red Hats: Paratroopers of the Second Indochina War; Elite Vietnamese Paratroopers and Their American Advisors.* Louisville, Ky.: Harmony House, 1995.

Nguyễn Cao Kỳ. *Twenty Years and Twenty Days.* New York: Stein & Day, 1976.

Nguyễn Cao Kỳ, with Marvin J. Wolf. *Buddha's Child: My Fight to Save Vietnam.* New York: St. Martin's Press, 2002.

Nguyễn Phú Đức. *The Viet-Nam Peace Negotiations: Saigon's Side of the Story.* Christiansburg, Va.: Dalley Book Service, 2005.

Nguyễn Tiến Hưng, and Jerrold Schecter. *The Palace File.* New York: Harper & Row, 1986.

Nguyễn Văn Tín. *Major General Nguyen Van Hieu, ARVN.* San Jose, Calif.: Writers Club Press, 2000.

Nguyễn Xuân Phong. *Hope and Vanquished Reality.* Philadelphia: Xlibris, 2001.

Penniman, Howard R. *Elections in South Vietnam.* Washington, D.C.: American Enterprise Institute, 1972.

Pham, Quang X. *A Sense of Duty: My Father, My American Journey.* New York: Ballantine, 2005.

Tambini, Anthony J. *F-5 Tigers over Vietnam.* Boston: Branden Books, 2001.

Topmiller, Robert J. *The Lotus Unleashed: The Buddhist Peace Movement in South Vietnam, 1964–1966.* Lexington, Ky.: University Press of Kentucky, 2002.

Trần Văn Đôn. *Our Endless War.* San Rafael, Calif.: Presidio Press, 1978.

Trần Văn Nhựt, with Christian L. Arevian. *An Loc: The Unfinished War.* Lubbock, Tex.: Texas Tech University Press, 2009.

Văn Nguyên Đường. *The Tragedy of the Vietnam War: A South Vietnamese Officer's Analysis.* Jefferson, N.C.: McFarland, 2008.

Wiest, Andrew. *Vietnam's Forgotten Army: Heroism and Betrayal in the ARVN.* New York: New York University Press, 2008.

Williams, Eleazar A. *The Election Process in Vietnam: The Road to a Functioning Polity.* Washington, D.C.: National War College, 1971.

DRV, PAVN, and NLF

Andrews, William R. *The Village War: Vietnamese Communist Revolutionary Activities in Dinh Tuong Province, 1960–1964.* Columbia, Mo.: University of Missouri Press, 1973.

Ang Cheng Guan. *Ending the Vietnam War: The Vietnamese Communists' Perspective.* New York: RoutledgeCurzon, 2004.

Beresford, Melanie. *Vietnam.* New York: Columbia University Press, 1988.

Boardman, Elizabeth J. *Phoenix Trip: Notes on a Quaker Mission to Haiphong.* Burnsville, N.C.: Celo Press, 1985.

Brigham, Robert K. *Guerrilla Diplomacy: The NLF's Foreign Relations and the Viet Nam War.* Ithaca, N.Y.: Cornell University Press, 1999.

Bùi Tín. *Following Ho Chi Minh: The Memoirs of a North Vietnamese Colonel.* Honolulu, Hawaii: University of Hawaii Press, 1995.

———. *From Enemy to Friend: A North Vietnamese Perspective on the War.* Annapolis, Md.: Naval Institute Press, 2002.

Burchett, Wilfred. *The Furtive War: The United States in Vietnam and Laos.* New York: International Publishers, 1963.

———. *Vietnam: Inside Story of the Guerrilla War.* New York: International Publishers, 1965.

———. *Vietnam North.* New York: International Publishers, 1966.

———. *Vietnam Will Win!* New York: Monthly Review Press, 1968.

———. *The Second Indochina War: Cambodia and Laos.* New York: International Publishers, 1970.

———. *Grasshoppers and Elephants: Why Viet Nam Fell.* New York: Urizen, 1977.

Cameron, James. *Here Is Your Enemy.* New York: Holt, Rinehart & Winston, 1966.

Chanoff, David, and Đoàn Văn Toại. *Portrait of the Enemy.* New York: Random House, 1986.

Đoàn Văn Toại, and David Chanoff. *The Vietnamese Gulag.* New York: Simon & Schuster, 1986.

Duiker, William J. *The Communist Road to Power in Vietnam.* Boulder, Colo.: Westview, 1996.

Emering, Edward J. *Viet Cong: A Photographic Portrait.* Atglen, Penn.: Schiffer Military History, 1999.

Fall, Bernard. *The Viet-Minh Regime: Government and Administration in the Democratic Republic of Vietnam.* Ithaca, N.Y.: Cornell University, 1954.

Gerassi, John. *North Vietnam: A Documentary.* Indianapolis, Ind.: Bobbs-Merrill, 1968.

Henderson, William D. *Why the Vietcong Fought: A Study of Motivation and Control in a Modern Army in Combat.* Westport, Conn.: Greenwood, 1979.

Hunt, David. *Vietnam's Southern Revolution: From Peasant Insurrection to Total War.* Amherst, Mass.: University of Massachusetts Press, 2008.

Kerkvliet, Benedict J. *The Power of Everyday Politics: How Vietnamese Peasants Transformed National Policy.* Ithaca, N.Y.: Cornell University Press, 2005.

Kerkvliet, Benedict J., and David Marr, eds. *Beyond Hanoi: Local Government in Vietnam.* Singapore: Institute of Southeast Asian Studies, 2004.

Kleinen, John. *Facing the Future, Reviving the Past: A Study of Social Change in a Northern Vietnamese Village.* Singapore: Institute of Southeast Asian Studies, 1999.

Lanning, Michael Lee, and Dan Cragg. *Inside the VC and the NVA: The Real Story of North Vietnam's Armed Forces.* New York: Fawcett, 1992.

Lockhard, Greg. *Nation in Arms: The Origins of the People's Army of Vietnam.* Sydney, NSW, Australia: Allen & Unwin, 1989.

Luong, Hy V., with Nguyen Dac Bang. *Revolution in the Village: Tradition and Transformation in North Vietnam, 1925–1988.* Honolulu, Hawaii: University of Hawaii Press, 1992.

Mallin, Jay, ed. *Strategy for Conquest: Communist Documents on Guerrilla Warfare.* Coral Gables, Fla.: University of Miami Press, 1970.

McCoy, James W. *Secrets of the Viet Cong.* New York: Hippocrene, 1992.

McGarvey, Patrick J., ed. *Visions of Victory: Selected Vietnamese Communist Military Writings, 1964–1968.* Stanford, Calif.: Hoover Institution, 1969.

Moise, Edwin E. *Land Reform in China and North Vietnam: Consolidating the Revolution at the Village Level.* Chapel Hill, N.C.: University of North Carolina Press, 1983.

Ninh, Kim Ngoc Bao. *A World Transformed: The Politics of Culture in Revolutionary Vietnam, 1945–1965*. Ann Arbor, Mich.: University of Michigan Press, 2002.

Pike, Douglas. *History of Vietnamese Communism, 1925–1976*. Stanford, Calif.: Hoover Institution, 1978.

Riboud, Marc. *The Face of North Vietnam*. New York: Holt, Rinehart & Winston, 1970.

Ton That Thiện. *The Foreign Politics of the Communist Party of Vietnam: A Study in Communist Tactics*. New York: Crane Russak, 1989.

Turley, William S., ed. *Vietnamese Communism in Comparative Perspective*. Boulder, Colo.: Westview, 1980.

Van Dyke, Jon M. *North Vietnam's Strategy for Survival*. Palo Alto, Calif.: Pacific Books, 1972.

DRV Allies

Ang Cheng Guan. *Vietnamese Communists' Relations with China and the Second Indochina Conflict, 1956–1962*. Jefferson, N.C.: McFarland, 1997.

Barnouin, Barbara, and Yu Changgen. *Chinese Foreign Policy during the Cultural Revolution*. London: Kegan Paul, 1998.

Burchett, Wilfred. *The China-Cambodia-Vietnam Triangle*. Chicago: Vanguard, 1981.

Chen, King C. *Vietnam and China, 1938–1954*. Princeton, N.J.: Princeton University Press, 1969.

Duiker, William. *China and Vietnam: The Roots of Conflict*. Berkeley, Calif.: Institute of East Asian Studies, 1986.

Gilks, Anne. *The Breakdown of the Sino-Vietnamese Alliance, 1970–1979*. Berkeley, Calif.: Institute of East Asian Studies, 1992.

Hood, Steven J. *Dragons Entangled: Indochina and the China-Vietnam War*. Armonk, N.Y.: M. E. Sharpe, 1992.

Lumbers, Michael. *Piercing the Bamboo Curtain: Tentative Bridge-Building to China during the Johnson Years*. Manchester, UK: Manchester University Press, 2008.

Olsen, Mari. *Soviet-Vietnam Relations and the Role of China, 1949–1964: Changing Alliances*. New York: Routledge, 2006.

Roberts, Priscilla, ed. *Behind the Bamboo Curtain: China, Vietnam, and the World beyond Asia*. Stanford, Calif.: Stanford University Press, 2006.

Smyser, W. R. *The Independent Vietnamese: Vietnamese Communism between Russia and China, 1956–1969*. Athens, Ohio: Ohio University Press, 1980.

Taylor, Jay. *China and Southeast Asia: Peking's Relations with Revolutionary Movements*. New York: Praeger, 1976.

Westad, Odd Orne, and Sophie Quinn-Judge, eds. *The Third Indochina War: Conflict between China, Vietnam and Cambodia, 1972–1979*. New York: Routledge, 2006.

Whiting, Allen. *The Chinese Calculus of Deterrence*. Ann Arbor, Mich.: University of Michigan Press, 1975.

Womack, Brantly. *China and Vietnam: The Politics of Asymmetry*. New York: Cambridge University Press, 2006.

Xia, Yafeng. *Negotiating with the Enemy: U.S.-China Talks during the Cold War, 1949–1972*. Bloomington, Ind.: Indiana University Press, 2006.

Zhai, Qiang. *China and the Vietnam Wars, 1950–1975*. Chapel Hill, N.C.: University of North Carolina Press, 2000.

Laos

Adams, Nina S., and Alfred W. McCoy, eds. *Laos: War and Revolution*. New York: Harper & Row, 1970.

Anthony, Victor B., and Richard R. Sexton. *The United States Air Force in Southeast Asia: The War in Northern Laos, 1954–1973*. Washington, D.C.: Center for Air Force History, 1993.

Branfman, Fred. *Voices from the Plain of Jars: Life under an Air War*. New York: Harper & Row, 1972.

Briggs, Thomas Leo. *Cash on Delivery: CIA Special Operations during the Secret War in Laos*. Rockville, Md.: Rosebank Press, 2009.

Brown, Mervyn. *War in Shangri-La: A Memoir of Civil War in Laos*. London: Radcliffe Press, 2001.

Castle, Timothy. *At War in the Shadow of Vietnam: United States Military Aid to the Royal Lao Government, 1955–75*. New York: Columbia University Press, 1993.

———. *One Day Too Long: Top Secret Site 85 and the Bombing of North Vietnam*. New York: Columbia University Press, 1999.

Churchill, Jan. *Classified Secret: Controlling Airstrikes in the Clandestine War in Laos*. Manhattan, Kans.: Sunflower University Press, 2000.

Conboy, Kenneth, with James Morrison. *Shadow War: The CIA's Secret War in Laos*. Boulder, Colo.: Paladin Press, 1995.

Curry, Robert. *Whispering Death: Our Journey with the Hmong in the Secret War for Laos*. Lincoln, Nebr.: iUniverse, 2004.

Défourneaux, René J. *The Winking Fox: Twenty-two Years in Military Intelligence*. Indianapolis, Ind.: Indiana Creative Arts, 1997.

Dommen, Arthur J. *Conflict in Laos: The Politics of Neutralization*. New York: Praeger, 1971.

———. *Laos: Keystone of Indochina*. Boulder, Colo.: Westview, 1985.

Drury, Richard S. *My Secret War*. New York: St. Martin's Press, 1986.

Fall, Bernard. *Anatomy of a Crisis: The Laotian Crisis of 1960–1961*. New York: Doubleday, 1969.

Field, Michael. *The Prevailing Wind: Witness in Indo-China*. London: Methuen, 1965.

Gettleman, Marvin, Susan Gettleman, Lawrence Kaplan, and Carol Kaplan, eds. *Conflict in Indo-China: A Reader on the Widening War in Laos and Cambodia*. New York: Random House, 1970.

Goldstein, Martin E. *American Policy toward Laos*. Rutherford, N.J.: Farleigh Dickinson University Press, 1999.

Goscha, Christopher E., and Soren Ivarsson. *Contesting Visions of the Lao Past: Lao Historiography at the Crossroads*. Copenhagen, Denmark: Nordic Institute of Asian Studies, 2003.

Halliday, John T. *Flying through Midnight: A Pilot's Dramatic Story of His Secret Missions over Laos during the Vietnam War*. New York: Scribner, 2005.

Halpern, Joel M., and William S. Turley, eds. *The Training of Vietnamese Communist Cadres in Laos: The Notes of Do Xuan Tao, Vietnamese Economics Specialist Assigned to the Pathet Lao in Xieng Khouang, Laos, 1968*. Christiansburg, Va.: Dalley Book Service, 1990.

Hamilton-Merritt, Jane. *Tragic Mountains: The Hmong, the Americans, and the Secret Wars for Laos, 1942–1992*. Bloomington, Ind.: Indiana University Press, 1993.

Hannah, Norman B. *The Key to Failure: Laos and the Vietnam War*. Lanham, Md.: Madison Books, 1987.

Khamkeo, Bounsang. *I Little Slave: A Prison Memoir from Communist Laos*. Spokane, Wash.: Eastern Washington University Press, 2006.

Kirk, Donald. *Wider War: The Struggle for Cambodia, Thailand, and Laos*. New York: Praeger, 1971.

Langer, Paul F., and Joseph J. Zasloff. *North Vietnam and the Pathet Lao: Partners in the Struggle for Laos*. Cambridge, Mass.: Harvard University Press, 1970.

Morrison, Gayle. *The Sky Is Falling: An Oral History of the CIA's Evacuation of the Hmong from Laos*. Jefferson, N.C.: McFarland, 1999.

Newman, Rick, and Don Shepperd. *Bury Us Upside Down: The Misty Pilots and the Secret Battle for the Ho Chi Minh Trail*. New York: Presidio Press, 2007.

Nolan, Keith W. *Into Laos: The Story of Dewey Canyon II/Lam Son 719, Laos 1971*. Novato, Calif.: Presidio Press, 1986.

Nyc, Frederick F., III. *Blind Bat: C-130 Night Forward Air Controller, Ho Chi Minh Trail*. Austin, Tex.: Eakin Press, 2000.

Parker, James E., Jr. *Codename Mule: Fighting the Secret War in Laos for the CIA*. Annapolis, Md.: Naval Institute Press, 1995.

Pratt, John Clark. *Laotian Fragments: The Chief Raven's Story*. New York: Viking, 1974.

Quincy, Keith. *Harvesting Pa Chay's Wheat: The Hmong and America's Secret War in Laos*. Seattle, Wa.: University of Washington Press, 2000.

Rantala, Judy A. *Laos Caught in the Web: The Vietnam War Years*. Bangkok, Thailand: Orchid Press, 2005.

Robbins, Christopher. *The Ravens*. New York: Crown, 1987.

Schanche, Don A. *Mister Pop*. New York: McKay, 1970.

Soutchay Vongsavanh. *RLG Military Operations and Activities in the Laotian Panhandle*. Washington, D.C.: Center of Military History, 1981.

Stevenson, Charles A. *The End of Nowhere: American Policy toward Laos since 1954*. Boston: Beacon Press, 1972.

Stieglitz, Perry. *In a Little Kingdom: The Tragedy of Laos, 1960–1980*. Armonk, N.Y.: M. E. Sharpe, 1990.

Stuart-Fox, Martin, and Mary Kooyman. *Historical Dictionary of Laos*. Lanham, Md.: Scarecrow Press, 2001.

Thee, Marek. *Notes of a Witness: Laos and the Second Indochina War*. New York: Random House, 1973.

Warner, Roger. *Back Fire: The CIA's Secret War in Laos and Its Link to the War in Vietnam*. New York: Simon & Schuster, 1995.

Weldon, Charles. *Tragedy in Paradise: A Country Doctor at War in Laos*. Bangkok, Thailand: Asia Books, 1999.

Cambodia

Ablin, David A., and Marlowe Hood, eds. *The Cambodian Agony*. Armonk, N.Y.: M. E. Sharpe, 1990.

Ayres, David M. *Anatomy of a Crisis: Education, Development, and the State in Cambodia, 1953–1998*. Honolulu, Hawaii: University of Hawaii Press, 2000.

Becker, Elizabeth. *When the War Was Over: The Voices of Cambodia's Revolution and Its People*. New York: Simon & Schuster, 1986.

Caldwell, Malcolm, and Lek Tan. *Cambodia in the Southeast Asian War*. New York: Monthly Review Press, 1973.

Chandler, David P. *The Tragedy of Cambodian History: Politics, War and Revolution since 1945*. New Haven, Conn.: Yale University Press, 1991.

———. *Brother Number One: A Political Biography of Pol Pot*. Boulder, Colo.: Westview, 1999.

———. *Voices from S-21: Terror and History in Pol Pot's Secret Prison*. Berkeley, Calif.: University of California Press, 1999.

Chanrithy Him. *When Broken Glass Floats: Growing Up under the Khmer Rouge*. New York: Norton, 2000.

Clymer, Kenton J. *The United States and Cambodia, 1870–1969: From Curiosity to Confrontation*. New York: Routledge, 2004.

Coleman, J. D. *Incursion*. New York: St. Martin's Press, 1991.

Deac, Wilfred P. *Road to the Killing Fields: The Cambodian War of 1970–1975*. College Station, Tex.: Texas A&M University Press, 1997.

Dith Pran and Kim Depaul. *Children of Cambodia's Killing Fields: Memoirs by Survivors*. New Haven, Conn.: Yale University Press, 1997.

Dudman, Richard. *Forty Days with the Enemy*. New York: Liveright, 1971.

Engelbert, Thomas, and Christopher E. Goscha. *Falling out of Touch: A Study on Vietnamese Communist Policy towards an Emerging Cambodian Communist Movement, 1930–1975*. Clayton, Australia: Monash Asia Institute, 1995.

Fielding, Leslie. *Before the Killing Fields: Witness to Cambodia and the Vietnam War*. London: I. B. Tauris, 2007.

Gouge, Robert J. *Raiding the Sanctuary: Redcatchers in Cambodia, May 12th–June 25th, 1970*. Bloomington, Ind.: AuthorHouse, 2006.

Guilmartin, John F., Jr. *A Very Short War: The Mayaguez and the Battle of Koh Tang*. College Station, Tex.: Texas A&M University Press, 1995.

Haas, Michael. *Cambodia, Pol Pot, and the United States: The Faustian Pact*. New York: Praeger, 1991.

Hinton, Alexander Laban. *Why Did They Kill? Cambodia in the Shadow of Genocide*. Berkeley, Calif.: University of California Press, 2005.

Kiernan, Ben. *How Pol Pot Came to Power: A History of Communism in Kampuchea, 1930–1975*. London: Verso, 1985.

Norodom Sihanouk. *My War with the CIA: The Memoirs of Prince Norodom Sihanouk*. New York: Pantheon, 1972.

———. *War and Hope: The Case for Cambodia*. New York: Pantheon, 1980.

Osborne, Milton. *Politics and Power in Cambodia: The Sihanouk Years.* Camberwell, Australia: Longman, 1973.

———. *Before Kampuchea: Preludes to Tragedy.* Sydney, NSW, Australia: Allen & Unwin, 1979.

———. *Sihanouk: Prince of Light, Prince of Darkness.* Honolulu, Hawaii: University of Hawaii Press, 1994.

Partridge, Larry. *Flying Tigers over Cambodia: An American Pilot's Memoir of the 1975 Phnom Penh Airlift.* Jefferson, N.C.: McFarland, 2001.

Punnee Soonthornpoct. *From Freedom to Hell: A History of Foreign Intervention in Cambodian Politics and Wars.* New York: Vantage Press, 2005.

Shaw, John M. *The Cambodian Campaign: The 1970 Offensive and America's Vietnam War.* Lawrence, Kans.: University Press of Kansas, 2005.

Shawcross, William. *Sideshow: Kissinger, Nixon, and the Destruction of Cambodia.* New York: Touchstone, 1987.

Simon, Sheldon W. *War and Politics in Cambodia: A Communications Analysis.* Durham, N.C.: Duke University Press, 1974.

Trần Đình Thọ. *The Cambodian Incursion.* Washington, D.C.: U.S. Army Center of Military History, 1979.

Wetterhahn, Ralph. *The Last Battle: The Mayaguez Incident and the End of the Vietnam War.* New York: Plume, 2002.

Widyono, Benny. *Dancing in Shadows: Sihanouk, the Khmer Rouge, and the United Nations in Cambodia.* Lanham, Md.: Rowman & Littlefield, 2007.

Wood, Richard. *Call Sign Rustic: The Secret Air War over Cambodia, 1970–1973.* Washington, D.C.: Smithsonian Institution Press, 2002.

Hồ Chí Minh Trail

Lễ Cao Đài. *The Central Highlands: A North Vietnamese Journal of Life on the Ho Chi Minh Trail, 1965–1973.* Hanoi: The Gioi, 2004.

Morris, Virginia, with Clive A. Hills. *A History of the Ho Chi Minh Trail: The Road to Freedom.* Bangkok, Thailand: Orchid Press, 2006.

Prados, John. *The Blood Road: The Ho Chi Minh Trail and the Vietnam War.* New York: Wiley, 1999.

Stevens, Richard L. *The Trail: A History of the Ho Chi Minh Trail and the Role of Nature in the War in Viet Nam.* Hamden, Conn.: Garland, 1993.

———. *Mission on the Ho Chi Minh Trail: Nature, Myth, and War in Viet Nam.* Norman, Okla.: University of Oklahoma Press, 1995.

SPECIAL OPERATIONS

Special Forces and Intelligence

Bass, Thomas A. *The Spy Who Loved Us: The Vietnam War and Pham Xuan An's Dangerous Game.* New York: PublicAffairs, 2009.

Berman, Larry. *Perfect Spy: The Incredible Double Life of Pham Xuan An, Time Magazine Reporter and Vietnamese Communist Agent*. Washington, D.C.: Smithsonian Books, 2007.

Blum, William. *Killing Hope: U.S. Military and CIA Interventions since World War II*. Monroe, Maine: Common Courage Press, 2008.

Currey, Cecil B. *Edward Lansdale: The Unquiet American*. Boston: Houghton Mifflin, 1988.

Edwards, Fred L., Jr. *The Bridges of Vietnam: From the Journals of a U.S. Marine Intelligence Officer*. Denton, Tex.: University of North Texas Press, 2000.

Generous, Kevin M. *Vietnam: The Secret War*. New York: Gallery Books, 1985.

Graham, Daniel O. *Confessions of a Cold Warrior*. Fairfax, Va.: Preview Press, 1995.

Hà Bình Nhưỡng. *Magnificent Camouflage: Stories of Secret Agents in the Saigon Administration*. Hanoi: Gioi Press, 2008.

Hobbs, Michael I. *Through Eyes of Stone: A Memoir*. Warrensburg, Mo.: Sweetgum Press, 2003.

Howey, William C. *Hard Knocks and Straight Talk: From the Jungles of Vietnam to the American Classroom*. Marco Island, Fla.: Keller Publishing, 2008.

Hubbard, Douglass H., Jr. *Special Agent, Vietnam: A Naval Intelligence Memoir*. Dulles, Va.: Potomac Books, 2006.

Hughes, R. Gerald, Peter Jackson, and Len Scott, eds. *Exploring Intelligence Archives: Enquiries into the Secret State*. New York: Routledge, 2008.

Lansdale, Edward G. *In the Midst of Wars: An American's Mission to Southeast Asia*. New York: Harper & Row, 1972.

Scott, Peter. *Lost Crusade: America's Secret Cambodian Mercenaries*. Annapolis, Md.: Naval Institute Press, 1998.

Smith, Eric McAllister. *Not by the Book: A Combat Intelligence Officer in Vietnam*. New York: Ivy Books, 1993.

Stanton, Shelby L. *Special Forces at War: An Illustrated History, Southeast Asia, 1957–1975*. Charlottesville, Va.: Howell Press, 1990.

Taylor, Richard. *Prodigals: A Vietnam Story*. Havertown, Penn.: Casemate, 2003.

Tourison, Sedgwick D., Jr. *Talking with Victor Charlie: An Interrogator's Story*. New York: Ivy Books, 1991.

Vandenbroucke, Lucien S. *Perilous Options: Special Operations as an Instrument of U.S. Foreign Policy*. New York: Oxford University Press, 1993.

Studies and Observations Group

Acre, James E. *Project Omega: Eye of the Beast*. Central Point, Ore.: Hellgate Press, 1999.

Conboy, Kenneth J., and Dale Andradé. *Spies and Commandos: How America Lost the Secret War in North Vietnam*. Lawrence, Kans.: University Press of Kansas, 2000.

Greco, Frank. *Running Recon: A Photo Journey with SOG Special Ops along the Ho Chi Minh Trail*. Boulder, Colo.: Paladin Press, 2004.

Jackson, Walter J. *Shades of Daniel Boone: A Personal View of Special Ops and the War in Vietnam*. Westminster, Md.: Eagle Editions, 2005.

Meyer, John Stryker, and John E. Peters. *On the Ground: The Secret War in Vietnam.* Oceanside, Calif.: Levin Publishing Group, 2007.
Miller, Franklin D., with Elwood J. C. Kureth. *Reflections of a Warrior.* Novato, Calif.: Presidio Press, 1991.
Nicholson, Thomas L. *15 Months in SOG: A Warrior's Tour.* New York: Ivy Books, 1999.
Plaster, John L. *SOG: The Secret Wars of America's Commandos in Vietnam.* New York: Simon & Schuster, 1997.
———. *SOG: A Photo History of the Secret Wars.* Boulder, Colo.: Paladin, 2000.
———. *Secret Commandos: Behind Enemy Lines with the Elite Warriors of SOG.* New York: Simon & Schuster, 2004.
Saal, Harve. *SOG: MACV Studies and Observations Group (Behind Enemy Lines).* Milwaukee, Wisc.: Jones Techno-Comm, 1990.
Sherman, Stephen. *Who's Who from MACV-SOG.* Houston, Tex.: Radix Press, 1996.
Shultz, Richard H., Jr. *The Secret War against Hanoi: Kennedy's and Johnson's Use of Spies, Saboteurs, and Covert Warriors in North Vietnam.* New York: HarperCollins, 1999.
Singlaub, John K., with Malcolm McConnell. *Hazardous Duty: An American Soldier in the Twentieth Century.* New York: Summit Books, 1991.
Tourison, Sedgwick D., Jr. *Secret Army, Secret War: Washington's Tragic Spy Operation in Vietnam.* Annapolis, Md.: Naval Institute Press, 1995.
Van Buskirk, Robert, and Fred Bauer. *Tailwind: A True Story.* Waco, Tex.: Word Books, 1983.

Army Special Forces

Archer, Chalmers, Jr. *Green Berets in the Vanguard: Inside Special Forces, 1953–1963.* Annapolis, Md.: Naval Institute Press, 2001.
Beckwith, Charlie A., and Ronald Knox. *Delta Force.* San Diego, Calif.: Harcourt Brace Jovanovich, 1983.
Benavidez, Roy P., and Oscar Griffin. *The Three Wars of Roy Benavidez.* San Antonio, Tex.: Corona, 1986.
Benavidez, Roy P., with John R. Craig. *Medal of Honor: A Vietnam Warrior's Story.* Dulles, Va.: Brassey's, 1995.
Bendell, Don. *Crossbow.* New York: Berkley, 1990.
———. *The B-52 Overture: The North Vietnamese Assault on Special Forces Camp A-242, Dak Pek.* New York: Dell, 1992.
———. *Valley of Tears: Assault into Plei Trap.* New York: Dell, 1993.
———. *Snake-Eater: Characters in and Stories about the U.S. Army Special Forces in the Vietnam War.* New York: Dell, 1994.
Billac, Pete. *The Last Medal of Honor.* New York: Swan, 1990.
Burruss, Lewis H. *Mike Force.* New York: Pocket Books, 1989.
Coppola, Vincent. *Uneasy Warriors: Coming Back Home; The Perilous Journey of the Green Berets.* Atlanta, Ga.: Longstreet, 1995.
Cornett, Alan G. *Gone Native: An NCO's Story.* New York: Ballantine, 2000.
Craig, William T. *Lifer! From Infantry to Special Forces.* New York: Ivy Books, 1994.

———. *Team Sergeant: A Special Forces NCO at Lang Vei and Beyond*. New York: Ivy Books, 1998.

Donahue, James C. *No Greater Love: A Day with the Mobile Guerrilla Force in Vietnam*. Canton, Ohio: Daring Books, 1988.

———. *Mobile Guerrilla Force: With the Special Forces in War Zone D*. Annapolis, Md.: Naval Institute Press, 1996.

———. *Blackjack-33: With Special Forces in the Viet Cong Forbidden Zone*. New York: Ivy Books, 1999.

Donlon, Roger H. C. *Beyond Nam Dong*. Leavenworth, Kans.: R & N Publishers, 1998.

Dooley, George E. *Battle for the Central Highlands*. New York: Ballantine, 2000.

Duncan, Donald. *The New Legions*. New York: Random House, 1967.

Foley, Dennis. *Special Men: A LRP's Recollections*. New York: Ivy Books, 1994.

Garner, Joe R., with Avrum M. Fine. *Code Name: Copperhead; My True-Life Exploits as a Special Forces Soldier*. New York: Simon & Schuster, 1994.

Gole, Henry G. *Soldiering: Observations from Korea, Vietnam, and Safe Places*. Dulles, Va.: Potomac Books, 2005.

Gritz, James "Bo." *Called to Serve*. Boulder City, Nev.: Lazarus, 1991.

Halberstadt, Hans. *War Stories of the Green Berets: The Viet Nam Experience*. Osceola, Wisc.: Motorbooks, 1994.

Ives, Christopher K. *US Special Forces and Counterinsurgency in Vietnam: Military Innovation and Institutional Failure, 1961–1963*. New York: Routledge, 2007.

Krasnoff, Stan. *Shadows on the Wall: The Adrenalin-Pumping, Heart-Yammering True Story of Project Rapid Fire*. St. Leonards, NSW, Australia: Allen & Unwin, 2003.

Marvin, Daniel. *Expendable Elite: One Soldier's Journey into Covert Warfare*. Walterville, Ore.: Trine Day, 2003.

Moore, Robin, and Henry Rothblatt. *Court-Martial*. Garden City, N.Y.: Doubleday, 1971.

Patton, Charles D. *Colt Terry, Green Beret*. College Station, Tex.: Texas A&M University Press, 2005.

Sasser, Charles W. *Always a Warrior: The Memoir of a Six-War Soldier*. New York: Pocket Books, 1994.

———. *Raider*. New York: St. Martin's Press, 2002.

Shackleton, Ronald. *Village Defense: Initial Special Forces Operations in Viet Nam*. Arvada, Colo.: Phoenix Press, 1975.

Simpson, Charles M., III. *Inside the Green Berets*. Novato, Calif.: Presidio Press, 1983.

Stanton, Shelby L. *Green Berets at War: US Army Special Forces in Southeast Asia, 1956–1975*. Novato, Calif.: Presidio Press, 1985.

Stein, Jeff. *A Murder in Wartime: Untold Spy Story That Changed the Course of the Vietnam War*. New York: St. Martin's Press, 1992.

Wade, Leigh. *Tan Phu: Special Forces Team A-23 in Combat*. New York: Ivy Books, 1997.

———. *Assault on Dak Pek: A Special Force A-Team in Combat, 1970*. New York: Ivy Books, 1998.

———. *The Protected Will Never Know*. New York: Ivy Books, 1998.

Yedinak, Steven M. *Hard to Forget: An American with the Mobile Guerrilla Force in Vietnam*. New York: Ivy Books, 1998.

Marines in Reconnaissance

Baumgardner, Randy, ed. *3rd Reconnaissance Battalion: Vietnam, 1965–1969*. Paducah, Ky.: Turner Publishing, 2003.

Delezen, John Edmund. *Eye of the Tiger: Memoir of a United States Marine, Third Force Recon Company, Vietnam*. Jefferson, N.C.: McFarland, 2003.

Finlayson, Andrew R. *Marine Advisors with the Vietnamese Provincial Reconnaissance Units, 1966–1970*. Quantico, Va.: History Division, United States Marine Corps, 2009.

Hildreth, Ray, and Charles W. Sasser. *Hill 488*. New York: Pocket Books, 2003.

Jacques, Maurice A., and Bruce H. Norton. *Sergeant Major, U.S. Marines*. New York: Ivy Books, 1995.

Lee, Alex. *Force Recon Command: A Special Marine Unit in Vietnam, 1969–1970*. Annapolis, Md.: Naval Institute Press, 1995.

Norton, Bruce H. *Force Recon Diary, 1970*. New York: Ivy Books, 1992.

———, ed. *Stingray*. New York: Ballantine, 2000.

Peters, Bill. *First Force Recon Company: Sunrise at Midnight*. New York: Ivy Books, 1999.

Rhodes, John R. *Rejoice or Cry: Diary of a Recon Marine, Vietnam, 1967–1968*. Danbury, Conn.: Economy Printing, 1996.

Vetter, Lawrence C., Jr. *Never without Heroes: Marine Third Reconnaissance Battalion in Vietnam, 1965–1970*. New York: Ivy Books, 1996.

Yerman, Ron. *Lead, Follow, or Get the Hell Out of the Way*. New York: Vantage Press, 1997.

Young, Paul R. *First Recon—Second to None: A Marine Reconnaissance Battalion, 1967–1968*. New York: Ivy Books, 1992.

Navy SEALs

Block, Mickey, and William Kimball. *Before the Dawn*. New York: Pocket Books, 1989.

Boehm, Roy, with Charles Sasser. *First SEAL*. New York: Pocket Books, 1997.

Bosiljevac, Tim L. *SEALs: UDT/SEAL Operations in Vietnam*. New York: Ivy Books, 1991.

Constance, Harry, with Randall Fuerst. *Good to Go: The Life and Times of a Decorated Member of the U.S. Navy's Elite SEAL Team Two*. New York: Morrow, 1997.

Cummings, Dennis. *The Men Behind the Trident: SEAL Team One in Vietnam*. Annapolis, Md.: Naval Institute Press, 1997.

Dockery, Kevin. *Free Fire Zones: The True Story of U.S. Navy SEAL Combat in Vietnam*. New York: HarperCollins, 2000.

———. *Navy SEALs: A History, Part II, The Vietnam Years*. New York: Berkley, 2002.

Dockery, Kevin, and Bill Fawcett, eds. *The Teams: An Oral History of the U.S. Navy Seals*. New York: Morrow, 1998.

Enoch, Barry W., with Gregory A. Walker. *Teammates: SEALs at War*. New York: Pocket Books, 1996.

Fawcett, Bill, ed. *Hunters and Shooters: An Oral History of the U.S. Navy SEALs in Vietnam*. New York: Morrow, 1995.

Gormly, Robert A. *Combat Swimmer: Memoirs of a Navy SEAL*. New York: NAL/Dutton, 1998.

Harper, W. Ivy. *Waltzing Matilda: The Life and Times of Nebraska Senator Robert Kerrey*. New York: St. Martin's Press, 1992.

Keith, Thomas H., and J. Terry Riebling. *SEAL Warrior: Death in the Dark; Vietnam, 1968–1972*. New York: St. Martin's Press, 2009.

Kerrey, Joseph Robert. *When I Was a Young Man*. New York: Harcourt, 2002.

Marcinko, Richard, with John Weisman. *Rogue Warrior*. New York: Pocket Books, 1992.

Miller, Rad, Jr. *Whattaya Mean I Can't Kill 'Em? A Navy SEAL in Vietnam*. New York: Ivy Books, 1998.

Smith, Gary R. *Master Chief: Diary of a Navy SEAL*. New York: Ivy Books, 1996.

Smith, Gary R., and Alan Maki. *Death in the Delta: Diary of a Navy SEAL*. New York: Ivy Books, 1996.

Vistica, Gregory L. *The Education of Lieutenant Kerrey*. New York: St. Martin's Press, 2003.

Walsh, Michael J., and Greg Walker. *SEAL!* New York: Pocket Books, 1995.

Waterman, Steven L. *Just a Sailor: A Navy Diver's Story of Photography, Salvage, and Combat*. New York: Ballantine, 2000.

Watson, James, and Kevin Dockery. *Point Man: Inside the Toughest and Most Deadly Unit in Vietnam by a Founding Member of Elite Navy SEALs*. New York: Morrow, 1993.

———. *Walking Point*. New York: Morrow, 1997.

Young, Darryl. *The Element of Surprise: Navy SEALs in Vietnam*. New York: Ivy Books, 1990.

Long-Range Reconnaissance Patrols

Ankony, Robert C. *Lurps: A Ranger's Diary of Tet, Khe Sanh, A Shau, and Quang Tri*. Lanham, Md.: University Press of America, 2006.

Burford, John. *LRRP Team Leader*. New York: Ivy Books, 1994.

Camper, Frank. *L.R.R.P.: The Professional*. New York: Dell, 1988.

Chambers, Larry. *Recondo: LRRPs in the 101st Airborne*. New York: Ivy Books, 1992.

———. *Death in the A Shau Valley: L Company LRRPs in Vietnam, 1969–1970*. New York: Ivy Books, 1998.

Christopher, Ronald Lee. *Above All Else*. Baltimore, Md.: PublishAmerica, 2006.

Ericson, Don, and John L. Rotundo. *Charlie Rangers*. New York: Ivy Books, 1989.

Ford, Gary Douglas. *4/4: A LRP's Narrative*. New York: Ivy Books, 1993.

Goshen, Bill. *War Paint*. New York: Ballantine, 2001.

Hall, Don C., and Annette R. Hall. *I Served*. Bellevue, Wa.: Trafford Publishing, 2006.

Johnson, Frank. *Diary of an Airborne Ranger: A LRRP's Year in the Combat Zone*. New York: Ballantine, 2001.

Jorgenson, Kregg P. J. *The Ghosts of the Highlands: 1st Cav LRRPs in Vietnam, 1966–1967*. New York: Ivy Books, 1999.

————. *LRRP Company Command: The Cav's LRP/Rangers in Vietnam, 1968–1969.* New York: Ballantine, 2000.

Lanning, Michael Lee. *Inside the LRRPs: Rangers in Vietnam.* New York: Ivy Books, 1988.

Linderer, Gary A. *Eyes Behind the Lines.* New York: Ivy Books, 1991.

————. *The Eyes of the Eagle.* New York: Ivy Books, 1991.

————. *Six Silent Men: 101st LRP/Rangers.* Vol. 3. New York: Ivy Books, 1997.

————. *Phantom Warriors: LRRPs, LRPs, and Rangers in Vietnam.* Vol. 1. New York: Ballantine, 2000.

————. *Phantom Warriors: LRRPs, LRPs, and Rangers in Vietnam.* Vol. 2. New York: Ballantine, 2001.

Martinez, Reynel. *Six Silent Men: 101st LRP/Rangers.* Vol. 1. N.Y.: Ivy Books, 1996.

Miller, Kenn. *Six Silent Men: 101st LRP/Rangers.* Vol. 2. N.Y.: Ivy Books, 1997.

Sallah, Michael, and Mitch Weiss. *Tiger Force: A True Story of Men and War.* Boston: Little, Brown, 2006.

Shanahan, Bill, and John P. Brackin. *Stealth Patrol: The Making of a Vietnam Ranger, 1968–1970.* Cambridge, Mass.: Da Capo, 2003.

Stanton, Shelby L. *Rangers at War: Combat Recon in Vietnam.* New York: Orion, 1992.

Walker, James W. *Fortune Favors the Bold: A British LRRP with the 101st.* New York: Ivy Books, 1998.

Phoenix Program

Andradé, Dale. *Ashes to Ashes: The Phoenix Program and the Vietnam War.* Lexington, Mass.: Lexington Books, 1990.

Cook, John L. *The Advisor.* Philadelphia: Dorrance, 1973.

Crowell, G. LaVerne. *ICEX Intelligence: Vietnam's Phoenix Program.* Baltimore, Md.: PublishAmerica, 2006.

Grant, Zalin. *Facing the Phoenix: The CIA and the Political Defeat of the United States in Vietnam.* New York: Norton, 1991.

Moyar, Mark. *Phoenix and the Birds of Prey: The CIA's Secret Campaign to Destroy the Viet Cong.* Lincoln, Nebr.: University of Nebraska Press, 2007.

Valentine, Douglas. *The Phoenix Program.* New York: Morrow, 1990.

SPECIAL TOPICS, MILITARY

Điện Biên Phủ and the 1954 Geneva Conference

Cable, James. *The Geneva Conference of 1954 on Indochina.* New York: St. Martin's Press, 1986.

Childs, Marquis. *The Ragged Edge: The Diary of a Crisis.* Garden City, N.Y.: Doubleday, 1955.

Fall, Bernard. *Hell in a Very Small Place.* Philadelphia: Lippincott, 1966.

Grauwin, Paul. *Doctor at Dien-Bien-Phu*. London: Hutchinson, 1955.

Gurtov, Melvin. *The First Vietnam Crisis: Chinese Communist Strategy and United States Involvement, 1953–1954*. New York: Columbia University Press, 1967.

Kaplan, Lawrence S., Denise Artaud, and Mark R. Rubin, eds. *Dien Bien Phu and the Crisis of Franco-American Relations, 1954–1955*. Wilmington, Del.: Scholarly Resources Books, 1990.

Keegan, John. *Dien Bien Phu*. New York: Ballantine, 1974.

Langlais, Pierre. *Dien Bien Phu*. Paris: Éditions France-Empire, 1963.

Mendes France, Pierre. *Face to Face with Asia*. New York: Liveright, 1974.

Morgan, Ted. *Valley of Death: The Tragedy at Dien Bien Phu That Led America into the Vietnam War*. New York: Random House, 2010.

Nordell, John R., Jr. *The Undetected Enemy: French and American Miscalculations at Dien Bien Phu, 1953*. College Station, Tex.: Texas A&M University Press, 1995.

Prados, John. *The Sky Would Fall*. New York: Dial, 1983.

Randle, Robert F. *Geneva 1954: The Settlement of the Indochinese War*. Princeton, N.J.: Princeton University Press, 1969.

Roy, Jules. *The Battle of Dien Bien Phu*. New York: Harper & Row, 1965.

Simpson, Howard R. *Dien Bien Phu: The Epic Battle America Forgot*. Dulles, Va.: Brassey's, 1994.

Stone, David. *Dien Bien Phu*. Dulles, Va.: Brassey's, 2004.

Võ Nguyên Giáp. *Dien Bien Phu*. Hanoi: Chính Trị Quốc Gia, 1998.

Western, Jon. *Selling Intervention and War: The Presidency, the Media, and the American Public*. Baltimore, Md.: Johns Hopkins University Press, 2005.

Windrow, Martin. *The Last Valley: Dien Bien Phu and the French Defeat in Vietnam*. Cambridge, Mass.: Da Capo, 2004.

Worth, Richard. *Dien Bien Phu*. Philadelphia: Chelsea House, 2002.

Gulf of Tonkin

Alvarez, Everett, Jr., and Anthony S. Pitch. *Chained Eagle*. New York: Fine, 1989.

Austin, Anthony. *The President's War*. New York: Lippincott, 1971.

Goulden, Joseph. *Truth Is the First Casualty: The Gulf of Tonkin Affair—Illusion and Reality*. Chicago: Rand McNally, 1969.

Halpern, Samuel E. *West Pac '64*. Boston: Branden Press, 1975.

Moïse, Edwin E. *Tonkin Gulf and the Escalation of the Vietnam War*. Chapel Hill, N.C.: University of North Carolina Press, 1996.

Siff, Ezra Y. *Why the Senate Slept: The Gulf of Tonkin Resolution and the Beginning of America's Vietnam War*. Westport, Conn.: Greenwood, 1999.

Windchy, Eugene G. *Tonkin Gulf*. New York: Doubleday, 1971.

Tết: The Year of Decision, 1968

Allison, William Thomas. *The Tet Offensive: A Brief History with Documents*. New York: Routledge, 2008.

Anderson, David L., ed. *Facing My Lai: Moving beyond the Massacre*. Lawrence, Kans.: University Press of Kansas, 1998.

Angers, Trent. *The Forgotten Hero of My Lai: The Hugh Thompson Story*. Lafayette, La.: Acadian House, 1999.

Belknap, Michal R. *The Vietnam War on Trial: The My Lai Massacre and the Court-Martial of Lieutenant Calley*. Lawrence, Kans.: University Press of Kansas, 2002.

Bilton, Michael, and Kevin Sim. *Four Hours in My Lai*. New York: Viking, 1992.

Blood, Jake. *The Tet Effect: Intelligence and the Public Perception of War*. New York: Routledge, 2005.

Brenner, Samuel, ed. *Vietnam War Crimes*. Farmington Hills, Mich.: Greenhaven Press, 2006.

Drez, Ronald J., and Douglas Brinkley. *Voices of Courage: The Battle for Khe Sanh, Vietnam*. New York: Bullfinch, 2005.

Ewing, Michael. *Khe Sanh*. New York: Bantam, 1987.

Ford, Ronnie E. *Tet 1968: Understanding the Surprise*. London: Frank Cass, 1995.

French, Peter A., ed. *Individual and Collective Responsibility: Massacre at My Lai*. Cambridge, Mass.: Schenkman, 1998.

Gershen, Martin. *Destroy or Die: The True Story of Mylai*. New Rochelle, N.Y.: Arlington House, 1971.

Gilbert, Marc Jason, and William Head, eds. *The Tet Offensive*. Westport, Conn.: Praeger, 1996.

Goldstein, Joseph, Burke Marshall, and Jack Schwartz. *The My Lai Massacre and Its Cover-up: Beyond the Reach of Law? The Peers Commission Report with a Supplement and Introductory Essay on the Limits of Law*. New York: Free Press, 1976.

Gott, Kendall W. *Breaking the Mold: Tanks in the Cities*. Fort Leavenworth, Kans.: Combat Studies Institute Press, 2006.

Greenhaw, Wayne. *The Making of a Hero: The Story of Lieutenant William Calley Jr.* Louisville, Ky.: Touchstone, 1971.

Greiner, Bernd. *War without Fronts: The USA in Vietnam*. London: Bodley Head, 2009.

Hammel, Eric. *Khe Sanh, Siege in the Clouds: An Oral History*. New York: Crown, 1989.
———. *Fire in the Streets: The Battle for Hue, Tet 1968*. Chicago: Contemporary Books, 1991.
———. *Marines in Hue City: A Portrait of Urban Combat, Tet 1968*. St. Paul, Minn.: Zenith Press, 2007.

Hammer, Richard. *One Morning in the War: The Tragedy at Son My*. New York: Coward-McCann, 1970.
———. *The Court-martial of Lt. Calley*. New York: Coward, McCann & Geoghagan, 1971.

Heonik Kwon. *After the Massacre: Commemoration and Consolation in Ha My and My Lai*. Berkeley, Calif.: University of California Press, 2006.

Herman, Edward S. *Atrocities in Vietnam: Myths and Realities*. Philadelphia: Pilgrim Press, 1970.

Hersh, Seymour M. *My Lai 4: A Report on the Massacre and Its Aftermath*. New York: Random House, 1970.
———. *Cover-Up*. New York: Random House, 1972.

Hoàng Ngọc Lung. *The General Offensives of 1968–1969*. McLean, Va.: General Research Corporation, 1978.

Nelson, Deborah. *The War behind Me: Vietnam Veterans Confront the Truth about U.S. War Crimes*. New York: Basic Books, 2008.

Nolan, Keith W. *Battle for Hue: Tet 1968*. Novato, Calif.: Presidio Press, 1983.

———. *The Battle for Saigon: Tet 1968*. New York: Pocket Books, 1996.

———. *House to House: Playing the Enemy's Game in Saigon, May 1968*. St. Paul, Minn.: Zenith Press, 2006.

Oberdorfer, Don. *Tet*. New York: Doubleday, 1971.

Oliver, Kendrick. *The My Lai Massacre in American History and Memory*. Manchester, UK: Manchester University Press, 2006.

Olson, James S., and Randy Roberts, *My Lai: A Brief History with Documents*. Boston: Bedford Books, 1998.

Peers, William R. *The My Lai Inquiry*. New York: Norton, 1979.

Phillips, William R. *Night of the Silver Stars: The Battle of Lang Vei*. Annapolis, Md.: Naval Institute Press, 1997.

Pisor, Robert. *The End of the Line: The Siege of Khe Sanh*. New York: Norton, 1982.

Prados, John, and Ray W. Stubbe. *Valley of Decision: The Siege of Khe Sanh*. Boston: Houghton Mifflin, 1991.

Ringler, Dale S. *How the North Vietnamese Won the War: Operational Art Bends but Does Not Break in Response to Asymmetry*. Ft. Leavenworth, Kans.: School of Advanced Military Studies, 2001.

Schmitz, David F. *The Tet Offensive: Politics, War, and Public Opinion*. Lanham, Md.: Rowman & Littlefield, 2005.

Stark, Judy Thornton. *Tete a Tet: Honeymoon under the Bed*. New York: Vantage, 2006.

Tiede, Tom. *Calley: Soldier or Killer?* New York: Pinnacle, 1971.

Willbanks, James H. *The Tet Offensive: A Concise History*. New York: Columbia University Press, 2006.

Pacification Efforts

Bergerud, Eric M. *The Dynamics of Defeat: The Vietnam War in Hau Nghia Province*. Boulder, Colo.: Westview, 1991.

Callison, Charles S. *Land-to-the-Tiller in the Mekong Delta: Economic, Social and Political Effects of Land Reform in Four Villages of South Vietnam*. Lanham, Md.: University Press of America, 1983.

Herrington, Stuart. *Silence Was a Weapon: The Vietnam War in the Villages*. Novato, Calif.: Presidio Press, 1982.

Hickey, Gerald C. *Village in Vietnam*. New Haven, Conn.: Yale University Press, 1964.

Hunt, Richard A. *Pacification: The American Struggle for Vietnam's Hearts and Minds*. Boulder, Colo.: Westview, 1995.

Lee, Eun Ho, and Yong Soon Yim. *The Politics of Military Civic Action: The Case of South Korean and South Vietnamese Forces in the Vietnam War*. Hong Kong: Asian Research Service, 1980.

Metzner, Edward P. *More Than a Soldier's War: Pacification in Vietnam.* College Station, Tex.: Texas A&M University Press, 1995.

Nighswonger, William A. *Rural Pacification in Vietnam.* New York: Praeger, 1966.

Sansom, Robert L. *The Economics of Insurgency in the Mekong Delta.* Cambridge, Mass.: MIT Press, 1970.

Schell, Jonathan. *The Village of Ben Suc.* New York: Knopf, 1967.

Tanham, George K., with W. Robert Warne, Earl J. Young, and William A. Nighswonger. *War without Guns: American Civilians in Rural Vietnam.* New York: Praeger, 1966.

Trullinger, James. *Village at War.* New York: Longman, 1980.

Walinsky, Louis J., ed. *Agrarian Reform as Unfinished Business: The Selected Papers of Wolf Ladejinsky.* New York: Oxford University Press, 1977.

Wiegersma, Nancy. *Vietnam—Peasant Land, Peasant Revolution: Patriarchy and Collectivity in the Rural Economy.* New York: St. Martin's Press, 1988.

Paris Peace Negotiations to the War's End

Asselin, Pierre. *A Bitter Peace: Washington, Hanoi, and the Making of the Paris Agreement.* Chapel Hill, N.C.: University of North Carolina Press, 2002.

Berman, Larry. *No Peace, No Honor: Nixon, Kissinger, and Betrayal in Vietnam.* New York: Free Press, 2001.

Bouscaren, Anthony T., ed. *All Quiet on the Eastern Front: The Death of South Vietnam.* Old Greenwich, Conn.: Devin-Adair, 1977.

Butler, David. *The Fall of Saigon.* New York: Simon & Schuster, 1985.

Engelmann, Larry. *Tears before the Rain: An Oral History of the Fall of Saigon.* New York: Oxford University Press, 1990.

Fenton, James. *All the Wrong Places: Adrift in the Politics of the Pacific Rim.* New York: Atlantic Monthly Press, 1988.

Haley, P. Edward. *Congress and the Fall of South Vietnam and Cambodia.* Rutherford, N.J.: Farleigh Dickinson University Press, 1982.

Herring, George C., ed. *Secret Diplomacy of the Vietnam War: The Negotiating Volumes of the Pentagon Papers.* Austin, Tex.: University of Texas Press, 1983.

Herschensohn, Bruce. *An American Amnesia: How the U.S. Congress Forced the Surrenders of South Vietnam and Cambodia.* New York: Beaufort Books, 2010.

Isaacs, Arnold. *Without Honor: Defeat in Vietnam and Cambodia.* Baltimore, Md.: Johns Hopkins University Press, 1983.

Kimball, Jeffrey. *Nixon's Vietnam War.* Lawrence, Kans.: University Press of Kansas, 1998.

———. *The Vietnam War Files: Uncovering the Secret History of Nixon-Era Strategy.* Lawrence, Kans.: University Press of Kansas, 2004.

Kraslow, David, and Stuart Loory. *The Secret Search for Peace in Vietnam.* New York: Random House, 1968.

Lee, J. Edward, and Toby Haynsworth, ed. *White Christmas in April: The Collapse of South Vietnam, 1975.* New York: Peter Lang, 1999.

Lưu Văn Lợi. *The Le Duc Tho–Kissinger Negotiations in Paris.* Hanoi: The Gioi, 1996.

Paolucci, Henry. *Public Image, Private Interest: Henry Kissinger's Foreign Policy Strategies in Vietnam.* Smyrna, Del.: Griffon House, 2002.

Peck-Barnes, Shirley. *The War Cradle: Vietnam's Children of War; Operation Babylift—The Untold Story.* Denver, Colo.: Vintage Pressworks, 2000.

Pilger, John. *The Last Day.* New York: Vintage Books, 1976.

Porter, D. Gareth. *A Peace Denied: The U.S., Vietnam, and the Paris Agreements.* Bloomington, Ind.: Indiana University Press, 1975.

Terzani, Tiziano. *Giai Phong! The Fall and Liberation of Saigon.* New York: St. Martin's Press, 1976.

Willbanks, James H. *Abandoning Vietnam: How America Left and South Vietnam Lost Its War.* Lawrence, Kans.: University Press of Kansas, 2004.

Technology and Weapons of War

Arnold, James R. *Artillery: Illustrated History of the Vietnam War.* New York: Bantam, 1987.

Dickson, Paul. *The Electronic Battlefield.* Bloomington, Ind.: Indiana University Press, 1976.

Dunstan, Simon. *Vietnam Tracks: Armor in Battle, 1945–1875.* Novato, Calif.: Presidio Press, 1982.

Emering, Edward J. *Weapons and Field Gear of the North Vietnamese Army and Viet Cong.* Atglen, Penn.: Schiffer Military History, 1998.

Ezell, Edward C. *Personal Firepower: Illustrated History of the Vietnam War.* New York: Bantam, 1988.

Gliedman, John. *Terror from the Sky: North Viet-Nam's Dikes and the U.S. Bombing.* Cambridge, Mass.: Vietnam Resource Center, 1972.

Kahaner, Larry. *AK-47: The Weapon That Changed the Face of Warfare.* New York: Wiley, 2006.

Mahnken, Thomas G. *Technology and the American Way of War since 1945.* New York: Columbia University Press, 2008.

Price, Alfred. *War in the Fourth Dimension: US Electronic Warfare from the Vietnam War to the Present.* Mechanicsburg, Penn.: Stackpole Books, 2001.

Tambini, Anthony J. *Wiring Vietnam: The Electronic Wall.* Lanham, Md.: Scarecrow Press, 2007.

POWs and MIAs

Allen, Michael J. *Until the Last Man Comes Home: POWs, MIAs, and the Unending Vietnam War.* Chapel Hill, N.C.: University of North Carolina Press, 2009.

Anton, Frank. *Why Didn't You Get Me Out?* Summit, Tex.: Summit, 1997.

Bailey, Lawrence R., Jr., with Ron Martz. *Solitary Survivor: The First American POW in Southeast Asia.* Dulles, Va.: Brassey's, 1995.

Blakey, Scott. *Prisoner at War: The Survival of Commander Richard A. Stratton.* New York: Doubleday, 1978.

Brace, Ernest C. *A Code to Keep: The True Story of America's Longest-held Civilian Prisoner of War in Vietnam*. New York: St. Martin's Press, 1988.

Burkett, B. G., and Glenna Whitley. *Stolen Valor: How the Vietnam Generation Was Robbed of Its Heroes and Its History*. Dallas, Tex.: Verity Press, 1998.

Certain, Robert G. *Unchained Eagle: From Prisoner of War to Prisoner of Christ*. Palm Springs, Calif.: ETC Publications, 2003.

Clarke, Douglas L. *The Missing Man: Politics and the MIA*. Washington, D.C.: National Defense University Press, 1979.

Coffee, Gerald. *Beyond Survival: Building on the Hard Times—A POW's Inspiring Story*. New York: Putnam, 1990.

Coram, Robert. *American Patriot: The Life and Wars of Colonel Bud Day*. Boston: Little, Brown, 2007.

Daly, James A., and Lee Bergman. *Black Prisoner of War: A Conscientious Objector's Vietnam Memoir*. Lawrence, Kans.: University Press of Kansas, 2000.

Denton, Jeremiah A., with Ed Brandt. *When Hell Was in Session*. New York: Reader's Digest Press, 1976.

Dockery, Kevin. *Operation Thunderhead: The True Story of Vietnam's Final POW Rescue Mission—and the Last Navy SEAL Killed in Country*. New York: Berkley Caliber, 2008.

Dramesi, John A. *Code of Honor*. New York: Norton, 1975.

Franklin, H. Bruce. *M.I.A. or Mythmaking in America*. Chicago: Lawrence Hill Books, 1992.

Gargus, John. *The Son Tay Raid: American POWs in Vietnam Were Not Forgotten*. College Station, Tex.: Texas A&M University Press, 2007.

Grant, Zalin. *Survivors*. New York: Norton, 1975.

Groom, Winston, and Duncan Spencer. *Conversations with the Enemy: The Story of PFC Robert Garwood*. New York: Putnam, 1983.

Grubb, Evelyn, and Carol Jose. *You Are Not Forgotten: A Family's Quest for Truth and the Founding of the National League of Families*. St. Petersburg, Fla.: Vandamere Press, 2008.

Gruner, Elliott. *Prisoners of Culture: Representing the Vietnam P.O.W.* New Brunswick, N.J.: Rutgers University Press, 1993.

Guarino, Larry. *A POW's Story: 2801 Days in Hanoi*. New York: Ivy Books, 1990.

Hawley, Thomas M. *The Remains of War: Bodies, Politics, and the Search for American Soldiers Unaccounted for in Southeast Asia*. Durham, N.C.: Duke University Press, 2005.

Hefley, James, and Marti Hefley. *No Time for Tombstones: Life and Death in the Vietnamese Jungle*. Wheaton, Ill.: Tyndale House, 1974.

Hirsch, James S. *Two Souls Indivisible: The Friendship That Saved Two POWs in Vietnam*. Boston: Houghton Mifflin, 2004.

Howes, Craig. *Voices of the Vietnam POWs: Witnesses to their Fight*. New York: Oxford University Press, 1993.

Hubbell, John G. *P.O.W.: A Definitive History of the American Prisoner-of-War Experience in Vietnam, 1964–1973*. New York: Reader's Digest Press, 1976.

Isby, David C. *Leave No Man Behind: Liberation and Capture Missions*. London: Weidenfeld & Nicolson, 2004.

Jensen-Stevenson, Monika, and William H. Stevenson. *Kiss the Boys Goodbye: How the United States Betrayed Its Own POWs in Vietnam*. New York: Dutton, 1990.

Keating, Susan K. *Prisoners of Hope: Exploiting the POW/MIA Myth in America*. New York: Random House, 1994.

McConnell, Malcolm. *Inside Hanoi's Secret Archives: Solving the MIA Mystery*. New York: Simon & Schuster, 1995.

Mulligan, James A. *The Hanoi Commitment*. Virginia Beach, Va.: RIF Marketing, 1981.

Philpott, Tom. *Glory Denied: The Saga of Jim Thompson, America's Longest-Held Prisoner of War*. New York: Norton, 2001.

Plumb, Charlie. *I'm No Hero: A POW Story as Told to Glen DeWerf.* Independence, Mo.: Independence Press, 1973.

Price, Donald L. *The First Marine Captured in Vietnam: A Biography of Donald G. Cook*. Jefferson, N.C.: McFarland, 2007.

Risner, Robinson. *The Passing of the Night: My Seven Years as a Prisoner of the North Vietnamese*. New York: Random House, 1973.

Robinson, Melissa B., and Maureen Dunn. *The Search for Canasta 404: Love, Loss, and the POW/MIA Movement*. Hanover, N.H.: University Press of New England, 2006.

Rochester, Stuart I., and Frederick Kiley. *Honor Bound: American Prisoners of War in Southeast Asia, 1961–1973*. Annapolis, Md.: Naval Institute Press, 1999.

Rowan, Stephen A. *They Wouldn't Let Us Die: The Prisoners of War Tell Their Story*. Middle Village, N.Y.: Jonathan David Publishers, 1973.

Rowe, James N. *Five Years to Freedom*. Boston: Little, Brown, 1971.

Sauter, Mark, and Jim Sanders. *The Men We Left Behind: Henry Kissinger, the Politics of Deceit and the Tragic Fate of POWs after the Vietnam War*. Washington, D.C.: National Press, 1993.

Schemmer, Benjamin F. *The Raid*. New York: Harper & Row, 1976.

Smith, George E. *P.O.W.: Two Years with the Vietcong*. Berkeley, Calif.: Ramparts Press, 1971.

Smith, Philip E., and Peggy Herz. *Journey into Darkness*. New York: Pocket Books, 1992.

Stern, Lewis M. *Imprisoned or Missing in Vietnam: Policies of the Vietnamese Government toward Captured and Detained United States Soldiers, 1969–1994*. Jefferson, N.C.: McFarland, 1995.

Stockdale, Jim, and Sybil Stockdale. *In Love and War*. New York: Harper & Row, 1984.

Swift, Earl. *Where They Lay: The Search for America's Lost Soldiers*. Boston: Houghton Mifflin, 2003.

Veith, George J. *Code-Name Bright Light: The Untold Story of U.S. POW Rescue Efforts during the Vietnam War*. New York: Free Press, 1998.

Central Intelligence Agency and the Secret Air War

Allen, George W. *None So Blind: A Personal Account of the Intelligence Failure in Vietnam*. Chicago: Ivan R. Dee, 2001.

Barrett, David M. *The CIA and Congress: The Untold Story from Truman to Kennedy*. Lawrence, Kans.: University Press of Kansas, 2005.

Bell, Larry A. *Dead Horses in the Sun*. Bloomington, Ind.: AuthorHouse, 2003.

Breckenridge, Scott. *CIA and the Cold War: A Memoir*. Westport, Conn.: Praeger, 1993.

Colby, William, and Peter Forbath. *Honorable Men: My Life in the CIA*. New York: Simon & Schuster, 1978.

Corn, David. *Blond Ghost: Ted Shackley and the CIA's Crusades*. New York: Simon & Schuster, 1994.

Davis, Charles O. *Across the Mekong: The True Story of an Air America Helicopter Pilot*. Charlottesville, Va.: Hildesigns, 1996.

DeForest, Orrin, and David Chanoff. *Slow Burn: The Rise and Bitter Fall of American Intelligence in Vietnam*. New York: Simon & Schuster, 1990.

DeSilva, Peer. *Sub Rosa: The CIA and the Uses of Intelligence*. New York: Times Books, 1978.

Gleason, Robert L. *Air Commando Chronicles: Untold Tales from Vietnam, Latin America, and Back Again*. Manhattan, Kans.: Sunflower University Press, 2000.

Helms, Richard. *A Look Over My Shoulder: A Life in the Central Intelligence Agency*. New York: Random House, 2003.

Kelly, Orr. *From a Dark Sky: The Story of U.S. Air Force Special Operations*. Novato, Calif.: Presidio Press, 1996.

Leary, William. *Perilous Missions: Civil Air Transport and CIA Covert Operations in Asia*. Tuscaloosa, Ala.: University of Alabama Press, 1984.

Love, Terry. *Wings of Air America: A Photo History*. Atglen, Penn.: Schiffer Military History, 1998.

McGarvey, Patrick. *CIA: The Myth and the Madness*. New York: Saturday Review Press, 1972.

McGehee, Ralph. *Deadly Deceits: My 25 Years in the CIA*. New York: Sheridan Square Publications, 1983.

Mehring, James A. *One Patriot's Saga: An Enlisted Man's Story of WWII, Korea, and Vietnam*. Raleigh, N.C.: Pentland Press, 1997.

Powers, Thomas. *The Man Who Kept the Secrets: Richard Helms and the CIA*. New York: Knopf, 1979.

Prados, John. *Lost Crusader: The Secret Wars of CIA Director William Colby*. New York: Oxford University Press, 2003.

Richardson, John H., Jr. *My Father the Spy: An Investigative Memoir*. New York: HarperCollins, 2005.

Robbins, Christopher. *Air America*. New York: Avon, 1985.

Secord, Richard, with Jay Wurts. *Honored and Betrayed*. New York: Wiley, 1992.

Shackley, Ted. *Spymaster: My Life in the CIA*. Dulles, Va.: Potomac Books, 2005.

Smith, Felix. *China Pilot: Flying for Chiang and Chennault*. Dulles, Va.: Brassey's, 1995.

Smith, Russell Jack. *The Unknown CIA: My Three Decades with the Agency*. Dulles, Va.: Brassey's, 1989.

Snepp, Frank. *Decent Interval: An Insider's Account of Saigon's Indecent End Told by the CIA's Chief Strategy Analyst in Vietnam*. New York: Random House, 1977.

———. *Irreparable Harm: A Firsthand Account of How One Agent Took on the CIA in an Epic Battle over Secrecy and Free Speech*. New York: Random House, 1999.

Sullivan, John F. *Of Spies and Lies: A CIA Lie Detector Remembers Vietnam*. Lawrence, Kans.: University Press of Kansas, 2002.

Trento, Joseph J. *The Secret History of the CIA*. Roseville, Calif.: Prima, 2001.

Trest, Warren A. *Air Commando One: Heinie Aderholt and America's Secret Wars*. Washington, D.C.: Smithsonian Institution Press, 2000.

Weber, Ralph E., ed. *Spymasters: Ten CIA Officers in Their Own Words*. Wilmington, Del.: Scholarly Resources Books, 1999.

Order of Battle Controversy

Adams, Sam. *War of Numbers: An Intelligence Memoir*. Hanover, N.H.: Steerforth Press, 1994.

Adler, Renata. *Reckless Disregard: Westmoreland v. CBS et al.; Sharon v. Time*. New York: Vintage Books, 1988.

Benjamin, Burton. *Fair Play: CBS, General Westmoreland, and How a Television Documentary Went Wrong*. New York: Harper & Row, 1988.

Brewin, Bob, and Sydney Shaw. *Vietnam on Trial: Westmoreland vs. CBS*. New York: Atheneum, 1987.

Dorland, Gil. *Legacy of Discord: Voices of the Vietnam War Era*. Dulles, Va.: Brassey's, 2002.

Hiam, C. Michael. *Who the Hell Are We Fighting? The Story of Sam Adams and the Vietnam Intelligence Wars*. Hanover, N.H.: Steerforth Press, 2006.

Jones, Bruce. *War without Windows*. New York: Vanguard, 1987.

Kowet, Don. *A Matter of Honor*. New York: Macmillan, 1984.

Rosenberg, Norman L. *Protecting the Best Men: An Interpretive History of the Law of Libel*. Chapel Hill, N.C.: North Carolina Press, 1986.

Roth, M. Patricia. *The Juror and the General*. New York: William Morrow, 1986.

Shields, Frederick L. *Preventable Disasters: Why Governments Fail*. Lanham, Md.: Rowman & Littlefield, 1991.

Smolla, Rodney A. *Suing the Press*. New York: Oxford University Press, 1986.

Wirtz, James J. *The Tet Offensive: Intelligence Failure in War*. Ithaca, N.Y.: Cornell University Press, 1991.

SPECIAL TOPICS, NONMILITARY

The Draft and Its Consequences

Appy, Christian G. *Working Class War: American Combat Soldiers and Vietnam*. Chapel Hill, N.C.: University of North Carolina Press, 1993.

Baskir, Lawrence M., and William A. Strauss. *Chance and Circumstance: The Draft, the War, and the Vietnam Generation*. New York: Knopf, 1978.

Flynn, George Q. *The Draft, 1940–1973*. Lawrence, Kans.: University Press of Kansas, 1993.

King, Edward L. *The Death of the Army: A Pre-mortem*. New York: Saturday Review Press, 1972.

Laurence, Janice H., and Peter F. Ramsberger. *Low-Aptitude Men in the Military: Who Profits, Who Pays?* New York: Praeger, 1991.

Leinwand, Gerald. *The Draft.* New York: Washington Square Press, 1970.

Tarr, Curtis W. *By the Numbers: The Reform of the Selective Service System, 1970–1972.* Washington, D.C.: National Defense University Press, 1981.

Morale and Discipline

Allison, William T. *Military Justice in Vietnam: The Rule of Law in an American War.* Lawrence, Kans.: University Press of Kansas, 2007.

Borch, Frederic L., III. *Vietnam: Army Lawyers in Southeast Asia, 1959–1975.* Fort Leavenworth, Kans.: U.S. Army Command and General Staff College Press, 2003.

Boyle, Richard. *Flower of the Dragon: The Breakdown of the U.S. Army in Vietnam.* San Francisco: Ramparts Press, 1972.

Crouchet, Jack. *Vietnam Stories: A Judge's Memoir.* Niwot, Colo.: University Press of Colorado, 1997.

Currey, Cecil Barr. *Self-Destruction: The Disintegration and Decay of the United States Army during the Vietnam Era.* New York: Norton, 1981.

———. *Long Binh Jail: An Oral History of Vietnam's Notorious U.S. Military Prison.* Dulles, Va.: Brassey's, 1999.

Henderson, Charles. *Jungle Rules: A True Story of Marine Justice in Vietnam.* New York: Berkley Caliber, 2006.

Kuzmarov, Jeremy. *The Myth of the Addicted Army: Vietnam and the Modern War on Drugs.* Amherst, Mass.: University of Massachusetts Press, 2009.

Prugh, George S. *Law at War: Vietnam, 1964–1973.* Washington, D.C.: United States Government Printing Office, 1975.

Women

Bartimus, Tad, Denby Fawcett, Jurate Kazickas, Edith Lederer, Ann Bryan Mariano, Anne Morrissy Merick, Laura Palmer, Kate Webb, and Tracy Wood. *War Torn: Stories of War from the Women Reporters Who Covered Vietnam.* New York: Random House, 2002.

Briand, Rena. *No Tears to Flow: Woman at War.* Melbourne, Australia: Heinemann, 1969.

Doughty, Marjorie. *Memoirs of an Insignificant Dragon.* Atlanta, Ga.: Allegro Press, 1999.

Fallaci, Oriana. *Nothing, and So Be It: A Personal Search for Meaning in War.* New York: Doubleday, 1972.

Fortin, Noonie. *Memories of Maggie: Martha Raye; A Legend Spanning Three Wars.* San Antonio, Tex.: LangMark Publishing, 1995.

———. *Potpourri of War.* San Antonio, Tex.: LangMark Publishing, 1998.

Lanier, Berneice. *A Rooster at Tet.* Huntington, W.Va.: University Editions, 1998.

Marshall, Kathryn. *In the Combat Zone: An Oral History of American Women in Vietnam, 1966–1975.* Boston: Little, Brown, 1987.

Merrell, Betty, and Priscilla Tunnell, eds. *Stories That Won't Go Away: Women in Vietnam, 1959–1975.* Birmingham, Ala.: New Hope, 1995.

Swerdlow, Amy. *Women Strike for Peace: Traditional Motherhood and Radical Politics in the 1960s*. Chicago: University of Chicago Press, 1993.

Taylor, Sandra C. *Vietnamese Women at War: Fighting for Ho Chi Minh and the Revolution*. Lawrence, Kans.: University Press of Kansas, 1999.

Turner, Karen Gottschang, with Phan Thanh Hào. *Even the Women Must Fight: Memories of War from North Vietnam*. New York: Wiley, 1998.

Van Devanter, Lynda, and Joan A. Furey, eds. *Visions of War, Dreams of Peace: Writings of Women in the Vietnam War*. New York: Warner Books, 1991.

Weaver, Gina Marie. *Ideologies of Forgetting: Rape in the Vietnam War*. Albany, N.Y.: State University of New York Press, 2010.

U.S. Ethnic Minorities

Astor, Gerald. *The Right to Fight: A History of African Americans in the Military*. Novato, Calif.: Presidio Press, 1998.

Becton, Julius W., Jr. *Autobiography of Becton, a Soldier and Public Servant*. Annapolis, Md.: Naval Institute Press, 2008.

Binkin, Martin, and Mark J. Eitelberg. *Blacks and the Military*. Washington, D.C.: The Brookings Institution, 1982.

Birdwell, Dwight W., and Keith William Nolan. *A Hundred Miles of Bad Road: An Armored Cavalryman in Vietnam, 1967–1968*. Novato, Calif.: Presidio Press, 1997.

Black, Samuel W. *Soul Soldiers: African Americans and the Vietnam Era*. Pittsburgh, Penn.: Senator John Heinz Pittsburgh Regional History Center, 2006.

Emanuel, Edwin L. *Soul Patrol*. New York: Presidio Press, 2003.

French, Albert. *Patches of Fire: A Story of War and Redemption*. New York: Anchor Doubleday, 1997.

Garcia, Manny. *An Accidental Soldier: Memoirs of a Mestizo in Vietnam*. Albuquerque, N.Mex.: University of New Mexico Press, 2003.

Gillam, James T. *War in the Central Highlands of Vietnam, 1968–1970: An Historian's Experience*. Lewiston, N.Y.: Edwin Mellen Press, 2006.

Goff, Stanley, and Robert Sanders. *Brothers: Black Soldiers in the Nam*. Novato, Calif.: Presidio Press, 1982.

Graham, Herman, III. *The Brothers' Vietnam War: Black Power, Manhood, and the Military Experience*. Gainesville, Fla.: University Press of Florida, 2003.

Guidry, Richard A. *The War in I Corps*. New York: Ivy Books, 1998.

Holm, Tom. *Strong Hearts and Wounded Souls: Native American Veterans and the Vietnam War*. Austin, Tex.: University of Texas Press, 1996.

Kimbrough, Natalie. *Equality or Discrimination? African Americans in the U.S. Military during the Vietnam War*. Lanham, Md.: University Press of America, 2007.

Kipp, Woody. *Viet Cong at Wounded Knee: The Trail of a Blackfeet Activist*. Lincoln, Nebr.: University of Nebraska Press, 2004.

Kusch, Frank. *All American Boys: Draft Dodgers in Canada from the Vietnam War*. Westport, Conn.: Praeger, 2001.

McDaniel, Norman A. *Yet Another Voice*. New York: Hawthorn, 1975.

Means, Howard. *Colin Powell: Soldier/Statesman–Statesman/Soldier*. New York: Fine, 1992.

MorningStorm, J. Boyd. *The American Indian Warrior Today: Native Americans in Modern U.S. Warfare*. Manhattan, Kans.: Sunflower University Press, 2004.

Moskos, Charles C., and John S. Butler. *All That We Can Be: Black Leadership and Racial Integration the Army Way*. New York: Basic Books, 1997.

Mullen, Robert W. *Blacks and Vietnam*. Washington, D.C.: University Press of America, 1981.

Parks, David. *GI Diary*. New York: Harper & Row, 1968.

Petersen, Frank E., with J. Alfred Phelps. *Into the Tiger's Jaw: America's First Black Marine Aviator*. Novato, Calif.: Presidio Press, 1998.

Powell, Colin, with Joseph E. Persico. *My American Journey*. New York: Random House, 1995.

Ramirez, Juan. *A Patriot After All: The Story of a Chicano Vietnam Vet*. Albuquerque, N.Mex.: University of New Mexico Press, 1999.

Taylor, Clyde. *Vietnam and Black America: An Anthology of Protest and Resistance*. Garden City, N.Y.: Anchor Press, 1973.

TeCube, Leroy. *Year in Nam: A Native American Soldier's Story*. Lincoln, Nebr.: University of Nebraska Press, 1999.

Terry, Wallace. *Bloods: An Oral History of the Vietnam War by Black Veterans*. New York: Ballantine, 1992.

———. *Missing Pages: Black Journalists of Modern America; An Oral History*. New York: Carroll & Graf, 2007.

Trujillo, Charley, ed. *Soldados: Chicanos in Viet Nam*. San Jose, Calif.: Chusma House Publications, 1990.

Vance, Samuel. *The Courageous and the Proud*. New York: Norton, 1970.

Ware, Ezell, and Joel Engel. *By Duty Bound: Survival and Redemption in a Time of War*. New York: Penguin, 2005.

Westheider, James E. *Fighting on Two Fronts: African Americans and the Vietnam War*. New York: New York University Press, 1997.

———. *The African American Experience in Vietnam: Brothers in Arms*. Lanham, Md.: Rowman & Littlefield, 2008.

Whelchel, Toshio. *From Pearl Harbor to Saigon: Japanese American Soldiers and the Vietnam War*. New York: Verso, 1999.

Ybarra, Lea. *Vietnam Veteranos: Chicanos Recall the War*. Austin, Tex.: University of Texas Press, 2004.

Chaplains at War

DeVeaux, Faith. *When Duty Calls*. San Jose, Calif.: Writer's Club Press, 2000.

Falabella, J. Robert. *Vietnam Memoirs: A Passage to Sorrow*. New York: Pageant Press International, 1971.

Hutchens, James M. *Beyond Combat*. Chicago: Moody, 1968.

Johnson, James D. *Combat Chaplain: A Thirty-Year Vietnam Battle*. Denton, Tex.: University of North Texas Press, 2001.

Johnson, Raymond. *Postmark: Mekong Delta*. Westwood, N.J.: Revell, 1968.

O'Connor, John J. *A Chaplain Looks at Vietnam*. New York: World, 1968.

Medical

Anderson, Doug. *Keep Your Head Down: Vietnam, the Sixties, and a Journey of Self-Discovery*. New York: Norton, 2009.

Bancoff, Carl. *A Forgotten Man*. New York: S.P.I. Books, 1992.

Bartecchi, Carl E. *Soc Trang: A Vietnamese Odyssey*. Boulder, Colo.: Rocky Mountain Writer's Guild, 1980.

Bennett, Marilyn Faye. *"Help! What Do I Do Now?": The Adventures of a Young Missionary Nurse in Vietnam*. Nashville, Tenn.: Southern Publishing Association, 1976.

Bey, Douglas. *Wizard 6: A Combat Psychiatrist in Vietnam*. College Station, Tex.: Texas A&M University Press, 2006.

Bigler, Philip. *Hostile Fire: The Life and Death of Lt. Sharon Lane*. Arlington, Va.: Vandamere, 1996.

Bradford, David. *The Gunners' Doctor: Vietnam Letters*. North Sydney, NSW, Australia: Random House Australia, 2007.

Byerly, Wesley G. *Nam Doc*. New York: Vantage, 1981.

———. *Trung Ta Bac Si*. Baltimore, Md.: Gateway Press, 1986.

Deardorff, Barbara, Ann Thompson, et al. *Another Kind of War Story: Army Nurses Look Back to Vietnam*. Lebanon, Penn.: A. Thompson, 1993.

Evans, Barbara. *Caduceus in Saigon: A Medical Mission to South Vietnam*. London: Hutchinson, 1968.

Evans, Daniel E., Jr., and Charles Sasser. *Doc: Platoon Medic*. New York: Pocket Books, 1998.

Ford, Herbert. *No Guns on Their Shoulders*. Nashville, Tenn.: Southern Publishing Association, 1968.

Freedman, Dan, and Jacqueline Rhoads, eds. *Nurses in Vietnam: The Forgotten Veterans*. Austin, Tex.: Texas Monthly Press, 1987.

Gloeckner, Fred. *A Civilian Doctor in Vietnam*. Philadelphia: Winchell, 1972.

Gruhzit-Hoyt, Olga. *A Time Remembered: American Women in the Vietnam War*. Novato, Calif.: Presidio Press, 1999.

Hall, Mike. *The Medic and the Mama-san*. Cortland, N.Y.: Hawkeye, 1994.

Hampton, Lynn. *The Fighting Strength: Memoirs of a Combat Nurse in Vietnam*. New York: Warner, 1992.

Hardaway, Robert M., ed. *Care of the Wounded in Vietnam*. Manhattan, Kans.: Sunflower University Press, 1988.

Hasselblad, Marva, with Dorothy Brandon. *Lucky-Lucky: A Nurse's Story of Life at a Hospital in Vietnam*. New York: Fawcett, 1967.

Herman, Jan K. *Navy Medicine in Vietnam: Oral Histories from Dien Bien Phu to the Fall of Saigon*. Jefferson, N.C.: McFarland, 2009.

Holley, Byron E. *Vietnam 1968–1969: A Battalion Surgeon's Journal*. New York: Ivy Books, 1993.

Hovis, Bobbi. *Station Hospital Saigon: A Navy Nurse in Vietnam, 1963–1964*. Annapolis, Md.: Naval Institute Press, 1992.

Kelsh, James Michael. *Triage: The Gathering Place*. New York: Carlton, 1977.

Kildea, John. *No Names, No Faces, No Pain: A Voice from Vietnam*. Westminster, Md.: Heritage Books, 2006.

Kinney, Charles M. *Borrowed Time: A Medic's View of the Vietnam War*. Victoria, British Columbia: Trafford, 2003.

McKeown, Bonni. *Peaceful Patriot: The Story of Tom Bennett*. Capon Springs, W.Va.: Peaceful Patriot Press.

McPartlin, Greg. *Combat Corpsman: The Vietnam Memoir of a Navy SEALs Medic*. New York: Berkley Caliber, 2005.

Mills, Randy K. *Troubled Hero: A Medal of Honor, Vietnam, and the War at Home*. Bloomington, Ind.: Indiana University Press, 2006.

Norman, Elizabeth M. *Women at War: The Story of Fifty Military Nurses Who Served in Vietnam*. Philadelphia: University of Pennsylvania Press, 1990.

Ordóñez, Robert L. *When I Was a Boy: One Year in Vietnam*. Lubbock, Tex.: CIMA, 1997.

Parrish, John A. *12, 20 & 5: A Doctor's Year in Vietnam*. New York: Bantam, 1986.

Powell, Mary Reynolds. *A World of Hurt: Between Innocence and Arrogance in Vietnam*. Cleveland, Ohio: Greenleaf, 2000.

Roberts, Craig. *Combat Medic: Vietnam*. New York: Pocket Books, 1991.

Rosenberger, Mary Sue. *Harmless as Doves: Witnessing for Peace in Vietnam*. Eglin, Ill.: Brethren Press, 1988.

Schulze, Gene. *The Third Face of War*. Austin, Tex.: Pemberton Press, 1970.

Sherman, Benjamin R. *Medic! The Story of a Conscientious Objector in the Vietnam War*. New York: Presidio Press, 2004.

Slone, Brady W. *Purple Smoke*. Pippa Passes, Ky.: Pippa Valley Printing, 1989.

Smith, Hilary. *Lighting Candles: Hospital Memories of Vietnam's Montagnards*. Barre, Vt.: Northlight Studio Press, 1988.

Smith, Winnie. *American Daughter Gone to War: On the Front Lines with an Army Nurse in Vietnam*. New York: Morrow, 1992.

Trembly, Diane L. *Petticoat Medic in Vietnam: Adventures of a Woman Doctor*. New York: Vantage, 1976.

Turpin, James W., with Al Hirshberg. *Vietnam Doctor: The Story of Project Concern*. New York: McGraw-Hill, 1966.

Van Devanter, Lynda. *Home Before Morning*. New York: Warner, 1984.

Vuic, Kara Dixon. *Officer, Nurse, Woman: The Army Nurse Corps in the Vietnam War*. Baltimore, Md.: Johns Hopkins University Press, 2010.

Walker, Keith. *A Piece of My Heart: The Stories of Twenty-six American Women who Served in Vietnam*. Novato, Calif.: Presidio Press, 1985.

Wilensky, Robert J. *Military Medicine to Win Hearts and Minds: Aid to Civilians in the Vietnam War*. Lubbock, Tex.: Texas Tech University Press, 2004.

Antiwar Movement

Adelson, Alan. *SDS*. New York: Scribner, 1972.

Adler, Margot. *Heretic's Heart: A Journey through Spirit and Revolution*. Boston: Beacon Press, 1997.

Albertson, Dean, ed. *Rebels or Revolutionaries? Student Movements of the 1960s.* New York: Simon & Schuster, 1975.

Ali, Tariq. *Street Fighting Years: An Autobiography of the Sixties.* London: Collins, 1987.

Ali, Tariq, and Susan Watkins. *1968: Marching in the Streets.* New York: Free Press, 1998.

Alonso, Karen. *The Chicago Seven Political Protest Trial: A Headline Court Case.* Berkeley Heights, N.J.: Enslow, 2002.

Anderson, Christopher. *Citizen Jane: The Turbulent Life of Jane Fonda.* New York: Henry Holt, 1990.

Anderson, Terry H. *The Movement and the Sixties.* New York: Oxford University Press, 1995.

———. *The Sixties.* New York: Longman, 1999.

Anson, Robert Sam. *McGovern: A Biography.* New York: Holt, Rinehart & Winston, 1972.

Aptheker, Herbert. *Mission to Hanoi.* New York: International Publishers, 1966.

Bannan, John F., and Rosemary S. Bannan. *Law, Morality and Vietnam: The Peace Militants and the Courts.* Bloomington, Ind.: Indiana University Press, 1974.

Barber, David. *A Hard Rain Fell: SDS and Why It Failed.* Jackson, Miss.: University Press of Mississippi, 2008.

Barkan, Steven E. *Protesters on Trial: Criminal Justice in the Southern Civil Rights and Vietnam Antiwar Movements.* New Brunswick, N.J.: Rutgers University Press, 1985.

Bates, Tom. *Rads.* New York: HarperCollins, 1992.

Bills, Scott L., ed. *Kent State/May 4: Echoes through a Decade.* Kent, Ohio: Kent State University Press, 1982.

Bloom, Alexander, and Winifred Breines, eds. *Takin' It to the Streets: A Sixties Reader.* New York: Oxford University Press, 1995.

Branch, Taylor. *At Canaan's Edge: America in the King Years, 1965–1968.* New York: Simon & Schuster, 2006.

Braudy, Susan. *Family Circle: The Boudins and the Aristocracy of the Left.* New York: Knopf, 2003.

Brinkley, Douglas. *Tour of Duty: John Kerry and the Vietnam War.* New York: Morrow, 2004.

Brody, Leslie. *Red Star Sister: Between Madness and Utopia.* St. Paul, Minn.: Hungry Mind Press, 1998.

Caputo, Philip. *13 Seconds: A Look Back at the Kent State Shootings.* New York: Chamberlain Brothers, 2005.

Casale, Ottavio M., and Louis Paskoff, eds. *The Kent Affair: Documents and Interpretations.* Boston: Houghton Mifflin, 1971.

Castellucci, John. *The Big Dance: The Untold Story of Kathy Boudin and the Terrorist Family that Committed the Brink's Robbery Murders.* New York: Dodd, Mead, 1986.

Chatfield, Charles. *The American Peace Movement: Ideals and Activism.* New York: Twayne, 1992.

Chomsky, Noam. *American Power and the New Mandarins.* New York: Pantheon, 1969.

———. *At War with Asia: Essays on Indochina.* New York: Random House, 1970.

———. *Towards a New Cold War: Essays on the Current Crisis and How We Got There.* New York: Pantheon, 1982.

Clardy, Brian K. *The Management of Dissent: Responses to the Post Kent State Protests at Seven Public Universities in Illinois.* Lanham, Md.: University Press of America, 2002.

Clark, Bronson P. *Not by Might: A Viet Nam Memoir.* Glastonbury, Conn.: Chapel Rock Publishers, 1997.

Clavir, Judy, and John Spitzer, eds. *The Conspiracy Trial.* Indianapolis, Ind.: Bobbs-Merrill, 1970.

Clinton, James W. *The Loyal Opposition: Americans in North Vietnam, 1965–1972.* Niwot, Colo.: University Press of Colorado, 1995.

Coffin, William Sloane, Jr. *Once to Every Man: A Memoir.* New York: Atheneum, 1977.

Cohen, Robert, and Reginald E. Zelnik, eds. *The Free Speech Movement: Reflections on Berkeley in the 1960s.* Berkeley, Calif.: University of California Press, 2002.

Curry, G. David. *Sunshine Patriots: Punishment and the Vietnam Offender.* South Bend, Ind.: University of Notre Dame Press, 1985.

Davies, Peter, et al. *The Truth about Kent State: A Challenge to the American Conscience.* New York: Farrar, Straus & Giroux, 1973.

Davis, James K. *Assault on the Left: The FBI and the Sixties Antiwar Movement.* Westport, Conn.: Praeger, 1997.

DeBenedetti, Charles, with Charles Chatfield. *An American Ordeal: The Antiwar Movement of the Vietnam Era.* Syracuse, N.Y.: Syracuse University Press, 1990.

Dellinger, David. *Revolutionary Nonviolence.* Indianapolis, Ind.: Bobbs-Merrill, 1970.

———. *More Power Than We Know: The People's Movement toward Democracy.* Garden City, N.Y.: Anchor Press, 1975.

———. *Vietnam Revisited: From Covert Action to Invasion to Reconstruction.* Boston: South End Press, 1986.

———. *From Yale to Jail: The Life Story of a Moral Dissenter.* New York: Pantheon, 1993.

D'Emilio, John. *Lost Prophet: The Life and Times of Bayard Rustin.* New York: Free Press, 2003.

Dickerson, James. *Dixie's Dirty Secret: The True Story of How the Government, the Media, and the Mob Conspired to Combat Integration and the Vietnam Antiwar Movement.* Armonk, N.Y.: M. E. Sharpe, 1998.

———. *North to Canada: Men and Women against the Vietnam War.* Westport, Conn.: Praeger, 1999.

Dohrn, Bernardine, Bill Ayers, and Jeff Jones, eds. *Sing a Battle Song: The Revolutionary Poetry, Statements, and Communiques of the Weather Underground, 1970–1974.* New York: Seven Stories Press, 2006.

Dumbrell, John, ed. *Vietnam and the Antiwar Movement: An International Perspective.* Brookfield, Vt.: Gower, 1989.

Eichel, Lawrence, Kenneth W. Jost, Robert D. Luskin, and Richard M. Neustadt. *The Harvard Strike*. Boston: Houghton Mifflin, 1970.

Elmer, Jerry. *Felon for Peace: The Memoir of a Vietnam-Era Draft Resister*. Nashville, Tenn.: Vanderbilt University Press, 2005.

Epstein, Jason. *The Great Conspiracy Trial: An Essay on Law, Liberty, and the Constitution*. New York: Random House, 1970.

Eszterhas, Joe, and Michael D. Roberts. *Thirteen Seconds: Confrontation at Kent State*. New York: Dodd, Mead, 1970.

Eymann, Marcia A., and Charles Wollenberg, eds. *What's Going On?: California and the Vietnam Era*. Berkeley, Calif.: University of California Press, 2004.

Ferber, Michael, and Staughton Lynd. *The Resistance*. Boston: Beacon Press, 1971.

Foley, Michael S. *Confronting the War Machine: Draft Resistance during the Vietnam War*. Chapel Hill, N.C.: University of North Carolina Press, 2003.

————, ed. *Dear Dr. Spock: Letters about the Vietnam War to America's Favorite Baby Doctor*. New York: New York University Press, 2005.

Fonda, Jane. *My Life So Far*. New York: Random House, 2005.

Frankfort, Ellen. *Kathy Boudin and the Dance of Death*. New York: Stein & Day, 1983.

Franks, Lucinda. *Waiting Out a War: The Exile of Private John Picciano*. New York: Coward, McCann & Geoghegan, 1974.

Friedland, Michael B. *Lift Up Your Voice Like a Trumpet: White Clergy and the Civil Rights and Antiwar Movements, 1954–1973*. Chapel Hill, N.C.: University of North Carolina Press, 1998.

Friedman, Leon, and Burt Neuborne. *Unquestioning Obedience to the President: The ACLU Case against the Legality of the War in Vietnam*. New York: Norton, 1972.

Frutkin, Mark. *Erratic North: A Vietnam Draft Resister's Life in the Canadian Bush*. Toronto: Dundurn Press, 2008.

Garfinkle, Adam. *Telltale Hearts: The Origins and Impact of the Vietnam Antiwar Movement*. New York: St. Martin's Press, 1995.

Gausman, William F. *Red Stains on Vietnam Doves*. Aurora, Colo.: Veracity Publications, 1989.

Gilbert, Marc Jason, ed. *The Vietnam War on Campus: Other Voices, More Distant Drums*. Westport, Conn.: Praeger, 2001.

Gioglio, Gerald R. *Days of Decision: An Oral History of Conscientious Objectors in the Military during the Vietnam War*. Trenton: Broken Rifle Press, 1989.

Gitlin, Todd. *The Whole World Is Watching: Mass Media in the Making and Unmaking of the New Left*. Berkeley, Calif.: University of California Press, 1980.

Goldstein, Warren. *William Sloane Coffin Jr.: A Holy Impatience*. New Haven, Conn.: Yale University Press, 2004.

Goodman, Adolph W. *A Victim of the Vietnam War: The Story of Virginia Hanly*. Raleigh, N.C.: Pentland Press, 2000.

Gordon, William A. *The Fourth of May: Killings and Coverups at Kent State*. Buffalo, N.Y.: Prometheus, 1990.

Gottlieb, Sherry Gershon. *Hell No, We Won't Go: Resisting the Draft during the Vietnam War*. New York: Viking, 1991.

Grant, Edward J., and Michael H. Hill. *I Was There: What Really Went on at Kent State, as Told by Former Ohio National Guardsmen Ed Grant and Mike Hill*. Lima, Ohio: C.S.S. Publishing, 1974.

Gurvis, Sandra. *Where Have All the Flower Children Gone?* Jackson, Miss.: University Press of Mississippi, 2006.

Guthman, Edwin O., and C. Richard Allen, eds. *RFK: Collected Speeches*. New York: Viking, 1993.

Hagan, John. *Northern Passage: American Vietnam War Resisters in Canada*. Cambridge, Mass.: Harvard University Press, 2001.

Hall, Mitchell K. *Because of Their Faith: CALCAV and Religious Opposition to the Vietnam War*. New York: Columbia University Press, 1990.

Hall, Simon. *Peace and Freedom: The Civil Rights and Antiwar Movements in the 1960s*. Philadelphia: University of Pennsylvania Press, 2004.

Halstead, Fred. *GIs Speak Out against the War: The Case of the Fort Jackson 8*. New York: Pathfinder Press, 1970.

———. *Out Now! A Participant's Account of the American Movement against the Vietnam War*. New York: Pathfinder Press, 1991.

Hamilton, Michael P., ed. *The Vietnam War: Christian Perspectives*. Grand Rapids, Mich.: Eerdman, 1967.

Harris, David. *Goliath*. New York: Sidereal Press, 1970.

———. *Our War: What We Did in Vietnam and What It Did to Us*. New York: Times Books, 1996.

Hart, Gary. *Right from the Start: A Chronicle of the McGovern Campaign*. New York: Quadrangle, 1973.

Hartke, Vance. *The American Crisis in Vietnam*. Indianapolis, Ind.: Bobbs-Merrill, 1968.

Hayden, Tom. *Reunion: A Memoir*. New York: Random House, 1988.

Hayes, Thomas Lee. *American Deserters in Sweden*. New York: Association Press, 1971.

Heath, G. Louis, ed. *Mutiny Does Not Happen Lightly: The Literature of the American Resistance to the Vietnam War*. Metuchen, N.J.: Scarecrow Press, 1976.

———. *Vandals in the Bomb Factory: The History and Literature of the Students for a Democratic Society*. Metuchen, N.J.: Scarecrow Press, 1976.

Heineman, Kenneth. *Campus Wars: The Peace Movement at American State Universities in the Vietnam Era*. New York: New York University Press, 1993.

Hensley, Thomas R., with James J. Best. *The Kent State Incident: Impact of Judicial Process on Public Attitudes*. Westport, Conn.: Greenwood, 1981.

Hershberger, Mary. *Traveling to Vietnam: American Peace Activists and the War*. Syracuse, N.Y.: Syracuse University Press, 1998.

———. *Jane Fonda's War: A Political Biography of an Antiwar Icon*. New York: New Press, 2005.

Herzog, Arthur. *McCarthy for President*. New York: Viking, 1969.

Hixson, Walter L., ed. *The Vietnam Antiwar Movement*. New York: Garland, 2000.

Hoffman, Abbie. *Revolution for the Hell of It*. New York: Dial Press, 1968.

———. *Soon to Be a Major Motion Picture*. New York: Putnam, 1980.

Hunt, Andrew. *The Turning: A History of Vietnam Veterans Against the War*. New York: New York University Press, 1999.

———. *David Dellinger: The Life and Times of a Nonviolent Revolutionary*. New York: New York University Press, 2006.

Hurwitz, Ken. *Marching Nowhere*. New York: Norton, 1971.

Jackson, Bruce. *Disorderly Conduct*. Urbana, Ill.: University of Illinois Press, 1992.

Jacobs, Ron. *The Way the Wind Blew: A History of the Weather Underground*. New York: Verso, 1997.

Jeffreys-Jones, Rhodri. *Peace Now! American Society and the Ending of the Vietnam War*. New Haven, Conn.: Yale University Press, 1999.

Jones, Thai. *A Radical Line: From the Labor Movement to the Weather Underground, One Family's Century of Conscience*. New York: Free Press, 2004.

Kahin, George McT. *Southeast Asia: A Testament*. New York: RoutledgeCurzon, 2003.

Kallen, Stuart A. *The Home Front: Americans Protest the War*. San Diego, Calif.: Lucent Books, 2001.

Kastenmeier, Robert W. *Vietnam Hearings: Voices from the Grass Roots*. New York: Doubleday, 1965.

Kelman, Steven. *Push Comes to Shove: The Escalation of Student Protest*. Boston: Houghton Mifflin, 1970.

Kelner, Joseph. *The Kent State Coverup*. New York: Harper & Row, 1980.

Kennan, George. *Democracy and the Student Left*. Boston: Little, Brown, 1968.

Kent, Stephen A. *From Slogans to Mantras: Social Protest and Religious Conversion in the Late Vietnam War Era*. Syracuse, N.Y.: Syracuse University Press, 2001.

Larner, Jeremy. *Nobody Knows: Reflections on the McCarthy Campaign of 1968*. New York: Macmillan, 1970.

Lens, Sidney. *Unrepentant Radical*. Boston: Beacon Press, 1980.

Levy, Howard, and David Miller. *Going to Jail: The Political Prisoner*. New York: Grove Press, 1970.

Lewes, James. *Protest and Survive: Underground GI Newspapers during the Vietnam War*. Westport, Conn.: Praeger, 2003.

Lieberman, Robbie. *Prairie Power: Voices of 1960s Midwestern Student Protest*. Columbia, Mo.: University of Missouri Press, 2004.

Lucas, Brad E. *Radicals, Rhetoric, and the War: The University of Nevada in the Wake of Kent State*. New York: Palgrave Macmillan, 2006.

Lukas, J. Anthony. *The Barnyard Epithet and Other Obscenities: Notes on the Chicago Conspiracy Trial*. New York: Harper & Row, 1970.

———. *Don't Shoot—We Are Your Children!* New York: Random House, 1971.

Lynd, Alice, ed. *We Won't Go: Personal Accounts of War Objectors*. Boston: Beacon Press, 1968.

Lynd, Staughton, and Thomas Hayden. *The Other Side*. New York: New American Library, 1966.

MacAfee, Norman, ed. *The Gospel According to RFK: Why It Matters Now*. Boulder, Colo.: Westview, 2004.

Mailer, Norman. *The Armies of the Night*. New York: New American Library, 1968.

————. *Miami and the Siege of Chicago: An Informal History of the Republican and Democratic Conventions of 1968*. New York: New American Library, 1968.

Maraniss, David. *They Marched into Sunlight: War and Peace, Vietnam and America, October 1967*. New York: Simon & Schuster, 2003.

Marshall, John Douglas. *Reconciliation Road: A Family Odyssey of War and Honor*. Syracuse, N.Y.: Syracuse University Press, 1993.

McCarthy, Eugene J. *The Year of the People*. Garden City, N.Y.: Doubleday, 1969.

————. *Parting Shots from My Brittle Bow: Reflections on American Politics and Life*. Golden, Colo.: Fulcrum, 2004.

McDonald, William P., and Jerry G. Smoke. *The Peasant's Revolt: McCarthy, 1968*. Mt. Vernon, Ohio: Noe-Bixby Publications, 1969.

McGill, William J. *The Year of the Monkey: Revolt on the Campus, 1968–1969*. New York: McGraw-Hill, 1982.

McGovern, George S. *A Time of War, A Time of Peace*. New York: Random House, 1968.

————. *An American Journey: The Presidential Campaign Speeches of George McGovern*. New York: Random House, 1974.

Melman, Seymour, et al. *In the Name of America: New York; Clergy and Laymen Concerned about Vietnam*. Annandale, Va.: Turnpike Press, 1968.

Michalek, Irene R. *When Mercy Seasons Justice: The Spock Trial*. Boston: Branden Press, 1972.

Michener, James A. *Kent State: What Happened and Why*. New York: Random House, 1971.

Miller, James. *Democracy Is in the Streets: From Port Huron to the Siege of Chicago*. New York: Simon & Schuster, 1987.

Miroff, Bruce. *The Liberals' Moment: The McGovern Insurgency and the Identity Crisis of the Democratic Party*. Lawrence, Kans.: University Press of Kansas, 2007.

Mitford, Jessica. *The Trial of Dr. Spock, William Sloane Coffin, Michael Ferber, Mitchell Goodman, and Marcus Raskin*. New York: Knopf, 1969.

Monhollon, Rusty L. *This Is America? The Sixties in Lawrence, Kansas*. New York: Palgrave Macmillan, 2004.

Moser, Richard. *The New Winter Soldiers: GI and Veteran Dissent during the Vietnam Era*. New Brunswick, N.J.: Rutgers University Press, 1996.

Mullen, Peg. *Unfriendly Fire: A Mother's Memoir*. Iowa City: University of Iowa Press, 1995.

Near, Holly, with Derk Richardson. *Fire in the Rain . . . Singer in the Storm: Holly Near, an Autobiography*. New York: William Morrow, 1990.

Nicosia, Gerald. *Home to War: A History of the Vietnam Veterans' Movement*. New York: Crown, 2001.

Oglesby, Carl. *Ravens in the Storm: A Personal History of the 1960s Antiwar Movement*. New York: Scribner, 2008.

Oropeza, Lorena. *¡Raza Sí! ¡Guerra No! Chicano Protest and Patriotism during the Viet Nam War Era*. Berkeley, Calif.: University of California Press, 2005.

Pardun, Robert. *Prairie Radical: A Journey through the Sixties*. Los Gatos, Calif.: Shire Press, 2001.

Payne, Cril. *Deep Cover: An FBI Agent Infiltrates the Radical Underground.* New York: Newsweek Books, 1979.

Perrin, Dick, with Tim McCarthy. *G.I. Resister: The Story of How One American Soldier and His Family Fought the War in Vietnam.* Victoria, B.C.: Trafford, 2001.

Polner, Murray. *When Can I Come Home? A Debate on Amnesty for Exiles, Antiwar Prisoners, and Others.* Garden City, N.Y.: Doubleday Anchor, 1972.

Rader, Dotson. *Blood Dues.* New York: Knopf, 1973.

Raskin, Jonah. *For the Hell of It.* Berkeley, Calif.: University of California Press, 1997.

Rhodes, Joel P. *The Voice of Violence: Performative Violence as Protest in the Vietnam Era.* Westport, Conn.: Praeger, 2001.

Rising, George. *Clean for Gene: Eugene McCarthy's 1968 Presidential Campaign.* Westport, Conn.: Praeger, 1997.

Robbins, Mary Susannah, ed. *Against the Vietnam War: Writings by Activists.* Syracuse, N.Y.: Syracuse University Press, 1999.

Rorabaugh, W. J. *Berkeley at War: The 1960s.* New York: Oxford University Press, 1989.

Rosenblatt, Roger. *Coming Apart: A Memoir of the Harvard Wars of 1969.* Boston: Little, Brown, 1997.

Rossiter, Caleb S. *The Chimes of Freedom Flashing: A Personal History of the Vietnam Anti-war Movement and the 1960s.* Washington, D.C.: TCA Press, 1996.

Rothrock, James. *Divided We Fall: How Disunity Leads to Defeat.* Bloomington, Ind.: AuthorHouse, 2006.

Rudd, Mark. *Underground: My Life with SDS and the Weathermen.* New York: William Morrow, 2009.

Sale, Kirkpatrick. *SDS.* New York: Random House, 1973.

Sandbrook, Dominic. *Eugene McCarthy: The Rise and Fall of Postwar American Liberalism.* New York: Knopf, 2004.

Schultz, John. *No One Was Killed: Documentation and Meditation; Convention Week, Chicago—August 1968.* Chicago: Big Table, 1969.

———. *Motion Will Be Denied: A New Report on the Chicago Conspiracy Trial.* New York: Morrow, 1972.

———. *The Chicago Conspiracy Trial.* New York: Da Capo, 1993.

Simons, Donald L. *I Refuse: Memories of a Vietnam War Objector.* Trenton, N.J.: Broken Rifle Press, 1992.

Smaby, Alpha. *Political Upheaval: Minnesota and the Vietnam War Protest.* Minneapolis, Minn.: Dillon Press, 1987.

Small, Melvin. *Covering Dissent: The Media and the Anti-Vietnam War Movement.* New Brunswick, N.J.: Rutgers University Press, 1994.

———. *Antiwarriors: The Vietnam War and the Battle for America's Hearts and Minds.* Wilmington, Del.: Scholarly Resources, 2002.

Small, Melvin, and William D. Hoover, eds. *Give Peace a Chance: Exploring the Vietnam Antiwar Movement.* Syracuse, N.Y.: Syracuse University Press, 1992.

Spann, Edward K. *Democracy's Children: The Young Rebels of the 1960s and the Power of Ideals.* Lanham, Md.: Rowman & Littlefield, 2003.

Stacewicz, Richard. *Winter Soldiers: An Oral History of the Vietnam Veterans Against the War*. New York: Twayne, 1997.

Stavis, Benedict. *We Were the Campaign: New Hampshire to Chicago for McCarthy*. Boston: Beacon Press, 1969.

Steel, Ronald. *In Love with Night: The American Romance with Robert Kennedy*. New York: Simon & Schuster, 2000.

Stevens, Franklin. *If This Be Treason: Your Sons Tell Their Own Stories of Why They Won't Fight for Their Country*. New York: P. H. Wyden, 1970.

Stone, Isidor Feinstein. *Polemics and Prophecies, 1967–1970*. New York: Random House, 1970.

———. *The Killings at Kent State; How Murder Went Unpunished*. New York: Vintage Books, 1971.

Strahs, James. *Seed Journal*. New York: Harper & Row, 1973.

Surrey, David S. *Choice of Conscience: Vietnam Era Military and Draft Resisters in Canada*. New York: Praeger, 1982.

Taylor, Stuart, et al. *Violence at Kent State, May 1 to 4, 1970: The Students' Perspective*. New York: College Notes & Texts, 1971.

Todd, Jack. *Desertion: In the Time of Vietnam*. Boston: Houghton Mifflin, 2001.

Tollefson, James W. *The Strength Not to Fight: An Oral History of Conscientious Objectors of the Vietnam War*. Boston: Little, Brown, 1993.

Tompkins, Phillip K., and Elaine Vanden Bout Anderson. *Communication Crisis at Kent State: A Case Study*. New York: Gordon & Breach, 1971.

Uhl, Michael. *Vietnam Awakening: My Journey from Combat to the Citizens' Commission of Inquiry on U.S. War Crimes in Vietnam*. Jefferson, N.C.: McFarland, 2007.

Useem, Michael. *Conscription, Protest and Social Conflict: The Life and Death of a Draft Resistance Movement*. New York: Wiley, 1973.

Varon, Jeremy. *Bringing the War Home: The Weather Underground, the Red Army Faction, and Revolutionary Violence in the Sixties and Seventies*. Berkeley, Calif.: University of California Press, 2004.

Vogelgesang, Sandy. *The Long Dark Night of the Soul: The American Intellectual Left and the Vietnam War*. New York: Harper & Row, 1974.

Warren, Bill, ed. *The Middle of the Country: The Events of May 4th as Seen by Students and Faculty at Kent State University*. New York: Avon, 1970.

Weil, Gordon Lee. *The Long Shot: George McGovern Runs for President*. New York: Norton, 1973.

Wells, Tom. *The War Within: America's Battle over Vietnam*. Berkeley, Calif.: University of California Press, 1994.

Whitmore, Terry, and Richard P. Weber. *Memphis, Nam, Sweden: The Autobiography of a Black American Exile*. Garden City, N.Y.: Doubleday, 1971.

Wiener, John, ed. *Conspiracy in the Streets: The Extraordinary Trial of the Chicago Eight*. New York: New Press, 2006.

Wilkerson, Cathy. *Flying Close to the Sun: My Life and Times as a Weatherman*. New York: Seven Stories Press, 2007.

Williams, Roger N. *The New Exiles: American War Resisters in Canada*. New York: Liveright, 1971.

Wilson, E. Raymond. *Uphill for Peace: Quaker Impact on Congress*. Richmond, Ind.: Friends United Press, 1975.

Woods, Randall B., ed. *Vietnam and the American Political Tradition: The Politics of Dissent*. New York: Cambridge University Press, 2003.

Zaroulis, Nancy, and Gerald Sullivan. *Who Spoke Up? American Protest against the War in Vietnam, 1963–1975*. New York: Doubleday, 1984.

Zinn, Howard. *Vietnam: The Logic of Withdrawal*. Boston: Beacon Press, 1967.

———. *You Can't be Neutral on a Moving Train: A Personal History of Our Times*. Boston: Beacon Press, 1994.

Agent Orange and the Effects of Chemical Warfare

Cecil, Paul. *Herbicidal Warfare*. New York: Praeger, 1986.

Gough, Michael. *Dioxin, Agent Orange: The Facts*. New York: Plenum Press, 1986.

Griffiths, Philip Jones. *Agent Orange: "Collateral Damage" in Vietnam*. London: Trolley, 2003.

Kelley, Charles. *Vietnam's Orange, White and Blue Rain: Agents and Weapons of Mass Destruction*. El Dorado Hills, Calif.: Corps Productions, 2005.

Lewallen, John. *Ecology of Devastation: Indochina*. Baltimore, Md.: Penguin Books, 1971.

Neilands, J. B., G. H. Orians, E. W. Pfeiffer, Alje Vennema, and Arthur Westing. *Harvest of Death: Chemical Warfare in Vietnam and Cambodia*. New York: Macmillan, 1972.

Schuck, Peter H. *Agent Orange on Trial: Mass Toxic Disasters in the Courts*. Cambridge, Mass.: Harvard University Press, 1987.

Scott, Wilbur J. *Vietnam Veterans since the War: The Politics of PTSD, Agent Orange, and the National Memorial*. Norman, Okla.: University of Oklahoma Press, 2004.

Westing, Arthur H., ed. *Herbicides in War: The Long-term Ecological and Human Consequences*. Philadelphia: Taylor & Francis, 1984.

Whiteside, Thomas. *The Withering Rain: America's Herbicidal Folly*. New York: Dutton, 1971.

Wilcox, Fred A. *Waiting for an Army to Die: The Tragedy of Agent Orange*. New York: Vintage Books, 1983.

Young, Alvin L., and Giuseppe M. Reggiani, eds. *Agent Orange and Its Associated Dioxin: Assessment of a Controversy*. Amsterdam, N.Y.: Elsevier, 1988.

The Media

Adams, Alyssa, ed. *Eddie Adams: Vietnam*. New York: Umbrage Editions, 2008.

Andrews, Owen, C. Douglas Elliot, and Laurence I. Levin. *Vietnam: Images from Combat Photographers*. Washington, D.C.: Starwood Publishing, 1991.

Anson, Robert Sam. *War News: A Young Reporter in Indochina*. New York: Simon & Schuster, 1989.

Arlen, Michael J. *Living Room War*. New York: Viking, 1969.

―――. *The View from Highway 1: Essays on Television.* New York: Farrar, Straus & Giroux, 1976.

Arnett, Peter. *Live from the Battlefield: From Vietnam to Baghdad, 35 Years in the World's War Zones.* New York: Simon & Schuster, 1994.

Baxter, Gordon. *13/13, Vietnam: Search and Destroy.* Cleveland, Ohio: World Publishing, 1967.

Behr, Edward. *Bearings: A Foreign Correspondent's Life behind the Lines.* New York: Viking, 1978.

Berry, Nicholas O. *Foreign Policy and the Press: An Analysis of the New York Times' Coverage of US Foreign Policy.* Westport, Conn.: Greenwood, 1990.

Bowden, Tim. *One Crowded Hour: Neil Davis, Combat Cameraman.* Sydney, NSW, Australia: Collins, 1987.

Braestrup, Peter. *Big Story: How the American Press and Television Reported and Interpreted the Crisis of Tet 1968 in Vietnam and Washington.* 2 vols. Boulder, Colo.: Westview, 1977.

―――. *Battle Lines: Report of the Task Force on the Military and the Media.* New York: Brookings Institution/Priority Press Publications, 1985.

Brelis, Dean, and Jill Krementz. *The Face of South Vietnam.* Boston: Houghton Mifflin, 1968.

Brinkley, David. *David Brinkley: 11 Presidents, 4 Wars, 22 Political Conventions, 1 Moon Landing, 3 Assassinations, 2,000 Weeks of News and Other Stuff on Television and 18 Years of Growing Up in North Cariolona.* New York: Knopf, 1995.

Browne, Malcolm W. *Muddy Boots and Red Socks: A Reporter's Life.* New York: Times Books, 1993.

Burrows, Larry. *Vietnam.* New York: Knopf, 2002.

Daugherty, Leo J., and Gregory Louis Mattson. *Nam: A Photographic History.* New York: Barnes & Noble, 2004.

Elwood-Akers, Virginia. *Women War Correspondents in the Vietnam War, 1961–1975.* Metuchen, N.J.: Scarecrow Press, 1988.

Emerson, Gloria A. *Winners & Losers: Battles, Retreats, Gains, Losses and Ruins from a Long War.* New York: Random House, 1977.

Faas, Horst, and Tim Page, eds. *Requiem: By the Photographers Who Died in Vietnam and Indochina.* New York: Random House, 1997.

Goldstein, Donald M., Katherine V. Dillon, and J. Michael Wenger. *The Vietnam War: The Story and Photographs.* Dulles, Va.: Brassey's, 1999.

Goulding, Phil G. *Confirm or Deny.* New York: Harper & Row, 1970.

Graham, Katharine. *Personal History.* New York: Knopf, 1997.

Griffiths, Philip Jones. *Vietnam Inc.* London: Phaidon Press, 2001.

Halberstam, David. *The Powers That Be.* New York: Knopf, 1979.

Hammond, William M. *Reporting Vietnam: Media and Military at War.* Lawrence, Kans.: University Press of Kansas, 1998.

Hoffmann, Joyce. *On Their Own: Women Journalists and the American Experience in Vietnam.* Cambridge, Mass.: Da Capo, 2008.

Howell, Haney. *Roadrunners: Combat Journalists in Cambodia.* Boulder, Colo.: Paladin Press, 1989.

Just, Ward. *To What End: Report from Vietnam*. Boston: Houghton Mifflin, 1968.

Kennerly, David. *Shooter*. New York: Newsweek Books, 1979.

Keogh, James. *President Nixon and the Press*. New York: Funk & Wagnalls, 1972.

Kern, Montague, Patricia W. Levering, and Ralph B. Levering. *The Kennedy Crisis: The Press, the Presidency, and Foreign Policy*. Chapel Hill, N.C.: University of North Carolina Press, 1983.

Laurence, John. *The Cat from Hué: A Vietnam War Story*. New York: Public Affairs, 2002.

Leroy, Catherine, ed. *Under Fire: Great Writers and Photographers in Vietnam*. New York: Random House, 2005.

Leslie, Jacques. *The Mark: A War Correspondent's Memoir of Vietnam and Cambodia*. New York: Four Walls Eight Windows, 1995.

Lucas, Jim G. *Dateline: Viet Nam*. New York: Award Books, 1968.

Lunn, Hugh. *Vietnam: A Reporter's War*. New York: Stein & Day, 1985.

MacDonald, J. Fred. *Television and the Red Menace: The Video Road to Vietnam*. New York: Praeger, 1985.

Maclear, Michael, and Hal Buell. *Vietnam: A Complete Photographic History*. New York: Tess Press, 2003.

McGrady, Mike. *A Dove in Vietnam*. New York: Funk & Wagnalls, 1968.

Minor, Dale. *The Information War*. New York: Hawthorn, 1970.

Moeller, Susan D. *Shooting War: Photography and the American Experience of Combat*. New York: Basic Books, 1989.

Ostroff, Roberta. *Fire in the Wind: The Life of Dickey Chapelle*. New York: Ballantine, 1992.

Page, Tim. *Page after Page: Memoirs of a War-Torn Photographer*. New York: Macmillan, 1988.

Palmos, Frank. *Ridding the Devils*. New York: Bantam, 1990.

Prochnau, William. *Once Upon a Distant War*. New York: Random House, 1995.

Pyle, Richard, and Horst Faas. *Lost over Laos: A True Story of Tragedy, Mystery, and Friendship*. Cambridge, Mass.: Da Capo, 2003.

Reston, James. *Deadline: A Memoir*. New York: Random House, 1991.

Safer, Morley. *Flashbacks: On Returning to Vietnam*. New York: Random House, 1990.

Salisbury, Harrison E. *Behind the Lines: Hanoi, December 23, 1966–January 7, 1967*. New York: Harper & Row, 1967.

———. *Without Fear or Favor: The New York Times and Its Times*. New York: Times Books, 1980.

———. *A Time of Change: A Reporter's Tale of Our Time*. New York: Harper & Row, 1988.

Smith, Howard K. *Events Leading up to My Death: The Life of a Twentieth-Century Reporter*. New York: St. Martin's Press, 1996.

Steinman, Ron. *Inside Television's First War: A Saigon Journal*. Columbia, Mo.: University of Missouri Press, 2002.

Swain, Jon. *River of Time*. New York: St. Martin's, 1997.

Trotta, Liz. *Fighting for Air: In the Trenches with Television News*. New York: Simon & Schuster, 1991.

Tuohy, William. *Dangerous Company*. New York: William Morrow, 1987.

Turner, Kathleen J. *Lyndon Johnson's Dual War: Vietnam and the Press*. Chicago: University of Chicago Press, 1985.

Utley, Garrick. *You Should Have Been Here Yesterday: A Life in Television News*. New York: Public Affairs, 2000.

Volkert, Kurt, and T. Jeff Williams. *A Cambodian Odyssey and the Deaths of 25 Journalists*. Le Vergne, Tenn.: Lightning Source, 2001.

Warner, Denis. *Reporting Southeast Asia*. Sydney, NSW, Australia: Angus & Robertson, 1966.

Webb, Kate. *On the Other Side: 23 Days with the Viet Cong*. New York: Quadrangle, 1972.

Williams, Marion. *My Tour in Vietnam: A Burlesque Shocker*. New York: Vantage, 1970.

Willwerth, James. *Eye in the Last Storm: A Reporter's Journal of One Year in Southeast Asia*. New York: Grossman, 1972.

Wyatt, Clarence R. *Paper Soldiers: The American Press and the Vietnam War*. New York: Norton, 1993.

Pentagon Papers Case

Ellsberg, Daniel. *Secrets: A Memoir of Vietnam and the Pentagon Papers*. New York: Viking, 2002.

Prados, John, and Margaret Pratt Porter, eds. *Inside the Pentagon Papers*. Lawrence, Kans.: University Press of Kansas, 2004.

Roberts, Chalmers M. *First Rough Draft: A Journalist's Journal of Our Times*. New York: Praeger, 1973.

Rudenstine, David. *The Day the Presses Stopped: A History of the Pentagon Papers Case*. Berkeley, Calif.: University of California Press, 1996.

Salter, Kenneth W. *The Pentagon Papers Trial*. Berkeley, Calif.: Editorial Justa Publications, 1975.

Schrag, Peter. *Test of Loyalty: Daniel Ellsberg and the Rituals of Secret Government*. New York: Simon & Schuster, 1974.

Shapiro, Martin M., ed. *The Pentagon Papers and the Courts: A Study in Foreign Policy-making and Freedom of the Press*. San Francisco: Chandler, 1972.

Ungar, Sanford J. *The Papers and the Papers: An Account of the Legal and Political Battle over the Pentagon Papers*. New York: Dutton, 1972.

Wells, Tom. *Wild Man: The Life and Times of Daniel Ellsberg*. New York: Palgrave, 2001.

OFFICIAL PERSONALITIES

General

Averch, Harvey. *The Rhetoric of War: Language, Argument, and Policy during the Vietnam War*. Lanham, Md.: University Press of America, 2002.

Ball, Moya Ann. *Vietnam-on-the-Potomac*. New York: Praeger, 1992.

Baral, Jaya Krishna. *The Pentagon and the Making of U.S. Foreign Policy*. Atlantic Highlands, N.J.: Humanities Press, 1978.

Barnet, Richard J. *Roots of War*. New York: Atheneum, 1972.

Berger, Graenum. *Not So Silent an Envoy*. New Rochelle, N.Y.: John Washburn Bleeker Hampton Publishing, 1992.

Burke, John P. *Honest Broker? The National Security Advisor and Presidential Decision Making*. College Station, Tex.: Texas A&M University Press, 2009.

Dean, Robert D. *Imperial Brotherhood: Gender and the Making of Cold War Foreign Policy*. Amherst, Mass.: University of Massachusetts Press, 2001.

Ellsberg, Daniel. *Papers on the War*. New York: Simon & Schuster, 1972.

Garrett, Stephen A. *Ideals and Reality: An Analysis of the Debate over Vietnam*. Washington, D.C.: University Press of America, 1978.

Griffiths, James M. *Vietnam Insights: Logic of Involvement and Unconventional Perspectives*. New York: Vantage, 2000.

Hulsey, Byron C. *Everett Dirksen and His Presidents: How a Senate Giant Shaped American Politics*. Lawrence, Kans.: University Press of Kansas, 2000.

Johnson, Robert David. *Congress and the Cold War*. New York: Cambridge University Press, 2006.

Kattenburg, Paul M. *The Vietnam Trauma in American Foreign Policy, 1945–1975*. New Brunswick, N.J.: Transaction Books, 1980.

Korb, Lawrence J. *The Joint Chiefs of Staff: The First Twenty-five Years*. Bloomington, Ind.: Indiana University Press, 1976.

Milstein, Jeffrey S. *Dynamics of the Vietnam War: A Quantitative Analysis and Predictive Computer Simulation*. Columbus, Ohio: Ohio State University Press, 1974.

Osborn, George K., Asa A. Clark, IV, Daniel J. Kaufman, and Douglas E. Lute, eds. *Democracy, Strategy, and Vietnam: Implications for American Policymaking*. Lexington, Mass.: Lexington Books, 1987.

Parker, F. Charles, IV. *Vietnam: Strategy for a Stalemate*. New York: Paragon House, 1989.

Perry, Mark. *Four Stars: The Inside Story of the Forty-Year Battle Between the Joint Chiefs of Staff and America's Civilian Leaders*. Boston: Houghton Mifflin, 1989.

Prados, John. *Keepers of the Keys: A History of the National Security Council from Truman to Bush*. New York: Morrow, 1991.

———, ed. *The White House Tapes: Eavesdropping on the President*. New York: New Press, 2003.

Sanders, Vivienne. *The USA and Vietnam, 1945–75*. London: Hodder & Stoughton, 2002.

Shapley, Deborah. *Promise and Power*. Boston: Little, Brown, 1993.

Small, Melvin. *At the Water's Edge: American Politics and the Vietnam War*. Chicago: Ivan R. Dee, 2005.

Stavins, Ralph, Richard J. Barnet, and Marcus G. Raskin. *Washington Plans an Aggressive War*. New York: Random House, 1971.

Steinberg, Blema S. *Shame and Humiliation: Presidential Decision Making on Vietnam*. Pittsburgh, Penn.: University of Pittsburgh Press, 1996.

Sullivan, Michael P. *The Vietnam War: A Study in the Making of American Foreign Policy*. Lexington, Ky.: University Press of Kentucky, 1985.

Tucker, Robert W. *Nation or Empire? The Debate over American Foreign Policy*. Baltimore, Md.: Johns Hopkins University Press, 1968.

Twing, Stephen W. *Myths, Models and U.S. Foreign Policy: The Cultural Shaping of Three Cold Warriors*. Boulder, Colo.: Lynne Rienner, 1998.

White, Ralph. *Nobody Wanted War: Misperception in Vietnam and Other Wars*. Garden City, N.Y.: Doubleday, 1968.

Wise, David. *The Politics of Lying: Government Deception, Secrecy, and Power*. New York: Random House, 1973.

Roosevelt and Truman Administrations

Beisner, Robert. *Dean Acheson: A Life in the Cold War*. Oxford: Oxford University Press, 2006.

Kuklick, Bruce. *Blind Oracles: Intellectuals and War from Kennan to Kissinger*. Princeton, N.J.: Princeton University Press, 2006.

McLellan, David. *Dean Acheson: The State Department Years*. New York: Dodd, Mead, 1976.

Eisenhower Administration

Brinkley, Douglas. *Dean Acheson: The Cold War Years, 1953–1971*. New Haven, Conn.: Yale University Press, 1992.

Gaddis, John Lewis. *Strategies of Containment: A Critical Appraisal of American National Security Policy during the Cold War*. New York: Oxford University Press, 2005.

Morgan, Joseph G. *The Vietnam Lobby: The American Friends of Vietnam, 1955–1975*. Chapel Hill, N.C.: University of North Carolina Press, 1997.

Ninkovich, Frank. *Modernity and Power: A History of the Domino Theory in the Twentieth Century*. Chicago: University of Chicago Press, 1994.

Tuunainen, Pasi. *The Role of Presidential Advisory Systems in US Foreign Policy-Making: The Case of the National Security Council and Vietnam, 1953–1961*. Helsinki, Finland: Suomalaisen Kirjallisuuden Seura, 2001.

Kennedy Administration

Abramson, Rudy. *Spanning the Century: The Life of W. Averell Harriman, 1891–1986*. New York: Morrow, 1992.

Acacia, John. *Clark Clifford: The Wise Man of Washington*. Lexington, Ky.: University Press of Kentucky, 2009.

Blair, Anne E. *Lodge in Vietnam: A Patriot Abroad*. New Haven, Conn.: Yale University Press, 1995.

Buzzanco, Robert. *Masters of War: Military Dissent and Politics in the Vietnam Era*. New York: Cambridge University Press, 1996.

Cohen, Warren I. *Dean Rusk*. Totowa, N.J.: Cooper Square, 1980.

Dietz, Terry. *Republicans and Vietnam: 1961–1968*. Westport, Conn.: Greenwood, 1986.

Halberstam, David. *The Best and the Brightest*. New York: Random House, 1972.

Herman, Edward S., and Richard B. DuBoff. *America's Vietnam Policy: The Strategy of Deception*. Washington, D.C.: Public Affairs Press, 1966.

Kochavi, Noam. *A Conflict Perpetuated: China Policy during the Kennedy Years*. Westport, Conn.: Praeger, 2002.

Schwab, Orrin. *Defending the Free World: John F. Kennedy, Lyndon Johnson, and the Vietnam War, 1961–1965*. Westport, Conn.: Praeger, 1998.

Johnson Administration

Anderson, David L., ed. *Shadow on the White House: Presidents and the Vietnam War, 1945–1975*. Lawrence, Kans.: University Press of Kansas, 1993.

Ashby, LeRoy, and Rod Gramer. *Fighting the Odds: The Life of Senator Frank Church*. Pullman, Wa.: Washington State University Press, 1994.

Barrett, David M. *Uncertain Warriors: Lyndon B. Johnson and His Vietnam Advisors*. Lawrence, Kans.: University Press of Kansas, 1993.

Berman, Larry. *Lyndon Johnson's War*. New York: Norton, 1989.

Berman, William C. *William Fulbright and the Vietnam War: The Dissent of a Political Realist*. Kent, Ohio: Kent State University Press, 1988.

Bill, James A. *George Ball: Behind the Scenes in U.S. Foreign Policy*. New Haven, Conn.: Yale University Press, 1997.

Bird, Kai. *The Color of Truth: McGeorge Bundy and William Bundy, Brothers in Arms*. New York: Simon & Schuster, 1998.

Blight, James G., and Janet M. Lang, eds. *The Fog of War: Lessons from the Life of Robert McNamara*. Lanham, Md.: Rowman & Littlefield, 2005.

Brands, Henry William. *The Wages of Globalism: Lyndon Johnson and the Limits of American Power*. New York: Oxford University Press, 1995.

Brown, Eugene. *J. William Fulbright: Advice and Dissent*. Iowa City, Iowa: University of Iowa Press, 1985.

Brown, Stuart G. *The Presidency on Trial: Robert Kennedy's 1968 Campaign and Afterwards*. Honolulu, Hawaii: University Press of Hawaii, 1972.

Burke, John P., and Fred I. Greenstein, with Larry Berman and Richard Immerman. *How Presidents Test Reality: Decisions on Vietnam, 1954 and 1965*. New York: Russell Sage Foundation, 1989.

Christofferson, Bill. *The Man from Clear Lake: Earth Day Founder Senator Gaylord Nelson*. Madison, Wisc.: University of Wisconsin Press, 2004.

Cohen, Warren I., and Nancy Bernkopf Tucker, eds. *Lyndon Johnson Confronts the World: American Foreign Policy, 1963–1968*. New York: Cambridge University Press, 1994.

Dallek, Robert. *Flawed Giant: Lyndon Johnson and His Times, 1961–1973*. New York: Oxford University Press, 1998.

Dauer, Richard P. *A North-South Mind in an East-West World: Chester Bowles and the Making of United States Cold War Foreign Policy, 1951–1969*. Westport, Conn.: Praeger, 2005.

DiLeo, David. *George Ball, Vietnam, and the Rethinking of Containment*. Chapel Hill, N.C.: University of North Carolina Press, 1991.

Dizard, Wilson P., Jr. *Inventing Public Diplomacy: The Story of the U.S. Information Agency*. Boulder, Colo.: Lynne Rienner, 2004.

Donovan, John C. *The Cold Warriors: A Policy-Making Elite*. Lexington, Mass.: Heath, 1974.

Donovan, Robert J. *Nemesis: Truman and Johnson in the Coils of War in Asia*. New York: St. Martin's Press, 1984.

Firestone, Bernard J., and Robert C. Vogt, eds. *Lyndon Johnson and the Uses of Power*. Westport, Conn.: Greenwood, 1988.

Fite, Gilbert C. *Richard B. Russell, Jr., Senator from Georgia*. Chapel Hill, N.C.: University of North Carolina Press, 1991.

Fry, Joseph. *Debating Vietnam: Fulbright, Stennis, and Their Senate Hearings*. Lanham, Md.: Rowman & Littlefield, 2006.

Goldberg, Robert Alan. *Barry Goldwater*. New Haven, Conn.: Yale University Press, 1995.

Goldstein, Gordon M. *Lessons in Disaster: McGeorge Bundy and the Path to War in Vietnam*. New York: Times Books, 2008.

Graff, Henry F. *The Tuesday Cabinet: Deliberation and Decision on Peace and War under Lyndon B. Johnson*. Englewood Cliffs, N.J.: Prentice-Hall, 1970.

Guthman, Edwin O., and Jeffrey Shulman, eds. *Robert Kennedy in His Own Words: The Unpublished Recollections of the Kennedy Years*. New York: Bantam, 1988.

Halberstam, David. *The Unfinished Odyssey of Robert Kennedy*. New York: Random House, 1968.

Hatcher, Patrick L. *The Suicide of an Elite: American Internationalists and Vietnam*. Stanford, Calif.: Stanford University Press, 1990.

Helsing, Jeffrey W. *Johnson's War/Johnson's Great Society: The Guns and Butter Trap*. Westport, Conn.: Praeger, 2000.

Hendrickson, Paul. *The Living and the Dead: Robert McNamara and Five Lives of a Lost War*. New York: Knopf, 1996.

Hilty, James W. *Robert Kennedy: Brother Protector*. Philadelphia: Temple University Press, 1997.

Hunt, Michael H. *Lyndon Johnson's War: America's Cold War Crusade in Vietnam, 1945–1965*. New York: Hill & Wang, 1996.

Isaacson, Walter, and Evan Thomas. *The Wise Men: Six Friends and the World They Made*. New York: Simon & Schuster, 1986.

Jervis, Robert, and Jack Snyder, eds. *Dominoes and Bandwagons: Strategic Beliefs and Great Power Competition in the Eurasian Rimland*. New York: Oxford University Press, 1991.

Johns, Andrew L. *Vietnam's Second Front: Domestic Politics, the Republican Party, and the War*. Lexington, Ky.: University Press of Kentucky, 2010.

Johnson, Robert David. *Ernest Gruening and the American Dissenting Tradition*. Cambridge, Mass.: Harvard University Press, 1998.

Kaiser, David. *American Tragedy: Kennedy, Johnson, and the Origins of the Vietnam War*. Cambridge, Mass.: Harvard University Press, 2000.

Kaufman, Robert Gordon. *Henry M. Jackson: A Life in Politics.* Seattle, Wa.: University of Washington Press, 2000.

Kearns, Doris. *Lyndon Johnson and the American Dream.* New York: Harper & Row, 1976.

Kenny, Henry J. *The American Role in Vietnam and East Asia: Between Two Revolutions.* New York: Praeger, 1984.

Kinnard, Douglas. *The Secretary of Defense.* Lexington, Ky.: University Press of Kentucky, 1980.

LaFeber, Walter. *The Deadly Bet: LBJ, Vietnam, and the 1968 Election.* Lanham, Md.: Rowman & Littlefield, 2005.

Longley, Kyle. *Senator Albert Gore, Sr.: Tennessee Maverick.* Baton Rouge, La.: Louisiana State University Press, 2004.

McFarland, Linda. *Cold War Strategist: Stuart Symington and the Search for National Security.* Westport, Conn.: Praeger, 2001.

McMaster, Herbert R. *Dereliction of Duty: Lyndon Johnson, Robert McNamara, the Joint Chiefs of Staff, and the Lies That Led to Vietnam.* New York: HarperCollins, 1997.

Milne, David. *America's Rasputin: Walt Rostow and the Vietnam War.* New York: Farrar, Straus & Giroux, 2008.

Newfield, Jack. *Robert Kennedy: A Memoir.* New York: Dutton, 1969.

Oberdorfer, Don. *Senator Mansfield: The Extraordinary Life of a Great American Statesman and Diplomat.* Washington, D.C.: Smithsonian Institution Press, 2003.

Olson, Gregory A. *Mansfield and Vietnam: A Study in Rhetorical Adaptation.* East Lansing, Mich.: Michigan State University Press, 1995.

Olson, James C. *Stuart Symington: A Life.* Columbia, Mo.: University of Missouri Press, 2003.

Palermo, Joseph A. *In His Own Right: The Political Odyssey of Senator Robert F. Kennedy.* New York: Columbia University Press, 2001.

Palmer, Gregory. *The McNamara Strategy and the Vietnam War: Program Budgeting in the Pentagon, 1960–1968.* Westport, Conn.: Greenwood, 1978.

Reedy, George. *Lyndon B. Johnson: A Memoir.* New York: Andrews McMeel Publishing, 1982.

Roherty, James. *Decisions of Robert S. McNamara: A Study of the Role of the Secretary of Defense.* Coral Gables, Fla.: University of Miami Press, 1970.

Ross, Douglas. *Robert F. Kennedy, Apostle of Change: A Review of His Public Record with Analysis.* New York: Pocket Books, 1968.

Rovere, Richard H. *Waist Deep in the Big Muddy: Personal Reflections on 1968.* Boston: Little, Brown, 1968.

Schaffer, Howard B. *Chester Bowles: New Dealer in the Cold War.* Cambridge, Mass.: Harvard University Press, 1993.

Schlesinger, Arthur, Jr. *Robert Kennedy and His Times.* Boston: Houghton Mifflin, 1978.

Shesol, Jeff. *Mutual Contempt: Lyndon Johnson, Robert Kennedy, and the Feud that Defined a Decade.* New York: Norton, 1997.

Stone, Gary. *Elites for Peace: The Senate and the Vietnam War, 1964–1968.* Knoxville, Tenn.: University of Tennessee Press, 2007.

Taylor, John M. *General Maxwell Taylor: The Sword and the Pen*. New York: Doubleday, 1989.

Thomas, Evan. *Robert Kennedy: His Life*. New York: Simon & Schuster, 2000.

Trewhitt, Henry L. *McNamara*. New York: Harper & Row, 1971.

Valenti, Jack. *A Very Human President*. New York: Norton, 1975.

Valeo, Francis R. *Mike Mansfield, Majority Leader: A Different Kind of Senate, 1961–1976*. Armonk, N.Y.: M. E. Sharpe, 1999.

Vandemark, Brian. *Into the Quagmire: Lyndon Johnson and the Escalation of the Vietnam War*. New York: Oxford University Press, 1991.

Vanden Heuvel, William, and William Gwirtzman. *On His Own: Robert F. Kennedy, 1964–1968*. Garden City, N.Y.: Doubleday, 1970.

Vandiver, Frank E. *Shadows of Vietnam: Lyndon Johnson's Wars*. College Station, Tex.: Texas A&M University Press, 1997.

Watson, W. Marvin, with Sherwin Markman. *Chief of Staff: Lyndon Johnson and His Presidency*. New York: St. Martin's Press, 2004.

Woods, Jeff. *Richard B. Russell: Southern Nationalism and American Foreign Policy*. Lanham, Md.: Rowman & Littlefield, 2006.

Woods, Randall B. *Fulbright: A Biography*. New York: Cambridge University Press, 1995.

———. *J. William Fulbright, Vietnam, and the Search for a Cold War Foreign Policy*. New York: Cambridge University Press, 1998.

———. *LBJ: Architect of American Ambition*. New York: Free Press, 2006.

Zeiler, Thomas W. *Dean Rusk: Defending the American Mission Abroad*. Wilmington, Del.: Scholarly Resources, 2000.

Nixon and Ford Administrations

Pike, Douglas, ed. *The Bunker Papers: Reports to the President from Vietnam, 1967–1973*. 3 vols. Berkeley, Calif.: Institute of East Asian Studies, 1990.

Schaffer, Howard B. *Ellsworth Bunker: Global Troubleshooter, Vietnam Hawk*. Chapel Hill, N.C.: University of North Carolina Press, 2003.

Serewicz, Lawrence W. *America at the Brink of Empire: Rusk, Kissinger, and the Vietnam War*. Baton Rouge, La.: Louisiana State University Press, 2007.

Small, Melvin. *Johnson, Nixon, and the Doves*. New Brunswick, N.J.: Rutgers University Press, 1988.

INTERNET RESOURCES

General and Reference

Australian involvement in Vietnam: www.hotkey.net.au/~marshalle

Battlefield: Vietnam: www.pbs.org/battlefieldvietnam

Congressional Medal of Honor Society: www.cmohs.org

Disabled American Veterans: www.dav.org

East Meets West Foundation: www.eastmeetswest.org

General Nguyễn Văn Hiếu Website: http://nguyentin.tripod.com
My Lai Court Case: www.law.umkc.edu/faculty/projects/ftrials/mylai/mylai.htm
Paralyzed Veterans of America: www.pva.org/site/PageServer
The American Experience, Vietnam Online: www.pbs.org/wgbh/amex/vietnam/
   index.html
The Friends of the Vietnam Veterans Memorial: www.vietwall.org
The Vietnam Conflict: www.deanza.fhda.edu/faculty/swensson/ewrt2vn.html
The Virtual Wall, Vietnam Veterans Memorial: www.virtualwall.org
The Wars for Vietnam: http://vietnam.vassar.edu
U.S. Army Center for Military History, Vietnam War: www.history.army.mil/html/
   bookshelves/resmat/vw.html
Vets with a Mission: History of Vietnam and the Vietnam War: www.vwam.com/vets/
   hisintro.html
Vietnam Veterans Home Page: www.vietvet.org
Vietnam Veterans Memorial Fund—Vietnam: Echoes from the War: www.teachvietnam
   .org
Vietnam War bibliography: http//www.clemson.edu/caah/history/FacultyPages
   /EdMoise/bibliography.htm
Vietnam War Internet Project: www.vwip.org/vwiphome.html
Vietnamese American Heritage Foundation: www.vietnameseamerican.org

Archival and Primary Documents

Fall of Saigon Stories: http://marianne_brems.tripod.com/Fall
Foreign Relations of the United States online:
www.state.gov/www/about_state/history/frusonline.html
International Cold War History Project Virtual Archive: www.wilsoncenter.org/index
   .cfm?topic_id=1409&fuseaction=va2.browse&sort=Collection
National Archives and Records Administration: www.archives.gov
National Security Archives: www.gwu.edu/~nsarchiv
Naval Historical Center: www.history.navy.mil
Pacifica Radio: University of California at Berkeley Social Activism Sound Record-
   ing Project: www.lib.berkeley.edu/MRC/pacificaviet.html
POW/MIA Database: http://lcweb2.loc.gov/pow/powhome.html
University of Wisconsin, Foreign Relations of the United States: www.state.gov/
   www/about_state/history/frus.html
Vietnam War Declassification Project: www.ford.utexas.edu/library/exhibits/vietnam/
   vietnam.htm
Virtual Vietnam Archive: www.vietnam.ttu.edu/virtualarchive

Military Units

1st Combat Evaluation Group Association: http://1cevga.com
1st Marine Division Association: www.usmc.org/7th

1/4th U.S. Cavalry: www.quarterhorsecav.org
2nd Brigade, 1st Air Cavalry Division, United States Army, Airmobile Infantry: www
 .ranger25.com
3rd Surgical Hospital: www.angelfire.com/ny5/msgfisher/3surg.htm
7th Engineer Battalion, 1st Marine Division: www.usmc.org/7th
9th Engineer Battalion (USMC) Association: http://9thengineers.com
11th Armored Cavalry's Veterans of Vietnam and Cambodia: http://11thcavnam.com
12th Cavalry Regiment Association: http://12thcav.us
15th Engineer Battalion (Combat) Association: www.15thcombatengineers.org
25th Infantry Association: www.25thida.com
29th Field Artillery: http://members.tripod.com/~msg_fisher/index.html
45th Surgical Hospital: http://the45thsurg.freeservers.com
46th Engineers: www.quarterhorsecav.org
1st Battalion, 69th Armor: www.rjsmith.com/my_unit.html#top
1/92nd Field Artillery Association, Vietnam: http://bravecannons.org
93rd Evacuation Hospital: http://members.tripod.com/~msg_fisher/93evac-5.html
173rd Airborne Brigade Association: http://skysoldiers.com
174th Assault Helicopter Company Association: www.174ahc.org
188th Assault Helicopter Company Association: www.blackwidows.net
327th Infantry, 101st Airborne Division Association: www.327infantry.org/about_us
458th Transportation Company (PBR): http://458thseatigers.homestead.com/pbr.html
611th Transportation Company: http://groups.yahoo.com/group/611thtransco
A Troop, 4/12th Cavalry (Vietnam Era) Association: www.atroop412cav.com
A-37 Association: http://a-37.org
AC-119 Gunship Association: www.ac-119gunships.com/welcome.htm
Air America Association: www.air-america.org
Alpha Company, 1st Battalion, 20th Infantry, 11th Light Infantry Brigade, Americal
 Division Association: http://alpha120.com
Americal Division Veterans Association: http://americal.org
Army Quartermaster Foundation: www.qmfound.com
Army Transportation Association: http://grambo.us/atav/default.html
B Troop, 2/17th Cavalry Association: www.vietnamproject.ttu.edu/banshee
B-2/501st Infantry, 101st Airborne Division: www.b2501airborne.com
C-7A Caribou Association: www.c-7acaribou.com
Combat Tracker Team: www.combattrackerteam.org
Company E (LRP) and Company C (Ranger) Association Inc.: http://e20-lrp-c75-rgr.org
Counterparts Association: www.counterparts.net
Delta Raiders of Vietnam Association (DROVA): www.blackied2501.com/drova.htm
Dustoff Association: www.dustoff.org
Echo Company, 2nd Battalion, 3rd Marines: http://echo23marines6569.org/
F Troop, 8th Cavalry Regiment Blue Ghost Association: www.blueghosts.com
Fleet Reserve Association: www.fra.org
Forward Air Controller Association: www.fac-assoc.org
FSB Ripcord Association: www.ripcordassociation.com
Gamewardens of Vietnam Association: www.tf116.org

HA(L)-3 Seawolf Association: www.seawolf.org/index.asp
India Company, 3rd Battalion, 5th Marines: www.aug.edu/~libwrw/vwar/vwar.htm
International Liaison Pilot and Aircraft Association: www.centercomp.com/ILPA
Khe Sanh Veterans Association: www.khesanh.org
Military Chaplains Association of the USA: www.mca-usa.org
Military Officers Association of America: www.moaa.org
Military Police of the Vietnam War: http://militarypolicevietnam.com
Military Police Sentry Dog Alumni: http://sentrydogalumni.us
Mobile Riverine Forces Association: www.mrfa.org
National Association of Medics and Corpsmen: www.medics-corpsmen.org
Naval Mobile Construction Battalion 121: http://mcb121.com
Navy Mobile Riverine Force: www.riverinesailor.com
PBR Forces Veterans Association: www.pbr-fva.org/betasite
Quiet Aircraft Association: http://quietaircraft.org
Rattler/Firebird Association: http://rattler-firebird.org
Society of Combat Search and Rescue (CSAR): www.combatsar.org
Society of the 1st Infantry Division: http://64.78.33.72/about/index.cfm
Southeast Asia Army Security Agency Association: www.oldspooksandspies.org
Swift Boat Sailors Association: www.swiftboats.org
Thailand, Laos, Cambodia Brotherhood: www.tlc-brotherhood.org
The 539th Transportation Company: http://hexmate.homestead.com
U.S. Army Otter Caribou Association: http://otter-caribou.org
U.S. Coast Guard in Vietnam: www.aug.edu/~libwrw/vwar/vwar.htm
U.S. Merchant Marine in Vietnam: www.aug.edu/~libwrw/vwar/vwar.htm
USMC Vietnam Helicopter Association: www.popasmoke.com/index.html
Veterans of the Vietnam War Inc.: www.vvnw.org
Vietnam Dog Handler Association: http://vdha.us
Vietnam Era Seabees Association: http://navymemorial.ibelong.com/site/Vietnam
    -Era-Seabees
Vietnam Helicopter Crew Member Association: www.vhcma.org
Vietnam Helicopter Flight Crew Network: www.vhfcn.org
Vietnam Helicopter Pilots Association: www.vhpa.org
Vietnam Veterans Association of Australia: www.vvaa.org.au
Vietnam Veterans of America: www.vva.org
Vietnam Women Veterans Association: http://vietnamwomenveterans.org
Vinh Long Outlaws Association: www.vinhlongoutlaws.com

About the Author

Ronald Bruce Frankum Jr. received his B.A. in history and political philosophy from Syracuse University, an M.A. in history from the University of Kentucky, and a Ph.D. in history from Syracuse University in 1997. Since then, he has served as the archivist and associate director of the Vietnam Center at Texas Tech University and is currently an associate professor of history at Millersville University of Pennsylvania where he teaches modern American diplomacy, military history, and the Vietnam War. He has also taught American foreign relations or the Vietnam War at Syracuse University and Texas Tech University, and in 1999 he conducted three workshops in Vietnam at the Vietnam National University (Đại Học Quốc Gia) in Hà Nội and Hồ Chí Minh City and at Cần Thơ University (Đại Học Cần Thơ). He is the author of *Silent Partners: The United States and Australia in Vietnam* (2001), *The Vietnam War for Dummies* [with Stephen Maxner] (2002), *Like Rolling Thunder: The Air War during the Vietnam War* (2005), and *Operation Passage to Freedom: The United States in Vietnam, 1954–1955* (2007), as well as several articles, book chapters, and reviews. He is currently engaged in writing an extensive history of Ngô Đình Diệm.